THE FORBIDDEN TEXTS - GOSPELS AND EPISTLES THAT WERE BANNED FROM THE BIBLE

By

Walter R. Cassels
Archbishop William Wake
J B Lightfoot

Cover Photograph: @jbtaylor

ISBN: 978-1-78139-216-4

© 2012 Benediction Classics, Oxford.

Contents

THE GOSPEL ACCORDING TO PETER - A STUDY

I 3

THE GOSPEL ACCORDING TO PETER

II 7
III 11
IV 18
V 28
VI 31
VII 37
VIII 41
IX 87
X 90
XI 103
XII 107
Appendix 109

ΕΥΑΓΓΕΛΙΟΝ ΚΑΤΑ ΠΕΤΡΟΝ

FORBIDDEN BOOKS OF THE NEW TESTAMENT.

PREFACE. 117

THE GOSPEL OF THE BIRTH OF MARY.

CHAPTER I. 121
CHAPTER II. 122
CHAPTER III. 124
CHAPTER IV. 125
CHAPTER V. 126
CHAPTER VI. 127
CHAPTER VII. 128
CHAPTER VIII. 130

THE GOSPEL CALLED THE PROTEVANGELION

CHAPTER I. 133
CHAPTER. II. 134
CHAPTER III. 135
CHAPTER IV. 135
CHAPTER V. 136
CHAPTER VI. 137
CHAPTER VII. 138
CHAPTER VIII. 139
CHAPTER IX. 140
CHAPTER X. 142
CHAPTER XI. 144
CHAPTER. XII. 145
CHAPTER XIII. 146
CHAPTER XIV. 147
CHAPTER XV. 149
CHAPTER XVI. 150

THE PROTEVANGELION. Note on the death of Zacharias in Chap. 16. 152
REFERENCES TO THE PROTEVANGELION. 153

THE FIRST GOSPEL OF THE INFANCY OF JESUS CHRIST.

CHAPTER I. 154
CHAPTER. II. 156
CHAPTER III. 157
CHAPTER IV. 158
CHAPTER V. 160
CHAPTER VI. 161
CHAPTER VII. 164
CHAPTER VIII. 167
CHAPTER IX. 168
CHAPTER X. 169
CHAPTER XI. 171
CHAPTER XII. 171
CHAPTER XIII. 173
CHAPTER XIV. 175
CHAPTER XV. 176
CHAPTER. XVI. 177
CHAPTER. XVII. 178
CHAPTER XVIII. 179
CHAPTER XIX. 181
CHAPTER XX. 183
CHAPTER XXI. 184
CHAPTER XXII. 186
REFERENCES TO THE FIRST GOSPEL OF THE INFANCY OF JESUS CHRIST 186

THE SECOND, OR ST. THOMAS'S GOSPEL OF THE INFANCY OF JESUS CHRIST.
CHAPTER I. 188
CHAPTER II. 189
CHAPTER III. 190
CHAPTER IV. 191

THE GOSPEL OF NICODEMUS, FORMERLY CALLED THE ACTS OF PONTIUS PILATE.
CHAPTER I. 192
CHAPTER II. 195
CHAPTER III. 196
CHAPTER IV. 197
CHAPTER. V. 198
CHAPTER VI. 202
CHAPTER. VII. 203
CHAPTER VIII. 204
CHAPTER IX. 206
CHAPTER X. 207
CHAPTER XI. 210
CHAPTER XII. 212
CHAPTER XIII. 214
CHAPTER XIV. 215
CHAPTER XV. 216
CHAPTER XVI. 218
CHAPTER XVII. 219
CHAPTER XVIII. 220
CHAPTER XIX. 222
CHAPTER XX. 223
CHAPTER XXI. 225
CHAPTER XXII. 226

THE EPISTLES OF JESUS CHRIST & ABGARUS KING OF EDESSA.

CHAPTER I. 230
CHAPTER II. 231

THE EPISTLE OF ST. PAUL THE APOSTLE TO THE LAODICEANS.

REFERENCES TO THE EPISTLE OF ST. PAUL THE APOSTLE TO THE LAODICEANS. 233

THE EPISTLES OF ST. PAUL THE APOSTLE TO SENECA, WITH SENECA'S TO PAUL.

CHAPTER I. 234
CHAPTER II. 235
CHAPTER III. 235
CHAPTER. IV. 235
CHAPTER V. 236
CHAPTER VI. 236
CHAPTER VII. 236
CHAPTER VIII. 237
CHAPTER IX. 237
CHAPTER X. 238
CHAPTER XI. 238
CHAPTER XII. 239
CHAPTER XIII. 239
CHAPTER XIV. 240

THE ACTS OF ST. PAUL AND THECLA.

CHAPTER I. 242
CHAPTER II. 244
CHAPTER III. 246
CHAPTER IV. 247
CHAPTER V. 248

CHAPTER VI. 249
CHAPTER VII. 251
CHAPTER VIII. 252
CHAPTER IX. 253
CHAPTER X. 256
CHAPTER XI. 258

THE FIRST EPISTLE OF CLEMENT TO THE CORINTHIANS.
CHAPTER I. 261
CHAPTER II. 262
CHAPTER III. 263
CHAPTER IV. 264
CHAPTER V. 266
CHAPTER VI. 267
CHAPTER VII. 268
CHAPTER VIII. 269
CHAPTER IX. 272
CHAPTER X. 273
CHAPTER. XI. 274
CHAPTER XII. 275
CHAPTER XIII. 277
CHAPTER XIV. 277
CHAPTER XV. 279
CHAPTER XVI. 280
CHAPTER XVII. 281
CHAPTER XVIII. 283
CHAPTER XIX. 285
CHAPTER XX. 287
CHAPTER XXI. 289
CHAPTER XXII. 291
CHAPTER XXIII. 293
CHAPTER XXIV. 295

THE SECOND EPISTLE OF CLEMENT TO THE CORINTHIANS

CHAPTER I. 297
CHAPTER II 298
CHAPTER III. 299
CHAPTER IV. 301
CHAPTER V. 303

THE GENERAL EPISTLE OF BARNABAS.

CHAPTER I. 305
CHAPTER II. 306
CHAPTER III. 308
CHAPTER IV. 309
CHAPTER V. 311
CHAPTER VI. 313
CHAPTER VII. 314
CHAPTER VIII. 315
CHAPTER IX. 317
CHAPTER X. 319
CHAPTER XI. 320
CHAPTER XII. 322
CHAPTER XIII. 324
CHAPTER XIV. 326
CHAPTER XV. 328

THE EPISTLE OF IGNATIUS TO THE EPHESIANS.

CHAPTER I. 331
CHAPTER II. 333
CHAPTER III. 334
CHAPTER IV. 336

THE EPISTLE OF IGNATIUS TO THE MAGNESIANS

CHAPTER I. 339
CHAPTER II. 340
CHAPTER III. 341
CHAPTER IV. 342

THE EPISTLE OF IGNATIUS TO THE TRALLIANS.

CHAPTER 1. 344

THE EPISTLE OF IGNATIUS TO THE ROMANS.

CHAPTER I. 349
CHAPTER. II. 350
CHAPTER III. 352

IGNATIUS TO THE PHILADELPHIANS.

CHAPTER I. 354
CHAPTER II. 355
CHAPTER III. 357

IGNATIUS TO THE SMYRNEANS.

CHAPTER I. 359
CHAPTER II. 360
CHAPTER III. 362

IGNATIUS TO POLYCARP

CHAPTER I. 365
CHAPTER II. 366
CHAPTER III. 367

THE EPISTLE OF POLYCARP TO THE PHILIPPIANS.

CHAPTER I. 370
CHAPTER II. 371

CHAPTER III. 373
CHAPTER IV. 374

THE FIRST PART OF THE BOOK OF HERMAS CALLED HIS VISION.

VISION I. 377
VISION II. 380
VISION III. 383
VISION IV. 393

THE SECOND PART OF THE BOOK OF HERMAS, CALLED HIS COMMANDS.

Introduction. 396
COMMAND I. 397
COMMAND II. 397
COMMAND III. 398
COMMAND IV. 399
COMMAND V. 402
COMMAND VI. 403
COMMAND VII. 405
COMMAND VIII. 405
COMMAND IX. 407
COMMAND X. 408
COMMAND XI. 410
COMMAND XII. 412

THE THIRD PART OF THE BOOK OF HERMAS, CALLED HIS SIMILITUDES.

SIMILITUDE I. 416
SIMILITUDE II. 417
SIMILITUDE III. 419
SIMILITUDE IV. 419
SIMILITUDE V. 420
SIMILITUDE VI. 426

SIMILITUDE VII. 430
SIMILITUDE VIII. 431
SIMILITUDE IX. 439
SIMILITUDE X. 462
REFERENCES TO THE BOOK OF HERMAS,
THE SHEPHERD. 465

THE DIDACHE OR TEACHING OF THE APOSTLES

1 469
2 470
3 470
4 471
5 472
6 473
7 473
8 473
9 474
10 474
11 475
12 476
13 476
14 477
15 477
16 477

THE DIDACHE – IN GREEK

ΔΙΔΑΧΗ ΤΩΝ ΔΩΔΕΚΑ ΑΠΟΣΤΟΛΩΝ

I 481
II 482
III 482
IV 483
V 483
VI 484
VII 484
VIII 484
IX 485
X 485
XI 485
XII 486
XIII 486
XIV 487
XV 487
XVI 487

THE GOSPEL ACCORDING TO PETER - A STUDY

By

Walter R. Cassels

Ἐπειδήπερ πολλοὶ ἐπεχείρησαν ἀνατάξασθαι διήγησιν περὶ τῶν πεπληροφορημένων ἐν ἡμῖν πραγμάτων .....

Forasmuch as many took in hand to draw up a narrative concerning the matters which have been fully believed among us....
LUKE i. 1

I

Egypt, in our days, ceasing to be any more the land of bondage, has, in more senses than one, become a veritable Land of Promise. It is a rich mine of historical and literary wealth, alas! most inadequately worked, and in that fine climate, with its clear dry air, the footprints of Time, leaving scarcely a trace, the treasures of an ancient civilisation, even of the most delicate texture, have been preserved to us with wonderful perfection. The habits of the peoples that have occupied the land have happily combined with the natural advantages of the climate, in transmitting to the modern world an inheritance of which we are now beginning to take possession. The dead have long been giving up their secrets, but it is only in recent times that we have been able to realise the fact that the tombs of Egypt may contain many a precious work, now known to us but in name, and many a writing which may change the current of controversy, and strangely modify many a cherished opinion. Without referring here to earlier discoveries in support of these remarks, we may at once pass to the more recent, with which we have particularly to do.

In the course of explorations carried on during the winter of 1886-87 by the order of M. Grébaut, then Director of the Museums of Egypt, two Greek manuscripts were discovered in the necropolis of Akhmîm, the ancient Panopolis, in Upper Egypt. The first of these was a papyrus, which was really found by some Fellahs who quarrelled regarding the partition of their precious booty and thus allowed the secret to leak out. It came to the knowledge of the Moudir, or Governor of the Province, who promptly settled the dispute by confiscating the papyrus, which he forwarded to the Museum of Gizeh at Boulaq. This MS. is a collection of problems in arithmetic and geometry, carefully written out, probably by a student, and buried with him as his highest and most valued achievement.

The second manuscript was of much higher interest. It was discovered in the tomb of a "monk." It consists of thirty-three pages in parchment, measuring 6 inches in height by 4-½ inches in breadth, without numbering, bound together in pasteboard covered with leather, which has become black with time. There is no date, nor any other indication of the approximate age of the MS. than that which is furnished by the characteristics of the writing and the part of the cemetery in which it was discovered. These lead to the almost certain conclusion, according to M. Bouriant, who first transcribed the text, that the MS. cannot be anterior to the eighth century or posterior to the twelfth. The ancient cemetery of Akhmîm stretches along to the north and west of the hill on which have been discovered tombs of the eighteenth to the twentieth dynasties, and it has served as a burial-place for the Christian inhabitants of the neighbourhood from the fifth to the fifteenth centuries, the more ancient part lying at the foot of the hill and extending gradually upward for about 700 metres. The tomb in which the MS. was found is in a position which approximately tallies, as regards age, with the date indicated by the MS. itself.[1] Of course, these indications refer solely to the date of the MS. itself, and not to the age of the actual works transcribed in its pages.

The thirty-three sheets of parchment, forming sixty-six pages, commence with an otherwise blank page, bearing a rough drawing of a Coptic cross, upon the arms of which rise smaller crosses of the same description, and the letters Ⲁ and Ⲱ stand the one on the left, the other on the right of the lower stem of the large cross. Over the page commences a fragment of the "Gospel of Peter," which continues to the end of page 10, where it abruptly terminates in the middle of a sentence. Pages 11 and 12 have been left blank. Pages 13 to 19 contain a fragment of the "Apocalypse of Peter," beginning and ending abruptly, and these have, either by accident or design, been bound in the volume upside down and in reverse order, so that, as they actually stand, the text commences at page 19 and ends at page 13. Page 20 is again blank, and the rest of the volume is made up of two fragments of the 'Book of Enoch,' the first extending from the 21st to the 50th page, and the second, written by a different hand, from the 51st to the 66th page. Finally, on the inside of the binding, and attached to it, is a sheet of parchment on which is written in uncials a fragment of the Greek "Acts of St. Julian," though which St. Julian amongst those in the Calendar does not appear.

---

[1] Fragments grecs du Livre d'Enoch, &c., publiés par les membres de la Mission archéol. française à Caire, Fasc. 3, 1893.

Walter R. Cassels

The French Archeological Mission published in 1892[1] the mathematical papyrus, edited by M. Baillet, but the much more interesting and important volume of fragments did not appear until 1393,[2] when they were edited by M. Bouriant. These precious works remained, therefore, practically hidden from the world for five or six years after their discovery, in consequence of what is vaguely, but truly, described as "vexatious delays," whilst the comparatively uninteresting arithmetical work preceded them by more than a year. The fragments of the "Gospel" and "Apocalypse" of Peter, long known by references or quotations by the Fathers, make us acquainted, for the first time, with the writings themselves, and the fragments of the "Book of Enoch" give us the Greek text of part of an early work quoted by the writer of the Epistle of Jude, hitherto only extant in an Ethiopian version.

Of almost greater interest than the actual discovery of these and other precious MSS. from time to time, in a similar way, is the possibility and probability opened out to us that we may yet recover from the dead still more precious works than these. The cemetery of Akhmîm stands near the ancient and very important city of Panopolis, and from a very early period it was the centre of a considerable Christian population. The custom of burying with the dead books which were a valued possession during life was probably a survival of the same primitive custom in accordance with which also a warrior's horse and dog and his weapons were interred with him to serve him again in the world of spirits. That books, at a time when their multiplication was so slow, should have been interred with their dead possessor is not only curious but very fortunate for us, and we may yet thank the cemetery of Akhmîm for preserving safely for us manuscripts which in no other way could have escaped the effects of time and the ravages of barbarism.

The fragments with which we are dealing present some peculiarities which deserve a moment's notice. The Gospel according to Peter commences in the middle of a sentence, but being at the top of a page it is probably only part of a manuscript of which the earlier portion was either lost or belonged to some one else. The fragment, however, ends abruptly in the middle of a phrase and, being followed by blank pages, the reasonable presumption is that the scribe intended to complete the transcription, but for some reason did not do so It is curious

---

[1] 1 Fasc.
[2] 3 Fasc.

THE GOSPEL ACCORDING TO PETER - A STUDY

that in a similar way the "Apocalypse of Peter" is only a fragment, beginning and ending abruptly, with a page left blank for continuation. Did the scribe hastily copy stray leaves of each work, which had fortuitously come in his way, leaving room for more should he be able to secure the rest? or did he break off his copy of the one to take up the other, and with equal restlessness leave it also unfinished? We shall never know exactly, but considering the value of books at that epoch, the probability seems to be that he hastily copied such portions of writings as had come into his possession, time or accident preventing the completion of his task.

The fragment of the "Gospel" of course does not bear any name or superscription—nor, indeed, does the "Apocalypse"—but the title is clearly deduced from the work itself, the writer saying directly "but I, Simon Peter," and thus proving that the narrative takes the form of a composition by that Apostle. It may be remarked, merely in passing, that it is a curious—if not in any way a significant—fact that the two Christian fragments in this little volume should both profess to have been written by the Apostle Peter. Are the peculiarities of the fragments which we have described due to the passage of some one having in his possession two works selected as being believed to emanate from the chief of the Apostles, from which there was only time to make these extracts? There is some reason for thinking that the parchment may have previously been used for some other writing, obliterated to make way for these fragments. The little volume has not altogether escaped injury in its long rest by the side of the dead, and parts of the text have had to be supplied by conjecture; but, on the whole, the writing is fairly legible and, by the invaluable aid of photography, it has been copied and published with complete fidelity. Before this was done, that the first transcription by M. Bouriant should have contained errors and omissions which led scholars into mistaken conclusions is very intelligible, but the text may now be considered fairly settled, and the following is a rather close and unpolished translation of the "Gospel according to Peter."

THE GOSPEL ACCORDING TO PETER[1]

II

(1) ... but of the Jews no man washed his hands, neither Herod nor any one of his judges; and as they were not minded to wash, Pilate rose. (2) And then Herod the King commandeth the Lord to be taken, saying unto them: "Whatsoever I commanded that ye should do, that do unto him." (3) But there was there Joseph, the friend of Pilate and of the Lord, and knowing that they are about to crucify him, he came to Pilate and asked the body of the Lord for burial. (4) And Pilate sent to Herod and asked for his body. (5) And Herod said: "Brother Pilate, even if no one had begged for him, we should have buried him; because the Sabbath is at hand; for it is written in the Law: 'The sun must not go down upon one put to death.'"

(6) And he delivered him to the people before the first day of the Unleavened bread of their feast. And taking the Lord they pushed him hurrying along, and said: "Let us drag along the Son of God as we have power over him." (7) And they clad him with purple and set him on a seat of judgment, saying: "Judge justly, King of Israel." (8) And one of them brought a crown of thorns and set it upon the head of the Lord. (9) And others standing by spat upon his eyes, and others smote him on the cheeks; others pierced him with a reed, and some scourged him, saying: "With this honour honour we the Son of God."

(10) And they brought two malefactors and crucified between them the Lord; but he kept silence as feeling no pain. (11) And as they set up the cross they wrote thereon: "This is the King of Israel." (12) And they laid the clothes before him and distributed them and cast lots for

---

[1] The Greek Text will be found in the Appendix.

them. (13) But one of these malefactors reproved them, saying: "We have suffered this for the evil which we wrought, but this man who has become the Saviour of men, what wrong hath he done you?" (14) And they were angry with him, and they commanded that his legs should not be broken, in order that he might die in torment.

(15) Now it was mid-day, and a darkness covered all Judaea, and they were troubled and anxious lest the sun should have set whilst he still lived, for it is written for them: "The sun must not go down upon one put to death." (16) And one of them said: "Give him to drink gall with vinegar;" and having mixed, they gave him to drink. (17) And they fulfilled all things and completed their sins upon their own head. (18) Now many went about with lights, thinking that it was night, and some fell. (19) And the Lord cried aloud, saying; "Power, my Power, thou hast forsaken me!" and having spoken, he was taken up. (20) And the same hour the veil of the temple of Jerusalem was torn in twain.

(21) And then they took out the nails from the hands of the Lord, and laid him upon the earth; and the whole earth quaked, and great fear came [upon them]. (22) Then did the sun shine out, and it was found to be the ninth hour. (23) Now the Jews were glad and gave his body to Joseph, that he might bury it, for he had beheld the good works that he did. (24) And he took the Lord and washed him, and wrapped him in linen, and brought him into his own grave, called "Joseph's Garden."

(25) Then the Jews and the elders and the priests, seeing the evil they had done to themselves, began to beat their breasts and to say: "Woe for our sins: judgment draweth nigh and the end of Jerusalem." (26) And I, with my companions, was mourning, and being pierced in spirit we hid ourselves; for we were sought for by them as malefactors, and as desiring to burn the temple. (27) Over all these things, however, we were fasting, and sat mourning and weeping night and day until the Sabbath.

(28) But the scribes and Pharisees and elders assembled themselves together, hearing that all the people murmured and beat their breasts, saying: "If at his death these great signs have happened, behold how just a one he is." (29) The elders were afraid and came to Pilate beseeching him and saying: (30) "Give us soldiers that we may watch his grave for three days, lest his disciples come and steal him, and the people believe that he rose from the dead and do us evil." (31) Pilate, therefore, gave them Petronius the centurion with soldiers to watch the tomb, and with them came the elders and scribes to the grave. (32) And they rolled a great stone against the centurion and the soldiers and

set it, all who were there together, at the door of the grave. (33) And they put seven seals; and setting up a tent there they kept guard. (34) And in the morning, at the dawn of the Sabbath, came a multitude from Jerusalem and the neighbourhood in order that they might see the sealed-up grave.

(35) Now, in the night before the dawn of the Lord's day, whilst the soldiers were keeping guard over the place, two and two in a watch, there was a great voice in the heaven. (36) And they saw the heavens opened and two men come down from thence with great light and approach the tomb. (37) And the stone which had been laid at the door rolled of itself away by the side, and the tomb was opened and both the young men entered.

(38) Then those soldiers, seeing this, awakened the centurion and the elders, for they also were keeping watch. (39) And whilst they were narrating to them what they had seen, they beheld again three men coming out of the tomb and the two were supporting the one, and a cross following them. (40) And the heads of the two indeed reached up to the heaven, but that of him that was led by (41) their hands rose above the heavens And they heard a voice from the heavens, saying: "Hast thou preached to them that are sleeping?" (42) And an answer was heard from the cross: "Yea." (43) These, therefore, took counsel together whether they should go and declare these things to Pilate. (44) And whilst they were still considering, the heavens again appeared opened, and a certain man descending and going into the grave.

(45) Seeing these things, the centurion and his men hastened to Pilate by night, leaving the tomb they were watching, and narrated all things they had seen, fearing greatly and saying: (46) "Truly he was a Son of God." Pilate answered and said, "I am pure of the blood of the Son of God, but thus it seemed good unto you." (47) Then they all came to him beseeching and entreating him that he should command the centurion and the soldiers to say nothing of what they had seen. (48) "For it is better," they said, "to lay upon us the greatest sins before God, and not to fall into the hands of the people of the Jews and be stoned." (49) Pilate, therefore, commanded the centurion and the soldiers to say nothing.

(50) In the morning of the Lord's day, Mary Magdalene, a disciple of the Lord (through fear of the Jews, for they burnt with anger, she had not done at the grave of the Lord that which women are accustomed to do for those that die and are loved by them), (51) took her women friends with her and came to the grave where he was laid. (52) And they feared lest the Jews should see them, and said: "If we could

not on that day in which he was crucified weep and lament, let us do these things even now at his grave. (53) But who will roll us away the stone that is laid at the door of the grave, in order that we may enter and set ourselves by him and do the things that are due? (54) For great was the stone, and we fear lest some one should see us. And if we should not be able to do it, let us at least lay down before the door that which we bring in his memory, and let us weep and lament till we come to our house." (55) And they went and found the tomb opened and, coming near, they stooped down and see there a certain young man sitting in the midst of the tomb, beautiful and clad in a shining garment, who said to them: (56) "Why are ye come? Whom seek ye? Him who was crucified? He is risen and gone away. But if ye do not believe, stoop down and see the place where he lay, that he is not there; for he is risen and gone away thither whence he was sent." (57) Then the women, frightened, fled.

(58) And it was the last day of the Unleavened bread, and many went forth, returning to their homes, the feast being ended. (59) But we, the twelve disciples of the Lord, wept and mourned, and each went to his home sorrowing for that which had happened. (60) But I, Simon Peter, and Andrew, my brother, took our nets and went to the sea, and there was with us Levi, the son of Alphaeus, whom the Lord....

III

No one can have studied this fragment of the Gospel according to Peter, with its analogy to, and still more striking divergence from, the canonical Gospels, without perceiving that we have here a most interesting work, well worth serious examination. The first question which naturally arises is connected with the date to be assigned to the fragment: Is this a part of the work used by many of the Fathers and well known amongst them as the Gospel according to Peter? We must first endeavour to form a correct judgment on this point.

Eusebius has preserved to us the earliest detailed notice of the Gospel according to Peter extant, in a quotation from Serapion, who became Bishop of Antioch about A.D. 190. Eusebius says:

> There is likewise another work written by him upon the so-called Gospel according to Peter, which he composed to refute the untruths contained in it, on account of certain in the community of Rhossus who were led away by this writing to heretical doctrines. It may be well to set forth some passages of this in which he expresses his opinion of the book:
>
> "For we, brethren, receive both Peter and the other Apostles even as Christ. But the false writings passing under their names we from experience reject, knowing that such things we have not received. When I was with you, I was under the impression that all held to the right faith and, without going through the Gospel put forward by them in the name of Peter, I said: 'If this is the only cause of difference amongst you, let it be read.' But now, having ascertained from information given to me that their minds were in some mist of heresy, I will hasten to come to you again; so, brethren, expect me shortly. We, therefore, brethren, knowing of what heresy was Marcianus, recognise how much he was in contradiction with

himself,[1] not comprehending that which he was saying, as you may perceive from what has been written unto you. For we borrowed this gospel from others who used it: that is to say, from the followers of those who introduced it before him, whom we call Docetae—for most of its thoughts are of this sect—having procured it from them, I was able to go through it, and to find, indeed, that most was according to the right teaching of the Saviour, but certain things were superadded, which we subjoin for you."[2]

There is little or no doubt that the writing before us is a fragment of this "Gospel according to Peter" of which Serapion writes.[3] It must always be remembered, as we examine the evidence for the work, that we have here only a short fragment, and that it would not be reasonable to expect to find in it materials for a perfect identification of the work with references to it in writings of the Fathers. Within the few

---

[1] The text of this sentence is faulty.
[2] ἡμεῖς γάρ, ἀδελφοί, καὶ Πέτρον καὶ τοὺς ἄλλους ἀποστόλους ἀποδεχόμεθα ὡς Χριστόν; τὰ δὲ ὀνόματι αὐτῶν ψευδεπίγραφα ὡς ἔμπειροι παραιτούμεθα, γινώσκοντες ὅτι τὰ τοιαῦτα οὐ παρελάβομεν. ἐγὼ γὰρ γενόμενος παρ' ὑμῖν ὑπενόουν τοὺς πάντας ὀρθῇ πίστει προσφέρεσθαι; καὶ μὴ διελθὼν τὸ ὑπ' αὐτῶν προφερόμενον ὀνόματι Πέτρου εὐαγγέλιον, εἶπον ὅτι Εἰ τοῦτό ἐστι μόνον τὸ δοκοῦν ὑμῖν παρέχειν μικροψυχίαν, ἀναγινωσκέσθω. νῦν δὲ μαθὼν ὅτι αἱρέσει τινὶ ὁ νοῦς αὐτῶν ἐνεφώλευεν ἐκ τῶν λεχθέντων μοι, σπουδάσω πάλιν γενέσθαι πρὸς ὑμάς; ὥστε, ἀδελφοί, προσδοκᾶτέ με ἐν τάχει. ἡμεῖς δέ, ἀδελφοί, καταλαβόμενοι ὁποίας ἦν αἱρέσεως ὁ Μαρκιανός, ὡς καὶ ἑαυτῷ ἠναντιοῦτο μὴ νοῶν ἃ ἐλάλει, ἃ μαθήσεσθε ἐξ ὧν ὑμῖν ἐγράφη. ἐδυνήθημεν γὰρ παρ' ἄλλων τῶν ἀσκησάντων αὐτὸ τοῦτο τὸ εὐαγγέλιον, τουτέστι παρὰ τῶν διαδόχων τῶν καταρξαμένων αὐτοῦ, οὓς Δοκητὰς καλοῦμεν (τὰ γὰρ φρονήματα τὰ πλείονα ἐκείνων ἐστὶ τῆς διδασκαλίας), χρησάμενοι παρ' αὐτῶν διελθεῖν καὶ εὑρεῖν τὰ μὲν πλείονα τοῦ ὀρθοῦ λόγου τοῦ σωτῆρος, τινὰ δὲ προσδιεσταλμένα, ἃ καὶ ὑπετάξαμεν ὑμῖν.—Euseb. H. E. vi. 12.
[3] Lods, De Evang. secundum Petrum, 1892, pp. 8 ff.; Harnack, Bruchstücke d. Evang. u.s.w. des Petrus, zweite Aufl. 1893, p. 41; Zahn, Das Ev. des Petrus, 1893, pp. 5 f., 70 ff.; Kunze, Das neu aufgef. Bruchstück des sogen. Petrusev. 1893, pp. 10 f.; Swete, The Akhmîm Fragment of the Apocr. Gospel of St. Peter, 1893, pp. xii f., xliv f.; Hilgenfeld, Zeitschr. wiss. Theol. 1893, ii. Heft. pp. 221 f., 239 ff.; J. Armitage Robinson, B.D., The Gospel according to Peter, &c., 1892, pp. 15 ff.; Martineau, The Nineteenth Century, 1893, pp. 906 ff.; J. R. Harris, Contemp. Rev. August 1893, p. 236; van Manen, Theol. Tijdschr. Juli 1893, p. 385.

pages which we possess, however, there is sufficient justification for concluding that they formed part of the Gospel current in Rhossus. Only one "Gospel according to Peter" is mentioned by early writers. This fragment distinctly pretends to be a narrative of Simon Peter; and its matter is generally such as must have satisfied Serapion's ideas of orthodox doctrine, if suspicion of Docetic tendencies had not made him believe that it contained a superadded leaven of heresy. This may not appear very clearly in the fragment, but we know from other sources, as we shall presently see, that they existed in the Gospel, and even here the representation that Jesus suffered no pain; that he is always called "the Lord," or the "Son of God;" that his one cry on the cross was susceptible of peculiar explanation, and that he was immediately "taken up," whilst his body subsequently presents aspects not common to the canonical Gospels, may have seemed to the careful bishop sufficiently Docetic to warrant at least his not very severe condemnation.

It is unnecessary to discuss minutely the details of Serapion's letter, which, if vague in parts and open to considerable doubt in some important respects, is at least sufficiently clear for our purpose in its general meaning. Nothing is known of the Marcianus to whom it refers. The bishop had evidently previously written of him, but the context has not been preserved. The Armenian version, made from a Syriac text, reads "Marcion" for "Marcianus," but it would be premature on this authority to associate the episode with that arch-heretic of the second century. It is clear from the bishop's words that on his previous visit to Rhossus, at the desire of part of the community, he sanctioned the public reading of the Gospel of Peter but, after personal acquaintance with its contents, he withdrew that permission. Zahn[1] maintains that the private reading by members of the Christian community, and not public reading at the services of the Church, is dealt with in this letter, but in this he stands alone. The *Index expurgatorius* had not been commenced in the second century, and it is impossible to think that the sanction of a bishop was either sought or required for the private reading of individuals. We have here only an instance of the diversity of custom, as regards the public reading of early writings, to which reference is made in the writings of the Fathers and in the Muratorian and other Canons. In this way the Epistle of the Roman

---

[1] L.c. p. 4 f.

THE GOSPEL ACCORDING TO PETER - A STUDY

Clement, as Eusebius[1] mentions, was publicly read in the churches; as were the Epistle of Soter to the Corinthians, the "Pastor" of Hermas,[2] the "Apocalypse of Peter,"[3] and various Gospels which did not permanently secure a place in the Canon. Eusebius, for instance, states that the Ebionites made use only of the "Gospel according to the Hebrews."[4]

Eusebius[5] mentions a certain number of works attributed to the Apostle Peter: the first Epistle, generally acknowledged as genuine, "but that which is called the second," he says, "we have not understood to be incorporated with the testament" (ἐνδιάθηκον). The other works are, the "Acts of Peter," the "Gospel according to Peter," the "Preaching of Peter," and the "Apocalypse of Peter," the last being doubtless the work of which a fragment has now been discovered in the little volume which contains the fragment of the Gospel which we are considering. Of these Eusebius says that he does not know of their being handed down as Catholic, or universally received by the Church.

The "Gospel according to Peter" is directly referred to by Origen in his Commentary on Matthew. He says: "Some say, with regard to the brethren of Jesus, from a tradition in the Gospel entitled according to Peter, or of the Book of James, that they were sons of Joseph by a former wife."[6] Although this statement does not in itself necessarily favour Docetic views, it is quite intelligible that it might be used in support of them and, therefore, might have been one of the passages which excited the suspicion of Serapion, more especially as a clear statement of this family relationship is not to be found in the canonical Gospels. The part of the Gospel referred to by Origen is not, unfortunately, contained in the fragment, and consequently cannot be verified, but it is quite in accordance with its general spirit, and at least we have here a distinct mention of the Gospel without any expression of unfa-

---

[1] H. E. iii. 16.
[2] H. E. iii. 3.
[3] Sozom. H. E. vii. 19; Canon Murat. Tregelles, p. 65.
[4] H. E. iii. 27.
[5] H. E. iii. 3.
[6] Comm. in Matt. T. x. 17: τοὺς δὲ ἀδελφοὺς Ἰησοῦ φασί τινες εἶναι, ἐκ παραδόσεωσ ὁρμώμενοι τοῦ ἐπιγεγραμμένου κατὰ Πέτρον εὐαγγελίου,)ἢ τῆσ βίβλου Ἰακώβου, υἱοὺς Ἰῳσὴφ ἐκ προτέρας γυναικὸς συνῳκηκυίας αὐτῷ πρὸ τῆς Μαρίας.

vourable opinion. What is more important still is the fact that Origen certainly made use of the Gospel, amongst others, himself.[1]

Jerome[2] likewise refers to it, after repeating the tradition that the Gospel was said to be Peter's, which Mark composed, who was his hearer and interpreter; and to the works ascribed to Peter, which Eusebius enumerates, he adds another—the "Judgment of Peter," of which little or nothing is known.

Theodoret says that the Nazarenes made use of the Gospel according to Peter.[3] Zahn and some others[4] argue against the correctness of this statement; but reasoning of this kind, based upon supposed differences of views, is not very convincing, when we consider that inferences to be drawn from peculiarities in the narrative in this Gospel are neither so distinct, nor so inevitable, as to be forced upon a simple and uncritical community, and probably that the anti-Judaistic tendency of the whole, the strongest characteristic of the composition, secured its acceptance, and diverted attention from any less marked tendencies.

A number of passages have been pointed out in the Didascalia and Apostolical Constitutions, Origen, Cyril of Jerusalem, Dionysius of Alexandria, and other ancient writers, showing the use of this Gospel according to Peter,[5] but into these later testimonies it is not necessary for us at present to go. That the work long continued to exercise considerable influence can scarcely be doubted. It is to the earlier history of the Gospel and its use in the second century that we must rather turn our attention.

A probable reference to the Gospel of Peter in Polycarp's "Epistle to the Corinthians" has been pointed out by Mr. F. C. Conybeare.[6] The writer speaks of "the testimony of the cross" (τὸ μαρτύριον τοῦ

---

[1] Cf. Murray, Expositor, January, 1893, pp. 55 ff.

[2] De Vir. illustr. i.

[3] οἱ δὲ Ναζωραῖοι Ἰουδαῖοί εἰσιν τὸν Χριστὸν τιμῶντες ὡς ἄνθρωπον δίκαιον καὶ τῷ καλουμένῳ κατὰ Πέτρον εὐαγγελίῳ κεχρημένοι. Haer. Fab. ii. 2.

[4] Zahn, Gesch. des N. T. Kanons, ii. 742 f.; Locs, l.c. pp. 14 ff. Zahn, however, admits that Theodoret's statement may at least be taken as testimony that the Gospel was in use amongst a sectarian community in Syria. Das Ev. d. Petrus, pp. 70 f.

[5] Harnack, l.c. pp. 40 ff.; Zahn, l.c. pp. 57 ff.; J. O. F. Murray, The Expositor, January 1893, pp. 55 ff.; Kunze, l.c. pp. 35 ff.; Hilgenfeld, l.c. pp. 242 ff.; Bernard, Academy, December 1892, September 30, 1893; Swete, l.c. p. xxxi.

[6] Academy, October 21, December 23, 1893.

σταυροῦ), an expression which has puzzled critics a good deal. No passage in our Gospels has hitherto explained it, but if it be referred to the answer made by the cross, in our fragment, to the question from Heaven: "Hast thou preached to them that are sleeping? And an it becomes at once intelligible. Mr. Taylor[1] suggests the question whether "the word of the cross" (ὁ λόγος τοῦ σταυροῦ) in 1 Cor. i. 18 is not also connected with the same tradition of the speaking cross and, as Mr. Conybeare points out, the context favours the idea, although he himself is not inclined to admit the interpretation. The words of Paul are worth quoting:

> For the word of the cross is to them that are perishing foolishness; but unto us which are being saved it is the power of God. 19. For it is written: "I will destroy the wisdom of the wise, and the prudence of the prudent will I reject;"

and so on. But although he cannot agree in the suggestion that Paul refers to this tradition, because, he says, "Such a view seems to me to be too bold and innovating in its character," Mr. Conybeare goes on to suggest that the incident in Peter, with this reply to the voice from heaven, may be

> one of the "three mysteries of crying" referred to by Ignatius, *ad Eph.* xix. "Ritschl and Lipsius," says Lightfoot, *ad locum* "agree that two of the three were, (1) the voice at the baptism, (2) the voice at the transfiguration. For the third ... Ritschl supposes that Ignatius used some other Gospel containing a third proclamation similar to the two others." The Peter Gospel seems here to supply just what is wanted.[2]

These suggestions are quoted here, in dealing with Polycarp, to show that the supposition that he refers to the answer of the cross in the Gospel of Peter is not without support in other early writings. When it is remembered that the doctrine of a descent into Hell has a place in the Creed of Christendom, it is not surprising that it should be dwelt on in early writings, and that a Gospel which proclaims it by a voice from Heaven, coupled with a miraculous testimony from the

---

[1] Guardian, November 29, 1893.
[2] Academy, December 23, 1893, p. 568.

cross, should be referred to. Of course it is impossible, in the absence of any explicit declaration, to establish by the passage we are discussing that the Gospel according to Peter was used by Polycarp, but there is some probability of it at least, since no other Gospel contains the episode to which the writer seems to refer.

IV

We may now consider whether Justin Martyr was acquainted with it, and here again it may be well to remind the reader that we have only a small fragment of the Gospel according to Peter to compare with the allusions to be found in writings of the Fathers. In these early works, few quotations are made with any direct mention of the source from which they were taken, and as only those parts of Patristic writings which deal with the trial, crucifixion and resurrection of Jesus can be expected to present analogies with our fragment, it will readily be seen how limited the range of testimony must naturally be. Justin Martyr is usually supposed to have died about A.D. 163-165,[1] and his first "Apology" may be dated A.D. 147, and the "Dialogue with Trypho" somewhat later. In these writings, Justin very frequently refers to facts, and to sayings of Jesus, making, indeed, some hundred and fifty quotations of this kind from certain "Memoirs of the Apostles" (ἀπομνημονεύματα τῶν ἀποστόλων), all of which differ more or less from our present canonical Gospels. He never mentions the name of any author of these Memoirs, if indeed he was acquainted with one, unless it be upon one occasion, which is of peculiar interest in connection with our fragment. The instance to which we refer is the following. Justin says: "The statement also that &c.[2] It was, of course, argued that the αὐτοῦ here does not refer to Peter but to Jesus; or that the word should be amended to αὐτῶν and applied to the Apostles; but

---

[1] The detailed statement of the case may be found in Supernatural Religion, complete ed. 1879, i. 283 ff. Hort (Journal of Philology, iii. 155 ff.) places it as early as a.d. 148.

[2] Καὶ τὸ εἰπεῖν μετωνομακέναι αὐτὸν Πέτρον ἕνα τῶν ἀποστόλων, καὶ γεγράφθαι ἐν τοῖς ἀπομνημονεύμασιν αὐτοῦ γεγενημένον καὶ τοῦτο, μετὰ τοῦ καὶ ἄλλους δύο ἀδελφούς, υἱοὺς Ζεβεδαίου ὄντας, μετωνομακέναι ὀνόματι τοῦ Βοανεργές, ὅ ἐστιν υἱοὶ βροντῆς, κ.τ.λ. Dial. cvi. The whole argument may be found in detail in Supernatural Religion, 1879, i. 416 ff.

the majority of critics naturally decided against such royal ways of removing difficulties, and were forced to admit a reference to "Memoirs of Peter." Hitherto, the apologetic explanation has been that the allusion of Justin must have been to the second Synoptic, generally referred to Mark, who was held by many of the Fathers to be the mere mouthpiece and "interpreter of Peter," and that this reference is supported by the fact that the Gospel according to Mark is the only one of the four canonical works which narrates these changes of name. This argument, however, is disposed of by the fact that our second Synoptic cannot possibly be considered the work referred to in the tradition of Papias.[1] Returning to Justin, we find that he designates the source of his quotations ten times as "Memoirs of the Apostles;" five times he calls it simply "Memoirs," and upon one occasion only explains that they were written "by his Apostles and their followers." He never speaks indefinitely of "Memoirs of Apostles," but always of the collective Apostles, except in the one instance which has been quoted above. In a single passage there occurs an expression which must be quoted. Justin says: "For the Apostles in the Memoirs composed by them, which are called Gospels," &c.[2] The ἃ καλεῖται εὐαγγέλια has very much the appearance of a gloss in the margin of some MS., which has afterwards been transferred to the text by a scribe, as scholars have before now suggested; but in any case it makes little difference in the argument.

It is obvious that the name "Memoirs" cannot with any degree of propriety be applied to our canonical Gospels; but the discovery of this fragment, which is distinctly written as a personal narrative, throws fresh light upon the subject, and the title "Memoirs of Peter," would exactly describe the form in which the Gospel is written. It may further be suggested whether it does not give us reason for conjecturing that the earlier documents, from which our Gospels were composed, were similarly personal narratives or memoirs of those who took part in early Christian development. The tradition preserved to us by Papias distinctly points in this direction:

> This also the Presbyter said: Mark having become the interpreter of Peter, wrote accurately whatever he remembered, though he did not arrange in order the things which

---

[1] See the argument, Supernatural Religion, i. 448 ff.
[2] Οἱ γὰρ ἀπόστολοι ἐν τοῖς γενομένοις ὑπ' αὐτῶν ἀπομνημονεύμασιν, ἃ καλεῖται εὐαγγέλια, κ.τ.λ. Apol. i. 66.

were either said or done by Christ. For he neither heard the Lord, nor followed him; but afterwards, as I said, accompanied Peter, who adapted his teaching to the occasion, and not as making a consecutive record of the Lord's oracles.[1]

There can be very little doubt that the first teaching of Apostles and early catechists must have taken the form of personal recollections of various episodes of Christian history and reports of discourses and parables, with an account of the circumstances under which they were delivered. This familiar and less impressive mode of tracing Christian history must gradually have been eliminated from successive forms of the story drawn up for the use of the growing Church, until, in the Gospels adopted into the Canon, it had entirely disappeared. In the fourth Gospel, a slight trace of it remains in the reference in the third person to the writer, and it is present in parts of the Apocalypse; but a more marked instance is to be found in the "Acts of the Apostles;" not so much in the prologue—which, of course, is not really part of the book—where the author distinctly speaks in the first person, as in the narrative after the call to Macedonia (xvi. 10-17), where the writer falls into the use of the first person plural (ἡμεῖς), resumes it after a break (xx. 5-15), and abandons it again, till it is recommenced in xxi. 1-18, xxvii. 1, xxviii. 16. As the author doubtless made use of written sources of information, like the writers of our Gospels, it is most probable that, in these portions of the Acts, he simply inserted portions of personal written narratives which had come into his possession. The Gospel according to Peter, which escaped the successive revisals of the canonical Gospels, probably presents the more original form of such histories. We are, of course, unable to say whether the change of names referred to by Justin was recorded in earlier portions of this Gospel which have not been recovered, but the use of the double name, "I, Simon Peter," favours the supposition that it was.

Without attaching undue importance to it, it may be well to point out—in connection with Origen's statement that, in the Gospel according to Peter, the brethren of Jesus are represented as being of a previous marriage—that the only genealogy of Jesus which is recognised by Justin is traced through the Virgin Mary, and excludes

---

[1] Eusebius, H. E. iii. 39.

Joseph.[1] She it is who is descended from Abraham, Isaac and Jacob, and from the house of David. The genealogy of Jesus in the canonical Gospels, on the contrary, is traced solely through Joseph, who alone is stated to be of the lineage of David. The genealogies of the first and third Synoptics, though differing in several important particulars, at least agree in excluding Mary. In the third Gospel Joseph goes to Judæa "unto the city of David, which is called Bethlehem, because he was of the house and lineage of David."[2] Justin simply states that Joseph went "to Bethlehem ... for his descent was from the tribe of Judah, which inhabited that region."[3] Justin could not, therefore, derive his genealogies from the canonical Gospels; and his Memoirs, from which he learns the Davidic descent through Mary only, to which he refers no less than eleven times, differed from them distinctly on this point. The Gospel according to Peter, which, according to Origen, contained a statement which separated Jesus from his brethren in the flesh, in all probability must have traced the Davidic descent through Mary. The Gospel of James, commonly called the "Protevangelium," to a form of which, at least, Origen refers at the same time as the Gospel according to Peter, states that Mary was of the lineage of David.[4] There are other peculiarities in Justin's account of the angelic announcement to Mary differing distinctly from our canonical Gospels,[5] regarding some of which Tischendorf was of opinion that they were derived from the "Protevangelium;" but there are reasons for supposing that they may have come from a still older work, and if it should seem that Justin made use of the Gospel according to Peter, these may also have been taken from it. In the absence of the rest of the Gospel, however, all this must be left for the present as mere conjecture.

The fragment begins with a broken sentence presenting an obviously different story of the trial of Jesus from that of the canonical Gospels. "... but of the Jews no man (τῶν δὲ Ἰουδαίων οὐδεὶς) washed his hands, neither Herod (οὐδὲ Ἡρῴδης) nor any of his judges.... Pilate rose up (ἀνέστη Πειλᾶτος). And then Herod the King (Ἡρῴδης ὁ βασιλεὺς) commandeth the Lord to be taken," &c. Justin in one place[6]

---

[1] Dial. xxiii., xliii. twice, xlv. thrice, c. twice, ci., cxx.; Apol. i. 32 cf. Supernatural Religion, i. 300 f.
[2] Luke ii. 4.
[3] Dial. lxxviii.
[4] Protevang. Jacobi, x.; Tischendorf, Evang. Apocr. p. 19 f.
[5] Cf. Supernatural Religion, i. 304 f.
[6] Apol. i. 40.

refers to this trial as foretold by the prophetic spirit, and speaks of what was done against the Christ "by Herod the King of the Jews, and the Jews themselves, and Pilate who was your governor among them, and his soldiers" (Ἡρώδου τοῦ βασιλέως Ἰουδαίων καὶ αὐτῶν Ἰουδαίων καὶ Πιλάτου τοῦ ὑμετέρου παρ᾽ αὐτοῖς γενομένου ἐπιτρόπου σὺν τοῖς αὐτοῦ στρατιώταις). This combination agrees with the representation of the fragment, and of course differs from that of the Gospels. In Dial. ciii. Justin repeats this to some extent, adding that he sent Jesus "bound" (δεδεμένον). This representation does not exist in Luke, but neither is it found in what we have of the Gospel according to Peter, though it may have occurred in the commencement of the scene to which we are so abruptly introduced.

Justin says in another place: "For as the prophet said, worrying him[1] (διασύροντες αὐτὸν), they set him (ἐκάθισαν) upon a judgment seat (ἐπὶ βήματος), and said, 'Judge for us' (Κρῖνον ἡμῖν)."[2] In the Gospel according to Peter we have: "They said, 'Let us drag along (σύρωμεν) the Son of God' ... and they set Him (ἐκάθισαν αὐτὸν) upon a seat of judgment (καθέδραν κρίσεως), saying, 'Judge justly (Δικαίως κρῖνε), King of Israel.'"[3] This representation is different from any in our Gospels, and it has some singular points of agreement with our fragment. It has frequently been suggested that Justin, in this passage, makes use of our canonical Gospels with a combination of the Septuagint version of Isaiah lviii. 2, 3, and that this is supported by the expression "as said the prophet." This does not sufficiently explain the passage, however. The Septuagint version of the part of Isaiah lviii. 2 referred to reads: αἰτοῦσίν με νῦν κρίσιν δικαίαν—"They ask me now for just judgment."

---

[1] The word used in the Gospel is σύρω, to drag along, but Justin's word is merely the same verb with the addition of δια, διασύρω, to worry, or harass with abuse. Although the English equivalent is thus changed, and conceals the analogy of the two passages, the addition of δια, strictly considered, cannot so change the meaning of σύρω, but rather should imply a continuance of the same action. This is also Dr. Martineau's view.
[2] Καὶ γάρ, ὡς εἶπεν ὁ προφήτης, διασύροντες αὐτὸν ἐκάθισαν ἐπὶ βήματος καὶ εἶπον; Κρῖνον ἡμῖν. Apol. i. 35.
[3] Ἔλεγον, Σύρωμεν τὸν υἱὸν τοῦ θεοῦ, ... καὶ ἐκάθισαν αὐτὸν ἐπὶ καθέδραν κρίσεως, λέγοντες Δικαίως κρῖνε, βασιλεῦ τοῦ Ἰσραήλ. Evang. Petri, 6. Hilgenfeld says regarding this, "Was fehlt noch zu dem Beweise, dass Justinus, wie ich schon 1850 ausgeführt habe, das Petrus-Evg. benutzt hat?" Zeitschr. 1893, ii. 251.

Justin drops the "just," which stands both in Isaiah and in the fragment, and therefore the omission may be considered equally unfavourable to both writings as the source. In other respects Justin is nearer the Gospel than the prophet. On the other hand, the proposed use of καθίζειν as a transitive verb would make the fourth Gospel, xix. 13, read: "Pilate ... brought Jesus out, and set him (ἐκάθισεν) upon a judgment seat (ἐπὶ βήματος)," &c.; and it is pretended that Justin may have taken it in this sense, and that by the use of the word βῆμα he betrays his indebtedness to the fourth Gospel. This use of the verb, however, can scarcely be maintained. It is impossible to suppose that Pilate himself set Jesus on a judgment seat, as this transitive use of ἐκάθισε would require us to receive; and we must, more especially in the absence of a distinct object, receive it as the Revisers of the New Testament have rightly done—intransitively: "He brought Jesus out and sat down."[1] In Justin it is not Pilate but the Jews who drag Jesus along, and put him on a judgment seat, and the use of the ordinary βῆμα for the expression of the fragment, "a seat of judgment" (καθέδρα κρίσεως), is not surprising in a writer like Justin, who is not directly quoting, but merely giving the sense of a passage. However this may be, the whole representation is peculiar, and the conclusion of many critics is that it proves Justin's dependence on the Gospel according to Peter.[2]

Justin, speaking of an incident of the crucifixion, says: "And those who were crucifying him parted his garments (ἐμερίσαν τὰ ἱμάτια αὐτοῦ) amongst themselves, casting lots (λαχμὸν βάλλοντες), each taking what pleased him, according to the cast of the lot (τοῦ κλήρου)."[3] In the Gospel according to Peter it is said: "And they laid the clothes (τὰ ἐνδύματα) before him, and distributed them (διεμερίσαντο), and cast lots (λαχμὸν ἔβαλον) for them." The use of the peculiar expression λαχμὸν βάλλειν both by the Gospel and Justin is undoubtedly striking, especially, as Dr. Swete properly points out,

---

[1] This passage has been discussed at some length by Dr. Martineau (Nineteenth Century, October 1893, pp. 647 ff.), in controversy with Mr. T. Rendel Harris (Contemp. Rev. August 1893, pp. 234 ff.), as it has frequently before been. Dr. Martineau seems to be in the right upon all points in connection with it.
[2] Hilgenfeld, Zeitschr. wiss. Theol. 1893, pp. 249 ff.; cf. Lods, De Evang. sec. Petrum, pp. 12 f.; Harnack, l.c. pp. 38 f., 63 f.; Martineau, Nineteenth Century, October 1893, pp. 650 f.; cf. Swete, l.c. p. xxxiv.
[3] Dial. xcvii.

as its use in this connection is limited, so far as we know, to the Gospel of Peter, Justin, and Cyril.[1] It is rendered more important by the fact that, both in the Gospel and Justin, the casting of lots is applied to all the clothes, in contradistinction to the fourth Gospel, in which it is connected with the coat alone, and that neither has any mention of the Johannine peculiarity that the coat was without seam.

Justin says that after he was crucified all the "acquaintances of Jesus forsook him" (οἱ γνώριμοι αὐτοῦ πάντες ἀπέστησαν);[2] and in another place that after his crucifixion "the disciples who were with him dispersed (διεσκεδάσθησαν) until he rose from the dead."[3] This representation is found in the first Synoptic only, but agrees still better with vv. 26, 27, and 59 of our fragment. Elsewhere, Justin, in agreement with the fragment, speaks of Herod, "King of the Jews."[4] Further, he says, more than once, that the Jews sent persons throughout the world to spread calumnies against Christians, amongst which was the story that "his disciples stole him by night from the grave (κλέψαντες αὐτὸν ἀπὸ τοῦ μνήματος νυκτός) where he had been laid when he was unloosed from the cross (ἀφηλωθεὶς ἀπὸ τοῦ σταυροῦ)."[5] The first Synoptic alone has the expression regarding the disciples stealing the body, using the same verb, but our fragment alone uses μνῆμα for the tomb and offers a parallel for the unloosing from the cross in v. 21. We must, however, point out that the statement regarding these emissaries from the Jews is not found at all in our canonical Gospels.[6]

It will be remembered that, in the fragment, the only cry from the cross is: " 'Power, my Power, thou hast forsaken me,' and having spoken, he was taken up." This is one of the most striking variations from the canonical Gospels. It is also claimed as, perhaps, the most Docetic representation of the fragment, for the idea was that one Christ suf-

---

[1] Swete, l.c. p. xxxiv. Mr. Rendel Harris says: "I regard it as certain that the reading λαχμὸς implies connection between Justin and Peter, either directly or through a third source accessible to both." Contemp. Rev. August 1893, p. 231.
[2] Apol. i. 50.
[3] Μετὰ γὰρ τὸ σταυρωθῆναι αὐτὸν οἱ σὺν αὐτῷ ὄντες μαθηταὶ αὐτοῦ διεσκεδάσθησαν, μέχρις ὅτου ἀνέστη ἐκ νεκρῶν. Dial. liii.; cf. Supernatural Religion, i. 330 ff.
[4] Dial. ciii.
[5] Dial. cviii.
[6] Cf. Supernatural Religion, i. 339.

fered and rose, and another flew up and was free from suffering.¹ It was believed by the Docetae that the Holy Spirit only descended upon the human Jesus, at his baptism, in the shape of a dove. Now one of the statements of Justin from his Memoirs, which has no existence in our Gospels, was that, when Jesus went to be baptized by John,

> As Jesus went down to the water, a fire was also kindled in the Jordan; and when he came up from the water, the Holy Spirit like a dove fell upon him, as the Apostles of this very Christ of ours wrote ... and at the same time a voice came from the heavens ... "Thou art my son, this day have I begotten thee."

Justin repeats his version of the words a second time in the same chapter.² The Synoptics make the voice say: "Thou art my beloved son; in thee I am well pleased," instead of the words from Psalm ii. 7. Now, although we have not the part of the Gospel according to Peter in which the earlier history of Jesus is related, it is not improbable that Justin's version, agreeing as it does with the later episode in the fragment and with the criticism of Serapion, was taken from this Gospel.

We refer to this point, however, for the purpose of introducing another statement of Justin, which may be worth a little consideration in connection with our fragment. One of the passages which are supposed most clearly to betray Docetic tendencies is the expression, *v.* 10, that when the Lord was crucified "he kept silence, as feeling no pain" (ὡς μηδὲν πόνον ἔχων). It is evident that these words may either be taken as simply representing the fortitude with which suffering was endured, or understood to support the view that no pain was really suffered, though this is by no means actually said. Now, Justin, in another chapter of his "Dialogue with Trypho," in which he again refers to the baptism and quotes the words of the voice as above, cites the agony in the garden to prove that "the Father wished his Son really to suffer (πάθεσιν ἀληθῶς) for our sakes, and that we may not say that he, being the Son of God, did not feel what was happening and being inflicted upon him."³ He goes on to say that the silence of Jesus, who returned no answer to any one in the presence of Pilate, was foretold in a pas-

---

¹ Cf. Irenaeus, Adv. Haer. iii. 12.
² Dial. lxxxviii.; cf Supernatural Religion, i. 316 ff.
³ Dial. ciii. There is another passage in Dial. cxxv., which may be compared: Ἀλλ' ἐπεὶ καὶ ναρκᾶν ἔμελλε, τουτέστιν ἐν πόνῳ καὶ ἐν ἀντιλήψει τοῦ πάθους, ὅτε σταυροῦσθαι ἔμελλεν, ὁ Χριστὸς ὁ ἡμέτερος, κ.τ.λ.

sage which he quotes. All this, in connection with representations not found in our canonical Gospels, may form another link with the Gospel according to Peter, as one of his Memoirs. Justin evidently made use of passages like the words at the baptism, to which he did not attach any Docetic interpretation, and it is quite natural that he should argue against the view that Jesus did not really suffer pain, and yet read quite naturally the words we are discussing, without directly referring to them. It was the practice of these early sects to twist passages, not originally intended to favour them, into evidence for their views, and an ordinary Christian might possess a Gospel containing them, in complete unconsciousness that it tended in the slightest degree to encourage heresy.[1] It is evident from several quotations which we have made, and from others which might be adduced, that Justin was an example of this very thing.

A number of small points might be added to these, but we do not go into them here. A majority of the critics who have discussed the question are of opinion that Justin made use of the Gospel according to Peter,[2] and even apologists, (who as a body seem agreed to depreciate the fragment), whilst refusing to admit its use by Justin, are not generally very decided in their denial nor, as we shall presently see, inclined to assign it a date which excludes the possibility. The case may be summed up in a few words. Justin undeniably quotes from his "Memoirs of the Apostles" facts and passages which are not found in our Gospels; he distinctly refers to statements as contained in certain "Memoirs of Peter;"[3] some of these variations from the canonical Gospels have linguistic and other parallels in our fragment, short as it is, and there is reason to suppose that others would have been found in it had the entire Gospel been extant for comparison; the style of the fragment precisely tallies with the peculiar name of "Memoirs," being a personal narrative in the first person singular; and finally, there is nothing in its composition or character which necessitates the assign-

---

[1] Mr. Murray, for instance, quotes a passage from Origen, using a similar expression to that in our fragment, that Jesus was silent as suffering no pain, with a comment which shows that he did not suspect a Docetic interpretation. Expositor, January 1893, pp. 55 f.
[2] Harnack, l.c. pp. 38 ff.; Lods, l.c. pp. 12 f.; Hilgenfeld, Zeitschr. wiss. Theol. 1893, pp. 221, 241, 267; van Manen, Theol. Tijdschrift, 1893, pp. 385 f., 551 ff.; Martineau, Nineteenth Century, June 1893, p. 910, October, pp. 643 f.; cf. J. Rendel Harris, Contemp. Rev. August 1893, pp. 227 ff., 231.
[3] Cf. Swete, l.c. pp. xxxiii. ff.

ment of such a date to the fragment as would exclude the possibility, or probability, of its use by Justin.

V

We may now consider whether there is any indication of the use of this Gospel according to Peter by the author of the "Epistle of Barnabas." The Epistle is variously dated between A.D. 70-132, apologists leaning towards the earlier date. The shortness of the fragment recovered, of course, diminishes greatly the probability of finding any trace of its use in so comparatively brief a work as this Epistle, but some indications may be pointed out. The fragment states that, being anxious lest the sun should set whilst he was still living and the law regarding one put to death be transgressed, "one of them said: 'Give him to drink gall with vinegar,' and having mixed they gave him to drink (Ποτίσατε αὐτὸν χολὴν μετὰ ὄξους; καὶ κεράσαντες ἐπότισαν).[1] ... Over all these things, however, we were fasting (ἐπὶ δὲ τούτοις πᾶσιν ἐνηστεύομεν)[2] ... the whole people ... beat their breasts (ὁ λαὸς ἅπας ... κόπτεται τὰ στήθη)."[3] This representation not only differs from the canonical Gospels in "gall with vinegar" being given to drink, but in the view that it was not given to relieve thirst, but as a potion to hasten death,[4] and there follow various statements regarding fasting and mourning. Now in Barnabas precisely the same representation is made. The Epistle says:

> But also when crucified, he had vinegar and gall given him to drink (ἀλλὰ καὶ σταυρωθεὶς ἐποτίζετο ὄξει καὶ χολῇ). Hear how, on this matter, the priests of the temple have revealed. Seeing that there is a commandment in

---

[1] Verse 16.
[2] Verse 27.
[3] Verse 28.
[4] Mr. Murray points out that Origen likewise regards the "gall" as baleful, as he likewise represents with our fragment the breaking of the limbs as an act of mercy (Expositor, January 1892, pp. 56 f.). Hilgenfeld is quite convinced that the Epistle derives the passage from Peter (Zeitschr. 1893, ii. 255 f.).

Scripture: "Whosoever shall not observe the fast shall surely die," the Lord commanded, because he was in his own person about to offer the vessel of his spirit for our sins ... "Since ye are to give me, who am to offer my flesh for the sins of my new people, gall with vinegar to drink, eat ye alone, while the people fasts and wails.... (μέλλετε ποτίζειν χολὴν μετὰ ὄξους ... τοῦ λαοῦ νηστεύοντος καὶ κοπτομένου)."[1]

There are three suppositions as the possible explanation of this similarity: (1) that the author of the Epistle derived his statement from the Gospel; (2) that the author of the Gospel derived it from the Epistle, or (3) that both drew it from a third and earlier source. Assigning as we do the later date to the Epistle of Barnabas, the first of these hypotheses seems to us the most natural and the correct one, although, of course, it is impossible to prove that both did not derive it from another source. The second explanation we must definitely reject, both because we consider that priority of date lies with the fragment, and because it does not seem probable that the representation originated in the Epistle. To admit this would be to suppose that the author first fabricated the statement that Jesus was given gall and vinegar to hasten death, and then proceeded immediately to explain the circumstance by means of the elaborate gnosis with which the Epistle is filled. It is quite undeniable that the whole narrative of the Gospels grew out of the suggestions of supposed prophetic passages in the Old Testament, but the author of the Epistle introduces the statement upon which his explanation is based, with a simplicity which seems to exclude the idea of its being his own fabrication: "But also, when crucified, he had

---

[1] The whole passage may be given here, as arguments are founded upon it: Ἀλλὰ καὶ σταυρωθεὶς ἐποτίζετο ὄξει καὶ χολῇ, ἀκούσατε πῶς περὶ τούτου πεφανέρωκαν οἱ ἱερεῖς τοῦ ναοῦ. γεγραμμένης ἐντολῆς; Ὃς ἂν μὴ νηστεύσῃ τὴν νηστείαν, θανάτῳ ἐξολεθρευθήσεται, ἐνετείλατο κύριος, ἐπεὶ καὶ αὐτὸς ὑπὲρ τῶν ἡμετέρων ἁμαρτιῶν ἔμελλεν τὸ σκεῦος τοῦ πνεύματος προσφέρειν θυσίαν, ἵνα καὶ ὁ τύπος ὁ γενόμενος ἐπὶ Ἰσαὰκ τοῦ προσενεχθέντος ἐπὶ τὸ θυσιαστήριον τελεσθῇ. τί οὖν λέγει ἐν τῷ προφήτῃ; Καὶ φαγέτωσαν ἐκ τοῦ τράγου τοῦ προσφερομένου τῇ νηστείᾳ ὑπὲρ πασῶν τῶν ἁμαρτιῶν. προσέχετε ἀκριβῶς καὶ φαγέτωσαν οἱ ἱερεῖς μόνοι πάντες τὸ ἔντερον ἄπλυτον μετὰ ὄξους. πρὸς τί; ἐπειδὴ ἐμέ, ὑπὲρ ἁμαρτιῶν μέλλοντα τοῦ λαοῦ μου τοῦ καινοῦ προσφέρειν τὴν σάρκα μου, μέλλετε ποτίζειν χολὴν μετὰ ὄξους, φάγετε ὑμεῖς μόνοι, τοῦ λαοῦ νηστεύοντος καὶ κοπτομένου ἐπὶ σάκκου καὶ σποδοῦ, κ.τ.λ. (vii. 3-5).

vinegar and gall given him to drink." There is not the ring here of a statement advanced for the first time, but if we suppose that the author had read it in such a work as the Gospel according to Peter, it would be quite natural. It is not to be understood that we doubt that the account in the fragment, or in our Gospels, was suggested by passages in the Old Testament, but simply that we do not believe that the representation originated in this Epistle, in immediate connection with the elaborate explanation given. A tradition, gradually influenced by such prophetic and other considerations, may have been embodied by the author of the Gospel in his narrative, and then the writer of the Epistle may have seized upon it and enlarged upon its typical signification, but it is not probable that he originated it himself.

VI

We do not propose to enter here upon an inquiry whether there is any evidence within our short fragment that the Gospel according to Peter was used by other early writers. The slight traces which alone we could hope to find, and which several able critics do find,[1] cannot be decisive of anything, and whilst there may be a faint literary interest in pursuing such researches, they need not detain us here. A short consideration may, however, be given to Tatian. Some critics, impressed apparently with the idea that no early Gospels can possibly be otherwise than dependent on our canonical works, yet having to explain the continuous divergence from the canonical narratives, advance the suggestion, that the writer of the Gospel according to Peter may have derived all the points which the fragment contains, in common with one or more of the canonical Gospels, from a Harmony of our Gospels. Now, the only Harmony of the second century which, they think, has survived is the so-called "Diatessaron" of Tatian. Of course, they find that the "Diatessaron" "might have furnished the writer of the fragment with all the incidents which he shares with any of the Four Gospels." Dr. Swete continues: "The order in Peter is not always the same as it seems to have been [2]

Not content with the conclusion that the Gospels, narrating the very same history, might have furnished the incidents which they have in common, Dr. Swete proceeds "to compare the 'Diatessaron' with our fragment, with the view of ascertaining whether Tatian would have provided the Petrine writer with the words which he seems to have adopted from the Four Gospels."[3]

---

[1] Harnack finds it almost certain that the Didache made use of this Gospel (l.c. pp. 58 f., 80); so also van Manen (Theol. Tijdschr. September 1893, pp. 353 f.) and others.
[2] L.c. pp. xxi f.
[3] L.c. pp. xxii f.

THE GOSPEL ACCORDING TO PETER - A STUDY

This is not the place to discuss again the identity of the supposed "Diatessaron," but it will be sufficient to point out that we have it only in an Arabic version, published and translated by Ciasca, and a translation of the supposed Armenian version of the Commentary upon it, ascribed to Ephraem, which again Moesinger, who edited the Latin version published in 1876, declares to be itself translated from the Syriac. In these varied transformations of the text, anything like verbal accuracy must be regarded as totally lost. The object in making the versions was not, of course, critical fidelity, and variations from canonical texts would, no doubt, often or always be regarded as accidental and to be corrected. Such translations can never, in textual criticism, be accepted as sufficient representations of the original. The process, however, by which Dr. Swete proceeds to ascertain whether the author of the fragment derives from Tatian the *words* which he seems to have adopted from the Four Gospels, is to place side by side with the Petrine narrative, in certain crucial passages, the corresponding portions of the "Diatessaron," approximately represented in Greek, and he selects the accounts of the mockery, the three hours, the burial, and the visit of the women to the tomb. He thus explains his system: "The plan adopted has been to substitute for Ciasca's translation of the Arabic Tatian the corresponding portions of the canonical Gospels. The text has been determined by a comparison of Ciasca's Latin with Moesinger's *Evangelii Concordantis Expositio, and the Curetonian Syriac of Luke xxiii., xxiv. It claims, of course, only to be an approximate and provisional representation of the text of the original work.*"[1]
However impartial Dr. Swete may have tried to be—and without doubt he did endeavour to be so—such a test is vitiated and rendered useless by the antecedent manipulation of the texts. The result at which he arrives is: "This comparison does not justify the conclusion that the writer of our fragment was limited to the use of the 'Diatessaron' "—the exact contents of which, in its original shape, be it noted, Dr. Swete, a few lines further on, admits that we do not know, "so that it would be unsafe to draw any negative inference" from certain exceptions.

On the whole we may perhaps claim to have established a strong presumption that the Petrine writer employed a Harmony which, in its general selection of extracts, and in some of its minuter arrangements, very

---

[1] L.c. p. xxii, n. 1.

nearly resembled the Harmony of Tatian. This is not equivalent to saying that he used Tatian, because there is some reason to think that there may have been a Harmony or Harmonies earlier than Tatian.... Thus the relation of the Petrine writer to Tatian remains for the present an open question; but enough has been said to render such a relation probable, if further inquiries should lead us to place the Gospel of Peter after the publication of the "Diatessaron."[1]

It must frankly be asserted that the whole of this comparison with Tatian, and the views so curiously expressed regarding the result, are the outcome of a preconceived idea that the Petrine author compiled his Gospel mainly from the canonical. The divergencies being so great, however, and the actual contradictions so strong, it becomes necessary to account for them in some way, and the theory of the use of a Harmony is advanced to see whether it may not overcome some of the difficulties. It would have been more to the purpose to have inquired whether the so-called "Diatessaron" did not make use of the Gospel according to Peter, amongst others.

In connection with this it may be well to refer to some remarkable observations of Professor J. Rendel Harris regarding the relation of the Gospel according to Peter and Tatian's Harmony. When the fragment was first discovered, he was naturally struck by its great importance. "The Gospel of Peter, even in the imperfect form in which it has come down to us, is the breaking of a new seal, the opening of a fresh door," he said, "to those who are engaged in the problems presented by Biblical and Patristic criticism,"[2] and he very rightly proceeded to try to find out "whether Peter has used Tatian, or Tatian Peter, or whether both of them are working upon common sources."[3] He first refers to "a curious addition to the story of the Crucifixion, which can be shown, with a very high probability, to have once stood in the Harmony of Tatian." The most interesting and instructive part of the reference is that Mr. Harris had made and published, some years before the discovery of the fragment before us, certain notes on the Harmony of Tatian, in which he had employed "the method of combination of passages in

---

[1] L.c. p. xxiv.
[2] A Popular Account of the newly recovered Gospel of Peter, 1893, pp. v, f.
[3] Ib. p. 75.

THE GOSPEL ACCORDING TO PETER - A STUDY

different writers who were known to have used the Harmony, or different texts which were suspected of having borrowed

> "They beat their breasts and said, Woe unto us, for the things which are done to-day for our sins; for the desolation of Jerusalem hath drawn nigh."[1]

It is unnecessary here to quote the way Mr. Harris arrived at this passage, which he frankly states, but at once go on to compare it with our fragment. He sums up:

> Now the reader will be interested to see that the missing sentence which I restored to Tatian's text has turned up in the Gospel of Peter, for we read that: "The Jews and the elders and the priests, when they saw what an evil deed they had done to themselves, began to beat their breasts and to say, Woe to our sins, for the judgment and the end of Jerusalem is at hand." Did the false Peter take this from Tatian, or was it the other way? or did both of them use some uncanonical writing or tradition?[2]

"There is nothing in what follows in the Arabic Harmony," Mr. Harris points out, "which suggests an allusion to the desolation of the city, or an imprecation upon, or lamentation over, themselves."[3]

Very few will feel any doubt that this is taken from our Gospel according to Peter, or possibly—for of course there is no absolute proof—from the tradition which the writer of that Gospel also used, and not by the writer from the Harmony; and it may be suggested that the omission of this and similar passages from versions of the Harmo-

---

[1] Ib. p. 76. It should be stated that the Syriac version of Cureton to Luke xxiii. 48 gives nearly this sentence, and that the old Latin Codex of St. Germain reads: "dicentes: Vae nobis, quae facta sunt hodie propter peccata nostra; appropinquavit enim desolatio Hierusalem." Mr. Harris of course refers to these passages. Harnack considers that this passage is derived from our Gospel according to Peter (l.c. p. 57).

[2] L.c. p. 81. It may be well to give the passage now in Moesinger's work: "'Vae fuit, vae fuit nobis, Filius Dei erat hic.' Quum autem eis sol naturalis defecisset, tunc per istas tenebras eis lucidum fiebat, excidium urbis suae advenisse: 'venerunt, ait, judicia dirutionis Jerosolymorum.' Quia itaque haec urbs non recepit eum qui eam aedificaverat, restabat ei ut ruinam suam videret." Evang. Concord. Expositio, 1876, pp. 245 f.

[3] L.c. p. 78.

ny may have been influenced by the fact that, not forming part of our Gospels, and not agreeing with the preconceived theory of a Harmony of our four Gospels, such passages were excluded as interpolations.

Another instance given by Mr. Harris is the statement in the fragment: "Then the sun shone out, and it was found to be the ninth hour," which he compares with the language of "Tatian's" commentator: "Three hours the sun was darkened, and afterwards it shone out again."[1] And further:

> Another case of parallelism is in the speech of the angel to Mary: *"He is not here, for he is risen, and has gone away to the place from whence he was sent."* At first sight this looks like a wilful expansion on the part of the writer of the Gospel; but on a reference to the Persian father Aphrahat, who is more than suspected of having used the text of Tatian, we find the words, "And the angels said to Mary, He is risen, and gone away to him that sent him," which is very nearly in coincidence with the text of the false Peter.[2]

Neither of these passages is found in the actual text of "Tatian." Finally, we may quote the other instance pointed out by Mr. Harris:

> The Docetic quotation from the Psalm "My Power, my Power, hast thou forsaken me?" is peculiar in this respect, that the second possessive pronoun is wanting, so that we ought to translate it "Power, my Power ..." Now, it is curious that Tatian's text had a similar peculiarity, for Ephrem gives it as "God, my God," and the Arabic Harmony as *Yaiil, Yaiili*, where the added suffix belongs to the possessive pronoun. This is a remarkable coincidence, and makes one suspect that Tatian had "Power, my Power" in his text, and that it has been corrected away. And it is significant that Ephrem in commenting on the passage, says: "The divinity did not so far depart from the humanity as to be cut off from it, but only as regards the *power of the divinity, which was hidden both from the Slain and the*

---

[1] L.c. pp. 81 f.
[2] L.c. pp. 83 f. Cf. Zahn, l.c. p. 65. Zahn considers it in the highest degree improbable that this was taken by Tatian from Peter, but the improbability is by no means made out.

slayers." This looks very suspicious that Ephrem found something in his text of Tatian differing from the words "God, my God."[1]

Mr. Harris reserves his final judgment on this relation between Tatian and the Gospel according to Peter; but as in a later article[2] he is not unwilling to allow the date of A.D. 130 to be assigned to the fragment, it is scarcely to be decided as Peter quoting Tatian. Mr. Harris throughout these passages, however, states the case in a most impartial manner, and the reader must form his own opinion.

We may, before leaving "Tatian," point out another instance of agreement to which Mr. Harris does not allude. In the Commentary there is the following passage: "*Et dederunt ei bibere acetum et fel. Acetum ei porrexerunt, pro felle autem magna ejus miseratio amaritudinem gentium dulcem fecit.*"[3] It will be remembered that this agrees with the representation of the fragment that they gave Jesus "vinegar and gall" to drink.

All these instances may, indeed, throw a new light upon the *Diapente* in the text of Victor, which has so exercised apologists, and lead to the opinion that Tatian's Harmony was not composed out of four Gospels, but out of five. If it be agreed, as it is by a majority of critics, that Justin made use of the Gospel of Peter, the probability that his pupil Tatian likewise possessed the same work, and used it for his Harmony, is immensely increased.

---

[1] L.c. pp. 82 f.
[2] Contemp. Rev. August 1893, p. 236.
[3] Ev. Concor. Expos. p. 245.

VII

We shall not attempt to fix any even approximate date to the Gospel according to Peter, although we shall presently have to consider its relation to our canonical Gospels in a way which will at least assign it a position in time relative to them. Harnack, in the preface to the second edition of his article on the fragment, suspends his judgment on its relation to our Gospels, and will not even undertake a sufficient examination of this important question, so long as there remains a hope of still recovering more of the Gospel. It is devoutly to be hoped that the Cemetery of Akhmîm may still give us more of this and other important early works; but there is no reason why we should not, even now, endeavour to derive what information we can from this instalment, and the worst—or the best—which can happen is that future acquisitions may enable us to correct the errors—or confirm the conclusions—of the present. So long as we confine ourselves to the legitimate inferences to be drawn from the actual fragment before us, we cannot go far wrong.

It is frequently possible to assign well-defined limits within which early works, whose authors are unknown, must have been composed, when a more precise date cannot with certainty be fixed. Direct references to the writing, or its use, by writers the period of whose literary work is known, may enable us to affirm that it was written at least before their time; and sometimes certain allusions or quotations in the work itself may, on the other hand, show that it must have been composed after a certain date; and thus limits, more or less narrow, become certain, within which its production must lie. The Gospel according to Peter, as we might expect, contains none of the allusions or quotations to which we refer, and we are therefore reduced to the one indication of age—reference to, or the use of it by, early writers, leaving the approximate date to which it may be set back wholly to conjecture. As we have already remarked above, the question whether it is dependent on, or independent of, our canonical Gospels has yet to be considered; but there is too much difference of opinion regarding the date of these Gospels themselves to render this more than a relative indication. So far, the opinions of critics assign the Gospel according to Peter to dates ranging from a period antecedent to our Gospels, in their present form, to about the middle of the second century.[1]

The indications of style and phraseology given by the fragment have of course to be taken into account, and it may be well, before proceeding further, to examine certain peculiarities which have been pointed out by writers who assert that the composition is decidedly later than our canonical Gospels.[2] The writer never speaks of "Jesus" simply, but always as "the Lord" (ὁ κύριος). He likewise refers to him as the "Saviour" (σωτήρ) in one place, and several times as "a Son of God" (υἱὸς τοῦ θεοῦ). Now, with regard to these expressions, they are in constant use throughout the New Testament writings, in the Gospels themselves, as well as in the Epistles of Paul and the Epistles popularly ascribed to him. For instance, ὁ κύριος: Matt. xxi. 3, xxviii. 6;[3] Mark xvi. 19;[4] Luke vii. 13, x. 1, xi. 39, xii. 42, xiii. 15, xvii. 5, 6, xviii. 6, xix. 8, 31, 34, xxii. 61, xxiv. 3, 34; John vi. 23, xi. 2, xiii. 13, 14, xx. 2, 13, 18, 20, 28, xxi. 7, 12. It is unnecessary to point out passages in the Acts and Epistles, for "the Lord," "the Lord Jesus," or "the Lord Jesus Christ," is everywhere used, and indeed no other form, it may be said, is adopted. "A Son of God" (υἱὸς τοῦ θεοῦ) is constantly used in the Gospels and Acts. A few instances may be given: Matt. viii. 29, xiv. 33, xvi. 16, xxvi. 63, xxvii. 40, 43, 54; Mark i. 1, iii. 11, v. 7, xv. 39; Luke i. 35, ix. 41, viii. 28, xxii. 70; John i. 34, 49, v. 25, x. 36, xi. 4, 27, xix. 7, xx. 31; Acts ix. 20. Of course, in the Epistles the

---

[1] Lods (before a.d. 150), Ev. sec. Petrum, 1893, pp. 26 f.; Robinson (before a.d. 160), The Gospel according to Peter, &c., 1892, p. 32; Harnack (beginning of second century), l.c. p. 80; Zahn (a.d. 140-145), Das Ev. des Petrus, 1893, p. 75; Kunze (about a.d. 170), Das neu aufgefund. Bruchstück des sogen. Petrusev. 1893, p. 47; Hilgenfeld (end of first century), Zeitschr. 1893, pp. 266 f.; Swete (a.d. 150-165), The Akhmîm Fragment, 1893, p. xlv; von Schubert (soon after middle of second century), Die Comp. des Pseudopetr. Ev. Fragments, 1893, p. 195; W. C. van Manen (older, rather than later, than our Gospels), Theol. Tijdschr. 5de Stuk, 1893, pp. 565 ff.; Martineau (a.d. 130), Nineteenth Century, June 1893, p. 925, September, p. 633; J. Rendel Harris (no objection to a.d. 130), Contemp. Rev. August 1893, p. 236.
[2] Zahn, l.c. pp. 18 ff.; Swete, l.c. pp. xliii, f.
[3] Zahn considers ὁ κύριος inauthentic in this place, but it stands in A C D, and many other codices, and it is adopted by the Revisers of the N. T.
[4] Although this is not part of the Gospel, it is very ancient.

expression is of frequent occurrence, as for instance, Rom. i. 4, 9, v. 10; 1 Cor. i. 9; 2 Cor. i. 19; Gal. ii. 20, and elsewhere. It is not necessary to show that "Saviour" is used, but the following may be pointed out: Luke ii. 11; John iv. 42; Acts v. 31, xiii. 23; and it more frequently occurs in the Epistles. All of these expressions are commonly employed in early Christian literature, such as the "Didache," Ignatian Epistles, Clement of Rome, Polycarp, "Pastor" of Hermas, and the "Apology" of Aristides.

The principal phrase upon which weight is laid by those who assign to the Gospel according to Peter, from this fragment, a later date than our canonical works, is the use of ἡ κυριακή without ἡμέρα to designate "the Lord's day"—Sunday; Dr. Swete calls it "the most decisive indication of the relatively late composition of our fragment."[1] After giving some instances of a similar expression, he states the case as follows:

> The name was therefore familiar amongst Eastern Greek-speaking Christians from the end of the first century. But Peter not only uses it freely, but seems to be unconscious that he is guilty of an anachronism when he imports this exclusively Christian term into the Gospel history. Ἡ κυριακή has so completely supplanted Ἡ μία τῶν σαββάτων, that it is twice used to describe the first Easter Day, in a document which usually manifests precision in such matters.[2]

It is not quite clear what Dr. Swete means when he says that Peter "uses it freely," but it would indeed be singular if he seemed to be conscious that he was guilty of an anachronism in making use of this or any word. The question, in fact, is whether it is an anachronism or not, and that it is so is very far from proved by any arguments yet brought forward. In the Apocalypse, i. 10, we have the use of the term "the Lord's day" (ἡ κυριακὴ ἡμέρα), A.D. 68-69. In the "Didache," which Dr. Lightfoot assigns to the first or the beginning of the second century, we meet with κυριακὴ κυρίου; and in the Ignatian Epistles, which those who believe in them date "in the early years of the second century," there is in one place[3] κατὰ κυριακήν. So far from its being

---

[1] L.c. p. xliii.
[2] L.c. pp. xliii, f.
[3] Magn. ix.

surprising that there should not be more authority for such an expression, however, it seems almost more remarkable that we should have any parallels at all, when we remember how few early writings are extant, and how few of these actually refer to the day thus designated. The Epistles, for this reason, may be set aside in a body, for they give no testimony either way, with the exception of 1 Cor. xvi. 2, where "the first day of the week" is referred to. The three Synoptics, following each other, and a common tradition, use ἡ μία τῶν σαββάτων each once, and the fourth Gospel has the same phrase twice, and the Acts once; but this use of another expression does not—in the face of the use of ἡ κυριακή in this fragment, and of ἡ κυριακὴ ἡμέρα, in the Apocalypse—at all show that, at the same period, the latter phrase was not also current, though it may not have supplanted "the first day of the week." The fact that Melito of Sardis, "about the middle of the second century," wrote a treatise περὶ κυριακῆς shows how general that expression had become; and even Dr. Swete, as we have seen above, recognises that it was "familiar amongst Eastern Greek-speaking Christians from the end of the first century." There is nothing whatever to warrant the conclusion that its use at the time when our Gospels were written would have been an anachronism, but the fact that a different expression happened to be used in a few writings. The author of the fragment employs the phrase twice only, and it is thoroughly consistent with his impressive style throughout the episode, that he should apply to the time when these astounding events are said to have taken place the appropriate term, already suggested by the author of the Apocalypse, of "the Lord's day," instead of "the first day of the week." There is nothing more difficult, as is proved every day in our time, than to fix the precise date at which words or expressions first came into use, and especially—in the absence of voluminous literature opposing the presumption—the denial of antiquity to a work, on the ground of its employing an expression supposed only to have come into general use a few years later than its otherwise probable date, is both rash and unjustifiable.

VIII

We now come to the most important part of our examination of this fragment, whether in regard to its approximate date or to its intrinsic value as an early Christian document—its relation to our canonical Gospels. The fragment begins and ends with a broken sentence, but taking it as it stands, in comparison with the same episodes in our four canonical Gospels, it contains about a fourth more matter. It will be seen that it is very far from a Harmony of the four narratives, and still less an abridgment of their common tradition, but it has markedly the character of an independent history drawn from similar, but varying, sources.

The fragment commences, "but of the Jews no man washed his hands, neither Herod nor any of his judges; and as they were not minded to wash, Pilate rose.[1] (2) And then Herod the King commandeth the Lord to be taken, saying unto them: 'Whatsoever I commanded that ye should do, that do unto him.'" It is clear from this that the tribunal before which it is represented that Jesus was taken for trial was quite different from that described in the canonical Gospels. Herod and other Jewish judges must, according to the writer, have sat along with Pilate, but the order given by "Herod the King" "to take the Lord" evidently shows that he is represented as playing the leading part. Although the episode of the washing of the hands (of which so much more is made by the author of the first Synoptic, who alone of the canonical Evangelists refers to it) must have been introduced, we have no means of knowing how far the two accounts may have agreed. Both, at least in one shape or another, adopt a tradition so incredible as that representing a Roman governor coerced into condemning an innocent man, and helplessly going through such a ceremony for the purpose of clearing himself from responsibility for gross injustice. The

---

[1] Cf. Ἀναστὰς δὲ ἀπὸ τοῦ βήματος ἐζήτει ἐξελθεῖν. Evang. Nicod. Pars 1. A. ix. 3; Tischendorf, Evang. Apocr. 1853, p. 229.

THE GOSPEL ACCORDING TO PETER - A STUDY

third Synoptist is the only one of the canonical Evangelists who prominently brings forward the share of Herod in judging Jesus (xxiii. 6-15), and he is in curious agreement with the spirit of Peter's account when he represents Pilate (xxiii. 6-7), on hearing that Jesus was a Galilean, recognising "that he was of Herod's jurisdiction," and sending him to Herod, "who himself also was at Jerusalem in these days." The statement also (xxiii. 12) that Herod and Pilate, having before been at enmity, became friends that day through this very act recognising Herod's jurisdiction, seems to point to a tradition coupling Herod with the trial, a form of which we have in the fragment. All the other Gospels are not only silent upon the point, but exclude his participation in the matter. When, according to our fragment, "Pilate rose," he seems to have passed out of all connection with the trial and condemnation of Jesus.

At this point, Peter represents the request for the body of Jesus as having been made but, before considering this part of his narrative, we must note the portions of the canonical account which he altogether omits. The first of these to which we must refer is the preference of Barabbas, which all of our four Evangelists carefully relate. Considering that his main object in writing this Gospel, according to some critics, was animosity to the Jews and a desire to cast upon them the whole guilt and responsibility of the death of Jesus, it is very remarkable that he should altogether exclude this picturesque episode, and sacrifice so favourable an opportunity of throwing upon them the odium of crying "Not this man, but Barabbas." There is strong presumptive evidence here of his entire independence of our four Gospels, for it is not reasonable to suppose that, if he had them before him, he could deliberately have passed over such striking material. A further indication of the same kind is to be found in the fact that he apparently knows nothing of the appeals made by Pilate to the people in favour of Jesus, so furiously rejected by them. It is distinctly a merit in the narrative of Peter that he does not, like the four Evangelists, give us the very extraordinary spectacle of a Roman Governor and Judge feebly expostulating with a noisy Jewish mob in favour of an accused person brought for trial before him, whom he repeatedly declares to be innocent, and at last allowing himself to be coerced against his will into scourging and crucifying him.

According to the four canonical Gospels,[1] the request of Joseph for the body of Jesus is made after he has expired on the cross. In Matthew (xxvii. 57 f.) he is a rich man from Arimathaea named Joseph, who also himself was a disciple of Jesus, and he goes to Pilate and asks for the body, which Pilate commands to be given to him. In Mark (xv. 43) Joseph of Arimathaea, a councillor of honourable estate, who also himself was looking for the kingdom of God, boldly goes in unto Pilate and asks for the body of Jesus. According to Matthew it is "When even was come" that he goes to Pilate; in Mark it is "When even was now come, because it was the Preparation, that is, the day before the Sabbath." In Matthew, Pilate simply commands that the body should be given; but in Mark it is further related (xv. 44): "And Pilate marvelled if he were already dead: and calling unto him the centurion, he asked him whether he had been any while dead. And when he learned it of the centurion he granted the corpse to Joseph." In Luke (xxiii. 50 f.): "A man named Joseph, who was a councillor, a good man and a righteous (he had not consented to their counsel and deed), of Arimathaea, a city of the Jews, who was looking for the kingdom of God: this man went to Pilate and asked for the body of Jesus." It is implied, but not said, that it was granted, and the time is mentioned further on (*v.* 54) "And it was the day of the Preparation, and the Sabbath drew on,"—which recalls Mark. In John (xix. 38): "After these things [the *crurifragium and piercing of the side], Joseph of Arimathaea, being a disciple of Jesus, but secretly for fear of the Jews, asked of Pilate that he might take away the body of Jesus: and Pilate gave him leave.*" In Peter, the request is made before Jesus is actually sent to be crucified, and the author is sometimes accused of perverting the narrative by introducing it at this time. It is impossible to see any object for so altering the sequence of events as given by the four canonical Gospels, on the supposition that he knew them, and it will be seen that the time in Peter's narrative is in perfect accord with the version which he gives of the trial. "Pilate rose," and it is to be inferred that he left the Praetorium. It is at this moment that Joseph seizes the opportunity of asking for the body: 3. "But there was there

---

[1] For the sake of brevity these Gospels will be called simply Matthew, Mark, Luke, and John.

THE GOSPEL ACCORDING TO PETER - A STUDY

Joseph the friend of Pilate[1] and of the Lord, and knowing that they are about to crucify (σταυρίσκειν) him, he came to Pilate and asked the body of the Lord for burial. 4. And Pilate sent to Herod and asked for his body; 5. and Herod said: 'Brother Pilate, even if no one had begged for him, we should have buried him, because the Sabbath is at hand, for it is written in the Law: The sun must not go down upon one put to death.' " It is to be noted that, whilst in the four canonical Gospels the request for the body is immediately followed by the entombment, in our fragment the request is made in anticipation, when a favourable moment for the request presented itself, and the actual reception of the body follows later, in its proper place. It is possible that the statement, in Luke (xxiii. 50-51), that Joseph was "a councillor" who had "not consented to their counsel and deed," which is here alone referred to, may indicate another tradition, of part of which Peter may have availed himself, and that it included his presence at the trial and consequently presented the opportunity of at once going to Pilate. That Pilate should send on the request to Herod is only in keeping with the representation that he had withdrawn from the trial, and would not himself further interfere in the matter. The mode of carrying on his narrative, by direct utterances put into the mouths of his personages, is particularly characteristic of the writer, and forms a remarkable feature of his style throughout. There is no sign of dependence upon the canonical Gospels in all this: but, on the contrary, the almost complete departure from their representations, in order and in substance, is only explicable on the hypothesis of a separate, though analogous, tradition.

If we look at the language, we find that critics point out one phrase which is common to the three Synoptics: "He went in unto Pilate [and] asked for the (προσελθὼν τῷ Πειλάτῳ ᾐτήσατο τὸ σῶμα τοῦ Ἰησοῦ,[2] Matthew and Luke; εἰσῆλθεν πρὸς τὸν Πειλᾶτον καὶ ᾐτήσατο τὸ σῶμα τοῦ Ἰησοῦ, Mark). In Peter we have: "He came to Pilate and asked for the body of the Lord" (ἦλθεν πρὸς τὸν Πειλᾶτον καὶ ᾔτησε τὸ σῶμα τοῦ κυρίου). It will be observed that the language of the three Synoptists is almost exactly the same, and although their interdependence throughout requires another explanation, which need not be entered

---

[1] Hilgenfeld conjectures that this abrupt mention of Joseph indicates that he must already have been mentioned in the Gospel of Peter. Zeitschr. 1893, 11. Heft, pp. 244 f.
[2] Cf. προσελθὼν τῷ Πιλάτῳ ᾐτήσατο τὸ σῶμα τοῦ Ἰησοῦ. Evang. Nicod. Pars I. A. xi. 3; Tischendorf, Evang. Apocr. 1853, p. 234.

into here, it is quite unreasonable to infer dependence on the part of Peter from similarity in these few words. It is the description of a perfectly simple action, in the most simple and natural language, and it is difficult to imagine what other words could be used without inflation. All the rest of the episode differs in every respect of language, order and substantial detail. It is right to add, however, that no great weight is attached by anyone to the point. On the other hand, it may be pointed out that σταυρίσκειν, in Peter, is a most uncommon word, not used in the New Testament at all, and that ταφή only occurs once in the New Testament, in Matt. xxvii. 7.

The fragment continues:

> And he delivered him to the people before the first day of the Unleavened bread of their feast (πρὸ μιᾶς τῶν ἀζύμων, τῆς ἑορτῆς αὐτῶν). 6. And taking the Lord they pushed him hurrying along, and said: "Let us drag along (σύρωμεν) the Son of God as we have power over him." 7. And they clad him with purple (πορφύραν αὐτὸν περιέβαλλον) and set him on a seat of judgment (καθέδραν κρίσεως), saying: "Judge justly (δικαίως κρῖνε), King of Israel." 8. And one of them brought a crown of thorns and set it upon the head of the Lord. 9. And others standing by spat in his eyes, and others smote him on the cheeks; others pierced him with a reed, and some scourged him, saying: "With this honour honour we the Son of God."

Before proceeding to compare this passage with our Gospels, it may be well to determine who the mockers in this fragment really are. It is argued by Zahn[1] and others, that Herod, according to this representation, hands Jesus over to the Jews, and that the people, and not the soldiers, as in the Gospels, conduct the mockery which is here described. It cannot be denied that the words used are, "he delivered him to the people" (παρέδωκεν αὐτὸν τῷ λαῷ), but the question is, whether the meaning is that he actually delivered him into the hands of the mob, and that the subsequent mockery, scourging, crucifixion and parting of the garments were performed by the people, or that, in delivering Jesus to the people, the meaning is not rather that he gave him up to their demands that he should be crucified, and that all the rest

---

[1] L.c. pp. 26 f.

followed between soldiers and people, as in the other narratives. We cannot but affirm that this latter interpretation is the true one. In Luke (xxiii. 25) the form of words used exactly expresses this: "but Jesus he delivered up to their will" (τὸν δὲ Ἰησοῦν παρέδωκεν τῷ θελήματι αὐτῶν). But a still more close representation of the case occurs in the fourth Gospel, where we read (xix. 16 f.): "Then, therefore, he delivered him unto them [the people and the chief priests] to be crucified. They took Jesus, therefore ... unto the place called, &c. ... where they crucified him." It is only in verse 23 that the narrative goes back and explains: "The soldiers, therefore, when they had crucified Jesus," &c. In the fragment, moreover, there is an important indication in the portion previously quoted, where we read: 2. "And then Herod the King commandeth the Lord to be taken, saying unto them: 'Whatsoever I commanded that ye should do, that do unto him.'" Who are indicated by the pronoun "them"?[1] Doubtless the context would have explained this and probably made clear all that follows, for the orders given must have been regarding the crucifixion, since in the following verse (3) it is said that Joseph, "knowing that they are about to crucify him," came to Pilate. Nothing had previously been said, in this fragment, of crucifixion. It is not possible to admit that the writer intends to represent that the people themselves carried out the crucifixion, or that the orders given by Herod were to the crowd. Herod, in all probability, is represented as commanding his own soldiers, which would accord with the statement in the third Synoptic (xxiii. 11), that Herod "with his soldiers set him at nought and mocked him," and so on. The doubt only proceeds from indefinite statement on the part of the writer, and preconceived ideas on the part of critics.

It is evident, from the statement that Jesus was delivered for crucifixion "before the first day of the Unleavened bread of their feast," that the Gospel of Peter adopts the same chronology as the fourth Gospel, in contradiction to that of the three Synoptics, and represents Jesus as put to death on the 14th Nisan. His agreement with the fourth Gospel, however, is limited to the mere matter of date, for on all other points

---

[1] Zahn, of course, argues that the commands of Herod can only have been given to the previously named Jews, the judges of Jesus, "and perhaps to their servants" (und etwa deren Diener), and he finds fault with Harnack for here bringing in "soldiers" from the canonical Gospels, without warrant from the text. He declares them to be directly excluded by the leading tendency of the Gospel of Peter (l.c. p. 27). This supposed "leading tendency," of hatred of the Jews, is a good deal exaggerated.

the author takes a widely different view. As Hilgenfeld points out, for him all the feasts prescribed by the Law are mere Jewish institutions, and he has none of the Johannine (xix. 33 f.) views as to the death of Jesus representing the Paschal offering, nor does he associate with that the circumstances regarding the breaking of the limbs, and the thrust of the spear in his side, which he altogether omits.[1]

The author of the fragment is reproached with the looseness of his narrative of the mockery, on the supposition that he represents the clothing in purple and the setting on the seat of judgment as occurring whilst Jesus is being dragged along by the Jews; but this is not the case. The hurrying along commences the mockery in verse 6. Then in verse 7 begins another episode. They clothe Jesus in purple and set him on the judgment seat. Now, before going into the details of this mockery, it is necessary to consider how the narrative in general accords with the account in the four canonical Gospels. In Peter, the whole of the mockery is represented as taking place after Jesus is delivered to be crucified. He is hustled along, clothed in purple and set upon a seat of judgment; the crown of thorns is put upon his head, they spit in his eyes and smite him on the cheeks, pierce him with a reed and scourge him. In the Synoptics, especially, the ill-usage is as much as possible lengthened and intensified. In Matthew, the mockery begins when Jesus is in the house of Caiaphas (xxvi. 67 f.): "Then did they spit in his face and buffet him; and some smote him with the palms of their hands, saying, Prophesy unto us, thou Christ: who is he that struck thee?" After Pilate causes Jesus to be scourged, and delivers him, the mockery begins afresh (xxvii. 27 ff.): "Then the soldiers of the governor took Jesus into the Palace and gathered unto him the whole band. And they stripped him, and put on him a scarlet robe. And they plaited a crown of thorns and put it upon his head, and a reed in his right hand; and they kneeled down before him and In Mark, the mockery also begins in the house of the high priest (xiv. 65 ff.): "And some began to spit on him, and to cover his face and to buffet him, and to say unto him: Prophesy: and the officers received him with blows of their hands." The mockery recommences after Jesus is scourged and delivered over to be crucified (xv. 16 ff.): "And the soldiers led him away within the court, which is the Praetorium; and they call together the whole band. And they clothe him with purple, and plaiting a crown of thorns, they put it on him; and they begin to salute him, Hail, King

---

[1] Zeitschr. 1893, ii. 248 f.

of the Jews! And they smote his head with a reed, and did spit upon him, and bowing their knees, worshipped him. And when they had mocked him, they took off from him the purple, and put on him his garments, and they led him out to crucify him." Of course it is unnecessary to point out how these two accounts depend upon each other. The same representation is made in the third Synoptic (xxii. 66 ff.): "And the men that held him mocked him and beat him. And they blindfolded him, and asked him, saying, Prophesy: who is he that struck thee? And many other things spake they against him, reviling him." This passes, as in the other Synoptics, in the house of the high priest, but the subsequent mocking does not take place after Pilate delivers Jesus to be crucified, but after he has been examined by Herod (xxiii. 11): "And Herod with his soldiers set him at nought, and mocked him, and arraying him in gorgeous apparel sent him back to Pilate." In the fourth Gospel there is only the one scene of mockery, and that is placed where Jesus is scourged by the order of Pilate (xix. 2): "And the soldiers plaited a crown of thorns and put it on his head, and arrayed him in a purple garment; and they came unto him, and said: Hail, King of the Jews! and they struck him with their hands." In many respects this is the most incredible of the four narratives, for the scene is reported as taking place in the presence of Pilate and before his final condemnation of Jesus; and in the very next verse (4) it is said: "And Pilate went out again, and saith unto them, Behold, I bring him out to you, that ye may know that I find no crime in him. Jesus therefore came out, wearing the crown of thorns and the purple garment. And Pilate saith unto them; Behold the man!" Although this scene, which has been the delight of artists ever since, is so picturesque, it is quite evident that it is opposed to all that we have in the Synoptics, as well as in our fragment, and that the representation of Pilate allowing his soldiers in his presence to act in such a way, not to speak of the scourging, to a man accused before him, of whom he so strongly declares, "I find no crime in him," is quite inadmissible. The narrative in Peter is at variance with all these accounts, whilst reproducing a similar tradition, and not varying more from our Gospels than they do from each other. The variation, however, is not that of a writer compiling a narrative from the canonical Gospels, but the distinct representation of one independently making use of similar, but separate, materials.

We have already discussed, in connection with Justin's reference, the passage of Peter in which it is said that "they clad him with purple and set him on a seat of judgment, saying: Judge justly, King of Israel." Of course it is argued by some that this is derived from the fourth Gospel, on the strength of the words just quoted: ἐκάθισαν αὐτὸν ἐπὶ καθέδραν κρίσεως, which are compared with the ἐκάθισεν ἐπὶ βήματος of the fourth Gospel. It is said that Archbishop Whately used to render these words "and set him on the judgment seat," understanding the verb καθίζειν to be used transitively, and thus stating that Pilate actually set Jesus in mockery upon a judgment seat. It is suggested that both Justin, as we have seen, and Peter may have misunderstood the passage, and based their statement upon it. Now, although it must be admitted that the Greek may be rendered in this way, yet it would be necessary to add αὐτὸν to justify such use of the verb. In connection with this argument they cite the words of Isaiah lviii. 2, in the Septuagint version, referred to by Justin: "For as the prophet said, they dragged him, and set him on the judgment seat, and said: Judge for us!" The Septuagint has: αἰτεῖτέ με νῦν κρίσιν δικαίαν ... λέγοντες. It is asserted that the idea of setting Jesus on the judgment seat came from the passage of the fourth Gospel which is quoted above, understood transitively. The representation that Pilate actually set Jesus on the judgment seat, if linguistically defensible, is rejected by most critics and, as has already been mentioned, amongst others by the Revisers of the New Testament. The words used for "seat of judgment" in the fragment, ἐπὶ καθέδραν κρίσεως, differ entirely from the ἐπὶ βήματος of the fourth Gospel. The analogous "Prophesy unto us, thou Christ: who is he that struck thee?" and the "Hail, King of the Jews," are, of course, widely different from the representation in Peter, in which the "Judge justly!" is evidently in mockery of the Messianic claims of Jesus, and the "King of Israel" a peculiarity of this Gospel to which we shall have to refer again further on. The statement that "others pierced him with a reed" is also a variation from the canonical Gospels, which only say, "they took the reed and smote him on the head." The fourth Gospel has alone the representation of the soldier piercing the side of Jesus with a spear "that the Scripture might be fulfilled.... They shall look on him whom they pierced," but in our fragment the representation is made casually and without any appearance of dogmatic intention. The crown of thorns is used merely incidentally, as in the case of the Synoptics, and without the artistic prominence given to it in the fourth Gospel.

There is no mention in Peter of any one bearing the cross, and in this there is a departure from the narrative both of the Synoptics and of the fourth Gospel. The Synoptics have in common, as usual, the story regarding its being laid on the shoulders of Simon of Cyrene (Matt.

xxvii. 32 f., Mark xv. 21 f., Luke xxiii. 26 f.), whom they compelled to carry it to Calvary. The fourth Gospel not only omits this episode, but contradicts it in good set terms (xix. 17): "They took Jesus, therefore; and he went out, bearing the cross for himself, unto the place called 'The place of a skull.'"

Peter does not enter into any intermediate detail, but at once says: 10. "And they brought two malefactors and crucified between them the Lord; but he kept silence, as feeling no pain." The canonical Gospels all narrate the crucifixion of the two malefactors, but the various terms in which this is done must be given for comparison. Matthew says (xxvii. 38): "Then are there crucified with him two robbers, one on the right hand, and one on the left." Mark uses almost the same words (xv. 27). Luke, with some exercise of his usual constructive style, says the same thing (xxiii. 32 f.): "And there were also two others, malefactors, led with The fourth Gospel reads (xix. 17 f.): "They took Jesus therefore; and he went out, bearing the cross for himself, unto the place called 'The place of a skull,' which is called in Hebrew Golgotha: where they crucified him, and with him two others, on either side one, and Jesus in the midst." The only remark necessary here is that in Peter the common tradition is given with independence and simplicity.

It is only in the last words of the verse that we have an important variation. "But he kept silence, as feeling no pain." We have already referred to this as one of the recognised Docetic passages of the fragment, although there is no necessity to read it in this sense. Mr. Murray has pointed out a passage in Origen in which that writer "gives them an innocent" (that is, not a Docetic) "interpretation."

> Et in his omnibus *unigenita virtus nocita non est, sicut nec passa est aliquid*, facta pro nobis maledictum, cum naturaliter benedictio esset; sed cum benedictio esset, consumpsit et solvit et dissipavit omnem maledictionem humanam. Orig. *in Mat.* 125.[1]

Although there is no exact parallel to this in our Gospels, it is worth a moment's notice that the silence of Jesus during the trial is mentioned as remarkable and as exciting wonder. We have not in our fragment, unfortunately, the earlier part of the trial, and cannot, therefore, see whether the words used have any reference to previous representations. In Matt. xxvii. 12 f., it is said: "And when he was ac-

---

[1] Murray, Expositor, January 1893, pp. 55 f.

cused by the chief priests and elders, he answered nothing Then saith An almost identical account is given in Mark. In Luke it is to the questioning of Herod that Jesus is silent (xxiii. 9): "And he [Herod] questioned him in many words; but he answered him nothing." In the fourth Gospel not only is nothing said of the silence of Jesus, but he is represented as answering freely—and in the tone of the discourses which characterise that Gospel—the questions of Pilate. Now, in the Synoptics, we have a silence described, which causes the governor to marvel greatly, that is not, however, when we go into detail, very marked in them, and is excluded by the fourth Gospel. Can a silence have been referred to, in the original tradition, which was connected with the trial, instead of the cross, because it began to receive a Docetic application, but which we have, in its earlier form, in Peter?

In our fragment, the narrative continues: 11. "And as they set up the cross they wrote thereon: 'This is the King of Israel.'" We have here a continuation of the indefinite "they," which it becomes at every step more impossible to identify otherwise than with the soldiers. It is a most curious circumstance, frequently pointed out. that no two of the Gospels agree even in so plain a matter as should be the inscription on the cross, and that the Gospel of Peter differs from them all. Matthew gives it (xxvii. 37): "This is Jesus, the King of the Jews;" Mark (xv. 26): "The King of the Jews;" Luke (xxiii. 38): "This is the King of the Jews," and John (xix. 19): "Jesus of Nazareth, the King of the Jews." The author of the fourth Gospel adds the statement that this title "was written in Hebrew, in and further gives a conversation between the "chief priests of the Jews" and Pilate, in which they complain of this superscription, and wish it to be put "that he said. I am King of the Jews," to which Pilate answered briefly, "What I have written, I have written." With so many forms to select from, is it reasonable to suppose that Peter would have invented another superscription, if these four Gospels had actually been before him?[1]

The author of the fragment continues: 12. "And they laid the clothes before him and distributed them and cast lots (λαχμὸν ἔβαλον) for them." In Matthew (xxvii. 35) it is said: "And when they had crucified him, they parted his garments among them, casting lots" (βάλλοντες κλῆρον); in Mark (xv. 24): "And they crucify him, and

---

[1] Van Manen conjectures that the author got this "King of Israel" from the independent use of some Hebrew or Aramaic source. Tijdschr. Juli 1893, p. 408.

part his garments among them, casting lots (βάλλοντες κλῆρον) upon them, what each should take." In Luke there is a similar statement (xxiii. 34): "And parting his garments among them, they cast lots" (ἔβαλον κλῆρον). In the fourth Gospel, as usual, we have further details (xix. 23 f.): "The soldiers therefore, when they had crucified Jesus, took his garments and made four parts, to every soldier a part; and also the coat: now the coat was without seam, woven from the top throughout. They said therefore one to another, Let us not rend it, but cast lots (λάχωμεν) for it, whose it shall be: that the scripture might be fulfilled, which saith, They parted my garments among them, and upon my vesture did they cast lots" (ἔβαλον κλῆρον). In discussing the connection of Justin with the Gospel of Peter, we have already partly dealt with this passage, and now confront it with all the four Gospels. It is obvious that the language of the three Synoptics is distinct from that of Peter, who uses the unusual word λαχμός, not found in any of the Gospels. The fourth Gospel has the common verb λαγχάνω, whilst the quotation from the Psalm (xxii. 18), from which the whole episode emanates, uses the expression common to the three Synoptics, ἔβαλον κλῆρον. There is no reason for supposing that Peter makes use of our Gospels here, and in the absence of other evidence, the λαχμός is decisive proof of his independence.

The author of our fragment, after the crucifixion, has none of the mocking speeches of the four Gospels, and he ignores the episode of the penitent thief, as it is told in the third Synoptic, but he relates, instead, how one of the malefactors rebuked the mockers: 13. "But one of these malefactors reproved them, saying: We have suffered this for the evil which we wrought, but this man who has become the saviour of men, what wrong hath he done you? 14. And they were angry with him, and they commanded that his legs should not be broken, in order that he might die in torment."

It will be remembered that the episode of the penitent thief is given in Luke only, and that the other Gospels do not mention any utterance of the two malefactors said to have been crucified with Jesus. Luke's narrative reads (xxiii. 39 f.): "And one of the malefactors which were hanged railed on him, saying: Art not thou the Christ? Save thyself and us. But the other answered, and rebuking him said, Dost thou not even fear God, seeing thou art in the same condemnation? And we indeed justly: for we receive the due reward of our deeds; but this man hath done nothing amiss. And he said, Jesus, remember me when thou comest in thy kingdom. And he said unto him, Verily, That all the other Gospels should have excluded an incident like this, supposing it to have really occurred, is very extraordinary, and the only conclusion to which we can come is either that it did not occur, or that they were ignorant of it. Peter has evidently got an earlier form of the story, without those much later touches with which the third Synoptist has embellished it. The malefactor rebukes the Jews and not his fellow, and if he display a piety which is not very natural under the circumstances, he is not in this more remarkable than his counterpart in the third Synoptic. That the author was not acquainted with the form in Luke, and is quite uninfluenced by it, seems to us manifest.

This is rendered all the more apparent by the continuation in Peter, in which, instead of any reply from Jesus, or any promise of Paradise, there is connected with the rebuke of the malefactor on the cross a view of the *crurifragium* which is quite foreign to the canonical Gospels. When the malefactor had spoken, instead of their being mollified, the fragment declares: "And they were angry with him, and they commanded that his legs should not be broken, in order that he might die in torment." Now, here, there is a point which demands examination. To whom does this sentence refer? to Jesus or the malefactor? It is at first sight, and apart from consideration of the style of the writer, a reference to the latter, but on closer examination it seems to us more probable that the writer intended it to apply to Jesus. In any case, it is a point in which so remarkable a version of the story is concerned that it cannot but be considered as very singular that most apologetic critics have passed it over without any notice whatever, and apparently treated the order not to break the legs as applying to the malefactor and not to Jesus.[1] In the first edition of his article on the fragment, Harnack took the view that more probably the malefactor was indicated here, but in his second edition he withdraws this, and adopts the conclusion that the reference of αὐτῷ to Jesus "appears more acceptable, both on account of John xix. 32 f., and also on account of the context."[2] Zahn considers the whole episode in Peter as a caricature of the Gospel tradition, through the author's hatred of the Jews, and refers only indirectly to the version of the *crurifragium* as drawn by the caricaturist from the "Motive" of the fourth Evangelist, but does not further go into the matter than to say, with mysterious reticence: "Whoever is of

---

[1] So, for instance, Swete, J. Rendel Harris, Robinson, and others. Others distinctly identify the αὐτῷ with the malefactor: as, for instance, Kunze, l.c. p. 22; Von Schubert, l.c. pp. 28 f.; cf. Lods, l.c. p. 21.
[2] L.c. p. 26.

another opinion should keep it to himself"![1] Hilgenfeld, who considers the whole passage as quite independent of our Gospels, regrets Harnack's change of view, and applies the αὐτῷ to the malefactor;[2] but many able critics, with equal decision, understand it as a reference to Jesus,[3] and Harnack himself, of course, sees that, even adopting his later view, there is a clear contradiction in the account in Peter to the representation of the fourth Gospel. To independent criticism, the result is a matter of indifference, and we shall merely state the reasons which seem to favour the view that the passage was intended to apply to Jesus, and then present the consequence if it be referred to the malefactor.

Throughout the whole of the fragment, the sustained purpose of the author is to present Jesus in the strongest light, and subordinate everything to the representation of his sufferings and resurrection. At the part we are considering, the narrative is of the closest and most condensed character: the crucifixion between the two malefactors; the silence as feeling no pain; the superscription on the cross, and the parting of the garments, are all told without wasting a word. The reproach of the malefactor, apparently addressed to those who are parting the garments, is more intended to increase our sympathy for Jesus than to excite it for the speaker, and it is certainly not the writer's purpose to divert our attention from the sufferings of Jesus by presenting those of the generous malefactor. Rather it is to show that the more the high character and mission of Jesus are set forth, the more bitter becomes the animosity and hatred of the Jews; so that, to the remonstrance of the malefactor, they reply by increasing the sufferings of Jesus. In short, the sense of the passage seems to be "And they, being angered at what was said, commanded that the legs of Jesus should not be broken, that he might die in torment." However, let us take the view that the command was given that the malefactor's legs should not be broken, that he might die in torment. It clearly follows that, if he was to be made to suffer more by not having *his* legs broken, the legs of the other two must on the contrary have been broken. The command not to break *his* legs necessarily implies that otherwise the legs of all would have been so broken. There is really no escape from this inference.

---

[1] "Wer anderer Meinung ist, sollte sie für sich behalten" (l.c. p. 55).
[2] Zeitschr. 1893, ii. 254.
[3] Van Manen, Theol. Tijdschrift, 4de Stuk, 1893, pp. 408 f.; Martineau, Nineteenth Century, June 1893, p. 911.

Now the *crurifragium* is here represented as an act of mercy and to hasten death, but in the immediate context we are told that they were troubled and anxious lest the sun should have set whilst Jesus still lived. No anxiety of this kind is felt lest the malefactors should still be alive, and why? Because if an exception to breaking the legs had been made in one case, and that exception had been Jesus, the malefactors would be supposed to be already dead. If, on the contrary, the legs of Jesus had been broken, they would not have feared his being alive, but rather the malefactor whose legs had not been broken. Jesus having been left to linger in torment is still alive, and the potion of vinegar and gall is given to him to produce death, and not to the malefactor. The whole context, therefore, shows that no means such as the *crurifragium* had been used with Jesus to hasten death, and that the potion was at last given for the purpose. If, on the other hand, the legs of Jesus were actually broken, and not those of the malefactor, a most complete contradiction of the account in the fourth Gospel is given, and of the Scripture which is said in it to have been fulfilled.

Let us now see how the account in Peter compares with that in the fourth Gospel, on the hypothesis that the writer intended to represent that, in order to lengthen his sufferings, the legs of Jesus were not broken. It would follow that the *crurifragium* was applied to the two malefactors, and that Jesus was left to a lingering death by the cruel animosity of his executioners. It will, of course, be remembered that the fourth Gospel is the only one which recounts the *crurifragium*. In this narrative it is not represented as an act of mercy to shorten the sufferings of the crucified. It is said (xix. 31 f.): "The Jews therefore, because it was the Preparation, that the bodies should not remain on the cross upon the Sabbath (for the day of that Sabbath was a high day), asked of Pilate that their legs might be broken, and that they might be taken away. The soldiers therefore came, and brake the legs of the first, and of the other which was crucified with him; but when they came to Jesus, and saw that he was dead already, The object of the author in relating this is obviously dogmatic, and to show the fulfilment of Scripture, but the way in which he brings the matter about is awkward, to say the least of it, and not so natural as that adopted by Peter. The soldiers brake the legs "of the first,"—and by this description they imply that they begin at one end—and proceed to the second, who would be Jesus; but not so, for having broken the legs "of the first, and of the other," they come to Jesus, whom they must have passed over. Is this passing over of Jesus in the first instance a slight indication of a tradition similar to that which has been reproduced in

Peter? However this may be, it is quite clear that, while the fourth Gospel deals with the episode purely from a dogmatic point of view, this is completely absent from Peter, who even leaves it in doubt, and as a problem for critics, whether the legs of Jesus were broken or not, and evidently does not give a thought to the Johannine representation of Jesus as the Paschal lamb. Whichever way the passage in Peter is construed, the entire independence of the writer from the influence of the fourth Gospel seems to be certain.

The fragment proceeds:

> 15. Now it was mid-day, and a darkness covered all Judaea, and they were troubled and anxious lest the sun should have set whilst he still lived, for it is written for them: "The sun must not go down upon one put to death." 16. And one of them said: "Give him to drink gall with vinegar;" and having mixed, they gave him to drink. 17. And they fulfilled all things, and completed their sins upon their own head. 18. Now many went about with lights, thinking that it was night, and some fell.[1]

The three Synoptics have an account of this darkness in words which nearly repeat each other. Matthew xxvii. 45: "Now from the sixth hour there was darkness over all the earth (ἐπὶ πᾶσαν τὴν γῆν) until the ninth hour." Mark (xv. 33): "And when the sixth hour was come, there was darkness over the whole earth (ἐφ' ὅλην τὴν γῆν) until the ninth hour." In Luke (xxiii. 44 f.) other details are, as usual, added: "And it was now about the sixth hour, and a darkness came over the whole earth (ἐφ' ὅλην τὴν γῆν) until the ninth hour, the sun failing [or rather 'being eclipsed,' τοῦ ἡλίου ἐκλειπόντος]."[2] It is a

---

[1] In the apocryphal work called Anaphora Pilati, an account of the crucifixion supposed to be sent by Pilate to the Emperor Tiberius, Pilate is represented as describing the darkness which comes over the whole earth, and saying that the Emperor could not be ignorant "that in all the world they lighted lamps from the sixth hour until evening" (ὅτι ἐν παντὶ τῷ κόσμῳ ἧψαν λύχνους ἀπὸ ἕκτης ὥρας ἕως ὀψίας). Anaphora Pilati, B. 7; Tischendorf, Evang. Apocr. 1853, p. 423.

[2] With regard to this addition of Luke, we may refer to a very interesting letter of Dr. Abbott's in the Spectator of October 21, 1893, from which we take the liberty of extracting the following passage: "In Luke (xxiii. 45) the correct reading is τοῦ ἡλίου ἐκλειπόντος, of which the natural interpretation is, the sun being eclipsed. Now, as it was well known that an eclipse could only

very extraordinary circumstance that, whether a miraculous eclipse or not, whether this darkness came over the whole land or the whole earth, the fourth Gospel has either not believed in it, or thought it unworthy of mention, for no reference to the astonishing phenomenon is found in it. Peter, in a manner quite different from the Synoptics, and in fuller detail, describes this darkness and its effect upon the people. For the second time, he refers to a portion of the Jewish law, interpreted from Deut. xxi. 23, to illustrate the anxiety which the supposed going down of the sun had excited. This expression does not favour any theory of his being acquainted with the third Synoptic.

The most important part of the passage is that in v. 16: "And one of them said: 'Give him to drink gall with vinegar;' and having mixed they gave him to drink." This proceeding is represented as the result of their anxiety at the sun going down whilst Jesus still lived, and the gall and vinegar are regarded as a potion to hasten death. This view is foreign to all of our Gospels. In Matthew xxvii. 48, when Jesus gives the loud cry, "My God, my God," &c., we read: "And straightway one of them ran and took a sponge and filled it with vinegar, and put it on a reed, and gave him to drink. And the rest said, Let be; let us see whether Elijah cometh to save him." In Mark (xv. 36) the representation is almost the same. In both of these cases death follows almost immediately. In Luke (xxiii. 36) a very different representation is made. There is no such cry connected with it, but it is simply said: "And the soldiers also mocked him, coming to him, offering him vine-

---

happen at new moon, and as Passover was at full moon, this would involve a portentous miracle. The probability is that Luke, who was by no means afraid of miracles, meant a miracle here. Not content with saying (with the Synoptics) 'darkness came over all the land,' he adds, in order to show that the darkness was miraculous, 'the sun being eclipsed.' But is this eclipse 'an invention of a conscious or unconscious romancer'? An examination of the parallel passages in Mark and Matthew will show that it is not. There we find that Jesus uttered a cry to God as abandoning Him. These words caused difficulty from the first. The words 'my God' were rendered by some (e.g. the Gospel of Peter) 'my Power;' by the fourth Gospel the words were omitted; our oldest manuscripts exhibit many variations: ἠλι, ἠλει, ἐλωι; the very bystanders are said to have interpreted the words as referring to Elias failing to help. Now 'Elias failing to help' might be, in Greek, ἠλείου ἐκλειπόντος, or quite as often ἠλίου ἐκλειπόντος, i.e. the sun being eclipsed. It seems extremely probable, then, that Luke is not here 'inventing' a miracle, but suggesting, or adopting, an edifying and miraculous interpretation of what seemed to him a non-edifying tradition" (pp. 546 f.).

gar, and saying, If thou art the King of the Jews, save thyself." In John the episode has quite another, and purely dogmatic, tendency (xix. 28 ff.). It commences immediately after the episode of the mother and the beloved disciple, and without any previous cry: "After this Jesus, knowing that all things are now finished, that the Scripture might be accomplished, saith, I thirst. There was set there a vessel full of vinegar; so they put a sponge full of vinegar upon Of course the Scripture which is represented as being thus fulfilled is Psalm lxix. 21: "... and in my thirst they gave me vinegar to drink." In all of these Gospels, the potion is simply vinegar, and being evidently associated with this Psalm, it is in no way connected with any baleful intention. The Psalm, however, commences: "They gave me also gall for my meat," and in connection with the combination of gall with vinegar in Peter, as a potion to hasten death, it may be mentioned that the word which is in the Psalm translated "gall" may equally well be rendered "poison"— as, indeed, is also the case with the Latin *"fel."* Peter, by what is said in *v.* 17—"And they fulfilled all things, and completed their sins upon their own head"—is more anxious to show that the Jews had put the final touch to their cruel work, in thus completing the death of Jesus, than to refer to the mere fulfilment of the Psalm. The only Gospel which mentions gall is the first Synoptic, in which it is said (xxvii. 34) that when they had brought Jesus to Golgotha before the crucifixion, "They gave him wine to drink mingled with gall; and when he had tasted it, he would not drink." This is a very different representation from that of Peter, and the potion was obviously that often offered to persons about to suffer, in order to dull sensation. The passage might almost be represented as Docetic, from the writer's intention to show that Jesus refused to adopt a usual method of diminishing pain. There does not seem to be any warrant for supposing that the author of the fragment derived the passage we are examining from our Gospels, from which it is in all essential points distinct.

The narrative of the fragment continues, *v.* 19: "And the Lord cried aloud, saying, 'Power, my Power, thou hast forsaken me!' (ἡ δύναμίς μου, ἡ δύναμις, κατέλειψάς με), and having spoken, he was taken up (ἀνελήφθη)." In this passage there is a very marked departure from the tradition followed by our four Gospels. Before considering the actual words of the cry recorded here, it may be desirable to form a general idea of the representations of the Synoptists and of the author of the fourth Gospel regarding the words spoken from the cross.

It might naturally have been supposed that, in describing the course of so solemn an event as the crucifixion, unusual care, securing unusual agreement, would have been exercised by Christian writers, and that the main facts—and still more the last words—of the great Master would have been collected. As we have already seen, however, in no portion of the history is there greater discrepancy in the accounts in the four Gospels, nor greater contradictions upon every point.

The same is the case with regard to what has still to be examined, and notably in the words and cries from the cross. In the first two Synoptics, with the exception of the inarticulate cry "with a loud voice" (Matt. xxvii. 50, Mark xv. 37) when yielding up his spirit, the only utterance recorded is one resembling that in Peter (Matt. xxvii. 46, Mark xv. 34): "Eloi, Eloi, lama sabachthani? that is, My God, my God, why hast thou forsaken me?"[1] (ἠλωί ἠλωί λαμὰ σαβαχθανεί; τοῦτ' ἔστιν; θεέ μου, θεέ μου, ἵνα τί με ἐγκατέλιπες?). It will be observed that here there is a demonstration of great accuracy, in actually giving the original words used and translating them, which is uncommon in the Gospels. It is all the more extraordinary that neither of the other Gospels gives this cry at all, but that they represent Jesus as uttering quite different words. The third Synoptist represents Jesus immediately after the crucifixion as saying (Luke xxiii. 34): "Father, forgive them; for they know not what they do." The other evangelists do not evince any knowledge of this, and as little of the episode of the penitent thief (xxiii. 39 ff.)—which we have already considered—in which Jesus uses the remarkable words (v. 43): "Verily I say unto thee, To-day shalt thou be with me in Paradise." In Luke, further, the inarticulate cry is interpreted (xxiii. 46): "And when Jesus had cried with a loud voice, he said, Father, into thy hands I commend my spirit; and having said this, he gave up the ghost." Of this the other Synoptists do not say anything. The author of the fourth Gospel has quite a different account to give from any of the Synoptists. He seems to be ignorant of the words which they report, and substitutes others of which they seem to know nothing. The episode of the penitent thief is replaced by the scene between Jesus and his mother and the disciple "whom he loved" (xix. 25 ff.). Not only is this touching episode apparently unknown to the Synoptists, but the proximity of the women to the cross is in direct contradiction to what we find in Matthew and Mark, for in the former (xxvii. 55 f.) it is said that many women, "among whom was Mary Magdalene, and Mary the mother of James and Joses, and the mother of the sons of Zebedee" were "beholding afar off;" and the latter (xv.

---

[1] Or "Why didst thou forsake me?"

40 f.) reports: "And there were also women beholding from afar: among whom were both Mary Magdalene and Mary the mother of James the less and of Joses, and Salome." In the fourth Gospel (xix. 28), Jesus is moreover reported to have said "I thirst," in order "that the Scripture might be accomplished"—a fact which is not recorded in any of the Synoptics—and having received vinegar upon hyssop, "he said, It is finished, and he bowed his head and gave up his spirit." The last words of Jesus, therefore, according to the fourth Gospel, are different from any found in the three Synoptics. The Gospel of Peter differs as completely from the four canonical Gospels as they do from each other, and the whole account of the agony on the cross given in it is quite independent of them.

The only words recorded by Peter as uttered on the cross are those quoted higher up: "Power, my Power, thou hast forsaken me," the second "my" being omitted, and the question of the two Synoptics, "Why hast thou forsaken me?" being changed into a declaration by the omission of ἵνα τί (or εἰς τί, Mark). We have already discussed the Docetic nature of this cry, and are now only considering it in relation to our Gospels. It is obvious that the substitution of "Power, my Power" for "My God, my God" introduces quite a different order of ideas, especially followed as it is by the remarkable statement: "He was taken up." Eusebius tells us that Aquila rendered the words of Psalm xxii. 1—whence the first two Synoptists take their cry—as ἰσχυρέ μου, ἰσχυρέ μου ("My strong one, my strong one"), but that the more exact sense was ἰσχύσ μου, ἰσχύς μου ("My strength, my strength");[1] but though this is interesting as in some degree connecting the cry with the Psalm, it does not lessen the discrepancy between Peter and the Gospels, or in the least degree favour the theory of acquaintance with them.

The expression used to describe what follows this cry completes the wide separation between them: "And having spoken, he was taken up" (ἀνελήφθη). In the first Synoptic, after his cry (xxvii. 50), "he yielded up the spirit" (ἀφῆκεν τὸ πνεῦμα), whilst the second and third say (Mark xv. 37, Luke xxiii. 46), "he gave up the ghost" ἐξέπνευσεν, and the fourth Gospel reads (xix. 30), "he delivered up the spirit" (παρέδωκεν τὸ πνεῦμα). The representation in Peter is understood to be that the divine descended upon the human Christ in the form of the dove at baptism, and immediately ascended to Heaven again at his

---

[1] Dem. Ev. x. 8, p. 494.

death. There is not here, however, any declaration of a double Christ, or any denial of the reality of the Christ's body, such as characterised the later Docetae; indeed, the fact that the dead body is still always spoken of as that of "the Lord" seems distinctly to exclude this, as does the whole subsequent narrative. Whatever Docetism there may be in this fragment is of the earliest type, if indeed its doctrines can be clearly traced at all; but undoubtedly when the sect had become pronounced heretics, orthodox Christians detected their subtle influence in much that was in itself very simple and harmless.

The fragment continues (v. 20): "And the same hour the veil of the Temple of Jerusalem was torn in twain" (διεράγη τὸ καταπέτασμα τοῦ ναοῦ τῆς Ἰερουσαλὴμ εἰς δύο). This expression the "temple of Jerusalem" is one of those which seem to indicate that the Gospel was written away from Palestine, but in this it probably differs little from most of the canonical Gospels. The statement regarding the veil of the temple is almost the same in the first two Synoptics (Matt. xxvii. 51, Mark xv. 38). "And behold, the veil of the temple was rent in twain from the top to the bottom" (τὸ καταπέτασμα τοῦ ναοῦ ἐσχίσθη ἀπ' ἄνωθεν ἕως κάτω εἰς δύο). In Luke (xxiii. 45) the rent is "in the midst" (μέσον), but otherwise the words are the same. The use of διεράγη instead of the ἐσχίσθη of the three Synoptics is characteristic. The fourth Gospel, strange to say, does not record at all this extraordinary phenomenon of the rending in twain of the veil of the temple. There are some further peculiarities which must be pointed out. The third Synoptist sets the rending of the veil before Jesus cried with a loud voice and gave up the ghost; whilst in Matthew and Mark it is after the cry and giving up the spirit. Moreover, in Matthew, it is associated with an earthquake, and the rending of the rocks and opening of tombs, and the astounding circumstance that many bodies of the saints that had fallen asleep were raised, and coming forth out of the tombs after his resurrection they entered into the holy city, and appeared unto many: of all of which the other three Gospels make no mention, nor does Peter in this connection.

The narrative in the fragment continues:

> 21. And then they took out the nails from the hands of the Lord, and laid him upon the earth; and the whole earth quaked, and great fear came [upon them]. 22. Then the sun shone out, and it was found to be the ninth hour. 23. Now the Jews were glad and gave his body to Joseph, that

he might bury it, for he had beheld the good works that he did.[1] 24. And he took the Lord and washed him, and wrapped him in linen, and brought him into his own grave, called "Joseph's Garden."

This passage is full of independent peculiarities. Although none of the canonical Gospels, except Matthew, says anything of an earthquake, and the first Synoptist associates it with the moment when Jesus "gave up the ghost," Peter narrates that when the body of the Lord was unloosed from the cross, the moment it was laid on the ground the whole earth quaked beneath the awful burden: a representation almost grander than anything in the four Gospels.

The canonical Gospels do not speak of the nails being taken out, and although Peter states that they were removed from the hands, he does not refer to the feet. The fourth is the only canonical Gospel that speaks of the nails at all, and there it is not in connection with the crucifixion, but the subsequent appearance to the disciples and the incredulity of Thomas (xx. 20, 25, 27). Here also, only the marks in the hands are referred to. The difference of the two representations is so great that there can really be no question of dependence, and those who are so eager to claim the use of the fourth Gospel simply because it is the only one that speaks of "nails" ("the print of the nails") might perhaps consider that the idea of crucifixion and the cross might well be independently associated with a reference to the nails by which the victim was generally attached. In the third Synoptic (xxiv. 39), the inference is inevitable that both hands and feet were supposed to be nailed. When the report, "The Lord is risen," is brought to the eleven, Jesus is represented as standing in their midst and assuring them that he was not a spirit, by saying: "See my hands and my feet, that it is I myself"—meaning of course the prints of the nails in both. The statement in Peter that on the occurrence of the earthquake "great fear came [upon them]" (φόβος μέγας ἐγένετο) is not even mentioned in Matthew when he narrates the earthquake, which he represents as occurring when Jesus expired. The expression is characteristic of the author, who uses it elsewhere.

The representation that the sun shone out and that the Jews were glad when they found it was the ninth hour, and that consequently their law, twice quoted by the author, would not be broken, is limited to the

---

[1] It is suggested that these words must be taken as sarcasm on the part of those who give the body to Joseph.

fragment; as is also the statement that they gave his body to Joseph that he might bury it, "for he had beheld the good works that he did." As we have already seen, the canonical Gospels represent Joseph as going to Pilate at this time and begging for the body of Jesus, and it will be remembered that, in Mark (xv. 44), it is said that "Pilate marvelled if he were already dead," and called the centurion to ascertain the fact before he granted the body. In Peter, the body was of course given in consequence of the previous order, when Pilate asked Herod for it.

Joseph is represented, here, as only washing the body and wrapping it in linen (λαβὼν δὲ τὸν κύριον ἔλουσε καὶ εἴλησε σινδόνι). The first Synoptist (xxvii. 59) says that Joseph took the body and "wrapped it in a clean linen cloth" (ἐνετύλιξεν αὐτὸ [ἐν] σινδόνι καθαρᾷ). Mark similarly describes that (xv. 46), bringing "a linen cloth and taking him down, he wound him in the linen cloth" (καθελὼν αὐτὸν ἐνείλησεν τῇ σινδόνι). The third Synoptist has nearly the same statement and words. The fourth Gospel has a much more elaborate account to give (xix. 38 ff.). Joseph goes to Pilate asking that he may take away the body, and Pilate gives him leave. He comes and takes away the body. "And there came also Nicodemus ... bringing a mixture of myrrh and aloes, about a hundred pound *weight. So they took the body of Jesus and bound it in linen clothes (καὶ ἔδησαν αὐτὸ ὀθονίοις) with the spices, as the custom of the Jews is to bury."* This account is quite different from that in the Synoptics, and equally so from Peter's, which approximates much more nearly to that in the latter.

Peter says that Joseph then "brought him into his own grave, called 'Joseph's Garden'" (εἰσήγαγεν εἰς ἴδιον τάφον καλούμενον Κῆπον Ἰωσήφ). The account of the tomb is much more minute in the canonical Gospels. In Matthew (xxvii. 60), Joseph is said to lay the body "in his own new tomb (μνημείῳ), which he had hewn out In Mark (xv. 46), he lays him "in a tomb (μνήματι) which had been hewn out of a rock; and he rolled a stone against the door of the tomb" (μνημείου). Luke has a new detail to chronicle (xxiii. 53): Joseph lays him "in a tomb (μνηματί) that was hewn in stone, where never man had yet lain." The first two Synoptists, it will be observed, say that Joseph rolls a stone against the entrance to the tomb: but neither Luke nor Peter has this detail, though the former leaves it to be inferred that it had been done, for (xxiv. 2) the women who came on the first day of the week find the stone rolled away from the tomb. In Peter, on the contrary, the stone is rolled against the tomb by the guard and others later, as we shall presently see.

THE GOSPEL ACCORDING TO PETER - A STUDY

In the fourth Gospel, the account has further and different details, agreeing, however, with the peculiar statement of Luke (xix. 41 f.): "Now in the place where he was crucified there was a garden (κῆπος), and in the garden a new tomb (μνημεῖον) wherein was never man yet laid. There then, because of the Jews' Preparation (for the tomb [μνημεῖον] was nigh at hand), they laid Jesus." Some stress has been laid upon the point that both Peter and the fourth Gospel use the word "garden," and that none of the Synoptics have it, and as these critics seem to go upon the principle that any statement in Peter which happens to be in any canonical Gospel, even although widely different in treatment, must have been derived from that Gospel, and not from any similar written or traditional source, from which that Gospel derived it, they argue that this shows dependence on the fourth Gospel. There is certainly no evidence of dependence here. In Peter, the grave (τάφος) is simply said to be called "Joseph's Garden" (Κῆπον Ἰωσηφ),[1] and described as "his own grave." The fourth Gospel does not identify the garden as Joseph's at all, but says that "in the place where he was crucified there was a garden," and in it "a tomb" (μνημεῖον), and the reason given for taking the body thither is not that it belonged to Joseph, but that the tomb "was nigh at hand," and that on account of the Jews' Preparation they laid it there. The whole explanation seems to exclude the idea that the writer knew that it belonged to Joseph. Peter simply contributes a new detail to the common tradition. There is no appearance of his deriving this from our canonical Gospels, from which he differs in substance and in language. Neither Peter nor the Synoptics know anything of the co-operation of Nicodemus.

The narrative in the fragment continues:

> 25. Then the Jews and the elders and the priests, seeing the evil they had done to themselves, began to beat their breasts (ἤρξαντο κόπτεσθαι) and to say: "Woe for our sins; judgment draweth nigh and the end of Jerusalem."

We have already discussed this passage in connection with the "Diatessaron," and have now only to consider it as compared with our Gospels. There is no equivalent in any of them, except that the third Synoptist (xxiii. 48) says that when Jesus gave up the ghost: "All the

---

[1] Harnack suggests that perhaps in the author's time Joseph's garden was a known locality (l.c. p. 28).

multitude that came together to this sight, when they beheld the things that were done, returned smiting their breasts (τύπτοντες τὰ στήθη ὑπέστρεφον)." The reason for this change of mood is, of course, the eclipse and consequent darkness in the third Synoptic, and the earthquake and darkness in Peter; but in the former "all the multitude" smite their breasts, and in the latter "the Jews and the elders and the priests." It may be suggested whether the words inserted in the ancient Latin Codex of St. Germain, "Vae nobis, quae facta sunt hodie propter peccata nostra, appropinquavit enim desolatio Hierusalem,"[1] may not have been taken from our Gospel of Peter, for an expansion of the original text of the third Synoptic, by the author of this version.

The common reference of the fragment is to "the Jews," "the Jews and the elders and the priests," "the scribes and Pharisees and elders," and "the elders and scribes." Throughout the same part of the narrative in Matthew, we have "the scribes and elders," "chief priests and elders of the people" (this, most frequently), "chief priests with the scribes and elders," and in speaking of the guard at the sepulchre, "the chief priests and the Pharisees." In Mark, the same leaders are named, whilst in Luke we have "the chief priests and captains of the Temple and elders," "the elders of the people and both the chief priests and scribes," and, repeatedly, the "chief priests and rulers." The fourth Gospel usually cites "the chief priests and Pharisees," "chief captains and officers of the Jews," "the Jews," and "the chief priests of the Jews." There is more analogy, in this respect, between the fragment and the fourth Gospel than between it and the Synoptics.

We come now to an important and characteristic part of the fragment:

> 26. And I, with my companions, was mourning, and being pierced in spirit we hid ourselves; for we were sought for by them as malefactors, and as desiring to burn the temple. 27. Over all these things, however, we were fasting, and sat mourning and weeping night and day until the Sabbath.

There is no parallel to this passage in our Gospels, but in the statement that the Apostles had hidden themselves (and—taken in connection with v. 59, where the same fact is again mentioned—this means all the twelve) we have here agreement with the narrative of the

---

[1] The Syriac version of Cureton has nearly the same reading.

first and second Synoptics (Matt. xxvi. 56; Mark xix. 50), that on the arrest of Jesus "all the disciples left him and fled." This passage seems to exclude the incident of the sword and Malchus which, as Hilgenfeld points out,[1] is also excluded by a passage in Justin; the denial of Peter, which Justin equally passes over unmentioned; and the episode of the "beloved disciple" by the cross. The reason given for hiding themselves, that they were accused of wishing to burn the temple, has some connection with the tradition, that testimony had been given against Jesus that he had said he could destroy this temple and build it in three days (Matt. xxvi. 60; Mark xiv. 58).[2] The passage is one of those in which the writer speaks in the first person and represents himself as an Apostle, which he still more clearly does, *v.* 60, where he distinctly calls himself Simon Peter.

The account that the Apostles were fasting and sat mourning and weeping "night and day until the Sabbath" (νυκτὸς καὶ ἡμέρας ἕως τοῦ σαββάτου) opens out an interesting problem. As a rule, the Greek expression would be ἡμέρας καὶ νυκτός, so if we are to take the words actually used as deliberately intended to represent the time, we should have to count at least one night and one day between the death of Jesus and the Sabbath, or in other words, that the crucifixion took place, not on Friday, but upon Thursday, which, according to the statement in *v.* 5, would really be the 13th Nisan. A great deal might be said in support of this view,[3] but it need not be entered into here. It is probable that, as Harnack suggests,[4] the author really thinks of the whole time from the Thursday night, when the arrest was made.

With the next portion of the fragment the narrative of the resurrection may be said to begin:

> 28. But the scribes and Pharisees and elders assembled themselves together (συναχθέντες πρὸς ἀλλήλους), hearing that all the people murmured and beat their breasts, saying, "If at his death these great signs have happened,

---

[1] Zeitschr. 1893, ii. 246.

[2] It will be remembered that the same accusation is brought against Stephen in Acts. The mockery of the passers-by (Matt. xxvii. 40), "Thou that destroyest the temple, and buildest it in three days, save thyself," is also in the same vein.

[3] There is an interesting discussion of the question by Van Manen, Theol. Tijdschr. 1893, 4de Stuk, pp. 423 ff.

[4] L.c. p. 28.

behold how just a one he is." 29. The elders were afraid (ἐφοβήθησαν) and came to Pilate (ἦλθον πρὸς Πειλᾶτον) beseeching him and saying. 30. "Give us soldiers that we may watch his grave for three days (ἵνα φυλάξωμεν τὸ μνῆμα αὐτοῦ ἐπὶ τρεῖς ἡμέρας), lest his disciples come and steal him, and the people believe that he rose from the dead and do us evil" (μήποτε ἐλθόντες οἱ μαθηταὶ αὐτοῦ κλέψωσιν αὐτὸν καὶ ὑπολάβῃ ὁ λαὸς ὅτι ἐκ νεκρῶν ἀνέστη, καὶ ποιήσωσιν ἡμῖν κακά). 31. Pilate, therefore, gave them Petronius the centurion with soldiers to watch the tomb (μετὰ στρατιωτῶν φυλάσσειν τὸν τάφον), and with them came the elders and scribes to the grave (τὸ μνῆμα). 32. And they rolled a great stone (κυλίσαντες λίθον μέγαν) against the centurion and the soldiers, and set it, all who were there together, at the door of the grave (μνήματος). 33. And they put seven seals (καὶ ἐπέχρισαν ἑπτὰ σφραγῖδας), and setting up a tent there they kept guard (ἐφύλαξαν). 34. And in the morning, at the dawn of the Sabbath, came a multitude from Jerusalem and the neighbourhood in order that they might see the sealed-up grave (τὸ μνημεῖον ἐσφραγισμένον).

There is no parallel to this narrative in any of our canonical Gospels except the first Synoptic, which alone mentions the circumstance that a watch was set over the sepulchre, a fact of which the other Gospels seem quite ignorant, and states that application was made to Pilate for a guard for that purpose. The account in Matthew is as follows (xxvii. 62 f.):

> Now on the morrow, which is *the day* after the Preparation, the chief priests and the Pharisees were gathered together (συνήχθησαν) unto Pilate, saying, Sir, we remember that that deceiver said, while he was yet alive, After three days I rise again. Command therefore that the sepulchre be made sure until the third day, lest haply his disciples come and steal him away, and say unto the people, He rose from the dead: and the last error will be worse than the first (ἀσφαλισθῆναι τὸν τάφον ἕως τῆς τρίτης ἡμέρας; μήποτε ἐλθόντες οἱ μαθηταὶ κλέψωσιν αὐτὸν, καὶ εἴπωσιν τῷ λαῷ, Ἠγέρθη ἀπὸ τῶν νεκρῶν; καὶ ἔσται ἡ ἐσχάτη πλάνη χείρων τῆς πρώτης). Pilate said unto them, Ye have a guard: go your way, make it as sure as

ye can. So they went, and made the sepulchre sure (ἠσφαλίσαντο τὸν τάφον), sealing the stone (σφραγίσαντες τὸν λίθον), the guard being with them (μετὰ τῆς κουστωδίας).

The fact that only one of the four canonical Gospels has any reference to this episode, or betrays the slightest knowledge of any precautions taken to guard the tomb, is remarkable. The analogies in the narrative in Peter with the general account, and the similarity of the language in certain parts, together with the wide variation in details and language generally, point to the conclusion that both writers derive the episode from a similar source, but independently of each other. The casual agreement with continuous dissimilarity of statement and style, are evidence of the separate treatment of a common tradition, and put the fragment upon a very different footing from the Synoptics in relation to each other. The absence of verisimilitude is pretty nearly equal in both Gospels, but these traditions grew up, and were unconsciously rounded by the contributions of pious imagination.

In the fragment it is "the scribes and Pharisees and elders" (οἱ γραμματεῖς καὶ Φαρισαῖοι καὶ πρεσβύτεροι) who meet together, but only the "elders" go to Pilate; in the Synoptic, "the chief Priests and the Pharisees" (οἱ ἀρχιερεῖς καὶ οἱ Φαρισαῖοι) meet and go to Pilate. Pilate gives them "Petronius the centurion with soldiers" to watch the tomb; in Matthew, he gives them "a guard," bidding them make it sure; so they go and seal the stone, the guard being with them. In Peter, the "elders and scribes" go to the grave, and themselves with the soldiers, "all who were there together," roll a great stone and set it at the door of the grave. Doubtless this trait is intended to convey an impression of the great size of the stone. A curious peculiarity occurs in the statement, "they roll the stone against the centurion and the soldiers," the intention of the words probably being that, in their suspicious mood, they thus protected themselves from possible fraud on the part even of the soldiers.[1] The motive for the application to Pilate, in the fragment, is fear on the part of the elders, in consequence of the murmuring and lamentation of the people, who are represented as being convinced by the great signs occurring at the death of Jesus "how just a one" he was. This is quite a variation from the Synoptic version, but both agree in the explanation given to Pilate of anxiety lest the disciples should steal the body, and say that Jesus had risen

---

[1] Dr. Swete also takes this view of the passage, l.c. p. 15, n. 4.

from the dead. In Matthew, they simply "seal the stone," but in the fragment they put or smear (ἐπέχρισαν) "seven seals" upon it. Some important peculiarities then occur in the narrative of Peter. They set up a tent beside the tomb and keep guard, and in the morning a multitude from Jerusalem and the neighbourhood come out to see the sealed-up grave. There is nothing corresponding to this in the Synoptic Gospel.

The narrative proceeds:

> 35. Now, in the night before the dawn of the Lord's day (ἡ κυριακή), whilst the soldiers were keeping guard over the place, two and two in a watch, there was a great voice in the heaven. 36. And they saw the heavens opened and two men come down from thence with great light and approach the tomb. 37. But the stone which had been laid at the door rolled of itself away by the side, and the tomb was opened and both the young men entered.

Here commences an account of the resurrection very different in every respect from that in our canonical Gospels, and the treatment of a tradition in some points necessarily common to all is evidently independent. In Matthew, the scene commences with an earthquake—earthquakes are, indeed, peculiar to the first Synoptist—(xxviii. 2 f.): "And behold there was a great earthquake; for an angel of the Lord descended from heaven, and came and rolled away the stone and sat upon it. His appearance was as lightning, and his raiment white as snow; and for fear of him the watchers did quake and become as dead men." Here only one angel comes down, whilst in Peter there are two men, whom some critics—amongst whom may be mentioned Nestle, with whom Harnack is inclined to agree, more especially as they are never called angels, but merely "two men"—identify as Moses and Elias. The angel rolls away the stone, which in Peter rolls away of itself, and sits upon it, whilst in Peter the two men enter into the tomb. No account is given in Mark of the opening of the tomb, the women simply finding the stone rolled away, and a young man (νεανίσκον) sitting on the right side arrayed in a white robe (xvi. 4 f.); the author does not mention any earthquake. In the third Synoptic (xxiv. 2 f.), the women also find the stone already rolled away from the tomb; there is no earthquake. When the women enter the tomb they do not find "the body of the Lord Jesus," but while they are perplexed two men stand by them in dazzling apparel. In the fourth Gospel (xx. 12 f.), Mary, coming to the sepulchre, sees two angels in white sitting—the one at the head, the other at the foot—where the body of Jesus had lain.

THE GOSPEL ACCORDING TO PETER - A STUDY

Thus, to sum up, in Matthew there is one angel, in Mark one young man, in Luke two men, in the fourth Gospel two angels, and in Peter two men descend from heaven to the tomb.

Peter goes on:

> 38. Then these soldiers, seeing this, awakened the centurion and the elders, for they also were keeping watch. 39. And whilst they were narrating to them what they had seen, they beheld again three men coming out of the tomb and the two were supporting the one, and a cross following them. 40. And the heads of the two indeed reached up to the heaven, but that of him that was led by their hands rose above the heavens. 41. And they heard a voice from the heavens saying, "Hast thou preached to them that are sleeping?" 42. And an answer was heard from the cross: "Yea."

Of course there is nothing corresponding to this in the canonical Gospels. In Matthew, the watchers quake and become as dead men, but no such alarm is here described. The elders and soldiers see the two men who had entered the tomb come out leading a third, and the stately appearance of the three is described with Oriental extravagance.[1] Following the three is a cross, a very singular representation, more especially as the cross presently speaks. Harnack says that Duhms, who supposes a Hebraic original, conjectures that the Hebrew word, which could as well stand for "crucified" as "cross," was misunderstood by the translator, and he adds that, if the original was Aramaic, the matter becomes still simpler. However, Harnack does not seem disposed to adopt the suggestion.[2] It is well known that in very early works the cross was identified with the crucified, and treated both as a type and as having a certain personality—the living and eloquent symbol of victory over death.[3]

---

[1] There are, of course, many instances of such exaggeration: Apoc. x. 1 f.; Hermas, Sim. ix. 6; 4 Esdras, ii. 43; Passio Perp. c. 10.

[2] L.c. p. 70.

[3] Cf. Justin, Apol. i. 55: Dial. lxxxvi. xci.; Irenaeus, C. Haer. ii. 24, 4; v. 17, 3 f. In the Ev. Nicod. ii. (Lat. B), in which the descent is fully treated, Jesus Christ is begged to make the sign of the cross: "Et factum est ita, posuitque dominus crucem suam in medio inferni, quae est signum victoriae et usque in aeternum permanebit" (Evang. Nicodemi, Pars ii. Latine B. cap. x. (xxvi.);

The words of the voice from the heavens are: " 'Hast thou preached to them that are sleeping?' and an answer was heard from the cross: 'Yea' " ('Εκήρυξας τοῖς κοιμωμένοις? καὶ ὑπακοὴ ἠκούετο ἀπὸ τοῦ σταυροῦ ὅτι Ναί). This is generally understood as a reference to the "descent into hell," which was early accepted as a dogma by the Church and has a place in the Creed, although its only clear mention in the New Testament occurs in 1 Peter iii. 18 f.: "Because Christ ... being put to death in the flesh, but quickened in the spirit, in which also he went and preached (ἐκήρυξεν) unto the spirits in prison, which aforetime were disobedient;" and (iv. 6): "For unto this end was the Gospel spoken unto the dead." It is a curious fact that the "Gospel according to Peter," the fragment of which is first discovered in a little volume along with a fragment of the "Apocalypse of Peter," should thus contain a reference to a doctrine, the only allusion to which in any of the canonical writings is contained in a so-called "Epistle of Peter." Hilgenfeld wishes to read κοινωμένοις instead of κοιμωμένοις, and disputes the rendering of ὑπακοή as "answer," although he admits that there is some support to this as a liturgical response.[1] He would render this passage: "Du verkündigtest den Profanirten und einem Gehorsam.[2] Von dem Kreuze her erschallt: Ja." He argues that there can be no question here of a descent into hell by one coming out of the grave who cannot even hold himself upright, but must be led; that, however much the inanimate body of Jesus may still be called "the Lord," his "Self" is already in death ascended to heaven; the selfless (*selbstlose*) body cannot possibly in the meantime have gone into Hades.[3] In this conclusion, however, he is at variance with almost all critics, who generally take the view rendered above.[4]

The passage which we have quoted from Matthew (xxvii. 52 f.) must be recalled, in which the first Synoptic alone of the four canoni-

---

Tischendorf, Evang. Apocr. 1853, p. 409; Ep. Barn. c. 12; Greg. Nyss. Adv. Jud. c. 7).

[1] Constitt. App. viii. 12, pp. 259, 13 f.
[2] The expression is so peculiar that we give it in the original.
[3] L.c. pp. 263 f. Dr. Martineau translates the passage: "Hast thou preached obedience to them that sleep?" Nineteenth Century, June 1893, pp. 917 f.
[4] Harnack, l.c. pp. 68 f.; Lods, l.c. p. 48, although with a ?; Zahn, l.c. pp. 22 f.; Robinson, l.c. pp. 24 f.; Swete, l.c. pp. xiv. 19. (Dr. Swete considers any reference to 1 Pet. iii. 19 improbable.) J. Rendel Harris, l.c. pp. 51 f., 89; von Schubert, l.c. pp. 101 f.; cf. van Manen, l.c. pp. 522 f.; Martineau, l.c. pp. 917 f.

cal Gospels has an account of astonishing events said to have occurred at the death of Jesus: an earthquake which rent the rocks and opened the tombs, "and many bodies of the saints that were sleeping (κεκοιμημένων) were raised; and coming forth out of the tombs after his resurrection, they entered into the holy city and appeared unto many." This resurrection of the saints "that were sleeping" is associated by Eusebius with the descent into hell,[1] and it is not improbable that the first Synoptist had it in his mind. It is not necessary to point out many early references to the descent into hell,[2] but an interesting passage may be quoted from Justin. He accuses the Jews of omitting from the prophecy of Jeremiah in their copies of the Septuagint the following verse: "The Lord God, the Holy one of Israel, remembered his dead who lay sleeping (κεκοιμημένων) in the earth, and descended to them to bring to them the good news of his salvation."[3] It is not known that the passage ever really existed in Jeremiah but, notwithstanding, Irenaeus quotes it no less than five times.[4]

The writer does not explain the representation of the three who came out of the tomb, two of whom were "supporting," or, as is subsequently said, leading him, or conducting him, but this figure, more stately than the others, of course, is intended to be recognised as Jesus. Too much has been said as to the weakness supposed to be here described, and Zahn, who as much as possible ridicules the whole contents of the fragment, says that "the raised Lazarus, in comparison with him, is a hero in strength and life." But is the intention here to depict weakness? No word is used which really demands that interpretation. As Dr. Swete rightly points out, "the support appears to be regarded as nominal only, since He is also said to be 'conducted' (χειραγωγούμενον)" (p. 18). It is true that χειραγωγεῖν is twice used in Acts (ix. 8, xxii. 11) to express Paul's helplessness when led by the hand after his vision on the way to Damascus, but it does not in itself imply weakness, and no other hint of feebleness is given in the fragment. The "touch me not" of the fourth Gospel, when Mary Magdalene stretches out her hand to Jesus, is quite as much a mark of weakness as this. It may not unfairly, on the other hand, be interpreted as a mark of honour, and nothing in Peter forbids this reading. If

---

[1] Dem. Ev. 500. This is referred to by Dr. Swete, l.c. p. 19, n. 2.
[2] For instance, Ignat. Ep. Magn. 9; Hermas, Sim. ix. 16.
[3] Dial. lxxii.
[4] Haer. iii. 20, 4; iv. 22, 1; 33, 1, 12; v. 31, 1.

weakness were indicated, it might be taken as a Docetic representation of the condition of the human body, deprived of the divine Christ, who had ascended from the cross.

The continuation of the narrative in Peter is as different from that of our canonical Gospels as its commencement:

> 43. These, therefore, took counsel together whether they should go and declare these things to Pilate. 44. And whilst they were still considering, the heavens again appeared opened, and a certain man descending and going into the grave. 45. Seeing these things, the centurion and his men hastened to Pilate by night, leaving the tomb they were watching, and narrated all things they had seen, fearing greatly, and saying: "Truly he was a Son of God" (ἀληθῶς υἱὸς ἦν θεοῦ). 46. Pilate answered and said, "I am pure of the blood of the Son of God, but thus it seemed good unto you" (ἐγὼ καθαρεύω τοῦ αἵματος τοῦ υἱοῦ τοῦ θεοῦ, ὑμῖν δὲ τοῦτο ἔδοξεν). 47. Then they all came to him beseeching and entreating him that he should command the centurion and the soldiers to say nothing of what they had seen, 48. "For it is better," they said, "to lay upon us the greatest sins before God, and not to fall into the hands of the people of the Jews and be stoned." 49. Pilate, therefore, commanded the centurion and the soldiers to say nothing.

As the first Synoptic is the only Gospel which relates the story of the application to Pilate for a guard and the watch at the sepulchre, so of course it is the only one which gives the sequel to that episode; but this differs in every respect from the account in Peter. It is as follows (xxviii. 11 f.):

> Some of the guard came into the city, and told unto the chief priests all the things that were come to pass. And when they were assembled with the elders, and had taken counsel, they gave large money unto the soldiers, saying, Say ye, His disciples came by night and stole him away while we slept. And if this come to the governor's ears, we will persuade him, and rid you of care. So they took the money, and did as they were taught: and this saying was spread abroad among the Jews, and continueth until this day.

THE GOSPEL ACCORDING TO PETER - A STUDY

When the centurion and soldiers in Peter go to Pilate after witnessing the events described as occurring at the resurrection, "fearing greatly" (ἀγωνιῶντες μεγάλως), they say, "Truly he was a Son of God" (ἀληθῶς υἱὸς ἦν θεοῦ). It will be remembered that, in the first Synoptic, when the centurion and they that were watching Jesus saw the earthquake and the things that were done when he expired, they "feared exceedingly" (ἐφοβήθησαν σφόδρα), and said, "Truly this was a Son of God" (ἀληθῶς θεοῦ υἱὸς ἦν οὗτος). The tradition of the astonished centurion bearing such testimony to Jesus is known to both writers, but under different circumstances, and independently treated. In similar fashion, the reply put into the mouth of Pilate in Peter, "I am pure of the blood (ἐγὼ καθαρεύω τοῦ αἵματος) of the Son of God, but thus it seemed good unto you," is, to a certain extent, the same as Pilate's declaration to the multitude after washing his hands (xxvii. 24 f.): "I am innocent of the blood of this righteous man (ἀθῷός εἰμι ἀπὸ τοῦ αἵματος τοῦ δικαίου τούτου): see ye to it;" but in this case, as well as the other, the details and the language show an independent use of a similar source. In the Synoptic, the centurion and soldiers do not go to Pilate at all, but are bribed by the chief priests and elders to say that his disciples stole him by night when they slept. They are warned by Pilate to be altogether silent, in Peter. As the desire of the author is represented to be to remove responsibility from Pilate and throw it all upon the Jews, it is difficult to conceive that, if he had this account before him, he could deliberately have left it unused, and preferred his own account.

We now come to the visit of the women to the sepulchre:

> 50. In the morning of the Lord's day, Mary Magdalene, a disciple of the Lord (through fear of the Jews, for they burnt with anger, she had not done at the grave of the Lord that which women are accustomed to do for those that die and are loved by them), 51. took her women friends with her and came to the grave where he was laid. 52. And they feared lest the Jews should see them, and said: "If we could not on that day on which he was crucified weep and lament, let us do these things even now at his grave. 53. But who will roll away the stone that is laid at the door of his grave (τίς δὲ ἀποκυλίσει ἡμῖν καὶ τὸν λίθον τὸν τεθέντα ἐπὶ τῆς θύρας τοῦ μνημείου) in order that we may enter and set ourselves by him and do the things that are due? 54. For great was the stone (μέγας γὰρ ἦν ὁ λίθος), and we fear lest some one should see us.

And if we should not be able to do it, let us at least lay down before the door that which we bring in his memory, and let us weep and lament till we come to our home " 55. And they went and found the tomb opened and, coming near, they stooped down and see there a certain young man sitting in the midst of the tomb, beautiful and clad in a shining garment (καὶ προσελθοῦσαι παρέκυψαν ἐκεῖ, καὶ ὁρῶσιν ἐκεῖ τινα νεανίσκον καθεζόμενον μέσῳ τοῦ τάφου, ὡραῖον καὶ περιβεβλημένον στολὴν λαμπροτάτην), who said to them: 56. "Why are ye come? Whom seek ye? Him who was crucified? He is risen and gone away But if ye do not believe, stoop down and see the place where he lay, that he is not there; for he is risen and gone away whence he was sent" (τί ἤλθατε; τίνα ζητεῖτε; μὴ τὸν σταυρωθέντα ἐκεῖνον; ἀνέστη καὶ ἀπῆλθεν; εἰ δὲ μὴ πιστεύετε, παρακύψατε καὶ ἴδατε τὸν τόπον ἔνθα ἔκειτο, ὅτι οὐκ ἔστιν; ἀνέστη γὰρ καὶ ἀπῆλθεν ἐκεῖ ὅθεναρυ ἀπεστάλη). Then the women, frightened, fled.

We need not remark that in all essential points the account given here is different from that in our Gospels.

In each of the three Synoptics, it is said that the women saw where Jesus was laid, and the first two name Mary Magdalene and Mary the mother of Jesus (Mark "the other Mary"), Matt. xxvii. 61, Mark xv. 47, Luke xxiii. 55. All four canonical Gospels relate their coming to the sepulchre: Matthew (xxviii. 1), "late on the Sabbath day, as it began to dawn toward the first day of the week;" Mark (xvi. 1), "when the Sabbath was past;" Luke (xxiv. 1), "on the first day of the week at early dawn;" but only the second and third state that they bring spices to anoint Jesus; in Matthew the purpose stated being merely "to see the sepulchre." In the fourth Gospel, only Mary Magdalene comes, and no reason is assigned. In Peter, Mary Magdalene only is named, but she takes her women friends, and though spices are not directly named, they are distinctly implied, and the object of the visit to the tomb, admirably described as "that which women are accustomed to do for those who die and are loved by them," which they had not been able to do on the day of the crucifixion, through fear of the Jews. Even now the same fear is upon them; but nothing is said of it in the four Gospels.

The only part of the words put into their mouths by the author which at all corresponds with anything in the canonical narratives is that regarding the opening of the sepulchre. "But who will roll us away the stone that is laid at the door of the grave?" (τίς δὲ ἀποκυλίσει ἡμῖν καὶ τὸν λίθον τὸν τεθέντα, ἐπὶ τῆς θύρας τοῦ μνημείου?). In Matthew, an angel had rolled away the stone, but in Mark the women are represented as asking the same question among themselves (xvi. 3), "Who shall roll us away the stone from the door of the grave?" (τίς ἀποκυλίσει ἡμῖν τὸν λίθον ἐκ τῆς θύρας τοῦ μνημείου?) practically in the same words. To appreciate the relative importance of the similarity in this detail it should be remembered that the same words are used with slight grammatical changes in the other two Synoptics: Matt. xxviii. 2, the angel "rolled away the stone" (ἀπεκύλισε τὸν λίθον); and Luke xxiv. 2, they found "the stone rolled away from the grave" (τὸν λίθον ἀποκεκυλισμένον ἀπὸ τοῦ μνημείου). The privilege of using a similar source of tradition must also be accorded to the author of the fragment.

The women in Peter, after a few more words explanatory of their purpose in going to the sepulchre, use an expression to which so much importance has been attached by Zahn that, to render it intelligible, it must be connected with the context just discussed. "But who will roll away the stone that is laid at the door of the grave, in order that we may enter and set ourselves by him, and do the things that are due? For great was the stone (μέγας γὰρ ἦν ὁ λίθος), and we fear lest some one should see us." Now in the second Synoptic (xvi. 4) we read that the women, looking up, "see that the stone (λίθος) is rolled back; for it was exceeding great" (ἦν γὰρ μέγας σφόδρα). Zahn says: "Just as certainly can the dependence of the Gospel of [1] To one so willing to be convinced, what might not be proved by many little words in the canonical Gospels? It must be remembered that none of our Synoptics sprang full-fledged from the original tradition, but, as is recognised by every critic competent to form an opinion, is based on previous works and records of tradition, which gradually grew into this more complete form. Any one who wishes to realise this should examine Rushbrooke's "Synopticon," which, at a glance, will show the matter and the language common to our first three Gospels, and leave little doubt as to the common origin of these works. It may be useful towards a proper understanding of the problem before us if we give a single illustration of the construction of the Synoptics taken from the

---

[1] L.c. p. 52.

very part of the narrative at which we have arrived. We shall arrange it in parallel columns for facility of comparison.

MATTHEW xxvii.	MARK xv.	LUKE xxiii.
55. And many women were there beholding from afar, which had followed Jesus from Galilee, ministering unto him: 56. among whom was Mary Magdalene, and Mary the mother of James and Joses, and the mother of the sons of Zebedee. 57. And when even was come, there came a rich man from Arimathaea, who also himself was Jesus' disciple: 58. this man went to Pilate, and asked for the body of Jesus.	40. And there were also women beholding from afar: among whom were both Mary Magdalene and Mary the mother of James the less and of Joses, and Salome; 41. who, when he was in Galilee, followed him, and ministered unto him.... 42. And when even was now come, ... 43. there came Joseph of Arimathaea, a councillor of honourable estate, who also himself was looking for the kingdom of God: and he boldly went in unto Pilate and asked for the body of Jesus.	49. And all his acquaintance, and the women that followed him from Galilee, stood afar off, seeing these things, xxiv. 10. Now they were Mary Magdalene and Joanna, and Mary [the mother] of James, and other women with them, xxiii. 50. 50. And behold a man named Joseph, who was a councillor, a good man and a righteous, 51. ... of Arimathaea, a city of the Jews, who was looking for the kingdom of God: 52. this man went to Pilate, and asked for the body of Jesus.
55. Ἦσαν δὲ ἐκεῖ γυναῖκες πολλαὶ ἀπὸ μακρόθεν θεωροῦσαι, αἵτινες ἠκολούθησαν τῷ Ἰησοῦ ἀπὸ τῆς Γαλιλαίας διακονοῦσαι αὐτῷ, (56) ἐν αἷς ἦν Μαρία ἡ Μαγδαληνή, καὶ Μαρία ἡ τοῦ	40. Ἦσαν δὲ καὶ γυναῖκες ἀπὸ μακρόθεν θεωροῦσαι, ἐν αἷς καὶ Μαρία ἡ Μαγδαληνὴ καὶ Μαρία ἡ Ἰακώβου τοῦ μικροῦ καὶ Ἰωσῆτος μήτηρ καὶ Σαλώμη, (41) αἳ ὅτε ἦν ἐν τῇ Γαλιλαίᾳ	49. Εἱστήκεισαν δὲ πάντες οἱ γνωστοὶ αὐτῷ ἀπὸ μακρόθεν, καὶ γυναῖκες αἱ συνακολουθοῦσαι αὐτῶ ἀπὸ τῆς Γαλιλαίας, ὁρῶσαι ταῦτα. (xxiv. 10) ἦσαν δὲ ἡ Μαγδαληνὴ Μαρία καὶ Ἰωάννα καὶ

Ἰακώβου καὶ Ἰωσὴ μήτηρ, καὶ ἡ μήτηρ τῶν υἱῶν Ζεβεδαίου. 57. Ὀψίας δὲ γενομένης ἦλθεν ἄνθρωπος πλούσιος ἀπὸ Ἀριμαθαίας, τοὔνομα Ἰωσήφ, ὃς καὶ αὐτὸς ἐμαθητεύθη τῷ Ἰησοῦ· 58. οὗτος προσελθὼν τῷ Πειλάτῳ ᾐτήσατο τὸ σῶμα τοῦ Ἰησοῦ.	ἠκολούθουν αὐτῷ καὶ διηκόνουν αὐτῷ, ... 42. καὶ ἤδη ὀψίας γενομένης, ... (43) ἐλθὼν Ἰωσὴφ ἀπὸ Ἀριμαθαίας, εὐσχήμων βουλευτής, ὃς καὶ αὐτὸς ἦν προσδεχόμενος τὴν βασιλείαν τοῦ θεοῦ, τολμήσας εἰσῆλθεν πρὸς τὸν Πειλᾶτον καὶ ᾐτήσατο τὸ σῶμα τοῦ Ἰησοῦ.	Μαρία ἡ Ἰακώβου καὶ αἱ λοιπαὶ σὺν αὐταῖς ... 50. Καὶ ἰδοὺ ἀνὴρ ὀνόματι Ἰωσὴφ βουλευτὴς ὑπάρχων, ἀνὴρ ἀγαθὸς καὶ δίκαιος, 51. ... ἀπὸ Ἀριμαθαίας πόλεως τῶν Ἰουδαίων. ὃς προσεδέχετο τὴν βασιλείαν τοῦ θεοῦ. 52. οὗτος προσελθὼν τῷ Πειλάτῳ ᾐτήσατο τὸ σῶμα τοῦ Ἰησοῦ. Ἰησοῦ.

Or take, for instance, a few verses giving the arrest of Jesus as narrated by the three Synoptists:

MATTHEW xxvi.	MARK xiv.	LUKE xxii.
47. And while he yet spake, lo, Judas, one of the twelve, came, and with him a great multitude with swords and staves, from the chief priests and elders of the people. 48. Now he that betrayed him gave them a sign, saying, Whomsoever I shall kiss, that is he: take him. 49. And straightway he came to Jesus, and said, Hail, Rabbi; and kissed him.	43. And straightway, while he yet spake, cometh Judas, one of the twelve, and with him a multitude with swords and staves, from the chief priests and the scribes and the elders. 44. Now he that betrayed him had given them a token, saying, Whomsoever I shall kiss, that is he; take him, 45. And when he was come, straightway he came to him and saith, Rabbi; and kissed him.	47. While he yet spake, lo, a multitude, and he that was called Judas, one of the twelve, went before them; and he drew near unto Jesus to kiss him.

50. And Jesus said unto him, Friend, do that for which thou art come.		48. But Jesus said unto him, Judas, betrayest thou the Son of man with a kiss?
Then they came and laid hands on Jesus and took him. 51. And lo, one of them that were with Jesus stretched out his hand, and drew his sword, and smote the servant of the high priest, and struck off his ear.	46. And they laid hands on him and took him. 47. But a certain one of them that stood by drew his sword, and smote the servant of the high priest, and struck off his ear.	(54. And they seized him and led him away.) 50 And a certain one of them smote the servant of the high priest, and struck off right ear.
47. Καὶ ἔτι αὐτοῦ λαλοῦντος, ἰδοὺ Ἰούδας εἷς τῶν δώδεκα ἦλθεν, καὶ μετ' αὐτοῦ ὄχλος πολὺς μετὰ μαχαιρῶν καὶ ξύλων ἀπὸ τῶν ἀρχιερέων καὶ πρεσβυτέρων τοῦ λαοῦ. 48. ὁ δὲ παραδιδοὺς αὐτὸν ἔδωκεν αὐτοῖς σημεῖον λέγων: ὃν ἂν φιλήσω, αὐτός ἐστιν: κρατήσατε αὐτόν. 49. Καὶ εὐθέως προσελθὼν τῷ Ἰησοῦ εἶπεν: χαῖρε ῥαββεί, καὶ κατεφίλησεν αὐτόν.	43. Καὶ εὐθὺς ἔτι αὐτοῦ λαλοῦντος παραγίνεται Ἰούδας εἷς τῶν δώδεκα, καὶ μετ' αὐτοῦ ὄχλος μετὰ μαχαιρῶν καὶ ξύλων παρὰ τῶν ἀρχιερέων καὶ τῶν γραμματέων καὶ πρεσβυτέρων. 44. δεδώκει δὲ ὁ παραδιδοὺς αὐτὸν σύσσημον αὐτοῖς λέγων: ὃν ἂν φιλήσω, αὐτός ἐστιν: κρατήσατε αὐτὸν καὶ ἀπάγετε ἀσφαλῶς. 45. Καὶ ἐλθὼν εὐθὺς προσελθὼν αὐτῷ λέγει: ῥαββεί, καὶ κατεφίλησεν αὐτόν.	47. ἔτι αὐτοῦ λαλοῦντος, ἰδοὺ ὄχλος, καὶ ὁ λεγόμενος Ἰούδας εἷς τῶν δώδεκα προήρχετο αὐτούς, καὶ ἤγγισεν τῷ Ἰησοῦ φιλῆσαι αὐτόν.

50. ὁ δὲ Ἰησοῦς εἶπεν αὐτῷ· ἑταῖρε, ἐφ' ὃ πάρει, τότε προσελθόντες ἐπέβαλον τὰς χεῖρας ἐπὶ τὸν Ἰησοῦν καὶ ἐκράτησαν αὐτόν.	46. οἱ δὲ ἐπέβαλαν τὰς χεῖρας αὐτῷ καὶ ἐκράτησαν αὐτόν.	48. Ἰησοῦς δὲ εἶπεν αὐτῷ· Ἰούδα, φιλήματι τὸν υἱὸν τοῦ ἀνθρώπου παραδίδως; (54. συλλαβόντες δὲ αὐτὸν ἤγαγον.)
51. Καὶ ἰδοὺ εἷς τῶν μετὰ Ἰησοῦ ἐκτείνας τὴν χεῖρα ἀπέσπασεν τὴν μάχαιραν αὐτοῦ, καὶ πατάξας τὸν δοῦλον τοῦ ἀρχιερέως ἀφεῖλεν αὐτοῦ τὸ ὠτίον.	47. εἷς δέ τις τῶν παρεστηκότων σπασάμενος τὴν μάχαιραν ἔπαισεν τὸν δοῦλον τοῦ ἀρχιερέως καὶ ἀφεῖλεν αὐτοῦ τὸ ὠτάριον.	50. καὶ ἐπάταξεν εἷς τις ἐξ αὐτῶν τοῦ ἀρχιερέως τὸν δοῦλον καὶ ἀφεῖλεν τὸ οὖς αὐτοῦ τὸ δεξιόν.

Such close similarity as this, with occasional astonishing omissions of matter and flagrant contradictions where independent narrative is attempted, runs through the whole of the three Synoptics. This is not the place to enter upon any discussion of these phenomena, or any explanation of the origin of our Gospels, but apologists may be invited to consider the fact before passing judgment on the Gospel of Peter. Any coincidence of statement in the narrative of the fragment with any one of the four Gospels is promptly declared to be decisive evidence of dependence on that Gospel; and even the use of a word which has a parallel in them is sufficient reason for denouncing the author as a plagiarist. It would almost seem as if such critics had never read the prologue to the third Synoptic, and forgotten the πολλοί to which its author refers, when they limit the Christian tradition to these Gospels, which again, upon examination, must themselves be limited to two—the Synoptic and the Johannine, which in so great a degree contradict each other.

To return now to the passage which we have to examine. It will be observed that the second Synoptic treats the episode of the women in a manner different from the other two, but in the same style, though with very differing details, as Peter. We shall show reason for believing that both have drawn from the same source, but that the fragment has probably adhered more closely to the original source. In Mark (xvi. 3 f.) the women are, as in Peter, represented as speaking: "And they were saying among themselves, 'Who shall roll us away the stone from the door of the tomb?'" Here the *spoken* words stop, and the writer continues to narrate: "And looking up, they see that the stone *is rolled back (ἀνακεκύλισται): for it was (ἦν) exceeding great.*" It is obvious that the "was" here is quite out of place, and it seems impossible to avoid the conclusion that, originally, it must have stood with a different context. That different context we have in Peter The women say amongst themselves: "Who will roll us away the stone that is laid at the door of the grave, in order that we may enter"—and, of course, in saying this they are supposed to have in their minds the stone which they had seen the evening before and, naturally, express their recollection of it in the past tense—"for it was exceeding great." If the phrase has been mechanically introduced, it has been so by the second Synoptist, in whose text it is more out of place than in Peter. A prescriptive right to early traditions of this kind cannot reasonably be claimed for any writer, simply because his compilation has happened to secure a place in the Canon.

When the women come to the tomb, they stoop down (παρέκυψαν) and see there (ὁρῶσιν ἐκεῖ) a certain young man (τινα νεανίσκον) sitting in the midst of the tomb, beautiful and clad in a shining garment (ὡραῖον καὶ περιβεβλημένον στολὴν λαμπροτάτην). This is the "certain man" who descended when the heavens were again opened, as described in *v.* 44. The realistic touch of the women stooping to look into the low entrance of the tomb is repeated when the "young man" bids them "stoop down" (παρακύψατε) and convince themselves that Jesus had risen. This does not occur in any of the Synoptics; but in the fourth Gospel (xx. 5), Peter, it is said, "stooping down" (παρακύψας) sees (βλέπει) the clothes. In Matthew, the angel sits upon the stone which he has rolled away, and not in the sepulchre, and his description is (xxviii. 3): "His appearance was as lightning, and his raiment white as snow" (ἦν δὲ ἡ εἰδέα αὐτοῦ ὡς ἀστραπή, καὶ τὸ ἔνδυμα αὐτοῦ λευκὸν ὡς χιών). In Mark (xvi. 8), they see a "young man" (νεανίσκον) sitting on the right side, and not in the middle, and he is "clad in a white robe" (περιβεβλημένον στολὴν λευκήν). In Luke (xxiv. 4), two men (ἄνδρες δύο) stand by the women "in dazzling apparel" (ἐν ἐσθῆτι ἀστραπτούσῃ). In the fourth Gospel (xx. 12), Mary sees two angels sitting, the one at the head, the other at the feet, where the body had lain, but they are simply said to be "in white" (ἐν λευκοῖς)

The "young man" says to the women in Peter: "Why are ye come? (τί ἤλθατε?) Whom seek ye? (τίνα ζητεῖτε?) Him who was crucified? (μὴ τὸν σταυρωθέντα ἐκεῖνον?) He is risen and gone away (ἀνέστη καὶ ἀπῆλθεν). But if ye do not believe, stoop down, and see the place where he lay (παρακύψατε καὶ ἴδατε τὸν τόπον ἔνθα ἔκειτο), that he is not there, for he is risen and gone away thither whence he was sent (ἀνέστη γὰρ καὶ ἀπῆλθεν ἐκεῖ ὅθεν ἀπεστάλη)." In Matthew (xxviii. 5 f.) the angel "answered and said unto the women" (who had not spoken to him, apparently) "Fear not ye: for I know that ye seek Jesus which hath been crucified (οἶδα γὰρ ὅτι Ἰησοῦν τὸν ἐσταυρωμένον ζητεῖτε). He is not here, for he rose (οὐκ ἔστιν ὧδε, ἠγέρθη γάρ), even as he said. Come, see the place where the Lord lay (δεῦτε ἴδετε τὸν τόπον ὅπου ἔκειτο). And go quickly, and tell his disciples he rose from the dead (ἠγέρθη ἀπὸ τῶν νεκρῶν); and lo, he goeth before you into Galilee; there shall ye see him: lo, I have told you." In Mark (xvi. 6 f.), this "young man" in the tomb says: "Be not amazed; ye seek Jesus the Nazarene which hath been crucified (Ἰησοῦν ζητεῖτε τὸν Ναζαρηνὸν τὸν ἐσταυρωμένον). He rose (ἠγέρθη); he is not here; behold, the place where they laid him! (οὐκ ἔστιν ὧδε; ἴδε ὁ τόπος ὅπου ἔθηκαν αὐτόν). But go tell his disciples and Peter, He goeth before you into Galilee: there shall ye see him, as he said unto you." The close resemblance of these two accounts in the first and second Gospels is striking, and scarcely less so is the resemblance, with important variations, of the third Synoptic (xxiv. 5 ff.). The "two say to the women, who stand with their faces bowed down towards the earth: "Why seek ye the living among the dead? He is not here, but he rose (οὐκ ἔστιν ὧδε, ἀλλὰ ἠγέρθη).[1] Remember how he spake unto you when he was yet in Galilee, saying, that the Son of man must be delivered up into the hands of sinful men, and be crucified, and the third day rise again." The complete change in the reference to Galilee here will be observed.

The peculiar ending of the words of the "young man" in Peter is nowhere found in our Gospels: "He is risen and gone away thither whence he was sent." Mr. Robinson compares with this a passage from the 20th Homily of Aphrahat (ed. Wright, p. 385): "And the angel said to Mary, he is risen and gone away to him that sent him." Mr. Robinson adds: "There is reason to believe that Aphrahat, a Syrian writer, used Tatian's Harmony: and thus we seem to have a second link between our Gospel and that important work."[2] But is it not rather a curious position in which to place the supposed "Diatessaron," to ar-

---

[1] Westcott and Hort put these words between double brackets, as almost certain interpolations, through the action of "Western influences."
[2] The Gospel according to Peter, p. 29, n. 1.

gue that a passage which it does not now contain was nevertheless in it because a Syrian writer who is supposed to have used the "Diatessaron" has quoted the passage? It shows how untrustworthy are all arguments regarding early works like the "Diatessaron." Looking at the other instances which could be pointed out, and to some of which we have referred, we see that everything not agreeing with the Gospels of the Church has been gradually eliminated or corrected into agreement, and that thus the very probable use of the Gospel according to Peter by Tatian may be concealed. As Mr. Robinson further points out, however, the words of the angel in Peter are in direct contradiction to those put into the mouth of Jesus in the fourth Gospel (xx. 17): "I am not yet ascended to the Father."

The conclusion of the whole episode in Peter is the short and comprehensive phrase: "Then the women, frightened, fled" (τότε αἱ γυναῖκες φοβηθεῖσαι ἔφυγον). In Matthew, in obedience to the order of the angel to go and tell his disciples, none of which is given in Peter, it is said (xxviii. 8): "And they departed quickly from the tomb with fear and great joy" (καὶ ἀπελθοῦσαι ταχὺ ἀπὸ τοῦ μνημείου μετὰ φόβου καὶ χαρᾶς μεγάλης), "and ran to bring his disciples word." In Mark (xvi. 8) it is said: "And they went out and fled from the tomb; for trembling and astonishment had come upon them (καὶ ἐξελθοῦσαι ἔφυγον ἀπὸ τοῦ μνημείου; εἶκεν γὰρ αὐτὰς τρόμος καί ἔκστασις). And they said nothing to anyone: for they were afraid" (ἐφοβοῦντο γάρ). The running to bring the disciples word, in the first, and the saying nothing to any one, of the second, Synoptic, is a case of curious contradiction in details. The third Gospel twice over repeats the statement that the women told what they had heard "to the eleven and to all the rest" (xxiv. 9, 10), but says nothing of the emotions excited by the interview, except the double statement (xxiv. 8), "And they remembered his words," and, 11, "And these words appeared in their sight as idle talk, and they disbelieved them."

In the first Synoptic, however (xxviii. 9 f.), as the women go, the risen Jesus himself meets them and delivers the same order to tell the disciples to depart into Galilee, where they shall see him. The genuine portion of the second Synoptic ends with the words quoted above, and it is only in the added conclusion (xvi. 9. 20) that we meet with an account of an appearance to Mary Magdalene in the morning. The third Synoptic relates no appearance to the women or any one that morning, but the fourth Gospel has the appearance of Jesus to Mary Magdalene, and a long interview between them. Now all this is quite distinctly excluded from the Gospel according to Peter, and those who argue for the dependence of the work on our Gospels have to explain this deliberate omission.

The fragment proceeds:

> 58. And it was the last day of the Unleavened bread, and many went forth, returning to their homes, the feast being ended. 59. But we, the twelve disciples of the Lord, wept and mourned, and each went to his home sorrowing for that which had happened. 60. But I, Simon Peter, and Andrew, my brother, took our nets and went to the sea, and there was with us Levi, the son of Alphaeus, whom the Lord....

And so, at a most interesting point, the fragment breaks off, in the middle of a phrase. This, it will be observed, distinctly excludes the vision to the two disciples in the country, mentioned Mark xvi. 12 f., supposing it to be that described in the third Synoptic (xxiv. 13 ff.), of which long narrative no hint is given in Peter. It also, of course, excludes the appearance to the disciples in the room, described in the fourth Gospel (xix. 20 ff.), and the breathing of the Holy Ghost upon them, of which very important episode the three Synoptics are equally ignorant, as well as the second appearance to them and the conviction of the unbelieving Thomas, which only this Gospel records. We may add that the appearance to the eleven as they sat at meat, related in the addition to the second Synoptic (xvi. 14 f.), with the mission of the apostles "into all the world," with miraculous powers endowed, which the other Gospels do not mention, is likewise excluded by Peter.

This is not all that is excluded, however, for in the fragment reference is distinctly made to the "twelve disciples," which is an explicit confirmation of the statement made in *v.* 26 f., "I and my companions ... were fasting and mourning," which makes no exception any more than the similar "We, the twelve disciples of the Lord" now quoted. Supposing this statement to be deliberately made, and we have no reason whatever from anything in the rest of the fragment to doubt it, this completely excludes the whole of the story of a betrayal of his master by Judas Iscariot. Various facts must be remembered in confirmation of the view that the "betrayal" of Jesus by Judas Iscariot was unknown to the older tradition. In the Apocalypse (xxi. 14) it is said that upon the twelve foundations of the Holy City, the New Jerusalem, are written "the twelve names of the twelve apostles of the Lamb." If, as is generally believed, this Apocalypse was written by John the Apostle, is it possible that, if Judas had betrayed his master in the manner described by the canonical Gospels, he could deliberately have written this, using twice over the "twelve," which includes that Apostle? Again, in the first epistle to the Corinthians (i. xv. 5), in relating the supposed "appearances" of Jesus, it is said that he first appeared to Cephas: "Then unto the twelve."[1] If the point be considered on the mere ground of historical probability, there is every reason to consider that the betrayal by Judas is a later product of the "evolved gnosis." Jesus is described as going about everywhere with his disciples, and nothing could have been easier, under the circumstances, than to follow and quietly arrest him, without any betrayal at all. In fact, there is no real need shown for such a betrayal, and the older Christian tradition probably did not contain it. It was just the trait which the "evolved gnosis" would add to the picture from such a passage as Psalm xli. 9: "Yea, mine own familiar friend, in whom I trusted, which did eat of my bread, hath lifted up his heel against me," and which was given its literal fulfilment in the detail mentioned in the first and second Synoptics (Matt. xxvi. 23, Mark. xiv. 20), "He that dipped his hand with me in the dish, the same shall betray me." It may be mentioned that Justin does not appear to have known anything of a betrayal of Jesus, and that, in places where, if he had been aware of the episode, he would certainly have referred to it, he passes over it in total silence.

According to the fragment, Simon Peter, and at least some of the disciples, must have gone into Galilee without any vision of the risen Jesus; and probably the last verse, which is broken off so abruptly, prepares the account of such an appearance as is described in the much-questioned last chapter of the fourth Gospel. It is worth pointing out, as perhaps an indication of the tradition which Peter follows, that both in the first and second Synoptic the order is given to the disciples to go into Galilee, where they are told that they are to see Jesus. In spite of this distinct order and statement, the author of the first Synoptic describes Jesus as immediately after appearing to the women, and giving the same direction to go into Galilee (xxviii. 7, 10), whilst in the spurious verses of Mark he nevertheless appears in Jerusalem to Mary Magdalene and to the Apostles. The third Synoptist gives a dif-

---

[1] In the passage 1 Cor. xi. 23 mention is made of a betrayal: "in the night in which he was betrayed," but without further detail, and it is quite consistent to suppose that the "betrayal" is not attributed to one of the Twelve. However, there is considerable reason for believing that this passage is an interpolation. It is a fact that a betrayal is not alluded to in any other place where we might expect to find it in these Epistles; e.g. Rom. iv. 25; viii. 32; Gal. ii. 20.

ferent turn to the mention of Galilee; but after the direction to go into Galilee, there to see Jesus, the visions described are a mere afterthought. In Peter, without any order, the disciples apparently go to Galilee, and there probably would be placed the first vision of the risen Jesus.

IX

We have now completed our comparison of the fragment with the canonical Gospels, and are able to form some opinion of its relative antiquity and relationship to our Gospels. Is it, as apologetic critics assert, a mere compilation from them, or can it take an independent position beside them, as a work derived from similar sources, and giving its own version of early Christian tradition? We have shown that it is not a compilation from our Gospels, but presents unmistakable signs of being an independent composition, and consequently a most interesting representation of Christian thought during the period when our Synoptic Gospels were likewise giving definite shape to the same traditions. Every part of this fragment has been set side by side with the corresponding narrative in the canonical Gospels, and it is simply surprising that a writing, dealing with a similar epoch of the same story, should have shown such freedom of handling. That there should be some correspondence between them was inevitable but the wonder is not that there should be so much agreement, but so much divergence; and this wonder increases in proportion as a later date is assigned to the fragment, and the authority of the canonical Gospels had become more established.

The theory of "tendency" was sure to be advanced as an explanation of differences of treatment of the same story, but this seems to us much exaggerated in what is said of the Gospel according to Peter. That early Docetic views might be supposed to be favoured by its representations is very possible; but these are far from being so pronounced as to render it unacceptable to those not holding such opinions, and the manner in which Justin and Origen make use of its statements is proof of this. As to its anti-Judaistic tone, a certain distinction has to be drawn. The expressions regarding "the Jews," "their feast" (used in reference to the Passover), and so on, may be put in the same category as the definition of the veil of the Temple "of Jerusalem," as indicating merely a work probably written out of Judaea, and for Gentile Christians; but in throwing upon the Jews, much more than on the Roman power, the odium of having crucified Jesus, the difference between Peter and the canonical Gospels is really infinitesimal. He certainly represents Pilate as retiring early from the trial, and leaving it to Herod, in whose "jurisdiction" it was, after washing his hands of the whole business; but this is a much more probable account, and perhaps an earlier tradition, than that which makes a Roman governor present the incredible and humiliating spectacle of a judge condemning and crucifying a man, in whom he finds no fault, at the dictation of a Jewish mob. The canonical Gospels, however, only accentuate the guilt of the Jews by representing the chief priests and elders, as well as the multitude, obstinately clamouring for his crucifixion, and finally overcoming Pilate's scruples. It is the chief priests and rulers who first seize Jesus and plot for his betrayal, who spit in his face, buffet and mock him, who prefer to him Barabbas, and cry: "His blood be on us and on our children" (Matt. xxvii. 25). The expressions of distinct antagonism to the Jews in the fourth Gospel far exceed any in the Gospel according to Peter. There is, therefore, no preconceived purpose conceivable to account for the characteristics of the narrative in this fragment.

That a writer who had our canonical Gospels before him should so depart from their lines, alter every representation without dogmatic purpose, insert contradictory statements, and omit episodes of absorbing interest and passages which would have enriched his narrative, is a theory which cannot be established. It is obvious that the feeling of the writer is one of intense devotion and reverence, and it is unreasonable to suppose that he could have passed over, altered, and contradicted so many points in the narrative of the Gospels, had he had those works before him.[1] In all probability he composed his work from earlier records and traditions, of the existence of which we have evidence in Luke i. 1, and the degree of resemblance on the one hand, and of discrepancy on the other, proceeds from independent use of these sources, from which the materials used in the canonical Gospels may have been drawn. It had not the good fortune of these Gospels, however, to be adopted by the Church and subjected, like them, to repeated revisal; but, drifting apart on the stream of time, it at last comes to us with all its original sins and imperfections on its head. Of course, any

---

[1] Harnack argues at considerable length that the Gospel according to Peter must have contained the episode of the woman taken in adultery, inserted into the fourth Gospel.

judgment now formed on the Gospel according to Peter is subject to the unfortunate limitation that we have only a fragment of the work in our hands; but should the rest be discovered, as we hope, it will not affect conclusions now based upon the part before us, whatever may be the final verdict on the whole.

X

We have still to consider objections raised by Mr. Rendel Harris, however, concerning the relation between this fragment and the Gospels accepted by the Church. In a long article in the "Contemporary Review" he tries to establish the thesis that *"The Gospel of Peter shows everywhere the traces of a highly evolved prophetic gnosis, and in particular most of the apparently new matter which it contains is taken from the Old Testament."*[1] It would not be possible, without wearying the most patient of parishioners, to illustrate in any adequate manner the perverse and hair-splitting ingenuity with which the "highly evolved prophetic gnosis" went to work, and which, in very parlous fashion, Mr. Harris applies to Peter; but, fortunately, this will not be necessary here. This gnosis doubtless began its operation early, and reached a climax towards the fourth century; but then it had ceased to be creative, and had become wildly analytical. Nothing then remained for it to do. Mr. Rendel Harris quotes, with admirable courage, a "significant sentence" from the "Peregrinatio ad Loca Sancta," a work of St. Sylvia of Aquitaine, or some other lady traveller of the fourth century, which has recently been published. She has been relating how the people were instructed in the mysteries of the faith by readings from the Scriptures, *imprimis*; of the Psalms predictive of the Messianic sufferings; then of passages from the Acts and Epistles which bear upon the interpretation of such predictions; further, the evidence of the prophets; and, to crown all, the story of the Passion itself from the Gospels. "The object of this service was, as Sylvia points out, that the people might understand by the Gospel record that whatever the psalmists and prophets had foretold concerning the Passion of the Lord had actually taken place." And now comes the "significant sentence" to which we referred above, italicised by Mr. Harris himself: "And so for the space of three hours the people is taught that *nothing took place*

---

[1] Contemp. Rev. August 1893, p. 217.

which had not been previously foretold, and nothing had been foretold which had not obtained its fulfilment." Mr. Harris supports the accuracy of Sylvia's description.[1]

But, whilst frankly admitting the application of this fundamental principle of the prophetic gnosis, more or less throughout all early Christian literature, Mr. Harris wishes to limit its influence upon works received into the canon, into which the two-edged weapon, however, pierces in spite of him to the sundering apart of soul and body. He says:

> Now no history is, in its ultimate analysis, so trustworthy as Christian history, but if we take the whole body of early literature, of which the canonical Gospels form the centre and crown, including Apocalypses, party-gospels, and the like, we shall find that there never was a body of history which was so overgrown with legend, and the major part of these legends result from the irregular study of the Old Testament, probably based on the synagogue methods of the time of the early Christian teachers. This reaction of the prophecy upon history colours the style of authors and affects their statements; and it is only by a close and careful study of the writers and their methods, that we are able to discriminate between what is a *bona fide* allusion in the Prophets, or what is a trick of style borrowed from the Prophets, or what is a pure legend invented out of the Prophets.[2]

The immediate object here, of course, is to lay the basis of an indictment against the fragment; but in this clear and excellent statement, a principle is enunciated, the application of which cannot be directed as the writer pleases, but is apt to be as deadly to friends as to foes. Mr. Harris may attempt to satisfy his doubts, in writing with the impartiality of a scholar, as he does, with the reservation that "no history is, in its ultimate analysis, so trustworthy as Christian history," but he has only to formulate the reasons for such a statement, to recognise their utter inadequacy. In so far as he gives us any glimpse of them here, they are of sad insufficiency. He speaks, a little further on, regarding "the real need of a critical method that can distinguish be-

---

[1] L.c. pp. 213 f.
[2] L.c. p. 215.

tween statements that are genuine history, and statements that are prophetic reflexes. For this discrimination," he says, "our main guide is the Canon, which expresses the judgment of the primitive Christian Church upon its literary materials; but I think it will be generally felt that we shall need finer-edged tools than Church customs or decrees in the more difficult parts of the problem; and certainly we must not assume *a priori in a critical investigation, that there is no trace of legendary accretion in the Gospel, and no element of genuine fact in what are called the Apocrypha.*"[1] Alas! is not the "main guide" a mere blind leader of the blind in regard to "the encroachment of prophetic interpretation upon the historical record"? We have no intention of maintaining here a very different view of the credibility of Christian history, the arguments against which we have elsewhere fully stated, but it is desirable, for reasons which will presently appear, that the fundamental principle of this attack on the Gospel according to Peter should be clearly understood. Mr. Harris goes on to affirm that the measure of this encroachment is, in the first two centuries, one of the best indications of documentary date we possess: "As a test, it will settle the period of many a document, and perhaps the measure of the appeal to prophecy will even determine the chronological order of the Gospels themselves: Mark, Luke, John, and Matthew."[2] This order will probably surprise a good many readers, and shake the faith they might perhaps be disposed to repose in the test which is supposed to have decided it. Mr. Harris applies the test in various instances to Peter, and we shall briefly examine his results.

It will be remembered that in *v.* 35 f. whilst the soldiers were keeping watch over the sepulchre, there was a great voice in the heavens, and they saw the heavens opened, and "two men" (δύο ἄνδρας) came down from thence with great light, and approach the tomb, and the stone which had been laid at the door rolled away, and they entered it, but presently they beheld again three men (τρεῖς ἄνδρας) coming out, and the two were supporting or conducting the other by the hand, and the lofty stature of the three is described. Now the "highly evolved prophetic gnosis" by which, according to Mr. Harris, this representation was composed is as follows, though only the main lines of the painful process can be given. In the prayer of Habakkuk (iii. 2), according to the Septuagint, the words which stand in our Bible, "In the

---

[1] L.c. p. 216.
[2] L.c. p. 216.

midst of the years make known" reads: "In the midst of *two lives*" (or of *two living creatures*) "thou shalt be known." This is referred in two ways: to "Christ's incarnation" and to his "Death and Resurrection." In the former case the two animals are the ox and the ass at the Nativity. The interpretation in the second case: the "living creatures" are the seraphim, two in number, because in Isaiah (vi. 3) "one called to the other and said:" "and we have only to find a situation in which Christ is seen between two angels, and the prophecy is fulfilled. This situation is made in the Gospel of Peter by Christ rising between two supporting angels." Mr. Harris endeavours to strengthen this by referring to Cyril of Alexandria's comment on the two living creatures (in the fourth century). Cyril is in doubt whether the two living creatures are the Father and the Holy Spirit, or the Old and New Testament, but recurs to the earlier interpretation that they are the Cherubim. Mr. Harris also cites the Targum of Jonathan Ben Uzziel on Zechariah iii. 7: "If thou wilt keep the observation of my word, *I will raise thee up in the resurrection of the dead, and set thy feet walking between the two cherubim.*" Then, as soon as this identification of the two living creatures had been made, it was easy, says Mr. Harris, to pass over to the ninety-ninth Psalm, which Justin[1] affirms to be a prediction of Christ.

> A little study of the opening words will show some interesting parallels with Peter. "The Lord hath reigned! Let the people be enraged! Sitting on the Cherubim, let the earth be shaken. The Lord in Zion is great and high above all the people." Here we have a parallel to the "Jews burning with rage," and to the enormous stature of the risen Christ, and, perhaps to the quaking of the earth. Nor is it without interest that Justin, having spoken of this great and high Christ, should turn immediately to another Psalm (xix.) where the sun is said to come forth as a bridegroom from his chamber, and to rejoice *as a giant* to run a race.[2]

In order to be as just as possible, all this has been given in greater detail than perhaps the case deserves. It seems rather a heavy avalanche of conjecture to bring down upon Peter, who simply narrates, without the most distant reference to any prophetic texts; and it is per-

---

[1] Dial. lxiv.
[2] L.c. pp. 219 ff.

haps a little hard that Justin, who in all probability had the Gospel already written and before him, should contribute in this casual way to the author's discomfiture. However, let us see what there is to be said upon the other side. The first general remark that may be made is, that it can scarcely be considered evidence of the later date of Peter to ascribe to him, as the source of this detail, an elaborate twisting of texts through the operation of gnosis, which has not been proved to have existed in this form before the epoch at which he wrote. This is said without any intention of casting doubt on the general operation of supposed prophetic passages on the evolution of Gospel history, but merely as questioning this particular explanation of the mode in which this representation was originally suggested, and more especially for the purpose of adding that, whatever reproach of this kind is cast upon the Gospel according to Peter, must equally be directed against the canonical gospels.

It will be remembered that, in the third Synoptic, "two men in shining apparel" assist at the resurrection, and that in the fourth Gospel Mary sees in the tomb "two angels in white sitting, the one at the head, the other at the feet, where the body of Jesus had lain." Here there is an occasion for applying with equal—or, as we shall presently see, greater—propriety the argument of "highly evolved prophetic gnosis" to the writers, and so explaining their representation. But there is more to be suggested in connection with the matter. In the first and second Synoptics, only one angel assists at the scene, who in the second Synoptic is called "a young man" (νεανίσκος). Now the "two men" of great stature in Peter only go into the tomb and come out again with Jesus; but subsequently the heavens were again opened (v. 44), and a certain man descends and goes into the tomb and remains there, for when the women come (v. 55) they see there "a certain young man" (νεανίσκος) "sitting in the midst of the tomb, beautiful and clad in a shining garment," who speaks to them as in the two Synoptics, and tells them that "Jesus is gone thither whence he was sent." This, then, is the angel who appears in Matthew and Mark. We have already mentioned that the two men of v. 36 have been identified by some critics as Moses and Elias. The account of the transfiguration is given in all the Synoptics, though it does not seem to have been known to the author of the fourth Gospel—although "John" was an actor in the scene—but that in the third Synoptic is fuller than the rest (ix. 28 ff). Jesus takes with him Peter and John and James, and goes up into the mountain to pray; and as he prays his countenance was altered, and his raiment becomes white and dazzling; "and behold there talked with him two men (ἄνδρες δύο), which were Moses and Elijah; who appeared in glory, *and spake of his decease which he was about to accomplish at Jerusalem."* When Peter and the others were fully awake, "they saw his glory and the two men (δύο ἄνδρας) that stood with him. And it came to pass, as they were parting from him, Peter said unto Jesus, Master, it is good for us to be here; and let us make three tabernacles; one for thee, and one for Moses and one for Elijah: *not knowing what he said. And while he said these things there came a cloud, and overshadowed them ... and a voice came out of the cloud, saying, This is my son, my chosen: hear ye him."* To this episode Mr. Harris might reasonably apply the test of the "highly evolved prophetic gnosis;" but in any case, the view that the two men of the fragment are intended to represent Moses and Elijah—the law and the prophets—who had so short a time before "spoken of and who now came, in stature reaching to the heavens, but less than his which rose above the heavens, and conducted Jesus the Christ forth from the tomb, in which that decease had been fulfilled, is in the highest degree probable. Much more might be said regarding this, but too much time has already been devoted to the point.

The second application of Mr. Harris's test is to the sealing of the stone at the sepulchre with seven seals. The Gospel of Peter simply states that the stone was sealed with seven seals, and Mr. Harris endeavours to find some abstruse meaning in the statement, which is peculiar to the fragment in so far as the number of seals is concerned. Where did Peter get the idea? Mr. Harris says, first from Zechariah iii. 9: "For behold the stone that I have set before Joshua; upon one stone are seven eyes; behold I will engrave the graving thereof, saith the Lord of hosts;" and the name Joshua is the Hebrew equivalent of Jesus. A reference is also made by the Fathers of the second century to passages to prove that Christ was the stone (of stumbling to the Jews, but the corner stone to believers). "Justin recognised Christ in the stone cut out without hands, of which Daniel speaks; in the stone which Jacob set for his pillow, and which he anointed with oil; in the stone on which Moses sat in the battle with Amalek," and the like. "Bearing in mind that there was an early tendency to connect the language of the 'Branch' passage with the resurrection, we can see that the interpretation took a second form, viz. to regard the stone before the face of Jesus as a prophecy of the stone which closed the tomb in the evangelic story." There is evidence, Mr. Harris says, that the seven eyes were early interpreted by Biblical Targumists to mean seven seals.

THE GOSPEL ACCORDING TO PETER - A STUDY

We need not be surprised, then, that the Peter Gospel speaks of the stone as sealed with seven seals; it is an attempt to throw the story into closer parallelism with Zechariah, no doubt for polemic purposes against the Jews. That he uses the curious word ἐπέχρισαν, which we are obliged, from the exigencies of language, to translate "they smeared" or "plastered" seven seals, but which to the writer meant much the same as if he were to say, "they on-christed seven seals," is due to the lurking desire to make a parallel with Christ and the stone directly, and with the anointed pillar of Jacob. The stone has a chrism.... But this is not all; in Zechariah (iv. 10) there is a passage, "they shall see the plummet in the hand of Zerubbabel," but in the Septuagint it runs, "they shall see the tin-stone." How is this to be connected with the "stone before the face of Joshua or Jesus"? The answer is found in the pages of the Peter Gospel: "a great crowd came from Jerusalem and the neighbourhood *to see the tomb which had been sealed.*" It only remains to identify the stone which they saw with the tin-stone. Symmachus retranslated the Hebrew word for "tin" as if it came from the root which means "to separate or divide," and in the Gospel of Peter, "the stone which had been laid on the door of the tomb withdrew (or separated) gradually" (ἐπεχώρησε παρὰ μέρος).

"The 'plummet' of Zerubbabel," Mr. Harris triumphantly concludes, "is used by Peter to make history square with prophecy."[1]

Now again the general remark has to be made that, in order to convict Peter of a late date, Mr. Harris takes all this "highly evolved gnosis" wherever he can find it, without consideration of epochs, and in some parts upon mere personal conjecture. He even confesses that he does not know the date of the translation of Symmachus, which he nevertheless uses as an argument. He observes, himself, that it is "a little awkward" that the stone, which at one time represents Jesus, has to be treated in the same breath as before the face of Jesus. The terribly complicated and involved process, by which it is suggested that the author of the Gospel according to Peter evolved a detail so apparently simple as the sealing of the sepulchre with seven seals, is difficult

---

[1] L.c. pp. 221 ff.

enough to follow, and must have been still more difficult to invent, but in his anxiety to assign a late date to the fragment, Mr. Harris forgets that, if the number seven is evidence of it, a large part of the New Testament must be moved back with the fragment. The Synoptics are full of it,[1] but it is quite sufficient to point to the Apocalypse, which has this typical number in almost every chapter: the message to the seven churches; the seven spirits before the throne; the seven golden candlesticks; the seven stars; seven lamps of fire burning; seven angels; seven trumpets; seven thunders; the dragon with seven heads, and seven diadems; the seven angels with seven plagues; the woman with seven heads, and so on. The most striking and apposite instance, which Mr. Harris indeed does not pass over, but mentions as having "a curious and suggestive connection" and "every appearance of being ultimately derived from the language of Zechariah,"[2] is the Book which is close sealed with seven seals, and the Lamb standing as though it had been slain, having seven horns and seven eyes, which are seven spirits of God, which is found worthy to take the book and open the seals.[3] Instead of giving the author of the fragment, who does not make the slightest claim to it, credit for so extraordinary a feat of synthetic exegesis, is it not more simple and probable that he used the number seven as a mere ordinary symbol of completeness? but if more than this be deemed requisite, and the detail has a deeper mystical sense, he can only be accused of "highly evolved prophetic gnosis," in company with the author of the Apocalypse and other canonical books, and this still gives him a position in the same epoch with them, more than which, probably, no one demands.

Another instance may be rapidly disposed of. The writer of Peter, Mr. Harris affirms, was not ignorant of the gnosis of the Cross wrought out by the Fathers from the Old Testament, on the "Wood" and the "Tree." One passage at which they laboured heavily is in Habakkuk ii. 11: "The stone cries out of the wall, and the cross-beam answers back to it." Mr. Harris proceeds:

> Now the author of the Peter Gospel has been at work on the passage; he wishes to make the cross talk, and not only talk, but answer back; accordingly, he introduces a

---

[1] E.g. Matt. xii. 45; xv. 34, 37; xxii. 25 f.; Mark viii. 5, 8, xii. 20 ff.; xvi. 9; Luke ii. 36; viii. 2; xi. 26; xx. 29 f.
[2] L.c. p. 222.
[3] Apoc. v. 1 ff.

question: "Hast thou preached to them that are asleep?" and the response is heard from the cross, "Yea." As far as I can suspect, the first speaker is Christ, the Stone; and the answer comes from the Cross, the Wood. It is then the Cross that has descended into Hades. But perhaps this is pressing the writer's words a little too far.[1]

Is it not also pressing the writer's thoughts a little too far to suggest such trains of childish interpretation as the origin of all his characteristic representations? Mr. Harris, by way of bringing the charge nearer to Peter, says that the passage of Habakkuk "is quoted by Barnabas, though no doubt from a corrupted text, with a positive assertion that the Cross is here intimated by the prophet."[2] This is not so. The passage in Barnabas (xii.) reads: "He defineth concerning the Cross in another prophet, who saith: 'And when shall these things be accomplished? saith the Lord. Whensoever a tree shall be bended and stand upright, and whensoever blood shall drop from a tree.' Again thou art taught concerning the cross and him that was to be crucified." This is not a quotation from Habakkuk, but from 4 Esdras v. 5. This is, however, not of much importance. It is of greater moment to observe that Mr. Harris, in applying this test, is only able to "suspect" that, in this episode in Peter, the speaker who asks the question is Christ the "stone," and the answer from the cross, the "wood;" but as the first "speaker" is a voice "out of the heavens," it is difficult to connect it with "Christ the Stone," to whom the question is actually addressed. According to this, he puts the question to himself. Such exegesis, applied to almost any conceivable statement, might prove almost any conceivable hypothesis.

The next instance requires us to turn to a passage in Amos (viii. 9-10, LXX): "And it shall come to pass in that day, saith the Lord God, that the sun shall set at midday, ... and I will turn your feasts into wailing and all your songs to lamentation, and I will lay sackcloth on all loins, and baldness on every head; and I will set him as the wailing for the beloved, and those that are with him as a day of grief." With it, we are told, must be taken the parallel verse in which Zechariah (xiv. 6, 7) predicts a day in which "there shall be no light, but cold and frost ... but towards evening there shall be light." This was one of the proofs with early Christians of the events which happened at the crucifixion,

---

[1] L.c. p. 224.
[2] Ibid.

and St. Cyprian, for instance, quotes it. It is also quoted in the sixth Homily of the Persian Father Aphrahat against the Jews. "The Gospel of Peter did not apparently possess the gnosis in such a highly evolved form as this," but works on the same lines. Mr. Harris then quotes passages from the fragment, which we shall give after him, with his inserted comments, but as he does not mark the intervals which occur between them, we shall take the liberty of inserting the verses from which they are taken between brackets.

> 15. It was mid-day and darkness over all the land of Judaea.... 22. then the sun shone out, and it was found to be the ninth hour [*at evening time it shall be light*]; 23. and the Jews rejoiced.... 25. and the Jews began to wail [*I will turn your feasts into mourning*].... 26. We also were fasting and sitting down (*i.e.* sitting on the ground in sackcloth[1]); [*I will lay sackcloth on all loins*]. 50. Mary Magdalene had not done at the tomb as women are wont to do over their dead beloveds, so she took her friends with her to wail [*I will set him as the Wailing for the Beloved*].
>
> The writer is, therefore, drawing on the details of prophecy, as suggested by the current testimonies against the Jews, and most likely on a written gnosis involving these testimonies. That he veils his sources simply shows that he is not one of the first brood of anti-Jewish preachers. If he had been early, he would not have been artificial or occult.[2]

Now, as before, Mr. Harris uses the eccentricities of a gnosis which he does not prove to have existed at the time the fragment may have been written and, for instance, he quotes St. Cyprian, who wrote in the second half of the third century, and the Persian Father Aphrahat, also a writer long after the Gospel of Peter was composed, and his remark that the writer "did not apparently possess the gnosis in so highly evolved a form" as Aphrahat, is not so much an admission in his favour as to prepare the reader to be content with inferior evidence. The

---

[1] This is not expressed in the text, which Mr. Harris rather strains for his purpose. The correct reading is: "We were fasting, and we sat mourning and weeping," καὶ ἐκαθεζόμεθα πενθοῦντες καὶ κλαίοντες.
[2] L.c. pp. 224 f.

THE GOSPEL ACCORDING TO PETER - A STUDY

test, however, quite as much applies to our Gospels as to the Gospel of Peter. In the previous working, of which the fragment says nothing, those who pass "wag their heads" and rail, in each of the Synoptics, in a jubilant way. The first Synoptic says (xxvii. 45 f.) "Now from the sixth hour there was darkness over all the land until the ninth The centurion and those who were watching "feared exceedingly." In Mark (xv. 33) there also "was darkness over the whole earth until the ninth hour," but in Luke (xxiii. 44 f.) the resemblance is still more marked. The darkness comes over the whole earth from the sixth until the ninth hour, "the sun's light failing." (48) "And all the multitudes that came together to this sight, when they beheld the things that were done, *returned smiting their breasts.*" In the fourth Gospel (xx. 11), Mary goes to the tomb weeping. We shall have more to say regarding the Gospels presently, but here we need only remark that, whether in exactly the same way or not, the "highly evolved prophetic gnosis" has certainly done its work in all of them. In this respect, the Gospel of Peter merely takes its place with the rest.

There is only one other instance to be noticed here. It refers to some of the details which the writer of the fragment introduces into the mockery which precedes the crucifixion. Some of the mockers "prick" Jesus with a reed; others spat on his eyes. This, Mr. Harris says, is connected with a view early taken regarding a change of Jewish feasts. In the Epistle of Barnabas, there is the best exposition of the doctrine that the Feast should be turned into mourning and the Passover at which Jesus suffered should be treated as if it had been the Day of Atonement. In Barnabas, the ritual of the great day is discussed in detail, and the rules of procedure for the Priests and the People, apparently taken, Mr. Harris thinks, from a Greek handbook, prove a variety of local usage such as would not have been suspected from the Scripture, read apart from the rest of the literature of the time. The "unwashed inwards" of one goat, offered at the fast for all sins, are to be eaten by the priests alone, with vinegar, while the people fast and wail in sackcloth and ashes. This goat is one of two over which lot is cast on the Day of Atonement; the other is the scape-goat, Azazel, which, according to Barnabas, was to be treated with contumely, and sent away into the wilderness: "All of you spit on him, and prick him, and put the scarlet wool on his head," &c. Now the two goats both represent Christ, according to Barnabas, "who twists these written regulations into prophecies of the first and second Advents, and of the details of the Passion."

The mention of vinegar to be eaten with the bitter portion of the goat, suggested the words of the Psalm: "Gall for my meat and vinegar for my drink;" the command to spit on the goat and prick (or pierce) him [which ill-usage, by the way, the Talmud admits to have been the practice of the Alexandrian Jews], is interpreted by Barnabas to be a type or a prophecy of Christ "set at naught and pierced and spat on." Is there any trace of the gnosis of the two goats in Peter? If we may judge from the conjunction of the words in the account of the Mockery, there is a decided trace: "Others stood and spat on his eyes ... others pricked him with a reed;" it is Christ as the goat Azazel.

Mr. Harris quotes "an almost contemporary Sibyllist," "They shall prick his side with a reed, *according to their law;*" and he continues: "If the Sybillist is quoting Peter, he is also interpreting him, and his interpretation is, they shall prick him, as is done to the goat Azazel."

To make Peter responsible for the ideas or interpretations of the Sybillist is a little hard. However, let us examine this matter. It is to be observed that the only innovation in Peter, regarding the spitting, is the expression that they "spat upon *his eyes*" instead of simply "upon him," or "in his face," as in the Gospels; but upon this nothing turns. The point is not even mentioned; so it may be dismissed. Regarding the reed, Peter says they "pierced" him with it, instead of "smote him" with it. Let us leave the "piercing" aside for the moment. In all other respects, the contumely is the same in the Gospels. Before the high priest, in Matthew and Mark (Matt. xxvi. 67, Mark xiv. 65), they spit in his face and buffet him, and smite him with the palms of their hands; and in Luke (xxii. 63 f.) they mock and beat him and revile him. It is curious that, according to the second Synoptist, all this was foretold, for he makes Jesus say (x. 33 f.): "Behold, we go up to Jerusalem; and the Son of man shall be delivered unto the chief priests and the scribes: and they shall condemn him to death, and shall deliver him unto the Gentiles: and they shall mock him, and shall spit upon him, and shall scourge him, and shall kill him, and after three days he shall rise again." After the trial before Pilate, in Mark (xv. 17 ff.), they put on him a purple robe, and the crown of thorns on his head, and a reed in his hand, and spit upon him, and take the reed and smite him on the head. In Peter, likewise, they clothe him in purple, put on his head the crown of thorns, spit upon his eyes, smite him on the cheeks, and pierce him with a reed.

What difference is there here except the mere piercing? Yes! there is a difference, for Mr. Harris has forgotten to refer to the scarlet wool put on the goat Azazel. There is nothing in Peter which corresponds with the scarlet wool. The robe that is put upon Jesus is purple. Now Barnabas, in the chapter from which Mr. Harris quotes all these passages, finds this point of the "scarlet wool" fulfilled in Jesus: "For they shall see him in that day wearing the long scarlet robe about his flesh."[1] But if we look in the first Synoptic we also find this, for we read (xxvii. 28): "And they stripped him, and put on him a scarlet robe" (χλαμύδα κοκκίνην). The mere detail of piercing with the reed instead of smiting with it is trifling compared with this, and in all essential points Mr. Harris's test more fitly applies to the first Synoptic than to Peter, and equally so to the other two.

As for the piercing with the reed, however, we have only to turn to the fourth Gospel, and we find its counterpart (xix. 34) where one of the soldiers with a spear pierced the side of Jesus. Why? (36) "That the Scripture might be fulfilled.... 'They shall look on him whom they pierced.' " Here is the "highly evolved prophetic gnosis" without any disguise. If one writer prefer to fulfil one part of Scripture, the other may select another without much difference in standing. Even Mr. Harris admits that "the gnosis on which Barnabas works is ultimately based on the same passage" as that quoted as fulfilled in the fourth Gospel[2]; then what distinction of date is possible when both apply the same gnosis based on the same texts?

---

[1] Barnabas, 7.
[2] L.c. p. 226.

XI

We have now discussed practically all the test instances advanced by Mr. Rendel Harris, and the result at which we arrive is, that he has not succeeded in proving that the Gospel of Peter betrays such traces of a "highly evolved prophetic gnosis" as require us to assign to it a later date than the canonical Gospels. If this system of elaborate and perverted ingenuity were applied to these Gospels, as it has been to the fragment, and every kind of false exegesis, childish reasoning, and wild interpretation, such as was current amongst the Fathers, brought forward to explain the construction of the four canonical works, the consequence would be terribly surprising to pious readers. That this exegesis began early is quite undeniable, and it is not too much to say that it is palpably visible on the very surface of most of the books of the New Testament. It had, as Mr. Harris must admit and does admit, practical effect on the composition of the Gospels as they have come down to us, but it is fully displayed in some of the Epistles of Paul, still more in those passing under his name, is supreme in the Epistle to the Hebrews, and as for the Acts, the Apostles are, from the very opening, made to express the highly evolved prophetic gnosis of the author. We do not, of course, argue that the writer of the fragment is free from it, but merely that he shares it equally with the other Evangelists, however much their canonicity, derived from the very Fathers who are steeped in this gnosis, may protect them from Mr. Harris's dangerous attack. Without going into an explanation of the genesis of various important points in the story, which would require a volume, we may just glance at some of the points at which the Evangelists frankly declare the source of the gnosis, and allow the process to be seen.

Let us take for instance the first Synoptic. The events previous to the birth of Jesus (i. 18 if.) take place "that it might be fulfilled which was spoken by the Lord through the prophet, saying, Behold, the virgin shall be with child, and shall bring forth a son, And they shall call his name Immanuel," and it is only an illustration of the *naïveté* of the period that two verses further on they call the son, not Immanuel, but

THE GOSPEL ACCORDING TO PETER - A STUDY

Jesus. The chief priests and scribes inform Herod (ii. 5 f.) that the Christ should be born in Bethlehem of Judaea, because it was written by the prophet: "And thou Bethlehem, land of Judah, Art in no wise least among the princes of Judah: For out of thee shall come forth a governor, Which shall be shepherd of my people Israel." Joseph takes the young child and his mother into Egypt (ii. 15 f.), "that it might be fulfilled which was spoken by the Lord through the prophet, saying, Out of Egypt did I call my son." Herod slays all the male children in Bethlehem and in all the borders thereof (ii. 16 f.) and "then was fulfilled that which was spoken through Jeremiah the prophet, saying, A voice was heard in Ramah, Weeping and great mourning, Rachel weeping for her children," &c. On returning from Egypt they settle in Galilee, in a city called Nazareth (ii. 23), "that it might be fulfilled which was spoken by the prophets, that he should be called a Nazarene." John the Baptist comes preaching "in the wilderness" (iii. 1 f.), "for this is he that was spoken of by Isaiah &c. The temptation of Jesus in the wilderness is based upon three texts: (iv. 1 ff.) "Man shall not live by bread alone," &c.; "He shall give his angels charge concerning thee," &c., and "Thou shalt worship the Lord thy God," &c. When John is delivered up (iv. 12 ff.) Jesus leaves Nazareth and dwells "in Capernaum, which is by the sea, in the borders of Zebulun and Naphtali: that it might be fulfilled which was spoken by Isaiah the prophet, saying, The land of Zebulun and the land of Naphtali, toward the sea, beyond Jordan, Galilee of the Gentiles, the people which sat in darkness saw a great light, and to them which sat in the region and shadow of death, to them did light spring up." In the episode of John in prison sending his disciples to Jesus (xi. 2 ff.), the whole reply is based indirectly on prophetic gnosis, and the *v.* 10 directly: "This is he, of whom it is written, Behold, I send my messenger before thy face, Who shall prepare thy way before thee," and *v.* 14, "And if ye are willing to receive it, this is Elijah, which is to come." When the Pharisees take counsel to destroy him (xii. 14 f.), and Jesus withdraws, healing the sick and enjoining them that they should not make him known, it is "that it might be fulfilled which was spoken by Isaiah the prophet, saying, Behold my servant," &c. There is an exhibition of "highly evolved prophetic gnosis" (xii. 39 ff.) when a sign is asked for, and the sign of Jonah the prophet is given, "for as Jonah was three days and three nights in the belly of the whale, so shall the Son of man be three days and three nights in the heart of the earth," a gnosis which helped to shape the representation of the entombment. The speaking in parables is justified, not originated (xiii. 14 f.), as a fulfilment of the prophecy of Isaiah, "By hearing ye shall hear, and &c, and (*v.* 35) "I will open my mouth in parables," &c. Of course, as Mr. Harris says, "no sane person would take St. Matthew's quotation as the cause of the Sermon on the Mount, or the parabolic discourse;"[1] but, as he admits, the prophetic passages were in the author's mind, and are amongst "the first faint shadows cast by the prophecy [?] upon the history," and they certainly led to the representation that those who heard the parabolic teaching, and notably the disciples, did not understand the most luminous discourses, and required a private explanation of the clearest allegories. The entry into Jerusalem (xxi. 2 f.) is arranged "that it might be fulfilled which was spoken by the prophet, saying, Tell ye the daughter of Zion, Behold, thy King cometh unto thee, meek, and riding upon an ass, and upon a colt the foal of an ass;" and the writer, not appreciating the duplication of Hebrew poetry, is literal enough to relate (*v.* 2) that Jesus tells the disciples they shall find "an ass tied, and a colt with her," which they are to bring, and (*v.* 7) "they brought the ass and the colt, and put on them their garments; *and he sat upon them*" (ἐπάνω αὐτῶν): a representation which has ever since given much trouble to pious commentators. It is not difficult to see that the "cleansing of the temple" (xxi. 12 f.) takes place because "it is written, My house shall be called a house of prayer, but ye make it a den of robbers." The trials when "the abomination of desolation (xxiv. 16 f.), which was spoken of by Daniel the prophet," is seen "standing in the holy place *(let him that readeth understand),*" is an example of the prophetic gnosis. The preparation for the passion commences (xxvi. 2), "Ye know that after two days the passover cometh, and the Son of man is delivered Jesus is represented (*v.* 31) as saying to the disciples: "All ye shall be offended in me this night: for it is written, I will smite the shepherd, and the sheep of the flock shall be scattered abroad;" and the curious phrase which follows is worth consideration: "But after I am raised up, I will go before you into Galilee," which seems to have slipped in here out of its place. The events which take place at the arrest, and their coming out with swords and staves as against a robber to take him (xxvi. 66), "All this is come to pass that the Scriptures of the prophets might be fulfilled;" and Jesus could not pray for legions of angels to help him, for (*v.* 66), "How then could the Scriptures be fulfilled?" The conduct of Judas after he had betrayed his master, when he took back the pieces of silver, the price of his betrayal, to the

---

[1] L.c. pp. 315 f.

priests (xxvii. 3 f.), fulfils "that which was spoken by Jeremiah the prophet, saying, And they took the thirty pieces of silver, the price of him that was priced, whom certain of the children of Israel did price; and they gave them for the potter's field, as the Lord appointed me."

XII

This need not be further pursued, however, though the principle applies quite as much to the other Gospels. Only one passage may be quoted from the last chapter of the third Synoptic. Jesus, when he appears to the disciples, after the episode of the fish to prove that he is not a spirit, but himself with flesh and bones (xxiv. 36 f.), is represented as saying:

> These are my words which I spake unto you, while I was yet with you, how that all things must needs be fulfilled, which are written in the law of Moses, and the prophets, and the psalms, concerning me. Then opened he their mind, that they might understand the Scriptures; and he said unto them, Thus it is written that the Christ should suffer, and rise again from the dead the third day: and that repentance and remission of sins should be preached in his name unto all the nations.

This is a direct justification of the gnosis, and it is no wonder that we find St. Sylvia some centuries later, recording the concrete principle upon which Gospel history is written: "Nothing took place which had not been previously foretold, and nothing had been foretold which had not obtained its fulfilment."

In so far as the Gospel according to Peter is concerned, the impartial verdict must be: It is neither better nor worse than the more fortunate works which have found a safe resting-place within the Canon of the Church. It is almost impossible now to judge of these works as we judge the fragment. Centuries of reverence, and individual habit of hearing their contents with docility and with bated criticism, have rendered most of us incapable of judging the effect which a good part of their contents would make upon us if, like the fragment of Akhmîm, they had been freshly discovered yesterday. There is no canonical glamour to veil its shortcomings, and it must not be forgotten that, in this short fragment, we have none of those parts of the Gospel, such as the Sermon on the Mount and some of the parables, which contain so much noble teaching and render the literature so precious. Then, as we have before pointed out, the canonical Gospels, in their greater circulation and in the process of reception by the Church, secured a gradual revision which might have smoothed away any roughness from the Gospel of Peter had it been equally fortunate. The three Synoptic Gospels are so closely dependent on each other, or on the same sources, as to be practically one work; and although this renders all the more remarkable certain indications of selection, some of which we have pointed out, it nevertheless limits our acquaintance with early belief. It is the merit of the fragment that it presents considerable variation in the original sources, and shows us the fluidity of the early reports of that which was supposed to take place during the period which it embraces. We have in it a primitive and less crystallised form of the Christian tradition.

Appendix

ΕΥΑΓΓΕΛΙΟΝ ΚΑΤΑ ΠΕΤΡΟΝ

(1) ... τῶν δὲ Ἰουδαίων οὐδεὶς ἐνίψατο τὰς χεῖρας, οὐδὲ Ἡρῴδης οὐδ᾽ εἷς τῶν κριτῶν αὐτοῦ· καὶ μὴ βουληθέντων νίψασθαι ἀνέστη Πειλᾶτος. (2) καὶ τότε κελεύει Ἡρῴδης ὁ βασιλεὺς παραλημφθῆναι τὸν κύριον, εἰπὼν αὐτοῖς ὅτι Ὅσα ἐκέλευσα ὑμῖν ποιῆσαι αὐτῷ, ποιήσατε. (3) Ἱστήκει δὲ ἐκεῖ Ἰωσὴφ ὁ φίλος Πειλάτου καὶ τοῦ κυρίου, καὶ εἰδὼς ὅτι σταυρίσκειν αὐτὸν μέλλουσιν, ἦλθεν πρὸς τὸν Πειλᾶτον καὶ ᾔτησε τὸ σῶμα τοῦ κυρίου πρὸς ταφήν. (4) καὶ ὁ Πειλᾶτος πέμψας πρὸς Ἡρῴδην ᾔτησεν αὐτοῦ τὸ σῶμα. (5) καὶ ὁ Ἡρῴδης ἔφη Ἀδελφὲ Πειλᾶτε, εἰ καὶ μή τις αὐτὸν ᾐτήκει, ἡμεῖς αὐτὸν ἐθάπτομεν, ἐπεὶ καὶ σάββατον ἐπιφώσκει· γέγραπται γὰρ ἐν τῷ νόμῳ ἥλιον μὴ δῦναι ἐπὶ πεφονευμένῳ.

(6) Καὶ παρέδωκεν αὐτὸν τῷ λαῷ πρὸ μιᾶς τῶν ἀζύμων, τῆς ἑορτῆς αὐτῶν. οἱ δὲ λαβόντες τὸν κύριον ὤθουν αὐτὸν τρέχοντες, καὶ ἔλεγον Σύρωμεν τὸν υἱὸν τοῦ θεοῦ, ἐξουσίαν αὐτοῦ ἐσχηκότες. (7) καὶ πορφύραν αὐτὸν περιέβαλλον, καὶ ἐκάθισαν αὐτὸν ἐπὶ καθέδραν κρίσεως, λέγοντες Δικαίως κρῖνε, βασιλεῦ τοῦ Ἰσραήλ. (8) καὶ τις αὐτῶν ἐνενκὼν στέφανον ἀκάνθινον ἔθηκεν ἐπὶ τῆς κεφαλῆς τοῦ κυρίου. (9) καὶ ἕτεροι ἑστῶτες ἐνέπτυον αὐτοῦ ταῖς ὄψεσι, καὶ ἄλλοι τὰς σιαγόνας αὐτοῦ ἐράπισαν· ἕτεροι καλάμῳ ἔνυσσον αὐτόν, καί τινες αὐτὸν ἐμάστιζον λέγοντες Ταύτῃ τῇ τιμῇ τιμήσωμεν τὸν υἱὸν τοῦ θεοῦ.

(10) Καὶ ἤνενκον δύο κακούργους, καὶ ἐσταύρωσαν ἀνὰ μέσον αὐτῶν τὸν κύριον· αὐτὸς δὲ ἐσιώπα, ὡς μηδὲν πόνον ἔχων. (11) καὶ ὅτε ὤρθωσαν τὸν σταυρόν, ἐπέγραψαν ὅτι Οὗτός ἐστιν ὁ βασιλεὺς τοῦ Ἰσραήλ. (12) καὶ τεθεικότες τὰ ἐνδύματα ἔμπροσθεν αὐτοῦ διεμερίσαντο, καὶ λαχμὸν ἔβαλον ἐπ᾽ αὐτοῖς. (13) εἷς δέ τις τῶν κακούργων ἐκείνων ὠνείδισεν αὐτοὺς λέγων Ἡμεῖς διὰ τὰ κακὰ ἃ

ἐποιήσαμεν οὕτω πεπόνθαμεν, οὗτος δὲ σωτὴρ γενόμενος τῶν ἀνθρώπων τί ἠδίκησεν ὑμᾶς; (14) καὶ ἀγανακτήσαντες ἐπ' αὐτῷ ἐκέλευσαν, ἵνα μὴ σκελοκοπηθῇ, ὅπως βασανιζόμενος ἀποθάνοι.

(15) Ἦν δὲ μεσημβρία, καὶ σκότος κατέσχε πᾶσαν τὴν Ἰουδαίαν; καὶ ἐθορυβοῦντο, καὶ ἠγωνίων μή ποτε ὁ ἥλιος ἔδυ, ἐπειδὴ ἔτι ἔζη; γέγραπται γὰρ αὐτοῖς ἥλιον μὴ δῦναι ἐπὶ πεφονευμένῳ. (16) καί τις αὐτῶν εἶπεν Ποτίσατε αὐτὸν χολὴν μετὰ ὄξους; (17) καὶ κεράσαντες ἐπότισαν. καὶ ἐπλήρωσαν πάντα, καὶ ἐτελείωσαν κατὰ τῆς κεφαλῆς αὐτῶν τὰ ἁμαρτήματα. (18) περιήρχοντο δὲ πολλοὶ μετὰ λύχνων, νομίζοντες ὅτι νύξ ἐστίν; [τινὲς δὲ] ἐπέσαντο.

(19) καὶ ὁ κύριος ἀνεβόησε λέγων Ἡ δύναμίς μου, ἡ δύναμις κατέλειψάς με; καὶ εἰπὼν ἀνελήφθη. (20) καὶ αὐτῆς ὥρας διεράγη τὸ καταπέτασμα τοῦ ναοῦ τῆς Ἰερουσαλὴμ εἰς δύο.

(21) Καὶ τότε ἀπέσπασαν τοὺς ἥλους ἀπὸ τῶν χειρῶν τοῦ κυρίου, καὶ ἔθηκαν αὐτὸν ἐπὶ τῆς γῆς; καὶ ἡ γῆ πᾶσα ἐσείσθη, καὶ φόβος μέγας ἐγένετο. (22) τότε ἥλιος ἔλαμψε καὶ εὑρέθη ὥρα ἐνάτη. (23) ἐχάρησαν δὲ οἱ Ἰουδαῖοι καὶ δεδώκασι τῷ Ἰωσὴφ τὸ σῶμα αὐτοῦ ἵνα αὐτὸ θάψῃ,

(24) ἐπειδὴ θεασάμενος ἦν ὅσα ἀγαθὰ ἐποίησεν. λαβὼν δὲ τὸν κύριον ἔλουσε καὶ εἴλησε σινδόνι καὶ εἰσήγαγεν εἰς ἴδιον τάφον καλούμενον Κῆπον Ἰωσήφ.

(25) Τότε οἱ Ἰουδαῖοι καὶ οἱ πρεσβύτεροι καὶ οἱ ἱερεῖς, γνόντες οἷον κακὸν ἑαυτοῖς ἐποίησαν, ἤρξαντο κόπτεσθαι καὶ λέγειν Οὐαὶ ταῖς ἁμαρτίαις ἡμῶν; ἤγγισεν ἡ κρίσις καὶ τὸ τέλος Ἰερουσαλήμ. (26) ἐγὼ δὲ μετὰ τῶν ἑταίρων μου ἐλυπούμην, καὶ τετρωμένοι κατὰ διάνοιαν ἐκρυβόμεθα; ἐζητούμεθα γὰρ ὑπ' αὐτῶν ὡς κακοῦργοι καὶ ὡς τὸν ναὸν θέλοντες ἐμπρῆσαι. (27) ἐπὶ δὲ τούτοις πᾶσιν ἐνηστεύομεν, καὶ ἐκαθεζόμεθα πενθοῦντες καὶ κλαίοντες νυκτὸς καὶ ἡμέρας ἕως τοῦ σαββάτου.

(28) Συναχθέντες δέ οἱ γραμματεῖς καὶ Φαρισαῖοι καὶ πρεσβύτεροι πρὸς ἀλλήλους, ἀκούσαντες ὅτι ὁ λαὸς ἅπας γογγύζει καὶ κόπτεται τὰ στήθη λέγοντες ὅτι Εἰ τῷ θανάτῳ αὐτοῦ ταῦτα τὰ μέγιστα σημεῖα γέγονεν, ἴδετε ὅτι πόσον δίκαιός ἐστιν; (29) ἐφοβήθησαν οἱ πρεσβύτεροι, καὶ ἦλθον πρὸς Πειλᾶτον δεόμενοι αὐτοῦ καὶ λέγοντες Παράδος ἡμῖν στρατιώτας, (30) ἵνα φυλάξω[μεν] τὸ μνῆμα αὐτοῦ ἐπὶ τρεῖς ἡμέρας, μήποτε ἐλθόντες οἱ μαθηταὶ αὐτοῦ κλέψωσιν αὐτὸν καὶ ὑπολάβῃ ὁ λαὸς ὅτι ἐκ νεκρῶν ἀνέστη, καὶ ποιήσωσιν ἡμῖν κακά. (31) ὁ δὲ Πειλᾶτος παραδέδωκεν αὐτοῖς Πετρώνιον τὸν κεντυρίωνα μετὰ στρατιωτῶν φυλάσσειν τὸν τάφον. καὶ σὺν αὐτοῖς ἦλθον πρεσβύτεροι καὶ γραμματεῖς ἐπὶ τὸ μνῆμα. (32) καὶ κυλίσαντες λίθον μέγαν κατὰ τοῦ κεντυρίωνος καὶ τῶν στρατιωτῶν ὁμοῦ πάντες οἱ ὄντες ἐκεῖ ἔθηκαν ἐπὶ τῇ θύρᾳ τοῦ μνήματος.

(33) καὶ ἐπέχρισαν ἑπτὰ σφραγῖδας, καὶ σκηνὴν ἐκεῖ πήξαντες ἐφύλαξαν. (34) πρωίας δέ, ἐπιφώσκοντος τοῦ σαββάτου, ἦλθεν ὄχλος ἀπὸ Ἰερουσαλὴμ καὶ τῆς περιχώρου ἵνα ἴδωσι τὸ μνημεῖον ἐσφραγισμένον.
(35) Τῇ δὲ νυκτὶ ᾗ ἐπέφωσκεν ἡ κυριακή, φυλασσόντων τῶν στρατιωτῶν ἀνὰ δύο δύο κατὰ φρουράν, μεγάλη φωνὴ ἐγένετο ἐν τῷ οὐρανῷ. (36) καὶ εἶδον ἀνοιχθέντας τοὺς οὐρανοὺς καὶ δύο ἄνδρας κατελθόντας ἐκεῖθεν, πολὺ φέγγος ἔχοντας καὶ ἐγγίσαντας τῷ τάφῳ. (37) ὁ δὲ λίθος ἐκεῖνος ὁ βεβλημένος ἐπὶ τῇ θύρᾳ ἀφ' ἑαυτοῦ κυλισθεὶς ἐπεχώρησε παρὰ μέρος, καὶ ὁ τάφος ἠνοίγη καὶ ἀμφότεροι οἱ νεανίσκοι εἰσῆλθον. (38) ἰδόντες οὖν οἱ στρατιῶται ἐκεῖνοι ἐξύπνισαν τὸν κεντυρίωνα καὶ τοὺς πρεσβυτέρους, παρῆσαν γὰρ καὶ αὐτοὶ φυλάσσοντες; (39) καὶ ἐξηγουμένων αὐτῶν ἃ εἶδον, πάλιν ὁρῶσιν ἐξελθόντας ἀπὸ τοῦ τάφου τρεῖς ἄνδρας, καὶ τοὺς δύο τὸν ἕνα ὑπορθοῦντας, καὶ σταυρὸν ἀκολουθοῦντα αὐτοῖς; (40) καὶ τῶν μὲν δύο τὴν κεφαλὴν χωροῦσαν μέχρι τοῦ οὐρανοῦ, τοῦ δὲ χειραγωγουμένου ὑπ' αὐτῶν ὑπερβαίνουσαν τοὺς οὐρανούς. (41) καὶ φωνῆς ἤκουον ἐκ τῶν οὐρανῶν λεγούσης Ἐκήρυξας τοῖς κοιμωμένοις? (42) καὶ ὑπακοὴ ἠκούετο ἀπὸ τοῦ σταυροῦ ὅτι Ναί. (43) Συνεσκέπτοντο οὖν ἀλλήλοις ἐκεῖνοι ἀπελθεῖν καὶ ἐνφανίσαι ταῦτα τῷ Πειλάτῳ.
(44) καὶ ἔτι διανοουμένων αὐτῶν φαίνονται πάλιν ἀνοιχθέντες οἱ οὐρανοὶ καὶ ἄνθρωπός τις κατελθὼν καὶ εἰσελθὼν εἰς τὸ μνῆμα.
(45) Ταῦτα ἰδόντες οἱ περὶ τὸν κεντυρίωνα νυκτὸς ἔσπευσαν πρὸς Πειλᾶτον, ἀφέντες τὸν τάφον ὃν ἐφύλασσον, καὶ ἐξηγήσαντο πάντα ἅπερ εἶδον, ἀγωνιῶντες μεγάλως καὶ λέγοντες Ἀληθῶς υἱὸς ἦν θεοῦ. (46) ἀποκριθεὶς ὁ Πειλᾶτος ἔφη Ἐγὼ καθαρεύω τοῦ αἵματος τοῦ υἱοῦ τοῦ θεοῦ, ὑμῖν δὲ τοῦτο ἔδοξεν. (47) εἶτα προσελθόντες πάντες ἐδέοντο αὐτοῦ καὶ παρεκάλουν κελεῦσαι τῷ κεντυρίωνι καὶ τοῖς στρατιώταις μηδὲν εἰπεῖν ἃ εἶδον; (48) συμφέρει γάρ, φασίν, ἡμῖν ὀφλῆσαι μεγίστην ἁμαρτίαν ἔμπροσθεν τοῦ θεοῦ, καὶ μὴ ἐμπεσεῖν εἰς χεῖρας τοῦ λαοῦ τῶν Ἰουδαίων καὶ λιθασθῆναι. (49) ἐκέλευσεν οὖν ὁ Πειλᾶτος τῷ κεντυρίωνι καὶ τοῖς στρατιώταις μηδὲν εἰπεῖν
(50) Ὄρθρου δὲ τῆς κυριακῆς Μαριὰμ ἡ Μαγδαληνή, μαθήτρια τοῦ κυρίου (φοβουμένη διὰ τοὺς Ἰουδαίους, ἐπειδὴ ἐφλέγοντο ὑπὸ τῆς ὀργῆς, οὐκ ἐποίησεν ἐπὶ τῷ μνήματι τοῦ κυρίου ἃ εἰώθεσαν ποιεῖν αἱ γυναῖκες ἐπὶ τοῖς ἀποθνήσκουσι καὶ τοῖς ἀγαπωμένοις αὐταῖς;) (51) λαβοῦσα μεθ' ἑαυτῆς τὰς φίλας ἦλθε ἐπὶ τὸ μνημεῖον ὅπου ἦν τεθείς. (52) καὶ ἐφοβοῦντο μὴ ἴδωσιν αὐτὰς οἱ Ἰουδαῖοι, καὶ ἔλεγον Εἰ καὶ μὴ ἐν ἐκείνῃ τῇ ἡμέρᾳ ᾗ ἐσταυρώθη ἐδυνήθημεν κλαῦσαι καὶ κόψασθαι, καὶ νῦν ἐπὶ τοῦ μνήματος αὐτοῦ ποιήσωμεν ταῦτα. (53) τίς δὲ

ἀποκυλίσει ἡμῖν καὶ τὸν λίθον τὸν τεθέντα ἐπὶ τῆς θύρας τοῦ μνημείου, ἵνα εἰσελθοῦσαι παρακαθεσθῶμεν αὐτῷ καὶ ποιήσωμεν τὰ ὀφειλόμενα? (54) μέγας γὰρ ἦν ὁ λίθος, καὶ φοβούμεθα μή τις ἡμᾶς ἴδῃ. καὶ εἰ μὴ δυνάμεθα, κἂν ἐπὶ τῆς θύρας βάλωμεν ἃ φέρομεν εἰς μνημοσύνην αὐτοῦ, κλαύσομεν καὶ κοψόμεθα ἕως ἔλθωμεν εἰς τὸν οἶκον ἡμων.

(55) Καὶ ἀπελθοῦσαι εὗρον τὸν τάφον ἠνεῳγμένον; καὶ προσελθοῦσαι παρέκυψαν ἐκεῖ, καὶ ὁρῶσιν ἐκεῖ τινα νεανίσκον καθεζόμενον μέσῳ τοῦ τάφου, ὡραῖον καὶ περιβεβλημένον στολὴν λαμπροτάτην, ὅστις ἔφη αὐταῖς Τί ἤλθατε? τίνα ζητεῖτε? (56) μὴ τὸν σταυρωθέντα ἐκεῖνον? ἀνέστη καὶ ἀπηλθεν; εἰ δὲ μὴ πιστεύετε, παρακύψατε καὶ ἴδατε τὸν τόπον ἔνθα ἔκειτο, ὅτι οὐκ ἔστιν; ἀνέστη γὰρ καὶ ἀπῆλθεν ἐκεῖ ὅθεν ἀπεστάλη. (57) τότε αἱ γυναῖκες φοβηθεῖσαι ἔφυγον.

(58) Ἦν δὲ τελευταία ἡμέρα τῶν ἀζύμων, καὶ πολλοί τινες ἐξήρχοντο, ὑποστρέφοντες εἰς τοὺς οἴκους αὐτῶν, τῆς ἑορτῆς παυσαμένης. (59) ἡμεῖς δὲ οἱ δώδεκα μαθηταὶ τοῦ κυρίου ἐκλαίομεν καὶ ἐλυπούμεθα, καὶ ἕκαστος λυπούμενος διὰ τὸ συμβὰν ἀπηλλάγη εἰς τὸν οἶκον αὐτοῦ. (60) ἐγὼ δὲ Σίμων Πέτρος καὶ Ἀνδρέας ὁ ἀδελφός μου λαβόντες ἡμῶν τὰ λίνα ἀπήλθαμεν εἰς τὴν θάλασσαν; καὶ ἦν σὺν ἡμῖν Λευεὶς ὁ τοῦ Ἀλφαίου, ὅν Κύριος ...

FORBIDDEN BOOKS OF THE NEW TESTAMENT.

BY
ARCHBISHOP WILLIAM WAKE
AND OTHER
LEARNED DIVINES

THE SUPPRESSED GOSPELS AND EPISTLES OF THE ORIGINAL NEW TESTAMENT OF JESUS THE CHRIST AND OTHER PORTIONS OF THE ANCIENT HOLY SCRIPTURES. NOW EXTANT, ATTRIBUTED TO HIS APOSTLES, AND THEIR DISCIPLES, AND VENERATED BY THE PRIMITIVE CHRISTIAN CHURCHES DURING THE FIRST FOUR CENTURIES, BUT SINCE, AFTER VIOLENT DISPUTATIONS FORBIDDEN BY THE BISHOPS OF THE NICENE COUNCIL, IN THE REIGN OF THE EMPEROR CONSTANTINE AND OMITTED FROM THE CATHOLICS AND PROTESTANT EDITIONS OF THE NEW TESTAMENT, BY ITS COMPILERS TRANSLATED FROM THE ORIGINAL TONGUES, WITH HISTORICAL REFERENCES TO THEIR AUTHENTICITY, BY ARCHBISHOP WAKE AND OTHER LEARNED DIVINES THE ORDER OF ALL THE FORBIDDEN BOOKS OF THE NEW TESTAMENT WITH THEIR PROPER NAMES, AND NUMBER OF CHAPTERS

PREFACE.

To uphold the "right of private judgment," and our "Christian liberty wherewith Christ hath made us free;" to add fuel to the fire of investigation, and in the crucible of deep inquiry, melt from the gold of pure religion, the dross of man's invention; to appeal from the erring tribunals of a fallible Priesthood, and restore to its original state the mutilated Testament of the Saviour; also to induce all earnest thinkers to search not a part, but the whole of the Scriptures, if therein they think they will find eternal life; I, as an advocate of free thought and untrammelled opinion, dispute the authority of those uncharitable, bickering, and ignorant Ecclesiastics who first suppressed these gospels and epistles; and I join issue with their Catholic and Protestant successors who have since excluded them from the New Testament, of which they formed a part; and were venerated by the Primitive Churches, during the first four hundred years of the Christian Era.

My opposition is based on two grounds; first, the right of every rational being to become a "Priest unto himself," and by the test of enlightened reason, to form his own unbiased judgment of all things natural and spiritual: second, that the reputation of the Bishops who extracted these books from the original New Testament, under the pretence of being Apocryphal, and forbade them to be read by the people, is proved by authentic impartial history too odious to entitle them to any deference. Since the Nicene Council, by a pious fraud, which I shall further allude to, suppressed these books, several of them have been reissued from time to time by various translators, who differed considerably in their versions, as the historical references attached to them in the following pages will demonstrate. But to the late Mr. William Hone we are indebted for their complete publication for the first time in one volume, about the year 1820; which edition, diligently revised, and purified of many errors both in the text and the notes attached thereto, I have re-published in numbers to enable all classes of the nation to purchase and peruse them. As, however, instead of being called by their own designation "Apocryphal," (which yet re-

PREFACE

mains to be proved), they were re-entitled THE FORBIDDEN BOOKS, and, from communications received, appear to have agitated a portion of the great mass of ignorant bigotry which mars the fair form of Religion in these sect-ridden dominions, I have modified the title to its present shape with the hope that in spite of illiberal clerical influence, my fellow Christians will read and inwardly digest the sublime precepts they inculcate;—as pure, as holy, and as charitable as those principles of Christianity taught in the Scriptures they; now read by permission; although their minds may, after mature reflection, doubt the truth of the miraculous records therein given.

To ensure these Gospels and Epistles an unprejudiced and serious attention, which they are entitled to, equally with those now patronised by Church authority, I will briefly refer to that disgraceful epoch in Roman Ecclesiastical Annals, when the New Testament was mutilated, and priestly craft was employed for excluding these books from its pages. HONE, in the preface to his first edition of the Apocryphal New Testament, so called, without satisfactory grounds, by the Council of Nice, in the reign of the Emperor Constantine, thus opens the subject:—

"After the writings contained in the New Testament were selected from the numerous Gospels and Epistles then in existence, what became of the Books that were rejected by the compilers?"

This question naturally occurs on every investigation as to the period when and the persons by whom the New Testament was formed. It has been supposed by many that the volume was compiled by the first Council of Nice, which, according to Jortin (Rem. on Eccl. vol. ii. p. 177), originated thus: Alexander, Bishop of Alexandria, and Arius, who was a presbyter in his diocese, disputed together about the nature of Christ; and the bishop being displeased at the notions of Arius, and finding that they were adopted by other persons, "was very angry." He commanded Arius to come over to his sentiments, and to quit his own; as if a man could change his opinions as easily as he can change his coat! He then called a Council of War, consisting of nearly, a hundred bishops, and deposed, excommunicated, and anathematized Arius, and with him several ecclesiastics, two of whom were bishops. Constantine sent a letter, in which he reprimanded the bishops for disturbing the church with their insignificant disputes. But the affair was gone too far to be thus composed. To settle this and other points, the Nicene Council was summoned, consisting of about 318 bishops. The first thing they did was to quarrel, and to express their resentments, and to present accusations to the Emperor against one another. "The Emperor burnt all their libels, and exhorted them to peace and unity." (See Mosheim's Eccle. Hist.) These were the kind of spiritual shepherds of whom Sabinus, the Bishop Heraclea affirms, that excepting Constantine himself, and Eusebius Pamphilus, they "were a set of illiterate creatures, that understood nothing." And now intelligent Catholics, especially Protestants who are content to read only the books of the Testament authorized by the Council of Nice, and agreed to ever since by your own bishops, although they and you profess to dissent from the Papacy, hear what Pappus in his Synodican to that Council says of their crafty contrivance when they separated the books of the original New Testament:—He tells us, that having "promiscuously put all the books that were referred to the Council for deliberation under the communion-table in a church, they besought the Lord that the inspired writings might get on the table, while the spurious ones remained underneath; and that it happened accordingly!" (See Com. Mace's N. T. p. 875.) Therefore, good reader, every Christian sect from the fourth century to the present period, have been blessed with the books that climbed upon the communion-table, and in consequence were deemed inspired and canonical; at the same time have been forbidden to read the Gospels and Epistles herein published, because they could not perform the same feat, but remained under the table, and were condemned accordingly, as uninspired and apocryphal writings. If you believe this popish legend, you will not read the good books I lay before you, but still continue to possess only HALF THE TESTAMENT, instead of the PERFECT ONE, which will enable you to burst the trammels of priestcraft, and by the light of God's whole truth become free. In conclusion, I implore you to examine for yourselves, and observe the testimony of Archbishop Wake and other learned divines and historians appended thereto; and subscribe myself,

Your well-wisher, EDWARD HANCOCK.

THE GOSPEL OF THE BIRTH OF MARY.

CHAPTER I.

1 The Parentage of Mary.
7 Joachim her father, and Anna her mother, go to Jerusalem to the feast of the dedication.
9 Issachar, the high priest, reproaches Joachim for being childless.

THE blessed and ever glorious Virgin Mary, sprung from the royal race and family of David, was born in the city of Nazareth, and educated at Jerusalem, in the temple of the Lord.

2 Her father's name was Joachim, and her mother's Anna. The family of her father was of Galilee and the city of Nazareth. The family of her mother was of Bethlehem.

3 Their lives were plain and right in the sight of the Lord, pious and faultless before men; for they divided all their substance into three parts;

4 One of which they devoted to the temple and officers of the temple; another they distributed among strangers, and persons in poor circumstances; and the third they reserved for themselves and the uses of their own family.

5 In this manner they lived for about twenty years chastely, in the favour of God, and the esteem of men, without any children.

6 But they vowed, if God should favour them with any issue, they would devote it to the service of the Lord; on which account they went at every feast in the year to the temple of the Lord.

THE GOSPEL OF THE BIRTH OF MARY.

7 And it came to pass, that when the feast of the dedication drew near, Joachim, with some others of his tribe, went up to Jerusalem, and at that time, Isachar was high-priest;

8 Who, when he saw Joachim along with the rest of his neighbours, bringing his offerings, despised both him and his offerings, and asked him,

9 Why he, who had no children, would presume to appear among those who had? Adding, that his offerings could never be acceptable to God, who was judged by him unworthy to have children; the Scripture having said, Cursed is every one who shall not beget a male in Israel.

10 He further said, that he ought first to be free from that curse by begetting some issue, and then come with his offerings into the presence of God.

11 But Joachim being much confounded with the shame of such reproach, retired to the shepherds who were with the cattle in their pastures;

12 For he was not inclined to return home, lest his neighbours, who were present and heard all this from the high-priest, should publicly reproach him in the same manner.

CHAPTER II.

1 An angel appears to Joachim,
9 and informs him that Anna shall conceive and bring forth a daughter, who shall be called Mary,
11 be brought up in the temple,
12 and while yet a virgin, in a way unparalleled, bring forth the Son of God:
13 Gives him a sign,
14 and departs.

BUT when he had been there for some time, on a certain day when he was alone, the angel of the Lord stood by him with a prodigious light.

2 To whom, being troubled at the appearance, the angel who had appeared to him, endeavouring to compose him, said:

3 Be not afraid, Joachim, nor troubled at the sight of me, for I am an angel of the Lord sent by him to you, that I might inform you that your prayers are heard, and your alms ascended in the sight of God.

ΔΙΔΑΧΗ ΤΩΝ ΔΩΔΕΚΑ ΑΠΟΣΤΟΛΩΝ

4 For he hath surely seen your shame, and heard you unjustly reproached for not having children: for God is the avenger of sin, and not of nature;

5 And so when he shuts the womb of any person, he does it for this reason, that he may in a more wonderful manner again open it, and that which is born appear to be not the product of lust, but the gift of God.

6 For the first mother of your nation, Sarah, was she not barren even till her eightieth year: and yet even in the end of her old age brought forth Isaac, in whom the promise was made of a blessing to all nations.

7 Rachel, also, so much in favour with God, and beloved so much by holy Jacob, continued barren for a long time, yet afterwards was the mother of Joseph, who was not only governor of Egypt, but delivered many nations from perishing with hunger.

8 Who among the judges was more valiant than Sampson, or more holy than Samuel? And yet both their mothers were barren.

9 But if reason will not convince you of the truth of my words, that there are frequent conceptions in advanced years, and that those who were barren have brought forth to their great surprise; therefore Anna your wife shall bring you a daughter, and you shall call her name Mary;

10 She shall, according to your vow, be devoted to the Lord from her infancy, and be filled with the Holy Ghost from her mother's womb;

11 She shall neither eat nor drink any thing which is unclean, nor shall her conversation be without among the common people, but in the temple of the Lord; that so she may not fall under any slander or suspicion of what is bad.

12 So in the process of her years, as she shall be in a miraculous manner born of one that was barren, so she shall, while yet a virgin, in a way unparalleled, bring forth the Son of the most High God, who shall, be called Jesus, and, according to the signification of his name, be the Saviour of all nations.

13 And this shall be a sign to you of the things which I declare, namely, when you come to the golden gate of Jerusalem, you shall there meet your wife Anna, who being very much troubled that you returned no sooner, shall then rejoice to see you.

14 When the angel had said this, he departed from him.

THE GOSPEL OF THE BIRTH OF MARY.

CHAPTER III.

1 The angel appears to Anna;
2 tells her a daughter shall be born unto her,
3 devoted to the service of the Lord in the temple,
5, who, being a virgin, and not knowing man, shall bring forth the Lord,
6 and gives her a sign therefore.
8 Joachim and Anna meet, and rejoice,
10 and praise the Lord.
11 Anna conceives, and brings forth a daughter called Mary.

AFTERWARDS the angel appeared to Anna his wife, saying; Fear not, neither think that which you see is a spirit;

2 For I am that angel who hath offered up your prayers and alms before God, and am now sent to you, that I may inform you, that a daughter will be born unto you, who shall be called Mary, and shall be blessed above all women.

3 She shall be, immediately upon her birth, full of the grace of the Lord, and shall continue during the three years of her weaning in her father's house, and afterwards, being devoted to the service of the Lord, shall not depart from the temple, till she arrive to years of discretion.

4 In a word, she shall there serve the Lord night and day in fasting and prayer, shall abstain from every unclean thing, and never know any man;

5 But, being an unparalleled instance without any pollution or defilement, and a virgin not knowing any man, shall ring forth a son, and a maid shall bring forth the Lord, who both by his grace and name and works, shall be the Saviour of the world.

6 Arise therefore, and go up to Jerusalem, and when you shall come to that which is called the golden gate (because it is gilt with gold), as a sign of what I have told you, you shall meet your husband, for whose safety you have been so much concerned.

7 When therefore you find these things thus accomplished, believe that all the rest which I have told you, shall also undoubtedly be accomplished.

ΔΙΔΑΧΗ ΤΩΝ ΔΩΔΕΚΑ ΑΠΟΣΤΟΛΩΝ

8 According therefore to the command of the angel, both of them left the places where they were, and when they came to the place specified in the angels prediction, they met each other.

9 Then, rejoicing at each other's vision, and being fully satisfied in the promise of a child, they gave due thanks to the Lord, who exalts the humble.

10 After having praised the Lord, they returned home, and lived in a cheerful and assured expectation of the promise of God.

11 So Anna conceived, and brought forth a daughter, and, according to the angel's command, the parents did call her name Mary.

CHAPTER IV.

1 Mary brought to the temple at three years old.
6 Ascends the stairs of the temple by miracle.
8 Her parents sacrifice and return home.

AND when three years were expired, and the time of her weaning complete, they brought the Virgin to the temple of the Lord with offerings.

2 And there were about the temple, according to the fifteen Psalms of degrees, fifteen stairs to ascend.

3 For the temple being built in a mountain, the altar of burnt-offering, which was without, could not be come near but by stairs;

4 The parents of the blessed Virgin and infant Mary put her upon one of these stairs;

5 But while they were putting off their clothes, in which they had travelled, and according to custom putting on some that were more neat and clean,

6 In the mean time the Virgin of the Lord in such a manner went up all the stairs one after another, without the help of any to lead her or lift her, that any one would have judged from hence, that she was of perfect age.

7 Thus the Lord did, in the infancy of his Virgin, work this extraordinary work, and evidence by this miracle how great she was like to be hereafter.

8 But the parents having offered up their sacrifice, according to the custom of the law, and perfected their vow, left the Virgin with other virgins in the apartments of the temple, who were to be brought up there, and they returned home.

THE GOSPEL OF THE BIRTH OF MARY.

CHAPTER V.

**2 Mary ministered unto by angels.
4 The high priest orders all virgins of fourteen years old to quit the temple and endeavour to be married.
5 Mary refuses,
6 having vowed her virginity to the Lord.
7 The high-priest commands a meeting of the chief persons of Jerusalem,
11 who seek the Lord for counsel in the matter.
13 A voice from the mercy-seat.
15 The high-priest obeys it by ordering all the unmarried men of the house of David to bring their rods to the altar,
17 that his rod which should flower, and on which the Spirit of God should sit, should betroth the Virgin.**

BUT the Virgin of the Lord, as she advanced in years, increased also in perfections, and according to the saying of the Psalmist, her father and mother forsook her, but the Lord took care of her.

2 For she every day had the conversation of angels, and every day received visitors from God, which preserved her from all sorts of evil, and caused her to abound with all good things;

3 So that when at length she arrived to her fourteenth year, as the wicked could not lay any thing to her charge worthy of reproof, so all good persons, who were acquainted with her, admired her life and conversation.

4 At that time the high-priest made a public order, That all the virgins who had public settlements in the temple, and were come to this age, should return home, and, as they were now of a proper maturity, should, according to the custom of their country, endeavour to be married.

5 To which command, though all the other virgins readily yielded obedience, Mary the Virgin of the Lord alone answered, that she could not comply with it,

6 Assigning these reasons, that both she and her parents had devoted her to the service of the Lord; and besides, that she had vowed virginity to the Lord, which vow she was resolved never to break through by lying with a man.

ΔΙΔΑΧΗ ΤΩΝ ΔΩΔΕΚΑ ΑΠΟΣΤΟΛΩΝ

7 The high-priest being hereby brought into a difficulty,

8 Seeing he durst neither on the one hand dissolve the vow, and disobey the Scripture, which says, Vow and pay,

9 Nor on the other hand introduce a custom, to which the people were strangers, commanded,

10 That at the approaching feast all the principal persons both of Jerusalem and the neighbouring places should meet together, that he might have their advice, how he had best proceed in so difficult a case.

11 When they were accordingly met, they unanimously agreed to seek the Lord, and ask counsel from him on this matter.

12 And when they were all engaged in prayer, the high-priest according to the usual way, went to consult God.

13 And immediately there was a voice from the ark, and the mercy seat, which all present heard, that it must be enquired or sought out by a prophecy of Isaiah, to whom the Virgin should be given and be betrothed;

14 For Isaiah saith, there shall come forth a rod out of the stem of Jesse, and a flower shall spring out of its root,

15 And the Spirit of the Lord shall rest upon him, the Spirit of Wisdom and Understanding, the Spirit of Counsel and Might, the Spirit of Knowledge and Piety, and the Spirit of the fear of the Lord shall fill him.

16 Then, according to this prophecy, he appointed, that all the men of the house and family of David, who were marriageable, and not married, should bring their several rods to the altar,

17 And out of whatsoever person's rod after it was brought, a flower should bud forth, and on the top of it the Spirit of the Lord should sit in the appearance of a dove, he should be the man to whom the Virgin should be given and be betrothed.

CHAPTER VI.

1 Joseph draws back his rod.
5 The dove pitches on it. He betroths Mary and returns to Bethlehem.
7 Mary returns to her parents' house at Galilee.

AMONG the rest there was a man named Joseph of the house and family of David, and a person very far advanced in years, who kept back his rod, when every one besides presented his.

THE GOSPEL OF THE BIRTH OF MARY.

2 So that when nothing appeared agreeable to the heavenly voice, the high-priest judged it proper to consult God again.

3 Who answered that he to whom the Virgin was to be betrothed was the only person of those who were brought together, who had not brought his rod.

4 Joseph therefore was betrayed.

5 For, when he did bring his rod, and a dove coming from Heaven pitched upon the top of it, every one plainly saw, that the Virgin was to be betrothed to him.

6 Accordingly, the usual ceremonies of betrothing being over, he returned to his own city of Bethlehem, to set his house in order, and make the needful provisions for the marriage.

7 But the Virgin of the Lord, Mary, with seven other virgins of the same age, who had been weaned at the same time, and who had been appointed to attend her by the priest, returned to her parents' house in Galilee.

CHAPTER VII.

7 The salutation of the Virgin by Gabriel, who explains to her that she shall conceive, without lying with a man, while a Virgin,
19 by the Holy Ghost coming upon her without the heats of lust.
21 She submits.

NOW at this time of her first coming into Galilee, the angel Gabriel was sent to her from God, to declare to her the conception of our Saviour, and the manner and way of her conceiving him.

2 Accordingly going into her, he filled the chamber where she was with a prodigious light, and in a most courteous manner saluting her, he said,

3 Hail, Mary! Virgin of the Lord most acceptable! O Virgin full of grace! The Lord is with you. You are blessed above all women, and you are blessed above all men, that have been hitherto born.

4 But the Virgin, who had before been well acquainted with the countenances of angels, and to whom such light from heaven was no uncommon thing,

ΔΙΔΑΧΗ ΤΩΝ ΔΩΔΕΚΑ ΑΠΟΣΤΟΛΩΝ

5 Was neither terrified with the vision of the angel, nor astonished at the greatness of the light, but only troubled about the angel's words,

6 And began to consider what so extraordinary a salutation should mean, what it did portend, or what sort of end it would have.

7 To this thought the angel, divinely inspired, replies;

8 Fear not, Mary, as though I intended anything inconsistent with your chastity in this salutation:

9 For you have found favour with the Lord, because you made virginity your choice.

10 Therefore while you are a Virgin, you shall conceive without sin, and bring forth a son.

11 He shall be great, because he shall reign from sea to sea, and from the rivers even to the ends of the earth?

12 And he shall be called the Son of the Highest; for he who is born in a mean state on earth, reigns in an exalted one in heaven.

13 And the Lord shall give him the throne of his father David, and he shall reign over the house of Jacob for ever, and of his kingdom there shall be no end.

14 For he is the King of Kings, and Lord of Lords, and his throne is forever and ever.

15 To this discourse of the angel the Virgin replied, not, as though she were unbelieving, but willing to know the manner of it.

16 She said, How can that be? For seeing, according to my vow, I have never known any man, how can I bear a child without the addition of a man's seed.

17 To this the angel replied and said, Think not, Mary, that you shall conceive in the ordinary way.

18 For, without lying with a man, while a Virgin, you shall conceive; while a Virgin, you shall bring forth; and while a Virgin shall give suck.

19 For the Holy Ghost shall come upon you, and the power of the Most High shall overshadow you, without any of the heats of lust.

20 So that which shall be born of you shall be only holy, because it only is conceived without sin, and being born, shall be called the Son of God.

21 Then Mary stretching forth her hands, and lifting her eyes to heaven, said, Behold the handmaid of the Lord! Let it be unto me according to thy word.

CHAPTER VIII.

**1 Joseph returns to Galilee, to marry the Virgin he had betrothed;
4 perceives she is with child,
5 is uneasy,
7 purposes to put her away privily,
8 is told by the angel of the Lord it is not the work of man but the Holy Ghost;
12 Marries her, but keeps chaste,
13 removes with her to Bethlehem,
15 where she brings forth Christ.**

JOSEPH therefore went from Judaea to Galilee, with intention to marry the Virgin who was betrothed to him:

2 For it was now near three months since she was betrothed to him.

3 At length it plainly appeared she was with child, and it could not be hid from Joseph:

4 For going to the Virgin in a free manner, as one espoused, and talking familiarly with her, he perceived her to be with child,

5 And thereupon began to be uneasy and doubtful, not knowing what course it would be best to take;

6 For being a just man, he was not willing to expose her, nor defame her by the suspicion of being a harlot, since he was a pious man:

7 He purposed therefore privately to put an end to their agreement, and as privately to send her away.

8 But while he was meditating these things, behold the angel of the Lord appeared to him in his sleep, and said, Joseph, son of David, fear not;

9 Be not willing to entertain any suspicion of the Virgin's being guilty of fornication, or to think any thing amiss of her, neither be afraid to take her to wife:

10 For that which is begotten in her and now distresses your mind, is not the work of man, but the Holy Ghost.

11 For she of all women is that only Virgin who shall bring forth the Son of God, and you shall call his name Jesus, that is, Saviour: for he will save his people from their sins.

12 Joseph thereupon, according to the command of the angel, married the Virgin, and did not know her, but kept her in chastity.

ΔΙΔΑΧΗ ΤΩΝ ΔΩΔΕΚΑ ΑΠΟΣΤΟΛΩΝ

13 And now the ninth month from her conception drew near, when Joseph took his wife and what other things were necessary to Bethlehem, the city from whence he came.

14 And it came to pass, while they were there, the days were fulfilled for her bringing forth.

15 And she brought forth her first-born son, as the holy Evangelists have taught, even our Lord Jesus Christ, who with the Father, Son, and Holy Ghost, lives and reigns to everlasting ages.

REFERENCES TO MARY'S GOSPEL

[In the primitive ages there was a Gospel extant bearing this name, attributed to St. Matthew, and received as genuine and authentic by several of the ancient Christian sects. It is to be found in the works of Jerome, a Father of the Church, who flourished in the fourth century, from whence the present translation is made. His contemporaries, Epiphanius, Bishop of Salamis, and Austin also mention a gospel under this title. The ancient copies differed from Jerome's, for from one of them the learned Faustus, a native of Britain, who became Bishop of Riez, in Provence, endeavoured to prove that Christ was not the Son of God till after his baptism; and that he was not of the house of David and tribe of Judah, because, according to the Gospel he cited, the Virgin herself was not of this tribe, but of the tribe of Levi; her father being a priest of the name of Joachim. It was likewise from this Gospel that the sect of the Collyridians established the worship and offering of manchet bread and cracknels, or fine wafers, as sacrificed to Mary, whom they imagined to have been born of a Virgin, as Christ is related in the Canonical Gospels to have been born of her. Epiphanius likewise cites a passage concerning the death of Zacharias, which is not in Jerome's copy, viz.: "That it was the occasion of the death of Zacharias in the temple, that when he had seen a vision, he, through surprise, was willing to disclose it, and his mouth was stopped. That which he saw was at the time of his offering incense, and it was a man standing in the form of an ass. When he was gone out, and had a mind to speak thus to the people, Woe unto you, whom do you worship? he who had appeared to him in the temple took away the use of his speech. Afterwards when he recovered it, and was able to speak, he declared this to the Jews; and they slew him. They add (viz. the Gnostics in this book), that on this very account the high-priest was appointed by their lawgiver (by God to Moses) to carry little bells, that whensoever he went into the temple to sacrifice he, whom they worshipped, hearing the noise of the bells, might have time enough to hide himself, and not be caught in that ugly shape and figure.' The princi-

THE GOSPEL OF THE BIRTH OF MARY.

pal part of this Gospel is contained in the Protevangelion of James which follows next in order.]

THE GOSPEL CALLED THE PROTEVANGELION

Or, an Historical Account of the BIRTH of CHRIST, and the perpetual VIRGIN MARY, his Mother, by JAMES THE LESSER, Cousin and Brother of the Lord Jesus, chief Apostle and first Bishop of the Christians in Jerusalem.

CHAPTER I.

1 Joachim, a rich man,
2 offers to the Lord,
3 is opposed by Reuben the high priest, because he has not begotten issue in Israel,
6 retires into the wilderness and fasts forty days and forty nights.

IN the history of the twelve tribes of Israel we read there was a certain person called Joachim, who being very rich, made double offerings to the Lord God, having made this resolution: My substance shall be for the benefit of the whole people, that I may find mercy from the Lord God for the forgiveness of my sins.

2 But at a certain great feast of the Lord, when the children of Israel offered their gifts, and Joachim also offered his, Reuben the highpriest opposed him, saying, it is not lawful for thee to offer thy gifts, seeing thou hast not begot any issue in Israel.

3 At this, Joachim being concerned very much, went away to consult the registries of the twelve tribes, to see whether he was the only person who had begot no issue.

4 But upon inquiry he found that all the righteous had raised up seed in Israel;

5 Then he called to mind the patriarch Abraham, How that God in the end of his life had given him his son Isaac; upon which he was exceedingly distressed, and would not be seen by his wife:

6 But retired into the wilderness, and fixed his tent there, and fasted forty days and forty nights, saying to himself,

7 I will not go down either to eat or drink, till the Lord my God shall look down upon me, but prayer shall be my meat and drink.

CHAPTER. II.

**1 Anna, the wife of Joachim mourns her Barrenness,
6 is reproached with it by Judith her maid,
9 sits under a laurel tree and prays to the Lord.**

IN the mean time his wife Anna was distressed and perplexed on a double account, and said, I will mourn both for my widowhood and my barrenness.

2 Then drew near a great feast of the Lord, and Judith her maid, said, How long will you thus afflict your soul? The feast of the Lord is now come, when it is unlawful for any one to mourn.

3 Take therefore this hood which was given by one who makes such things, for it is not fit that I, who am a servant should wear it, but it well suits a person of your greater character.

4 But Anna replied, Depart from me, I am not used to such things; besides, the Lord hath greatly humbled me.

5 I fear some ill-designing person hath given thee this, and thou art come to reproach me with my sin.

6 Then Judith her maid answered, what evil shall I wish you, when you will not hearken to me?

7 I cannot wish you a greater curse than you are under, in that God hath shut up your womb, that you should not be a mother in Israel.

8 At this Anna was exceedingly troubled, and having on her wedding garment, went about three o'clock in the afternoon to walk in her garden.

9 And she saw a laurel-tree and sat under it, and prayed unto the Lord, saying,

10 O God of my fathers, bless me and regard my prayer, as thou didst bless the womb of Sarah; and gavest her a son Isaac.

ΔΙΔΑΧΗ ΤΩΝ ΔΩΔΕΚΑ ΑΠΟΣΤΟΛΩΝ

CHAPTER III.

1 Anna perceiving a sparrow's nest in the laurels bemoans her barrenness.

AND as she was looking towards heaven she perceive a sparrow's nest in the laurel,

2 And mourning within herself, she said, Wo is me, who begat me? and what womb did bear me, that I should be thus accursed before the children of Israel, and that they should reproach and deride me in the temple of my God: Wo is me, to what can I be compared?

3 I am not comparable to the very beasts of the earth, for even the beasts of the earth are fruitful before thee, O Lord! Wo is me, to what can I be compared?

4 I am not compared to the brute animal, for even the brute animals are fruitful before thee, O Lord! Wo is me, to what am I comparable?

5 I cannot be comparable to these waters, for even the waters are fruitful before thee, O Lord! Wo is me, to what can I be compared?

6 I am not comparable to the waves of the sea; for these, whether they are calm, or in motion, with the fishes which are in them, praise thee, O Lord! Wo is me to what can I be compared?

7 I am not comparable to the very earth, for the earth produces its fruits, and praises thee, O Lord!

CHAPTER IV.

1 An Angel appears to Anna and tells her she shall conceive; two angels appear on the same errand.
5 Joachim sacrifices.
8 Anna goes to meet him,
9 rejoicing that she shall conceive.

THEN an angel of the Lord stood by her and said, Anna, Anna, the Lord hath heard thy prayer; thou shalt conceive and bring forth, and thy progeny shall be spoken of in all the world.

2 And Anna answered, As the Lord my God liveth, whatever I bring forth, whether it be male or female, I will devote it to the Lord my God and it shall minister to him in holy things, during its whole life.

3 And behold there appeared two angels, saying unto her, Behold Joachim thy husband is coming with his shepherds.

4 For an angel of the Lord hath also come down to him, and said, The Lord God hath heard thy prayer, make haste and go hence, for behold Anna thy wife shall conceive.

5 And Joachim went down and called his shepherds, saying, Bring me hither ten she-lambs without spot or blemish, and they shall be for the Lord my God.

6 And bring me twelve calves without blemish, and the twelve calves shall be for the priests and the elders.

7 Bring me also a hundred goats, and the hundred goats shall be for the whole people.

8 And Joachim went down with the shepherds, and Anna stood by the gate and saw Joachim coming with the shepherds.

9 And she ran, and hanging about his neck, said, Now I know that the Lord hath greatly blessed me:

10 For behold, I who was as a widow am no longer as a widow, and I who was barren shall conceive.

CHAPTER V.

1 Joachim abides the first day in his house but sacrifices on the morrow.
2 Consults the plate on the priests forehead,
3 and is without sin.
6 Anna brings forth a daughter,
9 whom she calls Mary.

AND Joachim abode the first day in his house, but on the morrow he brought his offerings, and said,

2 If the Lord be propitious to me let the plate which is on the priests forehead make it manifest.

3 And he consulted the plate which the priest wore, and saw it, and behold sin was not found in him.

4 And Joachim said, Now I know that the Lord is propitious to me, and hath taken away all my sins.

5 And he went down from the temple of the Lord justified, and he went to his own house.

6 And when nine months were fulfilled to Anna, she brought forth, and said to the midwife, What have I brought forth?

7 And she told her, A girl.

8 Then Anna said, The Lord hath this day magnified my soul; and she laid her in bed.

9 And when the days of her purification were accomplished, she gave suck to the child; and called her name Mary.

CHAPTER VI.

1 Mary at nine months old, walks nine steps.
3 Anna keeps her holy.
4 When she is a year old, Joachim makes a great feast.
7 Anna gives her the breast, and sings a song to the Lord.

AND the child increased in strength every day, so that when she was nine months old, her mother put her upon the ground, to try if she could stand; and when she had walked nine steps, she came again to her mother's lap.

2 Then her mother caught her up, and said, As the Lord my God liveth, thou shalt not walk again on this earth, till I bring thee into the temple of the Lord.

3 Accordingly she made her chamber a holy place, and suffered nothing uncommon or unclean to come near her, but invited certain undefiled daughters of Israel, and they drew her aside.

4 But when the child was a year old, Joachim made a great feast, and invited the priests, scribes, elders, and all the people of Israel;

5 And Joachim then made an offering of the girl to the chief-priests, and they blessed her, saying, The God of our fathers bless this girl, and give her a name famous and lasting through all generations. And all the people replied, So be it, Amen:

6 Then Joachim a second time offered her to the priests, and they blessed her, saying, O most high God, regard this girl, and bless her with an everlasting blessing.

7 Upon this her mother took her up, and gave her the breast, and sung the following song to the Lord.

8 I will sing a song unto the Lord my God, for he hath visited me, and taken away from me the reproach of mine enemies, and hath given me the fruit of his righteousness, that it may now be told the sons of Reuben, that Anna gives suck.

THE GOSPEL CALLED THE PROTEVANGELION

9 Then she put the child to rest in the room which she had consecrated, and she went out and ministered unto them.

10 And when the feast was ended, they went away rejoicing, and praising the God of Israel.

CHAPTER VII.

3 Mary being three years old, Joachim causes certain virgins to light each a lamp, and goes with her to the temple.
5 The high-priest places her on the third step of the altar, and sits dances with her feet.

BUT the girl grew, and when she was two years old, Joachim said to Anna, Let us lead her to the temple of the Lord, that we may perform our vow, which we have vowed unto the Lord God, lest he should be angry with us, and our offering be unacceptable.

2 But Anna said, Let us wait the third year, lest she should be at a loss to know her father. And Joachim said, Let us then wait.

3 And when the child was three years old, Joachim said, Let us invite the daughters of the Hebrews, who are undefiled, and let them take each a lamp, and let them be lighted, that the child may not turn back again, and her mind be set against the temple of the Lord,

4 And they did thus till they ascended into the temple of the Lord. And the high-priest received her, and blessed her, and said, Mary, the Lord God hath magnified thy name to all generations, and to the very end of time by thee will the Lord shew his redemption to the children of Israel.

5 And he placed her upon the third step of the altar, and the Lord gave unto her grace, and she dance with her feet, and all the house of Israel loved her.

ΔΙΔΑΧΗ ΤΩΝ ΔΩΔΕΚΑ ΑΠΟΣΤΟΛΩΝ

CHAPTER VIII.

2 Mary fed in the temple by angels.
3 When twelve years old the priests consult what to do with her.
6 The angel of the Lord warns Zacharias to call together all the widowers, each bringing a rod.
7 The people meet by sound of trumpet.
8 Joseph throws away his hatchet, and goes to the meeting.
11 A dove comes forth from his rod, and alights on his head.
12 He is chosen to betroth the Virgin,
13 refuses because he is an old man,
14 is compelled,
16 takes her home, and goes to mind his trade of building.

AND her parents went away filled with wonder, and praising God, because the girl did not return back to them.

2 But Mary continued in the temple as a dove educated there, and received her food from the hand of an angel.

3 And when she was twelve years of age, the priests met in a council, and said, Behold, Mary is twelve years of age, what shall we do with her, for fear lest the holy place of the Lord our God should be defiled?

4 Then replied the priests to Zacharias the high-priest, Do you stand at the altar of the Lord, and enter into the holy place, and make petitions concerning her, and whatsoever the Lord shall manifest unto you, that do.

5 Then the high-priest entered into the Holy of Holies, and taking away with him the breast-plate of judgment made prayers concerning her;

6 And behold the angel of the Lord came to him, and said, Zacharias, Zacharias, Go forth and call together all the widowers among the people, and let every one of them bring his rod, and he by whom the Lord shall shew a sign shall be the husband of Mary

7 And the criers went out through all Judaea, and the trumpet of the Lord sounded, and all the people ran and met together.

8 Joseph also throwing away his hatchet, went out to meet them; and when they were met, they went to the high-priest; taking every man his rod.

9 After the high-priest had received their rods, he went into the temple to pray;

10 And when he had finished his prayer, he took the rods, and went forth and distributed them, and there was no miracle attended them.

11 The last rod was taken by Joseph, said behold a dove proceeded out of the rod, and flew upon the head of Joseph.

12 And the high-priest said, Joseph, Thou art the person chosen to take the Virgin of the Lord, to keep her for him:

13 But Joseph refused, saying, I am an old man, and have children, but she is young, and I fear lest I should appear ridiculous in Israel.

14 Then the high-priest replied, Joseph, Fear the Lord thy God, and remember how God dealt with Dathan, Korah, and Abiram, how the earth opened and swallowed them up, because of their contradiction.

15 Now therefore, Joseph, fear God lest the like things should happen in your family.

16 Joseph then being afraid, took her unto his house, and Joseph said unto Mary, Behold, I have taken thee from the temple of the Lord, and now I will leave thee in my house; I must go to mind my trade of building. The Lord be with thee.

CHAPTER IX.

1 The priests desire a new veil for the temple,
3 seven virgins cast lots for making different parts of it,
4 the lot to spin the true purple falls to Mary.
5 Zacharias, the high priest, becomes dumb.
7 Mary takes a pot to draw water, and hears a voice,
8 trembles and begins to work,
9 an angel Appears and salutes her, and tells her she shall conceive by the Holy Ghost,
17 she submits.
19 Visits her cousin Elizabeth, whose child in her womb leaps.

AND it came to pass, in a council of the priests, it was said, Let us make a new veil for the temple of the Lord.

2 And the high-priest said, Call together to me seven undefiled virgins of the tribe of David.

ΔΙΔΑΧΗ ΤΩΝ ΔΩΔΕΚΑ ΑΠΟΣΤΟΛΩΝ

3 And the servants went and brought them into the temple of the Lord, and the high-priest said unto them, Cast lots before me now, who of you shall spin the golden thread, who the blue, who the scarlet, who the fine linen, and who the true purple.

4 Then the high-priest knew Mary; that she was of the tribe of David; and he called her, and the true purple fell to her lot to spin, and she went away to her own house.

5 But from that time Zacharias the high-priest became dumb, and Samuel was placed in his room till Zacharias spoke again.

6 But Mary took the true purple; and did spin it.

7 And she took a pot, and went out to draw water, and heard a voice saying unto her, Hail thou who art full of grace, the Lord is with thee; thou art blessed among women.

8 And she looked round to the right and to the left (to see) whence that voice came, and then trembling went into her house, and laying down the water-pot, she took the purple, and sat down in her seat to work it.

9 And behold the angel of the Lord stood by her, and said, Fear not, Mary, for thou hast found favour in the sight of God.

10 Which when she heard, she reasoned with herself what that sort of salutation meant.

11 And the angel said unto her, The Lord is with thee, and thou shalt conceive:

12 To which she replied, What! shall I conceive by the living God and bring forth as all other women do?

13 But the angel returned answer, Not so, O Mary, but the Holy Ghost shall come upon thee, and the power of the Most High shall overshadow thee:

14 Wherefore that which shall be born of thee shall be holy, and shall be called the Son of the Living God, and thou shalt call his name Jesus; for he shall save his people from their sins.

15 And behold thy cousin Elizabeth, she also hath conceived a son in her old age.

16 And this now is the sixth month with her, who was called barren: for nothing is impossible with God.

17 And Mary said, Behold the handmaid of the Lord; let it be unto me according to thy word.

18 And when she had wrought her purple, she carried it to the high-priest, and the high-priest blessed her, saying, Mary, the Lord God hath magnified thy name, and thou shalt be blessed in all the ages of the world.

19 Then Mary, filled with joy, went away to her cousin Elizabeth, and knocked at the door.

20 Which when Elizabeth heard, she ran and opened to her, and blessed her, and said, Whence is this to me, that the mother of my Lord should come unto me?

21 For lo! as soon as the voice of thy salutation reached my ears, that which is in me leaped and blessed thee.

22 But Mary, being ignorant of all those mysterious things which the archangel Gabriel had spoken to her, lifted up her eyes to heaven, and said, Lord! What am I, that all the generations of the earth should call me blessed?

23 But perceiving herself daily to grow big, and being afraid, she went home, and hid herself from the children of Israel; and was fourteen years old when all these things happened.

CHAPTER X.

1 Joseph returns from building houses, finds the Virgin grown big, being six months gone with child,
2 is jealous and troubled,
8 reproaches her,
10 she affirms her innocence,
13 he leaves her,
16 determines to dismiss her privately,
17 is warned in a dream that Mary is with child by the Holy Ghost,
20 and glorifies God who had shewn him such favour.

AND when her sixth month was come, Joseph returned from his building houses abroad, which was his trade, and entering into the house, found the Virgin grown big:

2 Then smiting upon his face, he said, With what face can I look up to the Lord my God? or, what shall I say concerning this young woman?

3 For I received her a Virgin out of the temple of the Lord my God, and have not preserved her such!

4 Who has thus deceived me? Who has committed this evil in my house, and seducing the Virgin from me, hath defiled her?

5 Is not the history of Adam exactly accomplished in me?

ΔΙΔΑΧΗ ΤΩΝ ΔΩΔΕΚΑ ΑΠΟΣΤΟΛΩΝ

6 For in the very instant of his glory, the serpent came and found Eve alone, and seduced her.

7 Just after the same manner it has happened to me.

8 Then Joseph arising from the ground, called her, and said, O thou who hast been so much favoured by God, why hast thou done this?

9 Why hast thou thus debased thy soul, who wast educated in the Holy of Holies, and received thy food from the hand of angels?

10 But she, with a flood of tears, replied, I am innocent, and have known no man.

11 Then said Joseph, How comes it to pass you are with child?

12 Mary answered, As the Lord my God liveth, I know not by what means.

13 Then Joseph was exceedingly afraid, and went ay from her, considering what he should do with her; and he thus reasoned with himself:

14 If I conceal her crime, I shall be found guilty by the law of the Lord;

15 And if I discover her to the children of Israel, I fear, lest she being with child by an angel, I shall be found to betray the life of an innocent person.

16 What therefore shall I do? I will privately dismiss her.

17 Then the night was come upon him, when behold an angel of the Lord appeared to him in a dream, and said,

18 Be not afraid to take that young woman, for that which is within her is of the Holy Ghost,

19 And she shall bring forth a son, and thou shalt call his name Jesus, for he shall save his people from their sins.

20 Then Joseph arose from his sleep, and glorified the God of Israel, who had shewn him such favour, and preserved the Virgin.

THE GOSPEL CALLED THE PROTEVANGELION

CHAPTER XI.

**3 Annas visits Joseph, perceives the Virgin big with child,
4 informs the high priest that Joseph had privately married her.
8 Joseph and Mary brought to trial on the charge.
17 Joseph drinks the water of the Lord as an ordeal, and receiving no harm, returns home.**

THEN came Annas the scribe, and said to Joseph, Wherefore have we not seen you since your return?

2 And Joseph replied, Because I was weary after my journey, and rested the first day.

3 But Annas turning about perceived the Virgin big with child.

4 And went away to the priest, and told him, Joseph in whom you placed so much confidence, is guilty of a notorious crime, in that he hath defiled the Virgin whom he received out of the temple of the Lord, and hath privately married her, not discovering it to the children of Israel.

5 Then said the priest, Hath Joseph done this?

6 Annas replied, If you send any of your servants you will find that she is with child.

7 And the servants went, and found it as he said.

8 Upon this both she and Joseph were brought to their trial, and the priest said unto her, Mary, what hast thou done?

9 Why hast thou debased thy soul, and forgot thy God, seeing thou wast brought up in the Holy of Holies, and didst receive thy food from the hands of angels, and heardest their songs?

10 Why hast thou done this?

11 To which with a flood of tears she answered, As the Lord my God liveth, I am innocent in his sight, seeing I know no man.

12 Then the priest said to Joseph, Why hast thou done this?

13 And Joseph answered, As the Lord my God liveth, I have not been concerned with her.

14 But the priest said, Lie not, but declare the truth; thou hast privately married her, and not discovered it to the children of Israel, and humbled thyself under the mighty hand (of God), that thy seed might be blessed:

15 And Joseph was silent.

16 Then said the priest (to Joseph), You must restore to the temple of the Lord the Virgin which you took thence.

17 But he wept bitterly, and the priest added, I will cause you both to drink the water of the Lord, which is for trial, and so your iniquity shall be laid open before you.—[bitter water that causeth the curse]

18 Then the priest took the water, and made Joseph drink, and sent him to a mountainous place,

19 And he returned perfectly well, and all the people wondered that his guilt was not discovered.

20 So the priest said, Since the Lord hath not made your sins evident, neither do I condemn you.

21 So he sent them away.

22 Then Joseph took Mary, and went to his house, rejoicing and praising the God of Israel.

CHAPTER. XII.

1 A decree from Augustus for taxing the Jews.
5 Joseph puts Mary on an ass, to return to Bethlehem,
6 she looks sorrowful,
7 she laughs,
8 Joseph inquires the cause of each,
9 she tells him she sees two persons, one mourning and the other rejoicing.
10 The delivery being near, he takes her from the ass, and places her in a cave.

AND it came to pass, that there went forth a decree from the Emperor Augustus, that all the Jews should be taxed, who were of Bethlehem in Judaea.

2 And Joseph said, I will take care that my children be taxed; but what shall I do with this young woman?

3 To have her taxed as my wife I am ashamed; and if I tax her as my daughter, all Israel knows she is not my daughter.

4 When the time of the Lord's appointment shall come, let him do as seems good to him.

5 And he saddled the ass, and put her upon it, and Joseph and Simon followed after her, and arrived at Bethlehem within three miles.

6 Then Joseph turning about saw Mary sorrowful, and said within himself, Perhaps she is in pain through that which is within her.

7 But when he turned about again, he saw her laughing, and said to her,

8 Mary, how happens it, that I sometimes see sorrow, and sometimes laughter and joy in thy countenance?

9 And Mary replied to him, I see two people with mine eyes, the one weeping and mourning, the other laughing and rejoicing.

10 And he went again across the way, and Mary said to Joseph, Take me down from the ass, for that which is in me presses to come forth.

11 But Joseph replied, Whither shall I take thee? for the place is a desert.

12 Then said Mary again to Joseph, take me down, for that which is within me mightily presses me.

13 And Joseph took her down.

14 And he found there a cave, and let her into it.

CHAPTER XIII.

1 Joseph seeks a Hebrew midwife,
2 perceives the owls stopping in their flight,
3 the working people at their food not moving,
8 the sheep standing still,
9 the shepherd fixed and immoveable,
10 and kids with their mouths touching the water but not drinking.

AND leaving her and his sons in the cave, Joseph went forth to seek a Hebrew midwife in the village of Bethlehem.

2 But as I was going (said Joseph), I looked up into the air, and I saw the clouds astonished, and the fowls of the air stopping in the midst of their flight.

3 And I looked down towards the earth, and saw a table spread, and working people sitting around it, but their hands were upon the table and they did not move to eat.

4 They who had meat in their mouths did not eat.

5 They who lifted their hands up to their heads did not draw them back,

6 And they who lifted them up to their mouths did not put any thing in;

7 But all their faces were fixed upwards.

8 And I beheld the sheep dispersed, and yet the sheep stood still.

9 And the shepherd lifted up his hand to smite them, and his hand continued up.

10 And I looked unto a river, and saw the kids with their mouths close to the water, and touching it, but they did not drink.

CHAPTER XIV.

1 Joseph finds a midwife.
10 A bright cloud overshadows the cave.
11 A great light in the cave, gradually increases until the infant is born.
13 The mid-wife goes out, and tells Salome that she has seen a virgin bring forth.
17 Salome doubts it.
20 her hand withers,
22 she supplicates the Lord,
28 is cured,
30 but warned not to declare what she had seen.

THEN I beheld a woman coming down from the mountains, and she said to me, Where art thou going, O man?

2 And I said to her, I go to enquire for a Hebrew midwife.

3 She replied to me, Where is the woman that is to be delivered?

4 And I answered, In the cave, and she is betrothed to me.

5 Then said the midwife, Is she not thy wife?

6 Joseph answered, It is Mary, who was educated in the Holy of Holies, in the house of the Lord, and she fell to me by lot, and is not my wife, but has conceived by the Holy Ghost.

7 The midwife said, Is this true?

8 He answered, Come and see.

9 And the midwife went along with him, and stood in the cave.

10 Then a bright cloud over- shadowed the cave and the mid- wife said, This day my soul is magnified, for mine eyes have seen surprising things, and salvation is brought forth to Israel.

11 But on a sudden the cloud became a great light in the cave, so that their eyes could not bear it.

12 But the light gradually decreased, until the infant appeared, and sucked the breast of his mother, Mary.

13 Then the midwife cried out, and said, How glorious a day is this, wherein mine eyes have seen this extraordinary sight!

14 And the midwife went out from the cave, and Salome met her.

15 And the midwife said to her, Salome, Salome, I will tell you a most surprising thing which I saw,

16 A virgin hath brought forth, which is a thing contrary to nature.

17 To which Salome replied, As the Lord my God liveth unless I receive particular proof of this matter, I will not believe that a virgin hath brought forth.

18 If Then Salome went in, and the midwife said, Mary, shew thyself, for a controversy is risen concerning thee.

19 And Salome received satisfaction.

20 But her hand was withered, and she groaned bitterly;

21 And said, Woe to me, because of mine iniquity; for I have tempted the living God, and my hand is ready to drop off.

22 Then Salome made her supplication to the Lord, and said, O God of my Fathers, remember me, for I am of the seed of Abraham, and Isaac, and Jacob.

23 Make me not a reproach among the children of Israel, but restore me sound to my parents.

24 For thou well knowest, O Lord, that I have performed many offices of charity in thy name, and have received my reward from thee.

25 Upon this an angel of the Lord stood by Salome, and said, The Lord God hath heard thy prayer, reach forth thy hand to the child, and carry him, and by that means thou shalt be restored.

26 Salome filled with exceeding joy, went to the child, and said, I will touch him.

27 And she purposed to worship him, for she said, This is a great king, which is born in Israel.

28 And straightway Salome was cured.

29 Then the midwife went out of the cave, being approved by God.

30 And lo! a voice came to Salome. Declare not the strange things which thou hast seen, till the child shall come to Jerusalem.

31 So Salome also departed, approved by God.

ΔΙΔΑΧΗ ΤΩΝ ΔΩΔΕΚΑ ΑΠΟΣΤΟΛΩΝ

CHAPTER XV.

1 Wise men come from the east.
3 Herod alarmed;
8 desires them if they find the child to bring him word.
10 They visit the cave and offer the child their treasure,
11 and being warned in a dream, do not return to Herod, but go home another way.

THEN Joseph was preparing to go away, because there arose a great disorder in Bethlehem by the coming of some wise men from the east,

2 Who said, Where is the King of the Jews born? For we have seen his star in the east, and are come to worship him.

3 When Herod heard this, he was exceedingly troubled, and sent messengers to the wise men, and to the priests, and enquired of them in the town-hall,

4 And said unto them, Where have you it written concerning Christ the king, or where should he be born?

5 Then they say unto him, In Bethlehem of Judaea; for thus it is written: And thou Bethlehem in the land of Judah, art not the least among the princes of Judah, for out of thee shall come a ruler, who shall rule my people Israel.

6 And having sent away the chief priests, he enquired of the wise men in the town-hall, and said unto them, What sign was it ye saw concerning the king that is born?

7 They answered him, We saw an extraordinary large star shining among the stars of heaven, and so out-shined all the other stars, as that they became not visible, and we knew thereby that a great king was born in Israel, and therefore we are come to worship him.

8 Then said Herod to them, Go and make diligent inquiry; and if ye find the child, bring me word again, that I may come and worship him also.

9 So the wise men went forth, and behold, the star which they saw in the east went before them, till it came and stood over the cave where the young child was with Mary his mother.

10 Then they brought forth out of their treasures, and offered unto him gold and frankincense, and myrrh.

11 And being warned in a dream by an angel, that they should not return to Herod through Judaea, they departed into their own country by another way.

CHAPTER XVI.

**1 Herod enraged, orders the infants in Bethlehem to be slain.
2 Mary puts her infant in an ox-manger.
3 Elizabeth flees with her son John to the mountains.
6 A mountain miraculously divides and receives them.
9 Herod incensed at the escape of John, causes Zacharias to be murdered at the altar.
23 The roofs of the temple rent, the body miraculously conveyed, and the blood petrified.
25 Israel mourns for him.
27 Simeon chosen his successor by lot.**

THEN Herod perceiving that he was mocked by the wise men, and being very angry, commanded certain men to go and to kill all the children that were in Bethlehem, from two years old and under.

2 But Mary hearing that the children were to be killed, being under much fear, took the child, and wrapped him up in swaddling clothes, and laid him in an ox- manger, because there was no room for them in the inn.

3 Elizabeth also, hearing that her son John was about to be searched for, took him and went up unto the mountains, and looked around for a place to hide him;

4 And there was no secret place to be found.

5 Then she groaned within herself, and said, O mountain of the Lord, receive the mother with the child.

6 For Elizabeth could not climb up,

7 And instantly the mountain was divided and received them.

8 And there appeared to them an angel of the Lord to preserve them.

9 But Herod made search after John, and sent servants to Zacharias, when he was (ministering) at the altar, and said unto him, Where hast thou hid thy son?

10 He replied, to them, I am a minister of God, and a servant at the altar: how should I know where my son is?

ΔΙΔΑΧΗ ΤΩΝ ΔΩΔΕΚΑ ΑΠΟΣΤΟΛΩΝ

11 So the servants went back, and told Herod the whole; at which he was incensed, and said, Is not this son of his like to be king of Israel?

12 He sent therefore again his servants to Zacharias, saying, Tell us the truth, where is thy son, for you know that your life is in my hand.

13 So the servants went and told him all this:

14 But Zacharias replied to them, I am a martyr for God, and if ye shed my blood, the Lord will receive my soul.

15 Besides know that ye shed innocent blood.

16 However Zacharias was murdered in the entrance of the temple said altar, and about the partition;

17 But the children of Israel knew not when he want killed.

18 Then at the hour of salutation the priests went into the temple but Zacharias did not according to custom, meet them and bless them.

19 Yet they still continued waiting for him to salute them;

20 And when they found he did not in a long time come, one of them ventured into the holy place where the altar was, and he saw blood lying upon the ground congealed:

21 When, beheld, a voice from heaven said, Zacharias is murdered, and his blood shall not be wiped away, until the revenger of his blood come.

22 But when he heard this, he was afraid; and went forth and told the priests what he had seen and heard; and they all went in, and saw the fact.

23 Then the roofs of the temple howled, and were rent from the top to the bottom:

24 And they could not find the body, but only blood made hard like stone.

25 And they went away, and told the people, that Zacharias was murdered, and all the tribes of Israel heard thereof, and mourned for him, and lamented three days:

26 Then the priests took council together concerning a person to succeed him.

27 And Simeon and the other priests cast lots, and the lot fell upon Simeon.

28 For he had been assured by the Holy Spirit, that he should not die, till he had seen Christ come in the flesh.

(I James wrote this History in Jerusalem: and when the disturbance was I retired into a desert place, until the death of Herod, and the disturbances ceased at Jerusalem. That which remains is, that I glorify God that he hath given me such wisdom to write unto you who are spiritual, and who love God: to whom (be ascribed) glory and dominion for ever and ever. Amen.)

THE PROTEVANGELION. Note on the death of Zacharias in Chap. 16.

There is a story both in the Jerusalem and Babylonish Talmud very similar to this. It is cited by Dr. Lightfoot, Talmud, Hierosol, in Taanith, fol. 69; and Talmud. Babyl. in Sanhedr., fol. 96. "O Rabbi Jochanan said, Eighty thousand priests were slain for the blood of Zacharias. Rabbi Judas asked Rabbi Achan, Where did they kill Zacharias? Was it in the woman's court, or in the court of Israel? He answered, Neither in the court of Israel, nor in the court of women, but in the court of the priests; and they did not treat his blood in the same manner as they were wont to treat the blood of a ram or young goat. For of these it is written, He shall pour out his blood, and cover it with dust. But it is written here, The blood is in the midst of her: she set it upon the top of a rock; she poured it not upon the ground. (Ezek. xxiv. 7.) But why was this? That it might cause fury to come up to take vengeance: I have set his blood upon the top of a rock, that it should not be covered. They committed seven evils that day: they murdered a priest, a prophet, and a king; they shed the blood of the innocent; they polluted the court: that day was the Sabbath: and the day of expiation. When therefore Nebuzaradan came there (viz. to Jerusalem,) he saw his blood bubbling, and said to them, What meaneth this? They answered, It is the blood of calves, lambs, and rams, which we have offered upon the altar. He commanded then, that they should bring calves, and lambs, and rams, and said I will try whether this be their blood: accordingly they brought and slew them, but the blood of Zacharias still bubbled, but the blood of these did not bubble. Then he said, Declare to me the truth of this matter, or else I will comb your flesh with iron combs. Then said they to him, He was a priest, prophet, and judge, who prophesied to Israel all these calamities which we have suffered from you; but we arose against him, and slew him. Then, said he, I will appease him; then he took the rabbis and slew them upon his (viz. Zacharias's) blood, and he was not yet appeased. Next he took the young boys from the schools, and slew them upon his blood; and yet it bubbled. Then he brought the young priests and slew them in the same place, and yet it still bubbled. So he slew at length ninety-four thousand persons upon his blood, and it did not as yet cease bubbling; then he drew near to it, and said, O Zacharias, Zacharias, thou halt occasioned the death of the chief of thy countrymen, shall I slay them all? then the blood ceased, and did bubble no more."

REFERENCES TO THE PROTEVANGELION.

[This Gospel is ascribed to James. The allusions to it in the ancient Fathers are frequent, and their expressions indicate that it had obtained a very general credit in the Christian world. The controversies founded upon it chiefly relate to the age of Joseph at the birth of Christ, and to his being a widower with children, before his marriage with the Virgin. It seems material to remark, that the legends of the latter ages affirm the virginity of Joseph, notwithstanding Epiphanius, Hilary, Chrysostom, Cyril, Euthymius, Thephylaet, Occumenius, and indeed all the Latin Fathers till Ambrose, and the Greek Fathers afterwards, maintain the opinions of Joseph's age and family, founded upon their belief in the authenticity of this book. It is supposed to have been originally composed in Hebrew. Postellus brought the MS. of this Gospel from the Levant, translated it into Latin, and sent it to Oporimus, a printer at Basil, where Bibliander, a Protestant Divine, and the Professor of Divinity at Zurich, caused it to be printed in 1552. Postellus asserts that it was publicly read as canonical in the eastern churches they making no doubt that James was the author, of it. It is, nevertheless considered apocryphal by some of the most learned divines in the Protestant and Catholic churches.]

THE FIRST GOSPEL OF THE INFANCY OF JESUS CHRIST.

CHAPTER I.

1 Caiphas relates that Jesus, when in his cradle, informed his mother that he was the Son of God.
5 Joseph and Mary going to Bethlehem to be taxed, Mary's time of bringing forth arrives, and she goes into a cave.
8 Joseph fetches in a Hebrew woman. The cave filled with great lights.
11 The infant born,
17 and cures the woman.
19 Arrival of the shepherds.

THE following accounts we found in the book of Joseph the high-priest, called by some Caiphas:

2 He relates, that Jesus spake even when he was in the cradle, and said to his mother:

3 Mary, I am Jesus the Son of God, that word, which thou didst bring forth according to the declaration of the angel Gabriel to thee, and my father hath sent me for the salvation of the world.

4 In the three hundred and ninth year of the era of Alexander, Augustus published a decree that all persons should go to be taxed in their own country.

5 Joseph therefore arose, and with Mary his spouse he went to Jerusalem, and then came to Bethlehem, that he and his family might be taxed in the city of his fathers.

ΔΙΔΑΧΗ ΤΩΝ ΔΩΔΕΚΑ ΑΠΟΣΤΟΛΩΝ

6 And when they came by the cave, Mary confessed to Joseph that her time of bringing forth was come, and she could not go on to the city, and said, Let us go into this cave.

7 At that time the sun was very near going down.

8 But Joseph hastened away, that he might fetch her a midwife; and when he saw an old Hebrew woman who was of Jerusalem, he said to her, Pray come hither, good woman, and go into that cave, and you will there see a woman just ready to bring forth.

9 It was after sunset, when the old woman and Joseph with her reached the cave, and they both went into it.

10 And behold, it was all filled with lights, greater than the light of lamps and candles, and greater than the light of the sun itself.

11 The infant was then wrapped up in swaddling clothes, and sucking the breasts of his mother St. Mary.

12 When they both saw this light, they were surprised; the old woman asked St. Mary, Art thou the mother of this child?

13 St. Mary replied, She was.

14 On which the old woman said, Thou art very different from all other women.

15 St. Mary answered, As there is not any child like to my son, so neither is there any woman like to his mother.

16 The old woman answered, and said, O my Lady, I am come hither that I may obtain an everlasting reward.

17 Then our Lady St. Mary said to her, Lay thine hands upon the infant, which, when she had done, she became whole.

18 And as she was going forth, she said, From henceforth, all the days of my life, I will attend upon and be a servant of this infant.

19 After this, when the shepherds came, and had made a fire, and they were exceedingly rejoicing, the heavenly host appeared to them, praising and adoring the supreme God.

20 And as the shepherds were engaged in the same employment, the cave at that time seemed like a glorious temple, because both the tongues of angels and men united to adore and magnify God, on account of the birth of the Lord Christ.

21 But when the old Hebrew woman saw all these evident miracles, she gave praises to God, and said, I thank thee, O God, thou God of Israel, for that mine eyes have seen the birth of the Saviour of the world.

THE FIRST GOSPEL OF THE INFANCY OF JESUS CHRIST.

CHAPTER. II.

1 The child circumcised in the cave,
2 and the old woman preserving his foreskin or navel-string in a box of spikenard, Mary afterwards anoints Christ with it.
5 Christ brought to the temple;
6 He shines,
7 and angels stand around him adoring.
8 Simeon praises Christ.

AND when the time of his circumcision was come: namely, the eighth day, on which the law commanded the child to be circumcised; they circumcised him in the cave.

2 And the old Hebrew woman took the foreskin (others say she took the navel-string), and preserved it in an alabaster-box of old oil of spikenard.

3 And she had a son who was a druggist, to whom she said, Take heed thou sell not this alabaster-box of spikenard-ointment, although thou shouldst be offered three hundred pence for it.

4 Now this is that alabaster-box which Mary the sinner procured, and poured forth the ointment out of it upon the head and the feet of our Lord Jesus Christ, and wiped them off with the hairs of her head.

5 Then after ten days they brought him to Jerusalem, and on the fortieth day from his birth they presented him in the temple before the Lord, making the proper offerings for him, according to the requirement of the law of Moses: namely, that every male which opens the womb shall be called holy unto God.

6 At that time old Simeon saw him shining as a pillar of light, when St. Mary the Virgin, his mother, carried him in her arms, and was filled with the greatest pleasure at the sight.

7 And the angels stood around him, adoring him, as a king's guards stand around him.

8 Then Simeon going near to St. Mary, and stretching forth his hands towards her, said to the Lord Christ, Now, O My Lord, thy servant shall depart in peace, according to thy word;

9 For mine eyes have seen thy mercy, which thou hast prepared for the salvation of all nations; a light to all people, and the glory of thy people Israel.

ΔΙΔΑΧΗ ΤΩΝ ΔΩΔΕΚΑ ΑΠΟΣΤΟΛΩΝ

10 Hannah the prophetess was also present, and drawing near, she gave praises to God, and celebrated the happiness of Mary.

CHAPTER III.

1 The wise men visit Christ. Mary gives them one of his swaddling clothes.
3 An angel appears to them in the form of a star.
4 They return and make a fire, and worship the swaddling cloth, and put it in the fire where it remains unconsumed.

AND it came to pass, when the Lord Jesus was born at Bethlehem, a city of Judaea, in the time of Herod the King;—the wise men came from the East to Jerusalem, according to the prophecy of Zoradascht, [Zoroaster] and brought with them offerings: namely, gold, frankincense, and myrrh, and worshipped him, and offered to him their gifts.

2 Then the Lady Mary took one of his swaddling clothes in which the infant was wrapped, and gave it to them instead of a blessing, which they received from her as a most noble present.

3 And at the same time there appeared to them an angel in the form of that star which had before been their guide in their journey; the light of which they followed till they returned into their own country.

4 On their return their kings and princes came to them inquiring, whom they had seen and done? What sort of journey and return they had? What Company they had on the road?

5 But they produced the swaddling cloth which St. Mary had given them, on account whereof they kept a feast.

6 And having, according to the custom of their country, made a fire, they worshipped it.

7 And casting the swaddling cloth into it, the fire took it and kept it.

8 And when the fire was put out, they took forth the swaddling cloth unhurt, as much as if the fire had not touched it.

9 Then they began to kiss it, and put it upon their heads and their eyes saying, This is certainly an undoubted truth, and it is really surprising that the fire could not burn it, and consume it.

10 Then they took it, and with the greatest respect laid it up among their treasures.

THE FIRST GOSPEL OF THE INFANCY OF JESUS CHRIST.

CHAPTER IV.

1 Herod intends to put Christ to death.
3 An angel warns Joseph to take the child and his mother into Egypt.
6 Consternation on their arrival.
13 The idols fall down.
15 Mary washes Christ's swaddling clothes, hangs them to dry on a post, and the son of a priest puts one on his head;
16 And being possessed of devils they leave him.

NOW Herod perceiving that the wise men did delay and not return to him, called together the priest and wise men, and said, Tell me in what place the Christ should be born.

2 And when they replied, in Bethlehem,—a city of Judaea, he began to contrive in his own mind the death of the Lord Jesus Christ.

3 But an angel of the Lord appeared to Joseph in his sleep, and said, Arise, take the child and his mother, and go into Egypt as soon as the cock crows. So he arose, and went.

4 And as he was considering with himself about his journey, the morning came upon him.

5 In the length of the journey the girts of the saddle broke.

6 And now he drew near to a great city, in which there was an idol, to which the priests of the other idols and gods of Egypt brought their offerings and vows.

7 And there was by this idol a priest ministering to it, who, as often as Satan spoke out of that idol, related the things he said to the inhabitants of Egypt, and those countries.

8 This priest had a son three years old, who was possessed with a great multitude of devils, who uttered many strange things and when the devils seized him, walked about naked with his clothes torn, throwing stones at those whom he saw.

9 Near to that idol was the inn of the city, into which when Joseph and St. Mary were come, and had turned into that inn, all the inhabitants of the city were astonished.

10 And all the magistrates and priests of the idols assembled before that idol, and made inquiry there, saying, What means all this consternation, and dread, which has fallen upon all our country?

ΔΙΔΑΧΗ ΤΩΝ ΔΩΔΕΚΑ ΑΠΟΣΤΟΛΩΝ

11 The idol answered them, The unknown God is come thither, who is truly God; nor is there any one besides him, who is worthy of divine worship for he is truly the Son of God.

12 At the fame of him this country trembled, and at his coming it is under the present commotion and consternation, and we ourselves are afrighted by the greatness of his power.

13 And at the same instant this idol fell down, and at his fall all the inhabitants of Egypt, besides others ran together.

14 But the son of the priest, when his usual disorder came upon him going into the inn, found there Joseph and St. Mary, whom all the rest had left behind and forsook.

15 And when the Lady St. Mary had washed the swaddling clothes of the Lord Christ, and hanged them out to dry upon a post, the boy possessed with the devil took down one of them, and put it upon his head.

16 And presently the devils began to come out of his mouth, and fly away in the shape of crows and serpents.

17 From that time the boy was healed by the power of the Lord Christ and he began to sing praises, and give thanks to the Lord who had healed him.

18 When his father saw him restored to his former state of health, he said, My son, what has happened to thee, and by what means wert thou cured?

19 The son answered, When the devils seized me, I went into the inn, and there found a very handsome woman with a boy, whose swaddling clothes she had just before washed, and hanged out upon a post.

20 One of these I took, and put it upon my head, and immediately the devils left me, and fled away.

21 At this the father exceedingly rejoiced, and said, My son, perhaps this boy is the son of the living God, who made the heavens and the earth.

22 For as soon as he came amongst us, the idol was broken, and all the gods fell down, and were destroyed by a greater power.

23 Then was fulfilled the prophecy which saith, Out of Egypt I have called my son.

THE FIRST GOSPEL OF THE INFANCY OF JESUS CHRIST.

CHAPTER V.

**1 Joseph and Mary leave Egypt.
3 Go to the Haunts of robbers,
4 Who hearing a mighty noise, as of a great army flee away.**

NOW Joseph and Mary when they heard that the idol was fallen down and destroyed, were seized with fear and, trembling, and said, When we Were in the land of Israel, Herod, intending to kill Jesus, slew for that purpose all the infants at Bethlehem, and that neighbourhood.

2 And there is no doubt but the Egyptians if they come to hear that this idol is broken and fallen down, will burn us with fire.

3 They went therefore hence to the secret places of robbers, who robbed travellers as they pass by, of their carriages and their clothes and carried them away bound.

4 These thieves upon their coming heard a great noise such as the noise of a king with a great army, and many horse and the trumpets sounding at his departure from his own city, at which they were so affrighted, as to leave all their booty behind them and fly away in haste.

5 Upon this the prisoners arose, and loosed each other's bonds, and taking each man his bags, they went way, and saw Joseph and Mary coming towards them, and inquired, Where is that king, the noise of whose approach the robbers heard, and left us, so that we are now come off safe?

6 Joseph answered, He will come after us.

ΔΙΔΑΧΗ ΤΩΝ ΔΩΔΕΚΑ ΑΠΟΣΤΟΛΩΝ

CHAPTER VI.

1 Mary looks on a woman in whom Satan had taken up his abode, and she becomes dispossessed.
5 Christ kissed by a bride made dumb by sorcerers, cures her.
11 Miraculously cures a gentlewoman in whom Satan had taken up his abode.
16 A leprous girl cured by the water in which he was washed, and becomes the servant of Joseph and Mary.
20 The leprous son of a prince's wife cured in like manner.
37 Has mother offers large gifts to Mary, and dismisses her.

THEN they went into another city where there was a woman possessed with a devil, and in whom Satan, that cursed rebel, had taken up his abode.

2 One night, when she went to fetch water, she could neither endure her clothes on, nor to be in any house; but as often as they tied her with chains or cords, she brake them, and went out into desert places, and sometimes standing where roads crossed, and in church yards, would throw stones at men.

3 When St. Mary saw this woman, she pitied her; where upon Satan presently left her, and fled away in the form of a young man, saying, Wo to me, because of thee, Mary, and thy son.

4 So the woman was delivered from her torment; but considering herself naked, she blushed, and avoided seeing any man and having put on her clothes, went home, and gave an account of her case to her father and relations who, as they were the best of the city, entertained St. Mary and Joseph with the greatest respect.

5 The next morning having received a sufficient supply of provisions for the road, they went from them, and about the evening of the day arrived at another town, where a marriage was then about to be solemnized; but by the arts of Satan and the practices of a sorcerers, the bride was become so dumb, that she could not so much as open her mouth.

6 But when this dumb bride saw the Lady St. Mary entering into the town, and carrying Lord Christ in her arms, she stretched out her hands to the Lord Christ, and took him in her arms, and closely hugging him, very often kissed him, continually moving him and, pressing him to her body.

THE FIRST GOSPEL OF THE INFANCY OF JESUS CHRIST.

7 Straightway the string of her tongue was loosed, and her ears were opened, and she began to sing praises unto God, who had restored her.

8 So there was great joy among the inhabitants of the town that night, who thought that God and his angels were come down among them.

9 In this place they abode three days, meeting with the greatest respect and most splendid entertainment.

10 And being then furnished by the people with provisions for the road, they departed and went to another city, in which they were inclined to lodge, because it was a famous place.

11 There was in this city a gentlewoman, who, as she went down one day to the river to bathe, behold cursed Satan leaped upon her in the form of a serpent.

12 And folded himself about her belly, and every night lay upon her.

13 This woman seeing the Lady St. Mary, and the Lord Christ the infant in her bosom, asked the Lady St. Mary, that she would give her the child to kiss, and carry in her arms.

14 When she had consented, and as soon as the woman had moved the child, Satan left her, and fled away, nor did the woman ever afterwards see him.

15 Hereupon all the neighbors praised the Supreme God, and the woman reward them with ample, beneficence.

16 On the morrow, the same woman brought perfumed water to wash the Lord Jesus; and when she had washed him, she preserved the water.

17 And there was a girl there, whose body was white with a leprosy, who being sprinkled with this water, and washed, was instantly cleansed from her leprosy.

18 The people therefore said Without doubt Joseph and Mary, and that boy are Gods, for they do not look like mortals.

19 And when they were making ready to go away, the girl, who had been troubled with the leprosy, came and desired they would permit her to go along with them; so they consented and the girl went with them till they came to a city in which was the palace of a great king, and whose house was not far from the inn.

20 Here they staid, and when the girl went one day to the prince's wife, and found her in a sorrowful and mournful condition, she asked her the reason of her tears.

ΔΙΔΑΧΗ ΤΩΝ ΔΩΔΕΚΑ ΑΠΟΣΤΟΛΩΝ

21 She replied, wonder not at my groans, for I am under a great misfortune, of which I dare not tell any one.

22 But, says the, girl, if you will entrust me with your private grievance, perhaps I may find you a remedy for it.

23 Thou, therefore, says the prince's wife, shall keep the secret, and not discover it to any one alive.

24 I have been married to this prince, who rules as king over large dominions, and lived long with him before he had any child by me.

25 At length I conceived by him, but alas! I brought forth a leprous son; which, when he saw him would not own to be his, but said to me,

26 Either do thou kill him, or send him to some nurse in such a place, that he may be never heard of; and now take care of yourself; I will never see you more.

27 So here I pine, lamenting my wretched and miserable circumstances. Alas, my son! alas, my husband; Have I disclosed it to you?

28 The girl replied I have found a remedy for your disease, which I promise you, for I also was leprous, but God hath cleansed me, even he who is called Jesus the son of the Lady Mary.

29 The woman inquiring where that God was, whom she spake of; the girl answered, He lodges with you here, in the same house.

30 But how can this be? says she; where is he? Behold, replied the girl, Joseph and Mary; and the infant who is, with them is called Jesus; and it is he who delivered me from my disease and torment.

31 But by what means, says she, were you cleansed from your leprosy? Will not you tell me that?

32 Why not? says the girl; I took the water with which his body had been washed, and poured it upon me, and my leprosy vanished.

33 The prince's wife then arose and entertained them, providing a great feast for Joseph among a large company of men.

34 And the next day took perfumed water to wash the Lord Jesus, and afterwards poured the same water upon her son, whom she had brought with her, and her son was instantly cleansed from his leprosy,

35 Then she sang thanks and unto God, and said, Blessed is the mother that bare thee, O Jesus!

36 Dost thou thus cure men of the same nature with thyself, with the water with which thy body is washed?

37 She then offered very large gifts to the Lady Mary, and sent her away with all imaginable respect.

THE FIRST GOSPEL OF THE INFANCY OF JESUS CHRIST.

CHAPTER VII.

**1 A man who could not enjoy his wife, freed from his disorder.
5 A young man who had been bewitched, and turned into a mule miraculously cured by Christ being put on his back,
28 and is married to the girl who had been cured of leprosy.**

THEY came afterwards to another city, and had a mind to lodge there.

2 Accordingly they went to a man's house, who was newly married but by the influence of sorcerers could not enjoy his wife.

3 But they lodging at his house that night, the man was freed of his disorder.

4 And when they were preparing early in the morning to go forward on their journey, the new-married person hindered them, and provided a noble entertainment for them.

5 But going forward on the morrow, they came to another city, and saw three women going from a certain grave with great weeping.

6 When St. Mary saw them, she spake to the girl who was their companion, saying, Go and inquire of them, what is the matter with them, and what misfortune has befallen them?

7 When the girl asked them, they made her no answer, but asked her again, Who are ye? and where are you going? For the day is far spent, and night is at hand.

8 We are travellers, saith the girl, and we are seeking for an inn to lodge at.

9 They replied, Go along with us, and lodge with us.

10 They then followed them, and were introduced into a new house, well furnished with all sorts of furniture.

11 Now it was winter-time, and the girl went into the parlour where these women were, and found them weeping and lamenting as before.

12 By them stood a mule, covered over with silk, and an ebony collar hanging down from his neck, whom they kissed and were feeding.

13 But when the girl said, How handsome, ladies, that mule is! they replied with tears, and said, This mule, which you see, was our brother, born of this same mother as we;

ΔΙΔΑΧΗ ΤΩΝ ΔΩΔΕΚΑ ΑΠΟΣΤΟΛΩΝ

14 For when our father died, and left us a very large estate, and we had only this brother, and we endeavoured to procure him a suitable match, and thought he should be married as other men, some giddy and jealous women bewitched him without our knowledge.

15 And we one night, a little before day, while the doors of the house were all shut fast, saw this our brother was changed into a mule, such as you now see him to be:

16 And we in the melancholy condition in which you see us, having no father to comfort us, have applied to all the wise men, magicians, and diviners in the world, but they have been of no service to us.

17 As often therefore as we find ourselves oppressed with grief, we rise and go with this our mother to our father's tomb, where, when we have cried sufficiently, we return home.

18 When the girl had heard this she said, Take courage, and cease your fears, for you have a remedy for your afflictions near at hand even amoung you and in the midst of your house.

19 For I was also leprous; but when I saw this woman, and this little infant with her, whose name is Jesus, I sprinkled my body with the water with which his mother had washed him and I was presently made well.

20 And I am certain that he is also capable of relieving you under your distress. Wherefore arise, go to my mistress Mary, and when you have brought her into your own parlour, disclose to her the secret, at the same time earnestly beseeching her to compassionate your case.

21 As soon as the women had heard the girl's discourse, they hastened away to the Lady St. Mary, introduced themselves to her, and sitting down before her, they wept.

22 And said, O our Lady St. Mary, pity your handmaids, for we have no head of our family, no one elder than us; no father or brother to go in or out before us.

23 But this mule, which you see, was our brother, which some women by witchcraft have brought into this condition which you see: we therefore entreat you to compassionate us.

24 Hereupon St. Mary was grieved at their case, and taking the Lord Jesus, put him upon the back of the mule.

25 And said to her son, O Jesus Christ, restore (or heal) according to thy extraordinary power this mule, and grant him to have again the shape of a man and a rational creature, as he had formerly.

THE FIRST GOSPEL OF THE INFANCY OF JESUS CHRIST.

26 This was scarce said by the Lady St. Mary, but the mule immediately passed into a human form, and became a young man without any deformity.

27 Then he and his mother and the sisters worshipped the Lady St. Mary, and lifting the child upon their heads, they kissed him, and said, Blessed is thy mother, O Jesus, O Saviour of the world! Blessed are the eyes which are so happy to see thee.

28 Then both the sisters told their mother, saying, Of a truth, our brother is restored to his former shape by the help of the Lord Jesus Christ, and the kindness of that girl who told us of Mary and her son.

29 And inasmuch as our brother is unmarried, it is fit that we marry him to this girl their servant.

30 When they had consulted Mary in this matter, and she had given her consent, they made a splendid wedding for this girl.

31 And so their sorrow being turned into gladness, and their mourning into mirth, they began to rejoice, and to make merry, and sing, being dressed in their richest attire, with bracelets.

32 Afterwards they glorified and praised God, saying, O Jesus, son of David, who changest sorrow into gladness, and mourning into mirth!

33 After this Joseph and Mary tarried there ten days, then went away, having received great respect from these people.

34 Who, when they took their leave of them, and returned home, cried,

35 But especially the girl.

ΔΙΔΑΧΗ ΤΩΝ ΔΩΔΕΚΑ ΑΠΟΣΤΟΛΩΝ

CHAPTER VIII.

1 Joseph and Mary pass through a country infested by robbers.
3 Titus a humane thief, offers Dumachus, his comrade, forty groats to let Joseph and Mary pass unmolested.
6 Jesus prophecies that the thieves Dumachus and Titus shall be crucified with him and that Titus shall go before him into paradise.
10 Christ causes a well to spring from a sycamore tree, and Mary washes his coat in it.
11 A balsam grows there from his sweat. They go to Memphis, where Christ works more miracles. Return to Judea.
15 Being warned, depart for Nazareth.

IN their journey from hence they came into a desert country and were told it was infested with robbers; so Joseph and St. Mary prepared to pass through it in the night.

2 And as they were going along, behold they saw two robbers asleep in the road, and with them a great number of robbers, who were their confederates, also asleep.

3 The names of these two were Titus and Dumachus; and Titus said to Dumachus, I beseech thee let these persons go along quietly, that our company may not perceive anything of them.

4 But Damachus refusing, Titus again said, I will give thee forty groats, and as a pledge take my girdle, which he gave him before he had done speaking, that he might not open his mouth or make a noise.

5 When the Lady St. Mary saw the kindness which this robber did shew them, she said to him, The Lord God will receive thee to his right hand and grant thee pardon of thy sins.

6 Then the Lord Jesus answered, and said to his mother. When thirty years are expired, O mother, the Jews will crucify me at Jerusalem;

7 And these two thieves shall be with me at the same time upon the cross, Titus on my right hand, and Dumachus on my left, and from that time Titus shall go before me into paradise;

8 And when she had said, God forbid this should be thy lot, O my son, they went on to a city in which were several idols; which, as soon as they came near to it, was turned into hills of sand.

THE FIRST GOSPEL OF THE INFANCY OF JESUS CHRIST.

9 Hence they went to that sycamore tree, which is now called Matarea.

10 And in Materea the Lord Jesus caused a well to spring forth, in which St. Mary washed his coat;

11 And a balsam is produced, or grows, in that country, from the sweat which ran down there from the Lord Jesus.

12 Thence they proceeded to Memphis, and saw Pharoah, and abode three years in Egypt.

13 And the Lord Jesus did very many miracles, in Egypt, which are neither to be found in Gospel of the Infancy nor in the Gospel of Perfection.

14 At the end of three years he returned out of Egypt, and when he came near to Judea, Joseph was afraid to enter;

15 For hearing that Herod was dead, and that Archelaus his son reigned in his stead, he was afraid.

16 And when he went to Judea, an, angel of God appeared to him, and said, O Joseph go into the city of Nazareth, and abide there.

17 It is strange indeed, that he, who is the Lord of all countries, should be thus carried backward and forward, through so many countries.

CHAPTER IX.

2 Two sick children cured by water wherein Christ was washed.

WHEN they came afterwards into the city of Bethlehem, they found there several very desperate distempers, which became so troublesome to children by seeing them, that most of them died.

2 There was there a woman who had a sick son, whom she brought, when he was at the point of death, to the Lady St. Mary, who saw her when she was washing Jesus Christ.

3 Then said the woman, O my Lady Mary, look down upon this my son, who is afflicted with most dreadful pains.

4 St. Mary hearing her, said, Take a little of that water with which I have washed my son, and sprinkle it upon him.

5 Then she took a little of that water, as St. Mary had commanded, and sprinkled it upon her son, who being wearied with his violent pains, was fallen asleep; and after he had slept a little, awaked perfectly well and recovered.

ΔΙΔΑΧΗ ΤΩΝ ΔΩΔΕΚΑ ΑΠΟΣΤΟΛΩΝ

6 The mother being abundantly glad of this success, went again to St. Mary, and St. Mary said to her, Give praise to God, who hath cured this thy son.

7 There was in the same place another woman, a neighbour of her, whose son was now cured.

8 This woman's son was afflicted with the same disease, and his eyes were now almost quite shut, and she was lamenting for him day and night.

9 The mother of the child which was cured, said to her, Why do you not bring your son to St. Mary, as I brought my son to her, when he was in the agonies of death; and he was cure by that water, with which the body of her son Jesus was washed?

10 When the woman heard her say this, she also went, and having procured the same water, washed her son with it, whereupon his body and his eyes were instantly restored to their former state.

11 And when she brought her son to St. Mary, and opened his case to her, she commanded her to give thanks to God for the recovery of her son's health, and tell no one what had happened.

CHAPTER X.

1 Two wives of one man, each have a son sick.
2 One of them named Mary, and whose son's name was Caleb, presents the Virgin with a handsome carpet, and Caleb is cured; but the son of the other wife dies,
4 which occasions a difference between the women.
5 The other wife puts Caleb into a hot oven, and he is miraculously preserved,
9 she afterwards throws him into a well, and he is again preserved;
11 his mother appeals to the Virgin against the other wife,
12 whose downfall the Virgin prophecies,
13 and who accordingly falls into the well,
14 therein fulfilling a saying of old.

THERE were in the same city two wives of one man, who had each a son sick. One of them was called Mary, and her son's name was Caleb.

2 She arose, and taking her son, went to the Lady St. Mary, the mother of Jesus, and offered her a very handsome carpet, saying, O my

THE FIRST GOSPEL OF THE INFANCY OF JESUS CHRIST.

Lady Mary accept this carpet of me, and instead of it give me a small swaddling cloth.

3 To this Mary agreed, and when the mother of Caleb was gone, she made a coat for her son of the swaddling cloth, put it on him, and his disease was cured; but the son of the other wife died.

4 Hereupon there arose between them a difference in doing the business of the family by turns, each her week;

5 And when the turn of Mary the mother of Caleb came, and she was heating the oven to bake bread, and went away to fetch the meal, she left her son Caleb by the oven;

6 Whom the other wife, her rival, seeing to be by himself, took and cast him into the oven, which was very hot, and then went away.

7 Mary on her return saw her son Caleb lying in the middle of the oven laughing, and the oven quite as cold as though it had not been before heated, and knew that her rival the other wife had thrown him into the fire.

8 When she took him out, she brought him to the Lady St. Mary, and told her the story, to whom she replied, Be quiet, I am concerned lest thou shouldest make this matter known.

9 After this her rival, the other wife, as she was drawing water at the well, and saw Caleb playing by the well, and that no one was near, took him, and threw him into the well.

10 And when some men came to fetch water from the well, they saw the boy sitting on the superficies of the water, and drew him out with ropes, and were exceedingly surprised at the child, and praised God.

11 Then came the mother and took him and carried him to the Lady St. Mary, lamenting and saying, O my Lady, see what my rival hath done to my son, and how she hath cast him into the well, and I do not question but one time or other she will be the occasion of his death.

12 St. Mary replied to her, God will vindicate your injured cause.

13 Accordingly a few days after, when the other wife came to the well to draw water, her foot was entangled in the rope, so that she fell headlong into the well, and they who ran to her assistance found her skull broken, and bones bruised.

14 So she came to a bad end, and in her was fulfilled that saying of the author, They digged a well, and made it deep, but fell themselves into the pit which they prepared.

ΔΙΔΑΧΗ ΤΩΝ ΔΩΔΕΚΑ ΑΠΟΣΤΟΛΩΝ

CHAPTER XI.

1 Bartholomew, when a child and sick, miraculously restored by being laid on Christ's bed.

ANOTHER woman in that city had likewise two son's sick.

2 And when one was dead, the other, who lay at the point of death, she took in her arms to the Lady St. Mary, and in a flood of tears addressed herself to her, saying,

3 O my Lady, help and relieve me; for I had two sons, the one I have just now buried, the other I see is fast at the point of death behold how I (earnestly) seek for your from God, and pray to him.

4 Then she said, O Lord, thou art gracious, and merciful, and kind; thou, hast given me two sons; one of them thou halt taken to thyself, O spare me this other.

5 St. Mary then perceiving the greatness of her sorrow, pitied her and said, Do thou place thy son in my son's bed, and cover him with his clothes.

6 And when she had placed him in the bed wherein Christ lay, at the moment when his eyes were just closed by death; as soon as ever the small of the garments of the Lord Jesus Christ reached the boy, his eyes were opened, and calling with a loud voice to his mother, he asked for bread, and when he had received it, he sucked it.

7 Than his mother said, O Lady Mary, now I am assured that the powers of God do dwell in you, so that thy son can cure children who are of the same sort as himself, as soon as they touch his garments.

8 This boy, who was thus cured, is the same who in the Gospel is called Bartholomew.

CHAPTER XII.

A leprous woman healed by Christ's washing water.
7 A princess healed by it and restored to her husband.

AGAIN, there was a leprous woman who went to the Lady St. Mary, the mother of Jesus, and said, O my Lady, help me.

2 St. Mary replied, What help does thou desire? Is it gold or silver, or that thy body be cured of its leprosy?

3 Who, says the woman, can grant me this?

THE FIRST GOSPEL OF THE INFANCY OF JESUS CHRIST.

4 St. Mary replied to her, Wait a little till I have washed my son Jesus, and put him to bed.

5 The woman waited, as she was commanded; and Mary when she had put Jesus in bed, giving her the water with which she had washed his body, said, Take some of the water, and pour it upon thy body;

6 Which when she had done, she instantly became clean, and praised God, and gave thanks to him.

7 Then she went away, after she had abode with her three days;

8 And going into the city, she saw a certain prince, who had married another princes daughter;

9 But when he came to see her, he perceived between her eyes the signs of leprosy like a star, and thereupon declared the marriage dissolved and void.

10 When the woman saw these persons in this condition, exceeding sorrowful, and shedding abundance of tears, she inquired of them the reason of their crying;

11 They replied, inquire not into our circumstances; for we are not able to declare our misfortunes to any, person, whatsoever.

12 But she still pressed and desired them to communicate their case to her; intimating, that she might be able to direct them to a remedy.

13 So when they showed the young woman to her, and the signs of the leprosy, which appeared between her eyes;

14 She said, I also whom ye see in this place, was afflicted with the same distemper, and going on some business to Bethlehem, I went into a certain cave, and saw a woman named Mary, who had a son called Jesus.

15 She seeing me to be leprous, was concerned for me, and gave me some water with which she had washed her son's body, with that I sprinkled my body, and became clean.

16 Then said these women, Will you Mistress, go along with us, and show the Lady St. Mary to us?

17 To which she consenting, they arose and went to the Lady St. Mary, taking with them very noble presents.

18 And when they came in and offered their presents to her, they showed the leprous young woman whom they brought with them to her.

19 Then said St. Mary, The mercy of the Lord Jesus Christ rest upon you;

ΔΙΔΑΧΗ ΤΩΝ ΔΩΔΕΚΑ ΑΠΟΣΤΟΛΩΝ

20 And giving them a little of that water, with which she had washed the body of Jesus Christ, she bade them wash the diseased person with it, which when they had done, she was presently cured;

21 So they, and all who were present, praised God; and being filled with joy, they went back to their own city, and gave praises to God on that account.

22 Then the prince hearing that his wife was cured, took her home and made a second marriage, giving thanks unto God for the recovery of his wife's health.

CHAPTER XIII.

1 A girl, whose blood Satan sucked receives one of Christ's swaddling clothes from the Virgin,
14 Satan comes like a dragon, and she shews it to him; flames and burning coals proceed from it and fall upon him;
19 he is miraculously discomfited, and leaves the girl.

THERE was also a girl, who was afflicted by Satan,

2 For that cursed spirit did frequently appear to her in the shape of a dragon, and was inclined to swallow her up, and had so sucked out all her blood, that she looked like a dead carcass.

3 As often as she came to herself, with her hands wringed about her head she would cry out, and say, Wo, Wo is me, that there is no one to be found, who can deliver me from that impious dragon!

4 Her father and mother, and all who were about her and saw her, mourned and wept over her;

5 And all who were present would especially be under sorrow and in tears, when they heard her bewailing and saying, My brethren and friends, is here no one who can deliver me from this murderer?

6 Then the prince's daughter, who had been cured of her leprosy, hearing the complaint of that girl, went upon the top of her castle, and saw her with her hands twisted about her head, pouring out a flood of tears, and all the people that were about her in tears.

7 Then she asked the husband of the possessed person, Whether his wife's mother was alive? He told her, That her father and mother were both alive,

THE FIRST GOSPEL OF THE INFANCY OF JESUS CHRIST.

8 Then she ordered her mother to be sent to her; to whom, when she saw her coming, she said, Is this possessed girl thy daughter? She moaning and bewailing said, Yes madam I bore her.

9 The prince's daughter answered, Disclose the secret of her case to me, for I confess to you that I was leprous, but the Lady Mary, the mother of Jesus Christ, healed me.

10 And if you desire your daughter to be restored to her former state, take her to Bethlehem, and inquire for Mary the mother of Jesus, and doubt not but your daughter will be cured; for I do not question but you will come home with great joy at your daughter's recovery.

11 As soon as ever she had done speaking, she arose and went with her daughter to the place appointed, and to Mary, and told her the case of her daughter.

12 When St. Mary had heard her story, she gave her a little of the water with which she had washed the body of her son Jesus, and bade her pour it upon the body of her daughter.

13 Likewise she gave her one of the swaddling cloths of the Lord Jesus, and said, Take this swaddling cloth, and shew it to thine enemy as often as thou seest him and she sent them away in peace.

14 After they bad left that city and returned home, and the time was come in which Satan was wont to seize her, in the same moment this cursed spirit appeared to her in the shape of a huge dragon, and the girl seeing him was afraid,

15 The mother said to her, Be not afraid, daughter; let him alone till he come nearer to thee! then shew him the swaddling cloth, which the Lady Mary gave us, and we shall see the event.

16 Satan then coming like a dreadful dragon, the body of the girl trembled for fear.

17 But as soon as she had put the swaddling cloth upon her head, and about her eyes, and chewed it to him, presently there issued forth from the swaddling cloth flames and burning coals, and fell upon the dragon.

18 Oh! how great a miracle was this, which was done: as soon as the dragon saw the swaddling cloth of the Lord Jesus, fire went forth and was scattered upon his head and eyes; so that he cried out with a loud voice, What have I to do with thee, Jesus, thou son of Mary? Whither shall I flee from thee?

19 So he drew back much affrighted, and left the girl.

ΔΙΔΑΧΗ ΤΩΝ ΔΩΔΕΚΑ ΑΠΟΣΤΟΛΩΝ

20 And she was delivered from this trouble, and sang praises and thanks to God, and with her all who were present at the working of the miracle.

CHAPTER XIV.

1 Judas when a boy possessed by Satan, and brought up by his parents to Jesus to be cured, whom he tries to bite, 7 but failing, strikes Jesus and makes him cry out. Whereupon Satan goes from Jesus in the shape of a dog.

ANOTHER woman likewise lived there, whose son was possessed by Satan,

2 This boy, named Judas, as often as Satan seized him, was inclined to bite all that were present; and if he found no one else near him, he would bite his own hands and other parts.

3 But the mother of this miserable boy, hearing of St. Mary and her son Jesus, arose presently and taking her son in her arms, brought him to the Lady Mary.

4 In the meantime, James and Joses had taken away the infant, the Lord Jesus, to play at a proper season with other children; and when they went forth, they sat down and the Lord Jesus with them.

5 Then Judas, who was possessed, came and sat down at the right hand of Jesus.

6 When Satan was acting upon him as usual, he went about to bite the Lord Jesus.

7 And because he could not do it, he struck Jesus on the right side, so that he cried out.

8 And in the same moment Satan went out of the boy, and ran away like a mad dog.

9 This same boy who struck Jesus, and out of whom Satan went in the form of a dog, was Judas Iscariot, who betrayed him to the Jews.

10 And that same side, on which Judas: struck him, the Jews pierced with a spear.

THE FIRST GOSPEL OF THE INFANCY OF JESUS CHRIST.

CHAPTER XV.

**1 Jesus and other boys play together, and make clay figures of animals.
4 Jesus causes them to walk,
6 also makes clay birds, which he causes to fly, and eat and drink.
7 The children's parents alarmed, and take Jesus for a sorcerer.
8 He goes to a dyer's shop, and throws all the cloths into the furnace, and works a miracle therewith.
15 Whereupon the Jews praise God.**

AND when the Lord Jesus was seven years of age, he was on a certain day with other boys his companions about the same age;

2 Who, when they were at play, made clay into several shapes, namely--asses, oxen, birds, and other figures;

3 Each boasting of his work, and endeavouring to exceed the rest.

4 Then the Lord Jesus said to the boys, I will command these figures which I have made to walk.

5 And immediately they moved, and when he commanded them to return, they returned.

6 He had also made the figures of birds and sparrows, which, when he commanded to fly, did fly, and when he commanded to stand still, did stand still; and if he gave them meat and drink, they did eat and drink.

7 When at length the boys went away, and related these things to their parents, their fathers said to them, Take heed, children, for the future of his company, for he is a sorcerer; shun and avoid him, and from henceforth never play with him.

8 On a certain day also, when the Lord Jesus was playing with the boys, and running about, he passed by a dyer's shop, whose name was Salem.

9 And there were in his shop many pieces of cloth belonging to the people of that city, which they designed to dye of several colours.

10 Then the Lord Jesus going into the dyer's shop, took all the cloths, and threw them into the furnace.

11 When Salem came home, and saw the cloths spoiled, he began to make a great noise, and to chide the Lord Jesus, saying,

ΔΙΔΑΧΗ ΤΩΝ ΔΩΔΕΚΑ ΑΠΟΣΤΟΛΩΝ

12 What hast thou done to me, O thou son of Mary? Thou hast injured both me and my neighbours; they all desired their cloths of a proper colour; but thou hast come and spoiled them all.

13 The Lord Jesus replied, I will change the colour of every cloth to what colour thou desirest.

14 And then he presently began to take the cloths out of the furnace, and they were all dyed of those same colours which the dyer desired.

15 And when the Jews saw this surprising miracle, they praised God.

CHAPTER. XVI.

1 Christ miraculously widens or contracts the gates, milk pails, sieves, or boxes, not properly made by Joseph,
4 he not being skilful at his carpenter's trade.
5 The King of Jerusalem gives Joseph an order for a throne.
6 Joseph works on it for two years in the king's palace, and makes it two spans too short. The king being angry with him,
10 Jesus comforts him,
13 commands him to pull one side of the throne, while he pulls the other, and brings it to its proper dimensions.
14 Whereupon the bystanders praise God.

AND Joseph, wheresoever he went in the city, took the Lord Jesus with him, where he was sent for to work to make gates, or milk-pails, or sieves, or boxes; the Lord Jesus was with him, wheresoever he went.

2 And as often as Joseph had anything in his work, to make longer, or shorter, or wider, or narrower, the Lord Jesus would stretch his hand towards it.

3 And presently it became as Joseph would have it:

4 So that he had no need to finish anything with his own hands, for he was not very skilful at his carpenter's trade.

5 On a certain time the King of Jerusalem sent for him, and said, I would have thee make me a throne of the same dimensions with that place in which I commonly sit.

6 Joseph obeyed, and forthwith began the work, and continued two years in the king's palace before he finished it.

THE FIRST GOSPEL OF THE INFANCY OF JESUS CHRIST.

7 And when he came to fix it in its place, he found it wanted two spans on each side of the appointed measure.

8 Which when the king saw, he was very angry with Joseph;

9 And Joseph afraid of the king's anger, went to bed without his supper, taking not any thing to eat.

10 Then the Lord Jesus asked him, What he was afraid of?

11 Joseph replied, Because I have lost my labour in the work which I have been about these two years.

12 Jesus said to him, Fear not, neither be cast down;

13 Do thou lay hold on one side of the throne, and I will the other, and we will bring it to its just dimensions.

14 And when Joseph had done as the Lord Jesus said, and each of them had with strength drawn his side, the throne obeyed, and was brought to the proper dimensions of the place:

15 Which miracle when they who stood by saw, they were astonished, and praised God.

16 The throne was made of the same wood which was in being in Solomon's time, namely, wood adorned with various shapes, and figures.

CHAPTER. XVII.

1 Jesus plays with boys at hide and seek.
3 Some women put his playfellows in a furnace,
7 where they are transformed by Jesus into kids.
10 Jesus calls them to go and play, and they are restored to their former shape.

ON another day the Lord Jesus going out into the street, and seeing some boys who were met to play, joined himself to their company.

2 But when they saw him, they hid themselves, and left him to seek for them;

3 The Lord Jesus came to the gate of a certain house, and asked some women who were standing there, Where the boys were gone?

4 And when they answered, That there was no one there; the Lord Jesus said, Who are those whom ye see in the furnace?

5 They answered, They were kids of three years old.

6 Then Jesus cried out aloud, and said, Come out hither, O ye kids, to your shepherd;

ΔΙΔΑΧΗ ΤΩΝ ΔΩΔΕΚΑ ΑΠΟΣΤΟΛΩΝ

7 And presently the boys came forth like kids, and leaped about him; which when the women saw, they were exceedingly amazed, and trembled,

8 Then they immediately worshipped the Lord Jesus, and beseeched him, saying, O our Lord Jesus, son of Mary, thou art truly that good shepherd of Israel! have mercy on thy handmaids, who stand before thee, who do not doubt, but that thou, O Lord, art come to save, and not to destroy.

9 After that, when the Lord Jesus said, the children of Israel are like Ethiopians among the people; the women said, Thou, Lord, knowest all things, nor is any thing concealed from thee: but now we entreat thee, and beseech of thy mercy, that thou wouldest restore those boys to their former state.

10 Then Jesus said, Come hither, O boys, that we may go and play; and immediately, in the presence of these women, the kids were changed, and returned into the shape of boys.

CHAPTER XVIII.

1 Jesus becomes the king of his playfellows, and they crown him with flowers;
4 miraculously causes a serpent who had bitten Simon the Canaanite, then a boy, to suck out all the poison again;
16 the serpent bursts, and Christ restores the boy to health.

IN the month Adar Jesus gathered together the boys, and ranked them as though he had been a king.

2 For they spread their garments on the ground for him to sit on; and having made a crown of flowers, put it upon his head, and stood on his right and left as the guards of a king.

3 And if any one happened to pass by, they took him by force, and said, Come hither, and worship the king, that you may have a prosperous journey.

4 In the mean time, while these things were doing, there came certain men, carrying a boy upon a couch;

5 For this boy having gone with his companions to the mountain to gather wood, and having found there a partridge's nest, and put his hand in to take out the eggs, was stung by a poisonous serpent, which leaped out of the nest; so that he was forced to cry out for the help of

THE FIRST GOSPEL OF THE INFANCY OF JESUS CHRIST.

his companions; who, when they came, found him lying upon the earth like a dead person.

6 After which his neighbours came and carried him back into the city.

7 But when they came to the place where the Lord Jesus, was sitting like a king, and the other boys stood around him like his ministers, the boys made haste to meet him, who was bitten by the serpent, and said to his neighbours, Come and pay your respects to the king;

8 But when, by reason of their sorrow, they refused to come, the boys drew them, and forced them against their wills to come.

9 And when they came to the Lord Jesus, he inquired, On what account they carried that boy?

10 And when they answered that a serpent had bitten him, the Lord Jesus said to the boys, Let us go and kill that serpent.

11 But when the parents of the boy desired to be excused, because their son lay at the point of death; the boys made answer, and said, Did not ye hear what the king said? Let us go and kill the serpent; and will not ye obey him?

12 So they brought the couch back again, whether they would or not.

13 And when they were come to the nest, the Lord Jesus said to the boys, Is this the serpent's lurking place? They said, It was.

14 Then the Lord Jesus calling the serpent, it presently came forth and submitted to him; to whom he said, Go and suck out all the poison which thou hast infused into that boy:

15 So the serpent crept to the boy, and took away all its poison again.

16 Then the Lord Jesus cursed the serpent, so that it immediately burst asunder, and died;

17 And he touched the boy with his hand to restore him to his former health;

18 And when he began to cry, the Lord Jesus said, Cease crying for hereafter thou shall be my disciple;

19 And this is that Simon the Canaanite, who is mentioned in the Gospel.

ΔΙΔΑΧΗ ΤΩΝ ΔΩΔΕΚΑ ΑΠΟΣΤΟΛΩΝ

CHAPTER XIX.

1 James being bitten by a viper, Jesus blows on the wound and cures him.
4 Jesus charged with throwing a boy from the roof of a house,
10 miraculously raises the dead boy to acquit him;
12 fetches water for his mother, breaks the pitcher and miraculously gathers the water in his mantle and brings it home;
16 makes fish pools on the Sabbath,
20 causes a boy to die who broke them down,
22 another boy runs against him, whom he also causes to die.

ON another day Joseph sent his son James to gather wood, and the Lord Jesus went with him;

2 And when they came to the place where the wood was, and James began to gather it, behold, a venomous viper bit him, so that he began to cry, and make a noise.

3 The Lord Jesus seeing him in this condition, came to him, and blowed upon the place where the viper had bit him, and it was instantly well.

4 On a certain day the Lord Jesus was with some boys, who were playing on the house-top, and one of the boys fell down, and presently died.

5 Upon which the other boys all running away, the Lord Jesus was left alone on the house-top.

6 And the boy's relations came to him and said to the Lord Jesus, Thou didst throw our son down from the house-top.

7 But he denying it, they cried out, Our son is dead, and this is he who killed him.

8 The Lord Jesus replied to them, Do not charge me with a crime of which you are not able to convict me, but let us go and ask the boy himself, who will bring the truth to light.

9 Then the Lord Jesus going down stood over the head of the dead boy, and said with a loud voice, Zeinunus, Zeinunus, who threw thee down from the housetop?

10 Then the dead boy answered, thou didst not throw me down, but such a one did.

THE FIRST GOSPEL OF THE INFANCY OF JESUS CHRIST.

11 And when the Lord Jesus bade those who stood by to take present praised God on account of that miracle.

12 On a certain time the Lady St. Mary had commanded the Lord Jesus to fetch her some water out of the well;

13 And when he had gone to fetch the water, the pitcher, when it was brought up full, brake;

14 But Jesus spreading his mantle gathered up the water again, and brought it in that to his mother;

15 Who, being astonished at this wonderful thing, laid up this, and all the other things which she had seen, in her memory.

16 Again on another day the Lord Jesus was with some boys by a river, and they drew water out of the river by little channels, and made little fish-pools.

17 But the Lord Jesus had made twelve sparrows, and placed them about his pool on each side, three on a side.

18 But it was the Sabbath day, and the son of Hanani a Jew came by, and saw them making these things, and said, Do ye thus make figures of clay on the Sabbath? And he ran to them, and broke down their fish-pools.

19 But when the Lord Jesus clapped his hands over the sparrows which he had made, they fled away chirping.

20 At length the son of Hanani coming to the fish-pool of Jesus to destroy it, the water vanished away, and the Lord Jesus said to him,

21 In like manner as this water had vanished, so shall thy life vanish; and presently the boy died.

22 Another time, when the Lord Jesus was coming home in the evening with Joseph, he met a boy, who ran so hard against him, that he threw him down;

23 To whom the Lord Jesus said, As thou hast thrown me down, so shalt thou fall, nor ever rise.

24 And that moment the boy fell down and died.

ΔΙΔΑΧΗ ΤΩΝ ΔΩΔΕΚΑ ΑΠΟΣΤΟΛΩΝ

CHAPTER XX.

4 Christ sent to school to Zaccheus to learn his letters, and teaches Zaccheus.
13 Sent to another schoolmaster,
14 refuses to tell his letters, and the schoolmaster going to whip him, his hand withers and he dies.

THERE was also at Jerusalem one named Zaccheus, who was a schoolmaster:

2 And he said to Joseph, Joseph, why dost thou not send Jesus to me, that he may learn his letters?

3 Joseph agreed, and told St. Mary;

4 So they brought him to that master; who, as soon as he saw him, wrote out an alphabet for him,

5 And he bade him say Aleph; and when he had said Aleph, the master bade him pronounce Beth.

6 Then the Lord Jesus said to him, Tell me first the meaning of the letter Aleph, and then I will pronounce Beth.

7 And when the master threatened to whip him, the Lord Jesus explained to him the meaning of the letters Aleph and Beth;

8 Also which were the straight figures of the letters, which the oblique, and what letters had double figures; which had points, and which had none; why one letter went before another; and many other things he began to tell him, and explain, of which the master himself had never heard, nor read in any book.

9 The Lord Jesus farther said to the master, Take notice how I say to thee; then he began clearly and distinctly to say Aleph, Beth, Gimel, Daleth, and so on to the end of the alphabet.

10 At this the master was so surprised, that he said, I believe this boy was born before Noah;

11 And turning to Joseph, he said, Thou hast brought a boy to me to be taught, who is more learned than any master.

12 He said also to St. Mary, This your son has no need of any learning.

13 They brought him then to a more learned master, who, when he saw him, said, say Aleph;

14 And when he had said Aleph, the master bade him pronounce Beth; to which the Lord Jesus replied, Tell me first the meaning of the letter Aleph, and then I will pronounce Beth.

15 But this master, when he did lift up his hand to whip him, had his hand presently withered, and he died.

16 Then said Joseph to St. Mary, Henceforth we will not allow him to go out of the house; for every one who displeases him is killed.

CHAPTER XXI.

[Compare Luke ii.
42, whose meagre account is deficient of the sublime details
    here given of the subjects disputed upon.]
1 Disputes learnedly with the doctors in the temple,
7 on law,
9 on astronomy,
12 on physics and metaphysics.
21 Is worshipped by a philosopher,
28 and fetched home by his mother.

AND when he was twelve years old, they brought him to Jerusalem to the feast; and when the feast was over, they returned.

2 But the Lord Jesus continued behind in the temple among the doctors and elders, and learned men of Israel; to whom he proposed several questions of learning, and also gave them answers:

3 For he said to them, Whose son is the Messiah? They answered, the son of David.

4 Why then, said he, does he in the spirit call him Lord? When he saith, The Lord said to my Lord, sit thou at my right hand, till I have made thine enemies thy foot-stool.

5 Then a certain principal Rabbi asked him, Hast thou read books?

6 Jesus answered, he had read both books, and the things which were contained in books.

7 And he explained to them the books of the law, and precepts, and statutes: and the mysteries which are contained in the books of the prophets; things which the mind of no creature could reach.

8 Then said that Rabbi, I never yet have seen or heard of such knowledge! What do you think that boy will be?

9 When a certain astronomer, who was present, asked the Lord Jesus, Whether he had studied astronomy?

10 The Lord Jesus replied, and told him the number of the spheres and heavenly bodies, as also their triangular, square, and sextile as-

ΔΙΔΑΧΗ ΤΩΝ ΔΩΔΕΚΑ ΑΠΟΣΤΟΛΩΝ

pect; their progressive and retrograde motion; their size and several prognostications; and other things which the reason of man had never discovered.

11 There was also among them a philosopher well skilled in physic and natural philosophy, who asked the Lord Jesus, Whether he had studied physic?

12 He replied, and explained to him physics and metaphysics.

13 Also those things which were above and below the power of nature;

14 The powers also of the body, its humours, and their effects.

15 Also the number of its members, and bones, veins, arteries, and nerves;

16 The several constitutions of body, hot and dry, cold and moist, and the tendencies of them;

17 How the soul operated upon the body;

18 What its various sensations and faculties, were;

19 The faculty of speaking, anger, desire;

20 And lastly the manner of its composition and dissolution; and other things, which the understanding of no creature had ever reached.

21 Then that philosopher arose, and worshipped the Lord Jesus, and said, O Lord Jesus, from henceforth I will be thy disciple and servant.

22 While they were discoursing on these and such like things, the Lady St. Mary came in, having been three days walking about with Joseph, seeking for him.

23 And when she saw him sitting among the doctors, and in his turn proposing questions to them, and giving answers, she said to him, My son, why hast thou done thus by us? Behold I and thy father have been at much pains in seeking thee.

24 He replied, Why did ye seek me? Did ye not know that I ought to be employed in my father's house?

25 But they understood not the words which he said to them.

26 Then the doctors asked Mary, Whether this were her son? And when she said, He was, they said, O happy Mary, who hast borne such a son.

27 Then he returned with them to Nazareth, and obeyed them in all things.

28 And his mother kept all these things in her mind;

29 And the Lord Jesus grew in stature and wisdom, and favour with God and man.

THE FIRST GOSPEL OF THE INFANCY OF JESUS CHRIST.

CHAPTER XXII.

**1 Jesus conceals his miracles,
2 studies the law,
3 and is baptized.**

NOW from this time Jesus began to conceal his miracles and secret works,

2 And gave himself to the study of the law, till he arrived to the end of his thirtieth year;

3 At which time the Father publicly owned him at Jordan, sending down this voice from heaven, This is my beloved son, in whom I am well pleased;

4 The Holy Ghost being also present in the form of a dove.

5 This is he whom we worship with all reverence, because he gave us our life and being, and brought us from our mother's womb, Glory to God,

6 Who, for our sakes, took a human body, and hath redeemed us, that so he might embrace us with everlasting mercy, and shew his free, large, bountiful grace and goodness to us.

7 To him be glory and praise, and power, and dominion, from henceforth said for evermore. Amen.

(The end of the whole Gospel of the Infancy, by the assistance of the Supreme God, according to what we found in the original.)

REFERENCES TO THE FIRST GOSPEL OF THE INFANCY OF JESUS CHRIST

[Mr. Henry Sike, Professor of Oriental Languages at Cambridge, first translated and published this Gospel in 1697. It was received by the Gnostics, a sect of Christians in the second century; and several of its relations were credited in the following ages by other Christians, viz., Eusebius, Athanasius, Epiphanius; Chrysostom. &c. Sozomen says, he was told by many, and he credits the relations, of the idols in Egypt falling down on Joseph, and Mary's flight thither with Christ; and of Christ making a well to wash his clothes in a sycamore-tree, from whence balsam afterwards proceeded; which stories are from this

ΔΙΔΑΧΗ ΤΩΝ ΔΩΔΕΚΑ ΑΠΟΣΤΟΛΩΝ

Gospel. Chemnitius, out of Stipulensis, who had it from Peter Martyr, Bishop of Alexandria, in the third century, says, that the place in Egypt where Christ was banished is now called Matarea, about ten miles beyond Cairo; that the inhabitants constantly burn a lamp in remembrance of it; and that there is a garden of trees yielding a balsam, which were planted by Christ when a boy. M. La Crosse cites a synod at Angamala, in the Mountain of Malabar, A. D. 1599, which shows this Gospel was commonly read by the Nestorians in the country. Ahmed Ibu Idris, a Mahometan divine, says, it was used by some Christians in common with the other four Gospels; and Ocobius de Castro mentions a Gospel of Thomas, which he says, he saw and had translated to him by an Armenian Archbishop at Amsterdam, that was read in very many churches of Asia and Africa, as the only rule of their faith. Fabricius takes it to be this Gospel. It has been supposed, that Mahomet and his coadjutors used it in compiling the Koran. There are several stories believed of Christ, proceeding from this Gospel; as that which Mr. Sike relates out of La Brosse's Persic Lexicon, that Christ practised the trade of a dyer, and his working a miracle with the colours; from whence the Persian dyers honour him as their patron, and call a dye-house the shop of Christ. Sir John Chardin mentions Persian legends concerning Christ's dispute with his schoolmaster about his ABC; and his lengthening the cedar-board which Joseph sawed too short.]

Note on the Miracles of Christ in the preceding Gospels.

A great void in the early life of the Saviour is filled up by these Gospels. In none of the Canonical Evangelists is any mention made of the childhood of Jesus. The Gospels of Matthew, Mark, Luke, and John, more rapidly than satisfactorily, pass over the period intervening between His birth and ministry. It is natural to suppose that the Infant Redeemer's earliest days were spent in the society of other young children, and it is quite consistent with every sincere Christians faith to believe that He had the power to perform the miracles here ascribed to him otherwise, a limit will be set to His divine attributes, doubts raised against His performance of the miracles related by the four Evangelists, in the authorised version of the Testament, and a denial given of the declaration therein, "With GOD nothing is impossible!"

THE SECOND, OR ST. THOMAS'S GOSPEL OF THE INFANCY OF JESUS CHRIST.

An Account of the ACTIONS and MIRACLES of our Lord and Saviour JESUS CHRIST in his INFANCY.

CHAPTER I.

2 Jesus miraculously clears the water after rain.
4 Plays with clay sparrows, which he animates on the Sabbath day.

I THOMAS, an Israelite, judged it necessary to make known to our brethren among the Gentiles, the actions and miracles of Christ in his childhood, which our Lord and God Jesus Christ wrought after his birth in Bethlehem in our country, at which I myself, was astonished; the beginning of which was as followeth.

2 When the child Jesus was five years of age, and there had been a shower of rain, which was now over, Jesus was playing with other Hebrew boys by a running stream; and the water running over the banks, stood in little lakes;

3 But the water instantly became clear and useful again; he having smote them only by his word, they readily obeyed him.

4 Then he took from the bank of the stream some soft clay, and formed out of it twelve sparrows; and there were other boys playing with him.

ΔΙΔΑΧΗ ΤΩΝ ΔΩΔΕΚΑ ΑΠΟΣΤΟΛΩΝ

5 But a certain Jew seeing the things which he was doing, namely, his forming clay into the figures of sparrows on the Sabbath day, went presently away, and told his father Joseph, and said,

6 Behold, thy boy is playing by the river side, and has taken clay, and formed it into twelve sparrows, and profaneth the Sabbath.

7 Then Joseph came to the place where he was, and when he saw him, called to him, and said, Why doest thou that which it is not lawful to do on the Sabbath day?

8 Then Jesus clapping together the palms of his hands, called to the sparrows, and said to them Go, fly away; and while ye live remember me.

9 So the sparrows fled away making a noise.

10 The Jews seeing this, were astonished, and went away, and told their chief persons what a strange miracle they had seen wrought by Jesus.

CHAPTER II.

2 Causes a boy to wither who broke down his fish-pools;
6 Partly restores him.
7 Kills another boy.
16 causes blindness to fall on his accusers,
18 for which, Joseph pulls him by the ear.

BESIDES this, the son of Annas the scribe, was standing there with Joseph, and took a bough of a willow tree, and scattered the waters which Jesus had gathered into lakes.

2 But the boy Jesus seeing what he had done, became angry, and said to him, Thou fool, what harm did the lake do thee, that thou shouldest scatter the water?

3 Behold, now thou shalt wither as a tree, and shalt not bring forth either leaves, or branches, or fruit.

4 And immediately he became withered all over.

5 Then Jesus went away home. But the parents of the boy who was withered, lamenting the misfortune of his youth, took and carried him to Joseph, accusing him, and said, Why dost thou keep a son who is guilty of such actions?

6 Then Jesus at the request of all who were present did heal him, leaving only some small member to continue withered, that they might take warning.

7 Another time Jesus went forth into the street, and a boy running by, rushed upon his shoulder;

8 At which Jesus being angry, said to him, Thou shalt go no farther;

9 And he instantly fell down dead:

10 Which when some persons saw, they said, Where was this boy born, that every thing which he says presently cometh to pass?

11 Then the parents of the dead boy going to Joseph, complained, saying, You are not fit to live with us, in our city, having such a boy as that:

12 Either teach him that he bless and not curse, or else depart hence with him, for he kills our children.

13 Then Joseph calling the boy Jesus by himself, instructed him, saying, Why doest thou such things to injure the people so, that they hate us and prosecute us?

14 But Jesus replied, I know that what thou sayest is not of thyself, but for thy sake I will say nothing;

15 But they who have said these things to thee, shall suffer everlasting punishment.

16 And immediately they who had accused him became blind,

17 And all they who saw it were exceedingly afraid and confounded, and said concerning him, Whatsoever he saith, whether good or bad, immediately cometh to pass and they were amazed.

18 And when they saw this action of Christ, Joseph arose, and plucked him by the ear, at which the boy was angry, and said to him, Be easy;

19 For if they seek for us, they shall not find us: thou hast done very imprudently.

20 Dost thou not know that I am thine? Trouble me no more.

CHAPTER III.

1 Astonishes his schoolmaster by his learning.

A CERTAIN schoolmaster named Zaccheaus, standing in a certain place, heard Jesus speaking these things to his father.

2 And he was much surprised, that being a child he should speak such things; and after a few days he came to Joseph, and said,

3 Thou hast a wise and sensible child, send him to me, that he may learn to read.

ΔΙΔΑΧΗ ΤΩΝ ΔΩΔΕΚΑ ΑΠΟΣΤΟΛΩΝ

4 When he sat down to teach the letters to Jesus, he began with the first letter Aleph;

5 But Jesus pronounced the second letter Mpeth (Beth) Cghimel (Gimel), and said over all the letters to him to the end.

6 Then opening a book, he taught his master the prophets but he was ashamed, and was at a loss to conceive how he came to know the letters.

7 And he arose and went home, wonderfully surprised at so strange a thing.

CHAPTER IV.

1 Fragment of an adventure at a dyer's.

AS Jesus was passing by a certain shop, he saw a young man dipping (or dyeing) some cloths and stockings in a furnace, of a sad colour, doing them according to every person's particular order;

2 The boy Jesus going to the young man who was doing this, took also some of the cloths ......

(Here endeth the fragment of Thomas's Gospel of the Infancy of Jesus Christ.)

REFERENCE TO ST. THOMAS'S GOSPEL OF THE INFANCY OF JESUS CHRIST.

[The original in Greek, from which this translation is made, will be found printed by Cotelerius, in his notes on the constitutions of the Apostles, from a MS. in the French King's Library, No. 2279.—It is attributed to St. Thomas, and conjectured to have been originally connected with the, Gospel of Mary. Unfortunately this ancient MS. was found torn at the second verse of the fourth chapter.]

THE GOSPEL OF NICODEMUS, FORMERLY CALLED THE ACTS OF PONTIUS PILATE.

The Gospel of NICODEMUS, the disciple, concerning the Sufferings and Resurrection of our Master and Saviour, JESUS CHRIST.

CHAPTER I.

**1 Christ accused to Pilate by the Jews of healing on the Sabbath.
9 Summoned before Pilate by a messenger who does him honour.
20 Worshipped by the standards bowing down to him.**

ANNAS and Caiphas, and Summas, and Datam, Gamaliel, Judas, Levi, Nepthalim, Alexander, Cyrus, and other Jews, went to Pilate about Jesus, accusing him with many bad crimes.

2 And said, We are assured that Jesus is the son of Joseph, the carpenter, and born of Mary, and that he declares himself the Son of God, and a king; and not only so, but attempts the dissolution of the Sabbath, and the laws of our fathers.

3 Pilate replied, What is it which he declares? and what is it which he attempts dissolving?

4 The Jews told him, We have a law which forbids doing cures on the Sabbath day; but he cures both the lame and the deaf, those afflicted with the palsy, the blind, the lepers, and demoniacs, on that day, by wicked methods.

ΔΙΔΑΧΗ ΤΩΝ ΔΩΔΕΚΑ ΑΠΟΣΤΟΛΩΝ

5 Pilate replied, How can he do this by wicked methods? They answered He is a conjurer, and casts out devils by the prince of the devils; and so all things, become subject to him.

6 Then said Pilate, Casting out devils seems not to be the work of an unclean spirit, but to proceed from the power of God.

7 The Jews replied to Pilate, We entreat your highness to summon him to appear before your tribunal, and hear him yourself.

8 Then Pilate called a messenger, and said to him, By what means will Christ be brought hither?

9 Then went the messenger forth, and knowing Christ, worshipped him; and having spread the cloak which he had in his hand upon the ground, he said, Lord, walk upon this, and go in, for the governor calls thee.

10 When the Jews perceived what the messenger had done, they exclaimed (against him) to Pilate, and said, Why did you not give him his summons by a beadle, and not by a messenger?—For the messenger, when he saw him, worshipped him, and spread the cloak which he had in his hand upon the ground before him, and said to him, Lord, the governor calls thee.

11 Then Pilate called the messenger, and said, Why hast thou done thus?

12 The messenger replied, When thou sentest me from Jerusalem to Alexander, I saw Jesus sitting in a mean figure upon a she-ass, and the children of the Hebrews cried out, Hosannah, holding boughs of trees in their hands.

13 Others spread their garments in the way, and said, Save us, thou who art in heaven; blessed is he who cometh in the name of the Lord.

14 Then the Jews cried out, against the messenger, and said, The children of the Hebrews made their acclamations in the Hebrew language; and how couldst thou, who art a Greek, understand the Hebrew?

15 The messenger answered them and said, I asked one of the Jews and said, What is this which the children do cry out in the Hebrew language?

16 And he explained it to me, saying, they cry out, Hosannah, which being interpreted, is, O Lord, save me; or, O Lord, save.

17 Pilate then said to them, Why do you yourselves testify to the words spoken by the children, namely, by your silence? In what has the messenger done amiss? And they were silent.

18 Then the governor said unto the messenger, Go forth and endeavour by any means to bring him in.

19 But the messenger went forth and did as before; and said, Lord come in, for the governor calleth thee.

20 And as Jesus was going in by the ensigns, who carried the standards, the tops of them bowed down and worshipped Jesus.

21 Whereupon the Jews exclaimed more vehemently against the ensigns.

22 But Pilate said to the Jews, I know it is not pleasing to you that the tops of the standards did of themselves bow and worship Jesus; but why do ye exclaim against the ensigns, as if they had bowed and worshipped?

23 They replied to Pilate, We saw the ensigns themselves bowing and worshipping Jesus.

24 Then the governor called the ensigns, and said unto them, Why did you do thus?

25 The ensigns said to Pilate, We are all Pagans and worship the gods in temples; and how should we think anything about worshipping him? We only held the standards in our hands, and they bowed themselves and worshipped him.

26 Then said Pilate to the rulers of the synagogue, Do ye yourselves choose some strong men, and let them hold the standards, and we shall see whether they will then bend of themselves.

27 So the elders of the Jews sought out twelve of the most strong and able old men, and made them hold the standards, and they stood in the presence of the governor.

28 Then Pilate said to the messenger, Take Jesus out, and by some means bring him in again. And Jesus and the messenger went out of the hall.

29 And Pilate called the ensigns who before had borne the standards, and swore to them, that if they had not borne the standards in that manner when Jesus before entered in, he would cut off their heads.

30 Then the governor commanded Jesus to come in again.

31 And the messenger did as he had done before, and very much entreated Jesus that he would go upon his cloak, and walk on it; and he did walk upon it, and went in.

32 And when Jesus went in, the standards bowed themselves as before, and worshipped him.

ΔΙΔΑΧΗ ΤΩΝ ΔΩΔΕΚΑ ΑΠΟΣΤΟΛΩΝ

CHAPTER II.

2 Is compassionated by Pilate's wife,
7 charged with being born in fornication.
12 Testimony to the betrothing of his parents.
15 Hatred of the Jews to him.

NOW when Pilate saw this, he was afraid, and was about to rise from his seat.

2 But while he thought to rise, his own wife who stood at a distance, sent to him, saying, Have thou nothing to do with that just man; for I have suffered much concerning him in a vision this night.

3 When the Jews heard this they said to Pilate, Did we not say unto thee, He is a conjuror? Behold, he hath caused thy wife to dream.

4 Pilate then calling Jesus, said, thou hast heard what they testify against thee, and makest no answer?

5 Jesus replied, If they had not a power of speaking, they could not have spoke; but because every one has the command of his own tongue, to speak both good and bad, let him look to it.

6 But the elders of the Jews answered, and said to Jesus, What shall we look to?

7 In the first place, we know this concerning thee, that thou wast born through fornication; secondly, that upon the account of thy birth the infants were slain in Bethlehem; thirdly, that thy father and mother Mary fled into Egypt, because they could not trust their own people.

8 Some of the Jews who stood by spake more favourably, We cannot say that he was born through fornication; but we know that his mother Mary was betrothed to Joseph, and so he was not born through fornication.

9 Then said Pilate to the Jews who affirmed him to be born through fornication, This your account is not true, seeing there was a betrothment, as they testify who are of your own nation.

10 Annas and Caiphas spake to Pilate, All this multitude of people is to be regarded, who cry out, that he was born through fornication, and is a conjurer; but they who deny him to be born through fornication, are his proselytes and disciples.

11 Pilate answered Annas and Caiphas, Who are the proselytes? They answered, They are those who are the children of Pagans, and are not become Jews, but followers of him

12 Then replied Eleazer, and Asterius, and Antonius, and James, Caras and Samuel, Isaac and Phinees, Crispus and Agrippa, Annas and

Judas, We are not proselytes, but children of Jews, and speak the truth, and were present when Mary was betrothed.

13 Then Pilate addressing himself to the twelve men who spake this, said to them, I conjure you by the life of Caesar, that ye faithfully declare whether he was born through fornication, and those things be true which ye have related.

14 They answered Pilate, We have a law whereby we are forbid to swear, it being a sin: Let them swear by the life of Caesar that it is not as we have said, and we will be contented to be put to death.

15 Then said Annas and Caiphas to Pilate, Those twelve men will not believe that we know him to be basely born, and to be a conjurer, although he pretends that he is the Son of God, and a king: which we are so far from believing, that we tremble to hear.

16 Then Pilate commanded every one to go out except the twelve men who said he was not born through fornication, and Jesus to withdraw to a distance, and said to them, Why have the Jews a mind to kill Jesus?

17 They answered him, They are angry because he wrought cures on the sabbath day. Pilate said, Will they kill him for a good work? They say unto him, Yes, Sir.

CHAPTER III.

1 Is exonerated by Pilate.
11 Disputes with Pilate concerning truth.

THEN Pilate, filled with anger, went out of the hall, and said to the Jews, I call the whole world to witness that I find no fault in that man.

2 The Jews replied to Pilate, If he had not been a wicked person, we had not brought him before thee.

3 Pilate said to them, Do ye take him and try him by your law.

4 Then the Jews said, It is not lawful for us to put any one to death.

5 Pilate said to the Jews, The command, therefore, thou shalt not kill, belongs to you, but not to me.

6 And he went again into the hall, and called Jesus by himself, and said to him, Art thou the king of the Jews?

7 And Jesus answering, said to Pilate, Dost thou speak this of thyself, or did the Jews tell it thee concerning me?

8 Pilate answering, said to Jesus, Am I a Jew? The whole nation and rulers of the Jews have delivered thee up to me. What hast thou done?

ΔΙΔΑΧΗ ΤΩΝ ΔΩΔΕΚΑ ΑΠΟΣΤΟΛΩΝ

9 Jesus answering, said, My kingdom is not of this world: if my kingdom were of this world, then would my servants fight, and I should not have been delivered to the Jews: but now my kingdom is not from hence.

10 Pilate said, Art thou a king then? Jesus answered, Thou sayest that I am a king: to this end was I born, and for this end came I into the world; and for this purpose I came, that I should bear witness to the truth; and every one who is of the truth, heareth my voice.

11 Pilate saith to him, What is truth?

12 Jesus said, Truth is from heaven.

13 Pilate said, Therefore truth is not on earth.

14 Jesus saith to Pilate, Believe that truth is on earth among those, who when they have the power of judgment, are governed by truth, and form right judgment.

CHAPTER IV.

1 Pilate finds no fault in Jesus.
16 The Jews demand his crucifixion.

THEN Pilate left Jesus in the hall, and went out to the Jews, and said, I find not any one fault in Jesus.

2 The Jews say unto him, But he said, I can destroy the temple of God, and in three days build it up again.

3 Pilate saith to them, What sort of temple is that of which he speaketh?

4 The Jews say unto him, That which Solomon was forty-six years in building, he said he would destroy, and in three days build up.

5 Pilate said to them again, I am innocent from the blood of that man! do ye look to it.

6 The Jews say to him, His blood be upon us and our children. Then Pilate calling together the elders and scribes, priests and Levites, saith to them privately, Do not act thus; I have found nothing in your charge (against him) concerning his curing sick persons, and breaking the sabbath, worthy of death.

7 The priests and Levites replied to Pilate, By the life of Caesar, if any one be a blasphemer, he is worthy of death; but this man hath blasphemed against the Lord.

8 Then the governor again commanded the Jews to depart out of the hall; and calling Jesus, said to him, What shall I do with thee?

9 Jesus answered him, Do according as it is written.

10 Pilate said to him, How is it written?

11 Jesus saith to him, Moses and the prophets have prophesied concerning my suffering and resurrection.

12 The Jews hearing this, were provoked, and said to Pilate, Why wilt thou any longer hear the blasphemy of that man?

13 Pilate saith to them, If these words seem to you blasphemy, do ye take him, bring him to your court, and try him according to your law.

14 The Jews reply to Pilate, Our law saith, he shall be obliged to receive nine and thirty stripes, but if after this manner he shall blaspheme against the Lord, he shall be stoned.

15 Pilate saith unto them, If that speech of his was blasphemy, do ye try him according to your law.

16 The Jews say to Pilate, Our law command us not to put any one to death. We desire that he may be crucified, because he deserves the death of the cross.

17 Pilate saith to them, It is not fit he should be crucified: let him be only whipped and sent away.

18 But when the governor looked upon the people that were present and the Jews, he saw many of the Jews in tears, and said to the chief priests of the Jews, All the people do not desire his death.

19 The elders of the Jews answered to Pilate, We and all the people came hither for this very purpose, that he should die.

20 Pilate saith to them, Why should he die?

21 They said to him, Because he declares himself to be the Son of God and a King.

CHAPTER. V.

1 Nicodemus speaks in defence of Christ, and relates his miracles.
12 Another Jew,
26 with Veronica,
34 Centurio, and others, testify of other miracles.

BUT Nicodemus, a certain Jew, stood before the governor, and said, I entreat thee, O righteous judge, that thou wouldst favour me with the liberty of speaking a few words.

2 Pilate said to him, Speak on.

ΔΙΔΑΧΗ ΤΩΝ ΔΩΔΕΚΑ ΑΠΟΣΤΟΛΩΝ

3 Nicodemus said, I spake to the elders of the Jews, and the scribes, and priests and Levites, and all the multitude of the Jews, in their assembly; What is it ye would do with this man?

4 He is a man who hath wrought many useful and glorious miracles, such as no man on earth ever wrought before, nor will ever work. Let him go, and do him no harm; if he cometh from God, his miracles, (his miraculous cures) will continue; but if from men, they will come to nought.

5 Thus Moses, when he was sent by God into Egypt, wrought the miracles which God commanded him, before Pharaoh king of Egypt; and though the magicians of that country, Jannes and Jambres, wrought by their magic the same miracles which Moses did, yet they could not work all which he did;

6 And the miracles which the magicians wrought, were not of God, as ye know, O Scribes and Pharisees; but they who wrought them perished, and all who believed them.

7 And now let this man go; because the very miracles for which ye accuse him, are from God; and he is not worthy of death.

8 The Jews then said to Nicodemus, Art thou become his disciple, and making speeches in his favour?

9 Nicodemus said to them, Is the governor become his disciple also, and does he make speeches for him? Did not Caesar place him in that high post?

10 When the Jews heard this they trembled, and gnashed their teeth at Nicodemus, and said to him, Mayest thou receive his doctrine for truth, and have thy lot with Christ!

11 Nicodemus replied, Amen; I will receive his doctrine, and my lot with him, as ye have said.

12 Then another certain Jew rose up, and desired leave of the governor to hear him a few words.

13 And the governor said, Speak, what thou hast a mind.

14 And he said, I lay for thirty-eight years by the sheep-pool at Jerusalem, labouring under a great infirmity, and waiting for a cure which should be wrought by the coming of an angel, who at a certain time troubled the water: and whosoever first after the troubling of the water stepped in, was made whole of whatsoever disease he had.

15 And when Jesus saw me languishing there, he said to me, Wilt thou be made whole? And I answered, Sir, I have no man, when the water is troubled, to put me into the pool.

16 And he said unto me, Rise, take up thy bed and walk. And I was immediately made whole, and took up my bed and walked

17 The Jews then said to Pilate, Our Lord Governor, pray ask him what day it was on which he was cured of his infirmity.

18 The infirm person replied, It was on the sabbath.

19 The Jews said to Pilate, Did we not say that he wrought his cures on the sabbath, and cast out devils by the prince of devils?

20 Then another certain Jew came forth, and said, I was blind, could hear sounds, but could not see any one; and as Jesus was going along, I heard the multitude passing by, and I asked what was there?

21 They told me that Jesus was passing by: then I cried out, saying, Jesus, Son of David, have mercy on me. And he stood still, and commanded that I should be brought to him, and said to me, What wilt thou?

22 I said, Lord, that I may receive my sight.

23 He said to me, Receive thy sight: and presently I saw, and followed him, rejoicing and giving thanks,

24 Another Jew also came forth, and said, I was a leper, and he cured me by his word only, saying, I will, be thou clean; and presently I was cleansed from my leprosy.

25 And another Jew came forth, and said I was crooked, and he made me straight by his word.

26 And a certain woman named Veronica, said, I was afflicted with an issue of blood twelve years, and I touched the hem of his garment, and presently the issue of blood stopped.

27 The Jews then said, We have a law, that a woman shall not be allowed as an evidence.

28 And, after other things, another Jew said, I saw Jesus invited to a wedding with his disciples, and there was a want of wine in Cana of Galilee;

29 And when the wine was all drank, he commanded the servants that they should fill six pots which were there with water, and they filled them up to the brim, and he blessed them and turned the water into wine, and all the people drank, being surprised at this miracle,

30 And another Jew stood forth, and said, I saw Jesus teaching in the synagogue at Capernaum; and there was in the synagogue a certain man who had a devil; and he cried out, saying, let me alone; what have we to do with thee, Jesus of Nazareth? Art thou come to destroy us? I know that thou art the Holy One of God.

31 And Jesus rebuked him, saying, Hold thy peace, unclean spirit, and come out of the man; and presently he came out of him, and did not at all hurt him.

ΔΙΔΑΧΗ ΤΩΝ ΔΩΔΕΚΑ ΑΠΟΣΤΟΛΩΝ

32 The following things were also said by a Pharisee: I saw that a great company came to Jesus from Galilee and Judea, and the sea-cost, and many countries about Jordan; and many infirm persons came to him, and he healed them all.

33 And I heard the unclean spirits crying out, and saying, Thou art the Son of God. And Jesus strictly charged them, that they should not make him known.

34 After this another person, whose name was Centurio, said, I saw Jesus in Capernaum, and I entreated him, saying, Lord, my servant lieth at home sick of the palsy.

35 And Jesus said to me, I will come and cure him.

36 But I said, Lord, I am not worthy that thou shouldst come under my roof; but only speak the word, and my servant shall be healed.

37 And Jesus said unto me, Go thy way; and as thou hast believed so be it done unto thee. And my servant was healed from that same hour.

38 Then a certain nobleman said, I had a son in Capernaum, who lay at the point of death; and when I heard that Jesus was come into Galilee, I went and besought him that he would come down to my house, and heal my son, for he was at the point of death.

39 He said to me, Go thy way, thy son liveth.

40 And my son was cured from that hour.

41 Besides these, also many others of the Jews, both men and Women, cried out and said, He is truly the Son of God, who cures all diseases only by his word, and to whom the devils are altogether subject.

42 Some of them farther said, This power can proceed from none but God.

43 Pilate said to the Jews, Why are not the devils subject to your doctors?

44 Some of them said, The power of subjecting devils cannot proceed but from God.

45 But others said to Pilate, That he had raised Lazarus from the dead, after he had been four days in his grave.

46 The governor hearing this, trembling, said to the multitude of the Jews, What will it profit you to shed innocent blood?

CHAPTER VI.

**1 Pilate dismayed by the turbulence of the Jews,
5 who demand Barabbas to be released, and Christ to be crucified.
9 Pilate warmly expostulates with them,
20 washes his hands of Christ's blood,
23 and sentences him to be whipped and crucified.**

THEN Pilate having called together Nicodemus, and the fifteen men who said that Jesus was not born through fornication, said to them, What shall I do, seeing there is like to be a tumult among the people.

2 They say unto him, We know not; let them look to it who raise the tumult.

3 Pilate then called the multitude again, and said to them, Ye know that ye have a custom, that I should release to you one prisoner at the feast of the passover:

4 I have a noted prisoner, a murderer, who is called Barabbas, and Jesus who is called Christ, in whom I find nothing that deserves death; which of them, therefore, have you a mind that I should release to you?

5 They all cry out, and say, Release to us Barabbas.

6 Pilate saith to them, What then shall I do with Jesus who is called Christ?

7 They all answer, Let him be crucified.

8 Again they cry out and say to Pilate, You are not the friend of Caesar, if you release this man; for he hath declared that he is the Son of God, and a king. But are you inclined that he should be king, and not Caesar?

9 Then Pilate filled with anger said to them, Your nation hath always been seditious, and you are always against those who have been serviceable to you.

10 The Jews replied, Who are those who have been serviceable to us?

11 Pilate answered them, Your God who delivered you from the hard bondage of the Egyptians, and brought you over the Red Sea as though it had been dry land, and fed you in the wilderness with manna and the flesh of quails, and brought water out of the rock, and gave you a law from heaven.

12 Ye provoked him all ways, and desired for yourselves a molten calf, and worshipped it, and sacrificed to it, and said, These are thy Gods, O Israel, which brought thee out of the land of Egypt:

13 On account of which your God was inclined to destroy you; but Moses interceded for you, and your God heard him, and forgave your iniquity.

14 Afterwards ye were enraged against, and would have killed your prophets, Moses and Aaron, when they fled to the tabernacle, and ye were always murmuring against God and his prophets.

15 And arising from his judgment seat, he would have gone out; but the Jews all cried out, We acknowledge Caesar to be king, and not Jesus;

16 Whereas this person, as soon as he was born, the wise men came and offered gifts unto him; which when Herod heard, he was exceedingly troubled, and would have killed him:

17 When his father knew this, he fled with him and his mother Mary into Egypt. Herod, when he heard he was born, would have slain him; and accordingly sent and slew all the children which were in Bethlehem, and in all the coasts thereof, from two years old and under.

18 When Pilate heard this account, he was afraid; and commanding silence among the people, who made a noise, he said to Jesus, Art thou therefore a king?

19 All the Jews replied to Pilate, he is the very person whom Herod sought to have slain.

20 Then Pilate taking water, washed his hands before the people and said, I am innocent of the blood of this just person; look ye to it.

21 The Jews answered and said, His blood be upon us and our children.

22 Then Pilate commanded Jesus to be brought before him, and spake to him in the following words;

23 Thy own nation hath charged thee as making thyself a king; wherefore I, Pilate, sentence thee to be whipped according to the laws of former governors; and that thou be first bound, then hanged upon a cross in that place where thou art now a prisoner; and also two criminals with thee, whose names are Dimas and Gestas.

CHAPTER. VII.

1 Manner of Christ's crucifixion with the two thieves.

THEN Jesus went out of the hall, and the two thieves with him.

2 And when they came to the place which is called Golgotha, they stript him of his raiment, and girt him about with a linen cloth, and put a crown of thorns upon his head, and put a reed in his hand.

3 And in like manner did they to the two thieves who were crucified with him, Dimas on his right hand and Gestas on his left.

4 But Jesus said, My Father, forgive them, For they know not what they do.

5 And they divided his garments, and upon his vesture they cast lots.

6 The people in the mean time stood by, and the chief priests and elders of the Jews mocked him, saying, He saved others, let him now save himself if he can; if he be the son of God, let him now come down from the cross.

7 The soldiers also mocked him, and taking vinegar and gall, offered it to him to drink, and said to him, If thou art king of the Jews, deliver thyself.

8 Then Longinus, a certain soldier, taking a spear, pierced his side, and presently there came forth blood and water.

9 And Pilate wrote the title upon the cross in Hebrew, Latin, and Greek letters, viz., THIS IS THE KING OF THE JEWS.

10 But one of the two thieves who were crucified with Jesus, whose name was Gestas, said to Jesus, If thou art the Christ, deliver thyself and us.

11 But the thief who was crucified on his right hand, whose name was Dimas, answering, rebuked him, and said, Dost not thou fear God, who art condemned to this punishment? We indeed receive rightly and justly the demerit of our actions; but this Jesus, what evil hath he done.

12 After this, groaning, he said to Jesus, Lord, remember me when thou comest into thy kingdom.

13 Jesus answering, said to him, Verily I say unto thee, that this day thou shalt be with me in Paradise.

CHAPTER VIII.

1 Miraculous appearance at his death.
10 The Jews say the eclipse was natural.
12 Joseph of Arimathaea embalms Christ's body and buries it.

AND it was about the sixth hour, and darkness was upon the face of the whole earth until the ninth hour.

ΔΙΔΑΧΗ ΤΩΝ ΔΩΔΕΚΑ ΑΠΟΣΤΟΛΩΝ

2 And while the sun was eclipsed, behold the veil of the temple was rent from the top, to the bottom; and the rocks also were rent, and the graves opened, and many bodies of saints, which slept, arose.

3 And about the ninth hour Jesus cried out with a loud voice, Eli, Eli, lama sabacthani? which being interpreted is, My God, My God, why hast thou forsaken me?

4 And after these things, Jesus said, Father, into thy hands I commend my spirit; and having said this, he gave up the ghost.

5 But when the centurion saw that Jesus thus crying out gave up the ghost, he glorified God, and said, Of a truth this was a just man.

6 And all the people who stood by, were exceedingly troubled at the sight; and reflecting upon what had passed, smote upon their breasts, and then returned to the city of Jerusalem.

7 The centurion went to the governor, and related to him all that had passed:

8 And when he had heard all these things, he was exceedingly sorrowful;

9 And calling the Jews together, said to them, Have ye seen the miracle of the sun's eclipse, and the other things which came to pass, while Jesus was dying?

10 Which when the Jews heard, they answered to the governor, The eclipse of the sun happened according to its usual custom.

11 But all those who were the acquaintance of Christ, stood at a distance, as did the women who had followed Jesus from Galilee, observing all these things.

12 And behold a certain man of Arimathaea, named Joseph, who was also a disciple of Jesus, but not openly so, for fear of the Jews, came to the governor, and entreated the governor that he would give him leave to take away the body of Jesus from the cross.

13 And the governor gave him leave.

14 And Nicodemus came, bringing with him a mixture of myrrh and aloes about a hundred pounds weight; and they took down Jesus from the cross with tears, and bound him in linen cloths with spices, according to the custom of burying among the Jews;

15 And placed him in a new tomb, which Joseph had built, and caused to be cut out of a rock, in which never any man had been put; and they rolled a great stone to the door of the sepulchre.

THE GOSPEL OF NICODEMUS

CHAPTER IX.

**1 The Jews angry with Nicodemus:
5 and with, Joseph of Arimathaea,
7 whom they imprison.**

WHEN the unjust Jews heard that Joseph had begged and buried the body of Jesus, they sought after Nicodemus, and those fifteen men who had testified before the governor, that Jesus was not born through fornication, and other good persons who had shown any good actions towards him.

2 But when they all concealed themselves through fear of the Jews, Nicodemus alone showed himself to them, and said, How can such persons as these enter into the synagogue?

3 The Jews answered him, But how durst thou enter into the synagogue, who wast a confederate with Christ? Let thy lot be along with him in the other world.

4 Nicodemus answered, Amen; so may it be, that I may have my lot with him in his kingdom.

5 In like manner Joseph, when he came to the Jews, said to them, Why are ye angry with me for desiring the body of Jesus of Pilate? Behold, I have put him in my tomb, and wrapped him up in clean linen, and put a stone at the door of the sepulchre:

6 I have acted rightly towards him; but ye have acted unjustly against that just person, in crucifying him, giving him vinegar to drink, crowning him with thorns, tearing his body with whips, and praying down the guilt of his blood upon you.

7 The Jews at the hearing of this were disquieted and troubled; and they seized Joseph, and commanded him to be put in custody before the Sabbath, and kept there till the Sabbath was over.

8 And they said to him, Make confession; for at this time it is not lawful to do thee any harm, till the first day of the week come. But we know that thou wilt not be thought worthy of a burial; but we will give thy flesh to the birds of the air, and the beasts of the earth.

9 Joseph answered, That speech is like the speech of proud Goliath, who reproached the living God in speaking against David. But ye scribes and doctors know that God saith by the prophet, Vengeance is mine, and I will repay to you evil equal to that which ye have threatened to me.

10 The God whom you have hanged upon the cross, is able to deliver me out of your hands. All your wickedness will return upon you.

ΔΙΔΑΧΗ ΤΩΝ ΔΩΔΕΚΑ ΑΠΟΣΤΟΛΩΝ

11 For the governor, when he washed his hands, said, I am clear from the blood of this just person. But ye answered and cried out, His blood be upon us and our children. According as ye have said, may ye perish for ever.

12 The elders of the Jews hearing these words, were exceedingly enraged; and seizing Joseph, they put him into a chamber where there was no window; they fastened the door, and put a seal upon the lock;

13 And Annas and Caiaphas placed a guard upon it, and took counsel with the priests and Levites, that they should all meet after the Sabbath, and they contrived to what death they should put Joseph.

14 When they had done this, the rulers, Annas and Caiaphas, ordered Joseph to be brought forth.

(In this place there is a portion of the Gospel lost or omitted, which cannot be supplied. It may, nevertheless, be surmised from the occurrence related in the next chapter, that the order of Annas and Caiaphas were rendered unnecessary by Joseph's miraculous escape, and which was announced to an assembly of people.)

CHAPTER X.

1 Joseph's escape.
2 The soldiers relate Christ's resurrection.
18 Christ is seen preaching in Galilee.
21 The Jews repent of their cruelty to him.

WHEN all the assembly heard this (about Joseph's escape), they admired and were astonished, because they found the same seal upon the lock of the chamber, and could not find Joseph.

2 Then Annas and Caiaphas went forth, and while they were all admiring at Joseph's being gone, behold one of the soldiers, who kept the sepulchre of Jesus, spake in the assembly,

3 That while they were guarding the sepulchre of Jesus, there was an earthquake; and we saw an angel of God roll away the stone of the sepulchre and sit upon it;

4 And his countenance was like lightning and his garment like snow; and we became through fear like persons dead.

5 And we heard an angel saying to the women at the sepulchre of Jesus, Do not fear; I know that you seek Jesus who was crucified; he is risen as he foretold;

6 Come and see the place where he was laid; and go presently, and tell his disciples that he is risen from the dead; and he will go before you into Galilee; there ye shall see him as he told you.

7 Then the Jews called together all the soldiers who kept the sepulchre of Jesus, and said to them, Who are those women, to whom the angel spoke? Why did ye not seize them.

8 The soldiers answered and said, We know not who the women were; besides we became as dead persons through fear, and how could we seize those women?

9 The Jews said to them, As the Lord liveth, we do not believe you;

10 The soldiers answering said to the Jews, when ye saw and heard Jesus working so many miracles, and did not believe him, how should ye believe us? Ye well said, As the Lord liveth, for the Lord truly does live.

11 We have heard that ye shut up Joseph, who buried the body of Jesus, in a chamber, under a lock which was sealed; and when ye opened it, found him not there.

12 Do ye then produce Joseph whom ye put under guard in the chamber, and we will produce Jesus whom we guarded in the sepulchre.

13 The Jews answered and said, We will produce Joseph, do ye produce Jesus. But Joseph is in his own city of Arimathaea.

14 The soldiers replied, If Joseph be in Arimathaea, and Jesus in Galilee, we heard the angel inform the women.

15 The Jews hearing this, were afraid, and said among themselves, If by any means these things should become public, then everybody will believe in Jesus.

16 Then they gathered a large sum of money, and gave it to the soldiers, saying, Do ye tell the people that the disciples of Jesus came in the night when ye were asleep, and stole away the body of Jesus; and if Pilate the governor should hear of this, we will satisfy him and secure you.

17 The soldiers accordingly took the money, and said as they were instructed by the Jews; and their report was spread abroad among all the people.

18 But a certain priest Phinees, Ada a schoolmaster, and a Levite, named Ageus, they three came from Galilee to Jerusalem, and told the chief priests and all who were in the synagogues, saying,

19 We have seen Jesus, whom ye crucified, talking with his eleven disciples, and sitting in the midst of them in Mount Olivet, and saying to them,

ΔΙΔΑΧΗ ΤΩΝ ΔΩΔΕΚΑ ΑΠΟΣΤΟΛΩΝ

20 Go forth into the whole world, preach the Gospel to all nations, baptizing them in the name of the Father, and the Son, and the Holy Ghost; and whosoever shall believe and be baptized, shall be saved.

21 And when he had said these things to his disciples, we saw him ascending up to heaven.

22 When the chief priests and elders, and Levites heard these things, they said to these three men, Give glory to the God of Israel, and make confession to him, whether those things are true, which ye say ye have seen and heard.

23 They answering said, As the Lord of our fathers liveth, the God of Abraham, and the God of Isaac, and the God of Jacob, according as we heard Jesus talking with his disciples, and according as we saw him ascending up to heaven, so we have related the truth to you.

24 And the three men farther answered, and said, adding these words, If we should not own the words which we heard Jesus speak, and that we saw him ascending into heaven, we should be guilty of sin.

25 Then the chief priests immediately rose up, and holding the book of the law in their hands, conjured these men, saying, Ye shall no more hereafter declare those things which ye have spoken concerning Jesus.

26 And they gave them a large sum of money, and sent other persons along with them, who should conduct them to their own country, that they might not by any means make any stay at Jerusalem.

27 Then the Jews did assemble all together, and having expressed the most lamentable concern said, What is this extraordinary thing which is come to pass in Jerusalem?

28 But Annas and Caiaphas comforted them, saying, Why should we believe the soldiers who guarded the sepulchre of Jesus, in telling us, that an angel rolled away the stone from the door of the sepulchre?

29 Perhaps his own disciples told them this, and gave them money that they should say so, and they themselves took away the body of Jesus.

30 Besides, consider this, that there is no credit to be given to foreigners, because they also took a large sum of us, and they have declared to us according to the instructions which we gave them. They must either be faithful to us or to the disciples of Jesus.

THE GOSPEL OF NICODEMUS

CHAPTER XI.

1 Nicodemus counsels the Jews.
6 Joseph found.
11 Invited by the Jews to return.
19 Relates the manner of his miraculous escape.

THEN Nicodemus arose, and said, Ye say right, O sons of Israel; ye have heard what those three men have sworn by the Law of God, who said, We have seen Jesus speaking with his disciples upon mount Olivet, and we saw him ascending up to heaven.

2 And the scripture teacheth us that the blessed prophet Elijah was taken up to heaven, and Elisha being asked by the sons of the prophets, Where is our father Elijah? He said to them, that he is taken up to heaven.

3 And the sons of the prophets said to him, Perhaps the spirit hath carried him into one of the mountains of Israel, there perhaps we shall find him. And they besought Elisha, and he walked about with them three days, and they could not find him.

4 And now hear me, O sons of Israel, and let us send men into the mountains of Israel, lest perhaps the spirit hath carried away Jesus, and there perhaps we shall find him, and be satisfied.

5 And the counsel of Nicodemus pleased all the people; and they sent forth men who sought for Jesus, but could not find him; and they returning, said, We went all about, but could not find Jesus, but we have found Joseph in his city of Arimathaea.

6 The rulers hearing this, and all the people, were glad, and praised the God of Israel, because Joseph was found, whom they had shut up in a chamber, and could not find.

7 And when they had formed a large assembly, the chief priests said, By what means shall we bring Joseph to us to speak with him?

8 And taking a piece of paper, they wrote to him, and said, Peace be with thee, and all thy family, We know that we have offended against God and thee. Be pleased to give a visit to us, your fathers, for we were perfectly surprised at your escape from prison.

9 We know that it was malicious counsel which we took against thee, and that the Lord took care of thee, and the Lord himself delivered thee from our designs. Peace be unto thee, Joseph, who art honourable among all the people.

10 And they chose seven of Joseph's friends, and said to them, When ye come to Joseph, salute him in peace, and give him this letter.

ΔΙΔΑΧΗ ΤΩΝ ΔΩΔΕΚΑ ΑΠΟΣΤΟΛΩΝ

11 Accordingly, when the men came to Joseph, they did salute him in peace, and gave him the letter.

12 And when Joseph had read it, he said, Blessed be the Lord God, who didst deliver me from the Israelites, that they could not shed my blood. Blessed be God, who hast protected me under thy wings.

13 And Joseph kissed them, and took them into his house. And on the morrow, Joseph mounted his ass, and went along with them to Jerusalem.

14 And when all the Jews heard these things, they went out to meet him, and cried out, saying, Peace attend thy coming hither, father Joseph.

15 To which he answered, Prosperity from the Lord attend all the people.

13 And they all kissed him; and Nicodemus took him to his house, having prepared a large entertainment.

17 But on the morrow, being a preparation-day, Annas, and Caiaphas, and Nicodemus, said to Joseph, Make confession to the God of Israel, and answer to us all those questions which we shall ask thee;

18 For we have been very much troubled, that thou didst bury the body of Jesus; and that when we had locked thee in a chamber, we could not find thee; and we have been afraid ever since, till this time of thy appearing among us. Tell us therefore before God, all that came to pass.

19 Then Joseph answering, said Ye did indeed put me under confinement, on the day of preparation, till the morning.

20 But while I was standing at prayer in the middle of the night, the house was surrounded with four angels; and I saw Jesus as the brightness of the sun, and fell down upon the earth for fear.

21 But Jesus laying hold on my hand, lifted me from the ground, and the dew was then sprinkled upon me; but he, wiping my face, kissed me, and said unto me, Fear not, Joseph; look upon me for it is I.

22 Then I looked upon him, and said, Rabboni Elias! He answered me, I am not Elias, but Jesus of Nazareth, whose body thou didst bury.

23 I said to him, show me the tomb in which I laid thee.

24 Then Jesus, taking me by the hand, led me unto the place where I laid him, and showed me the linen clothes, and napkin which I put round his head. Then I knew that it was Jesus, and worshipped him, and said; Blessed be he who cometh in the name of the Lord.

25 Jesus again taking me by the hand, led me to Arimathaea, to my own house, and said to me, Peace be to thee; but go not out of thy house till the fortieth day; but I must go to my disciples.

THE GOSPEL OF NICODEMUS

CHAPTER XII.

1 The Jews astonished and confounded.
16 Simeon's two sons, Charinus and Lenthius, rise from the dead at Christ's crucifixion.
19 Joseph proposes to get them to relate the mysteries of their resurrection.
21 They are sought and found,
22 brought to the synagogue,
23 privately sworn to secrecy,
25 and undertake to write what they had seen.

WHEN the chief priests and Levites heard all these things, they were astonished, and fell down with their faces on the ground as dead men, and crying out to one another, said, What is this extraordinary sign which is come to pass in Jerusalem? We know the father and mother of Jesus.

2 And a certain Levite said, I know many of his relations, religions persons, who are wont to offer sacrifices and burnt-offerings to the God of Israel, in the temple, with prayers.

3 And when the high-priest Simeon took him up in his arms, he said to him, Lord, now lettest thou thy servant depart in peace, according to thy word; for mine eyes have seen thy salvation, which then halt prepared before the face of all people; a light to enlighten the Gentiles, and the glory of thy people Israel.

4 Simeon in like manner blessed Mary the Mother of Jesus, and said to her, I declare to thee concerning that child; He is appointed for the fall and rising again of many, and for a sign which shall be spoken against;

5 Yea, a sword shall pierce through thine own soul also, and the thoughts of many hearts shall be revealed.

6 Then said all the Jews, Let us send to those three men, who said they saw him talking with his disciples in mount Olivet.

7 After this, they asked them what they had seen; who answered with one accord, In the presence of the God of Israel we affirm, that we plainly saw Jesus talking with his disciples in Mount Olivet, and ascending up to heaven.

8 Then Annas and Caiaphas took them into separate places, and examined them separately; who unanimously confessed the truth, and said, they had seen Jesus.

ΔΙΔΑΧΗ ΤΩΝ ΔΩΔΕΚΑ ΑΠΟΣΤΟΛΩΝ

9 Then Annas and Caiaphas said "Our law saith, By the mouth of two or three witnesses every word shall be established."

10 But what have we said? The blessed Enoch pleased God, and was translated by the word of God; and the burying-place of the blessed Moses is known.

11 But Jesus was delivered to Pilate, whipped, crowned with thorns, spit upon, pierced with a spear, crucified, died upon the cross, and was buried, and his body the honourable Joseph buried in a new sepulchre, and he testifies that he saw him alive.

12 And besides, these men have declared, that they saw him talking with his disciples on Mount Olivet, and ascending up to heaven.

13 Then Joseph rising up, said to Annas and Caiaphas, Ye may be justly under a great surprise, that you have been told, that Jesus is alive, and gone up to heaven.

14 It is indeed a thing really surprising, that he should not only himself arise from the dead, but also raise others from their graves, who have been seen by many in Jerusalem.

15 And now hear me a little We all knew the blessed Simeon, the high-priest, who took Jesus when an infant into his arms in the temple.

16 This same Simeon had two sons of his own, and we were all present at their death and funeral.

17 Go therefore and see their tombs, for these are open, and they are risen: and behold, they are in the city of Arimathaea, spending their time together in offices of devotion.

18 Some, indeed, have heard the sound of their voices in prayer, but they will not discourse with anyone, but they continue as mute as dead men.

19 But come, let us go to them, and behave ourselves towards them with all due respect and caution. And if we can bring them to swear, perhaps they will tell us some of the mysteries of their resurrection.

20 When the Jews heard this they were exceedingly rejoiced.

21 Then Annas and Caiaphas, Nicodemus, Joseph, and Gamaliel, went to Arimathaea, but did not find them in their graves; but walking about the city, they found them on their bended knees at their devotions:

22 Then saluting them with all respect and deference to God, they brought them to the synagogue at Jerusalem; and having shut the gates, they took the book of the law of the Lord,

23 And putting it in their hands, swore them by God Adonai, and the God of Israel, who spake to our fathers by the law and the prophets, saying, If ye believe him who raised you from the dead, to be

Jesus, tell us what ye have seen, and how ye were raised from the dead.

24 Charinus and Lenthius, the two sons of Simeon, trembled when they heard these things, and were disturbed, and groaned; and at the same time looking up to heaven, they made the sign of the cross with their fingers on their tongues,

25 And immediately they spake, and said, Give each of us some paper, and we will write down for you all those things which we have seen. And they each sat down and wrote, saying:—

CHAPTER XIII.

**1 The narrative of Charinus and Lenthius commences.
3 A great light in hell.
7 Simeon arrives, and announces the coming of Christ.**

O LORD Jesus and Father, who art God, also the resurrection and life of the dead, give us leave to declare thy mysteries, which we saw after death, belonging to thy cross; for we are sworn by thy name.

2 For thou hast forbidden thy servants to declare the secret things, which were wrought by thy divine power in hell.

3 When we were Placed with our fathers in the dept of hell, in the blackness of darkness, on a sudden there appeared the colour of the sun like gold, and a substantial purple-coloured light enlightening the place.

4 Presently upon this, Adam, the father of all mankind, with all the patriarchs and prophets, rejoiced and said, That light is the author of everlasting light, who hath promised to translate us to everlasting light.

5 Then Isaiah the prophet cried out and said, This is the light of the Father, and the Son of God, according to my prophecy, when I was alive upon earth.

6 The land of Zabulon, and the land of Nephthalim, beyond Jordan, a people who walked in darkness, saw a great light; and to them who dwelled in the region of the shadow of death, light is arisen. And now he is come, and hath enlightened us who sat in death.

7 And while we were all rejoicing in the light which shone upon us, our father Simeon came among us, and congratulating all the company, said, Glorify the Lord Jesus Christ the Son of God.

8 Whom I took up in my arms when an infant in the temple, and being moved by the Holy Ghost, said to him, and acknowledged, That now mine eyes have seen thy salvation, which thou hast prepared be-

ΔΙΔΑΧΗ ΤΩΝ ΔΩΔΕΚΑ ΑΠΟΣΤΟΛΩΝ

fore the face of all people; a light to enlighten the Gentiles, and the glory of thy people Israel.

9 All the saints who were in the depth of hell, hearing this, rejoiced the more.

10 Afterwards there came forth one like a little hermit, and was asked by every one, Who art thou?

11 To which he replied, I am the voice of one crying in the wilderness, John the Baptist, and the prophet of the Most High, who went before his coming to prepare his way, to give the knowledge of salvation to his people for the forgiveness of sins.

12 And I, John, when I saw Jesus coming to me, being moved by the Holy Ghost, I said, Behold the Lamb of God, behold him who takes away the sins of the world.

13 And I baptized him in the river Jordan, and saw the Holy Ghost descending upon him in the form of a dove, and heard a voice from heaven saying, This is my beloved Son, in whom I am well pleased.

14 And now while I was going before him, I came down hither to acquaint you, that the Son of God will next visit us, and, as the dayspring from on high, will come to us, who are in darkness and the shadow of death.

CHAPTER XIV.

1 Adam causes Seth to relate what he heard from Michael the archangel, when he sent him to Paradise to entreat God to anoint his head in his sickness.

BUT when the first man our father Adam heard these things, that Jesus was baptized in Jordan, he called out to his son Seth, and said,

2 Declare to your sons, the patriarchs and prophets, all those things, which thou didst hear from Michael, the archangel, when I sent thee to the gates of Paradise, to entreat God that he would anoint my head when I was sick.

3 Then Seth, coming near to the patriarchs and prophets, said, I, Seth, when I was praying to God at the gates of Paradise, beheld the angel of the Lord, Michael, appear unto me, saying, I am sent unto thee from the Lord; I am appointed to preside over human bodies.

4 I tell thee, Seth, do not pray to God in tears, and entreat him for the oil of the tree of mercy wherewith to anoint thy father Adam for his head-ache;

5 Because thou canst not by any means obtain it till the last day and times, namely, till five thousand and five hundred years be past.

6 Then will Christ, the most merciful Son of God, come on earth to raise again the human body of Adam, and at the same time to raise the bodies of the dead, and when he cometh he will be baptized in Jordan;

7 Then with the oil of his mercy he will anoint all those who believe in him; and the oil of his mercy will continue to future generations, for those who shall be born of the water and the Holy Ghost unto eternal life.

8 And when at that time the most merciful Son of God, Christ Jesus, shall come down on earth, he will introduce our father Adam into Paradise, to the tree of mercy.

9 When all the patriarchs and prophets heard all these things from Seth, they rejoiced more.

CHAPTER XV.

1 Quarrel between Satan and the prince of hell, concerning the expected arrival of Christ in hell.

WHILE all the saints were rejoicing, behold Satan, the prince and captain of death, said to the prince of hell,

2 Prepare to receive Jesus of Nazareth himself, who boasted that he was the Son of God, and yet was a man afraid of death, and said, My soul is sorrowful even to death.

3 Besides he did many injuries to me and to many others; for those whom I made blind and lame and those also whom I tormented with several devils, he cured by his word; yea, and those whom I brought dead to thee, he by force takes away from thee.

4 To this the prince of hell replied to Satan, Who is that so powerful prince, and yet a man who is afraid of death?

5 For all the potentates of the earth are subject to my power, whom thou broughtest to subjection by thy power.

6 But if he be so powerful in his human nature, I affirm to thee for truth, that he is almighty in his divine nature, and no man can resist his power:

7 When therefore he said he was afraid of death, he designed to ensnare thee, and unhappy it will be to thee for everlasting ages,

8 Then Satan replying, said to the prince of hell, Why didst thou express a doubt, and wast afraid to receive that Jesus of Nazareth, both thy adversary and mine?

ΔΙΔΑΧΗ ΤΩΝ ΔΩΔΕΚΑ ΑΠΟΣΤΟΛΩΝ

9 As for me, I tempted him and stirred up my old people the Jews with zeal and anger against him;

10 I sharpened the spear for his suffering; I mixed the gall and vinegar, and commanded that he should drink it; I prepared the cross to crucify him, and the nails to pierce through his hands and feet; and now his death is near at hand, I will bring him hither, subject both to thee and me.

11 Then the prince of hell answering, said, Thou saidst to me just now, that he took away the dead from me by force.

12 They who have been kept here till they should live again upon earth, were taken away hence, not by their own power, but by prayers made to God, and their almighty God took them from me.

13 Who then is that Jesus of Nazareth that by his word hath taken away the dead from me without prayer to God?

14 Perhaps it is the same who took away from me Lazarus, after he had been four days dead, and did both stink and was rotten, and of whom I had possession as a dead person, yet he brought him to life again by his power.

15 Satan answering, replied to the prince of hell, It is the very same person, Jesus of Nazareth.

16 Which when the prince of hell heard, he said to him, I adjure thee by the powers which belong to thee and me, that thou bring him not to me.

17 For when I heard of the power of his word, I trembled for fear, and all my impious company were at the same disturbed;

18 And we were not able to detain Lazarus, but he gave himself a shake, and with all the signs of malice he immediately went away from us; and the very earth, in which the dead body of Lazarus was lodged, presently turned him out alive.

19 And I know now that he is Almighty God who could perform such things, who is mighty in his dominion, and mighty in his human nature, who is the Saviour of mankind.

20 Bring not therefore this person hither, for he will set at liberty all those whom I hold in prison under unbelief, and bound with the fetters of their sins, and will conduct them to everlasting life.

CHAPTER XVI.

**1 Christ's arrival at hell-gates; the confusion thereupon.
19 He descends into hell.**

AND while Satan and the Prince of hell were discoursing thus to each other, on a sudden there was a voice as of thunder, and the rushing of winds, saying, Lift up your gates, O ye princes; and be ye lift up, O everlasting gates, and the King of Glory shall come in.

2 When the prince of hell heard this, he said to Satan, Depart from me, and begone out of my habitations; if thou art a powerful warrior, fight with the King of Glory. But what hast thou to do with him?

3 And he cast him forth from his habitations.

4 And the prince said to his impious officers, Shut the brass gates of cruelty, and make them fast with iron bars, and fight courageously, lest we be taken captives.

5 But when all the company of the saints heard this they spake with a loud voice of anger to the prince of hell,

6 Open thy gates, that the King of Glory may come in.

7 And the divine prophet David cried out, saying, Did not I, when on earth, truly prophesy and say, O that men would praise the Lord for his goodness, and for his wonderful works to the children of men!

8 For he hath broken the gates of brass, and cut the bars of iron in sunder. He hath taken them because of their iniquity, and because of their unrighteousness they are afflicted.

9 After this, another prophet, namely, holy Isaiah, spake in like manner to all the saints, Did not I rightly prophesy to you when I was alive on earth?

10 The dead men shall live, and they shall rise again who are in their graves, and they shall rejoice who are in the earth; for the dew which is from the Lord, shall bring deliverance to them.

11 And I said in another place, O grave, where is thy victory? O death, where is thy sting?

12 When all the saints heard these things spoken by Isaiah, they said to the prince of hell, Open now thy gates, and take away thine iron bars; for thou wilt now be bound, and have no power.

13 Then was there a great voice, as of the sound of thunder, saying, Lift up your gates, O princes; and be ye lifted up, ye gates of hell, and the King of Glory will enter in.

14 The prince of hell perceiving the same voice repeated, cried out, as though he had been ignorant, Who is that King of Glory?

ΔΙΔΑΧΗ ΤΩΝ ΔΩΔΕΚΑ ΑΠΟΣΤΟΛΩΝ

15 David replied to the prince of hell, and said, I understand the words of that voice, because I spake them in his spirit. And now, as I have before said, I say unto thee, the Lord strong and powerful, the Lord mighty in battle: he is the King of Glory, and he is the Lord in heaven and in earth.

16 He hath looked down to hear the groans of the prisoners, and to set loose those that are appointed to death.

17 And now, thou filthy and stinking prince of hell, open thy gates, that the King of Glory may enter in; for he is the Lord of heaven and earth.

18 While David was saying this, the mighty Lord appeared in the form of a man, and enlightened those places which had ever before been in darkness.

19 And broke asunder the fetters which before could not be broken; and with his invincible power visited those who sate in the deep darkness by iniquity, and the shadow of death by sin.

CHAPTER XVII.

1 Death and the devils in great horror at Christ's coming.
13 He tramples on death, seizes the prince of hell, and takes Adam with him to Heaven.

IMPIOUS death and her cruel officers hearing these things, were seized with fear in their several kingdoms, when they saw the clearness of the light,

2 And Christ himself on a sudden appearing in their habitations, they cried out therefore, and said, We are bound by thee; thou seemest to intend our confusion before the Lord.

3 Who art thou, who has no signs of corruption, but that bright appearance which is a full proof of thy greatness, of which yet thou seemest to take no notice?

4 Who art thou, so powerful, and so weak, so great and so little; mean, and yet a soldier of the first rank, who can command in the form of a servant and a common soldier?

5 The king of Glory, dead and alive, though once slain upon the cross?

6 Who layest dead in the grave, and art come down alive to us, and in thy death all the creatures trembled, and all the stars were moved; and now hast thy liberty among the dead, and givest disturbance to our legions?

7 Who art thou, who dost release the captives that were held in chains by original sin, and bringest them into their former liberty?

8 Who art thou, who dost spread so glorious and divine a light over those who were made blind by the darkness of sin?

9 In like manner all the legions of devils were seized with the like horror, and with the most submissive fear cried out, and said,

10 Whence comes it, O thou Jesus Christ, that thou art a man so powerful and glorious in majesty so bright as to have no spot, and so pure as to have no crime? For that lower world of earth, which was ever till now subject to us, and from whence we received tribute, never sent us such a dead man before, never sent such presents as these to the princes of hell.

11 Who therefore art thou, who with such courage enterest among our abodes, and art not only not afraid to threaten us with the greatest punishments, but also endeavourest to rescue all others from the chains in which we hold them?

12 Perhaps thou art that Jesus, of whom Satan just now spoke to our prince, that by the death of the cross thou wert about to receive the power of death.

13 Then the King of Glory trampling upon death, seized the prince of hell, deprived him of all his power, and took our earthly father Adam with him to his glory.

CHAPTER XVIII.

1 Beelzebub, prince of hell, vehemently upbraids Satan for persecuting Christ and bringing him to hell.
14 Christ gives Beelzebub dominion over Satan forever, as a recompence for taking away Adam and his sons.

THEN the prince of hell took Satan, and with great indignation said to him, O thou prince of destruction, author of Beelzebub's defeat and banishment, the scorn of God's angels and loathed by all righteous persons! What inclined thee to act thus?

2 Thou wouldst crucify the King of Glory, and by his destruction, hast made us promises of very large advantages, but as a fool wert ignorant of what thou wast about.

3 For behold now that Jesus of Nazareth, with the brightness of his glorious divinity, puts to flight all the horrid powers of darkness and death;

4 He has broke down our prisons from top to bottom, dismissed all the captives, released all who were bound, and all who were wont formerly to groan under the weight of their torments, have now insulted us, and we are like to be defeated by their prayers.

5 Our impious dominions are subdued, and no part of mankind is now left in our subjection, but on the other hand, they all boldly defy us;

6 Though, before, the dead never durst behave themselves insolently towards us, nor being prisoners, could ever on any occasion be merry.

7 O Satan, thou prince of all the wicked, father of the impious and abandoned, why wouldest thou attempt this exploit, seeing our prisoners were hitherto always without the least hope of salvation and life?

8 But now there is not one of them does ever groan, nor is there the least appearance of a tear in any of their faces.

9 O prince Satan, thou great keeper of the infernal regions, all thy advantages which thou didst acquire by the forbidden tree, and the loss of Paradise, thou hast now lost by the wood of the cross;

10 And thy happiness all then expired, when thou didst crucify Jesus Christ the King of Glory.

11 Thou hast acted against thine own interest and mine, as thou wilt presently perceive by those large torments and infinite punishments which thou art about to suffer.

12 O Satan, prince of all evil, author of death, and source of all pride, thou shouldest first have inquired into the evil crimes of Jesus of Nazareth, and then thou wouldest have found that he was guilty of no fault worthy of death.

13 Why didst thou venture, without either reason or justice, to crucify him, and hast brought down to our regions a person innocent and righteous, and thereby hast lost all the sinners, impious and unrighteous persons in the whole world?

14 While the prince of hell was thus speaking to Satan, the King of Glory said to Beelzebub the prince of hell, Satan the prince shall be subject to thy dominions for ever, in the room of Adam and his righteous sons, who are mine,

CHAPTER XIX.

1 Christ takes Adam by the hand, the rest of the saints join hands, and they all ascend with him to Paradise.

THEN Jesus stretched forth his hand, and said, Come to me, all ye my saints, who were created in my image, who were condemned by the tree of the forbidden fruit, and by the devil and death;

2 Live now by the wood of my cross; the devil, the prince of this world, is overcome, and death is conquered,

3 Then presently all the saints were joined together under the hand of the most high God; and the Lord Jesus laid hold on Adam's hand, and said to him, Peace be to thee, and all thy righteous posterity, which is mine.

4 Then Adam, casting himself at the feet of Jesus, addressed himself to him with tears, in humble language, and a loud voice, saying,

5 "I will extol thee, O Lord, for thou halt lifted me up, and hast not made my foes to rejoice over me. O Lord my God, I cried unto thee, and thou hast healed me."

6 "O Lord thou hast brought up my soul from the grave; thou hast kept me alive, that I should not go down to the pit."

7 "Sing unto the Lord, all ye saints of his, and give thanks at the remembrance of his holiness, for his anger endureth but for a moment; in his favour is life."

8 In like manner all the saints, prostrate at the feet of Jesus, said with one voice, Thou art come, O Redeemer of the world, and hast actually accomplished all things, which thou didst foretell by the law and thy holy prophets.

9 Thou hast redeemed the living by thy cross, and art come down to us, that by the death of the cross thou mightest deliver us from hell, and by thy power from death.

10 O Lord, as thou hast put the ensigns of thy glory in heaven, and hast set up the sign of thy redemption, even thy cross on earth; so, Lord, set the sign of the victory of thy cross in hell, that death may have dominion no longer.

11 Then the Lord stretching forth his hand, made the sign of the cross upon Adam, and upon all his saints.

12 And taking hold of Adam by his right hand, he ascended from hell, and all the saints of God followed him.

ΔΙΔΑΧΗ ΤΩΝ ΔΩΔΕΚΑ ΑΠΟΣΤΟΛΩΝ

13 Then the royal prophet, David, boldly cried, and said, O sing unto the Lord a new song, for he hath done marvellous things; his right hand and his holy arm have gotten him the victory.

14 The Lord hath made known his salvation, his righteousness hath he openly shewn in the sight of the heathen.

15 And the whole multitude of saints answered, saying, This honour have all his saints, Amen, Praise ye the Lord.

16 Afterwards, the prophet Habbakuk cried out, and said, Thou wentest forth for the salvation of thy people, even for salvation with thine anointed.

17 And all the saints said, Blessed is he who cometh in the name of the Lord; for the Lord hath enlightened us. This is our God for ever and ever; he shall reign over us to everlasting ages. Amen.

18 In like manner all the prophets spake the sacred things of his praise, and followed the Lord.

CHAPTER XX.

1 Christ delivers Adam to Michael the archangel.
3 They meet Enoch and Elijah in heaven,
5 and also the blessed thief, who relates how he came to Paradise.

THEN the Lord, holding Adam by the hand, delivered him to Michael the archangel; and he led them into Paradise, filled with mercy and glory;

2 And two very ancient men met them, and were asked by the saints, Who are ye, who have not yet been with us in hell, and have had your bodies placed in Paradise?

3 One of them answering, said, I am Enoch, who was translated by the word of God: and this man who is with me, is Elijah the Tishbite, who was translated in a fiery chariot.

4 Here we have hitherto been, and have not tasted death, but are now about to return at the coming of Antichrist, being armed with divine signs and miracles, to engage with him in battle, and to be slain by him at Jerusalem, and to be taken up alive again into the clouds, after three days and a half.

5 And while the holy Enoch and Elias were relating this, behold there came another man in a miserable figure, carrying the sign of the cross upon his shoulders.

6 And when all the saints saw him, they said to him, Who art thou? For thy countenance is like a thief's; and why dost thou carry a cross upon thy shoulders?

7 To which he answering, said, Ye say right, for I was a thief, who committed all sorts of wicked. ness upon earth.

8 And the Jews crucified me with Jesus; and I observed the surprising things which happened in the creation at the crucifixion of the Lord Jesus.

9 And I believed him to be the Creator of all things, and the Almighty King; and I prayed to him, saying, Lord remember me, when thou comest into thy kingdom.

10 He presently regarded my supplication, and said to me, Verily I say unto thee, this day thou shalt be with me in Paradise.

11 And he gave me this sign of the cross, saying, Carry this, and go to Paradise; and if the angel who is the guard of Paradise will not admit thee, show him the sign of the cross, and say unto him Jesus Christ who is now crucified, hath sent me hither to thee.

12 When I did this and told the angel who is the guard of Paradise all these things, and he heard them, he presently opened the gates, introduced me, and placed me on the right hand in Paradise,

13 Saying, Stay here a little time, till Adam, the father of all mankind, shall enter in, with all his sons, who are the holy and righteous servants of Jesus Christ, who was crucified.

14 When they heard all this account from the thief, all the patriarchs said with one voice, Blessed be thou, O Almighty God, the Father of everlasting goodness, and the Father of mercies, who hast shown such favour to those who were sinners against him, and hast brought them to the mercy of Paradise, and hast placed them amidst thy large and spiritual provisions, in a spiritual and holy life. Amen.

ΔΙΔΑΧΗ ΤΩΝ ΔΩΔΕΚΑ ΑΠΟΣΤΟΛΩΝ

CHAPTER XXI.

**1 Charinus and Lenthius being only allowed three days to remain on earth,
7 deliver in their narratives, which miraculously correspond; they vanish,
13 and Pilate records these transactions.**

THESE are the divine and sacred mysteries which we saw and heard. We, Charinus and Lenthius are not allowed to declare the other mysteries of God, as the archangel Michael ordered us,

2 Saying, ye shall go with my brethren to Jerusalem, and shall continue in prayers, declaring and glorifying the resurrection of Jesus Christ, seeing he hath raised you from the dead at the same time with himself.

3 And ye shall not talk with any man, but sit as dumb persons till the time come when the Lord will allow you to relate the mysteries of his divinity.

4 The archangel Michael farther commanded us to go beyond Jordan, to an excellent and fat country, where there are many who rose from the dead along with us for the proof of the resurrection of Christ.

5 For we have only three days allowed us from the dead, who arose to celebrate the passover of our Lord with our parents, and to bear our testimony for Christ the Lord, and we have been baptized in the holy river of Jordan. And now they are not seen by any one.

6 This is as much as God allowed us to relate to you; give ye therefore praise and honour to him, and repent, and he will have mercy upon you. Peace be to you from the Lord God Jesus Christ, and the Saviour of us all. Amen, Amen, Amen.

7 And after they had made an end of writing, and had written on two distinct pieces of paper, Charinus gave what he wrote into the hands of Annas, and Caiaphas, and Gamaliel.

8 Lenthius likewise gave what he wrote into the hands of Nicodemus and Joseph; and immediately they were changed into exceeding white forms and were seen no more.

9 But what they had written was found perfectly to agree, the one not containing one letter more or less than the other.

10 When all the assembly of the Jews heard all these surprising relations of Charinus and Lenthius, they said to each other, Truly all

these things were wrought by God, and blessed be the Lord Jesus for ever and ever, Amen.

11 And they went all out with great concern, and fear, and trembling, and smote upon their breasts and went away every one to his home.

12 But immediately all these things which were related by the Jews in their synagogues concerning Jesus, were presently told by Joseph and Nicodemus to the governor.

13 And Pilate wrote down all these transactions, and placed all these accounts in the public records of his hall.

CHAPTER XXII.

1 Pilate goes to the temple; calls together the rulers, and scribes, and doctors.
2 Commands the gates to be shut; orders the book of the Scriptures; and causes the Jews to relate what they really knew concerning Christ.
14 They declare that they crucified Christ in ignorance, and that they now know him to be the Son of God, according to the testimony of the Scriptures; which, after they put him to death, were examined.

AFTER these things Pilate went to the temple of the Jews, and called together all the rulers and scribes, and doctors of the law, and went with them into a chapel of the temple.

2 And commanding that all the gates should be shut, said to them, I have heard that ye have a certain large book in this temple; I desire you, therefore, that it may be brought before me.

3 And when the great book, carried by four ministers of the temple, and adorned with gold and precious stones, was brought, Pilate said to them all, I adjure you by the God of your Fathers, who made and commanded this temple to be built, that ye conceal not the truth from me.

4 Ye know all the things which are written in that book; tell me therefore now, if ye in the Scriptures have found any thing of that Jesus whom ye crucified, and at what time of the world he, ought to have come: show it me.

5 Then having sworn Annas and Caiaphas, they commanded all the rest who were with them to go out of the chapel.

ΔΙΔΑΧΗ ΤΩΝ ΔΩΔΕΚΑ ΑΠΟΣΤΟΛΩΝ

6 And they shut the gates of the temple and of the chapel, and said to Pilate, Thou hast made us to swear, O judge, by the building of this temple, to declare to thee that which is true and right.

7 After we had crucified Jesus, not knowing that he was the Son of God, but supposing he wrought his miracles by some magical arts, we summoned a large assembly in this temple.

8 And when we were deliberating among one another about the miracles which Jesus had wrought, we found many witnesses of our own country, who declared that they had seen him alive after his death, and that they heard him discoursing with his disciples, and saw him ascending into the height of the heavens, and entering into them;

9 And we saw two witnesses, whose bodies Jesus raised from the dead, who told us of many strange things which Jesus did among the dead, of which we have a written account in our hands.

10 And it is our custom annually to open this holy book before an assembly, and to search there for the counsel of God.

11 And we found in the first of the seventy books, where Michael the archangel is speaking to the third son of Adam the first man, an account that after five thousand five hundred years, Christ the most beloved son of God was to come on earth,

12 And we further considered, that perhaps he was the very God of Israel who spoke to Moses, Thou shalt make the ark of the testimony; two cubits and a half shall be the length thereof, and a cubit and a half the breadth thereof, and a cubit and a half the height thereof.

13 By these five cubits and a half for the building of the ark of the Old Testament, we perceived and knew that in five thousand years and half (one thousand) years, Jesus Christ was to come in the ark or tabernacle of a body;

14 And so our Scriptures testify that he is the Son of God, and the Lord and King of Israel.

15 And because after his suffering, our chief priests were surprised at the signs which were wrought by his means, we opened that book to search all the generations down to the generation of Joseph and Mary the mother of Jesus, supposing him to be of the seed of David;

16 And we found the account of the creation, and at what time he made the heaven and the earth, and the first man Adam, and that from thence to the flood, were two thousand seven hundred and forty- eight years.

17 And from the flood to Abraham, nine hundred and twelve. And from Abraham to Moses, four hundred and thirty. And from Moses to David the King, five hundred and ten.

THE GOSPEL OF NICODEMUS

18 And from David to the Babylonish captivity five hundred years. And from the Babylonish captivity to the incarnation of Christ, four hundred years.

19 The sum of all which amounts to five thousand and half (a thousand.)

20 And so it appears, that Jesus whom we crucified, is Jesus Christ the Son of God, and true Almighty God. Amen.

(In the name of the Holy Trinity, thus end the acts of our Saviour Jesus Christ, which the Emperor Theodosius the Great found at Jerusalem, in the hall of Pontius Pilate, among the public records; the things were acted in the nineteenth year of Tiberius Caesar, Emperor of the Romans, and in the seventeenth year of the government of Herod, the son of Herod and of Galilee, on the eighth of the calends of April, which is the twenty-third day of the month of March, in the CCIId Olympiad, when Joseph and Caiaphas were rulers of the Jews; being a History written in Hebrew by Nicodemus, of what happened after our Saviour's crucifixion.)

REFERENCES TO THE GOSPEL OF NICODEMUS, FORMERLY CALLED THE ACTS OF PONTIUS PILATE.

[Although this Gospel is, by some among the learned, supposed to have been really written by Nicodemus, who became a disciple of Jesus Christ, and conversed with him; others conjecture that it was a forgery towards the close of the third century by some zealous believer, who, observing that there had been appeals made by the Christians of the former age, to the acts of Pilate, but that such acts could not be produced, imagined it would be of service to Christianity to fabricate and publish this Gospel; as it would both confirm the Christians under persecution, and convince the Heathens of the truth of the Christian religion. The Rev. Jeremiah Jones says, that such pious frauds were very common among Christians even in the first three centuries; and that a forgery of this nature, with the view above-mentioned, seems natural and probable. The same author, in noticing that Eusebius in his Ecclesiastical History, charges the Pagans with having forged and published a book, called "The Acts of Pilate," takes occasion to observe that the internal evidence of this Gospel shows it was not the work of any Heathen, but that if in the latter end of the third century we find it in use among Christians (as it was then certainly in some churches), and about the same time find a forgery of the Heathens under the same title, it seems exceedingly probable that some Christians, at that time, should publish such a piece as this, in order partly to confront the spurious one of the Pagans, and partly to support those appeals which had

ΔΙΔΑΧΗ ΤΩΝ ΔΩΔΕΚΑ ΑΠΟΣΤΟΛΩΝ

been made by former Christians to the Acts of Pilate; and Mr. Jones says, he thinks so more particularly as we have innumerable instances of forgeries by the faithful in the primitive ages, grounded on less plausible reasons. Whether it be canonical or not, it is of very great antiquity, and is appealed to by several of the ancient Christians. The present translation is made from the Gospel, published by Grynaeus in the Orthodoxographa, vol. i, tom, ii, p. 613.]

Notwithstanding the diversity of opinions here alluded to, the majority of the learned believe that the internal evidence of the authenticity of this Gospel is manifested in the correct details of that period of Christ's life on which it treats, while it far excels the canonical Evangelists narrative of the trial of our Saviour before Pilate, with more minute particulars of persons, evidence, circumstance, &c.

THE EPISTLES OF JESUS CHRIST & ABGARUS KING OF EDESSA.

CHAPTER I.

A copy of a letter written by King Abgarus to Jesus; and sent to him by Ananius, his footman, to Jerusalem,
5 inviting him to Edessa.

ABGARUS, king of Edessa, to Jesus the good Saviour, who appears at Jerusalem, greeting.

2 I have been informed concerning you and your cures, which are performed without the use of medicines and herbs.

3 For it is reported, that you cause the blind to see, the lame to walk, do both cleanse lepers, and cast out unclean spirits and devils, and restore them to health who have been long diseased; and raiseth up the dead;

4 All which when I heard, I was persuaded of one of these two, namely, either that you are God himself descended from heaven; who do these things, or the Son of God.

5 On this account therefore I have written to you, earnestly to desire you would take the trouble of a journey hither, and cure a disease which I am under.

6 For I hear the Jews ridicule you and, intend you mischief.

7 My city is indeed small, but neat, and large enough for us both.

ΔΙΔΑΧΗ ΤΩΝ ΔΩΔΕΚΑ ΑΠΟΣΤΟΛΩΝ

CHAPTER II.

The answer of Jesus by Ananias the footman to Abgarus the king,
3 declining to visit Edessa.

ABGARUS, you are happy, forasmuch as you have believed on me, whom you have not seen.

2 For it is written concerning me, that those who have seen me should not believe on me, that they who have not seen might believe and live.

3 As to that part of your letter, which relates to my giving you a visit, I must inform you, that I must fulfil all the ends of my mission in this country, and after that be received up again to him who sent me.

4 But after my ascension I will send one of my disciples, who will cure your disease, and give life to you, and all that are with you.

REFERENCES TO THE EPISTLES OF JESUS CHRIST AND ABGARUS KING OF EDESSA.

[The first writer who makes any mention of the Epistles that passed between Jesus Christ and Abgarus, is Eusebius, Bishop of Caesarea, in Palestine, who flourished in the early part of the fourth century. For their genuineness, he appeals to the public registers and records of the City of Edessa in Mesopotamia, where Abgarus reigned, and where he affirms that he found them written in the Syriac language. He published a Greek translation of them, in his Ecclesiastical History. The learned world has been much divided on this subject; but, notwithstanding the erudite Grabe, with Archbishop Cave, Dr, Parker, and other divines, have strenuously contended for their admission into the canon of Scripture, they are deemed apocryphal. The Rev. Jeremiah Jones observes, that the common people in England have this Epistle in their houses in many places, fixed in a frame, with the picture of Christ before it; and that they generally, with much honesty and devotion, regard it as the word of God, and the genuine Epistle of Christ.]

THE EPISTLE OF ST. PAUL THE APOSTLE TO THE LAODICEANS.

1 He salutes the brethren;
3 exhorts them to persevere in good works,
4 and not to be moved by vain speaking.
6 Rejoices in his bonds,
10 desires them to live in the fear of the Lord.

PAUL an Apostle, not of men, neither by man, but by Jesus Christ, to the brethren which are at Laodicea.

2 Grace be to you, and peace from God the Father and our Lord Jesus Christ.

3 I thank Christ in every prayer of mine, that ye may continue and persevere in good works, looking for that which is promised in the day of judgment.

4 Let not the vain speeches of any trouble you, who pervert the truth, that they may draw you aside from the truth of the Gospel which I have preached.

5 And now may God grant, that my converts may attain to a perfect knowledge of the truth of the Gospel, be beneficent, and doing good works which accompany salvation.

6 And now my bonds, which I suffer in Christ, are manifest, in which I rejoice and am glad. For I know that this shall turn to my salvation for ever, which shall be through your prayer, and the supply of the Holy Spirit.

8 Whether I live or die, to live shall be a life to Christ, to die will be joy.

9 And our Lord will grant us his mercy, that ye may have the same love, and be like-minded.

ΔΙΔΑΧΗ ΤΩΝ ΔΩΔΕΚΑ ΑΠΟΣΤΟΛΩΝ

10 Wherefore, my beloved, as ye have heard of the coming of the Lord, so think and act in fear, and it shall be to you life eternal;
11 For it is God, who worketh in you:
12 And do all things without sin.
13 And what is best, my beloved rejoice in the Lord Jesus Christ and avoid all filthy lucre.
14 Let all your requests be made known to God, and be steady in the doctrine of Christ.
15 And whatsoever things are sound and true, and of good report, and chaste, and just, and lovely, these things do.
16 Those things which ye have heard, and received, think on these things, and peace shall be with you.
17 All the saints salute you.
18 The grace of our Lord Jesus Christ be with your spirit. Amen.
19 Cause this Epistle to be read to the Colossians, and the Epistle of the Colossians to be read among you.

REFERENCES TO THE EPISTLE OF ST. PAUL THE APOSTLE TO THE LAODICEANS.

[This Epistle has been highly esteemed by several learned men of the church of Rome and others. The Quakers have printed a translation, and plead for it, as the reader may see, by consulting Poole's Annotation on Col. vi. 16. Sixtus Senensis mentions two MSS., the one in the Sorbonne Library at Paris, which is a very ancient copy, and the other in the Library of Joannes a Viridario, at Padua, which he transcribed and published; and which is the authority for the following translation. There is a very old translation of this Epistle in the British Museum, among the Harleian MSS., Cod. 1212.]

THE EPISTLES OF ST. PAUL THE APOSTLE TO SENECA, WITH SENECA'S TO PAUL.

CHAPTER I.

ANNAEUS SENECA to PAUL Greeting.

I SUPPOSE, Paul, you have been informed of that conversation, which passed yesterday between me and my Lucilius, concerning hypocrisy and other subjects; for there were some of your disciples in company with us;

2 For when we were retired into the Sallustian gardens, through which they were also passing, and would have gone another way, by our persuasion they joined company with us.

3 I desire you to believe, that we much wish for your conversation;

4 We were much delighted with your book of many Epistles, which you have written to some cities and chief towns of provinces, and contain wonderful instructions for moral conduct:

5 Such sentiments, as I suppose you were not the author of, but only the instrument of conveying, though sometimes both the author and the instrument,

6 For such is the sublimity of those, doctrines, and their grandeur, that I suppose the age of a man is scarce sufficient to be instructed and perfected in the knowledge of them. I wish your welfare, my brother. Farewell.

ΔΙΔΑΧΗ ΤΩΝ ΔΩΔΕΚΑ ΑΠΟΣΤΟΛΩΝ

CHAPTER II.

PAUL to SENECA Greeting.

I RECEIVED your letter yesterday with pleasure, to which I could immediately have written an answer, had the young man been at home, whom I intended to have sent to you:

2 For you know when, and by whom, at what seasons, and to whom I must deliver everything which I send.

3 I desire therefore you would not charge me with negligence, if I wait for a proper person.

4 I reckon myself very happy in having the judgment of so valuable a person, that you are delighted with my Epistles:

5 For you would not be esteemed a censor, a philosopher, or be the tutor of so great a prince, and a master of everything, if you were not sincere. I wish you a lasting prosperity.

CHAPTER III.

ANNAEUS SENECA to PAUL Greeting.

I HAVE completed some volumes and divided them into their proper parts.

2 I am determined to read them to Caesar, and if any favourable opportunity happens, you also shall be present, when they are read;

3 But if that cannot be, I will appoint and give you notice of a day, when we will together read over the performance.

4 I had determined, if I could with safety, first to have your opinion of it, before I published it to Caesar, that you might be convinced of my affection to you. Farewell, dearest Paul.

CHAPTER. IV.

PAUL to SENECA Greeting.

AS often as I read your letters, I imagine you present with me; nor indeed do I think any other, than that you are always with us.

2 As soon therefore as you begin to come, we shall presently see each other. I wish you all prosperity.

CHAPTER V.

ANNAEUS SENECA to PAUL Greeting.

WE are very much concerned at your too long absence from us.

2 What is it, or what affairs are they, which obstructs your coming?

3 If you fear the anger of Caesar because you have abandoned your former religion, and made proselytes also of others, you have this to plead, that your acting thus proceeded not from inconstancy, but judgment. Farewell.

CHAPTER VI.

PAUL to SENECA and LUCILIUS Greeting.

CONCERNING those things, about which ye wrote to me, it is not proper for me to mention anything in writing with pen and ink: the one of which leaves marks, and the other evidently declares things.

2 Especially since I know that there are near you, as well as me, those who will understand my meaning.

3 Deference is to be paid to all men, and so much the more, as they are more likely to take occasions of quarrelling.

4 And if we show a submissive temper, we shall overcome effectually in all points, if so be they are, who are capable of seeing and acknowledging themselves to have been in the wrong. Farewell.

CHAPTER VII.

ANNAEUS SENECA to PAUL Greeting.

I PROFESS myself extremely pleased with the reading your letters to the Galatians, Corinthians, and people of Achaia.

2 For the Holy Ghost has in them by you delivered those sentiments which are very lofty, sublime, deserving of all respect, and beyond your own invention.

3 I could wish therefore, that when you are writing things so extraordinary, there might not be wanting an elegancy of speech agreeable to their majesty.

4 And I must own, my brother, that I may not at once dishonestly conceal anything from you, and be unfaithful to my own conscience,

ΔΙΔΑΧΗ ΤΩΝ ΔΩΔΕΚΑ ΑΠΟΣΤΟΛΩΝ

that the emperor is extremely pleased with the sentiments of your Epistles;

5 For when he heard the beginning of them read, he declared, that he was surprised to find such notions in a person, who had not had a regular education.

6 To which I replied, That the Gods sometimes made use of mean (innocent) persons to speak by, and gave him an instance of this in a mean countryman named Vatienus, who, when he was in the country of Reate, had two men appeared to him, called Castor and Pollux, and received a revelation from the gods. Farewell.

CHAPTER VIII.

PAUL to SENECA Greeting.

ALTHOUGH I know the emperor is both an admirer and favourer of our religion, yet give me leave to advise you against your suffering any injury (by showing favour to us).

2 I think indeed you ventured upon a very dangerous attempt, when you would declare (to the emperor) that which is so very contrary to his religion, and way of worship; seeing he is a worshipper of the heathen gods.

3 I know not what you particularly had in view, when you told him of this; but I suppose you did it out of too great respect for me.

4 But I desire that for the future you would not do so; for you had need be careful, lest by showing your affection for me, you should offend your master:

5 His anger indeed will do us no harm, if he continue a heathen; nor will his not being angry be of any service to us:

6 And if the empress act worthy of her character, she will not be angry; but if she act as a woman, she will be affronted. Farewell.

CHAPTER IX.

ANNEUS SENECA to PAUL Greeting.

KNOW that my letter, wherein I acquainted you, that I had read to the Emperor your Epistles, does not so much affect you as the nature of the things (contained in them.)

ST. PAUL THE APOSTLE TO SENECA

2 Which do so powerfully divert men's minds from their former manners and practices, that I have always been surprised, and have been fully convinced of it by many arguments heretofore.

3 Let us therefore begin afresh; and if any thing heretofore has been imprudently acted, do you forgive.

4 I have sent you a book decopia verborum. Farewell, dearest Paul.

CHAPTER X.

PAUL to SENECA Greeting.

AS often as I write to you, and place my name before yours, I do a thing both disagreeable to myself, and contrary to our religion:

2 For I ought, as I have often declared, to become all things to all men, and to have that regard to your quality, which the Roman law has honoured all senators with; namely, to put my name last in the (inscription of the) Epistle, that I may not at length with uneasiness and shame be obliged to do that which it was always my inclination to do. Farewell, most respected master. Dated the fifth of the calends of July, in the fourth Consulship of Nero, and Messala.

CHAPTER XI.

ANNAEUS SENECA to PAUL Greeting.

ALL happiness to you, my dearest Paul.

2 If a person so great, and every way agreeable as you are, become not only a common, but a most intimate friend to me, how happy will be the case of Seneca!

3 You therefore, who are so eminent, and so far exalted above all, even the greatest, do not think yourself unfit to be first named in the inscription of an Epistle;

4 Lest I should suspect you intend not so much to try me, as to banter me; for you know yourself to be a Roman citizen.

5 And I could wish to be in that circumstance or station which you are, and that you were in the same that I am. Farewell, dearest Paul. Dated the tenth of the calends of April, in the Consulship of Aprianus and Capito.

ΔΙΔΑΧΗ ΤΩΝ ΔΩΔΕΚΑ ΑΠΟΣΤΟΛΩΝ

CHAPTER XII.

ANNAEUS SENECA to PAUL Greeting.

ALL happiness to you, my dearest Paul. Do you not suppose I am extremely concerned and grieved that your innocence should bring you into sufferings?

2 And that all the people should suppose you (Christians) so criminal, and imagine all the misfortunes that happen to the city, to be caused by you?

3 But let us bear the charge with a patient temper, appealing for our innocence to the court above, which is the only one our hard fortune will allow us to address to, till at length our misfortunes shall end in unalterable happiness.

4 Former ages have produced (tyrants) Alexander the son of Philip, and Dionysius; ours also has produced Caius Caesar; whose inclinations were their only laws.

5 As to the frequent burnings of the city of Rome, the cause is manifest; and if a person in my mean circumstances might be allowed to speak, and one might declare these dark things without danger, every one should see the whole of the matter.

6 The Christians and Jews are indeed commonly punished for the crime of burning the city; but that impious miscreant, who delights in murders and butcheries, and disguises his villainies with lies, is appointed to, or reserved till, his proper time.

7 And as the life of every excellent person is now sacrificed instead of that one person (who is the author of the mischief), so this one shall be sacrificed for many, and he shall be devoted to be burnt with fire instead of all.

8 One hundred and thirty-two houses, and four whole squares (or islands) were burnt down in six days: the seventh put an end to the burning. I wish you all happiness.

9 Dated the fifth of the calends of April, in the Consulship of Frigius and Bassus.

CHAPTER XIII.

ANNAEUS SENECA to PAUL Greeting.

ALL happiness to you, my dearest Paul.

2 You have written many volumes in an allegorical and mystical style, and therefore such mighty matters and business being committed to you, require not to be set off with any rhetorical flourishes of speech, but only with some proper elegance.

3 I remember you often said, that many by affecting such a style do injury to their subjects, and lose the force of the matters they treat of.

4 But in this I desire you to regard me, namely, to have respect to true Latin, and to choose just words, that so you may the better manage the noble trust which is reposed in you.

5 Farewell. Dated the fifth of the nones of July, Leo and Savinus Consuls.

CHAPTER XIV.

PAUL to SENECA Greeting.

YOUR serious consideration is requited with those discoveries, which the Divine Being has granted but to few;

2 I am thereby assured that I sow the most strong seed in a fertile soil, not anything material, which is subject to corruption, but the durable word of God, which shall increase and bring forth fruit to eternity.

3 That which by your wisdom you have attained to, shall abide without decay for ever.

4 Believe that you ought to avoid the superstitions of Jews and Gentiles.

5 The things which you have in some measure arrived to, prudently make known to the emperor, his family, and to faithful friends;

6 And though your sentiments will seem disagreeable, and not be comprehended by them, seeing most of them will not regard your discourses, yet the Word of God once infused into them, will at length make them become new men, aspiring towards God.

7 Farewell Seneca, who art most dear to us. Dated on the calends of August, in the Consulship of Leo and Savinus.

REFERENCES TO THE EPISTLES OF ST. PAUL THE APOSTLE TO SENECA, WITH SENECA'S TO PAUL.

[Several very learned writers have entertained a favourable opinion of these Epistles. They are undoubtedly of high antiquity. Salmeron

ΔΙΔΑΧΗ ΤΩΝ ΔΩΔΕΚΑ ΑΠΟΣΤΟΛΩΝ

cites them to prove that Seneca was one of Caesar's household, referred to by Paul, Philip iv. 22, as saluting the brethren at Philippi. In Jerome's enumeration of illustrious men, he places Seneca, on account of these Epistles, amongst the ecclesiastical and holy writers of the Christian Church. Sixtus Senensis has published them in his Bibliotheque, p 89, 90; and it is from thence that the present translation is made. Baronius, Bellarmine, Dr. Cave, Spanheim, and others, contend that they are not genuine.]

THE ACTS OF ST. PAUL AND THECLA.

The martyrdom of the holy and glorious first Martyr and Apostle Thecla.

CHAPTER I.

1 Demas and Hermogenes become Paul's companions.
4 Paul visits Onesiphorus.
8 Invited by Demos and Hermogenes.
11 Preaches to the household of Onesiphorus.
12 His sermon.

WHEN Paul went up to Iconium, after his flight from Antioch, Demas and Hermogenes became his companions, who were then full of hypocrisy.

2 But Paul looking only at the goodness of God, did them no harm, but loved them greatly.

3 Accordingly he endeavoured to make agreeable to them all the oracles and doctrines of Christ, and the design of the Gospel of God's well-beloved son; instructing them in the knowledge of Christ, as it was revealed to him.

4 And a certain man named Onesiphorus, hearing that Paul was come to Iconium, went out speedily to meet him, together with his wife Lectra, and his sons Simmia and Zeno, to invite him to their house.

5 For Titus had given them a description of Paul's personage, they as yet not knowing him in person, but only being acquainted with his character.

ΔΙΔΑΧΗ ΤΩΝ ΔΩΔΕΚΑ ΑΠΟΣΤΟΛΩΝ

6 They went in the king's highway to Lystra, and stood there waiting for him, comparing all who passed by with that description which Titus had given them.

7 At length they saw a man coming (namely Paul), of a low stature, bald on the head; with crooked thighs, handsome legs, hollow-eyes; and a crooked nose; full of grace, for sometimes he appeared as a man, sometimes he had the countenance of an angel. And Paul saw Onesiphorus, and was glad.

8 And Onesiphorus said: Hail, thou servant of the blessed God. Paul replied, The grace of God be with thee and thy family.

9 But Denies and Hermogenes were moved with envy, and, under a show of great religion, Demas said, And are not we also servants of the blessed God? Why didst thou not salute us?

10 Onesiphorus replied, Because I have not perceived in you the fruits of righteousness; nevertheless, if ye are of that sort, ye shall be welcome to my house also.

11 Then Paul went into the house of Onesiphorus, and there was great joy among the family on that account: and they employed themselves in prayer, breaking of bread, and hearing Paul preach the word of God concerning temperance and the resurrection, in the following manner:

12 Blessed are the pure in heart; for they shall see God.

13 Blessed are they who keep their flesh undefiled (or pure); for they shall be the temple of God.

14 Blessed are the temperate (or chaste); for God will reveal himself to them.

15 Blessed are they who abandon their worldly enjoyments; for they shall be accepted of God.

16 Blessed are they who have wives, as though they had them not; for they shall be made angels of God.

17 Blessed are they who tremble at the word of God; for they shall be comforted.

18 Blessed are they who keep their baptism pure; for they shall find peace with the Father, Son, and Holy Ghost.

19 Blessed are they who pursue the wisdom or doctrine of Jesus Christ; for they shall be called the sons of the Most High.

20 Blessed are they who observe the instructions of Jesus Christ; for they shall dwell in eternal light.

21 Blessed are they, who for the love of Christ abandon the glories of the world, for they shall judge angels, and be placed at the right hand of Christ, and shall not suffer the bitterness of the last judgment.

22 Blessed are the bodies and souls of virgins; for they are acceptable to God, and shall not lose the reward of their virginity; for the word of their (heavenly) Father shall prove effectual to their salvation in the day of his Son, and they shall enjoy rest for evermore.

CHAPTER II.

1 Thecla listens anxiously to Paul's preaching.
5 Thamyris, her admirer, concerts with Theoclia her mother to dissuade her,
12 in vain.
14 Demas and Hermogenes vilify Paul to Thamyris.

WHILE Paul was preaching this sermon in the church which was in the house of Onesiphorus, a certain virgin named Thecla (whose mother's name was Theoclia, and who was betrothed to a man named Thamyris) sat at a certain window in her house.

2 From whence, by the advantage of a window in the house where Paul was, she both night and day heard Paul's sermons concerning God, concerning charity, concerning faith in Christ, and concerning prayer;

3 Nor would she depart from the window, till with exceeding joy she was subdued to the doctrines of faith.

4 At length, when she saw many women and virgins going into Paul, she earnestly desired that she might be thought worthy to appear in his presence, and hear the word of Christ; for she had not yet seen Paul's person, but only heard his sermons, and that alone.

5 But when she would not be prevailed upon to depart from the window, her mother sent to Thamyris, who came with the greatest pleasure, as hoping now, to marry her. Accordingly he said to Theoclia, Where is my Thecla?

6 Theoclia replied, Thamyris, I have something very strange to tell you; for Thecla, for the space of three days, will not move from the window, not so much as to eat or drink, but is so intent in hearing the artful and delusive discourses of a certain foreigner, that I perfectly wonder Thamyris, that a young woman of her known modesty, will suffer herself to be so prevailed upon.

7 For that man has disturbed the whole city of Iconium, and even your Thecla, among others. All the women and young men flock to him to receive his doctrine; who, besides all the rest, tells them that

there is but one God, who alone is to be worshipped, and that we ought to live in chastity.

8 Notwithstanding this, my daughter Thecla, like a spider's web fastened to the window, is captivated, by the discourses of Paul, and attends' upon them with prodigious eagerness, and vast delight; and thus, by attending on what he says, the young woman is seduced. Now then do you go, and speak to her, for she is betrothed to you.

9 Accordingly Thamyris went, and having saluted her, and taking care not to surprise her, he said, Thecla, my spouse, why sittest thou in this melancholy posture? What strange impressions are made upon thee? Turn to Thamyris, and blush.

10 Her mother also spake to her after the same manner, and said, Child, why dost thou sit so melancholy, and, like one astonished, makest no reply?

11 Then they wept exceedingly, Thamyris, that he had lost his spouse; Theoclia, that she had lost her daughter; and the maids, that they had lost their mistress; and there was an universal mourning in the family.

12 But all these things made no impression upon Thecla, so as to incline her so much as to turn to them, and take notice of them; for she still regarded the discourses of Paul.

13 Then Thamyris ran forth into the street to observe who they were that went in to Paul, and came out from him; and he saw two men engaged in a very warm dispute, and said to them;

14 Sirs, what business have you here? and who is that man within, belonging to you, who deludes the minds of men, both young men and virgins, persuading them, that they ought not to marry, but continue as they are?

15 I promise to give you a considerable sum, if ye will give me a just account of him; for I am the chief person of this city.

16 Demas and Hermogenes replied, We cannot so exactly tell who he is; but this we know, that he deprives young men of their (intended) wives, and virgins of their (intended) husbands, by teaching, There can be no future resurrection, unless ye continue in chastity, and do not defile your flesh.

THE ACTS OF ST. PAUL AND THECLA.

CHAPTER III.

1 They betray Paul.
7 Thamyris arrests him with officers.

THEN said Thamyris, Come along with me to my house, and refresh yourselves. So they went to a very splendid entertainment, where there was wine in abundance, and very rich provision.

2 They were brought to a table richly spread, and made to drink plentifully by Thamyris, on account of the love he had for Thecla and his desire to marry her.

3 Then Thamyris said, I desire ye would inform me what the doctrines of this Paul are, that I may understand them; for I am under no small concern about Thecla, seeing she so delights in that stranger's discourses, that I am in danger of losing my intended wife.

4 Then Demas and Hermogenes answered both together, and said, Let him be brought before the governor Castellius, as one who endeavours to persuade the people into the new religion of the Christians, and he, according to the order of Caesar, will put him to death, by which means you will obtain your wife;

5 While we at the same time will teach her, that the resurrection which he speaks of is already come, and consists in our having children; and that we then arose again, when we came to the knowledge of God.

6 Thamyris having this account from them, was filled with hot resentment:

7 And rising early in the morning he went to the house of Onesiphorus, attended by the magistrates, the Jailor, and a great multitude of people with staves, and said to Paul;

8 Thou hast perverted the city of Iconium, and among the rest, Thecla, who is betrothed to me, so that now she will not marry me. Thou shalt therefore go with us to the governor Castellius.

9 And all the multitude cried out, Away with this imposter, for he has perverted the minds of our wives, and all the people hearken to him.

ΔΙΔΑΧΗ ΤΩΝ ΔΩΔΕΚΑ ΑΠΟΣΤΟΛΩΝ

CHAPTER IV.

**1 Paul accused before the governor by Thamyris.
5 Defends himself.
9 Is committed to prison,
10 and visited by Thecla.**

THEN Thamyris standing before the governor's judgment-seat, spake with a loud voice in the following manner.

2 O governor, I know not whence this man cometh; but he is one who teaches that matrimony is unlawful. Command him therefore to declare before you for what reason he publishes such doctrines.

3 While he was saying thus, Demas and Hermogenes (whispered to Thamyris, and) said; Say that he is a Christian, and he will presently be put to death.

4 But the governor was more deliberate, and calling to Paul, he said, Who art thou? What dost thou teach? They seem to lay gross crimes to thy charge.

5 Paul then spake with a loud voice, saying, As I am now called to give an account, O governor, of my doctrines, I desire your audience.

6 That God, who is a God of vengeance, and who stands in need of nothing but the salvation of his creatures, has sent me to reclaim them from their wickedness, and corruptions; from all (sinful) pleasures, and from death; and to persuade them to sin no more.

7 On this account, God sent his Son Jesus Christ, whom I preach, and in whom I instruct men to place their hopes, as that person who only had such compassion on the deluded world, that it might not, O governor, be condemned, but have faith, the fear of God, the knowledge of religion, and the love of truth.

8 So that if I only teach those things which I have received by revelation from God, where is my crime?

9 When the governor heard this, he ordered Paul to be bound, and to be put in prison, till he should be more at leisure to hear him more fully.

10 But in the night, Thecla taking off her ear-rings, gave them to the turnkey of the prison, who then opened the door to her, and let her in;

11 And when she made a present of a silver looking-glass to the jailor, was allowed to go into the room where Paul was; then she set down at his feet, and heard from him the great things of God.

12 And as she perceived Paul not to be afraid of suffering, but that by divine assistance he behaved himself with courage, her faith so far increased that she kissed his chains.

CHAPTER V.

**1 Thecla sought and found by her relations.
4 Brought with Paul before the governor.
9 Ordered to be burnt, and Paul to be whipt.
15 Thecla miraculously saved.**

AT length Thecla was missed and sought for by the family and by Thamyris in every street, as though she had been lost; till one of the porter's fellow-servants told them, that she had gone out in the night-time.

2 Then they examined the porter, and he told them, that she was gone to the prison to the strange man.

3 They went therefore according to his direction, and there found her; and when they came out, they got a mob together, and went and told the governor all that had happened.

4 Upon which he ordered Paul to be brought before his judgment seat.

5 Thecla in the mean time lay wallowing on the ground in the prison, in that same place where Paul had sat to teach her; upon which the governor also ordered her to be brought before his judgment-seat; which summons she received with joy, and went.

6 When Paul was brought thither, the mob with more vehemence cried out, He is a magician, let him die.

7 Nevertheless the governor attended with pleasure upon Paul's discourses of the holy works of Christ; and, after a council called, he summoned Thecla, and said to her, Why do you not, according to the law of the Iconians, marry Thamyris?

8 She stood still, with her eyes fixed upon Paul; and finding she made no reply, Theoclia, her mother cried out saying, Let the unjust creature be burnt; let her be burnt in the midst of the theatre, for refusing Thamyris, that all women may learn from her to avoid such practices.

9 Then the governor was exceedingly concerned, and ordered Paul to be whipt out of the city, and Thecla to be burnt.

10 So the governor arose, and went immediately into the theatre; and all the people went forth to see the dismal sight.

11 But Thecla, just as a lamb in the wilderness looks every way to see his shepherd, looked around for Paul;

12 And as she was looking upon the multitude, she saw the Lord Jesus in the likeness of Paul, and said to herself, Paul is come to see me in my distressed circumstances. And she fixed her eyes upon him; but he instantly ascended up to heaven, while she looked on him.

13 Then the young men and women brought wood and straw for the burning of Thecla; who being brought naked to the stake, extorted tears from the governor, with surprise beholding the greatness of her beauty.

14 And when they had placed the wood in order, the people commanded her to go upon it; which she did, first making the sign of the cross.

15 Then the people set fire to the pile; though the flame was exceeding large, it did not touch her; for God took compassion on her, and caused a great eruption from the earth beneath, and a cloud from above to pour down great quantities of rain and hail;

16 Insomuch that by the rupture of the earth, very many were in great danger, and some were killed, the fire was extinguished, and Thecla preserved.

CHAPTER VI.

1 Paul with Onesiphorus in a cave.
7 Thecla discovers Paul;
12 proffers to follow him:
13 he exhorts her not for fear of fornication.

IN the mean time Paul, together with Onesiphorus, his wife and children, was keeping a fast in a certain cave, which was in the road from Iconium to Daphne.

2 And when they had fasted for several days, the children said to Paul, Father, we are hungry, and have not wherewithal to buy bread; for Onesiphorus had left all his substance to follow Paul with his family.

3 Then Paul, taking off his coat, said to the boy, Go, child, and buy bread, and bring it hither.

4 But while the boy was buying the bread, he saw his neighbour Thecla, and was surprised, and said to her, Thecla, where are you going?

THE ACTS OF ST. PAUL AND THECLA.

5 She replied, I am in pursuit of Paul, having been delivered from the flames.

6 The boy then said, I will bring you to him, for he is under great concern on your account, and has been in prayer and fasting these six days.

7 When Thecla came to the cave, she found Paul upon his knees praying and saying, O holy Father, O Lord Jesus Christ, grant that the fire may not touch Thecla; but be her helper, for she is thy servant.

8 Thecla then standing behind him, cried out in the following words: O sovereign Lord Creator of heaven and earth, the Father of thy beloved and holy Son, I praise thee that thou hast preserved me from the fire, to see Paul again.

9 Paul then arose, and when he saw her, said, O God, who searchest the heart, Father of my Lord Jesus Christ, I praise thee that thou hast answered my prayer.

10 And there prevailed among them in the cave an entire affection to each other; Paul, Onesiphorus, and all that were with them being filled with joy.

11 They had five loaves, some herbs and water, and they solaced each other in reflections upon the holy works of Christ.

12 Then said Thecla to Paul, If you be pleased with it, I will follow you whithersoever you go.

13 He replied to her, Persons are now much given to fornication, and you being handsome, I am afraid lest you should meet with greater temptation than the former, and should Not withstand, but be overcome by it.

14 Thecla replied, Grant me only the seal of Christ, and no temptation shall affect me.

15 Paul answered, Thecla, wait with patience, and you shall receive the gift of Christ.

ΔΙΔΑΧΗ ΤΩΝ ΔΩΔΕΚΑ ΑΠΟΣΤΟΛΩΝ

CHAPTER VII.

**1 Paul and Thecla go to Antioch.
2 Alexander, a magistrate, falls in love with Thecla:
4 kisses her by force:
5 she resists him:
6 is carried before the governor, and condemned to be thrown to wild beasts.**

THEN Paul sent back Onesiphorus and his family to their own home, and taking Thecla along with him, went for Antioch;

2 And as soon as they came in to the city, a certain Syrian, named Alexander, a magistrate in the city, who had done many considerable services for the city during his magistracy, saw Thecla, and fell in love with her, and endeavoured by many rich presents to engage Paul in his interest.

3 But Paul told him, I know not the woman of whom you speak, nor does she belong to me.

4 But he being a person of great power in, Antioch, seized her in the street and kissed her: which Thecla would not bear, but looking about for Paul, cried out in a distressed loud tone, Force me not, who am a stranger; force me not, who am a servant of God; I am one of the principal persons of Iconium, and was obliged to leave that city because I would not be married to Thamyris.

5 Then she laid hold on Alexander, tore his coat, and took his crown off his head, and made him appear ridiculous before all the people.

6 But Alexander, partly as he loved her, and partly being ashamed of what had been done, led her to the governor, and upon her confession of what she had done, he condemned her to be thrown among the beasts.

THE ACTS OF ST. PAUL AND THECLA.

CHAPTER VIII.

**2 Thecla entertained by Trifina;
3 brought out to the wild beasts; a she-lion licks her feet.
5 Trifina upon a vision of her deceased daughter, adopts Thecla,
11 who is taken to the amphitheatre again.**

WHICH when the people saw, they said: The judgments passed in this city are unjust. But Thecla desired the favour of the governor, that her chastity might not be attacked, but preserved till she should be cast to the beasts.

2 The governor then inquired, Who would entertain her; upon which a certain very rich widow, named Trifina, whose daughter was lately dead, desired that she might have the keeping of her; and she began to treat her in her house as her own daughter.

3 At length a day came, when the beasts were to be brought forth to be seen; and Thecla was brought to the amphitheatre, and put into a den in which was an exceeding fierce she-lion, in the presence of a multitude of spectators.

4 Trifina; without any surprise, accompanied Thecla, and the she-lion licked the feet of Thecla. The title written which denoted her crime, was Sacrilege. Then the women cried out, O God, the judgments of this city are unrighteous.

5 After the beasts had been shown, Trifina took Thecla home with her, and they went to bed; and behold, the daughter of Trifina, who was dead, appeared to her mother, and said; Mother, let the young woman, Thecla, be reputed by you as your daughter in my stead; and desire her that she should pray for me, that I may be translated to a state of happiness.

6 Upon which Trifina, with a mournful air, said, My daughter Falconilla has appeared to me, and ordered me to receive you in her room; wherefore I desire, Thecla, that you would pray for my daughter, that she may be translated into a state of happiness, and to life eternal.

7 When Thecla heard this, she immediately prayed to the Lord, and said: O Lord God of heaven and earth, Jesus Christ, thou Son of the Most High, grant that her daughter Falconilla may live forever. Trifina hearing this, groaned again, and said: O unrighteous judgments! O un-

reasonable wickedness! that such a creature should (again) be cast to the beasts!

8 On the morrow, at break of day, Alexander came to Trifina's house, and said: The governor and the people are waiting; bring the criminal forth.

9 But Trifina ran in so violently upon him, that he was affrighted, and ran away. Trifina was one of the royal family, and she thus expressed her sorrow, and said; Alas! I have trouble in my house on two accounts, and there is no one who will relieve me, either under the loss of my daughter, or my being unable to save Thecla. But now, O Lord God, be thou the helper of Thecla thy servant.

10 While she was thus engaged, the governor sent one of his own officers to bring Thecla. Trifina took her by the hand, and, going with her, said: I went with Falconilla to her grave, and now must go with Thecla to the beasts.

11 When Thecla heard this, she weeping prayed, and said: O Lord God, whom I have made my confidence and refuge, reward Trifina for her compassion to me, and preserving my chastity.

12 Upon this there was a great noise in the amphitheatre; the beasts roared, and the people cried out, Bring in the criminal.

13 But the women cried out, and said: Let the whole city suffer for such crimes; and order all of us, O governor, to the same punishment. O unjust judgment! O cruel sight!

14 Others said, Let the whole city be destroyed for this vile action. Kill us all, O governor. O cruel sight! O unrighteous judgment.

CHAPTER IX.

1 Thecla thrown naked to the wild beasts;
2 but they all refuse to attack her.
8 She baptizes herself in a pit of water.
10 Other wild beasts refuse to injure her.
11 Tied to wild bulls.
13 Miraculously saved.
21. Released.
24 Entertained by Trifina,

THEN Thecla was taken out of the hand of Trifina, stripped naked, had a girdle put on, and thrown into the place appointed for fighting with the beasts: and the lions and the bears were let loose upon her.

THE ACTS OF ST. PAUL AND THECLA.

2 But a she-lion, which was of all the most fierce, ran to Thecla, and fell down at her feet. Upon which the multitude of women shouted aloud.

3 Then a she-bear ran fiercely towards her, but the she lion met the bear, and tore it in pieces.

4 Again a he-lion, who had been wont to devour men, and which belonged to Alexander, ran towards her; but the she-lion encountered the he-lion, and they killed each other.

5 Then the women were under a greater concern, because the she-lion, which had helped Thecla, was dead.

6 Afterwards they brought out many other wild beasts; but Thecla stood with her hands stretched towards heaven, and prayed; and when she had done praying, she turned about, and saw a pit of water, and said, Now it is a proper time for me to be baptized.

7 Accordingly she threw herself into the water, and said, In thy name, O my Lord Jesus Christ, I am this last day baptized. The women and the people seeing this, cried out and said, Do not throw yourself into the water. And the governor himself cried out, to think that the fish (sea-calves) were like to devour so much beauty.

8 Notwithstanding all this, Thecla threw herself into the water, in the name of our Lord Jesus Christ.

9 But the fish (sea-calves) when they saw the lightning and fire, were killed, and swam dead upon the surface of the water, and a cloud of fire surrounded Thecla; so that as the beasts could not come near her, so the people could not see her nakedness.

10 Yet they turned other wild beasts upon her; upon which they made a very mournful outcry; and some of them scattered spikenard, others cassia, others amomus (a sort of spikenard, or the herb of Jerusalem, or ladies rose), others ointment; so that the quantity of ointment was large, in proportion to the number of people; and upon this all the beasts lay as though they had been fast asleep, and did not touch Thecla.

11 Whereupon Alexander said to the governor, I have some very terrible bulls; let us bind her to them. To which the governor, with concern, replied, You may do what you think fit.

12 Then they put a cord round Thecla's waist, which bound also her feet, and with it tied her to the bulls, to whose privy-parts they applied red-hot irons, that so they being the more tormented, might more violently drag Thecla about, till they had killed her.

13 The bulls accordingly tore about, making a most hideous noise; but the flame which was about Thecla, burnt off the cords which were

fastened to the members of the bulls, and she stood in the middle of the stage, as unconcerned as if she had not been bound.

14 But in the mean time Trifina, who sat upon one of the benches, fainted away and died; upon which the whole city was under a very great concern.

15 And Alexander himself was afraid, and desired the governor, saying: I entreat you, take compassion on me and the city, and release this woman, who has fought with the beasts; lest both you and I, and the whole city, be destroyed;

16 For if Caesar should have any account of what has passed now, he will certainly immediately destroy the city, because Trifina, a person of royal extract, and a relation of his, is dead upon her seat.

17 Upon this the governor called Thecla from among the beasts to him, and said to her, Who art thou? and what are thy circumstances, that not one of the beasts will touch thee?

18 Thecla replied to him; I am a servant of the living God; and as to my state, I am a believer on Jesus Christ his Son, in whom God is well pleased; and for that reason none of the beasts could touch me.

19 He alone is the way to eternal salvation, and the foundation of eternal life. He is a refuge to those who are in distress; a support to the afflicted, hope and defence to those who are hopeless; and in a word, all those who do not believe on him, shall not live, but suffer eternal death.

20 When the governor heard these things, he ordered her clothes to be brought, and said to her, Put on your clothes.

21 Thecla replied: May that God who clothed me when I was naked among the beasts, in the day of judgment clothe your soul with the robe of salvation. Then she took her clothes, and put them on; and the governor immediately published an order in these words: I release to you Thecla the servant of God.

22 Upon which the women cried out together with a loud voice, and with one accord gave praise unto God, and said; There is but one God, who is the God of Thecla; the one God who hath delivered Thecla.

23 So loud were their voices, that the whole city seemed to be shaken; and Trifina herself heard the glad tidings, and arose again, and ran with the multitude to meet Thecla; and embracing her, said: Now I believe there shall be a resurrection of the dead; now I am persuaded that my daughter is alive. Come therefore home with me, my daughter Thecla, and I will make all over that I have to you.

THE ACTS OF ST. PAUL AND THECLA.

24 So Thecla went with Trifina, and was entertained there a few days, teaching her the word of the Lord, whereby many young women were converted; and there was great joy in the family of Trifina.

25 But Thecla longed to see Paul, and inquired and sent every where to find him; and when at length she was informed that he was at Myra, in Lycia, she took with her many young men and women; and putting on a girdle, and dressing herself in the habit of a man, she went to him to Myra in Lycia, and there found Paul preaching the word of God; and she stood by him among the throng.

CHAPTER X.

1 Thecla visits Paul;
6 visits Onesiphorus;
8 and visits her Mother
9 who repulses her.
14 Is tempted by the devil.
16 Works miracles.

BUT it was no small surprise to Paul when he saw her and the people with her; for he imagined some fresh trial was coming upon them;

2 Which when Thecla perceived, she said to him: I have been baptized, O Paul; for he who assists you in preaching, has assisted me to baptize.

3 Then Paul took her, and led her to the house of Hermes; and Thecla related to Paul all that had befallen her in Antioch, insomuch that Paul exceedingly wondered, and all who heard were confirmed in the faith, and prayed for Trifina's happiness.

4 Then Thecla arose, and said to Paul, I am going to Iconium. Paul replied to her: Go and teach the word of the Lord.

5 But Trifina had sent large sums of money to Paul, and also clothing by the hands of Thecla, for the relief of the poor.

6 So Thecla went to Iconium. And when she came to the house of Onesiphorus, she fell down upon the floor where Paul had sat and preached, and, mixing tears with her prayers, she praised and glorified God in the following words:

7 O Lord the God of this house, in which I was first enlightened by thee; O Jesus, son of the living God, who wast my helper before the governor, my helper in the fire, and my helper among the beasts; thou alone art God for ever and ever, Amen.

ΔΙΔΑΧΗ ΤΩΝ ΔΩΔΕΚΑ ΑΠΟΣΤΟΛΩΝ

8 Thecla now (on her return) found Thamyris dead, but her mother living. So calling her mother, she said to her: Theoclia, my mother, is it possible for you to be brought to a belief, that there is but one Lord God, who dwells in the heavens? If you desire great riches, God will give them to you by me; if you want your daughter again, here I am.

9 These and many other things she represented to her mother, (endeavouring) to persuade her (to her own opinion). But her mother Theoclia gave no credit to the things which were said by the martyr Thecla.

10 So that Thecla perceiving, she discoursed to no purpose, signing her whole body with the sign (of the cross), left the house and went to Daphne; and when she came there, she went to the cave, where she had found Paul with Onesiphorus, and fell down upon the ground; and wept before God.

11 When she departed thence, she went to Seleucia, and enlightened many in the knowledge of Christ.

12 And a bright cloud conducted her in her journey.

13 And after she had arrived at Seleucia she went-to a place out of the city, about the distance of a furlong, being afraid of the inhabitants, because they were worshippers of idols.

14 And she was lead (by the cloud) into a mountain called Calamon, or Rodeon. There she abode many years, and underwent a great many grievous temptations of the devil, which she bore in a becoming manner, by the assistance which she had from Christ.

15 At length certain gentle-women hearing of the virgin Thecla, went to her, and were instructed by her in the oracles of God, and many of them abandoned this world, and led a monastic life with her.

16 Hereby a good report was spread everywhere of Thecla, and she wrought several (miraculous) cures, so that all the city and adjacent countries brought their sick to that mountain, and before they came as far as the door of the cave, they were instantly cured of whatsoever distemper they had.

17 The unclean spirits were cast out, making a noise; all received their sick made whole, and glorified God, who had bestowed such power on the virgin Thecla;

18 Insomuch that the physicians of Seleucia were now of no more account, and lost all the profit of their trade, because no one regarded them; upon which they were filled with envy, and began to contrive what methods to take with this servant of Christ.

THE ACTS OF ST. PAUL AND THECLA.

CHAPTER XI.

**1 Thecla is attempted to be ravished,
12 escapes by a rock opening,
17 and closing miraculously.**

THE devil then suggested bad advice to their minds; and being on a certain day met together to consult, they reasoned among each other thus: The virgin is a priestess of the great goddess Diana, and whatsoever she requests from her, is granted, because she is a virgin, and so is beloved by all the gods.

2 Now then let us procure some rakish fellows, and after we have made them sufficiently drunk, and given them a good sum of money, let us order them to go and debauch this virgin, promising them, if they do it, a larger reward.

3 (For they thus concluded among themselves, that if they be able to debauch her, the gods will no more regard her nor Diana cure the sick for her).

4 They proceeded according to this resolution, and the fellows went to the mountain, and as fierce as lions to the cave, knocking at the door.

5 The holy martyr Thecla relying upon the God in whom she believed, opened the door, although she was before apprised of their design, and said to them, Young men, what is your business?

6 They replied, Is there any one within, whose name is Thecla? She answered, What would you have with her? They said, We have a mind to lie with her.

7 The blessed Thecla answered, Though I am a mean old woman, I am the servant of my Lord Jesus Christ; and though you have a vile design against me, ye shall not be able to accomplish it. They replied, Is it impossible? but we must be able to do with you what we have a mind,

8 And while they were saying this, they laid hold on her by main force, and would have ravished her. Then she with the (greatest) mildness said to them: Young men have patience, and see the glory of the Lord.

9 And while they held her, she looked up to heaven and said: O God most reverend, to whom none can be likened; who makest thyself glorious over thine enemies; who didst deliver me from the fire, didst not give me up to Thamyris, and didst not give me up to Alexander: who deliveredst me from the wild beasts; who didst preserve me in the

deep waters; who hast everywhere been my helper, and hast glorified thy name in me;

10 Now also deliver me from the hands of these wicked and unreasonable men nor suffer them to debauch my chastity which I have hitherto preserved for thy honour; for I love thee, and long for thee, and worship thee, O Father, Son, and Holy Ghost, for evermore. Amen.

11 Then came a voice from heaven, saying, Fear not Thecla, my faithful servant, for I am with thee. Look and see the place which is opened for thee; there thy eternal abode shall be; there thou shalt receive the (beatific) vision.

12 The blessed Thecla observing, saw the rock opened to as large a degree as that a man might enter in; she did as she was commanded, bravely fled from the vile crew, and went into the rock, which instantly so closed, that there was not any crack visible where it had opened.

13 The men stood perfectly astonished at so prodigious a miracle, and had no power to detain the servant of God; but only catching hold of her veil (or hood), they tore off a piece of it;

14 And even that was by the permission of God, for the confirmation of their faith, who should come to see this venerable place; and to convey blessings to those in succeeding ages, who should believe on our Lord Jesus Christ from a pure heart.

15 Thus suffered that first martyr and apostle of God, and virgin, Thecla, who came from Iconium at eighteen years of age; afterwards, partly in journeys and travels, and partly in a monastic life in the cave, she lived seventy- two years; so that she was ninety years old when the Lord translated her.

16 Thus ends her life.

17 The day which is kept sacred to her memory, is the twenty-fourth of September, to the glory of the Father, and the Son, and the Holy Ghost, now and for evermore. Amen.

REFERENCES TO THE ACTS OF ST. PAUL AND THECLA.

[Tertullian says that this piece was forged by a Presbyter of Asia, who being convicted, "confessed that he did it out of respect to Paul," and Pope Gelasius, in his Decree against apocryphal books, inserted it among them. Notwithstanding this, a large part of the history was credited and looked upon as genuine among the primitive Christians. Cyprian, Eusebius, Epiphanius, Austin, Gregory, Nagianzen. Chrysostom, and Severus Sulpitius, who all lived within the fourth century mention Thecla or refer to her history. Basil of Seleucia wrote her acts, sufferings and victories, in verse; and Euagrius Scholasticus an eccle-

THE ACTS OF ST. PAUL AND THECLA.

siastical historian, about 590, relates that "after the Emperor Zeno, had abdicated his empire, and Basilik had taken possession of it, he had a vision of the holy and excellent martyr Thecla, who promised him the restoration of his empire; for which, when it was brought about, he erected and dedicated a most noble and sumptuous temple to this famous martyr, Thecla, at Seleucia, a city of Isauria, and bestowed upon it very noble endowments, which (says the author) are preserved even till this day." Hist. Ecel. lib. 3 cap. 8.—Cardinal Barenius, Locrinus, Archbishop Wake, and others; and also the learned Grabe, who edited the Septuagint, and revived the Acts of Paul and Thecla, consider them as having been written in the Apostolic age; as containing nothing superstitious, or disagreeing from the opinions and belief of those times; and, in short, as a genuine and authentic history. Again, it is said, that this is not the original book of the early Christians; but however that may be, it is published from the Greek MS. in the Bodleian Library at Oxford, which Dr. Mills copied and transmitted to Dr. Grabe.]

THE FIRST EPISTLE OF CLEMENT TO THE CORINTHIANS.

CHAPTER I.

Clement commends them for their excellent order and piety in Christ, before their schism broke out.

THE Church of God which is at Rome, to the Church of God which is at Corinth, elect, sanctified by the will of God, through Jesus Christ our Lord: grace and peace from the Almighty God, by Jesus Christ, be multiplied unto you.

2 Brethren, the sudden and unexpected dangers and calamities that have fallen upon us, have, we fear, made us the more slow in our consideration of those things which you inquired of us:

3 As also of that wicked and detestable sedition, so unbecoming the elect of God, which a few headstrong and self-willed men have fomented to such a degree of madness, that your venerable and renowned name, so worthy of all men to be beloved, is greatly blasphemed thereby.

4 For who that has ever been among you has not experienced the firmness of your faith, and its fruitfulness in all good works; and admired the temper and moderation of your religion in Christ; and published abroad the magnificence of your hospitality; and thought you happy in your perfect and certain knowledge of the Gospel?

5 For ye did all things without respect of persons, and walked according to the laws of God; being subject to those who had the rule over you, and giving the honour that was fitting to the aged among you.

6 Ye commanded the young men to think those things that were modest and grave.

7 The women ye exhorted to do all things with an unblameable, and seemly, and pure conscience; loving their own husbands, as was fitting: and that keeping themselves within the bounds of a due obedience, they should order their houses gravely, with all discretion.

8 Ye were all of you humble- minded, not boasting of anything desiring rather to be subject than to govern; to give than to receive; being a content with the portion God hath dispensed to you:

9 And hearkening diligently to his word, ye were enlarged in your bowels, having his sufferings always before your eyes.

10 Thus a firm, and blessed, and profitable peace was given unto you: and an unsatiable desire of doing good; and a plentiful effusion of the Holy Ghost was upon all of you.

11 And being full of good designs, ye did with, great readiness of mind, and with a religious confidence stretch forth your hands to God Almighty; beseeching him to be merciful unto you, if in anything ye had unwillingly sinned against him.

12 Ye contended day and night for the whole brotherhood; that with compassion and a good conscience, the number of his elect might be saved.

13 Ye were sincere, and without offence towards each other; not mindful of injuries; all sedition and schism was an abomination unto you.

14 Ye bewailed every one his neighbours' sins, esteeming their defects your own.

15 Ye were kind one to another without grudging; being ready to every good work. And being adorned with a conversation altogether virtuous and religious, ye did all things in the fear of God; whose I commandments were written upon the tables of your heart.

CHAPTER II.

How their divisions began.

ALL honour and enlargement was given unto you; and so was fulfilled that which is written, my beloved did eat and drink, he was enlarged and waxed fat, and he kicked.

2 From hence came emulation, and envy, and strife, and sedition; persecution and disorder, war and captivity.

ΔΙΔΑΧΗ ΤΩΝ ΔΩΔΕΚΑ ΑΠΟΣΤΟΛΩΝ

3 So they who were of no renown, lifted up themselves against the honourable; those of no reputation against those who were in respect; the foolish against the wise; the young men against the aged.

4 Therefore righteousness and peace are departed from you, because every one hath forsaken the fear of God; and is grown blind in his faith; nor walketh by the rule of God's commandments nor liveth as is fitting in Christ:

5 But every one follows his own wicked lusts: having taken up an unjust and wicked envy, by which death first entered into the world.

CHAPTER III.

Envy and emulation the original of all strife and disorder. Examples of the mischiefs they have occasioned.

FOR thus it is written, And in process of time it came to pass, that Cain brought of the fruit of the ground an offering unto the Lord. And Abel, he also brought of the firstlings of his flock, and of the fat thereof:

2 And the Lord had respect unto Abel, and to his offering. But unto Cain and unto his offering he had not respect. And Cain was very sorrowful, and his countenance fell.

3 And the Lord said unto Cain, Why art thou sorrowful? And why is thy countenance fallen? If thou shalt offer aright, but not divide aright, hast thou not sinned? Hold thy peace: unto thee shall be his desire, and thou shalt rule over him.

4 And Cain said unto Abel his brother, Let us go down into the field. And it came to pass, as they were in the field, that Cain rose up against Abel his brother, and slew him.

5 Ye see, brethren, how envy and emulation wrought the death of a brother. For this, our father Jacob fled from the face of his brother Esau.

6 It was this that caused Joseph to be persecuted even unto death, and to come into bondage. Envy forced Moses to flee from the face of Pharoah king of Egypt, when he heard his own countryman ask him, "Who made thee a Judge, and a ruler over us? Wilt thou kill me as thou didst the Egyptian yesterday?"

7 Through envy Aaron and Miriam were shut out of the camp, from the rest of the congregation seven days.

8 Emulation's sent Dathan and Abiram quick into the grave because they raised up a sedition against Moses the servant of God.

9 For this, David was not only hated of strangers, but was persecuted even by Saul the king of Israel.

10 But not to insist upon ancient examples, let us come to those worthies that have been nearest to us; and take the brave examples of our own age.

11 Through zeal and envy, the most faithful and righteous pillars of the church have been persecuted even to the most grievous deaths.

12 Let us set before our eyes, the holy Apostles; Peter by unjust envy underwent not one or two, but many sufferings; till at last being martyred, he went to the place of glory that was due unto him.

13 For the same cause did Paul in like manner receive the reward of his patience. Seven times he was in bonds; he was whipped, was stoned; he preached both in the East and in the West; leaving behind him the glorious report of his faith:

14 And so having taught the whole world righteousness, and for that end travelled even to the utmost bounds of the West; he at last suffered martyrdom by the command of the governors,

15 And departed out of the world, and went unto his holy place; having become a most eminent pattern of patience unto all ages.

16 To these Holy Apostles were joined a very great number of others, who having through envy undergone in like manner many pains and torments, have left a glorious example to us.

17 For this, not only men but women have been persecuted; and having suffered very grievous and cruel punishments, have finished the course of their faith with firmness; and though weak in body, yet received a glorious reward.

18 This has alienated the minds even of women from their husbands; and changed what was once said by our father Adam; This is now bone of my bones, and flesh of my flesh.

19 In a word, envy and strife, have overturned whole cities, and rooted out great nations from off the earth.

CHAPTER IV.

4 He exhorts them to live by holy rules, and repent of their divisions, and they shall be forgiven.

THESE things, beloved, we write unto you, not only for your instruction, but also for our own remembrance.

2 For we are all in the same lists, and the same combat is prepared for us all.

ΔΙΔΑΧΗ ΤΩΝ ΔΩΔΕΚΑ ΑΠΟΣΤΟΛΩΝ

3 Wherefore let us lay aside all vain and empty cares; and let us come up to the glorious and venerable rule of our holy calling.

4 Let us consider what is good, and acceptable and well-pleasing in the sight of him that made us.

5 Let us look steadfastly to the blood of Christ, and see how precious his blood is in the sight of God: which being shed for our salvation, has obtained the grace of repentance for all the world.

6 Let us search into all the ages that have gone before us; and learn that our Lord has in every one of them still given place for repentance to all such as would turn to him.

7 Noah preached repentance; and as many as hearkened to him were saved. Jonah denounced destruction against the Ninevites.

8 Howbeit they repenting of their sins, appeased God by their prayers: and were saved, though they were strangers to the covenant of God.

9 Hence we find how all the ministers of the grace of God have spoken by the Holy Spirit of repentance. And even the Lord of all, has himself declared with an oath concerning it;

10 As I live, saith the Lord, I desire not the death of a sinner, but that he should repent. Adding farther this good sentence, saying Turn from your iniquity, O house of Israel.

11 Say unto the children of my people, though your sins should reach from earth to heaven; and though they shall be redder than scarlet, and blacker than sackcloth yet if ye shall turn to me with all your heart, and shall call me father, I will hearken to you, as to a holy people.

12 And in another place he saith on this wise: wash ye, make you clean; put away the evil of your doings from before mine eyes; cease to do evil, learn to do well; seek judgment, relieve the oppressed, judge the fatherless, plead for the widow.

13 Come now and let us reason together, saith the Lord: though your sins be as scarlet, they shall be as white as snow; though they be as red as crimson, they shall be as wool.

14 If ye be willing and obedient ye shall eat the good of the land but, if ye refuse and rebel, ye shall be devoured with the sword; for the mouth of the Lord hath spoken it.

15 These things has God established by his Almighty will, desiring that all his beloved should come to repentance.

THE FIRST EPISTLE OF CLEMENT TO THE CORINTHIANS.

CHAPTER V.

1 He sets before them the examples of holy men, whose piety is recorded in the Scripture.

WHEREFORE let us obey his excellent and glorious will; and imploring his mercy and goodness, let us fall down upon our faces before him, and cast ourselves upon his mercy; laying aside all vanity, and contention, and envy which leads unto death.

2 Let us look up to those who have the most perfectly ministered to his excellent glory. Let us take Enoch for our example; who being found righteous in obedience, was translated, and his death was not known.

3 Noah being proved to be faithful, did by his ministry, preach regeneration to the world; and the Lord saved by him all the living creatures, that went with one accord into the ark.

4 Abraham, who was called God's friend, was in like manner found faithful; inasmuch as he obeyed the commands of God.

5 By obedience he went out of his own country, and from his own kindred, and from his father's house; that so forsaking a small country, and a weak affinity, and a little house, he might inherit the promises of God.

6 For thus God said unto him; "get thee out of thy country, and from thy kindred, and from thy father's house, unto a land that I will show thee."

7 "And, I will make thee a great nation, and will bless thee, and make thy name great, and thou shalt be blessed. And I will bless them that bless thee, and curse them that curse thee; and in thee shall all families of the earth be blessed,"

8 And again when he separated himself from Lot, God said unto him; I Lift up now thine eyes, and look from the place where thou art northward, and southward, and eastward, and westward, for all the land which thou seest, to thee will I give it, and to thy seed for ever.

9 And I will make thy seed as the dust of the earth, so that if a man can number the dust of the earth, then shall thy seed also be numbered.

10 And again he saith: and God brought forth Abraham, and said unto him; look now toward heaven, and tell the stars, if thou be able to number them: so shall thy seed be.

11 And Abraham believed God, and it was counted to him for righteousness.

ΔΙΔΑΧΗ ΤΩΝ ΔΩΔΕΚΑ ΑΠΟΣΤΟΛΩΝ

12 Through faith and hospitality he had a son given him in his old age; and through obedience he offered him up in sacrifice to God, upon one of the mountains which God showed into him.

CHAPTER VI.

1 Redemption for such as have been eminent for their faith, kindness, and charity to their neighbours.

BY hospitality and goodliness was Lot saved out of Sodom, when all the country round about was destroyed by fire and brimstone.

2 The Lord thereby making it manifest, that he will not forsake those that trust in him; but will bring the disobedient to punishment and correction.

3 For his wife who went out with him, being of a different mind, and not continuing in the same obedience, was for that reason set forth for an example, being turned into a pillar of salt unto this day.

4 That so all men may know, that those who are double minded, and distrustful of the power of God, are prepared for condemnation, and to be a sign to all succeeding ages.

5 By faith and hospitality was Rahab the harlot saved. For when the spies were sent by Joshua the son of Nun to search out Jericho, and the king of Jericho knew that they were come to spy out his country, he sent men to take them, so that they might be put to death.

6 Rahab therefore, being hospitable, received them, and hid them under the stalks of flax, on the top of her house.

7 And when the messengers that were sent by the king came unto her, and asked her, saying, There came men unto thee to spy out the land, bring them forth, for so hath the king commanded: She answered, The two men whom ye seek came unto me, but presently they departed, and are gone: Not discovering them unto them.

8 Then she said to the spies, I know that the Lord your God has given this city into your hands; for the fear of you is fallen upon all that dwell therein. When, therefore, ye shall have taken it, ye shall save me and my father's house.

9 And they answered her, saying, It shall be as thou hast spoken unto us, Therefore, when thou shalt know that we are near, thou shalt gather all thy family together, upon the house-top and they shall be saved: but all that shall be found without thy house shall be destroyed.

10 And they gave her moreover a sign, that she should hang out of her house a scarlet rope, showing thereby, that by the blood of our

THE FIRST EPISTLE OF CLEMENT TO THE CORINTHIANS.

Lord, there should be redemption to all that believe and hope in God. Ye see, beloved, how there was not only faith, but prophesy too in this woman.

CHAPTER VII.

1 What rules are given for leading a holy life.

LET us, therefore, humble ourselves, brethren, laying aside all pride, and boasting, and foolishness, and anger: And let us do as it is written.

2 For thus saith the Holy Spirit; Let not the wise man glory in his wisdom, nor the strong man in his strength, nor the rich man in his riches; but let him that glorieth, glory in the Lord, to seek him, and to do judgment and justice.

3 Above all, remembering the words of the Lord Jesus, which he spake concerning equity and long suffering, saying,

4 Be ye merciful, and ye shall obtain mercy; forgive, and ye shall be forgiven; as ye do, so shall it be done unto you; as ye give, so shall it be given unto you; as ye judge, so shall ye be judged; as ye are kind to others, so shall God be kind to you; with what measure ye mete, with the same shall it be measured to you again.

5 By this command, and by these rules, let us establish ourselves, that so we may always walk obediently to his holy words; being humble minded:

6 For so says the Holy Scripture; upon whom shall I look, even upon him that is poor and of a contrite spirit, and that trembles at my word.

7 It is, therefore, just and righteous, men and brethren, that we should become obedient unto God, rather than follow such as through pride and sedition, have made themselves the ring-leaders of a detestable emulation.

8 For it is not an ordinary harm that we shall do ourselves, but rather a very great danger that we shall run, if we shall rashly give up ourselves to the wills of men, who promote strife and seditions, to turn us aside from that which is fitting.

9 But let us be kind to one another, according to the compassion and sweetness of him that made us.

10 For it is written, The merciful shall inherit the earth; and they that are without evil shall be left upon it: but the transgressors shall perish from off the face of it.

ΔΙΔΑΧΗ ΤΩΝ ΔΩΔΕΚΑ ΑΠΟΣΤΟΛΩΝ

11 And again he saith, I have seen the wicked in great power and spreading himself like the cedar of Libanus. I passed by, and lo! he was not; I sought his place, but it could not be found.

12 Keep innocently, and do the thing that is right, for there shall be a remnant to the peaceable man.

13 Let us, therefore, hold fast to those who religiously follow peace; and not to such as only pretend to desire.

14 For he saith in a certain place, This people honoureth me with their lips, but their heart is far from me.

15 And again, They bless with their mouths, but curse in their hearts.

16 And again he saith, They loved him with their mouths, and with their tongues they lied to him. For their heart was not right with him, neither were they faithful in his covenant.

17 Let all deceitful lips become dumb, and the tongue that speaketh proud things. Who have said, with our tongue will we prevail; our lips are our own, who is Lord over us?

18 For the oppression of the poor, for the sighing of the needy, now will I arise saith the Lord; I will set him in safety, I will deal confidently with him.

CHAPTER VIII.

He advises then, to be humble, and, follow the examples of Jesus, and of holy men in all ages.

FOR Christ is theirs who are humble, and not who exalt themselves over his flock. The sceptre of the majesty of God, our Lord Jesus Christ, came not in the show of pride and arrogance, though he could have done so; but with humility as the Holy Ghost had before spoken concerning him.

2 For thus he saith, Lord, who hath believed our report, and to whom is the arm of the Lord revealed; For he shall grow up before him as a tender plant, and as a root out of a dry ground;

3 He hath no form or comeliness, and when we shall see him, there is no beauty that we should desire him.

4 He is despised and rejected of men; a man of sorrows and acquainted with grief.

5 And we hid, as it were, our faces from him; he was despised, and we esteemed him not.

THE FIRST EPISTLE OF CLEMENT TO THE CORINTHIANS.

6 Surely he hath borne our griefs, and carried our sorrows yet we did esteem him stricken, smitten of God, and afflicted.

7 But he was wounded for our transgressions; he was bruised for our iniquities; the chastisement of our peace was upon him; and with his stripes we are healed.

8 All we like sheep have gone astray; we have turned every one to his own way; and the Lord hath laid on him the iniquity of us all.

9 He was oppressed, and he was afflicted, yet he opened not his mouth: he is brought as a lamb to the slaughter; and as a sheep before her shearers is dumb, so he openeth not his mouth.

10 He was taken from prison and from judgment; and who shall declare this generation? For he was cut off out of the land of the living: for the transgression of my people was he stricken.

11 And he made his grave with the wicked, and with the rich in his death; because he had done no violence, neither was any deceit in his mouth.

12 Yet it pleased the Lord to bruise him; he hath put him to grief: when thou shalt make his soul an offering for sin, he shall see his seed, he shall prolong his days, and the pleasure of the Lord shall prosper in his hand.

13 He shall see of the travail of his soul, and shall be satisfied: by his knowledge shall my righteous servant justify many; for he shall bear their iniquities.

14 Therefore will I divide him a portion with the great, and he shall divide the spoil with the strong; because he hath poured out his soul unto death; and he was numbered with the transgressors, and he bare the sin of many, and made intercession for the transgressors.

15 And again he himself saith, I am a worm and no man, a reproach of men, and despised of the people. All they that see me laugh me to scorn; they shoot out their lips, they shake their heads, saying; He trusted in the Lord that he would deliver him, let him deliver him seeing he delighted in him.

16 Ye see, beloved, what the pattern is that has been given to us. For if the Lord thus humbled himself, what should we do who are brought by him under the yoke of his grace?

17 Let us be followers of those who went about in goat-skins, and sheep-skins; preaching the coming of Christ.

18 Such were Elias, and Eliaxus, and Ezekiel, the prophets, And let us add to these, such others as have received the like testimony.

ΔΙΔΑΧΗ ΤΩΝ ΔΩΔΕΚΑ ΑΠΟΣΤΟΛΩΝ

19 Abraham has been greatly witnessed of; having been called the friend of God. And yet he steadfastly beholding the glory of God, says with all humility, I am dust and ashes.

20 Again of Job, it is thus written, That he was just, and without blame, true; one that served God, and abstained from all evil. Yet he accusing himself, said, No man is free from pollution, no, not though he should live but one day.

21 Moses was called faithful in all God's House; and by his conduct the Lord punished Israel by stripes and plagues.

22 And even this man, though thus greatly honoured, spake not greatly of himself; but when the oracle of God was delivered to him out of the bush, he said, Who am I, that thou dost send me? I am of a slender voice, and a slow tongue.

23 And again he saith, I am as the smoke of the pot.

24 And what shall we say of David, so highly testified of in the Holy Scriptures? To whom God said, I have found a man after my own heart, David the son of Jesse, with my holy oil have I anointed him.

25 But yet he himself saith unto God, Have mercy upon me, O God, according to thy loving kindness; according unto the multitude of thy tender mercies, blot out my transgressions.

26 Wash me thoroughly from mine iniquity, and cleanse me from my sin. For I acknowledge my transgressions, and my sin is ever before me.

27 Against Thee only have I sinned, and done this evil in thy sight; that thou mightest be justified when thou speakest; and be clear when thou judgest.

28 Behold I was shapen in iniquity, and in sin did my mother conceive me.

29 Behold, thou desirest truth in the inward parts; and in the hidden part thou shalt make me to know wisdom.

30 Purge me with hyssop, and I shall be clean: wash me, and I shall be whiter than snow.

31 Make me to hear joy and gladness, that the bones which thou hast broken may rejoice.

32 Hide thy face from my sins, and blot out all mine iniquities. Create in me a clean heart O God; and renew a right spirit within me.

34 Cast me not away from thy presence, and take not thy holy spirit from me.

35 Restore unto me the joy of thy salvation, and uphold me with thy free spirit.

36 Then will I teach transgressors thy ways, and sinners shall be converted unto thee.
37 Deliver me from blood-guiltiness, O God, thou God of my salvation; and my tongue shall sing aloud of thy righteousness.
38 O Lord open thou my lips, and my mouth shall show forth thy praise.
39 For thou desirest not sacrifice, else would I give it; thou delightest not in burnt-offerings.
40 The sacrifices of God are a broken spirit; a broken and a contrite heart, O God, thou wilt not despise.

CHAPTER IX.

He again persuades them to compose their divisions.

THUS has the humility and godly fear of these great and excellent men recorded in the Scriptures, through obedience, made not only us, but also the generations before us better; even as many as have received his holy oracles with fear and truth.
2 Having therefore so many, and such great and glorious examples, let us return to that peace which was the mark that from the beginning was set before us;
3 Let us look up to the Father and Creator of the whole world; and let us hold fast to his glorious and exceeding gifts and benefits of peace.
4 Let us consider and behold with the eyes of our understanding his long suffering will; and think how gentle and patient he is towards his whole creation.
5 The heavens moving by his appointment, are subject to him in peace.
6 Day and night accomplish the courses that he has allotted unto them, not disturbing one another.
7 The sun and moon, and all the several companies and constellations of the stars, run the courses that he has appointed to them in concord, without departing in the least from them.
8 The fruitful earth yields its food plentifully in due season both to man and beast, and to all animals that are upon it, according to his will; not disputing, nor altering any thing of what was ordered by him.
9 So also the unfathomable and unsearchable floods of the deep, are kept in by his command;

ΔΙΔΑΧΗ ΤΩΝ ΔΩΔΕΚΑ ΑΠΟΣΤΟΛΩΝ

10 And the conflux of the vast sea, being brought together by his order into its several collections, passes not the bounds that he has set to it;

11 But as he appointed it, so it remains. For he said, Hitherto shalt then come, and thy floods shall be broken within thee.

12 The ocean impassable to mankind, and the worlds that are beyond it are governed by the same commands of their great master.

13 Spring and summer, autumn and winter, give place peaceably to each other.

14 The several quarters of the winds fulfil their work in their seasons, without offending one another.

15 The ever-flowing fountains, made both for pleasure and health, never fail to reach out their breasts to support the life of men.

16 Even the smallest creatures live together in peace and concord with each other.

17 All these has the Great Creator and Lord of all, commanded to observe peace and concord; being good to all.

18 But especially to us who flee to his mercy through our Lord Jesus Christ; to whom be glory and majesty for ever and ever. Amen.

CHAPTER X.

He exhorts them to obedience, from the consideration of the goodness of God, and of his presence in every place.

TAKE heed, beloved, that his many blessings be not to our condemnation; except we shall walk worthy of him, doing with one consent what is good and pleasing in his sight.

2 The spirit of the Lord is a candle, searching out the inward parts of the belly.

3 Let us therefore consider how near he is to us; and how that none of our thoughts, or reasonings which we frame within ourselves, are hid from him,

4 It is therefore just that we should not forsake our rank, by doing contrary to his will.

5 Let us choose to offend a few foolish and inconsiderate men, lifted up and glorying in their own pride, rather than God.

6 Let us reverence our Lord Jesus Christ whose blood was given for us.

7 Let us honour those who are set over us; let us respect the aged that are amongst us; and let us instruct the younger men, in the discipline and fear of the LORD.

8 Our wives let us direct, to do that which is good.

9 Let them show forth a lovely habit of purity, in all their conversation; with a sincere affection of meekness.

10 Let the government of their tongues be made manifest by their silence.

11 Let their charity be without respect of persons, alike towards all such as religiously fear God.

12 Let your children be bred up in the instruction of Christ:

13 And especially let them learn how great a power humility has with God; how much a pure and holy charity avails with him; how excellent and great his fear is; and how it will save all such as turn to him with holiness in a pure mind.

14 For he is the searcher of the thoughts and counsels of the heart; whose breath is in us, and when he pleases he can take it from us.

CHAPTER. XI.

Of faith: and particularly what we are to believe as to the Resurrection.

BUT all these things must be confirmed by the faith which is in Christ; for so He himself bespeaks us by the Holy Ghost;

2 Come ye children and hearken unto me, and I will teach you the fear of the Lord. What man is there that desireth life, and loveth to see good days?

3 Keep thy tongue from evil, and thy lips that they speak no guile.

4 Depart from evil and do good; seek peace and pursue it.

5 The eyes of the Lord are upon the righteous, and his ears are open unto their prayers.

6 But the face of the Lord is against them that do evil, to cut off the remembrance of them from the earth.

7 The righteous cried, and the Lord heard him, and delivered him out of all his troubles.

8 Many are the troubles of the wicked; but they that trust in the Lord mercy shall encompass them about.

9 Our all-merciful and beneficent Father hath bowels of compassion towards them that fear him: and kindly and lovingly bestows his graces upon all such as come to him with a simple mind.

ΔΙΔΑΧΗ ΤΩΝ ΔΩΔΕΚΑ ΑΠΟΣΤΟΛΩΝ

10 Wherefore let us not waver, neither let us have any doubt in our hearts, of his excellent and glorious gifts.

11 Let that be far from us which is written, Miserable are the double-minded, and those who are doubtful in their hearts;

12 Who say these things have we heard, and our fathers have told us these things. But behold we are grown old, and none of them has happened unto us.

13 O ye fools consider the trees: take the vine for an example. First it sheds its leaves; then it buds; after that it spreads its leaves; then it flowers; then come the sour grapes; and after them follows the ripe fruit. See now in a little time the fruit of the trees comes to maturity.

14 Of a truth yet a little while and his will shall suddenly be accomplished.

15 The Holy Scripture itself bearing witness, that He shall quickly come and not tardy, and that the Lord shall suddenly come to his temple, even the 3 holy ones whom ye look for.

16 Let us consider, beloved, how the Lord does continually show us, that there shall be a future resurrection; of which he has made our Lord Jesus Christ the first fruits, raising him from the dead.

17 Let us contemplate, beloved, the resurrection that is continually made before our eyes.

18 Day and night manifest a resurrection to us. The night lies down, and the day arises: again the day departs and the night comes on.

19 Let us behold the fruits of the earth. Every one sees how the seed is sown. The sower goes forth, and casts it upon the earth; and the seed which when it was sown fell upon the earth dry and naked, in time dissolves.

20 And from the dissolution, the great power of the providence of the Lord rises it again; and of one seed many arise, and bring forth fruit.

CHAPTER XII.

The Resurrection further proved.

LET us consider that wonderful type of the resurrection which is seen in the Eastern countries: that is to say, in Arabia.

2 There is a certain bird called a Phoenix; of this there is never but one at a time: and that lives five hundred years. And when the time of its dissolution draws near, that it must die, it makes itself a nest of

frankincense, and myrrh, and other spices into which when its time is fulfilled it enters and dies.

3 But its flesh putrefying, breeds a certain worm, which being nourished with the juice of the dead bird brings forth feathers; and when it is grown to a perfect state, it takes up the nest in which the bones of its parent lie, and carries it from Arabia into Egypt, to a city called Heliopolis:

4 And flying in open day in the sight of all men, lays it upon the altar of the sun, and so returns from whence it came.

5 The priests then search into the records of the time: and find that it returned precisely at the end of five hundred years.

6 And shall we then think it to be any very great and strange thing for the Lord of all to raise up those that religiously serve him in the assurance of a good faith, when even by a bird he shows us the greatness of his power to fulfil his promise?

7 For he says in a certain place, Thou shalt raise me up and I shall confess unto thee.

8 And again, I laid me down and slept, and awaked, because thou art with me.

9 And again, Job says, Thou shalt raise up this flesh of mine, that has suffered all these things.

10 Having therefore this hope, let us hold fast to him who is faithful in all his promises, and righteous in all his judgments; who has commanded us not to lie, how much more will he not himself lie?

11 For nothing is impossible with God but to lie.

12 Let his faith then be stirred up again in us; and let us consider that all things are nigh unto him.

13 By the word of his power he made all things: and by the same word he is able, (whenever he will,) to destroy them.

14 Who shall say unto him, what dost thou? or who shall resist the power of his strength?

15 When, and as he pleased, he will do all things; and nothing shall pass away of all that has been determined by him.

16 All things are open before him; nor can anything be hid from his counsel.

17 The heavens declare the glory of God, and the firmament showeth his handy work. Day unto day uttereth speech, and night unto night showeth knowledge. There is no speech nor language where their voice is not heard.

ΔΙΔΑΧΗ ΤΩΝ ΔΩΔΕΚΑ ΑΠΟΣΤΟΛΩΝ

CHAPTER XIII.

It is impossible to escape the vengeance of God, if we continue in sin.

SEEING then all things are seen and heard by God, let us fear him, and let us lay aside our wicked works which proceed from ill desires; that through his mercy we may be delivered from the condemnation to come.

2 For whither can any of us flee from his mighty hand? Or what world shall receive any of those who run away from him?

3 For thus saith the Scripture in a certain place. Whither shall I flee from thy spirit, or where shall I hide myself from thy presence?

4 If I ascend up into heaven, thou art there; if I shall go to the uttermost parts of the earth, there is thy right hand: if I shall make my bed in the deep, thy Spirit is there.

5 Whither then shall any one go; or whither shall he run from him that comprehends all things?

6 Let us therefore come to him with holiness of heart, lifting up chaste and undefiled hands unto him; loving our gracious and merciful Father, who has made us to partake of his election.

7 For so it is written, When the Most High divided the nations; when he separated the sons of Adam, he set the bounds of the nations, according to the number of his angels; his people Jacob became the portion of the Lord, and Israel the lot of his inheritance.

8 And in another place he saith, Behold the Lord taketh unto himself a nation, out of the midst of the nations, as a man taketh the firstfruits of his flour; and the Most Holy shall come out of that nation.

CHAPTER XIV.

How we must live that we may please God.

WHEREFORE we being apart of the Holy One: let us do all those things that pertain unto holiness:

2 Fleeing all evil-speaking against one another; all filthy and impure embraces, together with all drunkenness, youthful lusts, abominable concupiscences, detestable adultery, and execrable pride.

3 For God saith, he resisteth the proud, but giveth grace to the humble.

THE FIRST EPISTLE OF CLEMENT TO THE CORINTHIANS.

4 Let us therefore hold fast to those to whom God has given his grace.

5 And let us put on concord, being humble, temperate; free from all whispering and detraction; and justified by our actions, not our words.

6 For he saith, Doth he that speaketh and heareth many things, and is of a ready tongue, suppose that he is righteous? Blessed is he that is born of a woman, that liveth but a few days: use not therefore much speech.

7 Let our praise be of God, not of ourselves; for God hateth those that commend themselves.

8 Let the witness of our good actions be given to us by others, as it was given to the holy men that went before us.

9 Rashness, and arrogance, and confidence, belong to them who are accursed of God: but equity, and humility, and mildness, to such as are blessed by him.

10 Let us then lay hold of his blessing, and let as consider what are the ways by which we may attain unto it.

11 Let us look back upon those things that have happened from the beginning.

12 For what was our Father Abraham blessed? Was it not because that through faith he wrought righteousness and truth?

13 Isaac being fully persuaded of what he knew was to come, cheerfully yielded himself up for a sacrifice. Jacob with humility departed out of his own country, fleeing from his brother, and went unto Laban and served him; and so the sceptre of the twelve tribes of Israel was given unto him.

14 Now what the greatness of this gift was, will plainly appear, if we shall take the pains distinctly to consider all the parts of it.

15 For, from him came the priests and Levites; who all ministered at the altar of God.

16 From him came our Lord Jesus Christ, according to the flesh.

17 From him came the kings, and princes, and rulers in Judah.

18 Nor were the rest of his tribes in any little glory: God having promised that their seed shall be as the stars of heaven.

19 They were all therefore greatly glorified, not for their own sake, or for their own works, or for the righteousness that they themselves wrought, but through his will.

20 And we also being called by the same will in Christ Jesus, are not justified by ourselves, neither by our own wisdom, or knowledge, or piety, or the works which we have done in the holiness of our hearts.

ΔΙΔΑΧΗ ΤΩΝ ΔΩΔΕΚΑ ΑΠΟΣΤΟΛΩΝ

21 But by that faith, by which God Almighty has justified all men from the beginning; to whom be glory for ever and ever, Amen.

CHAPTER XV.

We are justified by faith; yet this must not lessen our care to live a virtuous life, nor our pleasure in it.

WHAT shall we do therefore, brethren? Shall we be slothful in well-doing, and lay aside our charity? God forbid that any such thing should be done by us.

2 But rather let us hasten with all earnestness and readiness of mind, to perfect every good work. For even the Creator and Lord of all things himself rejoices in his own works.

3 By his Almighty power he fixed the heavens, and by his incomprehensible wisdom he adorned them.

4 He also divided the earth from the water, with which it is encompassed: and fixed it as a secure tower, upon the foundation of his own will.

5 He also by his appointment, commanded all the living creatures that are upon it, to exist.

6 So likewise the sea, and all the creatures that are in it; having first created them, he enclosed them therein by his power.

7 And above all, he with his holy and pure hands, formed man, the most excellent; and, as to his understanding, truly the greatest of all other creatures; the character of his own image.

8 For thus God says; Let us make man in our image, after our own likeness; so God created man, male and female created he them.

9 And having thus finished all these things, he commended all that he had made, and blessed them, and said, increase and multiply.

10 We see how all righteous men have been adorned with good works Wherefore even the Lord himself, having adorned himself with his works, rejoiced.

11 Having therefore such an example, let us without delay, fulfil his will; and with all our strength, work the work of righteousness.

CHAPTER XVI.

A virtuous life enforced from the examples of the holy angels, and from the exceeding greatness of that reward which God has prepared for us.

THE good workman with confidence receives the bread of his labour; but the sluggish and lazy cannot look him in the face that set him on work.

2 We must therefore be ready and forward in well-doing: for from him are all things.

3 And thus he foretells us, behold the Lord cometh, and his reward is with him, even before his face, to render to everyone according to his work.

4 He warns us therefore beforehand, with all his heart to this end, that we should not be slothful and negligent in well-doing.

5 Let our boasting, therefore, and our confidence be in God let us submit ourselves to his will, Let us consider the whole multitude of his angels, how ready they stand to minister unto his will.

6 As saith the Scripture, thousands of thousands stood before him and ten thousand times ten thousand ministered unto him. And they cried, saying, Holy, holy, holy is the Lord of hosts; The whole earth is full of his glory.

7 Wherefore let us also, being conscientiously gathered together in concord with one another; as it were with one mouth, cry, earnestly unto him, that he would make us partakers of his great and glorious promises.

8 For he saith, a Eye hath not seen, nor ear heard, neither have entered into the heart of man, the things which God has prepared for them that wait for him,

ΔΙΔΑΧΗ ΤΩΝ ΔΩΔΕΚΑ ΑΠΟΣΤΟΛΩΝ

CHAPTER XVII.

1 We must attain the gifts of God by faith and obedience, which we must carry on in an orderly pursuing of the duties of our several stations, without envy or contention.
24 The necessity of different orders among men.
33 We have none of us anything but what we received of God: whom therefore we ought in every condition thankfully to obey.

HOW blessed and wonderful, beloved, are the gifts of God.

2 Life in immortality! brightness in righteousness! truth in full assurance! faith in confidence! temperance in holiness!

3 And all this has God subjected to our understandings:

4 What therefore shall those things be which he has prepared for them that wait for him?

5 The Creator and Father of spirits, the Most Holy; he only knows both the greatness and beauty of them,

6 Let us therefore strive with all earnestness, that we may be found in the number of those that wait for him, that so we may receive the reward which he has promised.

7 But how, beloved, shall we do this? We must fix our minds by faith towards God, and seek those things that are pleasing and acceptable unto him.

8 We must act conformably to his holy will; and follow the way of truth, casting off from us all unrighteousness and iniquity, together with all covetousness, strife, evil manners, deceit, whispering, detractions; all hatred of God, pride and boasting; vain-glory and ambition;

9 For they that do these things are odious to God; and not only they that do them, but also all such as approve of those that do them.

10 For thus saith the Scripture, But unto the wicked, God said, What hast thou to do to declare my statute, or that thou shouldst take my covenant in thy mouth? Seeing that thou hatest instruction, and castest my words behind thee.

11 When thou sawest a thief, then thou consentedst with him; thou hast been partaker with adulterers, Thou givest thy mouth to evil, and thy tongue frameth deceit. Thou sittest and speakest against thy brother; thou slanderest thine own mother's son.

THE FIRST EPISTLE OF CLEMENT TO THE CORINTHIANS.

12 These things hast thou done and I kept silence; thou thoughtest that I was altogether such a one as thyself: but I will reprove thee, and set them in order before thine eyes.

13 Now consider this ye that forget God, lest I tear you in pieces, and there be none to deliver.

14 Whose offereth praise, glorifieth me; And to him that disposeth his way aright, will I show the salvation of God.

15 This is the way, beloved, in which we may find our Saviour, even Jesus Christ, the high-priest of all our offerings, the defender and helper of our weakness.

16 By him we look up to the highest heavens; and behold, as in a glass, his spotless and most excellent visage.

17 By him are the eyes of our hearts opened; by him our foolish and darkened understanding rejoiceth to behold his wonderful light.

18 By him would God have us to taste the knowledge of immortality: who being the brightness of his glory, is by so much greater than the angels, as he has by inheritance obtained a more excellent name than they.

19 For so it is written, who maketh his angels spirits, and his ministers a flame of fire:

20 But to his son, thus saith the Lord, Thou art my Son, to-day have I begotten thee.

21 Ask of me and I will give thee the heathen for thy inheritance, and the utmost parts of the earth for thy possession.

22 And again he saith unto him, Sit thou on my right hand until I make thine enemies thy foot-stool.

23 But who are his enemies? even the wicked, and such who oppose their own wills to the will of God.

24 Let us therefore march-on, men and brethren, with all earnestness in his holy laws.

25 Let us consider those who fight under our, earthly governors How orderly, how readily, and with what exact obedience they perform those things that are commanded them.

26 All are not generals, nor colonels, nor captains, nor inferior officers:

27 But everyone in his respective rank does what is commanded him by the king, and those who have the authority over him.

28 They who are great, cannot subsist without those that are little; nor the little without the great;

29 But there must be a mixture in all things, and then there will be use and profit too.

ΔΙΔΑΧΗ ΤΩΝ ΔΩΔΕΚΑ ΑΠΟΣΤΟΛΩΝ

30 Let us, for example, take our body: the head without the feet is nothing, neither the feet without the head.

31 And even the smallest members of our body are yet both necessary and useful to the whole body.

32 But all conspire together, and are subject to one common use, namely, the preservation of the whole body.

33 Let therefore our whole body by saved in Christ Jesus; and let everyone be subject to his neighbour, according to the order in which he is placed by the gift of God.

34 Let not the strong man despise the weak; and let the weak see that he reverence the strong.

35 Let the rich man distribute to the necessity of the poor; and let the poor bless God, that he has given one unto him, by whom his want may be supplied.

36 Let the wise man show forth his wisdom, not in words, but in good works.

37 Let him that is humble, not bear witness to himself, but let him leave it to another to bear witness of him.

38 Let him that is pure in the flesh, not grow proud of it, knowing that it was from another that he received the gift of continence.

39 Let us consider therefore, brethren, whereof we are made; who, and what kind of men we came into the world, as it were cut of a sepulchre, and from outer darkness.

40 He hath made us, and formed us, brought us into his own world; having presented us with his benefits, even before we were born.

41 Wherefore, having received all these things from him, we ought in everything to give thanks unto him, to whom be glory for ever and ever. Amen.

CHAPTER XVIII.

Clement therefore exhorts them to do everything orderly in the Church, as the only way to please God.

FOOLISH and unwise men, who have neither prudence, nor learning, may mock and deride us; being willing to set up themselves in their own conceits.

2 But what can a mortal man do? Or what strength is there in him that is made out of the dust?

3 For it is written, there was no shape before mine eyes; only I heard a sound and a voice.

THE FIRST EPISTLE OF CLEMENT TO THE CORINTHIANS.

4 For what? Shall man be pure before the Lord? Shall he be blameless in his works?

5 Behold, he trusteth not in his servants; and his angels he chargeth with folly.

6 Yes, the heaven is not clean in his sight, how much less they that dwell in houses of clay; of which also we ourselves were made?

7 He smote them as a moth: and from morning even unto the evening they endure not. Because they were not able to help themselves, they perished; he breathed upon them and they died, because they had no wisdom.

8 Call now if there be any that will answer thee; and to which of the angels wilt thou look?

9 For wrath killeth the foolish man, and envy slayeth him that is in error.

10 I have seen the foolish taking root, but lo, their habitation was presently consumed.

11 Their children were far from safety, they perished at the gates of those who were lesser than themselves: and there was no man to help them.

12 For what was prepared for them, the righteous did eat; and they shall not be delivered from evil.

13 Seeing then these things are manifest unto us, it will behove us to take care that looking into the depths of the divine knowledge, we do all things in order, whatsoever our Lord has commanded us to do.

14 And particularly that we perform our offerings and service to God, at their appointed seasons for these he has commanded to be done, not rashly and disorderly, but at certain determinate times and hours.

15 And therefore he has ordained by his supreme will and authority, both where, and by what persons, they are to be performed; that so all things being piously done unto all well-pleasing, they may be acceptable unto him.

16 They therefore who make their offerings at the appointed seasons, are happy and accepted; because through obeying the commandments of the Lord, they are free from sin.

17 And the same care must be had of the persons that minister unto him.

18 For the chief-priest has his proper services; and to the priest their proper place is appointed; and to the Levites appertain their proper ministries; and the layman is confined within the bounds of what is commanded to laymen.

ΔΙΔΑΧΗ ΤΩΝ ΔΩΔΕΚΑ ΑΠΟΣΤΟΛΩΝ

19 Let every one of you therefore, brethren, bless God in his proper station, with a good conscience, and with all gravity, not exceeding the rule of his service that is appointed to him.

20 The daily sacrifices are not offered everywhere; nor the peace-offerings, nor the sacrifices appointed for sins and transgressions; but only at Jerusalem: nor in any place there, but only at the altar before the temple; that which is offered being first diligently examined by the high-priest and the other minister we before mentioned.

21 They therefore who do any thing which is not agreeable to his will, are punished with death.

22 Consider, brethren, that by how much the better knowledge God has vouchsafed unto us, by so much the greater danger are we exposed to.

CHAPTER XIX.

The orders of Ministers in Christ's Church established by the Apostles, according to Christ's command,
7 after the example of Moses.
16 Therefore they who have been duly placed in the ministry according to their order, cannot without great sin be put out of it.

THE Apostles have preached to us from the Lord Jesus Christ Jesus Christ from God.

2 Christ therefore was sent by God, the Apostles by Christ; so both were orderly sent, according to the will of God.

3 For having received their command, and being thoroughly assured by the resurrection of our Lord Jesus Christ, and convinced by the word of God, with the fulness of the Holy Spirit, they went abroad, publishing, That the kingdom of God was at hand.

4 And thus preaching through countries and cities, they appointed the first fruits of their conversion to be bishops and ministers over such as should afterwards believe, having first proved them by the Spirit.

5 Nor was this any new thing; seeing that long before it was written concerning bishops and deacons.

6 For thus saith the Scripture, in a certain place; I will appoint their overseers in righteousness, and their ministers in faith.

THE FIRST EPISTLE OF CLEMENT TO THE CORINTHIANS.

7 And what wonder if they, to whom such a work was committed by God in Christ, established such officers as we before mentioned; when even that blessed and faithful servant in all his house, Moses, set down in the Holy Scriptures all things that were commanded him.

8 Whom also all the rest of the prophets followed, bearing witness with one consent to those things that were appointed by him.

9 For he, perceiving an emulation to arise among the tribes concerning the priesthood, and that there was a strife about it, which of them should be adorned with that glorious name; commanded their twelve captains to bring to him twelve rods; every tribe being written upon its rod, according to its name,

10 And he took them and bound them together, and sealed them with the seals of the twelve princes of the tribes: and laid them up in the tabernacle of witness, upon the table of God.

11 And when he had shut the door of the tabernacle, he sealed up the keys of it, in like manner as he had done the rods; and said unto them, Men and brethren, whichsoever tribe shall have its rod blossom, that tribe has God chosen to perform the office of a priest, and to minister unto him in holy things.

12 And when the morning was come, he called together all Israel, six hundred thousand men; and showed to the princes their seals and opened the tabernacle of witness; and brought forth the rods.

13 And the rod of Aaron was found not only to have blossomed, but also to have fruit upon it.

14 What think you, beloved? Did not Moses before know what should happen?

15 Yes verily: but to the end there might be no division, nor tumult in Israel, he did in this manner, that the name of the true and only God might be glorified; to whom be honour for ever and ever, Amen.

16 So likewise our Apostles knew by our Lord Jesus Christ, that there should contentions arise, upon account of the ministry.

17 And therefore having a perfect fore-knowledge of this, they appointed persons, as we have before said, and then a gave direction, how, when they should die, other chosen and approved men should succeed in their ministry.

18 Wherefore we cannot think that those may justly be thrown out of their ministry, who were either appointed by them, or afterwards chosen by other eminent men, with the consent of the whole church; and who have with all lowliness and innocency ministered to the flock of Church, in peace, and without self-interest, and were for a long time commended by all.

19 For it would be no small sin in us, should we cast off those from their ministry, who holily and without blame fulfil the duties of it.

20 Blessed are those priests, who having finished their course before these times, have obtained a fruitful and perfect dissolution for they have no fear, lest any one should turn them out of the place which is now appointed for them.

21 But we see how you have put out some, who lived reputably among you, from the ministry, which by their innocence they had adorned.

CHAPTER XX.

He exerts them to peace from examples out of the Holy Scriptures,
20 particularly from St. Paul's exhortation to them.

YE are contentious, brethren, and zealous for things that pertain not unto salvation.

2 Look into the Holy Scriptures, which are the true words of the Holy Ghost. Ye know that there is nothing unjust or counterfeit written in them.

3 There you shall not find that righteous men were ever cast off by such as were good themselves.

4 They were persecuted, but it was by the wicked and unjust.

5 They were cast into prison, but they were cast in by those that were unholy.

6 They were stoned, but it was by transgressors.

7 They were killed, but by accursed men, and such as had taken up an unjust envy against them.

8 And all these things they underwent gloriously.

9 For what shall we say, brethren? Was Daniel cast into the den of lions, by men fearing God? Shadrach, Meshach, and Abednego, were they cast into the fiery furnace by men, professing the excellent and glorious worship of the Most High? God forbid.

10 What kind of persons then were they that did these things? They were men abominable, full of all wickedness; who were incensed; to so great a degree, as to bring those into sufferings, who with a holy and unblameable purpose of mind worshipped God: not knowing that the Most High is the protector and defender of all such as with a pure conscience serve his holy name: to whom be glory for ever and ever, Amen.

THE FIRST EPISTLE OF CLEMENT TO THE CORINTHIANS.

11 But they who with a full persuasion have endured these things, are made partakers of glory and honour: and are exalted and lifted up by God for a memorial throughout all ages, Amen.

12 Wherefore it will behove us also, brethren, to follow such examples as these; for it is written, Hold fast to such as are holy; for they that do so shall be sanctified.

13 And again in another place he saith, With the pure, thou shalt be pure (and with the elect thou shalt be elect,) but with, the perverse man thou shalt be perverse.

14 Let us therefore join ourselves to the innocent and righteous; for such are the elect of God.

15 Wherefore are there strifes, and anger, and divisions, and schisms, and wars, among us?

16 Have we not all one God, and one Christ? Is not one spirit of grace poured out upon us all? Have we not one calling in Christ.

17 Why then do we rent and tear in pieces the members of Christ; and raise seditious against our own body? And are come to such a height of madness, as to forget that we were members one of another?

18 Remember the words of our Lord Jesus, (how he said, Woe to that man by whom offences come). It, were better for him that he had never been born, than that he should have offended one of my elect. It were better for him, that a mill-stone should be tied about his neck, and he should be cast into the sea, than that he should offend one of my little ones.

19 Your schism has perverted many, has discouraged many: it has caused diffidence in many, and grief in us all. And yet your sedition continues still.

20 Take the Epistle of the blessed Paul the Apostle into your hands; What was It that he wrote to you at his first preaching the Gospel among you?

21 Verily he did by the spirit admonish you concerning himself, and Cephas, and Apollos, because that even then ye had begun to fall into parties and factions among yourselves.

22 Nevertheless your partiality then led you into a much less sin forasmuch as ye placed your affections upon Apostles, men of eminent reputation in the church; and upon another, who was greatly tried and approved of by them.

23 But consider, we pray you, who are they that have now led you astray; and lessened the reputation of that brotherly love that was so eminent among you;

ΔΙΔΑΧΗ ΤΩΝ ΔΩΔΕΚΑ ΑΠΟΣΤΟΛΩΝ

24 It is a shame, my beloved, yea, a very great shame, and unworthy of your Christian profession, to hear that the most firm and ancient church of the Corinthians should, by one or two persons, be led into a sedition against its priests.

25 And this report is come not only to us, but to those also that differ from us.

26 Insomuch that the name of the Lord is blasphemed through your folly; and even ye yourselves are brought into danger by it.

27 Let us therefore with all haste put an end to this sedition; and let us fall down before the Lord, and beseech him with tears that he would be favourably reconciled to us, and restore us again to a seemly and holy course of brotherly love.

28 For this is the gate of righteousness, opening unto life: As it is written, I Open unto me the gates of righteousness; I will go into them and will praise the Lord. This is the gate of the Lord, the righteous shall enter into it.

29 Although therefore many gates are opened, yet this gate of righteousness is that gate in Christ at which blessed are they that enter in, and direct their way in holiness and righteousness; doing all things without disorder.

30 Let a man be faithful, let him be powerful in the utterance of knowledge; let him be wise in making an exact judgment of words; let him be pure in all his actions.

31 But still by how much the more he seems to be above others, by reason of these things, by so much the more will it behove him to be humble-minded; and to seek what is profitable to all men, and not his own advantage.

CHAPTER XXI.

1 The value which God, puts upon love and unity: the effects of a true charity,
8 which is the gift of God, and must be obtained by prayer.

HE that has the love that is in Christ, let him keep the commandments of Christ.

2 For who is able to express the obligation of the love of God? What man is sufficient to declare, and is fitting, the excellency of its beauty?

3 The height to which charity leads, is inexpressible.

THE FIRST EPISTLE OF CLEMENT TO THE CORINTHIANS.

4 Charity unites us to God; charity covers the multitude of sins: charity endures all things; is long-suffering in all things.

5 There is nothing base and sordid in charity: charity lifts not itself up above others; admits of no divisions; is not seditious; but does all things in peace and concord.

6 By charity were all the elect of God made perfect: Without it nothing is pleasing and acceptable in the sight of God.

7 Through charity did the Lord join us into himself; whilst for the love that he bore towards us, our Lord Jesus Christ gave his own blood for us, by the will of God; his flesh for our flesh; his soul for our souls.

8 Ye see, beloved, how great and wonderful a thing charity is; and how that no expressions are sufficient to declare its perfection.

9 But who is fit to be found in it? Even such only as God shall vouchsafe to make so.

10 Let us therefore pray to him, and beseech him, that we may be worthy of it; that so we may live in charity; being unblameable, without human propensities, without respect of persons.

11 All the ages of the world, from Adam, even unto this day, are passed away; but they who have been made perfect in love, have by the grace of God obtained a place among the righteous; and shall be made manifest in the judgment of the kingdom of Christ.

12 For it is written, Enter into thy chambers for a little space, till my anger and indignation shall pass away: And I will remember the good day, and, will raise you up out of your graves.

13 Happy then shall we be, beloved, if we shall have fulfilled the commandments of God, in the unity of love; that so, through love, our sins may be forgiven us.

14 For so it is written, Blessed are they whose iniquities are forgiven, and whose sins are covered. Blessed is the man to whom the Lord imputeth no sin, and in whose mouth there is no guile.

15 Now this blessing is fulfilled in those who are chosen by God through Jesus Christ our Lord, to whom be glory for ever and ever, Amen.

ΔΙΔΑΧΗ ΤΩΝ ΔΩΔΕΚΑ ΑΠΟΣΤΟΛΩΝ

CHAPTER XXII.

1 He exhorts such as have been concerned in these divisions to repent, and return to their unity, confessing their sin to God,
7 which he enforces from the example of Moses,
10 and of many among the heathen,
23 and of Judith and Esther among the Jews.

LET us therefore, as many as have transgressed by any of the suggestions of the adversary, beg God's forgiveness.

2 And as for those who have been the heads of the sedition and faction among you, let them look to the common end of our hope.

3 For as many as are endued with fear and charity, would rather they themselves should fall into trials than their neighbours: And choose to be themselves condemned, rather than that the good and just charity delivered to us, should suffer.

4 For it is seemly for a man to confess wherein he has transgressed.

5 And not to harden his heart, as the hearts of those were hardened, who raised up sedition against Moses the servant of God whose punishment was manifest unto all men, for they went down alive into the grave; death swallowed them up.

6 Pharaoh and his host, and all the rulers of Egypt, their chariots also and their horsemen, were for no other cause drowned in the bottom of the Red Sea, and perished; but because they hardened their foolish hearts, after so many signs done in the land of Egypt, by Moses the servant of God.

7 Beloved, God is not indigent of anything; nor does he demand anything of us, but that we should confess our sins unto him.

8 For so says the Holy David, I will confess unto the Lord, and it shall please him better than a young bullock that hath horns and hoof. Let the poor see it and be glad.

9 And again he saith, Offer unto God the sacrifice of praise, and pay thy vows unto the Most Highest. And call upon me in the day of trouble, and I will deliver thee, and thou shalt glorify me. The sacrifice of God is a broken spirit.

10 Ye know, beloved, ye know full well, the Holy Scriptures; and have thoroughly searched into the oracles of God: call them therefore to your remembrance.

THE FIRST EPISTLE OF CLEMENT TO THE CORINTHIANS.

11 For when Moses went up into the mount, and tarried there forty days and forty nights in fasting and humiliation; God said unto him, Arise, Moses, and get thee down quickly from hence, for thy people whom thou broughtest out of the land of Egypt, have committed wickedness: they have soon transgressed the way that I commanded them, and have made to themselves graven images.

12 And the Lord said unto him, I have spoken unto thee several times, saying, I have seen this people, and behold it is a stiff- necked people: let me therefore destroy them, and put out their name from under heaven. And I will make unto thee a great and a wonderful nation, that shall be much larger than this.

13 But Moses said, Not so, Lord: Forgive now this people their sin; or if thou wilt not, blot me also out of the book of the living. O admirable charity! O insuperable perfection! The servant speaks freely to his Lord: He beseeches him either to forgive the people, or to destroy him together with them.

14 Who is there among you that is generous? Who that is compassionate? Who that has any charity? Let him say, if this sedition, this contention, and these schisms, be upon my account, I am ready to depart; to go away whithersoever you please; and do whatsoever ye shall command me: Only let the flock of Christ be in peace, with the elders that are set over it.

15 He that shall do this, shall get to himself a very great honour in the Lord; and there is no place but what will be ready to receive him: For the earth is the Lord's, and the fulness thereof.

16 These things, they who have their conversation towards God not to be repented of, both have done, and will always be ready to do.

17 Nay and even the Gentiles themselves have given us examples of this kind.

18 For we read, How many kings and princes, in times of pestilence, being warned by their oracles, have given up themselves unto death; that by their own blood, they might deliver their country from destruction.

19 Others have forsaken their cities, so that they might put an end to the seditions of them.

20 We know how many among ourselves, have given up themselves unto bonds, that thereby they might free others from them.

21 Others have sold themselves into bondage, that they might feed their brethren with the price of themselves.

22 And even many women, being strengthened by the grace of God, have done many glorious and manly things on such occasions.

ΔΙΔΑΧΗ ΤΩΝ ΔΩΔΕΚΑ ΑΠΟΣΤΟΛΩΝ

23 The blessed Judith, when her city was besieged, desired the elders, that they would suffer her to go into the camp of their enemies; and she went out exposing herself to danger, for the love she bare to her country and her people that were besieged: and the Lord delivered Holofernes into the hands of a woman.

24 Nor did Esther, being perfect in faith, expose herself to any less hazard, for the delivery of the twelve tribes of Israel, in danger of being destroyed. For by fasting and humbling herself, she entreated the Great Maker of all things, the God of spirits; so that beholding the humility of her soul, he delivered the people, for whose sake she was in peril.

CHAPTER XXIII.

The benefit of mutual advice and correction. He entreats them to follow that which is here given to them.

WHEREFORE let us also pray for such as are fallen into sin. That being endued with humility and moderation, they may submit not unto us, but to the wish of God.

2 For by this means they shall obtain a fruitful and perfect remembrance, with mercy, both in our prayers to God, and in our mention of them before his saints.

3 Let us receive correction, at which no man ought to repine.

4 Beloved, the reproof and the correction which we exercise towards one another, is good, and exceeding profitable: for it unites us the more closely to the will of God.

5 For, so says the Holy Scripture, The Lord corrected me, but he did not deliver me over unto death. For whom the Lord loveth he chasteneth, and scourgeth every son whom he receiveth.

6 The righteous, saith he, shall instruct me in mercy and reprove me; but let not oil of sinners make fat my head.

7 And again he saith, Happy is the man whom God correcteth; therefore despise not thou the chastening of the Almighty.

8 For he maketh gore and bindeth up; he woundeth and his hands make whole.

9 He shall deliver thee in six troubles; yea in seven there shall no evil touch thee. In famine he shall redeem thee from death; and in war from the power of the sword.

10 Thou shalt be hid from the scourge of the tongue; neither shalt thou be afraid of destruction when it cometh.

11 Thou shalt laugh at the wicked and sinners; neither shalt thou be afraid of the beasts of the earth. The wild beast shall be at peace with thee.

12 Then shalt thou know that thy house shall be in peace; and the habitation of thy tabernacle shall not err. Then shalt know also that thy seed shall be great and thy offspring as the grass of the earth.

13 Thou shalt come to thy grave as the ripe corn, that is taken in due time: like as a shock of corn cometh in, in its season.

14 Ye see, beloved, how there shall be a defence to those that are corrected of the Lord. For being a good instructor, he is willing to admonish us by his holy discipline.

15 Do ye therefore who laid the first foundation of this sedition, submit yourselves unto your priests; and be instructed unto repentance, bending the knees of your hearts.

16 Learn to be subject, laying aside all proud and arrogant boasting of your tongues.

17 For it is better for you to be found little, and approved, in the sheepfold of Christ, than to seem to yourselves better than others, and be cast out of his fold.

18 For thus speaks the excellent and all-virtuous wisdom, Behold I will pour out the word of my spirit upon you, I will make known my speech unto you.

19 Because I called and ye would not hear, I stretched out my hand and ye regarded not.

20 But ye have set at nought all my counsel, and would none of my reproof. I will also laugh at your calamity, and mock when your fear cometh.

21 When your fear cometh as desolation, and your destruction as a whirlwind, when distress and anguish cometh upon you.

22 Then shall ye call upon me but I will not hear you: the wicked shall seek me but they shall not find me. For that they hated knowledge, and did not seek the fear of the Lord.

23 They would not hearken unto my counsel: they despised all my reproof. Therefore shall they eat of the fruit of their own ways; and be filled with their own wickedness.

ΔΙΔΑΧΗ ΤΩΝ ΔΩΔΕΚΑ ΑΠΟΣΤΟΛΩΝ

CHAPTER XXIV.

1 Recommends them to God. Desires speedily to hear that this Epistle has had a good effect upon them. 4 Conclusion.

NOW God, the inspector of all things, the Father of Spirits, and the Lord of all flesh, who hath chosen our Lord Jesus Christ, and us by him, to be his peculiar people;

2 Grant to every soul of man that calleth upon his glorious and holy name, faith, fear, peace, long-suffering, patience, temperance, holiness and sobriety, unto all well-pleasing in his sight; through our High-Priest and Protector Jesus Christ, by whom be glory and majesty, and power, and honour unto him now and for ever more, Amen.

3 The messengers whom we have sent unto you, Claudius, Ephebus, and Valerios Bito, with Fortunatus, send back to us again with all speed, in peace and with joy, that they may the sooner acquaint us with your peace and concord, so much prayed for and desired by us: and that we may rejoice in your good order.

4 The grace of our Lord Jesus Christ be with you, and with all that are any where called by God through him: To whom be honour and glory, and might and majesty, and eternal dominion, by Christ Jesus, from everlasting to everlasting, Amen.

REFERENCES TO CLEMENT'S FIRST EPISTLE TO THE CORINTHIANS.

[Clement was a disciple of Peter, and afterwards Bishop of Rome. Clemens Alexandrinus calls him an apostle. Jerome says he was an apostolic man, and Rafinus that he was almost an apostle. Eusebius calls this the wonderful Epistle of St. Clement, and says that it was publicly read in the assemblies of the primitive church. It is included in one of the ancient collections of the Canon Scripture. Its genuineness has been much questioned, particularly by Photius, patriarch of Constantinople in the ninth century, who objects that Clement speaks of worlds beyond the ocean: that he has not written worthily of the divinity of Christ; and that to prove the possibility of a future resurrection, he introduces the fabulous story of the phoenix's revival from its own ashes. To the latter objection, Archbishop Wake replies that the generality of the ancient Fathers have made use of the same instance in proof of the same point; and asks, if St. Clement really believed that there was such a bird, and that it did revive out of the cinders of the body after burning, where was the great harm either in giving credit to

THE FIRST EPISTLE OF CLEMENT TO THE CORINTHIANS.

such a wonder, or, believing it, to make rich a use as he here does of it?—The present is the Archbishop's translation from the ancient Greek copy of the Epistle, which is at the end of the celebrated Alexandrine MS. of the Septuagint and New Testament, presented by Cyril, patriarch of Alexandria, to King Charles the First, now in the British Museum. The Archbishop, in prefacing his translation, esteems it a great blessing that this "Epistle" was at last so happily found out, for the increase and confirmation both of our faith and our charity.]

THE SECOND EPISTLE OF CLEMENT TO THE CORINTHIANS

CHAPTER I.

That we ought to value our salvation; and to show that we do by a sincere obedience.

BRETHREN, we ought so to think of Jesus Christ as of God: as of the judge of the living, and the dead; nor should we think any less of our salvation.

2 For if we think meanly of him, we shall hope only to receive some small things from him.

3 And if we do so, we shall sin; not considering from whence we have been called, and by whom, and to what place; and how much Jesus Christ vouchsafed to suffer for our sakes.

4 What recompense then shall we render unto him? Or what fruit that may be worthy of what he has given to us?

5 For indeed how great are those advantages which we owe to him in relation to our holiness? He has illuminated us; as a father, he has called us his children; he has saved us who were lost and undone.

6 What praise shall we give to him? Or what reward that may be answerable to those things which we have received.

7 We were defective in our understandings; worshipping stones, and wood; gold, and silver, and brass, the work of men's hands; and our whole life was nothing else but death.

8 Wherefore being encompassed with darkness, and having such a mist before our eyes, we have looked up, and through his will have laid aside the cloud wherewith we were surrounded.

9 For he had compassion upon us, and being moved in his bowels towards us, he saved us; having beheld in us much error, and destruction; and seeing that we had no hope of salvation, but only through him.

10 For he called us, who were not; and was pleased from nothing to give us being.

CHAPTER II.

1 That God had before prophesied by Isaiah, that the Gentiles should be saved;
8 And that this ought to engage, such especially to live well; without which they will still miscarry.

REJOICE, thou barren, that bearest not, break forth and cry thou that travailest not; for she that is desolate hath many more children than she that hath a husband.

2 In that saying, Rejoice thou barren that bearest not, he spake of us: for our church was barren before children were given unto it.

3 And again; when he said, Cry thou that travailest not: he implied thus much: That after the manner of a woman in travail, we should not cease to put up our prayers unto God abundantly.

4 And for what follows, because she that is desolate hath more children than she that hath a husband; it was therefore added, because our people which seemed to have been forsaken by God, now believing in him, are become more than they who seemed to have God.

5 And another Scripture saith, a I came not to call the righteous but sinners (to repentance). The meaning of which is this; that those who were lost must be saved:

6 For that is, indeed, truly great and wonderful, not to confirm those things that are yet standing, but those which are falling,

7 Even so did it seem good to Christ to save what was lost; and when he came into the world, he saved many, and called us who were already lost.

8 Seeing then he has showed so great mercy towards us; and chiefly for that we who are alive, do now no longer sacrifice to dead Gods, nor pay any worship to them, but have by him been brought to the knowledge of the Father of truth.

9 Whereby shall we show that we do indeed know him, and by not denying him by whom we have come to the knowledge of him.

ΔΙΔΑΧΗ ΤΩΝ ΔΩΔΕΚΑ ΑΠΟΣΤΟΛΩΝ

10 For even he himself saith, Whosoever shall confess me before men, him will I confess before my Father. This therefore is our reward, if we shall confess him by whom we have been saved.

11 But, wherein must we confess him?—Namely, in doing those things which he saith, and not disobeying his commandments by worshipping him not with our lips only, but with all our heart, and with all our mind. For he saith in Isaiah; This people honoureth me with their lips, but their heart is far from me.

12 Let us then not only call him Lord; for that will not save us. For he saith: Not everyone that saith unto me Lord, Lord, shall be saved, but he that doth righteousness.

13 Wherefore, brethren, let us confess him by our works; by loving one another; in not committing adultery, not speaking evil against each other, not envying one another; but by being temperate, merciful, good.

14 Let us also have a mutual sense of one another's sufferings; and not be covetous of money; but let us, by our good works, confess God, and not by those that are otherwise.

15 Also let us not fear men: but rather God. Wherefore, if we should do such wicked things, the Lord hath said; Though ye should be joined unto me, even in my very bosom, and not keep my commandments, I would cast you off, and say unto you; Depart from me; I know not whence you are, ye workers of iniquity.

CHAPTER III.

1 That, whilst we secure the other world, we need not fear what can befall its in this.
5 That, if we follow the interests of this present world, we cannot escape the punishment of the other.
10 Which ought to bring us to repentance and holiness,
14 and that presently: because in this world is the only time for repentance.

THEREFORE brethren, leaving willingly for conscience sake our sojourning in this world, let us do the will of him who has called us, and not fear to depart out of this world.

2 For the Lord saith, Ye shall be as sheep in the midst of wolves. Peter answered and said, What if the wolves shall tear in pieces the sheep? Jesus said unto Peter, Let not the sheep fear the wolves after

THE SECOND EPISTLE OF CLEMENT TO THE CORINTHIANS

death: And ye also fear not those that kill you, and after that have no more than they can do unto you; but fear him who after you are dead, has power to cast both soul and body into hell-fire.

3 For consider, brethren, that the sojourning of this flesh in the present world, is but little, and of a short continuance, but the promise of Christ is great and wonderful, even the rest of the kingdom that is to come, and of eternal life.

4 What then must we do that we may attain unto it?—We must order our conversation, holy and righteously, and look upon all the things of this world as none of ours, and not desire them. For, if we desire to possess them we fall from the way of righteousness.

5 For thus saith the Lord, No servant can serve two masters. If therefore we shall desire to serve God and Mammon, it will be without profit to us. For what will it profit, if one gain the whole world, and lose his own soul?

6 Now this world and that to come are two enemies. This speaketh of adultery and corruption, of covetousness and deceit; but that renounces these things.

7 We cannot, therefore, be the friends of both; but we must resolve by forsaking the one, to enjoy the other. And we think it is better to hate the present things, as little, short-lived, and corruptible; and to love those which are to come, which are truly good and incorruptible.

8 For, if we do the will of Christ, we shall find rest: but if not, nothing shall deliver us from eternal punishment if we shall disobey his commands. For even thus saith the Scripture in the prophet Ezekiel, If Noah, Job, and Daniel should rise up, they shall not deliver their children in captivity.

9 Wherefore, if such righteous men are not able by their righteousness to deliver their children; how can we hope to enter into the kingdom of God, except we keep our baptism holy and undefiled? Or who shall be our advocate, unless we shall be found to have done what is holy and just?

10 Let us, therefore, my brethren, contend with all earnestness, knowing that our combat is at hand; and that many go long voyages to encounter for a corruptible reward.

11 And yet all are not crowned, but they only that labour much, and strive gloriously. Let us, therefore, so contend, that we may all be crowned. Let us run in the straight road, the race that is incorruptible: and let us in great numbers pass unto it, and strive that we may receive the crown. But if we cannot all be crowned, let us come as near to it as we are able.

ΔΙΔΑΧΗ ΤΩΝ ΔΩΔΕΚΑ ΑΠΟΣΤΟΛΩΝ

12 Moreover, we must consider, that he who contends in a corruptible combat; if he be found doing anything that is not fair, is taken away and scourged, and cast out of the lists. What think ye then that he shall suffer, who does anything that is not fitting in the combat of immortality?

13 Thus speaks the prophet concerning those who keep not their seal; Their worm shall not die, and their, fire shall not be quenched; and they shall be for a spectacle unto all flesh.

14 Let us therefore repent, whilst we are yet upon the earth: for we are as clay in the hand of the artificer. For the potter if he make a vessel, and it be turned amiss in his hands, or broken, again forms it anew; but if he has gone so far as to throw it into the furnace of fire, he can no more bring any remedy to it.

15 So we, whilst we are in this world should repent with our whole heart for whatsoever evil we have done in the flesh; while we have yet the time of repentance, that we may be saved by the Lord.

16 For after we shall have departed out of this world, we shall no longer be able either to confess our sins or repent in the other.

17 Wherefore, brethren, let us, doing the will of the Father, and keeping our flesh pure, and observing the commandments of the Lord, lay hold on eternal life: for the Lord saith in the Gospel, If ye have not kept that which was little, who will give you that which is great?— For I say unto you, he that is faithful in that which is least, is faithful also in much.

18 This, therefore, is what he saith; keep your bodies pure, and your seal without spot, that ye may receive eternal life.

CHAPTER IV.

We shall rise, and be judged, in our bodies; therefore we must live well in them;
6 that we ought, for our own interest, to live well; though few seem to mind what, really is for their advantage;
10 and we should not deceive ourselves: seeing God will certainly judge us, and render to all of us according to our works.

AND let not any one among you say, that this very flesh is not judged, neither raised up. Consider, in what were you saved in what did you look up, if not whilst you were in the flesh?

2 We must, therefore, keep our flesh as the temple of God. For in like manner as ye were called in the flesh, ye shall also come to judgment in the flesh. Our one Lord Jesus Christ, who has saved us, being first a spirit, was made flesh, and so called us; even so we also shall in this flesh receive the reward.

3 Let us, therefore, love one another, that we may attain unto the kingdom of God. Whilst we have time to be healed, let us deliver up ourselves to God our physician, giving our reward unto him.

4 And what reward shall we give?—Repentance out of a pure heart. For he knows all things beforehand, and searches out our very hearts.

5 Let us, therefore, give praise unto him: not only with our mouths, but with all our souls; that he may receive us as children. For so the Lord hath said; They are my brethren, who do the will of my father.

6 Wherefore, my brethren, let us do the will of the Father, who hath called us, that we may live. Let us pursue virtue, and forsake wickedness, which leadeth us into sins; and let us flee all ungodliness, that evils overtake us not.

7 For, if we shall do our diligence to live well, peace shall follow us. And yet how hard is it to find a man that does this? For almost all are led by human fears, choosing rather the present enjoyments, than the future promise.

8 For they know not how great a torment the present enjoyments bring with them; nor what delights the future promise.

9 And if they themselves only did this, it might the more easily be endured; but now they go on to infect innocent souls with their evil doctrines; not knowing that both themselves, and those that hear them, shall receive a double condemnation.

10 Let us, therefore, serve God with a pure heart, and we shall be righteous: but if we shall not serve him, because we do not believe the promise of God, we shall be miserable.

11 For thus saith the prophet; Miserable are the double-minded, who doubt in their heart, and say, these things we have heard, even. in the time of our fathers, but we have seen none of them, though we have expected them from day to day.

12 O ye fools! compare yourselves to a tree; take the vine for an example. First it sheds its leaves, then it buds, then come the sour grapes, then the ripe fruit; even so my people has borne its disorders and afflictions, but shall hereafter receive good things.

13 Wherefore my brethren, let us not doubt in our minds, but let us expect with hope, that we may receive our reward; for he is faithful,

ΔΙΔΑΧΗ ΤΩΝ ΔΩΔΕΚΑ ΑΠΟΣΤΟΛΩΝ

who has promised that he will render to everyone a reward according to his works.

14 If, therefore, we shall do what is just in the sight of God we shall enter into his kingdom, and shall receive the promises; Which neither eye has seen, nor ear heard, nor have entered into the heart of man.

15 Wherefore let us every hour expect the kingdom of God in love and righteousness: because we know not the day of God's appearing.

CHAPTER V.

A FRAGMENT.

Man's immortal nature a type of the Lord's kingdom.

1 * * * For the Lord himself, being asked by a certain person, When his kingdom should come? answered, When two shall be one, and that which is without as that which is within; and the male with the female, neither male nor female.

2 Now two are one, when we speak the truth to each other, and there is (without hypocrisy) one seal in two bodies:

3 And that which is without as that which, is within;—He means this; he calls the soul that which is within, and the body that which is without. As therefore thy body appears, so let thy soul be seen by its good works.

4 And the male with, the female, neither Male nor female;—He means this; he calls our anger the male, our concupiscence the female.

5 When therefore a man is come to such a pass that he is subject neither to the one nor the other of these (both of which, through the prevalence of custom, and an evil education, cloud and darken the reason,)

6 But rather, having dispelled the mist arising from them, and being full of shame, shall by repentance have united both his soul and spirit in the obedience of reason; then, as Paul says, there is in us neither male nor female.

REFERENCE TO THE SECOND EPISTLE THE CORINTHIANS.

[Archbishop Wake is the translator of this Second Epistle, which he says was not of so great reputation among the primitive Fathers as the first. He defends it notwithstanding; and in answer to those who objected to Clement's First Epistle, that it did not duly honour the

THE SECOND EPISTLE OF CLEMENT TO THE CORINTHIANS

Trinity; the Archbishop refers to this as containing proof of the writer's fulness of belief on that point.]

THE GENERAL EPISTLE OF BARNABAS.

CHAPTER I.

Preface to the Epistle.

ALL happiness to you my sons and daughters, in the name of our Lord Jesus Christ, who loved us, in peace.

2 Having perceived abundance of knowledge of the great and excellent laws of God to be in you, I exceedingly rejoice in your blessed and admirable souls, because ye have so worthily received the grace which was grafted in you.

3 For which cause I am full of joy, hoping the rather to be saved; inasmuch as I truly see a spirit infused into you, from the pure fountain of God:

4 Having this persuasion, and being fully convinced thereof, because that since I have begun to speak unto you, I have had a more than ordinary good success in the way of the law of the Lord, which is in Christ,

5 For which cause brethren, I also think verily that I love you above my own soul; because that therein dwelleth the greatness of faith and charity, as also the hope of that life which is to come

6 Wherefore considering this, that if I shall take care to communicate to you a part of what I have received, it shall turn to my reward, that I have served such good souls. I gave diligence to write in a few words unto you; that together with your faith, your knowledge also may be perfect.

7 There are therefore three things ordained by the Lord; the hope of life, the beginning, and the completion of it.

8 For the Lord hath both declared unto us, by the prophets, those things that are past; and opened to us the beginnings of those that are to come.

9 Wherefore, it will behove us, as he has spoken, to come more holily, and nearer to his altar.

10 I therefore, not as a teacher but as one of you, will endeavour to lay before you a few things by which you may, on many accounts, become the more joyful.

CHAPTER II.

That God has abolished the legal sacrifices, to introduce the spiritual righteousness of the Gospel.

SEEING then the days are exceedingly evil, and the adversary has got the power of this present world we ought to give the more diligence to inquire into the righteous judgments of the Lord.

2 Now the assistants of our faith are fear and patience; our fellow-combatants, long suffering and continence.

3 Whilst these remain pure in what relates unto the Lord, wisdom, and understanding, and science, and knowledge, rejoice together with them.

4 For God has manifested to us by all the prophets, that he has no occasion for our sacrifices, or burnt-offerings, or oblations: saying thus; To what purpose is the multitude of your sacrifices unto me, saith the Lord.

5 I am full of the burnt-offerings of rams, and the fat of fed beasts; and I delight not in the blood of bullocks, or of he-goats.

6 When ye come to appear before me, who hath required this at your hands? Ye shall no more tread my courts.

7 Bring no more vain oblations, incense is an abomination unto me your new moons and sabbaths, and the calling of assemblies I cannot bear with, it is iniquity, even the solemn meeting; your new moons and your appointed feasts my soul hateth.

8 These things therefore hath God abolished, that the new law of our Lord Jesus Christ, which is without the yoke of any such necessity, might have the spiritual offering of, men themselves.

9 For so the Lord saith again to those heretofore; Did I at all command your fathers when they came out of the land of Egypt concerning burnt-offerings of sacrifices?

ΔΙΔΑΧΗ ΤΩΝ ΔΩΔΕΚΑ ΑΠΟΣΤΟΛΩΝ

10 But this I commanded them, saying, Let none of you imagine evil in your hearts against his neighbour, and love no false oath.

11 Forasmuch then as we are not without understanding, we ought to apprehend the design of our merciful Father. For he speaks to us, being willing that we who have been in the same error about the sacrifices, should seek and find how to approach unto him.

12 And therefore he thus bespeaks us, The sacrifice of God (is a broken spirit,) a broken and contrite heart—God will not despise.

13 Wherefore brethren, we ought the more diligently to inquire after those things that belong to our salvation, that the adversary may not have any entrance into us, and deprive us of our spiritual life.

14 Wherefore he again speaketh to them, concerning these things; Ye shall not fast as ye do this day, to make your voice to be heard on high.

15 Is it such a fast that I have chosen? A day for a man to afflict his soul? Is it to bow down his head like a bulrush, and to spread sackcloth and ashes under him? Wilt thou call this a fast, and an acceptable day to the Lord?

16 But to us he saith on this wise: Is not this the fast that I have chosen, to loose the bands of wickedness, to undo the heavy burdens, and to let the oppressed go free: and that ye break every yoke?

17 Is it not to deal thy bread to the hungry, and that thou bring the poor that are cast out to thy house? When thou seest the naked that thou cover him, and that thou hide not thyself from thy own flesh.

18 Then shall thy light break forth as the morning, and thy health shall spring forth speedily; and thy righteousness shall go before thee; the glory of the Lord shall be thy reward.

19 Then shalt thou call and the Lord shall answer; thou shalt cry and he shall say, Here I am; if thou put away from the midst of thee the yoke: the putting forth of the finger, and speaking vanity; and if thou draw out thy soul to the hungry; and satisfy the afflicted soul.

20 In this, therefore, brethren, God has manifested his foreknowledge and love for us; because the people which he has purchased to his beloved Son were to believe in sincerity; and therefore he has shown these things to all of us, that we should not run as proselytes to the Jewish Law.

THE GENERAL EPISTLE OF BARNABAS.

CHAPTER III.

The prophecies of Daniel concerning the ten kings, and the coming of Christ.

WHEREFORE it is necessary that searching diligently into those things which are soon to come to pass, we should write to you what may serve to keep you whole.

2 To which end, let us flee from every evil work and hate the errors of the present time, that we may be happy in that which is to come.

3 Let us not give ourselves the liberty of disputing with the wicked and sinners; lest we should chance in time to become like unto them.

4 For the consummation of sin is come, as it is written, as the prophet Daniel says. And for this end the Lord hath shortened the times and the days, that his beloved might hasten his coming to his inheritance.

5 For so the prophet speaks; There shall ten kings reign in the heart, and there shall rise last of all another little one, and he shall humble three kings.

6 And again Daniel speaks in like manner concerning the kingdoms; and I saw the fourth beast dreadful and terrible, and strong exceedingly; and it had ten horns. I considered the horns, and behold there came up among them another little horn, before which were three of the first horns plucked up by the roots.

7 We ought therefore to understand this also: And I beseech you, as one of your own brethren, loving you all beyond my own life, that you look well to yourselves, and be not like to those who add sin to sin, and say; That their covenant is ours also. Nay, but it is ours only: for they have forever lost that which Moses received.

8 For thus saith the Scripture And Moses continued fasting forty days and forty nights in the Mount; and he received the covenant from the Lord, even the two tables of stone, written by the hand of God.

9 But having turned themselves to idols they lost it; as the Lord also said to Moses; Moses, go down quickly, for thy people which thou hast brought forth out of Egypt, have corrupted themselves, and turned aside from the way which I commanded them. And Moses cast the two tables out of his hands; and their covenant was broken; that the love of Jesus might be sealed in your hearts, unto the hope of his faith.

10 Wherefore let us give heed unto the last times. For all the time past of our life and our faith, will profit us nothing; unless we continue

ΔΙΔΑΧΗ ΤΩΝ ΔΩΔΕΚΑ ΑΠΟΣΤΟΛΩΝ

to hate what is evil, and to withstand the future temptations. So the Son of God tells us; Let us resist all iniquity and hate it.

11 Wherefore consider the works of the evil way. Do not withdraw yourselves from others as if you were already justified; but coming altogether into one place, inquire what is agreeable to and profitable for the beloved of God. For the Scripture saith; Woe unto them that are wise in their own eyes; and prudent in their sight.

12 Let us become spiritually a perfect temple to God. As much as in us lies let us meditate upon the fear of God; and strive to the utmost of our power to keep his commandments; that we may rejoice in his righteous judgments.

13 For God will judge the world without respect of persons and everyone shall receive according to his works.

14 If a man shall be good, his righteousness shall go before him if wicked, the reward of his wickedness shall follow him.

15 Take heed therefore lest sitting still now, that when we are called, we fall asleep in our sins; and the wicked one getting the dominion over us, stir us up, and shut us out of the kingdom of the Lord.

16 Consider this also: although you have seen so great signs and wonders done among the people of the Jews, yet this notwithstanding the Lord hath forsaken them.

17 Beware, therefore, lest it happen to us; as it is written There may be many called, but few chosen.

CHAPTER IV.

That Christ was to suffer is proved from the prophecies concerning him.

For this cause did our Lord vouchsafe to give up his body to destruction, that through the forgiveness of our sins we might be sanctified; that is, by the sprinkling of his blood.

2 Now for what concerns the things that are written about him, some belong to the people of the Jews, and some to us.

3 For thus saith the Scripture; He was wounded for our transgressions, he was bruised for our iniquities, and by his blood we are healed. He was led as a lamb to the slaughter, and as a sheep before his shearers is dumb, so he opened not his mouth.

4 Wherefore we ought the more to give thanks unto God, for that he hath both declared unto us what is passed, and not suffered us to be without understanding of those things that are to come.

THE GENERAL EPISTLE OF BARNABAS.

5 But to them he saith; The nets are not unjustly spread for the birds.

6 This he spake, because a man will justly perish, if having the knowledge of the way of truth, he shall nevertheless not refrain himself from the way of darkness.

7 And for this cause the Lord was content to suffer for our souls, although he be the Lord of the whole earth; to whom God said before the beginning of the world, Let us make man after our own image and likeness.

8 Now how he suffered for us, seeing it was by men that he underwent it, I will shew you.

9 The prophets having received from him the gifts of prophecy, spake before concerning him:

10 But he, that he might abolish death, and make known the resurrection from the dead, was content, as it was necessary, to appear in the flesh, that he might make good the promise before given to our fathers, and preparing himself a new people, might demonstrate to them whilst he was upon earth, that after the resurrection he would judge the world.

11 And finally, teaching the people of Israel, and doing many wonders and signs among them, he preached to them, and shewed the exceeding great love which he bare towards them.

12 And when he chose his apostles, which were afterwards to publish his Gospel, he took men who had been very great sinners; that thereby he might plainly shew That he came not to call the righteous but sinners to repentance.

13 Then he clearly manifested himself to be the Son of God. For had he not come in the flesh, how should men have been able to look upon him, that they might be saved?

14 Seeing that if they beheld only the sun, which was the work of his hands, and shall hereafter cease to be, they are not able to endure steadfastly to look against the rays of it;

15 Wherefore the Son of God came in the flesh for this cause, that he might fill up the measure of their iniquity, who have persecuted his prophets unto death. And for the same reason also he suffered.

16 For God hath said of the stripes of his flesh, that they were from them. And, I will smite the shepherd, and the sheep of the flock shall be scattered.

17 Thus he would suffer, because it behoved him to suffer upon the cross.

ΔΙΔΑΧΗ ΤΩΝ ΔΩΔΕΚΑ ΑΠΟΣΤΟΛΩΝ

18 For thus one saith, prophesying concerning him; Spare my soul from the sword. And again, My flesh trembleth for fear.

19 And again, the congregation of wicked doers rose up against me, (They have pierced my hands and my feet).

20 And again he saith, I gave my back to the smiters, and my face I set as a hard rock.

CHAPTER V.

The subject continued.

And when he had fulfilled the commandment of God, What says he? Who will contend with me? Let him stand against me or who is he that will implead me? Let him draw near to the servant of the Lord. Woe be to you! Because ye shall all wax old as a garment, the moth shall eat you up.

2 And again adds the prophet, He is put for a stone of stumbling. Behold I lay in Zion for a foundation, a precious stone a choice cornerstone; an honourable stone. And what follows? And he that hopeth in him shall live for ever.

3 What then? Is our hope built upon a stone? God forbid. But because the Lord hath hardened his flesh against sufferings, he saith, I have put me as a firm rock.

4 And again the prophet adds; The stone which the builders refused has become the head of the corner. And again he saith This is the great and wonderful day which the Lord hath made. a I write these things the more plainly to you that ye may understand: I For indeed I could be content even to die for your sakes.

5 But what saith the prophet again; The counsel of the wicked encompassed me about. They came about me, as bees about the honeycomb: and, Upon my vesture they cast lots.

6 Forasmuch then as our Saviour was to appear in the flesh and suffer, his passion was hereby foretold.

7 For thus saith the prophet against Israel: "Woe be to their soul because they have taken wicked counsel against themselves, saying; let us lay snares for the righteous, because he is unprofitable to us."

8 Moses also in like manner speaketh to them; Behold thus saith the Lord God; Enter ye into the good land of which the Lord hath sworn to Abraham, and Isaac, and Jacob, that he would give it you, and possess it; a land flowing with milk and honey.

9 Now what the spiritual meaning of this is, learn; It is as if it had been said, Put your trust in Jesus, who shall be manifested to you in the flesh. For man is the earth which suffers: forasmuch as out of the substance of the earth Adam was formed.

10 What therefore does he mean when he says, Into a good land flowing with milk and honey? Blessed be our Lord, who has given us wisdom, and a heart to understand his secrets. For so says the prophet, "Who shall understand the hard sayings of the Lord? But he that is wise, and intelligent, and that loves his Lord."

11 Seeing therefore he has renewed us by the remission of our sins, he has put us into another frame, that we should have souls like those of children, forming us again himself by the spirit.

12 For thus the Scripture saith concerning us, where it introduceth the Father speaking to the Son; Let us make man after our likeness and similitude; and let them have dominion over the beasts of the earth, and over the fowls of the air, and the fish of the sea.

13 And when the Lord saw the man which he had formed, that behold he was very good; he said, Increase and multiply, and replenish the earth. And this he spake to his son.

14 I will now show you, how he made us a new creature, in the latter days.

15 The Lord saith; Behold I will make the last as the first. Wherefore the prophet thus spake, Enter into the land flowing with milk and honey, and have dominion over it.

16 Wherefore ye see how we are again formed anew; as also he speaks by another prophet; Behold saith the Lord, I will take from them; that is, from those whom the spirit I of the Lord foresaw, their hearts of stone, and I will put into them hearts of flesh.

17 Because he was about to be made manifest in the flesh and to dwell in us.

18 For, my brethren, the habitation of our heart is a 'holy temple unto the Lord. For the prophet saith again, In what place shall I appear before the Lord my God, and be glorified?

19 He answers I will confess unto thee in the congregation in the midst of my brethren; and will sing unto thee in the church of the saints:

20 Wherefore we are they whom he has brought into that good land.

21 But what signifies the milk and honey? Because as the child is nourished first with milk, and then with honey; so we being kept alive

ΔΙΔΑΧΗ ΤΩΝ ΔΩΔΕΚΑ ΑΠΟΣΤΟΛΩΝ

by the belief of his promises and his word, shall live and have dominion over the land.

22 For he foretold before, saying, increase and multiply, and have dominion over the beasts, fishes, and birds.

23 But who is there that is now able to have this dominion over the wild beasts, or fishes, or fowls of the air? For you know that to rule, is to have power; that a man should be set over what he rules.

24 But forasmuch as this we have not now, he tells us when we shall have it; namely, when we shall become perfect, that we may be made the inheritors of the covenant of the Lord.

CHAPTER VI.

The sacrifice of Jesus, and of a goat, an evident type of Christ crucified.

UNDERSTAND then my beloved children, that the good God hath before manifested all things unto us, that we might know to whom we ought always to give thanks and praise.

2 If therefore the Son of God who is the Lord of all, and shall come to judge both the quick and dead, hath suffered, that by his stripes we might live; let us believe that the Son of God could not have suffered but for us. But being crucified, they gave him vinegar and gall to drink.

3 Hear therefore how the priests of the temple did foreshow this also: the Lord by his command which was written, declared that whosoever did not fast the appointed fast he should die the death: because he also was himself one day to offer up his body for our sins; that so the type of what was done in Isaac might be fulfilled, who was offered upon the altar.

4 What therefore is it that he says by the prophet? And let them eat of the goat which is offered in the day of the fast for all their sins. Hearken diligently, (my brethren,) and all the priests, and they only shall eat the inwards not washed with vinegar.

5 Why so? because I know that when I shall hereafter offer my flesh for the sins of a new people, ye will give me vinegar to drink mixed with gall; therefore do ye only eat, the people fasting the while, and lamenting in sackcloth and ashes.

6 And that he might foreshow that he was to suffer for them, hear then how he appointed it.

7 Take, says he, two goats, fair and alike, and offer them; and let the high priest take one of them for a burnt offering. And what shalt be done with the other? Let it, says he, be accursed.

8 Consider how exactly this appears to have been a type of Jesus. And let all the congregation spit upon it, and prick it; and put the scarlet wool about its head; and thus let it be carried forth into the wilderness.

9 And this being done, he that was appointed to convey the goat, led it into the wilderness, and took away the scarlet wool, and put it upon a thorn bush, whose young sprouts, when we find them in the field, we are wont to eat: so the fruit of that thorn only is sweet.

10 And to what end was this ceremony? Consider; one was offered upon the altar, the other was accursed.

11 And why was that which was accursed crowned? Because they shall see Christ on that day having a scarlet garment about his body; and shall say: Is not this he whom we crucified; having despised him, pierced him, mocked him? Certainly, this is he, who then said, that he was the Son of God.

12 As therefore he shall be then like to what he was on earth, so were the Jews heretofore commanded, to take two goats fair and equal; that when they shall see (our Saviour) hereafter coming (in the clouds of heaven), they may be amazed at the likeness of the goats.

13 Wherefore ye here again see a type of Jesus who was to suffer for us.

14 But what then signifies this, That the wool was to be put into the midst of the thorns?

15 This also is a figure of Jesus, set out to the church. For as he who would take away the scarlet wool must undergo many difficulties, because that thorn was very sharp, and with difficulty get it: So, says Christ, they that will see me, and come to my kingdom, must through many afflictions and troubles attain unto me.

CHAPTER VII.

The red heifer, another type of Christ.

BUT what type do ye suppose it to have been, where it is commanded to the people of Israel, that grown persons in whom sins are come to perfection, should offer an heifer, and after they had killed it should burn the same;

ΔΙΔΑΧΗ ΤΩΝ ΔΩΔΕΚΑ ΑΠΟΣΤΟΛΩΝ

2 But then young men should take up the ashes and put them in vessels; and tie a piece of scarlet wool and hyssop upon a stick, and so the young men should sprinkle every one of the people, and they should be clear from their sins?

3 Consider how all these are delivered in a figure to us.

4 This heifer is Jesus Christ; the wicked men that were to offer it are those sinners who brought him to death; who afterwards have no more to do with it: for the sinners have no more the honour of handling it:

5 But the young men that performed the sprinkling, signified those who preach to us the forgiveness of sins, and the purification of the heart, to whom the Lord gave authority to preach his Gospel: being at the beginning twelve, to signify the tribes, because there were twelve tribes of Israel.

6 But why were there three young men appointed to sprinkle? To denote Abraham, and Isaac, and Jacob, because they were great before God.

7 And why was the wool put upon a stick? Because the kingdom of Jesus was founded upon the cross; and therefore they that put their trust in him, shall live for ever.

8 But why was the wool and hyssop put together? To signify that in the kingdom of Christ there shall be evil and filthy days, in which however, we shall be saved; and because he that has any disease in the flesh by some filthy humours, is cured by hyssop.

9 Wherefore these things being thus done, are to us indeed evident, but to the Jews they are obscure; because they hearkened not unto the voice of the Lord.

CHAPTER VIII.

Of the circumcision of the ears and how in the first institution of circumcision Abraham mystically foretold Christ by name.

AND therefore the Scripture again speaks concerning our ears, that God has circumcised them, together with our hearts. For thus saith the Lord by the holy prophet: By the hearing of the ear they obeyed me.

2 And again, They who are afar off, shall hear and understand what things I have done. And again, Circumcise your hearts, saith the Lord.

THE GENERAL EPISTLE OF BARNABAS.

3 And again he saith, Hear O Israel! For thus saith the Lord thy God. And again the Spirit of God prophesieth, saying: Who is there that would live for ever, let him hear the voice of my Son.

4 And again, Hear, O Heavens, and give ear O Earth! Because the Lord has spoken these things for a witness.

5 And again, he saith, Hear the word of the Lord, ye princes of the people. And again, Hear O children! The voice of one crying in the wilderness.

6 Wherefore he has circumcised our ears, that we should hear his word, and believe. But as for that circumcision, in which the Jews trust, it is abolished: for the circumcision of which God spake, was not of the flesh.

7 But they have transgressed his commands, because the evil one hath deceived them. For thus God bespeaks them; Thus saith the Lord your God, (Here I find the new law) Sow not among thorns; but circumcise yourselves to the Lord your God. And what doth he mean by this saying? Hearken unto your Lord.

8 And again he saith, Circumcise the hardness of your heart, and harden not your neck. And again, Behold, saith the Lord, all the nations are uncircumcised, (they have not lost their fore-skin): but this people is uncircumcised in heart.

9 But you will say the Jews were circumcised for a sign. And so are all the Syrians and Arabians, and all the idolatrous priests: but are they therefore of the covenant of Israel? And even the Egyptians themselves are circumcised.

10 Understand therefore, children, these things more fully, that Abraham was the first, that brought in circumcision, looking forward in the Spirit, to Jesus; circumcised, having received the mystery of three letters.

11 For the Scripture says that Abraham circumcised three hundred and eighteen men of his house. But what therefore was the mystery that was made known unto him!

12 Mark, first the eighteen, and next the three hundred. For the numeral letters of ten and eight are T H. And these denote Jesus.

13 And because the cross was that by which we were to find grace, therefore he adds, three hundred; the note of which is T (the figure of his cross). Wherefore by two letters he signified Jesus, and by the third his cross.

14 He who has put the engrafted gift of his doctrine within us, knows that I never taught to anyone a more certain truth: but I trust that ye are worthy of it.

ΔΙΔΑΧΗ ΤΩΝ ΔΩΔΕΚΑ ΑΠΟΣΤΟΛΩΝ

CHAPTER IX.

That the commands of Moses concerning clean and unclean beasts, were all designed for a spiritual signification.

BUT why did Moses say Ye shall not eat of the swine, neither the eagle nor the hawk; nor the crow; nor any fish that has not a scale upon him?—I answer that, in the spiritual sense, he comprehended three doctrines, that were to be gathered from thence.

2 Besides which he says to them in the book of Deuteronomy, And I will give my statutes unto this people. Wherefore it is not the command of God that they should not eat these things; but Moses in the spirit spake unto them.

3 Now the sow he forbad them to eat, meaning thus much: Thou shalt not join thyself to such persons as are like unto swine, who, whilst they live in pleasure, forget their God; but when any want pinches them, then they know the Lord: as the sow when she is full knows not her master, but when she is hungry she makes a noise; and being again fed, is silent.

4 Neither, says he, shalt thou eat the eagle, nor the hawk, nor the kite, nor the crow; that is, thou shalt not keep company with such kind of men as know not how by their labour and sweat to get themselves food; but injuriously ravish away the things of others, and watch how to lay snares for them; when at the same time they appear to live in perfect innocence.

3 So these birds alone (seek not food for themselves,) but sitting idle, seek how they may eat of the flesh others have provided being destructive through their wickedness.

6 Neither, says he, shalt thou eat the lamprey, nor the polypus, nor the cuttle-fish; that is thou shalt not be like such men, by seeking to converse with them who are altogether wicked and adjudged to death. For so those fishes are alone accursed, that wallow in the mire, nor swim as other fishes, but tumble in the dirt at the bottom of the deep.

7 But, he adds, neither shalt thou eat of the hare. To what end?—To signify this to us; Thou shalt not be an adulterer, nor liken thyself to such persons. For the hare every year multiplies the places of its conception; and as many years as it lives, so many it has

8 Neither shalt thou eat of the hyena: that is, again, be not an adulterer, nor a corrupter of others; neither be like to such. And wherefore so?—Because that creature every year changes its kind, which is sometimes male and sometimes female.

9 For which cause also he justly hated the weazel; to the end that they should not be like such persons who with their mouths commit wickedness by reason of their uncleanness; nor join themselves with those impure women, who with their mouths commit wickedness. Because that animal conceives with its mouth.

10 Moses, therefore, speaking as concerning meats, delivered indeed three great precepts to them in the spiritual signification of those commands. But they according to the desires of the flesh, understood him as if he had only meant it of meats.

11 And therefore David took aright the knowledge of his three-fold command, saying in like manner:

12 Blessed is the man that hath not walked in the counsel of the ungodly; as the fishes before mentioned in the bottom of the deep, in darkness.

13 Nor stood in the way of sinners, as they who seem to fear the Lord, but yet sin, as the sow.

14 And hath not sat in the seat of the scorners; as those birds who sit and watch that they may devour.

15 Here you have the law concerning meat perfectly set forth and according to the true knowledge of it.

16 But, says Moses, ye shall eat all that divideth the hoof, and cheweth the cud. Signifying thereby such an one as having taken his food, knows him that nourisheth him; and resting upon him, rejoiceth in him.

17 And in this he spake well, having respect to the commandment. What, therefore, is it that he says?—That we should hold fast to them that fear the Lord; with those who meditate on the command of the word which they have received, in their heart; with those that declare the righteous judgments of the Lord, and keep his commandments;

18 In short, with those who know that to meditate is a work of pleasure, and therefore exercise themselves in the word of the Lord.

19 But why might they eat those that clave the hoof? Because the righteous liveth in this present world; but his expectation is fixed upon the other. See, brethren, how admirably Moses commanded these things.

20 But how should we thus know all this, and understand it? We, therefore, understanding aright the commandments, speak as the Lord would have us. Wherefore he has circumcised our ears and our hearts, that we might know these things.

ΔΙΔΑΧΗ ΤΩΝ ΔΩΔΕΚΑ ΑΠΟΣΤΟΛΩΝ

CHAPTER X.

Baptism and the cross of Christ foretold in figures under the law.

LET us now inquire whether the Lord took care to manifest anything beforehand concerning water and the cross.

2 Now for the former of these, it is written to the people of Israel how they shall not receive that baptism which brings to forgiveness of sins; but shall institute another to themselves that cannot.

3 For thus saith the prophet: Be astonished, O Heaven! and let the earth tremble at it, because this people have done two great and wicked things: they have left me, the fountain of living water, and have digged for themselves broken cisterns, that can hold no water.

4 Is my holy mountain of Zion, a desolate wilderness? For ye shall be as a young bird when its nest is taken away.

5 And again the prophet saith, I will go before thee, and will make plain the mountains, and will break the gates of brass, and will snap in sunder the bars of iron; and will give thee dark, and hidden, and invisible treasures, that they may know that I am the Lord God.

6 And again: he shall dwell in the high den of the strong rock. And then, what follows in the same prophet? His water is faithful; ye shall see the king with glory, and your soul shall learn the fear of the Lord.

7 And again he saith in another prophet: He that does these things; I shall be like a tree planted by the currents of water, which shall give its fruit in its season. Its leaf also shall not wither, and whatsoever he doth it shall prosper.

8 As for the wicked it is not so with them; but they are as the dust which the wind scattereth away from the face of the earth.

9 Therefore the ungodly shall not stand in the judgment, neither the sinners in the council of the righteous. For the Lord knoweth the way of the righteous, and the way of the ungodly shall perish.

10 Consider how he has joined both the cross and the water together.

11 For this he saith: Blessed are they who put their trust in the cross, and descend into the water; for they shall have their reward in due time: then, saith he, will I give it them.

12 But as concerning the present time, he saith, their leaves shall not fall: meaning thereby, that every word that shall go out of your mouth, shall through faith and charity be to the conversion and hope of many.

13 In like manner doth another prophet speak. And the land of Jacob was the praise of all the earth; magnifying thereby the vessel of his spirit.

14 And what follows?—And there was a river running on the right hand, and beautiful trees grew up by it; and he that shall eat of them shall live for ever. The signification of which is this that we go down into the water full of sins and pollutions, but come up again, bringing forth fruit; having in our hearts the fear and hope which is in Jesus, by the spirit. And whosoever shall eat of them shall live for ever.

15 That is, whosoever shall hearken to those who call them, and shall believe, shall live for ever.

CHAPTER XI.

The subject continued.

IN like manner he determines concerning the cross in another prophet, saying: And when shall these things be fulfilled?

2 The Lord answers: When the tree that is fallen shall rise, and when blood shall drop down from the tree. Here you have again mention made, both of the cross, and of him that was to be crucified upon it.

3 And yet farther he saith by Moses; (when Israel was fighting with, and beaten by, a strange people; to the end that God might put them in mind how that for their sins they were delivered unto death) yea, the holy spirit put it into the heart of Moses, to represent both the sign of the cross, and of him that was to suffer: that so they might know that if they did not believe in him, they should be overcome for ever.

4 Moses therefore I piled up armour upon armour in the middle of a rising ground, and standing up high above all of them, stretched forth his arms, and so Israel again conquered.

5 But no sooner did he let down his hands, but they were again slain. And why so?—To the end they might know, that except they trust in him they cannot be saved.

6 And in another prophet, he saith, I have stretched out my hands all the day long to a people disobedient, and speaking against my righteous way.

7 And again Moses makes a type of Jesus, to show that he was to die, and then that he, whom they thought to be dead, was to give life to others; in the type of those that fell in Israel.

ΔΙΔΑΧΗ ΤΩΝ ΔΩΔΕΚΑ ΑΠΟΣΤΟΛΩΝ

8 For God caused all sorts of serpents to bite them, and they died: forasmuch as by a serpent transgression began in Eve; that so he might convince them that for their transgressions they shall be delivered into the pain of death.

9 Moses then himself, who had commanded them, saying, Ye shall not make to yourselves any graven or molten image, to be your God yet now did so himself, that he might represent to them the figure of the Lord Jesus.

10 For he made a brazen serpent, and set it up on high, and called the people together by a proclamation: where being come, they entreated Moses that he would make an atonement for them, and pray that they might be healed.

11 Then Moses spake unto them, saying: when any one among you shall be bitten, let him come unto the serpent that is set upon the pole; and let him assuredly trust in him, that though he be dead, yet he is able to give life, and presently he shall be saved; and so they did. See therefore how here also you have in this the glory of Jesus; and that in him and to him are all things.

12 Again; What says Moses to Joshua, the Son of Nun, when he gave that name unto him, as being a prophet, that all the people might hear him alone? Because the father did manifest all things concerning his son Jesus, in Joshua, the Son of Nun; and gave him that name when he sent him to spy out the land of Canaan, saying; Take a book in thine hands, and write what the Lord saith. Forasmuch as Jesus the Son of God shall in the last days cut off by the roots all the house of Amalek, see here again Jesus, not the son of man, but the Son of God, made manifest in a type, and in the flesh.

13 But because it might hereafter be said that Christ was the Son of David; therefore David fearing and well knowing the errors of the wicked, saith; the Lord said unto my Lord, sit thou on my right hand until I make thine enemies thy footstool.

14 And again Isaiah speaketh on this wise, The Lord said unto Christ my Lord, I have laid hold on his right hand, that the nations should obey before him, and I will break the strength of kings.

15 Behold, how doth David and Isaiah call him Lord, and the Son of God.

CHAPTER XII.

The Promise of God not made to the Jews only, but to the Gentiles also, and fulfilled to us by Jesus Christ.

BUT let us go yet further, and inquire whether this people be the heir, or the former; and whether the covenant be with us or with them.

2 And first, as concerning the people, hear now what the Scripture saith:

3 Isaac prayed for his wife Rebekah, because she was barren; and she conceived. Afterwards Rebekah went forth to inquire of the Lord.

4 And the Lord said unto her; There are two nations in thy womb, and two people shall come from thy body; and the one shall have power over the other, and the greater shall serve the lesser. Understand here who was Isaac; who Rebekah; and of whom it was foretold, this people shall be greater than that.

5 And in another prophecy Jacob speaketh more clearly to his son Joseph, saying; Behold the Lord hath not derived me of seeing thy face, bring me thy sons that I may bless them. And he brought unto his father Manasseh and Ephraim, desiring that he should bless Manasseh, because he was the elder.

6 Therefore Joseph brought him to the right hand of his father Jacob. But Jacob by the spirit foresaw the figure of the people that was to come.

7 And what saith the Scripture? And Jacob crossed his hands, and put his right hand upon Ephraim, his second, and the younger son, and blessed him. And Joseph said unto Jacob; Put thy right hand upon the head of Manasseh, for he is my first-born son. And Jacob said unto Joseph; I know it, my son, I know it; but the greater shall serve the lesser; though he also shall be blessed.

8 Ye see of whom he appointed it, that they should be the first people, and heirs of the covenant.

9 If therefore God shall have yet farther taken notice of this, by Abraham too; our understanding of it will then be perfectly established.

10 What then saith the Scripture of Abraham, when I be believed, and it was imputed unto him for righteousness? Behold I have made thee a father of the nations, which without circumcision believe in the Lord.

11 Let us therefore now inquire whether God has fulfilled the covenant, which he sware to our fathers, that he would give this people?

ΔΙΔΑΧΗ ΤΩΝ ΔΩΔΕΚΑ ΑΠΟΣΤΟΛΩΝ

Yes, verily, he gave it; but they were not worthy to receive it by reason of their sins.

12 For thus saith the prophet And Moses continued fasting in mount Sinai, to receive the covenant of the Lord with the people, forty days and forty nights.

13 And he received of the Lord two tables written with the finger of the Lord's hand, in the Spirit. And Moses, when he had received them, brought them down that he might deliver them to the people.

14 And the Lord said unto Moses; Moses, Moses, get thee down quickly, for the people which thou broughtest out of the land of Egypt have done wickedly.

15 And Moses understood that they had again set up a molten image: and he cast the two tables out of his hands; and the tables of the covenant of the Lord were broken. Moses therefore received them, but they were not worthy.

16 Now then learn how we have received them. Moses, being a servant, took them; but the Lord himself has given them unto us, that we might be the people of his inheritance; having suffered for us.

17 He was therefore made manifest; that they should fill up the measure of their sins, and that we being made heirs by him, should receive the covenant of the Lord Jesus.

18 And again the prophet saith Behold, I have set thee for a light unto the Gentiles; to be the saviour of all the ends of the earth, saith the Lord; the God who hath redeemed thee.

19 Who for that very end was prepared, that by his own appearing he might redeem our hearts, already devoured by death, and delivered over to the irregularity of error, from darkness; and establish a covenant with us by his word.

20 For so it is written that the father commanded him by delivering us from darkness, to prepare unto himself a holy people.

21 Wherefore the prophet saith I the Lord thy God have called thee in righteousness, and I will take thee by thy hand, and will strengthen thee, and give thee for a covenant of the people; for a light to the Gentiles. To open the eyes of the blind, to bring out the prisoners from the prison, and them that sit in darkness out of the prison house.

22 Consider, therefore, from whence we have been redeemed. And again the prophet saith The spirit of the Lord is upon me, because he hath anointed me: he hath sent me to preach glad tidings to the lowly; to heal the broken in heart; to preach remission to the captives, and give sight unto the blind; to proclaim the acceptable year of the Lord, and the day of restitution; to comfort all that mourn.

THE GENERAL EPISTLE OF BARNABAS.

CHAPTER XIII.

That the sabbath of the Jews was but a figure of a more glorious sabbath to come, and their temple, of the spiritual temples of God.

FURTHERMORE it is written concerning the sabbath, in the Ten Commandments, which God spake in the mount Sinai to Moses, face to face: Sanctify the sabbath of the Lord with pure hands, and with a clean heart.

2 And elsewhere he saith; If thy children shall keep my Sabbaths, then will I put my mercy upon them.

3 And even in the beginning of the creation he makes mention of the sabbath. And God made in six days the works of his hands, and he finished them on the seventh day; and he rested the seventh day, and sanctified it.

4 Consider, my children, what that signifies, he finished them in six days. The meaning of it is this: that in six thousand years the Lord God will bring all things to an end.

5 For with him one day is a thousand years; as himself testifieth, saying, Behold this day shall be as a thousand years. Therefore, children, in six days, that is, in six thousand years, shall a all things be accomplished.

6 And what is that he saith, And he rested the seventh day he meaneth this: that when his Son shall come, and abolish the season of the Wicked One, and judge the ungodly; and shall change the sun and the moon, and the stars; then he shall gloriously rest on that seventh day,

7 He adds, lastly: Thou shalt sanctify it with clean hands and a pure heart. Wherefore we are greatly deceived if we imagine that anyone can now sanctify that day which God has made holy, without having a heart pure in all things.

8 Behold, therefore, he will then truly sanctify it with blessed rest, when we (having received the righteous promise, when iniquity shall be no more, all things being renewed by the Lord) shall be able to sanctify it, being ourselves first made holy;

9 Lastly, he saith unto them Your new moons and your Sabbaths I cannot bear them. Consider what he means by it; the Sabbaths, says he, which ye now keep are not acceptable unto me, but those which I have made; when resting from all things I shall begin the eight day, that is, the beginning of the other world.

ΔΙΔΑΧΗ ΤΩΝ ΔΩΔΕΚΑ ΑΠΟΣΤΟΛΩΝ

10 For which cause we observe the eight day with gladness, in which Jesus rose from the dead; and having manifested himself to his disciples, ascended into heaven.

11 It remains yet that I speak to you concerning the temple: how those miserable men being deceived have put their trust in the house, and not in God himself who made them, as if it were the habitation of God.

12 For much after the same manner as the Gentiles, they consecrated him in the temple.

13 But learn therefore how the Lord speaketh, rendering the temple vain: Who has measured the heaven with a span, and the earth with his hand? Is it not I? Thus with the Lord, Heaven is my throne, and the earth is my footstool. What is the house that ye will build me? Or what is the place of my rest? Know therefore that all their hope is vain.

14 And again he speaketh after this manner: Behold they that destroy this temple, even they shall again build it up. And so it came to pass; for through their wars it is now destroyed by their enemies; and the servants of their enemies build it up.

15 Furthermore it has been made manifest, how both the city and the temple, and the people of Israel should be given up. For the scripture saith; And it shall come to pass in the last days, that the Lord will deliver up the sheep of his pasture, and their fold, and their tower unto destruction. And it is come to pass, as the Lord hath spoken.

16 Let us inquire therefore, whether there be any temple of God? Yes there is: and there where himself declares that he would both make and perfect it. For it is written: And it shall be that as soon as the week shall be completed, the temple of the Lord shall be gloriously built in the name of the Lord.

17 I find therefore that there is a temple. But how shall it be built in the name of the Lord? I will shew you.

18 Before that we believed in God, the habitation of our heart was corruptible, and feeble, as a temple truly built with hands.

19 For it was a house full of idolatry, a house of devils; inasmuch as there was done in it whatsoever was contrary unto God But it shall be built in the name of the Lord.

20 Consider, how that the temple of the Lord shall be very gloriously built; and by what means that shall be, learn.

21 Having received remission of our sins, and trusting in the name of the Lord, we are become renewed, being again created as it were from the beginning. Wherefore God truly dwells in our house, that is, in us.

22 But how does he dwell in us? By the word of his faith, the calling of his promise, the wisdom of his righteous judgments and the commands of his doctrine. He himself prophesies within us, he himself dwelleth in us, and openeth to us who were in bondage of death the gate of our temple, that is, the mouth of wisdom, having given repentance unto us; and by this means has brought us to be an incorruptible temple.

23 He therefore that desires to be saved looketh not unto the man, but unto him that dwelleth in him, and speaketh by him; being struck with wonder, forasmuch as he never either heard him speaking such words out of his mouth, nor ever desired to hear them.

24 This is that spiritual temple that is built unto the Lord.

CHAPTER XIV.

Of the way of light; being a summary of what a Christian is to do, that he maybe happy for ever.

AND thus I trust, I have declared to you as much, and with as great simplicity as I could, those, things which provide for your salvation, so as not to have omitted any thing that might be requisite thereunto.

2 For should I speak farther of the things that now are, and of those that are to come, you would not yet understand them, seeing they lie in parables. This therefore shall suffice as to these things.

3 Let us now go on to the other kind of knowledge and doctrine. There are two ways of doctrine and power; the one of light, the other of darkness.

4 But there is a great deal of difference between these two ways for over one are appointed the angels of God, the leaders of the way of light; over the other, the angels of Satan. And the one is the Lord from everlasting to everlasting; the other is the prince of the time of unrighteousness.

5 Now the way of light is this: If any one desires to attain to the place that is appointed for him, and will hasten thither by his works. And the knowledge that has been given to us for walking in it, to this effect: Thou shalt love him that made thee: thou shalt glorify him that hath redeemed thee from death.

6 Thou shalt be simple in heart, and rich in the spirit. Thou shalt not cleave to those that walk in the way of death. Thou shalt hate to do anything that is not pleasing unto God. Thou shalt abhor all dissimulation. Thou shalt not neglect any of the commands of the Lord.

ΔΙΔΑΧΗ ΤΩΝ ΔΩΔΕΚΑ ΑΠΟΣΤΟΛΩΝ

7 Thou shalt not exalt thyself, but shalt be humble. Then shalt not take honour to thyself. Thou shalt not enter into any wicked counsel against thy neighbour. Thou shalt not be over confident in thy heart.

8 Thou shaft not commit fornication, nor adultery. Neither shalt thou corrupt thyself with mankind. Thou shalt not make use of the word of God, to any impurity,

9 Thou shalt not except any man's person, when thou reprovest any one's faults. Thou shalt be gentle. Thou shalt be quiet. Thou shalt tremble at the words which thou hast heard. Thou shalt not keep any hatred in thy heart against thy brother. Thou shalt not entertain any doubt whether it shall be or not.

10 Thou shalt not take the name of the Lord in vain. Thou shalt love thy neighbour above thy own soul,

11 Thou shalt not destroy thy conceptions, before they are brought forth; nor kill them after they are born.

12 Thou shalt not withdraw thy hand from thy son, or from thy daughter; but shall teach them from their youth the fear of the Lord.

13 Thou shalt not covet thy neighbour's goods; neither shalt thou be an extortioner. Neither shall thy heart be joined to proud men; but thou shalt be numbered among the righteous and the lowly. Whatever events shall happen unto thee, thou shalt receive them as good.

14 Thou shalt not be double- minded or double-tongued; for a double tongue is the snare of death. Thou shalt be subject unto the Lord and to inferior masters as to the representatives of God, in fear and reverence.

15 Thou shalt not be bitter in thy commands towards any of thy servants that trust in God; lest thou chance not to fear him who is over both; because he came not to call any with respect of persons, but whomsoever the spirit had prepared.

16 Thou shalt communicate to thy neighbour of all thou hast; thou shalt not call anything thine own: for if ye partake of such things as are incorruptible, how much more should you do it in those that are corruptible?

17 Thou shalt not be forward to speak; for the mouth is the snare of death. Strive for thy soul with all thy might. Reach not out thine hand to receive, and withhold it not when thou shouldest give.

18 Thou shalt love, as the apple of thine eye, everyone that speaketh unto thee the Word of the Lord. Call to thy remembrance, day and night, the future judgment.

19 Thou shalt seek out every day, the persons of the righteous; and both consider and go about to exhort others by the word, and meditate how thou mayest save a soul.

20 Thou shaft also labour with thy hands to give to the poor, that thy sins may be forgiven thee, Thou shalt not deliberate whether thou shouldst give; nor having given, murmur at it.

21 Give to everyone that asks so shalt thou know who is the good rewarder of thy gifts.

22 Keep what thou hast received; thou shalt neither add to it nor take from it.

23 Let the wicked be always thy aversion. Thou shalt judge with righteous judgment. Thou shalt never cause divisions; but shalt make peace between those that are at variance, and bring them together.

24 Thou shalt confess thy sins; and not come to thy prayer with an evil conscience.

25 This is the way of light.

CHAPTER XV.

Of the way of darkness; that is, what kind of persons shall be for ever cast out of the kingdom of God.

BUT the way of darkness is crooked, and full of cursing. For it is the way of eternal death, with punishment; in which they that walk meet those things that destroy their own souls.

2 Such are; idolatry, confidence, pride of power, hypocrisy, double-mindedness, adultery, murder, rapine, pride, transgression, deceit, malice, arrogance, witchcraft, covetousness, and the want of the fear of God.

3 In this, walk those, who are the persecutors of them that are good; haters of truth; lovers of lies; who know not the reward of righteousness, nor cleave to any thing that is good.

4 Who administer not righteous judgment to the widow and orphan; who watch for wickedness, and not for the fear of the Lord;

5 From whom gentleness and patience are far off: who love vanity, and follow after rewards; having no compassion upon the poor; nor take any pains for such as are heavy laden and oppressed.

6 Ready to evil speaking, not knowing him that made them; murderers of children; corrupters of the creature of God; that turn away from the needy; oppress the afflicted; are the advocates of the rich, but unjust judges of the poor; being altogether sinners.

ΔΙΔΑΧΗ ΤΩΝ ΔΩΔΕΚΑ ΑΠΟΣΤΟΛΩΝ

7 It is therefore fitting that learning the just commands of the Lord, which we have before mentioned, we should walk in them. For he who does such things shall be glorified in the kingdom of Hod.

8 But he that chooses the other part, shall be destroyed, together with his works. For this cause there shall be both a resurrection, and a retribution.

9 I beseech those that are in high estate among you, (if so be you will take the counsel which with a good intention I offer to you,) you have those with you towards whom you may do good; do not forsake them.

10 For the day is at hand in which all things shall be destroyed, together with the wicked one. The Lord is near, and his reward is with him.

11 I beseech you, therefore, again, and again, Be as good lawgiver's to one Another; continue faithful counsellors do each other remove from among you all hypocrisy.

12 And may God, the Lord of all the world, give you wisdom, knowledge, counsel, and understanding of his judgments in patience:

13 Be ye taught of God; seeking what it is the Lord requires of you, and doing it; that ye may be saved in the day of judgment.

14 And if there be among you any remembrance of what is good, think of me; meditating on these things, that both my desire and my watching for you may turn to a good account.

15 I beseech you; I ask it as a favour of you; whilst you are in this beautiful tabernacle of the body, be wanting in none of these things; but without ceasing seek them, and fulfil every command, For these things are fitting and worthy to be done.

16 Wherefore I have given the more diligence to write unto you according to my ability, that you might rejoice. Farewell, children of love and peace.

17 The Lord of glory and of all grace, be with your spirit, Amen.

[The end of the Epistle of Barnabas the Apostle, and fellow-traveller of St. Paul the Apostle.]

REFERENCES TO THE GENERAL EPISTLE OF BARNABAS.

[Barnabas was a companion and fellow-preacher with Paul. This Epistle lays a greater claim to canonical authority than most others. It has been cited by Clemens, Alexandrinus, Origen, Eusebius, and Jerome, and many ancient Fathers. Cotelerius affirms that Origen and Jerome esteemed it genuine and canonical; but Cotelerius himself did not believe it to be either one or the other; on the contrary, he supposes it was written for the benefit of the Ebionites, (the christianized Jews,) who were tenacious of rites and ceremonies. Bishop Fell feared to own expressly what he seemed to be persuaded of, that it ought to be treated with the same respect as several of the books of the present canon. Dr. Bernard, Savilian professor at Oxford, not only believed it to be genuine, but that it was read throughout in the churches of Alexandria, as the canonical Scriptures were. Dodwell supposed it to have been published before the Epistle of Jude, and the writings of both the Johns. Vossius, Dupuis, Dr. Cane, Dr. Mill, Dr, S. Clark, Whitson, and Archbishop Wake also esteemed it genuine: Menardus, Archbishop Land, Spanheim, and others deemed it apocryphal.]

THE EPISTLE OF IGNATIUS TO THE EPHESIANS.

CHAPTER I.

1 Ignatius commends the brethren for sending Onesimus and other members of the church to him.
8 Exhorts them to unity;
13 by a due subjection to their bishop;

IGNATIUS, who is also called Theophorus, to the church which is at Ephesus in Asia; most deservedly happy: being blessed through the greatness and fullness of God the Father, and predestinated before the world began; that it should be always unto an enduring and unchangeable glory; united and chosen through his true passion, according to the will of the Father, and Jesus Christ our God; all happiness, by Jesus Christ, and his undefiled grace.

2 I have heard of your name much beloved in God; which ye have very justly attained by a habit of righteousness, according to the faith and love which is in Jesus Christ our Saviour.

3 How that being followers of God, and stirring up yourselves by the blood of Christ ye have perfectly accomplished the work that was con-natural unto you.

4 For hearing that I came bound from Syria, for the common name and hope, trusting through your prayers to fight with beasts at home; so that by suffering I may become indeed the disciple of him who gave himself to God, an offering and sacrifice for us; ye hastened to see me. I received, therefore, in the name of God, your whole multitude in Onesimus;

THE EPISTLE OF IGNATIUS TO THE EPHESIANS.

5 Who by: inexpressible love is ours, but according to the flesh is our bishop; whom I beseech you, pray Jesus Christ, to love: and that you would all strive to be like unto him. And blessed be God, who has granted unto you, who are so worthy of him, to enjoy such an excellent bishop.

6 For what concerns my fellow servant Burrhus, and your most blessed deacon in things pertaining to God; I entreat you that he may tarry longer, both for yours, and your bishop's honour.

7 And Crocus also worthy of both our God and you, whom I have received as the pattern of your love, has in all things refreshed me, as the Father of our Lord Jesus Christ shall also refresh him; together with Onesimus, and Burrhus, and Euplus, and Fronto, in whom I have, as to your charity, seen all of you, And may always, have joy of you, if I shall be worthy of it.

8 It is therefore fitting that you should by all means glorify Jesus Christ, who hath glorified you that by a uniform obedience ye may be perfectly joined together in the same mind, and in the same judgment; and may all speak the same things concerning everything:

9 And that being, subject to your bishop, and the presbytery, ye may be wholly and thoroughly sanctified.

10 These things I prescribe to you, not as if I were somebody extraordinary: for though I am bound for his name, I am not yet perfect in Christ Jesus. But now I begin to learn, and I speak to you as fellow disciples together with me.

11 For I ought to have been stirred up by you, in faith: in admonition; in patience; in long- suffering; but forasmuch as charity suffers me not to be silent towards you, I have first taken upon me to exhort you, that ye would all run together, according to the will of God.

12 For even Jesus Christ, our inseparable life, is sent by the will of the Father; as the bishops, appointed unto the utmost bounds of the earth, are by the will of Jesus Christ.

13 Wherefore it will become you to run together according to the will of your bishop, as also ye do,

14 For your famous presbytery, worthy of God, is fitted as exactly to the bishop, as the strings are to the harp.

15 Therefore in your concord and agreeing charity, Jesus Christ is sung; and every single person among you makes up the chorus:

16 That so being all consonant in love, and taking up the song of God, ye may in a perfect unity with one voice, sing to the Father by Jesus Christ; to the end that he may both hear you, and perceive by your works, that ye are indeed the members of his son.

ΔΙΔΑΧΗ ΤΩΝ ΔΩΔΕΚΑ ΑΠΟΣΤΟΛΩΝ

17 Wherefore it is profitable for you to live in an unblameable unity, that so ye may always have a fellowship with God.

CHAPTER II.

1 The benefit of subjection.
4 The bishop not to be respected the less because he is not forward in exacting it:
8 warns brethren against heretics; bidding them cleave to Jesus, whose divine and human mature is declared: commends them for their care to keep themselves from false teachers: and shews them the way to God.

FOR if I in this little time have had such a familiarity with your bishop, I mean not a carnal, but spiritual acquaintance with him; how much more must I think you happy who are so joined to him, as the church is to Jesus Christ, and Jesus Christ to the Father; so that all things may agree in the same unity.

2 Let no man deceive himself; if a man be not within the altar, he is deprived of the bread of God. For if the prayer of one or two be of such force, as we are told; how much more powerful shall that of the bishop and the whole church be?

3 He therefore that does not come together in the same place with it, is proud, and has already condemned himself; for it is written, God resisteth the proud. Let us take heed therefore, that we do not set ourselves against the bishop, that we may be subject to God.

4 The more any one sees his bishop silent, the more let him revere him. For whomsoever the master of the house sends to be over his own household, we ought in like manner to receive him, as we do him that sent him. It is therefore evident that we ought to look upon the bishop, even as we do upon the Lord himself.

5 And indeed Onesimus himself does greatly commend your good order in God: that you all live according to the truth, and that no heresy dwells among you. For neither do ye hearken to anyone more than to Jesus Christ speaking to you in truth.

6 For some there are who carry about the name of Christ in deceitfulness, but do things unworthy of God; whom ye must flee, as ye would do so many wild beasts. For they are raving dogs, who bite secretly; against whom ye must guard yourselves, as men hardly to be cured.

THE EPISTLE OF IGNATIUS TO THE EPHESIANS.

7 There is one Physician, both fleshy and spiritual; made and not made; God incarnate; true life in death; both of Mary and of God: first passible, then impassible; even Jesus Christ our Lord.

8 Wherefore let no man deceive you; as indeed neither are ye deceived, being wholly the servants of God. For inasmuch as there is no contention nor strife among you, to trouble you, ye must needs live according to God's will. My soul be for yours; and I myself, the expiatory offering for your church of Ephesus; so famous throughout the world.

9 They that are of the flesh cannot do the works of the spirit; neither they that are of the spirit the works of the flesh; as he that has faith cannot be an infidel; nor he that is an infidel have faith. But even those things which ye do according to the flesh are spiritual; forasmuch as ye do all things in Jesus Christ.

10 Nevertheless I have heard of some who have passed by you, having perverse doctrine; whom ye did not suffer to sow among you; but stopped your ears, that ye might not receive those things that were sown by them: because being the stones of the temple of the Father, prepared for his building; and drawn up on high by the Cross of Christ, as by an engine;

11. Using the Holy Ghost as the rope: your faith being your support; and your charity the way that leads unto God.

12 Ye are therefore, with all your companions in the same journey full of God; his spiritual temples, full of Christ, and of holiness: adorned in all things with the commands of Christ.

13 In whom also I rejoice that I have been thought worthy by this present epistle to converse, and joy together with you; that with respect to the other life, ye love nothing but God only.

CHAPTER III.

1 Exhorts them to prayer; to be unblamable.
5 To be careful of salvation;
11 frequent in public devotion;
13 and to live in charity.

PRAY also without ceasing for other men; for there is hope of repentance in them, that they may attain unto God. Let them therefore at least be instructed by your works, if they will be no other way.

2 Be ye mild at their anger; humble at their boasting; to their blasphemies return your prayers to their error, your firmness in the faith;

ΔΙΔΑΧΗ ΤΩΝ ΔΩΔΕΚΑ ΑΠΟΣΤΟΛΩΝ

when they are cruel, be ye gentle; not endeavouring to imitate their ways.

(3 Let us be their brethren in all kindness and moderation, but let us be followers of the Lord; for who was ever more unjustly used? More destitute? More despised?).

4 That so no herb of the devil may be found in you: but ye may remain in all holiness and sobriety both of body and spirit, in Christ Jesus.

5 The last times are come upon us: let us therefore be very reverent, and fear the long- suffering of God, that it be not to us unto condemnation.

6 For let us either fear the wrath that is to come, or let us love the grace that we at present enjoy; that by the one or other of these, we may be found in Christ Jesus, unto true life

7 Besides him, let nothing be worthy of you; for whom also I bear about these bonds; those spiritual jewels, in which I would to God that I might arise through your prayers.

8 Of which I entreat you to make me always partaker, that I may be found in the lot of the Christians of Ephesus, who have always agreed with the Apostles, through the power of Jesus Christ.

9 I know both who I am, and to whom I write: I, a person condemned; ye, such as have obtained mercy; I, exposed to danger; ye confirmed against danger.

10 Ye are the passage of those that are killed for God; the companions of Paul in the mysteries of the Gospel; the holy, the martyr, the deservedly most happy Paul: at whose feet may I be found, when I shall have attained unto God; who throughout all his epistles, makes mention of you in Christ Jesus.

11 Let it be your care therefore to come more fully together, to the praise and glory of God; for when ye meet fully together in the same place, the powers of the devil are destroyed, and his mischief is dissolved by the unity of your faith.

12 And indeed, nothing is better than peace, by which all war both spiritual and earthly is abolished.

13 Of all which, nothing is hid from you, if ye have perfect faith and charity in Christ Jesus, which are the beginning and end of life.

14 For the beginning is faith; the end is charity. And these two joined together, are of God; but all other things which concern a holy life, are the consequences of these.

15 No man professing a true faith, sinneth; neither does he who has charity hate any.

16 The tree is made manifest by its fruit; so they who profess themselves to be Christians are known by what they do.

17 For Christianity is not the work of an outward profession; but shows itself in the power of faith, if a man be found faithful unto the end.

18 It is better for a man to hold his peace, and be; than to say, he is a Christian, and not to be.

19 It is good to teach; if what he says he does likewise.

20 There is therefore one master who spake, and it was done; and even those things which he did without speaking, are worthy of the Father.

21 He that possesses the word of Jesus, is truly able to bear his very silence. That he may be perfect, he will do according to what he speaks, and be known by those things of which he is silent.

22 There is nothing hid from God, but even our secrets are nigh unto him.

23 Let us therefore do all things, as becomes those who have God dwelling in them; that we maybe his temples; and he may be our God as also he is, and will manifest himself before our faces, by those things for which we justly love him.

CHAPTER IV.

1 To have a care for the Gospel.
9 The virginity of Mary, the incarnation, and the death of Christ, were hid from the Devil.
11 How the birth of Christ was revealed.
16 Exhorts to unity.

BE not deceived, my brethren: those that corrupt families by adultery, shall not inherit the kingdom of God.

2 If therefore they who do this according to the flesh, have suffered death; how much more shall he die, who by his wicked doctrine corrupts the faith of God, for which Christ was crucified?

3 He that is thus defiled, shall depart into unquenchable fire, and so also shall he that hearkens to him.

4 For this cause did the Lord suffer the ointment to be poured on his head; that he might breathe the breath of immortality unto his church.

ΔΙΔΑΧΗ ΤΩΝ ΔΩΔΕΚΑ ΑΠΟΣΤΟΛΩΝ

5 Be not ye therefore anointed with the evil savour of the doctrine of the prince of this world: let him not take you captive from the life that is set before you.

6 And why are we not all wise, seeing we have received the knowledge of God, which is Jesus Christ? Why do we suffer ourselves foolishly to perish; not considering the gift which the Lord has truly sent to us?

7 Let my life be sacrificed for the doctrine of the cross; which is indeed a scandal to the unbelievers, but to us is salvation and life eternal.

8 Where is the wise man? Where is the disputer? Where is the boasting of those who are called wise?

9 For our Lord Jesus Christ was according to the dispensation of God, conceived in the womb of Mary, of the seed of David, by the Holy Ghost. He was born and baptized, that through his passion he might purify water, to the washing away of sin.

10 Now the Virginity of Mary, and he who was born of her, was kept in secret from the prince of this world; as was also the death of our Lord: three of the mysteries the most spoken of throughout the world, yet done in secret by God.

11 How then was our Saviour manifested to the world? A star shone in heaven beyond all the other stars, and its light was inexpressible, and its novelty struck terror into men's minds. All the rest of the stars, together with the sun and moon, were the chorus to this star; but that sent out its light exceedingly above them all.

12 And men began to be troubled to think whence this new star came so unlike to all the others.

13 Hence all the power of magic became dissolved; and every bond of wickedness was destroyed: men's ignorance was taken away; and the old kingdom abolished; God himself appearing in the form of a man, for the renewal of eternal life.

14 From thence began what God had prepared: from thence. forth things were disturbed; forasmuch as he designed to abolish death.

15 But if Jesus Christ shall give me grace through your prayers, and if it be his will, I purpose in a second epistle which I will suddenly write unto you, to manifest to you more fully the dispensation of which I have now begun to speak, about the new man, which is Jesus Christ; both in his faith, and charity; in his suffering, and in his resurrection.

16 Especially if the Lord shall make known unto me, that ye all by name come together united in one faith, and in Jesus Christ; who was

THE EPISTLE OF IGNATIUS TO THE EPHESIANS.

of the race of David according to the flesh; the Son of man, and son of God; obeying your bishop and the presbytery with an entire affection; breaking one and the same bread, which is the medicine of immortality; our antidote that we should not die, but live for ever in Christ Jesus.

17 My soul be for yours, and theirs whom ye have sent, to the glory of God; even unto Smyrna, from whence also I write to you; giving thanks unto the Lord and loving Polycarp even as I do you. Remember me, as Jesus Christ does remember you.

18 Pray for the church which is in Syria from whence I am carried bound to Rome; being the least of all the faithful which are there, as I have been thought worthy to be found, to the glory of God.

19 Fare ye well in God the Father, and in Jesus Christ, our common hope. Amen.

THE EPISTLE OF IGNATIUS TO THE MAGNESIANS

CHAPTER I.

4 Ignatius mentions the arrival of Damas, their bishop, and others,
6 whom he exhorts them to reverence notwithstanding he was a young man.

IGNATIUS, who is also called Theophorus, to the blessed church, by the grace of God the Father, in Jesus Christ our Saviour; through whom I salute the church which is at Magnesia, near the Maeander: and wish it all joy in God the Father, and in Jesus Christ.

2 When I heard of your well- ordered love and charity in God, being full of joy, I desired much to speak unto you in the faith of Jesus Christ.

3 For having been thought worthy to obtain a most excellent name, in the bonds which I carry about, I salute the churches; wishing in them a union both of the body and spirit of Jesus Christ, our eternal life: as also of faith and charity, to which nothing is preferred: but especially of Jesus and the Father; in whom if we undergo all the injuries of the prince of this present world, and escape, we shall enjoy God,

4 Seeing, then, I have been judged worthy to see you, by Damas your most excellent bishop; and by your worthy presbyters, Bassus and Apolonius; and by my fellow-servant Sotio, the deacon;

5 In whom I rejoice, forasmuch as he is subject unto his bishop as to the grace of God; and to the presbytery as to the law of Jesus Christ; I determined to write unto you.

THE EPISTLE OF IGNATIUS TO THE MAGNESIANS

6 Wherefore it will become you also not to use your bishop too familiarly upon the account of his youth; but to yield all reverence to him according to the power of God the Father; as also I perceive that your holy presbyters do: not considering his age, which indeed to appearance is young; but as becomes those who are prudent in God, submitting to him, or rather not to him but to the Father of our Lord Jesus Christ, the bishop of us all.

7 It will therefore behove you with all sincerity, to obey your bishop; in honour of him whose pleasure it is that ye should do so.

8 Because he that does not do so, deceives not the bishop whom he sees, but affronts him that is invisible. For whatsoever of this kind is done, it reflects not upon man, but upon God, who knows the secrets of our hearts.

9 It is therefore fitting, that we should not only be called christians, but be so.

10 As some call indeed their governor, bishop; but yet do all things without him.

11 But I can never think that such as these have a good conscience, seeing that they are not gathered together thoroughly according to God's commandment.

CHAPTER II.

1 That as all must die,
4 he exhorts them to live orderly and in unity.

SEEING then all things have an end, there are these two indifferently set before us, death and life: and everyone shall depart unto his proper place.

2 For as there are two sorts of coins, the one of God, the other of the world, and each of these has its proper inscription engraven upon it; so also is it here.

3 The unbelievers are of this world; but the faithful, through charity have the character of God the Father by Jesus Christ: by whom if we are not readily disposed to die after the likeness of his passion, his life is not in us.

4 Forasmuch, therefore, as I have in the persons before mentioned, seen all of you in faith and charity; I exhort you that ye study to do all things in a divine concord:

5 Your bishop presiding in the place of God; your presbyters in the place of the council of the Apostles; and your deacons most dear to

ΔΙΔΑΧΗ ΤΩΝ ΔΩΔΕΚΑ ΑΠΟΣΤΟΛΩΝ

me, being entrusted with the ministry of Jesus Christ; who was the Father before all ages, and appeared in the end to us.

6 Wherefore taking the same holy course, see that ye all reverence one another, and let no one look upon his neighbour after the flesh; but do ye all mutually love each other in Jesus Christ.

7 Let there be nothing that may be able to make a division among you; but be ye united to your bishop, and those who preside over you, to be your pattern and direction in the way to immortality.

8 As therefore the Lord did nothing without the Father, being united to him; neither by himself nor yet by his Apostles, so neither do ye do anything without your bishop and presbyters:

9 Neither endeavour to let anything appear rational to yourselves apart;

10 But being come together into the same place, have one common prayer; one supplication; one mind; one hope; one in charity, and in joy undefiled.

11 There is one Lord Jesus Christ, than whom nothing is better. Wherefore come ye all together, as unto one temple of God; as to one altar; as to one: Jesus Christ, who proceeded from one Father, and exists in one; and is returned to one.

CHAPTER III.

1 He cautions them against false opinions.
3 Especially those of Ebion and the Judaising Christians.

BE not deceived with strange doctrines; nor with old fables which are unprofitable. For if we still continue to live according to the Jewish law, we do confess ourselves not to have received grace. For even the most holy prophets lived according to Christ Jesus.

2 And for this cause were they persecuted, being inspired by his grace to convince the unbelievers and disobedient that there is one God who has manifested himself by Jesus Christ his Son; who is his eternal word, not coming forth from silence; who in all things pleased him that sent him.

3 Wherefore if they who were brought up in these ancient laws, came nevertheless to the newness of hope; no longer observing sabbaths, but keeping the Lord's day in which also our life is sprung up by him, and through his death, whom yet some deny:

4 (By which mystery we have been brought to believe and therefore wait that we maybe found the disciples of Jesus Christ, our only master:)

5 How shall we be able to live different from him; whose disciples the very prophets themselves being, did by the spirit expect him as their master;

6 And therefore he whom they justly waited for, being come, raised, them up from the dead.

7 Let us not then be insensible of his goodness; for should he have dealt with us according to our works, we had not now had a being.

8 Wherefore being become his disciples, let us learn to live according to the rules of Christianity; for whosoever is called by any other name besides this, he is not of God.

9 Lay aside therefore the old and sour, and evil leaven; and be ye changed into the new leaven, which is Jesus Christ.

10 Be ye salted in him, lest any one among you should be corrupted; for by your Savior ye shall be judged.

11 It is absurd to name Jesus Christ, and to Judaize. For the christian religion did not embrace the Jewish, but the Jewish the christian; that so every tongue that believed might be gathered together unto God.

12 These things, my beloved, I write unto you; not that I know of any among you that lie under this error: but as one of the least among you, I am desirous to forewarn you, that ye fall not into the snares of false doctrine.

13 But that ye be fully instructed in the birth, and suffering, and resurrection of Jesus Christ, our hope; which was accomplished in the time of the government of Pontius Pilate, and that most truly and certainly: and from which God forbid that any among you should be turned aside.

CHAPTER IV.

1 Commends their faith and piety; exhorts them to persevere;
10 desires their prayers for himself and the church at Antioch.

MAY I therefore have joy of you in all things, if I shall be worthy of it. For though I am bound, yet am I not worthy to be compared to one of you that are at liberty.

ΔΙΔΑΧΗ ΤΩΝ ΔΩΔΕΚΑ ΑΠΟΣΤΟΛΩΝ

2 I know that ye are not puffed up; for ye have Jesus Christ in your hearts.

3 And especially when I commend you, I know that ye are ashamed, as it is written, The just man condemneth himself.

4 Study therefore to be confirmed in the doctrine of our Lord, and of his Apostles; that so whatever ye do, ye may prosper both in body and spirit, in faith and charity, in the Son, and in the Father, and in the Holy Spirit; in the beginning, and in the end:

5 Together with your most worthy bishop, and the well-wrought spiritual crown of your presbytery, and your deacons, which are according to God.

6 Be subject to your bishop, and to one another, as Jesus Christ was to the Father, according to the flesh; and the Apostles, both to Christ, and to the Father; and to the Holy Ghost: that so ye may be united both in body and spirit

7 Knowing you to be full of God, I have the more briefly exhorted you.

8 Be mindful of me in your prayers, that I may attain unto God, and of the church that is in Syria, from which I am not worthy to be called.

9 For I stand in need of your joint prayers in God, and of your charity, that the church which is in Syria may be thought worthy to be nourished by your church.

10 The Ephesians from Smyrna salute you, from which place I write unto you; (being present here to the glory of God, in like manner as you are,) who have in all things refreshed me, together with Polycarp, the bishop of the Smyrneans.

11 The rest of the churches in the honour of Jesus Christ salute you.

12 Farewell, and be ye strengthened in the concord of God; enjoying his inseparable spirit, which is Christ Jesus.

THE EPISTLE OF IGNATIUS TO THE TRALLIANS.

CHAPTER 1.

1 Acknowledges the coming of their bishop.
5 Commends them for their subjection to their bishop, priests, and deacons; and exhorts them to continue in it:
15 is afraid even of his over-great desire to suffer, lest it should be prejudicial to him.

IGNATTUS, who is also called Theophorus, to the holy church which is at Tralles in Asia: beloved of God, the Father of Jesus Christ; elect and worthy of God, having peace through the flesh and blood, and passion of Jesus Christ our hope; in the resurrection which is by him: which also I salute in its fullness, continuing in the apostolical character, wishing all joy and happiness unto it.

2 I have heard of your blameless and constant disposition through patience, which not only appears in your outward conversation, but is naturally rooted and grounded in you.

3 In like manner as Polybius your bishop has declared unto me, who came to me to Smyrna, by the will of God and Jesus Christ, and so rejoiced together with me in my bonds for Jesus Christ, that in effect I saw your whole church in him.

4 Having therefore received testimony of your good will towards me for God's sake, by him; I seemed to find you, as also I knew that ye were the followers of God.

5 For whereas ye are subject to your bishop as to Jesus Christ, ye appear to one to live not after the manner of men, but according to Je-

ΔΙΔΑΧΗ ΤΩΝ ΔΩΔΕΚΑ ΑΠΟΣΤΟΛΩΝ

sus Christ who died for us, that so believing in his death, ye might escape death.

6 It is therefore necessary, that as ye do, so without your bishop you should do nothing: also be ye subject to your presbyters, as to the Apostles of Jesus Christ our hope; in whom if we walk, we shall be found in him.

7 The deacons also, as being the ministers of the mysteries of Jesus Christ, must by all means please ye. For they are not the ministers of meat and drink, but of the church of God. Wherefore they must avoid all offences, as they would do fire.

8 In like manner let us reverence the deacons as Jesus Christ; and the bishop as the Father; and the presbyters as the Sanctuary of God, and college of the Apostles.

9 Without these there is no church; concerning all which, I am persuaded that ye think after the very same manner; for I have received, and even now have with me, the pattern of your love, in your bishop.

10 Whose very look is instructive; and whose mildness powerful: whom I am persuaded, the very Atheists themselves cannot but reverence.

11 But because I have a love towards you, I will not write any more sharply unto you about this matter, though I very well might but now I have done so, lest being a condemned man, I should seem to prescribe to you as an Apostle.

12 I have great knowledge in God; but I refrain myself, lest I should perish in my boasting.

13 For now I ought the more to fear, and not to hearken to those that would puff me up.

14 For they that speak to me, in my praise, chasten me.

15 For I indeed desire to suffer, but I cannot tell whether I am worthy so to do.

16 And this desire, though to others it does not appear, yet to myself it is for that very reason the more violent. I have, therefore, need of moderation; by which the prince of this world is destroyed.

17 Am I not able to write to you of heavenly things?—But I fear lest I should harm you, who are yet but babes in Christ; (excuse me this care;) and lest perchance being not able to receive them, ye should be choken with them.

18 For even I myself, although I am in bonds, yet am not therefore able to understand heavenly things;

THE EPISTLE OF IGNATIUS TO THE TRALLIANS.

19 As the assembly of angels, and the several companies of them, under their respective princes; things visible and invisible: but in these I am yet a learner.

20 For many things are wanting to us, that we come not short of God.

CHAP. II.

1 Warns them against heretics, 4 exhorts them to humility and unity, 10 and briefly sets before them the true doctrine concerning Christ.

EXHORT you therefore, or rather not I, but the love of Jesus Christ; that ye use none but christian nourishment; abstaining from pasture which is of another kind, I mean heresy.

2 For they that are heretics, confound together the doctrine of Jesus Christ, with their own poison: whilst they seem worthy of belief:

3 As men give a deadly potion mixed with sweet wine; which he who drinks of, does with the treacherous pleasure sweetly drink in his own death.

4 Wherefore guard yourself against such persons; and that you will do, if you are not puffed up; but continue inseparable from Jesus Christ our God, and from your bishop, and from the commands of the Apostles.

5 He that is within the altar, is pure; but he that is without, namely, does anything without the bishop, the presbyters, and deacons, is not pure in his conscience.

6 Not that I know there is any thing of this nature among you; but I fore-arm you, as being greatly beloved by me, foreseeing the snares of the devil.

7 Wherefore putting on meekness, renew yourselves in faith, which is the flesh of the Lord; and in charity, which is the blood of Jesus Christ.

8 Let no man have any grudge against his neighbour. Give no occasion to the Gentiles; lest by means of a few foolish men, the whole congregation of God be evil spoken of.

9 For woe to that man through whose vanity my name is blasphemed by any.

10 Stop your ears therefore, as often as any one shall speak contrary to Jesus Christ, who was of the race of David; by the Virgin Mary.

11 Who was truly born, and did eat and drink; was truly persecuted under Pontius Pilate; was truly crucified and dead; both those in heaven and on earth, and under the earth, being spectators of it:

ΔΙΔΑΧΗ ΤΩΝ ΔΩΔΕΚΑ ΑΠΟΣΤΟΛΩΝ

12 Who, was also truly raised from the dead by his Father, after the same manner as HE will also raise up us who believe in him by Christ Jesus; without whom we have no true life.

13 But if, as some who are Atheists, that is to say infidels, pretend, that he seemed to suffer, (they themselves only seeming to exist) why then am I bound?— Why do I desire to fight with beasts?—Therefore do I die in vain: therefore I will not speak falsely against the Lord.

14 Flee therefore these evil sprouts which bring forth deadly fruit; of which if any one taste, he shall presently die.

15 For these are not the plants of the Father; seeing if they were, they would appear to be the branches of the cross, and their fruit would be incorruptible; by which he invites you through his passion, who are members of him.

16 For the head cannot be without its members, God having promised a union with himself.

CHAP. III.

He again exhorts to unity, and desires their prayers for himself, and for his church at Antioch.

I SALUTE you from Smyrna, together with the churches of God that are present with me; who have refreshed me in all things, both in the flesh and in the spirit.

2 My bonds, which I carry about me for the sake of Christ, (beseeching him that I may attain unto God) exhort you that you continue in concord among yourselves, and in prayer with one another.

3 For it becomes everyone of you, especially the presbyters, to refresh the bishop, to the honour of the Father of Jesus Christ, and of the Apostles.

4 I beseech you, that you hearken to me in love; that I may not by those things which I write, rise up in witness against you.

5 Pray also for me; who, through the mercy of God, stand in need of your prayers, that I may be worthy of the portion which I am about to obtain, and that I be not found a reprobate.

6 The love of those who are at Smyrna and Ephesus salute you. Remember in your prayers the church of Syria, from which I am not worthy to be called, being one of the least of it.

7 Fare ye well in Jesus Christ; being subject to your bishop as to the command of God; and so like. wise to the presbytery.

8 Love every one his brother with an unfeigned heart. My soul be your expiation, not only now, but when I shall have attained unto God; for I am yet under danger.

THE EPISTLE OF IGNATIUS TO THE TRALLIANS.

9 But the Father is faithful in Jesus Christ, to fulfil both mine and your petition; in whom may ye be found unblameable.

THE EPISTLE OF IGNATIUS TO THE ROMANS.

CHAPTER I.

Ignatius testifies his desire to see, and his hopes of suffering for Christ
5 which he earnestly entreats them not to prevent,
10 but to pray for him, that God would strengthen him to the combat.

IGNATIUS, who is also called Theophorus, to the church which has obtained mercy from the majesty of the Most High Father, and his only begotten Son Jesus Christ; beloved, and illuminated through the will of him who willeth all things which are according to the love of Jesus Christ our God; which also presides in the place of the region of the Romans; and which I salute in the name of Jesus Christ, as being united both in flesh and spirit to all his commands, and filed with the grace of God; with all joy in Jesus Christ our God.

2 Forasmuch as I have at last obtained through my prayers to God, permission to see your faces, which I much desired to do; being bound in Jesus Christ, I hope ere long to salute you, if it shall be the will of God to grant me to attain unto the end I long for.

3 For the beginning is well disposed, if I shall but have grace, without hindrance, to receive what is appointed for me.

4 But I fear your love, lest it do me an injury; for it is easy for you to do what you please; but it will be hard for me to attain unto God, if you spare me.

5 But I would not that ye should please men, but God; whom also ye do, please. For neither shall I hereafter have such an opportunity of

THE EPISTLE OF IGNATIUS TO THE ROMANS.

going unto God; nor will you, if ye shall now be silent, ever be entitled to a better work. For if you, shall be silent in my behalf, I shall be made partaker of God.

6 But if you shall love my body, I shall have my course again to run. Wherefore ye cannot do me a greater kindness, than to suffer me to be sacrificed unto God, now that the altar is already prepared:

7 That when ye shall be gathered together in love, ye nay give thanks to the Father through Christ Jesus, that he has vouchsafed to bring a bishop of Syria unto you, being called from the east unto the west.

8 For it is good for me to turn from the world, unto God; that I may rise again unto him.

9 Ye have never envied any one; ye have taught others. I would therefore that ye should now do those things yourselves, which in your instructions you have prescribed to others.

10 Only pray for me, that God would give me both inward and outward strength, that I may not only say, but will; nor be only called a christian, but be found one.

11 For if I shall be found a christian, I may then deservedly be called one; and be thought faithful, when I shall no longer appear to the world.

12 Nothing is good, that is seen.

13 For even our God, Jesus Christ, now that he is in the Father, does so much the more appear.

14 A christian is not a work of opinion; but of greatness of mind, especially when he is hated by the world.

CHAPTER. II.

Expresses his great desire and determination to suffer martyrdom.

I WRITE to the churches, and signify to them all, that I am willing to die for God, unless you hinder me.

2 I beseech you that you show not an unseasonable good will towards me. Suffer me to be food to the wild beasts, by whom I shall attain unto God.

3 For I am the wheat of God, and I shall be ground by the teeth of the wild-beasts, that I may be found the pure bread of Christ. Rather encourage the beasts, that they may became my sepulchre, and may let

ΔΙΔΑΧΗ ΤΩΝ ΔΩΔΕΚΑ ΑΠΟΣΤΟΛΩΝ

live nothing of my body; that being dead I may not be troublesome to any.

5 Then shall I be truly the disciple of Jesus Christ, when the world shall not see so much as my body. Pray therefore unto Christ for me, that by these instruments I may be made the sacrifice of God.

6 I do not, as Peter and Paul, command you. They were Apostles, I a condemned man; they were free, but I am even to this day a servant:

7 But if I shall suffer, I shall then become the freeman of Jesus Christ, and shall rise free. And now, being in bonds I learn not to desire any thing.

8 From Syria even unto Rome, I fight with beasts both by sea and land; both night and day: being bound to ten leopards, that is to say, to such a band of soldiers, who, though treated with all manner of kindness, are the worse for it.

9 But I am the more instructed by their injuries; yet am I not therefore justified.

10 May I enjoy the wild beasts that are prepared for me; which also I wish may exercise all their fierceness upon me.

11 And whom for that end I will encourage, that they may be sure to devour me, and not serve me as they have done some, whom out of fear they have not touched. But if they will not do it willingly, I will provoke them to it.

12 Pardon me in this matter; I know what is profitable for me, now I begin to be a disciple. Not shall any thing move me whether visible or invisible, that I may attain to Jesus Christ.

13 Let fire and the cross; let the companies of wild beasts; let breakings of bones, and tearing of members; let the shattering in pieces of the whole body, and all the wicked torments of the devil come upon me; only let me enjoy Jesus Christ.

14 All the ends of the world, and the kingdoms of it, will profit me nothing: I would rather die for Jesus Christ, than rule to the utmost ends of the earth. Him I seek who died for us; him I desire who rose again for us. This is the gain that is laid up for me.

15 Pardon me, my brethren, ye shall not hinder me from living; nor seeing I desire to go to God, may you separate me from him, for the sake of this world;—nor induce me by any of the desires of it. Suffer me to enter into pure light, where being come, I shall be indeed the servant of God.

16 Permit me to imitate the passion of my God. If any one has God within himself, let him consider what I desire; and let him have compassion on me, as knowing how I am straightened.

THE EPISTLE OF IGNATIUS TO THE ROMANS.

CHAPTER III.

Further expresses his desire to suffer.

THE prince of this world would fain carry me away, and corrupt my resolution towards my God. Let none of you therefore help him; rather do ye join with me, that is, with God.

2 Do not speak with Jesus Christ, and yet covet the world. Let not any envy dwell with you; no, not though I myself, when I shall be come unto you, should exhort you to it, yet do not ye hearken to me; but rather believe what I now write to you.

3 For though I am alive at the writing of this, yet my desire is to die. My love is crucified; and the fire that is within me does not desire any water; but being alive and springing within me, says, Come to the Father.

4 I take no pleasure in the food of corruption, nor in the pleasures of this life.

5 I desire the bread of God which is the flesh of Jesus Christ, of the seed of David; and the drink that I long for is his blood, which is incorruptible love.

6 I have no desire to live any longer after the manner of men; neither shall I, if you consent. Be ye therefore willing, that ye yourselves also maybe pleasing to God. I exhort you in a few words; I pray you believe me.

7 Jesus Christ will shew you that I speak truly. My mouth is without deceit, and the Father hath truly spoken by it. Pray therefore for me, that I may accomplish what I desire.

8 I have not written to you after the flesh, but according to the will of God. If I shall suffer, ye have loved me: but if I shall be rejected, ye have hated me.

9 Remember in your prayers the church of Syria, which now enjoys God for its shepherd instead of me. Let Jesus Christ only oversee it, and your charity.

10 But I am even ashamed to be reckoned as one of them; for neither am I worthy, being the least among them, and as one born out of due season. But through mercy I have risen to be somebody, if I shall get unto God.

11 My spirit salutes you; and the charity of the churches that have received me in the name of Jesus Christ; not as a passenger, for even they that were not near to me in the way, have gone before me to the next city to meet me.

ΔΙΔΑΧΗ ΤΩΝ ΔΩΔΕΚΑ ΑΠΟΣΤΟΛΩΝ

12 These things I write to you from Smyrna, by the most worthy of the church of Ephesus.

13 There is now with me, together with many others, Crocus, most beloved of me. As for those which are come from Syria, and are gone before me to Rome, to the glory of God, I suppose you are not ignorant of them.

14 Ye shall therefore signify to them that I draw near, for they, are all worthy both of God and of you: Whom it is fit that you refresh in all things.

15 This have I written to you, the day before the ninth of the, calends of September. Be strong unto the end, in the patience of Jesus Christ.

IGNATIUS TO THE PHILADELPHIANS.

CHAPTER I.

Commends their bishop, whom they had sent unto him, warns them against division and schism.

IGNATIUS, who is also called Theophorus, to the church of God the Father, and our Lord Jesus Christ, which is at Philadelphia in Asia; which has obtained mercy, being fixed in the concord of God, and rejoicing evermore in the passion of our Lord, and being fulfilled in all mercy through his resurrection: Which also I salute in the blood of Jesus Christ, which is our eternal and undefiled joy; especially if they are at unity with the bishop, and presbyters who are with him, and the deacons appointed according to the mind of Jesus Christ; whom he has settled according to his own will in all firmness by his Holy Spirit:

2 Which bishop I know obtained that great ministry among you, not of himself, neither by men, nor out of vain glory; but by the love of God the Father, and our Lord Jesus Christ.

3 Whose moderation I admire; who by his silence is able to do more than others with all their vain talk. For he is fitted to the commands, as the harp to its strings.

4 Wherefore my soul esteems his mind towards God most happy, knowing it to be fruitful in all virtue, and perfect; full of constancy, free from passion, and according to all the moderation of the living God.

5 Wherefore as becomes the children both of the light and of truth; flee divisions and false doctrines; but where your shepherd is, there do ye, as sheep, follow after.

ΔΙΔΑΧΗ ΤΩΝ ΔΩΔΕΚΑ ΑΠΟΣΤΟΛΩΝ

6 For there are many wolves who seem worthy of belief, that with a false pleasure lead captive those that run in the course of God; but in the concord they shall find no place.

7 Abstain therefore from those evil herbs which Jesus Christ does not dress: because such are not the plantation of the Father. Not that I have found any division among you, but rather all manner of purity.

8 For as many as are of God, and of Jesus Christ, are also with their bishop. And as many as shall with repentance return into the unity of the church, even these shall also be the servants of God, that they may live according to Jesus Christ.

9 Be not deceived brethren; if any one follows him that makes a schism in the church, he shall not inherit the kingdom of God. If any one walks after any other opinion, he agrees not with the passion of Christ.

10 Wherefore let it be your endeavour to partake all of the same holy eucharist.

11 For there is but one flesh of our Lord Jesus Christ; one cup in the unity of his blood; and one altar;

12 As also there is one bishop, together with his presbytery, and the deacons my fellow servants that so whatsoever ye do, ye may do it according to the will of God.

CHAPTER II.

Desires their prayers, and to be united, but not to Judaize.

MY brethren, the love I have towards you makes me the more large; and having a great joy in you, I endeavour to secure you against danger; or rather not I, but Jesus Christ; in whom being bound, I the more fear, as being yet only on the way to suffering.

2 But your prayer to God shall make me perfect, that I may attain to that portion, which by God's mercy is allotted to me Fleeing to the Gospel as to the flesh of Christ; and to the Apostles as to the presbytery of the church.

3 Let us also love the prophets, forasmuch as they have led us to the Gospel, and to hope in Christ, and to expect him.

4 In whom also believing they were saved in the unity of Jesus Christ; being holy men, worthy to be loved, and had in wonder;

5 Who have received testimony from Jesus Christ, and are numbered in the Gospel of our common hope.

IGNATIUS TO THE PHILADELPHIANS.

6 But if any one shall preach the Jewish law unto you, hearken not unto him; for it is better to receive the doctrine of Christ from one that has been circumcised, than Judaism from one that has not.

7 But if either the one, or other, do not speak concerning Christ Jesus; they seem to me to be but as monuments and sepulchres of the dead, upon which are written only the names of men.

8 Flee therefore the wicked arts and snares of the prince of this world; lest at any time being oppressed by his cunning, ye grow cold in your charity. But come altogether into the same place, with an undivided heart.

9 And I bless my God that I have a good conscience towards you, and that no one among you has whereof to boast either openly or privately, that I have been burthensome to him in much or little.

10 And I wish to all, among whom I have conversed, that may not turn to a witness again them.

11 For although some would have deceived me according to the flesh, yet the spirit, being from God, is not deceived: for it knows, both whence it comes and whither it goes, and reproves the secrets of the heart.

12 I cried whilst I was among you; I spake with a loud voice: attend to the bishop, and to the presbytery, and to the deacons.

13 Now some supposed that I spake this as foreseeing the division that should come among you.

14 But he is my witness for whose sake I am in bonds that I know nothing from any man. But the spirit spake, saying on this wise: Do nothing without the bishop:

15 Keep your bodies as the temples of God: Love unity; Flee divisions; Be the followers of Christ, as he was of his Father.

16 I therefore did as became me, as a man composed to unity for where there is division, and wrath, God dwelleth not.

17 But the Lord forgives all that repent, if they return to the unity of God, and to the council of the bishop.

18 For I trust in the grace Jesus Christ that he will free you from every bond.

19 Nevertheless I exhort you that you do nothing out of strife but according to the instruction of Christ.

20 Because I have heard some who say; unless I find written in the originals, I will not believe it to be written in the Gospel. And when I said, It is written; they answered from what lay before them in the corrupted copies.

ΔΙΔΑΧΗ ΤΩΝ ΔΩΔΕΚΑ ΑΠΟΣΤΟΛΩΝ

21 But to me Jesus Christ instead of all the uncorrupted monuments in the world; together with those undefiled monuments, his cross, and death, and resurrection, and the faith which is by him; by which I desire, through your prayers, to be justified.

22 The priests indeed are good; but much better is the High Priest to whom the Holy of Holies has been committed; and who alone has been intrusted with the secrets of God.

23 He is the door of the Father; by which Abraham, and Isaac, and Jacob, and all the prophets, enter in; as well as the Apostles, and the church.

24 And all these things tend to the unity which is of God. Howbeit the Gospel has somewhat in it far above all other dispensations; namely, the appearance of our Saviour, the Lord Jesus Christ, his passion and resurrection.

25 For the beloved prophets referred to him; but the Gospel is the perfection of incorruption. All therefore together are good, if ye believe with charity.

CHAPTER III.

Informs them he had heard that the persecution was stopped at Antioch: and directs them to send a messenger thither to congratulate with the church.

NOW as concerning the church of Antioch which is in Syria, seeing I am told that through your prayers and the bowels which ye have towards it in Jesus Christ, it is in peace; it will become you, as the church of God, to ordain some I deacon to go to them thither as the ambassador of God; that he may rejoice with them when they meet together, and glorify God's name.

2 Blessed be that man in Jesus, Christ, who shall be found worthy of such a ministry; and ye yourselves also shall be glorified.

3 Now if you be willing, it is not impossible for you to do this for the grace of God; as also the other neighbouring churches have sent them some bishops, some priests and some deacons.

4 As concerning Philo the deacon of Cilicia, a most worthy man, he still ministers unto me in the word of God: together with Rheus of Agathopolis a singular good person, who has followed me even from Syria, not regarding his life: These also bear witness unto you.

IGNATIUS TO THE PHILADELPHIANS.

5 And I myself give thanks to God for you, that you receive them as the Lord shall receive you. But for those that dishonoured them, may they be forgiven through the grace of Jesus Christ.

6 The charity of the brethren that are at Troas salutes you: from whence also I now write by Burrhurs, who was sent together with me by those of Ephesus and Smyrna, for respect sake.

7 May our Lord Jesus Christ honour them; in whom they hope, both in flesh, and soul, and spirit; in faith, in love, in unity. Fare-well in Christ Jesus our common hope.

IGNATIUS TO THE SMYRNEANS.

CHAPTER I.

**1 Declares his joy for their firmness in the Gospel.
4 Enlarges on the person of Christ, against such as pretend that Christ did not suffer.**

IGNATIUS, who is also called Theophorus, to the church of God the Father, and of the beloved Jesus Christ, which God hath mercifully blessed with every good gift; being filled with faith and charity, so that it is wanting in no gift; most worthy of God, and fruitful in saints; the church which is at Smyrna in Asia; all through his immaculate spirit, through word of God.

2 I glorify God, even Jesus Christ, who has given you such wisdom.

3 For I have observed that you are settled in an immoveable faith, as if you were nailed to the cross of our Lord Jesus Christ, both in the flesh and in the spirit; and are confirmed in love through the blood of Christ; being fully persuaded of those things which relate unto our Lord.

4 Who truly was of the race of David according to the flesh, but the Son of God according to the will and power of God; truly born of the Virgin, and baptised of John; that so all righteousness might be fulfilled by him.

5 He was also truly crucified by Pontius Pilate, and Herod the Tetrarch, being nailed for us in the flesh; by the fruits of which we are, even by his most blessed Passion;

6 That he might set up a token for all ages through his resurrection, to all his holy and faithful servants, whether they be Jews or Gentiles, in one body of his church.

7 Now all these things he suffered for us that we might be saved; and he suffered truly, as he also truly raised up himself; and not, as some unbelievers say, that he only seemed to suffer; they themselves 'only seeming to be.'

8 And as they believe so shall it happen unto them, when being divested of the body they shall become mere spirits.

9 But I know that even after his resurrection he was in the flesh; and I believe that he is still so.

10 And when he came to those who were with Peter, he said unto them, Take, handle me, and see that I am not an incorporeal daemon. And straightway they felt and believed; being convinced both by his flesh and spirit.

11 For this cause they despised death, and were bound to be above it.

12 But after his resurrection he did eat and drink with them, as he was flesh; although as to his Spirit he was united to the Father.

CHAPTER II.

1 Exhorts them against heretics.
8 The danger of their doctrine.

NOW these things, beloved, I put you in mind of, not questioning but that you yourselves also believe that they are so.

2 But I arm you before-hand against certain beasts in the shape of men, whom you must not only not receive, but if it be possible must not meet with.

3 Only you must pray for them, that if it be the will of God they may repent; which yet will be very hard. But of this our Lord Jesus Christ has the power, who is our true life.

4 For if all these things were done only in show by our Lord, then do I also seem only to be bound:

5 And why have I given up myself to death, to the fire, to the sword, to wild beasts?

6 But now the nearer I am to the sword, the nearer I am to God: when I shall come among the wild beasts, I shall come to God.

7 Only in the name of Jesus Christ, I undergo all, to suffer together with him; he who was made a perfect man strengthening, me.

8 Whom some not knowing, do deny; or rather have been denied by him, being the advocates of death, rather than of the truth. Whom

ΔΙΔΑΧΗ ΤΩΝ ΔΩΔΕΚΑ ΑΠΟΣΤΟΛΩΝ

neither the prophecies, nor the law of Moses have persuaded; nor the Gospel itself, even to this day; nor the sufferings of every one of us.

9 For they think also the same things of us. For what does a man profit me, if he shall praise me, and blaspheme my Lord; not confessing that he was truly made man?

10 Now he that doth not say this, does in effect deny him, and is in death. But for the names of such as do this, they being unbelievers, I thought it not fitting to write them unto you.

11 Yea, God forbid that I should make any mention of them, till they shall repent to a true belief of Christ's passion, which is our resurrection.

12 Let no man deceive himself; both the things which are in heaven, and the glorious angels, and princes, whether visible or invisible, if they believe not in the blood of Christ, it shall be to them, unto condemnation.

13 He that is able to receive this, let him receive it. Let no man's place or state in the world puff him up: that which is worth all his faith and charity, to it nothing is to be preferred.

14 But consider those who are of a different opinion from us, as to what concerns the grace of Jesus Christ which is come unto us, how contrary they are to the design of God.

15 They have no regard to charity, no care of the widow, the fatherless, and the oppressed; of the bond or free, of the hungry or thirsty.

16 They abstain from the eucharist, and from the public offices; because they confess not the eucharist to be the flesh of our Saviour Jesus Christ which suffered for our sins, and which the Father of his goodness raised again from the dead.

17 And for this cause contradicting the gift of God, they die in their disputes; but much better would it be for them to receive it, that they might one day rise through it.

18 It will therefore become you. to abstain from such persons, and not to speak with them, neither in public nor in private.

19 But to hearken to the prophets, and especially to the Gospel, in which both Christ's passion is manifested unto us, and his resurrection perfectly declared.

20 But flee all divisions, as the beginning of evils.

IGNATIUS TO THE SMYRNEANS.

CHAPTER III.

**1 Exhorts them to follow their bishop and pastors; but especially their bishop.
6 Thanks them for their kindness,
11 and acquaints them with the ceasing of the persecution at Antioch.**

SEE that ye all follow your bishop, as Jesus Christ, the Father; and the presbytery, as the Apostles; and reverence the deacons, as the command of God.

2 Let no man do any thing of what belongs to the church separately from the bishop.

3 Let that eucharist be looked upon as well established, which is either offered by the bishop, or by him to whom the bishop has given. his consent.

4 Wheresoever the bishop shall appear, there let the people also be: as where Jesus Christ is, there is the Catholic church.

5 It is not lawful without the bishop; neither to baptize, nor to celebrate the Holy Communion but whatsoever he shall approve of, that is also pleasing unto God; that so whatever is done, may be sure and well done.

6 For what remains, it is very reasonable that we should repent whilst there is yet time to return unto God.

7 It is a good thin to have a due regard both to God, and to the bishop: he that honours the bishop, shall be honoured of God; but he that does any thing without his knowledge, ministers unto the devil.

8 Let all things therefore abound to you in charity; seeing that ye are worthy.

9 Ye have refreshed me in all things; so shall Jesus Christ you. Ye have loved me both when I was present with you, and now being absent, ye cease not to do so.

10 May God be your reward, for whom whilst ye undergo all things, ye shall attain unto him.

11 Ye have done well in that ye have received Philo, and Rheus Agathopus, who followed me for the word of God, as the deacons of Christ our God.

12 Who also gave thanks unto the Lord for you, forasmuch as ye have refreshed them in all things. Nor shall any thing that you have done be lost to you.

ΔΙΔΑΧΗ ΤΩΝ ΔΩΔΕΚΑ ΑΠΟΣΤΟΛΩΝ

13 My soul be for yours, and my bonds which ye have not despised, nor been ashamed of. Wherefore neither shall Jesus Christ, our perfect faith, be ashamed of you.

14 Your prayer is come to the church of Antioch, which is in Syria. From whence being sent bound with chains becoming God. I salute the churches; being not worthy to be called from thence, as being the least among them.

15 Nevertheless by the will of God I have been thought worthy of this honour; not for that I think I have deserved it, but by the grace of God;

16 Which I wish may be perfectly given unto me, that through your prayers I may attain unto God.

17 And therefore, that your work may be fully accomplished, both upon earth and in heaven; it will be fitting, and for the honour of God, that your church appoint some worthy delegate, who being come as far as Syria, may rejoice together with them that they are in peace; and that they are again restored to their former state, and have again received their proper body.

18 Wherefore I should think it a worthy action, to send some one from you with an epistle, to congratulate with them their peace in God; and that through your prayers, they have now gotten to their harbour.

19 For inasmuch as ye are perfect yourselves, you ought to think those things that are perfect. For when you are desirous to do well, God is ready to enable you there, unto.

20 The love of the brethren that are at Troas salute you; from whence I write to you by Burrhus whom ye sent with me, together with the Ephesians, your brethren; and who has in all Things refreshed me.

21 And I would to God that all would imitate him, as being a pattern of the ministry of God. May his grace fully reward him.

22 I salute your very worthy bishop, and your venerable presbytery; and your deacons, my fellow-servants; and all of you in general, and every one in particular, in the name of Jesus Christ, and in his flesh and blood; in his passion and resurrection both fleshly and spiritually; and in the unity of God with you.

23 Grace be with you, and mercy, and peace, and patience, for evermore.

24 I salute the families of my brethren, with their wives and children; and the virgins that are called widows. Be strong in the power of the Holy Ghost. Philo, who is present with me salutes you.

IGNATIUS TO THE SMYRNEANS.

25 I salute the house of Tavias, and pray that it may be strengthened in faith and charity, both of flesh and spirit.

26 I salute Alce my well-beloved, together with the incomparable Daphnus, and Eutechnus, and all by name.

27 Farewell in the grace of God.

IGNATIUS TO POLYCARP

CHAPTER I.

Ignatius blesses God for the firm, establishment of Polycarp in the faith, and gives him particular directions for improving it.

IGNATIUS, who is also called Theophorus, to Polycarp, bishop of the church which is at Smyrna; their overseer, but rather himself overlooked by God the Father, and the Lord Jesus Christ; all happiness.

2 Having known that thy mind towards God, is fixed as it were upon an immoveable rock; I exceedingly give thanks, that I have been thought worthy to behold thy blessed face, in which may I always rejoice in God.

3 Wherefore I beseech thee by the grace of God with which thou art clothed, to press forward in thy course, and to exhort all others that they may be saved.

4 Maintain thy place with all care both of flesh and spirit: Make it thy endeavour to preserve unity, than which nothing is better. Bear with all men even as the Lord with thee.

5 Support all in love, as also thou dost. Pray without ceasing ask more understanding than what thou already hast. Be watchful, having thy spirit always awake.

6 Speak to every one according as God shall enable thee. Bear the infirmities of all, as a perfect combatant; where the labour is great, the gain is the more.

7 If thou shalt love the good disciples, what thank is it? But rather do thou subject to thee those that are mischievous, in meekness.

8 Every wound is not healed with the same plaister: if the accessions of the disease be vehement, modify them with soft remedies: be in all things wise as a serpent, but harmless as a dove.

9 For this cause thou art composed of flesh and spirit; that thou mayest modify those things that appear before thy face.

10 And as for those that are not seen, pray to God that he would reveal them into thee, that so thou mayest be wanting in nothing, but mayest abound in every gift.

11 The times demand thee, as the pilots the winds; and he that is tossed in a tempest, the haven where he would be.

12 That thou mayest attain unto God, be sober as the combatant of God. The crown proposed to thee is immortality, and eternal life: concerning which thou art also fully persuaded. I will be thy surety in all things, by my bonds, which thou halt loved.

13 Let not those that seem worthy of credit, but teach other doctrines, disturb thee. Stand firm and immoveable, as an anvil when it is beaten upon.

14 It is the part of a brave combatant to be wounded, and yet overcome. But especially we ought to endure all things for God's sake, that he may bear with us.

15 Be every day better than others; consider the times, and expect him, who is above all time, eternal; invisible, though for our sakes made visible: impalpable, and impassible, yet for us subjected to sufferings; enduring all manner of ways for our salvation.

CHAPTER II.

1 Continues his advice,
6 and teaches him how to advise others.
12 Enforces unity and subjection to the bishop.

LET not the widows be neglected: be thou after God, their Guardian.

2 Let nothing be done without thy knowledge and consent; neither do thou anything but according to the will of God; as also thou dost, with all constancy.

3 Let your assemblies be more full: inquire into all by name.

4 Overlook not the men and maid servants; neither let them be puffed up: but rather let them be the more subject to the glory of God, that they may obtain from him a better liberty.

ΔΙΔΑΧΗ ΤΩΝ ΔΩΔΕΚΑ ΑΠΟΣΤΟΛΩΝ

5 Let them not desire to be set free at the public cost, that they be not slaves to their own lusts.

6 Flee evil arts; or rather make not any mention of them.

7 Say to my sisters, that they love the Lord; and be satisfied with their own husbands, both in the flesh and spirit.

8 In like manner, exhort my brethren in the name of Jesus Christ, that they love their wives, even as the Lord the church.

9 If any man can remain in a virgin state, to the honour of the flesh of Christ, let him remain without boasting; but if he boast, he is undone. And if he desire to be more taken notice of than the bishop he is corrupted.

10 But it becomes all such as are married, whether men or women, to come together with the consent of the bishop, that so their marriage may be according to godliness, and not in lust.

11 Let all things be done to the honour of God.

12 Hearken unto the bishop, that God also may hearken unto you. My soul be security for them that submit to their bishop, with their presbyters and deacons. And may my portion be together with theirs in God.

13 Labour with one another; contend together, run together, suffer together; sleep together, and rise together; as the stewards, and assessors, and ministers of God.

14 Please him under whom ye war; and from whom ye receive your wages. Let none of you be found a deserter; but let your baptism remain, as your arms; your faith, as your helmet; your charity, as your spear; your patience, as your whole armour.

15 Let your works be your charge, that so you may receive a suitable reward. Be long suffering therefore towards each other in meekness; as God is towards you.

16 Let me have joy of you in all things.

CHAPTER III.

1 Greets Polycarp on the peace of the church at Antioch:
2 and desires him to write to that and other churches.

NOW forasmuch as the church of Antioch in Lyria is, as I am told, in peace through your prayers; I also have been the more comforted, and without care in God; if so be that by suffering, I shall attain unto God; and through your prayers I may be found a disciple of Christ.

IGNATIUS TO POLYCARP

2 It will be very fit, O most worthy Polycarp, to call a select council, and choose some one whom ye particularly love, and who is patient of labour: that he may be the messenger of God; and that going unto Syria, he may glorify your incessant love, to the praise of Christ.

3 A Christian has not the power of himself; but must be always at leisure for God's service. Now this work is both God's and our's; when ye shall have perfected it.

4 For I trust through the grace of God that ye are ready to every good work that is fitting for you in the Lord.

5 Knowing therefore your earnest affection for the truth, I have exhorted you by these short letters.

6 But forasmuch as I have not been able to write to all the churches, because I must suddenly sail from Troas to Neapolis; (for so is the command of those to whose pleasure I am subject;) do you write to the churches that are near you, as being instructed in the will of God, that they also may do in like manner.

7 Let those that are able send messengers; and let the rest send their letters by those who shall be sent by you: that you may be glorified to all eternity, of which you are worthy.

8 I salute all by name; particularly the wife of Epitropus with all her house and children. I salute Attalus my well-beloved.

9 I salute him who shall be thought worthy to be sent by you into Syria. Let grace be ever with him, and with Polycarp who sends him.

10 I wish you all happiness in our God, Jesus Christ; in whom continue, in the unity and protection of God.

11 I salute Alce my well- beloved. Farewell in the Lord.

REFERENCES TO THE SEVEN EPISTLES OF IGNATIUS.

[The Epistles of Ignatius are translated by Archbishop Wake from the text of Vossius. He says that there were considerable difference in the editions; the best for a long time extant containing fabrications, and the genuine being altered and corrupted. Archbishop Usher printed old Latin translations of them at Oxford, in 1644. At Amsterdam, two years afterwards, Vossius printed six of them in their ancient and pure Greek; and the seventh, greatly amended from the ancient Latin version, was Printed at Paris, by Ruinart, in 1689, in the Acts and Martyrdom of Ignatius, from a Greek uninterpolated copy. These are supposed to form the collection that Polycarp made of the Epistles of Ignatius, mentioned by Irenaes, Origen, Eusebius, Jerome, Athanasius, Theodoret, and other ancients: but many learned men have imagined all of them to be apocryphal. This supposition, the piety of Archbishop Wake, and his persuasion of their utility to the faith of the church, will

ΔΙΔΑΧΗ ΤΩΝ ΔΩΔΕΚΑ ΑΠΟΣΤΟΛΩΝ

not permit him to entertain: hence he has taken great pains to render the present translation acceptable, by adding numerous readings and references to the Canonical Books.]

THE EPISTLE OF POLYCARP TO THE PHILIPPIANS.

[The genuineness of this Epistle is controverted, but implicitly believed by Archbishop Wake, whose translation is below. There is also a translation by Dr. Cave attached to his life of Polycarp.]

CHAPTER I.

Polycarp commends the Philippians for their respect to those who suffered for the Gospel; and for their own faith.

POLYCARP, and the presbyters that are with him, to the church of God which is at Philippi; mercy unto you, and peace from God Almighty, and the Lord Jesus Christ our Saviour, be multiplied.

2 I rejoiced greatly with you in our Lord Jesus Christ, that ye received the images of a true love, and accompanied, as it behoved you, those who were in bonds, becoming saints; which are the crowns of such as are truly chosen by God and our Lord:

3 As also that the root of the faith which was preached from ancient times, remains firm in you to this day; and brings forth fruit to our Lord Jesus Christ, who suffered himself to be brought even to the death for our sins:

4 Whom God hath raised up, having loosed the pains of death. Whom having not seen, ye love; in whom though now ye see him not, yet believing, ye rejoice with joy unspeakable and full of glory.

5 Into which many desire to enter; I knowing that by grace ye are saved; not by works, but by the will of God through Jesus Christ.

6 Wherefore girding up the loins of your minds; I serve the Lord with fear, and in truth; laying aside all empty and vain speech, and the

ΔΙΔΑΧΗ ΤΩΝ ΔΩΔΕΚΑ ΑΠΟΣΤΟΛΩΝ

errors of many; believing in him that raised up our Lord Jesus Christ from the dead, and hath given him glory and a throne at his right hand.

7 To whom all things are made subject, both that are in heaven, and that are in earth; whom every living creature shall worship; who shall come to be the judge of the quick and dead: whose blood God shall require of them that believe not in him.

8 But he that raised up Christ from the dead, shall also raise up us in like manner, if we do his will, and walk according to his commandments; and love those things which he loved:

9 Abstaining from all unrighteousness; inordinate affection, and love of money; from evil. speaking; false witness; not rendering evil for evil, or railing for railing, or striking for striking, or cursing for cursing:

10 But remembering what the Lord has taught us saying, Judge not, and ye shall not be judged; forgive and ye shall be forgiven; be ye merciful, and ye shall obtain mercy; for with the same measure that ye meet withal, it shall be measured to you again.

11 And again; Blessed are the poor, and they that are persecuted for righteousness sake; for theirs is the kingdom of God.

CHAPTER II.

2 Exhorts to Faith, Hope, and Charity.
5 Against covetousness, and as to the duties of husbands, wives, widows,
9 deacons, young men, virgins, and presbyters.

THESE things, my brethren, I took not the liberty of myself to write unto you concerning righteousness, but you yourselves before encouraged me to it.

2 For neither can i, nor any other such as I am, come up to the wisdom of the blessed and renowned Paul; who being himself in person with those who then lived, did with all exactness and soundness teach the word of truth: and being gone from you wrote an epistle to you.

3 Into which if you look, you will be able to edify yourselves in the faith that has been delivered unto you, which is the mother of us all; being followed with hope, and led on by a general love, both towards God and towards Christ, and towards our neighbour.

4 For if any man has these things, he has fulfilled the law of righteousness: for he that has charity is far from all sin.

THE EPISTLE OF POLYCARP TO THE PHILIPPIANS.

5 But the love of money is the root of all evil. Knowing therefore that as we brought nothing into this world, so neither may we carry any thing out; let us arm ourselves with the armour of righteousness.

6 And teach ourselves first to walk according to the commandments of the Lord; and then your wives to walk likewise according to the faith that is given to them; in charity, and in purity; loving their own husbands, with all sincerity, and all others alike, with all temperance; and to bring up their children in the instruction and fear of the Lord.

7 The widows likewise teach that they be sober as to what concerns the faith of the Lord: praying always for all men; being far from all detraction, evil speaking, false witness; from covetousness, and from all evil.

8 Knowing that they are the altars of God, who sees all blemishes, and from whom nothing is hid; who searches out the very reasonings, and thoughts, and secrets of our hearts.

9 Knowing therefore that God is not mocked, we ought to walk worthy both of his command and of his glory.

10 Also the deacons must be blameless before him, as the ministers of God in Christ, and not of men. Not false mousers, not double tongued, not lovers of money; but moderate in all things; compassionate, careful; walking according to the truth of the Lord, who was the servant of all.

11 Whom if we please in this present world, we shall also be made partakers of that which is to come, according as he has promised to us, that he will raise us from the dead; and that if we shall walk worthy of him, we shall also reign together with him, if we believe.

12 In like manner the younger men must be unblameable in all things; above all, taking care of their purity, and to restrain themselves from all evil. For it is good to be cut off from the lusts that are in the world; because every such lust warreth against the spirit: and neither fornicators, nor effeminate, nor abusers of themselves with mankind, shall inherit the kingdom of God; nor they who do such things as are foolish and unreasonable.

13 Wherefore ye must needs abstain from all these things, being subject to the priests and deacons, as unto God and Christ.

14 The virgins admonish to walk in a spotless and pure conscience.

15 And let the elders be compassionate and merciful towards all; turning them from their errors; seeking out those that are weak; not forgetting the widows, the fatherless, and the poor; but always providing what is good both in the sight of God and man.

ΔΙΔΑΧΗ ΤΩΝ ΔΩΔΕΚΑ ΑΠΟΣΤΟΛΩΝ

16 Abstaining from all wrath, respect of persons, and unrighteous judgment; and especially being free from all covetousness.

17 Not easy to believe anything against any; not severe in judgment; knowing that we are all debtors in point of sin

18 If therefore we pray to the Lord that he would forgive us, we ought also to forgive others; for we are all in the sight of our Lord and God; a and must all stand before the judgment-seat of Christ; and shall every one give an account of himself.

19 Let us therefore serve him in fear, and with all reverence as both himself hath commanded; and as the Apostles who have preached the Gospel unto us, and the prophets who have foretold the coming of our Lord have taught us:

20 Being zealous of what is good; abstaining from all offence, and from false brethren; and from those who bear the name of Christ in hypocrisy; who deceive vain men.

CHAPTER III.

1 As to faith in our Saviour Christ; his nature and sufferings, the resurrection and judgment.
3 Exhorts to prayer
5 and steadfastness in the faith, from the examples of Christ,
7 and Apostles and saints, and exhorts to carefulness in all well-doing.

FOR whosoever does not confess that Jesus Christ is come in the flesh, he is Antichrist: and whoever does not confess his suffering upon the cross, is from the devil.

2 And whosoever perverts the oracles of the Lord to his own lusts, and says that there shall. neither be any resurrection, nor judgment, he is the first-born of Satan.

3 Wherefore leaving the vanity of many, and their false doctrines; let us return to the word that was delivered to us from the beginning: Watching unto prayer; and persevering in fasting;

4 With supplication beseeching the all seeing God not to lead us into temptation; as the Lord hath said, The spirit is truly willing, but the flesh is weak.

5 Let us therefore without ceasing hold steadfastly to him who is our hope, and the earnest of our righteousness, even Jesus Christ; Who, his own self, bare our sins in his own body on the tree: who did

THE EPISTLE OF POLYCARP TO THE PHILIPPIANS.

no sin, neither was guile found in his mouth; but suffered all for us that we might live through him.

6 Let us therefore imitate his patience; and if we suffer for his name, let us glorify him; for this example he has given us by himself, and so have we believed.

7 Wherefore I exhort all of you that ye obey the word of righteousness, and exercise all patience; which ye have seen set forth before your eyes, not only in the blessed Ignatius, and Zozimus, and Rufus; but in others among yourselves; and in Paul himself, and the rest of the Apostles:

8 Being confident of this, that all these have not run in vain, but in faith and righteousness; and are gone to the place that was due to them from the Lord; with whom also they suffered.

9 For they loved not this present world; but him who died, and was raised again by God for us.

10 Stand therefore in these things, and follow the example of the Lord; being firm and immutable in the faith, lovers of the brotherhood, lovers of one another: companions together in the truth, being kind and gentle towards each other, despising none.

11 When it is in your power to do good defer it not, for charity delivered from death.

12 Be all of you subject one to another, having your conversation honest among the Gentiles; that by your good works, both ye yourselves may receive praise, and the Lord may not be blasphemed through you. But woe be to him by whom the name of the Lord is blasphemed.

13 Therefore teach all men sobriety; in which do ye also exercise yourselves.

CHAPTER IV.

Valens, a presbyter, having fallen into the sin of covetousness, he exhorts them against it.

I am greatly afflicted for Valens, who was once a presbyter among you; that he should so little understand the place that was given to him in the church, Wherefore I admonish you that ye abstain from covetousness; and that ye be chaste, and true of speech.

2 Keep yourselves from all evil. For he that in these things cannot govern himself, how shall he be able to prescribe them to another?

ΔΙΔΑΧΗ ΤΩΝ ΔΩΔΕΚΑ ΑΠΟΣΤΟΛΩΝ

3 If a man does not keep himself from covetousness, he shall be polluted with idolatry, and be judged as if he were a Gentile.

4 But who of you are ignorant of the judgment of God? Do we not know that the saints shall judge the world, as Paul teaches?

5 But I have neither perceived nor heard anything of this kind in you, among whom the blessed Paul laboured; and who are named in the beginning of his Epistle.

6 For he glories of you in all the churches who then only knew God; for we did not then know him. Wherefore, my brethren, I am exceedingly sorry both for him and for his wife; to whom God grant a true repentance.

7 And be ye also moderate upon this occasion; and look not upon such as enemies, but call them back as suffering and erring members, that ye may save your whole body: for by so doing, ye shall edify your own selves.

8 For I trust that ye are well exercised in the Holy Scriptures, and that nothing is hid from you but at present it is not granted unto me to practise that which is written, Be angry and sin not; and again, Let not the sun go down upon your wrath.

9 Blessed be he that believeth and remembereth these things; which also I trust you do.

10 Now the God and Father of our Lord Jesus Christ, and he himself who is our everlasting high-priest, the Son of God, even Jesus Christ, build you up in faith and in truth, and in all meekness and lenity; in patience and long- suffering, in forbearance and chastity:

11 And grant unto you a lot and portion among his saints, and us with you; and to all that are under the heavens, who shall believe in our Lord Jesus Christ, and in his Father who raised him from the dead.

12 Pray for all the saints: pray also for kings, and all that are in authority; and for those who persecute you, and hate you, and for the enemies of the cross; that your fruit may be manifest in all: and that ye may be perfect in Christ.

13 Ye wrote to me, both ye, and also Ignatius, that if any one went from hence into Syria, he should bring your letters with him; which also I will take care of, as soon as I shall have a convenient opportunity; either by myself, or him whom I shall send upon your account.

14 The Epistle of Ignatius, which he wrote unto us, together with what others of his have come to our hands, we have sent to you, according to your order; which are subjoined to this Epistle:

15 By which we may be greatly profited; for they treat of faith and patience, and of all things that pertain to edification in the Lord Jesus.

THE EPISTLE OF POLYCARP TO THE PHILIPPIANS.

16 What you know certainly of Ignatius, and those that are with him, signify to us.

17 These things have I written unto you by Crescens, whom by this present Epistle I have recommended to you, and do now again commend.

18 For he has had his conversation without blame among us; and I suppose also with you.

19 Ye will also have regard unto his sister when she shall come unto you.

20 Be ye safe in the Lord Jesus Christ; and in favour with all yours. Amen.

THE FIRST PART OF THE BOOK OF HERMAS CALLED HIS VISION.

VISION I.

**1 Against filthy and proud thoughts;
20 also the neglect of Hermas in chastising his children.**

HE who had bred me up sold a certain young maid at Rome; whom when I saw many years after, I remembered her, and began to love her as a sister. It happened some time afterwards, that I saw her washing in the river Tyber; and I reached out my hand unto her, and brought her out of the river,

2 And when I saw her I thought with myself, saying, How happy should I be if I had such a wife, both for beauty and manners. This I thought with myself; nor did I think any thing more. But not long after, as I was walking, and musing on these thoughts, I began to honour this creature of God, thinking with myself; how noble and beautiful she was.

3 And when I had walked a little, I fell asleep; and the spirit caught me away, and carried me through a certain place towards the right hand, through which no man could pass. It was a place among rocks, very steep, and unpassable for water.

4 When I was past this place, I came into a plain; and there falling down upon my knees, I began to pray unto the Lord, and to confess my sins.

5 And as I was praying, the heaven was opened, and I saw the woman which I had coveted, saluting me from heaven, and saying, Hermas, hail! and I looking upon her, answered, Lady, what dost thou

do here? She answered me, I am taken up hither to accuse thee of sin before the Lord.

6 Lady, said I, wilt thou convince me? No, said she: but hear the words which I am about to speak unto thee. God who dwelleth in heaven, and hath made all things out of nothing, and hath multiplied them for his holy church's sake, is angry with thee because thou hast sinned against me.

7 And I answering said unto her, Lady, if I have sinned against thee, tell me where, or in what place, or when did I ever speak an unseemly or dishonest word unto thee?

8 Have I not always esteemed thee as a lady? Have I not always reverenced thee as a sister? Why then dost thou imagine these wicked things against me?

9 Then she, smiling upon me, said: the desire of naughtiness has risen up in thy heart. Does it not seem to thee to be an ill thing for a righteous man to have an evil desire rise up in his heart.

10 It is indeed a sin, and that a very great sin, to such a one; for a righteous man thinketh that which is righteous. And whilst he does so, and walketh uprightly, he shall have the Lord in heaven favourable unto him in all his business.

11 But as for those who think wickedly in their hearts, they take to themselves death and captivity; and especially those who love this present world, and glory in their riches, and regard not the good things that are to come; their souls wander up and down and know not where to fix.

12 Now this is the case of such as are double-minded, who trust not in the Lord, and despise and neglect their own life.

13 But do thou pray unto the Lord, and he will heal thy sins, and the sins of thy whole house, and of all his saints.

14 As soon as she had spoken these words the heaven were shut, and I remained utterly swallowed up with sadness and fear: and said within myself, if this be laid against me for sin, how can I be saved.

15 Or how should I ever be able to entreat the Lord for my many and great sins? With what words shall I beseech him to be merciful unto me?

16 As I was thinking over these things, and meditating in myself upon them, behold a chair was set over against me of the whitest wool, as bright as snow.

17 And there came an old woman in a bright garment, having a book in her hand, and sat alone, and saluted me, saying, Hermas, hail! and I being full of sorrow and weeping, answered, Hail Lady!

ΔΙΔΑΧΗ ΤΩΝ ΔΩΔΕΚΑ ΑΠΟΣΤΟΛΩΝ

18 And she said unto me, Why art thou sad, Hermas, who wert wont to be patient, and modest, and always cheerful? I answered, and said to her, Lady, a reproach has been laid to my charge by an excellent woman, who tells me that I have sinned against her.

19 She replied. Far be any such thing from the servant of God. But it may be the desire of her has risen up in thy heart? For indeed such a thought maketh the servants of God guilty of sin.

20 Nor ought such a detestable thought to be in the servant of God: nor should he who is approved by the Spirit desire that which is evil; but especially Hermas, who contains himself from all wicked lusts, and is full of all simplicity, and of great innocence.

21 Nevertheless the Lord is not so much angry with thee for thine own sake, as upon the account of thy house, which has committed wickedness against the Lord, and against their parents.

22 And for that out of thy fondness towards thy sons, thou hast not admonished thy house, but hast permitted them to live wickedly; for this cause the Lord is angry with thee: but he will heal all the evils that are done in thy house. For through their sins and iniquities, thou art wholly consumed in secular affairs.

23 But now the mercy of God hath taken compassion upon thee, and upon thine house, and hath greatly comforted thee. Only as for thee, do not wander, but be of an even mind, and comfort thy house.

24 As the workman bringing forth his work, offers it to whomsoever he pleaseth; so shalt thou by teaching every day what is just, cut off a great sin. Wherefore cease not to admonish thy sons, for the Lord knows that they will repent with all their heart, and they shall be written in the book of life.

25 And when she had said this, she added unto me; Wilt thou hear me read? I answered her, Lady, I will.

26 Hear then, said she; and opening the book she read, gloriously, greatly and wonderfully, such things as I could not keep in my memory. For they were terrible words, such as no man could bear.

27 How it be I committed her last words to my remembrance; for they were but few, and of great use to us:—

28 Behold the mighty Lord, who by his invisible power, and with his excellent wisdom made the world, and by his glorious counsel beautified his creature, and with the word of his strength fixed the heaven, and founded the earth upon the waters; and by his powerful virtue established the Holy Church, which he hath blessed.

29 Behold he will remove the heavens, and the mountains, the hills, and the seas; and all things shall be made plain for his elect; that he

may render unto them the promise which he has promised, with much honour and joy; if so be that they shall keep the commandments of God, which they have received with great faith.

30 And when she had made an end of reading, she rose out of the chair; and behold four young men came, and carried the chair to the east.

31 And she called me unto her, and touched my breast, and said unto me, Did my reading please thee? I answered, Lady, these last things please me; but what went before was severe and hard.

32 She said unto me, these last things are for the righteous, but the foregoing for the revolters and heathen.

33 And as she was talking with me, two men appeared, and took her upon their shoulders, and went to the east where the chair was.

34 And she went cheerfully away; and as she was going, said unto me, Hermas, be of good cheer.

VISION II.

Again, of his neglect in correcting his talkative wife; and of his lewd sons.

AS I was on the way to Cuma, about the same time that I went the year before, I began to call to mind the vision I formerly had. And again the spirit carried me away, and brought me into the same place, in which I had been the year before.

2 And when I was come into the place, I fell down upon my knees, and began to pray unto the Lord, and to glorify his name, that he had esteemed me worthy, and had manifested unto me my former sins.

3 And when I arose from prayer, behold I saw over against me the old woman whom I had seen the last year, walking and reading in a certain book.

4 And she said unto me, Canst thou tell these things to the elect of God? I answered and said unto her, Lady, I cannot retain so many things in my memory, but give me the book, and I will write them down.

5 Take it, says she, and see that thou restore it again to me.

6 As soon as I had received it, I went aside into a certain place of the field, and transcribe every letter, for I found no syllables.

7 And as soon as I had finished what was written in the book, the book was suddenly caught out of my hand, but by whom I saw not.

ΔΙΔΑΧΗ ΤΩΝ ΔΩΔΕΚΑ ΑΠΟΣΤΟΛΩΝ

8 After fifteen days, when I had fasted, and entreated the Lord with all earnestness, the knowledge of the writing was revealed unto me. Now the writing was this:—

9 Thy seed, O Hermas! hath sinned against the Lord, and have betrayed their parents, through their great wickedness. And they have been called the betrayers of their parents, and have gone on in their treachery.

10 And now have they added lewdness to their other sins, and the pollutions of their naughtiness: thus have they filled up the measure of their iniquities. But do thou upbraid thy sons with all these words; and thy wife, who shall be as thy sister; and let her learn to refrain her tongue, with which she calumniates.

11 And when she shall hear these things, she will refrain herself, and shall obtain mercy.

12 And they also shall be instructed, when thou shalt have reproached them with these words, which the Lord has commanded to be revealed unto them.

13 Then shall their sins be forgiven, which they have heretofore committed, and the sins of all the saints who have sinned even unto this day; if they shall repent with all their hearts, and remove all doubts out of their hearts.

14 For the Lord hath sworn by his glory concerning his elect, having determined this very time, that if any one shall even now sin, he shall not be saved.

15 For the repentance of the righteous has its end; the days of repentance are fulfilled to all the saints; but to the heathen, there is repentance even unto the last day.

16 Thou shalt therefore say to those who are over the church, that they order their ways in righteousness; so that they may fully receive the promise with much glory.

17 Stand fast therefore ye that work righteousness and continue to do it, that your departure may be with the holy angels.

18 Happy are ye, as many as shall endure the great trial that is at hand, and whosoever shall not deny his life.

19 For the Lord hath sworn by his Son, that whoso, denieth his Son and HIM, being afraid of his life, he will also deny him in the world that is to come.

20 But those who shall never deny him, he will of his exceeding great mercy be favourable unto them.

THE FIRST PART OF THE BOOK OF HERMAS

21 But thou, O Hermas! remember not the evils which thy sons have done, neither neglect thy sister, but take care that they amend of their former sins.

22 For they will be instructed by this doctrine, if thou shalt not be mindful of what they have done wickedly.

23 For the remembrance of evils worketh death, but the forgetting of them eternal life.

24 But thou, O Hermas! hast undergone a great many worldly troubles for the offences of thy house, because thou hast neglected them, as things that did not belong unto thee; and thou art wholly taken up with thy great business.

25 Nevertheless, for this cause shalt thou be saved, that thou hast not departed from the living God, and thy simplicity and singular continency shall preserve thee, if thou shalt continue in them.

26 Yes, they shall save all such as do such things, and walk in innocence and simplicity.

27 They who are of this kind shall prevail against all impiety, and continue until life eternal.

28 Happy are all they that do righteousness, they shall not be consumed for ever.

29 But thou wilt say, Behold there is a great trial coming. If it seem good to thee, deny him again.

30 The Lord is nigh to them that turn to him, as it is written in the book of Heldam and Modal, who prophesied to the people of Israel in the wilderness.

31 Moreover, brethren, it was revealed to me, as I was sleeping, by a very goodly young man, saying unto me, What thinkest thou of that old woman from whom thou receivedst the book; who is she? I answered, a Sybil.

32 Thou art mistaken said he, she is not. I replied, Who is she then, sir? He answered me, It is the church of God.

33 And I said unto him, Why then does she appear old? She is therefore, said he, an old woman, because she was the first of all the creation, and the world was made for her.

34 After this I saw a vision at home in my own house, and the old woman, whom I had seen before, came to me and asked me whether I had yet delivered her book to the elders of the church? And I answered, that I had not yet.

35 She replied, Thou hast well done, for I have certain words more to tell thee. But when I shall have finished all the words, they shall be clearly understood by the elect.

ΔΙΔΑΧΗ ΤΩΝ ΔΩΔΕΚΑ ΑΠΟΣΤΟΛΩΝ

36 And thou shalt write two books, and send one to Clement and one to Grapte. For Clement shall send it to the foreign cities, because it is permitted to him so to do: but Grapte shall admonish the widows and orphans.

37 But thou shalt read in this city with the elders of the church.

VISION III.

Of the building of the church triumphant, and of the several sorts of reprobates.

THE vision which I saw, brethren, was this.

2 When I had often fasted and prayed unto the Lord, that he would manifest unto me the revelation, which he had promised by the old woman to show unto me; the same night she appeared unto me, and said unto me,

3 Because thou dost thus afflict thyself, and art so desirous to know all things, come into the field, where thou wilt, and about the sixth hour, I will appear unto thee, and show thee what thou must see.

4 I asked her, saying; Lady, into what part of the field? She answered, wherever thou wilt, only choose a good and a private place. And before I began to speak and tell her the place, she said unto me; I will come where thou wilt.

5 I was therefore, brethren in the field and I observed the hours, and came into the place where I had appointed her to come.

6 And I beheld a bench placed; it was a linen pillow, and over it spread a covering of fine linen.

7 When I saw these things ordered in this manner, and that there was nobody in the place, I began to be astonished, and my hair stood on end, and a kind of horror seized me; for I was alone.

8 But being come to myself, and calling to mind the glory of God, and taking courage, I fell down upon my knees and began again to confess my sins as before.

9 And whilst I was doing this, the old woman came thither with the six young men whom I had seen before, and stood behind me as I was praying, and heard me praying and confessing my sins unto the Lord.

10 And touching me, she said; Leave off praying now only for thy sins; pray also for righteousness, that thou mayest receive a part of it in thy house.

11 And she lifted me up from the place, and took me by the hand, and brought me to the seat; and said to the young men, go, and build.

12 As soon as they were departed, and we were alone, she said unto me; sit here. I answered her; Lady, let those who are elder sit first. She replied, Sit down as I bid you.

13 And when I would have sat on the right side, she suffered me not, but made a sign to me with her hand, that I should sit on the left.

14 As I was therefore musing, and full of sorrow, that she would not suffer me to sit on the right side, she said unto me, Hermas, why art thou sad?

15 The place which is on the right hand is theirs who have already attained unto God, and have suffered for his name-sake. But there is yet a great deal remaining unto thee, before thou canst sit with them.

16 But continue as thou doest, in thy sincerity, and thou shalt sit with them; as all others shall, who do their works, and shall bear what they have borne.

17 I said to her; Lady, I would know what it is that they have suffered? Hear then, said she: wild beasts, scourgings, imprisonments, and crosses for his name-sake.

18 For this cause the right hand of holiness belongs to them, and to all others as many as shall suffer for the name of God; but the left belongs to the rest.

19 Howbeit the gifts and the promises belong to both, to them on the right, and to those on the left hand; only that sitting on the right hand they have some glory above the others.

20 But thou art desirous to sit on the right hand with them, and yet thy defects are many. But thou shalt be purged from thy defects, as also all who doubt not shall be cleansed from all the sins which they have committed unto this day.

21 And when she had said this she would have departed.

22 Wherefore, falling down before her feet, I began to entreat her, for the Lord's sake, that she would show me the vision which she had promised.

23 Then she again took me by the hand, and lifted me up, and made me sit upon the seat at the left side; and holding up a certain bright wand, said unto me, Seest thou that great thing? I replied, Lady, I see nothing.

24 She answered, Dost thou not see over against thee a great tower, which is built upon the water with bright square stones?

25 For the tower was built upon a square by these six young men that came with her.

26 But many thousand of other men brought stones; some drew them out of the deep, others carried them from the ground, and gave them to the six young men; and they took them and built.

ΔΙΔΑΧΗ ΤΩΝ ΔΩΔΕΚΑ ΑΠΟΣΤΟΛΩΝ

27 As for those stones which were drawn out of the deep, they put them all into the building; for they were polished, and their squares exactly answered one another, and so one was joined in such wise to the other, that there was no space to be seen where they joined, insomuch that the whole tower appeared to be built as it were of one stone.

28 But as for the other stones that were taken off from the ground, some of them they rejected, others they fitted into the building.

29 As for those which were rejected, some they cut out, and cast them at a distance from the tower; but many others of them lay round about the tower, which they made no use of in the building.

30 For some of these were rough, others had clefts in them, others were white and round, not proper for the building of the tower.

31 But I saw the other stones cast afar off from the tower, and falling into the high-way, and yet not continuing in the way, but were rolled from the way into a desert place.

32 Others I saw falling into the fire and burning; others fell near the water, yet could not roll themselves into it, though very desirous to fall into the water.

33 And when she had showed me these things she would have departed; but I said to her, Lady, what doth it profit me to see these things, and not understand what they mean?

34 She answered and said unto me; You are very cunning, in that you are desirous to know those things which relate to the tower. Yea, said I, lady, that I may declare them unto the brethren, and they may rejoice, and hearing these things may glorify God with great glory.

35 Then she said, Many indeed shall hear them, and when they shall have heard them, some shall rejoice, and others weep. And yet even these, if they shall repent, shall rejoice too.

36 Hear therefore what I shall say concerning the parable of the tower, and after this be no longer importunate with me about the revelation.

37 For these revelations have an end, seeing they are fulfilled. But thou dost not leave off to desire revelations, for thou art very urgent.

38 As for the tower which thou seest built, it is myself, namely, the church, which have appeared to thee both now and heretofore. Wherefore ask what thou wilt concerning the tower, and I will reveal it unto thee, that thou mayest rejoice with the saints.

39 I said unto her, Lady, because thou hast thought me once worthy to receive from thee the revelation of all these things, declare them unto me.

THE FIRST PART OF THE BOOK OF HERMAS

40 She answered me, Whatsoever is fit to be revealed unto thee shall be revealed: only yet thy heart be with the Lord, and doubt not, whatsoever thou shalt see.

41 I asked her, Lady, why is the tower built upon the water? She replied, I said before to thee that thou wert very wise to inquire diligently concerning the building, therefore thou shalt find the truth.

42 Hear therefore why the tower is built upon the water: because your life is and shall be saved by water. For it is founded by the word of the almighty and honourable name, and is supported by the invisible power and virtue of God.

43 And I answering, said unto her, These things are very admirable; but, lady, who are those six young men that build?

44 They are, said she, the angels of God, who were first appointed, and to whom the Lord has delivered all his creatures, to frame and build them up, and to rule over them. For by these the building of the tower shall be finished.

45 And who are the rest who bring them stones?

46 They also are the holy angels of the Lord; but the others are more excellent than these. Wherefore when the whole building of the tower shall be finished, they shall all feast together beside the tower, and shall glorify God, because the structure of the tower is finished.

47 I asked her, saying, I would know the condition of the stones, and what the meaning of them is?

48 She answering, said unto me, Art thou better than all others that this should be revealed unto thee? For others are both before thee and better than thou art, to whom these visions should be made manifest.

49 Nevertheless, that the name of God may be glorified, it has been shown and shall be revealed unto thee, for the sake of those who are doubtful, and think in their hearts whether these things are so or not.

50 Tell them that all these things are true, and that there is nothing in them that is not true but all are firm and truly established.

51 Hear now then concerning the stones that are in the building.

52 The square and white stones which agree exactly in their joints, are the apostles, and bishops, and doctors, and ministers, who through the mercy of God have come in, and governed, and taught and ministered holily and modestly to the elect of God, both they that have fallen asleep, and which yet remain; and have always agreed with them, and have had peace within themselves, and have heard each other.

53 For which cause their joints exactly meet together in the building of the tower.

ΔΙΔΑΧΗ ΤΩΝ ΔΩΔΕΚΑ ΑΠΟΣΤΟΛΩΝ

54 They which are drawn out of the deep and put into the building, and whose joints agree with the other stones which are already built, are those which are already fallen asleep, and have suffered for the sake of the Lord's name.

55 And what are the other stones, lady, that are brought from the earth? I would know what are they.

56 She answered, They which lie upon the ground and are not polished, are those which God has approved, because they have walked in I the law of the Lord, and directed their ways in his commandments.

57 They which are brought and put in the building of the tower, are the young in faith and the faithful. And these are admonished by the angels to do well because iniquity is not found in them.

58 But who are those whom they rejected, and laid beside the tower?

59 They are such as have sinned and are willing to repent; for which cause they are not cast far from the tower, because they will be useful for the building, if they shall repent.

60 They therefore that are yet to repent, if they repent they shall become strong in the faith; that is, if they repent now, whilst the tower is building. For if the building shall be finished there will then be no place for them to be put in, but they shall be rejected; for he only has this privilege who shall now be put into the tower.

61 But would you know who they are that were cut out, and cast afar off from the tower? Lady said I, I desire it.

62 They are the children of iniquity, who believed only in hypocrisy, and departed not from their evil ways; for this cause they shall not be saved, because they are not of any use in the building by reason of their sins.

63 Wherefore they are cut out, and cast afar off, because of the anger of the Lord, and because they have provoked him to anger against them.

64 As for the great number of other stones which thou hast seen placed about the tower, but now put into the building; those which are rugged, are they who have known the truth, but have not continued in it, nor been joined to the saints, and therefore are unprofitable.

65 Those that have clefts in them, are they that keep up discord in their hearts against each other, and live not in peace; that are friendly when present with their brethren, but as soon as they are departed from one another, their wickedness still continues in their hearts: these are the clefts which are seen in those stones.

66 Those that are maimed and short, are they who have believed indeed, but still are in great measure full of wickedness; for this cause they are maimed and not whole.

67 But what are the white and round stones, lady, and which are not proper for the building of the tower?

68 She answering said unto me: How long wilt thou continue foolish and without understanding, asking everything and discerning nothing?

69 They are such as have faith indeed, but have withal the riches of this present world. When therefore any troubles arise, for the sake of their riches and traffic, they deny the Lord.

70 I answering, said unto her, When therefore will they be profitable to the Lord? When their riches shall be cut away, says she, in which they take delight, then they will be profitable unto the Lord for his building.

71 For as a round stone, unless it be cut away and is cast somewhat of its bulk, cannot be made square, so they who are rich in this world; unless their riches be pared off; cannot be made profitable unto the Lord.

72 Learn this from thy own experience: when thou wert rich, thou wast unprofitable; but now thou art profitable, and fit for the life which thou hast undertaken; for thou also once was one of those stones.

73 As for the rest of the stones which thou sawest cast afar off from the tower, and running in the way, and tumbled out of the way into desert places; they are such as have believed indeed, but through their doubting have forsaken the true way, thinking that they could find a better. But they wander and are miserable, going into desolate ways.

74 Then for those stones which fell into the fire and were burnt, they are those who have for ever departed from the living God; nor doth it ever come into their hearts to repent, by reason of the affection which they bear to their lusts and wickedness which they commit.

75 And what are the rest which fell by the water, and could not roll into the water?

76 They are such as have heard the word, and were willing to be baptised in the name of the Lord; but considering the great holiness which the truth requires, have withdrawn themselves, an walked again after wicked lusts.

77 Thus she finished the explanation of the tower.

78 But I being still urgent, asked her, Is there repentance allowed to all those stones which are thus cast away, and were not suitable to the building of the tower; and shall they find place in this tower?

ΔΙΔΑΧΗ ΤΩΝ ΔΩΔΕΚΑ ΑΠΟΣΤΟΛΩΝ

79 They may repent, said she, yet they cannot come into this tower; but, they shall be placed in a much lower rank, and then only after they shall have been afflicted and fulfilled the days of their sins.

80 And for this cause they shall be removed, because they have received the word of righteousness: and then they shall be translated from their afflictions, if they shall have a true sense in their hearts of what they have done amiss.

81 But if they shall not have this sense in their hearts, they shall not be saved by reason of the hardness of their hearts.

82 When therefore I had done asking her concerning all these things, she said unto me, Wilt thou see something else? And being desirous of seeing it, I became very cheerful of countenances.

83 She therefore looking back upon me, and smiling a little, said unto me, Seest thou seven women about the tower? Lady, said I, I see them.

84 This tower, replied she, is supported by them, according to the command of the Lord: hear therefore the effects of them.

85 The first of them, which holds fast with her hand, is called Faith; The next, which is girt up, and looks manly, is named Abstinence: she is the daughter of Faith.

86 Whosoever therefore shall follow her shall be happy in all his life, because he shall abstain from all evil works, believing that if he shall contain himself from all concupiscence, he shall be the heir of eternal life. And what, lady, said I, are the other five?

87 They are, replied she, the daughters of one another. The first of them is called Simplicity; the next Innocence; the third Modesty; then Discipline; and the last of all is Charity. When therefore thou shalt have fulfilled the works of their mother, thou shalt be able to do all things.

88 Lady, said I, I would know what particular virtue every one of these has.

89 Hear then, replied she; they have equal virtues, and their virtues are knit together, and follow one another as they were born.

90 From Faith proceeds Abstinence; from Abstinence, Simplicity; from Simplicity, Innocence; from Innocence, Modesty; from Modesty, Discipline and Charity. Therefore the works of these are holy, and chaste, and right.

91 Whoever therefore shall serve these, and hold fast to their works, he shall have his dwelling in the tower with the saints of God.

92 Then I asked her concerning the times, whether the end were now at hand?

THE FIRST PART OF THE BOOK OF HERMAS

93 But she cried out with a loud voice, saying, O foolish man! Dost thou not see the tower yet a building? When therefore the tower shall be finished, and built, it shall have an end; and indeed it shall soon be accomplished.

94 But do not ask me any more questions. What has been said may suffice thee and all the saints for the refreshment of your spirits. For these things have not been revealed to thee only, but that thou mayest make them manifest unto all.

95 For therefore, O Hermas, after three days thou must understand these words which I begin to speak unto thee, that thou mayest speak them in the ears of the saints; that when thou shall have heard and done them, they may be cleansed from their iniquities, and thou together with them.

96 Hear me therefore, O my sons! I have bred you up in much simplicity, and innocency, and modesty, for the love of God, which has dropped down upon you in righteousness, that you should be sanctified and justified from all sin and wickedness; but ye will not cease from your evil doings.

97 Now therefore hearken unto me, and have peace one with another, and visit one another, and receive one another, and do not enjoy the creatures of God alone.

98 Give freely to them that are in need. For some by too free feeding contract an infirmity in their flesh, and do injury to their bodies; whilst the flesh of others, who have not food, withers away, because they want sufficient nourishment, and the bodies are consumed.

99 Wherefore this intemperance is hurtful to you, who have, and do not contribute to them that want. Prepare for the judgment that is about to come upon you.

100 Ye that are the more eminent, search out them that are hungry, whilst the tower is yet unfinished. For when the tower shall be finished, ye shall be willing to do good, and shall not find any place in it.

101 Beware, therefore, ye that glory in your riches, lest perhaps they groan who are in want, and their sighing come up unto God, and ye be shut out with your goods without the gate of the tower.

102 Behold I now warn you who are set over the church, and love the highest seats, be not ye like unto those that work mischief.

103 And they indeed carry about their poison in boxes, but ye contain your poison and infection in your hearts, and will not purge them, and mix your sense with a pure heart, that ye might find mercy with the Great King.

104 Take heed, my children, that your dissensions deprive you not of your lives. How will ye instruct the elect of God, when ye your-

ΔΙΔΑΧΗ ΤΩΝ ΔΩΔΕΚΑ ΑΠΟΣΤΟΛΩΝ

selves want correction? Wherefore admonish one another, and be at peace among yourselves, that I, standing before your Father, may give an account of you unto the Lord.

105 And when she had made an end of talking with me, the six young men that built, came and carried her to the tower; and four others took up the seat on which she sat, and they also went away again to the tower. I saw not the faces of these, for their backs were towards me.

106 As she was going away, I asked her, that she would reveal to me what concerned the three forms, in which she had appeared unto me.

107 But she answering said unto me, concerning these things thou must ask some other, that they may be revealed unto thee.

108 Now, brethren, in the first vision the last year, she appeared unto me exceedingly old, and sitting in a chair.

109 In another vision, she had indeed a youthful face, but her flesh and hair were old; but she talked with me standing, and was more cheerful than the first time.

110 In the third vision, she was in all respects much younger, and comely to the eye; only she had the hair of an aged person: yet she looked cheerful, and sat upon a seat.

111 I was therefore very sad concerning these things, until I might understand the vision.

112 Wherefore I saw the same old woman in a vision of the night saying unto me, All prayer needeth humiliation. Fast, therefore, and thou shalt learn from the Lord that which thou dost ask. I fasted therefore one day.

113 The same night a young man appeared to me and said, Why dost thou thus often desire Revelations in thy prayers? Take heed that by asking many things, thou hurt not the body. Let these Revelations suffice thee.

114 Canst thou see more notable Revelations than those which thou hast already received?

115 I answered and said unto him, Sir, I only ask this one thing upon the account of the three figures of the old woman that appeared to me, that the Revelation may be complete.

116 He answered me, You are not without understanding, but your doubts make you so; for as much as you have not your heart with the Lord.

117 I replied and said, But we shall learn these things more carefully from you.

THE FIRST PART OF THE BOOK OF HERMAS

118 Hear then, says he, concerning the figures about which you inquire.

119 To begin; in the first vision she appeared to thee in the shape of an old woman sitting in, a chair, because your old spirit was decayed, and without strength, by reason of your infirmities, and the doubtfulness of your heart.

120 For as they who are old have no hope of renewing themselves, nor expect any thing but their departure; so you being weakened through your worldly affairs gave yourself up to sloth, and cast not away your solicitude from yourself upon the Lord: and your sense was confused, and you grew old in your sadness.

121 But, sir, I would know why she sat upon a chair?

122 He answered, because every one that is weak sitteth upon a chair by reason of his infirmity, that his weakness may be upheld. Behold therefore the figure of the first vision.

123 In the second vision you saw her standing, and having a youthful face, and more cheerful than her former; but her flesh and her hair were ancient. Hear, said he, this parable also.

124 When any one grows old, he despairs of himself by reason of his infirmity and poverty, and expects nothing but the last day of his life.

125 But on a sudden an inheritance is left to him, and he hears of it, and rises: and being become cheerful, he puts on new strength. And now he no longer sits down, but stands, and is delivered from his former sorrow; and sits not, but acts manfully.

126 So you, having heard the Revelation which God revealed unto you, because God had compassion upon you, and renewed your spirit, both laid aside your infirmities, and strength came to you, and you grew strong in the faith; and God, seeing your strength, rejoiced.

127 For this cause he showed you the building of the tower, and will show other things unto you, if you shall have peace with all your heart among each other.

128 But in the third vision you saw her yet younger, fair and cheerful, and of a serene countenance.

129 For, as if some good news comes to him that is sad, he straightway forgets his sadness, and regards nothing else but the good news which he has heard; and for the rest he is comforted, and his spirit is renewed through the joy which he has received even so you have been refreshed in your spirit by seeing these good things.

130 And for that you saw her sitting upon a bench, it denotes a strong position; because a bench has four feet, and stands strongly. And even the world itself is upheld by the four elements.

ΔΙΔΑΧΗ ΤΩΝ ΔΩΔΕΚΑ ΑΠΟΣΤΟΛΩΝ

131 They therefore that repent perfectly, shall be young; and they that turn from their sins with their whole heart, shall be established.

132 And now you have the Revelation fully, ask no more to have any thing farther revealed unto you.

133 But if any thing is to be revealed, it shall be made manifest unto you.

VISION IV.

Of the trial, and tribulation that is about to come upon men.

I SAW a vision brethren, twenty days after the former vision; a representation of the tribulation that is at hand. I was walking in the field way.

2 Now from the public way to the place whither I went is about ten furlongs; it is a way very little frequented:

3 And as I was walking alone, I entreated the Lord that he would confirm the Revelations which he had shown unto me by his Holy Church.

4 And would grant repentance to all his servants who had been offended, that his great and honourable name might be glorified, and because he thought me worthy to whom he might show his wonders, and, that I might honour him, and give thanks unto him.

5 And behold somewhat like a voice answered me; Doubt not, Hermas. Wherefore I began to think, and say within myself, why should I doubt, seeing I am thus settled by the Lord, and have seen such glorious things?

6 I had gone but a little farther, brethren, when behold I saw a dust rise up to heaven. I began to say within myself, is there a drove of cattle coming, that rises such a dust?

7 It was about a furlong off from me. And behold I saw the dust rise more and more, insomuch that I began to suspect that there was somewhat extraordinary in it.

8 And the sun shone a little; and behold I saw a great beast, as it were a whale; and fiery locusts came out of his mouth. The height of the beast was about a hundred feet, and he had a head like a large earthen vessel.

9 I began to weep, and to pray unto the Lord that he would deliver me from it. Then I called to mind the word which I had heard; Doubt not, Hermas.

THE FIRST PART OF THE BOOK OF HERMAS

10 Wherefore, brethren, putting on a divine faith, and remembering who it was that had taught me great things, I delivered myself bodily unto the beast.

11 Now the beast came on in such a manner, as if it could at once have devoured a city.

12 I came near unto it, and the beast extended its whole bulk upon the ground, and put forth nothing but its tongue, nor once moved itself till I had quite passed by it.

13 Now the beast had upon its head four colours; first black, then a red and bloody colour, then a golden, and then a white.

14 After that I had passed by it, and was gone forward about thirty feet, behold there met me a certain virgin, well adorned as if she had been just come out of her bride-chamber; all in white, having on white shoes, and a veil down her face, and covered with shining hair.

15 Now I knew by my former visions that it was the church, and thereupon grew the more cheerful. She saluted me, saying, Hail, O Man! I returned the salutation, saying, Lady, Hail!

16 She answering said unto me, Did nothing meet you, O man! I replied, Lady, there met me such a beast, as seemed able to devour a whole people; but by the power of God, and through his singular mercy, I escaped it.

17 Thou didst escape it well, said she, because thou didst cast thy whole care upon God, and opened thy heart unto him, believing that thou couldst be safe by no other than by his great and honourable name.

18 For this cause the Lord sent his angel, who is over the beast, whose name is Hegrin, and stopped his mouth, that he should not devour thee, Thou hast escaped a great trial through thy faith, and because thou didst not doubt for such a terrible beast.

19 Go, therefore, and relate to the elect of God the great things that he hath done for thee. And thou shalt say unto them, that this beast is the figure of the trial that is about to come.

20 If, therefore, ye shall have prepared yourselves, ye may escape it, if your hearts be pure and without spot; and if ye shall serve God all the rest of your days without complaint.

21 Cast all your care upon the Lord, and he will direct them. Believe in God, ye doubtful, because he can do all things; he can both turn away his wrath from you, and send you help and security.

22 Woe to the doubtful, to those who shall hear these words, and shall despise them: it had been better for them that they had not been born.

ΔΙΔΑΧΗ ΤΩΝ ΔΩΔΕΚΑ ΑΠΟΣΤΟΛΩΝ

23 Then I asked her concerning the four colours which the beast had upon its head. But she answered me saying; Again thou art curious in that thou asketh concerning these things. But I said to her, Lady, chew me what they are?

24 Hear, said she; The black which thou sawest denotes the world in which you dwell. The fiery and bloody colour signifies that this age must be destroyed by fire and blood.

25 The golden part are ye, who have escaped out of it; for as gold is tried by the fire, and is made profitable, so are ye also in like manner tried who dwell among the men of this world.

26 They therefore, that shall endure to the end, and be proved by them, shall be purged. And as gold, by this trial, is cleansed and loses its dross, so shall ye also cast away all sorrow and trouble, and be made pure for the building of the tower.

27 But the white colour denotes the time of the world which is to come, in which the elect of God shall dwell: because the elect of God shall be pure and without spot until life eternal.

28 Wherefore do not thou cease to speak these thing in the ears of the saints. Here ye have the figure of the great tribulation that is about to come; which, if you please, shall be nothing to you.

29 When she had spoken thus much, she departed; but I saw not whither she went. But suddenly I heard a noise, and I turned back, being afraid, for I thought that the beast was coming toward me.

THE SECOND PART OF THE BOOK OF HERMAS, CALLED HIS COMMANDS.

Introduction.

WHEN I had prayed at home, and was sat down upon the bed, a certain man came in to me with a reverend look, in the habit of a Shepherd, clothed with a white cloak, having his bag upon his back, and his staff in his hand, and saluted me.

2 I returned his salutation, and immediately he sat down by me, and said unto me, I am sent by that venerable messenger, that I should dwell with thee all the remaining days of thy life.

3 But I thought that he was come to try me, and said unto him, Who are you? For I know to whom I am committed. He said unto me, Do you not know me? I answered no. I am, said he, that shepherd to whose care you are delivered.

4 Whilst he was yet speaking, his shape was changed; and when I knew that it was he to whom I was committed, I was ashamed, and a sudden fear came upon me, and I was utterly overcome with sadness, because I had spoken so foolishly unto him.

5 But he said unto me, Be not ashamed, but receive strength in thy mind, through the commands which I am about to deliver unto thee. For, said he, I am sent to show unto thee all those things again, which thou hast seen before, but especially such of them as may be of most use unto thee.

6 And first of all write my Commands and Similitudes, the rest thou shall so write as I shall show unto thee. But I therefore bid thee first of all write my Commands and Similitudes, that by often reading of them thou mayest the more easily keep them in memory.

ΔΙΔΑΧΗ ΤΩΝ ΔΩΔΕΚΑ ΑΠΟΣΤΟΛΩΝ

7 Whereupon I wrote his Commands and Similitudes, as he bade me.

8 Which things if when you have heard, ye shall observe to do them, and shall walk according to them, and exercise yourselves in them with a pure mind, ye shall receive from the Lord those things which he has promised unto you.

9 But if having heard them ye shall not repent, but shall still go on to add to your sins, ye shall be punished by him.

10 All these things that Shepherd, the angel of repentance, commanded me to write.

COMMAND I.

Of believing in one God.

FIRST of all believe that there is one God who created and brought all things out of nothing into existence.

2 He comprehends all things, and is only INFINITE, not to be comprehended by any.

3 Who can neither be defined by any words, nor conceived by the mind.

4 Therefore believe in him, and fear him; and fearing him abstain from all evil.

5 Keep these things, and cast all lust and iniquity far from thee, and put on righteousness, and thou shalt live to God, if thou shalt keep his commandment.

COMMAND II.

That we must avoid detraction, and do our alms-deeds with simplicity.

HE said unto me, Be innocent and without disguise; so shalt thou be like an infant who knows no malice which destroys the life of man.

2 Especially see that thou speak evil of none, nor willingly hear any one speak evil of others.

3 For if thou observest not this, thou also who hearest shall be partaker of the sin of him that speaketh evil, by believing the slander, and thou also shalt have sin, because thou believedst him that spoke evil of thy brother.

4 Detraction is a pernicious thing; an inconstant, evil spirit; that never continues in peace, but is always in discord. Wherefore refrain thyself from it, and keep peace ever more with thy brother.

5 Put on an holy constancy, in which there are no sins, but all is full of joy; and do good of thy labours.

6 Give without distinction to all that are in want, not doubting to whom thou givest.

7 But give to all, for God will have us give to all, of all his own gifts. They therefore that receive shall give an account to God, both wherefore they received and for what end.

8 And they that receive without real need, shall give an account for it; but he that gives shall be innocent.

9 For he has fulfilled his duty as he received it from God; not making any choice to whom he should give, and to whom not. And this service he did with simplicity and to the glory of God.

10 Keep therefore this command according as I have delivered it into thee: that thy repentance nay be found to be sincere, and that good may come to thy house; and have a pure heart.

COMMAND III.

Of avoiding lying, and the repentance of Hermas for his dissimulation.

MOREOVER he said unto me love truth; and let all the speech be true which proceeds out of thy mouth.

2 That the spirit which the Lord hath given to dwell in thy flesh may be found true towards all men; and the Lord be glorified, who hath given such a spirit unto thee: because God is true in all his words, and in him there is no lie.

3 They therefore that lie, deny the Lord, and become robbers of the Lord, not rendering to God what they received from him.

4 For they received the spirit free from lying: If therefore they make that a liar, they defile what was committed to them by the Lord, and become deceivers.

5 When I heard this, I wept bitterly; and when he saw me weeping, he said unto me, Why weepest thou? And I said, Because, sir, I doubt whether I can be saved.

6 He asked me, Wherefore? I replied, Because, sir, I never spake a true word in my life; but always lived in dissimulation, and affirmed a lie for truth to all men; and no man contradicted me, but all gave credit to my words. How then can I live, seeing I have done in this manner?

ΔΙΔΑΧΗ ΤΩΝ ΔΩΔΕΚΑ ΑΠΟΣΤΟΛΩΝ

7 And he said unto me, Thou thinkest well and truly; for thou oughtest, as the servant of God, to have walked in the truth, and not have joined an evil conscience with the spirit of truth, nor have grieved the holy and true Spirit of God.

8 And I replied unto him, Sir, I never before hearkened so diligently to these things. He answered, Now thou hearest them Take care from henceforth, that even those things which thou hast formerly spoken falsely for the sake of thy business, may, by thy present truth receive pardon.

9 For even those things may be forgiven, if for the time to come thou shalt speak the truth; and by so doing thou mayest attain unto life.

10 And whosoever shall hearken unto this command, and do it, and shall depart from all lying, he shall live unto God.

COMMAND IV.

Of putting away one's wife for adultery.

FURTHERMORE, said he, I command thee, that thou keep thyself chaste; and that thou suffer not any thought of any other marriage, or of fornication, to enter into thy heart; for such a thought produces great sin.

2 But be thou at all times mindful of the Lord, and thou shalt never sin. For if such an evil thought should arise in thy heart, then thou shall be guilty of a great sin; and they who do such things, follow the way of death.

3 Look therefore to thyself, and keep thyself from such a thought; for where chastity remains in the heart of a righteous man, there an evil thought ought never to arise.

4 And I said unto him, Sir, suffer me to speak a little to you. He bade me say on. And I answered, Sir, if a man that is faithful in the Lord shall have a wife, and shall catch her in adultery; doth a man sin that continues to live still with her?

5 And he said unto me, As long as he is ignorant of her sin, he commits no fault in living with her; but if a man shall know his wife to, have offended, and she shall not repent of her sin, but go on still in her fornication, and a man shall continue nevertheless to live with her, he shall become guilty of her sin, and partake with her in her adultery.

6 And I said unto him, What therefore is to be done, if the woman continues on in her sin? He answered, Let her husband put her away,

and let him continue by himself; but if he shall put away his wife and marry another, he also doth commit adultery.

7 And I said, What, if the woman that is so put away, should repent, and be willing to return to her husband, shall she not be received by him? He said unto me, Yes; and if her husband shall not receive her, he will sin, and commit a great offence against himself; for he ought to receive the offender, if she repents: only not often.

8 For, to the servants of God, there is but one repentance; and for this cause a man that putteth away his wife ought not to take another, because she may repent.

9 This act is alike both in the man and in the woman. Now they commit adultery, not only who pollute their flesh, but who also make an image. If therefore a woman perseveres in any thing of this kind, and repents not, depart from her; and live not with her, otherwise thou also shalt be partaker of her sin.

10 But it is therefore commanded that both the man and the woman should remain unmarried, because such persons may repent.

11 Nor do I in this administer any occasion for the doing of these things; but rather that whoso has offended, should not offend any more.

12 But for their former sins, God who has the power of healing will give a remedy; for he has the power of all things.

13 I asked him again, and said, Seeing the Lord hath thought me worthy that thou shouldest dwell with me continually, speak a few words unto me, because I understand nothing, and my heart is hardened through my former conversation; and open my understanding because I am very dull, and apprehend nothing at all.

14 And he answering said unto me, I am the minister of repentance, and give understanding to all that repent. Does it not seem to thee to be a very wise thing to repent? Because he that does so gets great understanding.

15 For he is sensible that he hath sinned and done wickedly in the sight of the Lord, and he remembers within himself that he has offended, and repents and does no more wickedly, but does that which is good, and humbles his soul and afflicts it, because he has offended. You see therefore that repentance is great wisdom.

16 And I said unto him, For this cause, sir, I inquire diligently into all things, because I am a sinner, that I may know what I must do that I may live; because my sins are many.

17 And he said unto me, Thou shalt live if thou shalt keep these my commandments. And whosoever shall hear and do these commands shall live unto God.

ΔΙΔΑΧΗ ΤΩΝ ΔΩΔΕΚΑ ΑΠΟΣΤΟΛΩΝ

18 And I said unto him, I have even now heard from certain teachers, that there is no other repentance beside that of baptism, when we go down into the water, and receive the forgiveness of our sins; and that after that, we must sin no more, but live in purity.

19 And he said unto me, Thou hast been rightly informed. Never-the-less seeing now thou inquirest diligently into all things, I will manifest this also unto thee; yet not so as to give any occasion of sinning, either to those who shall hereafter believe, or to those who have already believed in the Lord.

20 For neither they who have newly believed, or shall hereafter believe, have any repentance of sins, but forgiveness of them.

21 But as to those who have been called to the faith, and since that are fallen into any gross sin, the Lord hath appointed repentance, because God knoweth the thoughts of all men's hearts, and their infirmities, and the manifold wickedness of the devil, who is always contriving something against the servants of God, and maliciously lays snares for them.

22 Therefore our merciful Lord had compassion towards his creature, and appointed that repentance, and gave unto me the power of it. And therefore I say unto thee, if any one after that great and holy calling shall be tempted by the devil and sin, he has one repentance. But if he shall often sin and repent, it shall not profit such a one; for he shall hardly live unto God.

23 And I said, Sir, I am restored again to life since I have thus diligently hearkened to these commands. For I perceive that if I shall not hereafter add any more of my sins, I shall be saved.

24 And he said, Thou shalt be saved: and so shall all others, as many as shall observe these commandments.

25 And again I said unto him, Sir, seeing thou hearest me patiently, show me yet one thing more. Tell me, saith he, what it is.

26 And I said, If a husband or a wife die, and the party which survives marry again, does he sin in so doing? He that marries says he, sins not: howbeit, if he shall remain single, he shall thereby gain to himself great honour before the Lord.

27 Keep therefore thy chastity and modesty, and thou shalt live unto God. Observe from henceforth those things which I speak with thee, and command thee to observe, from the time that I have been delivered unto thee, and dwell in thy house.

28 So shall thy former sins be forgiven, if thou shalt keep these my commandments. And in like manner shall all others be forgiven, who shall observe these my commandments.

THE SECOND PART OF THE BOOK OF HERMAS
COMMAND V.

Of the sadness of the heart, and of patience.

Be patient, says he, and long- suffering; so shalt thou have dominion over all wicked works, and shall fulfil all righteousness.

2 For if thou shalt be patient, the Holy Spirit which dwelleth in thee shall be pure, and not be darkened by any evil spirit; but being full of joy shall be enlarged, and feast in the body in which it dwells, and serve the Lord with joy, and in great peace.

3 But if any anger shall overtake thee, presently the Holy Spirit which is in thee will be straightened and seek to depart from thee.

4 For he is choked by the evil spirit, and has not the liberty of serving the Lord as he would; for he is grieved by anger. When, therefore, both these spirits dwell together, it is destructive to a man.

5 As if one should take a little wormwood, and put it into a vessel of honey, the whole honey would be spoiled; and a great quantity of honey is corrupted by a very little wormwood, and loses the sweetness of honey, and is no longer acceptable to its Lord because the whole honey is made bitter, and loses its use.

6 But if no wormwood be put into the honey, it is sweet and profitable to its Lord. Thus is forbearance sweeter than honey, and profitable to the Lord who dwelleth in it.

7 But anger is unprofitable. If therefore anger shall be mixed with forbearance, the soul is distressed, and its prayer is not profitable with God.

8 And I said unto him, Sir, I would know the sinfulness of anger, that I may keep myself from it. And he said unto me, Thou shall know it; and if thou shalt not keep thyself from it, thou shalt lose thy hope with all thy house. Wherefore depart from it.

9 For I the messenger of righteousness am with thee, and all that depart from it: as many as shall repent with all their hearts, shall live unto God; and I will be with them, and will keep them all.

10 For all such as have repented have been justified by the most holy messenger, who is a minister of salvation.

11 And now, says he, hear the wickedness of anger; how evil and hurtful is is, and how it overthrows the servants of God; for it cannot hurt those that are full of faith because the power of God is with them; but it overthrows the doubtful, and those that are destitute of faith.

12 For as often as it sees such men, it casts itself into their hearts; and so a man or woman is in bitterness for nothing: for the things of life, or for sustenance, or for a vain word, if any should chance to fall

ΔΙΔΑΧΗ ΤΩΝ ΔΩΔΕΚΑ ΑΠΟΣΤΟΛΩΝ

in; or by reason of any friend, or for a debt, or for any other superfluous things of the like nature.

13 For these things are foolish, and superfluous, and vain to the servants of God. But equanimity is strong, and forcible; and of great power, and sitteth in great enlargement; is cheerful, rejoicing in peace; and glorifying God at all times I with meekness.

14 And this long-suffering dwells with those that are full of faith. But anger is foolish, and light, and empty. Now bitterness is bred through folly; by bitterness, anger; by anger, fury; and this fury arising from so many evil principles, worketh a great and incurable sin.

15 For when all these things, are in the same man in which the Holy Spirit dwells, the vessel cannot contain them, but runs over: and because the Spirit being tender cannot tarry with the evil one; it departs and dwells with him that is meek.

16 When, therefore, it is departed from the man in whom it dwelt, that man becomes destitute of the Holy Spirit, and is afterwards filled with wicked spirits, and is blinded with evil thoughts. Thus doth it happen to all angry men.

17 Wherefore depart then from anger, and put on equanimity, and resist: wrath; so then shalt be found with modesty and chastity by God. Take good heed, therefore, that thou neglect not this commandment.

18. For if thou shalt obey this command, then thou shalt also be able to observe the other commandments which I shall command thee.

19 Wherefore strengthen thyself now in these commands, that then mayest live unto God. And whosoever shall observe these commandments shall live unto God.

COMMAND VI.

That every man has two angels and of the suggestions of both.

I COMMANDED thee, said he, in my first commandments, that thou shouldst keep faith and fear, and repentance. Yes, sir, said I.

2 He continued. But now I will shew thee the virtues of these commands, that then mayest know their effects; how they are prescribed alike to the just and unjust.

3 Do thou therefore believe the righteous, but give no credit to the unrighteous. For righteousness keepeth the right way, but unrighteousness the wicked way.

4 Do thou therefore keep the right way, and leave that which is evil. For the evil way has not a good end, but hath many stumbling-blocks; it is rugged and full of thorns, and leads to destruction; and it is hurtful to all such as walk in it.

5 But they who go in the right way walk with evenness, and without offence; because it is not rough nor thorny.

6 Thou seest therefore how it is best to walk in this way. Thou shalt therefore go, says he, and all others, as many as believe in God with all their heart, shall go through it.

7 And now, says he, I understand first of all what belongs to faith. There are two angels with man; one of righteousness, the other of iniquity.

8 And I said unto him, Sir, how shall I know that there are two such angels with man? Hear, says he, and understand.

9 The angel of righteousness, is mild and modest, and gentle, and quiet. When, therefore, he gets into thy heart, immediately he talks with thee of righteousness, of modesty, of chastity, of bountifulness, of forgiveness, of charity, and piety.

10 When all these things come into thy heart, know then that the angel of righteousness is with thee. Wherefore hearken to this angel and to his works.

11 Learn also the works of the angel of iniquity. He is first of all bitter, and angry, and foolish; and his works are pernicious, and overthrow the servants of God. When therefore these things come into thine heart; thou shalt know by his works, that this is the angel of iniquity.

12 And I said unto him, Sir, how shall I understand these things? Hear, says he, and understand; When anger overtakes thee, or bitterness, know that he is in thee:

13 As also, when the desire of many things, and of the best meats, and of drunkenness; when the love of what belongs to others, pride, and much speaking, and ambition; and the like things, come upon thee.

14 When therefore these things arise in thine heart, know that the angel of iniquity is with thee. Seeing therefore thou knowest his works, depart from them all, and give no credit to him: because his works are evil, and become not the servants of God.

15 Here therefore thou hast the works of both these angels. Understand now and believe the angel of righteousness, because his instruction is good.

16 For let a man be never so happy; yet if the thoughts of the other angel arise in his heart, that man or woman must needs sin.

ΔΙΔΑΧΗ ΤΩΝ ΔΩΔΕΚΑ ΑΠΟΣΤΟΛΩΝ

17 But let man or woman be never so wicked, if the works of the angel of righteousness come into their hearts, that man or woman must needs do some good.

18 Thou seest therefore how it is good to follow the angel of righteousness. If therefore thou shall follow him, and submit to his works, thou shalt live unto God. And as many as shall submit to his work shall live also unto God.

COMMAND VII.

That we must fear God but not the Devil.

FEAR God, says he, and keep his commandments. For if thou keepest his commandments thou shalt be powerful in every work, and all thy works shall be excellent. For by fearing God, thou shalt do everything well.

2 This is that tear with which thou must be affected that thou mayest be saved. But fear not the Devil: for if thou fearest the Lord, thou shalt have dominion over him; because there is no power in him.

3 Now if there be no power in him, then neither is he to be feared: for every one that has power, is to be feared. But he that has no power is despised by every one.

4 Fear the works of the Devil, because they are evil. For by fearing the Lord, thou wilt fear and do not the works of the Devil, but keep thyself from them.

5 There is therefore a twofold fear; if thou wilt not do evil, fear the Lord and thou shalt not do it. But if thou wilt do good, the fear of the Lord is strong, and great and glorious.

6 Wherefore, fear God and thou shalt live: and whosoever shall fear him, and keep his commandments, their life is with the Lord. But they who keep them not, neither is there life in them.

COMMAND VIII.

That we must flee from evil, and do good works.

I HAVE told thee, said he, that there are two kinds of creatures of the Lord, and that there is a two-fold abstinence. From some things therefore thou must abstain, and from others not.

2 I answered, Declare to me, sir, from what I must abstain, and from what not. Hearken, said he, Keep thyself from evil, and do it not;

yet abstain not from good, but do it. For if thou shalt abstain from what is good, and not do it, thou shalt sin. Abstain therefore from all evil, and thou shalt know all righteousness.

3 I said, What evil things are they from which I must abstain? Hearken, said he; from adultery, from drunkenness, from riots, from excess of eating, from daintiness and dishonesty, from pride, from fraud, from lying, from detraction, from hypocrisy, from remembrance of injuries, and from all evil speaking.

4 For these are the works of iniquity, from which the servant of God must abstain. For he that cannot keep himself from these things, cannot live unto God.

5 But hear, said he, what follows of these kind of things: for indeed many more there are from which the servant of God must abstain. From theft, and cheating; from false witness, from covetousness, from boasting, and all other things of the like nature.

6 Do these things seem to thee to be evil or not? Indeed they are very evil to the servants of God, Wherefore the servant of God must abstain from all these works.

7 Keep thyself therefore from them, that thou mayest live unto God, and be written among those that abstain from them. And thus have I shown thee what things thou must avoid: now learn from what thou must not abstain.

8 Abstain not from any good works, but do them. Hear, said he, what the virtue of those good works is which thou must do, that thou mayest be saved. The first of all is faith; the fear of the Lord; charity; concord; equity; truth; patience; chastity.

9 There is nothing better than these things in the life of men; who shall keep and do these things in their life. Hear next what follow these.

10 To minister to the widows; not to despise the fatherless and poor; to redeem the servants of God from necessity; to be hospitable (for in hospitality there is sometimes great fruit); not to be contentious, but be quiet.

11 To be humble above all men; to reverence the aged; to labour to be righteous; to respect the brotherhood; to bear affronts; to be long-suffering; not to cast away those that have fallen from the faith, but to convert them, and make them be of good cheer: to admonish sinners; not to oppress those that are our debtors; and all other things of a like kind.

12 Do these things seem to thee to be good or not? And I said, What can be better than these words? Live then, said he, in these commandments, and do not depart from them. For if thou shalt keep

all these commandments, thou shalt live unto God. And all they that shall keep these commandments shall live unto God.

COMMAND IX.

That we must ask of God daily; and without doubting.

AGAIN he said unto me; remove from thee all doubting; and question nothing at all when thou askest any thing of the Lord; saying within thyself, how shall I be able to ask any thing of the Lord and receive it, seeing I have so greatly sinned against him?

2 Do not think thus, but turn unto the Lord with all thy heart, and ask of him without doubting, and thou shalt know the mercy of the Lord; bow that he will not forsake thee, but will fulfil the request of thy soul.

3 For God is not as men, mindful of the injuries he has received; but he forgets injuries, and has compassion upon his creature.

4 Wherefore purify thy heart from all the vices of this present world; and observe the commands I have before delivered unto thee from God; and thou shall receive whatsoever good things thou shalt ask, and nothing shall be wanting unto thee of all thy petitions; if thou shalt ask of the Lord without doubting.

5 But they that are not such, shall obtain none of those things which they ask. For they that are full of faith, ask all things with confidence, and receive from the Lord, because they ask without doubting. But he that doubts, shall hardly live unto God, except he repent.

6 Wherefore purify thy heart from doubting, and put on faith, and trust in God, and thou shall receive all that thou shalt ask. But if thou shouldest chance to ask something, and not immediately receive it, yet do not therefore doubt, because thou hast not presently received the petition of thy soul.

7 For it may be thou shalt not presently receive it for thy trial, or else for some sin which thou knowest not. But do not thou leave off to ask, and then thou shalt receive. Else if thou shalt cease to ask, thou must complain of thyself, and not of God, that he has not given unto thee what thou didst desire.

8 Consider therefore this doubting how cruel and pernicious it is; and how it utterly roots out many from the faith, who were very faithful and firm. For this doubting is the daughter of the Devil, and deals very wickedly with the servants of God.

9 Despise it therefore, and thou shalt rule over it on every occasion. Put on a firm and powerful faith: for faith promises all things and perfects all things. But doubting will not believe that it shall obtain any thing by all that it can do.

10. Thou seest therefore, says he, how faith cometh from above from God; and hath great power. But doubting is an earthly spirit, and proceedeth from the Devil, and has no strength.

11 Do thou therefore keep the virtue of faith, and depart from doubting, in which is no virtue, and thou shalt live unto God. And all shall live unto God, as many as do these things.

COMMAND X.

Of the sadness of the heart; and that we must take, heed not to grieve the spirit of God that is in us.

PUT all sadness far from thee; for it is the sister of doubting and of anger. How, sir, said I is it the sister of these? For sadness, and anger, and doubting, seem to me to be very different from one another.

2 And he answered: Art thou without sense that thou dost not understand it? For sadness is the most mischievous of all spirits, and the worst to the servants of God: It destroys the spirits of all men, and torments the Holy Spirit, and it saves again.

3 Sir, said I, I am very foolish, and understand not these things. I cannot apprehend how it can torment, and yet save. Hear, said he, and understand. They who never sought out the truth, nor inquired concerning the majesty of God, but only believed, are involved in the affairs of the heathen.

4 And there is another lying prophet that destroys the minds of the servants of God; that is of those that are doubtful, not of those that fully trust in the Lord. Now those doubtful persons come to him, as to a divine spirit, and inquire of him what shall befall them.

5 And this lying prophet, having no power in him of the Divine Spirit, answers them according to their demands, and fills their souls with promises according as they desire. Howbeit that prophet is vain, and answers vain things to those who are themselves vain.

6 And whatsoever is asked of him by vain men, he answers them vainly; nevertheless he speaketh some things truly. For the Devil fills him with his spirit, that he may overthrow some of the righteous.

7 Whosoever therefore are strong in the faith of the Lord, and have put on the truth; they are not joined to such spirits, but depart from

ΔΙΔΑΧΗ ΤΩΝ ΔΩΔΕΚΑ ΑΠΟΣΤΟΛΩΝ

them. But they that are doubtful, and often repenting, like the heathens, consult them, and heap up to themselves great sin, serving idols.

8 As many therefore as are such, inquire of them upon every occasion; worship idols, and are foolish; and void of the truth. For every spirit that is given from God needs not to be asked: but having the power of divinity speaks all things of itself, because he comes from above; from the power of God.

10 But he, that being asked speaks according to men's desires and concerning many other affairs of this present world, understands not the tidings which relate unto God. For these spirits are darkened through such affairs, and corrupted, and broken.

11 As good vines if they are neglected, are oppressed with weeds and thorns, and at last killed by them; so are the men who believe such spirits.

12 They fall into many actions and businesses, and are void of sense, and when they think of things pertaining unto God, they understand nothing at all; but at any time they chance to hear any thing concerning the Lord, their thoughts are upon their business.

13 But they that have the fear of the Lord, and search out the truth concerning God, having all their thoughts towards the Lord; apprehend whatsoever is said to them, and forthwith understand it, because they have the fear of the Lord in them.

14 For where the spirit of the Lord dwells, there is also much understanding added. Wherefore join thyself to the Lord, and thou shalt understand all things.

15 Learn now, O unwise man! how sadness troubleth the Holy Spirit, and how it saves. When a man that is doubtful is engaged in any affair, and does not accomplish it by reason of his doubting; this sadness enters into him, and grieves the Holy Spirit, and makes him sad.

16 Again anger, when it over, takes any man for any business he is greatly moved; and then again sadness entereth into the heart of him, who was moved with anger, and he is troubled for what he hath done, and repenteth, because he hath done amiss.

17 This sadness therefore seemeth to bring salvation, because he repenteth of his evil deed. But both the other things, namely, doubting and sadness, such as before was mentioned, vex the spirit: doubting, because his work did not succeed; and sadness, because he angered the Holy Spirit.

18 Remove therefore sadness from thyself, and afflict not the Holy Spirit which dwelleth in thee, lest he entreat God, and depart from

thee. For the spirit of the Lord which is given to dwell in the flesh, endureth no such sadness.

19 Wherefore clothe thyself with cheerfulness, which has always favour with the Lord, and thou shalt rejoice in it. For every cheerful man does well; and relishes those things that are good, and despises sadness.

20 But the sad man does always wickedly. First, he doth wickedly, because he grieveth the Holy Spirit, which is given to man being of a cheerful nature. And again he does ill, because be prays with sadness unto the Lord, and maketh not first a thankful acknowledgment unto him of former mercies, and obtains not of God what he asks.

21 For the prayer of a sad man has not always efficacy to come up to the altar of God. And I said unto him, Sir, why has not the prayer of a sad man virtue to come up to the altar of God? Because, said he, that sadness remaineth in his heart.

22 When therefore a man's prayer shall be accompanied with sadness, it will not suffer his requests to ascend pure to the altar of God. For as wine when it is mingled with vinegar, has not the sweetness it had before; so sadness being mixed with the Holy Spirit, suffers not a man's prayer to be the same as it would be otherwise.

23 Wherefore cleanse thyself from sadness, which is evil, and thou shalt live unto God. And all others shall live unto God, as many as shall lay aside sadness, and put on cheerfulness.

COMMAND XI.

That the spirits and prophets are to be tried by their works; and of a twofold, spirit.

HE showed me certain men sitting upon benches, and one sitting in a chair: and he said unto me; Seest thou those who sit upon the benches? Sir, said I, I see them. He answered, They are the faithful; and he who sits in the chair is an earthly spirit.

2 For he cometh not into the assembly of the faithful, but avoids it. But he joins himself to the doubtful and empty; and prophesies to them in corners and hidden places; and pleases them by speaking according to all the desires of their hearts.

3 For he placing himself among empty vessels, is not broken, but the one fitteth the other. But when he cometh into the company of just men, who are full of the spirit of God, and they pray unto the Lord; that man is emptied, because that earthly spirit flies from him, and he is dumb, and cannot speak anything.

ΔΙΔΑΧΗ ΤΩΝ ΔΩΔΕΚΑ ΑΠΟΣΤΟΛΩΝ

4 As if in a store-house you shall stop up wine or oil, and among those vessels place an empty jar; and when afterwards you come to open it, you shall find it empty as you stopped it up; so those empty prophets when they come among the spirits of the just, are found to be such as they came.

5 I said, How then shall a man be able to discern them? Consider what I am going to say concerning both kinds of men; and as I speak unto thee so shalt thou prove the prophet of God, and the false prophet.

6 And first try the man who hath the spirit of God, because the spirit which is from above is humble, and quiet, and departs from all wickedness; and from the vain desires of the present world; and makes himself more humble than all men; and answers to none when he is asked; nor to every one singly: for the Spirit of God doth not speak to a man when he will, but when God pleases.

7 When therefore a man who hath the Spirit of God hath come into the church of the righteous, who have the faith of God, and they pray unto the Lord; then the holy angel of God fills that man with the blessed Spirit, and he speaks in the congregation as he is moved of God.

8 Thus therefore is the spirit, of God known, because whosoever speaketh by the Spirit of God, speaketh as the Lord will.

9 Hear now concerning the earthly spirit, which is empty and foolish, and without virtue. And first of all the man who is supposed to have the Spirit, (whereas he hath it not in reality), exalteth himself, and desires to have the first seat, and is wicked, and full of words.

10 And spends his time in pleasure, and in all manner of voluptuousness, and receives the reward of his divination; which if he receives not, he does not divine.

11 Should the Spirit of God receive reward, and divine? It doth not become a prophet of God so to do.

12 Thus you seethe life of each of these kind of prophets. Wherefore prove that man by his life and works, who says that he hath the Holy Spirit. And believe the Spirit which comes from God, and has power as such. But believe not the earthly and empty spirit, which is from the devil, in whom there is no faith nor virtue.

13 Hear now the similitude which I am about to speak unto thee. Take a stone, and throw it up towards heaven; or take a spout of water, and mount it up thitherward; and see if thou canst reach unto heaven.

14 Sir; said I, how can this be done? For neither of those things which you have mentioned, are possible to be done. And he answered,

Therefore as these things cannot be done, so is the earthy spirit without virtue, and without effect.

15 Understand yet farther the power which cometh from above, in this similitude. The grains of hail that drop down are exceedingly small; and yet when they fall upon the head of a man, how do they cause pain to it.

16 And again, consider, the droppings of a house; how the little drops falling upon the earth, work a hollow in the stones.

17 So in like manner the least things which come from above, and fall upon the earth, have great force. Wherefore join thyself to this spirit, which has the power; and depart from the other which is empty.

COMMAND XII.

Of a two fold desire: that the commands of God, are not impossible: and that the devil is not to be feared by them that believe.

AGAIN he said unto me; remove from thee all evil desires, and put on good and holy desires. For having put on a good desire, thou shalt hate that which is evil, and bridle it as thou wilt. But an evil desire is dreadful, and hard to be tamed.

2 It is very horrible and wild; and by its wildness consumes men. And especially if a servant of God shall chance to fall into it, except he be very wise, he is ruined by it. For it destroys those who have not the garment of a good desire and are engaged in the affairs of this present world; and delivers them unto death.

3 Sir, said I, what are the works of an evil desire, which bring men unto death? Shew them to me that I may depart from them. Hear, said he, by what works an evil desire bringeth the servants of God unto death.

4 First of all, it is an evil desire to covet another man's wife, or for a woman to covet another's husband; as also to desire the dainties of riches; and multitude of superfluous meats; and drunkenness; and many delights.

5 For in much delicacy there is folly; and many pleasures are needless to the servants of God. Such lusting therefore is evil and pernicious, which brings to death the servants of God. For all such lusting is from the devil.

6 Whosoever therefore shall depart from all evil desires, shall live unto God; but they that are subject unto them shall die forever. For this evil lusting is deadly. Do thou therefore put on the desire of righteous-

ness, and being armed with the fear of the Lord resist all wicked lusting.

7 For this fear dwelleth in good desires; and, when evil coveting shall see thee armed with the fear of the Lord, and resisting it; it will fly far from thee, and not appear before thee, but be afraid of thy armour.

8 And thou shall have the victory, and be crowned for it; and shall attain to that desire which is good; and shall give the victory which thou hast obtained unto God, and shall serve him in doing what thou thyself wouldest do.

9 For if thou shalt serve good desires, and be subject to them; then thou shalt be able to get the dominion over thy wicked lustings; and they will be subject to thee, as thou wilt.

10 And I said, Sir, I would know how to serve that desire which is good? Hearken, said he, Fear God, and put thy trust in him, and love truth, and righteousness, and do that which is good.

10 If thou shalt do these things, thou shall be an approved servant of God, and serve him; and all others who shall in like manner serve a good desire, shall live unto God.

12 And when he had fulfilled these twelve commands, he said unto me, Thou hast now these commands, walk in them, and exhort those that hear them, to repent, and that they keep their repentance pure all the remaining days of their life.

13 And fulfil diligently this ministry which I commit to thee, and thou shalt receive great advantage by it, and find favour with all such as shall repent and believe thy words. For I am with thee, and will force them to believe.

14 And I said unto him, Sir, these commands are great and excellent, and able to cheer the heart of that man that shall be able to keep them. But, Sir, I cannot tell, whether they can be observed by any man?

15 He answered, Thou shalt easily keep these commands, and they shall not be hard: howbeit, if thou shalt suffer it once to enter into thine heart that they cannot be kept by any one, thou shalt not fulfil them.

16 But now I say unto thee, if thou shalt not observe these commands, and shall neglect them, thou shalt not be saved, nor thy children, nor thy house: because thou hast judged that these commands cannot be kept by man.

THE SECOND PART OF THE BOOK OF HERMAS

17 These things he spake very angrily unto me, insomuch that he greatly affrighted me, for he changed his countenance so that a man could not bear his anger.

18 And when he saw me altogether troubled and confounded, he began to speak more moderately and cheerfully, saying, O foolish, and without understanding!

19 Unconstant, not knowing the majesty of God how great and wonderful he is; who created the world for man, and hath made every creature subject unto him; and given him all power, that he should be able to fulfil all these commands.

20 He is able, said he, to fulfil all these commands, who has the Lord in his heart; but they who have the Lord only in their mouths, their hearts are hardened, and they are far from the Lord: to such persons these commands are hard and difficult.

21 Therefore, ye that are empty and light in the faith, put the Lord your God in your hearts; and ye shall perceive how that nothing is more easy than these commands, nor more pleasant, nor more gentle and holy.

22 And turn yourselves to the Lord your God, and forsake the devil and his pleasures, because they are evil, and bitter, and impure. And fear not the devil, because he has no power over you.

23 For I am with you, the messenger of repentance, who have the dominion over him. The devil doth indeed affright men but his terror is vain. Wherefore fear him not, and he will flee from you.

24 And I said unto him; Sir, hear me speak a few words unto you. He answered, Say on: A man indeed desires to keep the commandments of God, and there is no one but what prays unto God, that he may be able to keep his commandments;

25 But the devil is hard, and by his power rules over the servants of God. And he said; He cannot rule over the servants of God, who trust in him with all their hearts.

26 The devil may strive, but he cannot overcome them.

27 For if ye resist him, he will flee away with confusion from you. But they that are not full in the faith, fear the devil, as if he had some great power. For the devil tries the servants of God and if he finds them empty, he destroys them.

28 For as man, when he fills up vessels with good wine, and among them puts a few vessels half full, and comes to try and taste of the vessels, doth not try those that are full, because he knows that they are good, but tastes those that are half full, lest they should grow sour; (for vessels half full soon grow sour, and lose the taste of wine:) so the devil comes to the servants of God to try them.

ΔΙΔΑΧΗ ΤΩΝ ΔΩΔΕΚΑ ΑΠΟΣΤΟΛΩΝ

29 They that are full of faith resist him stoutly, and he departs from them, because he finds no place where to enter into them then he goes to those that are not full of faith, and because he has a place of entrance he goes into them, and does what he will with them, and they become his servants.

30 But I, the messenger of repentance, say unto you, fear not the devil, for I am sent unto you, that I may be with you, as many as shall repent with your whole heart, and that I may confirm you in the faith.

31 Believe therefore, ye who by reason of your transgressions have forgot God and your own salvation; and adding to your sins have made your life very heavy.

32 That if ye shall turn to the Lord with your whole hearts, and shall serve him according to his will; he will heal you of your former sins, and ye shall have dominion over all the works of the devil.

33 Be not then afraid in the least of his threatenings, for they are without force, as the nerves of a dead man. But hearken unto me, and fear the Lord Almighty, who is able to save and to destroy you; and keep his commands, that ye may live unto God.

34 And I said unto him; Sir, I am now confirmed in all the commands of the Lord whilst you are with me, and I know that you will break all the powers of the devil.

35 And we also shall overcome him, if we shall be able, through the help of the Lord, to keep these commands which you have delivered.

36 Thou shalt keep them, said he, if thou shalt purify thy heart towards the Lord. And all they also shall keep them who shall cleanse their hearts from the vain desires of the present world, and shall live unto God.

THE THIRD PART OF THE BOOK OF HERMAS, CALLED HIS SIMILITUDES.

SIMILITUDE I.

That seeing we have no abiding city in this world, we ought to look after that which is to come.

AND he said onto me; Ye know that ye who are the servants of the Lord, live here as in a pilgrimage; for your city is far off from this city.

2 If, therefore, ye know your city in which ye are to dwell, why do ye here buy estates, and provide yourselves with delicacies, and stately buildings, and superfluous houses? For he that provides himself these things in this city, does not think of returning into his own city.

3 O foolish, and doubtful, and wretched man; who understandest not that all these things belong to other men, and are under the power of another. For the Lord of this city saith unto thee; Either obey my laws, or depart out of my city.

4 What therefore shalt thou do who art subject to a law in thine own city? Canst thou for thy estate, or for any of those things which thou hast provided, deny thy law? But if thou shalt deny it, and wilt afterwards return into thy own city, thou shalt not be received, but shall be excluded thence.

5 See therefore, that like a man in another country, thou procure no more to thyself than what is necessary, and sufficient for thee; and be ready, that when the God or Lord of this city shall drive thee out of it thou mayest oppose his law, and go into thine own city; where thou mayest with all cheerfulness live according to thine own law with no wrong.

ΔΙΔΑΧΗ ΤΩΝ ΔΩΔΕΚΑ ΑΠΟΣΤΟΛΩΝ

6 Take heed therefore ye that serve God, and have him in your hearts: work ye the works of God, being mindful both of his commands and of his promises, which he has promised; and be assured that he will make them good unto you; if ye shall keep his commandments.

7 Instead therefore of the possessions that ye would otherwise purchase, redeem those that are in want from their necessities, as every one is able; justify the widows; judge the cause of the fatherless; and spend your riches and your wealth in such works as these.

8 For this end has God enriched you, that ye might fulfil these kind of services. It is much better to do this, than to buy lands or houses; because all such things shall perish with this present time.

9 But what ye shall do for the name of the Lord, ye shall find in your city, and shall have joy without sadness or fear. Wherefore covet not the riches of the heathen; for they are destructive to the servants of God.

10 But trade with your own riches which you possess, by which ye may attain unto everlasting joy.

11 And do not commit adultery, nor touch any other man's wife, nor desire her; but covet that which is thy own business, and thou shalt be saved.

SIMILITUDE II.

As the vine is supported by the elm, so is the rich man helped by the prayers of the poor.

AS I was walking into the field, and considered the elm and the vine, and thought with myself of their fruits, an angel appeared unto me, and said unto me; What is it that thou thinkest upon thus long within thyself?

2 And I said unto him, Sir, I think of this vine and this elm because their fruits are fair. And he said unto me; These two trees are set for a pattern to the servants of God.

3 And I said unto him, Sir, I would know in what the pattern of these trees which thou mentionest, does consist. Hearken, saith he; seest thou this vine and this elm? Sir, said I, I see them.

4 This vine, saith he, is fruitful, but the elm is a tree without fruit. Nevertheless this vine unless it were set by this elm, and supported by it, would not bear much fruit; but lying along upon the ground, would

THE THIRD PART OF THE BOOK OF HERMAS

bear but ill fruit, because it did not hang upon the elm; whereas, being supported upon the elm, it bears fruit both for itself and for that.

5 See, therefore, how the elm gives no less, but rather more fruit, than the vine. How, Sir, said I, does it bear more fruit than the vine? Because, said he, the vine being supported upon the elm gives both much and good fruit; whereas, if it lay along upon the ground, it would bear but little, and that very ill too.

6 This similitude, therefore, is set forth to the servants of God; and it represents the rich and poor man. I answered, Sir, make this manifest unto me. Hear, said he; the rich man has wealth: howbeit towards the Lord he is poor; for he is taken up about his riches, and prays but little to the Lord; and the prayers which he makes are lazy and without force.

7 When therefore, the rich man reaches out to the poor those things which he wants, the poor man prays unto the Lord for the rich; and God grants unto the rich man all good things, because the poor man is rich in prayer; and his requests have great power with the Lord.

8 Then the rich man ministers all thing to the poor, because he perceives that he is heard by the Lord; and he the more willingly and without doubting, affords him what he wants, and takes care that nothing be lacking to him.

9 And the poor man gives thanks unto the Lord for the rich; because they both do their work from the Lord.

10 With men, therefore, the elm is not thought to give any fruit; and they know not, neither understand that its company being added to the vine, the vine bears a double increase, both for itself and for the elm.

11 Even so the poor praying unto the Lord for the rich, are heard by him; and their riches are increased, because they minister to the poor of their wealth. They are, therefore, both made partakers of each other's good works.

12 Whosoever, therefore, shall do these things, he shall not be forsaken by the Lord, but shall be written in the book of life.

13 Happy are they who are rich, and perceive themselves to be increased: for he that is sensible of this, will be able to minister somewhat to others.

ΔΙΔΑΧΗ ΤΩΝ ΔΩΔΕΚΑ ΑΠΟΣΤΟΛΩΝ

SIMILITUDE III.

As the great trees in the winter cannot be distinguished from the dry; so neither can the righteous from the wicked in this present world.

AGAIN he showed me many trees whose leaves were shed, and which seemed to me to be withered, for they were all alike. And he said unto me, Seest thou these trees? I said, Sir, I see that they look like dry trees.

2 He answering, said unto me; These trees are like unto the men who live in the present world. I replied: Sir, why are they like unto dried trees? Because, said he, neither the righteous, nor unrighteous, are known from one another; but all are alike in this present world.

3 For this world is as the winter to the righteous men, because they are not known, but dwell among sinners.

4 As in the winter all the trees having lost their leaves, are like dry trees; nor can it be discerned which are dry and which are green: so in this present world neither the righteous, nor wicked are discerned from each other; but they are all alike.

SIMILITUDE IV.

As in the summer the living trees are distinguished from the dry by their fruit and green leaves; so in the world to come the righteous shall be distinguished from the unrighteous by their happiness.

AGAIN he showed me many other trees, of which some had leaves, and others appeared dry and withered. And he said unto me, Seest thou these trees I answered, Sir, I see them; some are dry, and others full of leaves.

2 These trees, saith be, which are green, are the righteous, who shall possess the world to come. For the world to come, is the summer to the righteous; but to sinners it is the winter.

3 When, therefore, the mercy of the Lord shall shine forth, then they who serve God shall be made manifest, and plain unto all. For as in the summer the fruit of every tree is shown and made manifest. so also the works of the righteous shall be declared and made manifest, and they shall all be restored in that world merry and joyful.

4 For the other kind of men, namely the wicked, like the trees which thou rawest dry, shall, as such, be found dry and without fruit in that other world; and like dry wood shall be burnt; and it shall be made manifest that they have done evil all the time of their life;

5 And they shall be burnt because they have sinned and have not repented of their sins. And also all the other nations shall be burnt, because they have not acknowledged God their Creator.

6 Do then, therefore, bring forth good fruit, that in the summer thy fruit may be known; and keep thyself from much business, and thou shalt not offend. For they who are involved in much business, sin much; because they are taken up with their affairs, and serve not God.

7 And how can a man that does not serve God, ask anything of God, and receive it? But they who serve him, ask and receive what they desire.

8 But if a man has only one thing to follow, he may serve God, because his mind is not taken off from God, but he serves him with a pure mind.

9 If, therefore, thou shalt do this, thou mayest have fruit in the world to come; and as many as shall do in like manner, shall bring forth fruit.

SIMILITUDE V.

Of a true fast, and the rewards of it: also of the cleanliness of the body.

AS I was fasting, and sitting down in a certain mountain, and giving thanks unto God for all the things that he had done unto me; behold, I saw the Shepherd, who was wont to converse with me, sitting by me, and saying unto me: What has brought thee hither thus early in the morning? I answered, Sir, to-day I keep a station.

2 He answered, What is a station; I replied, it is a fast. He said, What is that fast? I answered, I fast as I have been wont to do. Ye know not, said he, what it is to fast unto God; nor is this a fast which ye keep, profiting nothing with God.

3 Sir, said I, what makes you speak thus? He replied, I speak it, because it is not the true fast which you think that you keep; but I will show you what that is which is a complete fast, and acceptable unto God.

4 Hearken, said he, The Lord does not desire such a needless fast; for by fasting in this manner, thou advancest nothing in righteousness.

ΔΙΔΑΧΗ ΤΩΝ ΔΩΔΕΚΑ ΑΠΟΣΤΟΛΩΝ

5 But the true fast is this: Do nothing wickedly in thy life, but serve God with a pure mind; and keep his commandments, and walk according to his precepts, nor suffer any wicked desire to enter into the mind.

6 But trust in the Lord, that if thou dost these things, any feares: him, and abstaineth from every evil work, thou shall live unto God.

7 If thou shalt do this, thou shall perfect a great fast, and an acceptable one unto the Lord.

8 Hearken unto the similitude which I am about to propose unto thee, as to this matter.

9 A certain man having a farm, and many servants, planted a vineyard in a certain part of his estate for his posterity:

10 And taking a journey into a far country, chose one of his servants which he thought the most faithful and approved, and delivered the vineyard into his care; commanding him that he should stake up the vines. Which if he did, and fulfilled his command, he promised to give him his liberty. Nor did he command him to do any thing more; and so went into a far country.

11 And after that servant had taken that charge upon him, he did whatsoever his lord commanded him. And when he had staked the vineyard, and found it to be full of weeds, he began to think within himself, saying:

12 I have done what my lord commanded me, I will now dig this vineyard, and when it is digged, it will be more beautiful; and the weeds being pulled up, it will bring forth more fruit and not be choked by the weeds.

13 So setting about this work he digged it, and plucked up all the weeds that were in it; and so the vineyard became very beautiful and prosperous, not being choked with weeds.

14 After some time the lord of the vineyard comes and goes into the vineyard, and when he saw that it was handsomely staked and digged, and the weeds plucked up that were in it, and the vines flourishing, he rejoiced greatly at the care of his servant.

15 And calling his son whom he loved, and who was to be his heir, and his friends with whom he was wont to consult; he tells them what he had commanded his servant to do, and what his servant had done more; and they immediately congratulated that servant, that he had received so full a testimony from his lord.

16 Then he said to them, I indeed promised this servant his liberty, if he observed the command which I gave him; and he observed it, and besides has done a good work to my vineyard, which has exceedingly pleased me.

THE THIRD PART OF THE BOOK OF HERMAS

17 Wherefore, for this work which he hath done, I will make him my heir together with my son; because that when he saw what was good, he neglected it not, but did it.

18 This design of the lord both his son and his friends approved, namely, that his servant should be heir together with his son.

19 Not long after this the master of the family calling together, his friends, sent from his supper several kinds of food to that servant.

20 Which when he had received, he took so much of them as was sufficient for himself, and divided the rest among his fellow-servants.

21 Which when they had received, they rejoiced; and wished that he might find yet greater favour with his lord, for what he had done to them.

22 When his lord heard all these things, he was again filled with great joy: and calling again his friends and his son together, he related to them what his servant had done with the meats which he had sent unto him.

23 They therefore so much the more assented to the master of the household; and he ought to make that servant his heir together with his son.

24 I said unto him, sir, I know not these similitudes, neither can I understand them, unless you expound them unto me. I will, says he, expound, all things unto thee whatsoever I have talked with thee, or shown unto thee.

25 Keep the commandments of the Lord and thou shalt be approved, and shall be written in the number of those that keep his commandments. But if besides those things which the Lord hath commanded, thou shalt add some good thing; thou shall purchase to thyself a greater dignity, and be in more favour with the Lord than thou shouldst otherwise have been.

26 If therefore thou shalt keep the commandments of the Lord, and shalt add to them these stations, thou shall rejoice; but especially if thou shalt keep them according to my commands.

27 I said unto him, sir, whatsoever thou shall command me, I will observe; for I know that thou wilt be with me. I will, said he, be with thee who hast taken up such a resolution; and I will be with all those who purpose in like manner.

28 This fast, saith he, whilst thou dost also observe the commandments of the Lord, is exceeding good; therefore thus shalt thou keep it.

29 First of all, take heed to thyself, and keep thyself from every wicked act, and from every filthy word, and from every hurtful desire; and purify thy mind from all the vanity of this present world. If thou shalt observe these things, this fast shall be right.

ΔΙΔΑΧΗ ΤΩΝ ΔΩΔΕΚΑ ΑΠΟΣΤΟΛΩΝ

30 Thus therefore do. Having performed what is before written, that day on which thou fastest thou shalt taste nothing at all but bread and water; and computing the quantity of food which thou art want to eat upon other days, thou shalt lay aside the expense which thou shouldest have made that day, and give it unto the widow, the fatherless, and the poor.

31 And thus thou shalt perfect the humiliation of thy soul; that he who receives of it may satisfy his soul, and his prayer come up to the Lord God for thee.

32 If therefore thou shalt thus accomplish thy fast, as I command thee, thy sacrifice shall be acceptable unto the Lord, and thy fast shall be written in his book.

33 This station, thus performed, is good and pleasing and acceptable unto the Lord. These things if thou shalt observe with thy children and with all thy house, thou shalt be happy.

34 And whosoever, when they hear these things, shall do them, they also shall be happy; and whatsoever they shall ask of the Lord they shall receive it.

35 And I prayed him that he would expound unto me the similitude of the farm, and the Lord, and of the vineyard, and of the servant that had staked the vineyard; and of the weeds that were plucked out of the vineyard; and of his son and his friends which he took into counsel with him; for I understand that that was a similitude

36 He said unto me, Thou art very bold in asking; for thou oughtest not to ask any thing; because if it be fitting to show it unto thee, it shall be showed unto thee.

37 I answered him; Sir, whatsoever thou shalt show me, without explaining it unto me, I shall in vain see it, if I do not understand what it is. And if thou shalt propose any similitudes, and not expound them, I shall in vain hear them.

38 He answered me again, saying: Whosoever is the servant of God, and has the Lord in his heart, he desires understanding of him, and receives it; and he explains every similitude, and understands the words of the Lord which need an inquiry.

39 But they that are lazy and slow to pray, doubt to seek from the Lord: although the Lord be of such an extraordinary goodness, that without ceasing he giveth all things to them that ask of him.

40 Thou therefore who art strengthened by that venerable messenger, and hast received such a powerful gift of prayer; seeing thou art not slothful, why dost thou not now ask understanding of the Lord, and receive it?

THE THIRD PART OF THE BOOK OF HERMAS

41 I said unto him; seeing I have thee present, it is necessary that I should seek it of thee, and ask thee; for thou shewest all things unto me, and speakest to me when thou art present.

42 But if I should see or hear these things when thou wert not present, I would then ask the Lord that he would chew them unto me.

43 And he replied, I said a little before that thou wert subtle and bold, in that thou asketh the meaning of these similitudes.

44 But because thou still persistest, I will unfold to thee this parable which then desirest, that thou mayest make it known unto all men.

45 Hear, therefore, said he, and understand. The farm before mentioned denotes the whole earth. The Lord of the farm is he, who created and finished all things; and gave virtue unto them.

46 His son is the Holy Spirit; the servant is the Son of God: the vineyard is the people whom he saves. The stakes are the messengers which are set oven them by the Lord, to support his people. The weeds that are plucked up out of the vineyard, are the sins which the servants of God had committed.

47 The food which he sent him from his supper, are the commands which he gave to his people by his Son. The friends whom he called to counsel with him, are the holy angels whom he first created. The absence of the master of the household, is the time that remains unto his coming.

48 I said unto him, Sir, all these things are very excellent, and wonderful, and good. But, continued I, could I or any other man besides, though never so wise, have understood these things?

49 Wherefore now, sir, tell me, what I ask. He replied, ask me what thou wilt. Why, said I, is the Son of God in this parable, put in the place of a servant.

50 Hearken, he said: the Son of God is not put in the condition of a servant, but in great power and authority. I said unto him, how, sir? I understand it not.

51 Because, said he, the Son set his messengers over those whom the Father delivered unto him, to keep every one of them; but he himself laboured very much, and suffered much, that he might blot out their offences.

52 For no vineyard can be digged without much labour and pains. Wherefore having blotted out the sins of his people, he showed to them the paths of life, giving them the law which he had received of the Father.

53 You see, said he, that he is the Lord of his people, having received all power from his Father. But why the lord did take his son

ΔΙΔΑΧΗ ΤΩΝ ΔΩΔΕΚΑ ΑΠΟΣΤΟΛΩΝ

into counsel, about dividing the inheritance, and the good angels, hear now.

54 That Holy Spirit, which was created first of all, he placed in the body in which God should dwell; namely, in a chosen body, as it seemed good to him. This body therefore into which the Holy Spirit was brought, served that Spirit, walking rightly and purely in modesty; nor ever defiled that Spirit.

55 Seeing therefore the body at all times obeyed the Holy Spirit, and laboured rightly and chastely with him, nor faltered at anytime; that body being wearied conversed indeed servilely, but being mightily approved to God with the Holy Spirit, was accepted by him.

56 For such a stout course pleased God, because he was not defiled in the earth, keeping the Holy Spirit. He called therefore to counsel his Son, and the good angels, that there might be some place of standing given to this body which had served the Holy Spirit without blame; lest it should seem to have lost the reward of its service.

57 For every pure body shall receive its reward; that is found without spot, in which the Holy Spirit has been appointed to dwell. And thus you have now the exposition of this parable also.

58 Sir, said I, I now understand your meaning, since I have heard this exposition. Hearken farther, said he: keep this thy body clean and pure, that the Spirit which shall dwell in it may bear witness unto it, and be judged to have been with thee.

59 Also take heed that it be not instilled into thy mind that this body perishes, and thou abuse it to any lust. For if thou shalt defile thy body, thou shalt also at the same time defile the Holy Spirit; and if thou shalt defile the Holy Spirit, thou shall not live.

60 And I said, What if through ignorance this should have been already committed, before a man heard these words; How can he attain into salvation, who has thus defiled his body?

61 He replied. As for men's former actions which through ignorance they have committed, God only can afford a remedy unto them; for all the power belongeth unto him.

62 But now guard thyself; and seeing God is almighty and merciful, he will grant a remedy to what thou hast formerly done amiss, if for the time, to come thou shalt not defile thy body and spirit:

63 For they are companions together, and the one cannot be defiled but the other will be so too. Keep therefore both of them pure, and thou shalt live unto God.

THE THIRD PART OF THE BOOK OF HERMAS
SIMILITUDE VI.

Of two sorts of voluptuous men, and of their death and defection; and of the continuance of their pains.

AS I was sitting at home, and praising God for all the things which I had seen; and was thinking concerning the commands, that they were exceedingly good, and great, and honest, and pleasant, and such as were able to bring a man to salvation; I said thus within myself, I shall be happy if I walk according to these commands; and whosoever shall walk in them shall live unto God.

2 Whilst I was speaking on this wise within myself, I saw him whom I had before been wont to see, sitting by me; and he spake thus unto me:

3 What doubtest thou concerning my commands which I have delivered unto thee? They are good, doubt not, but trust in the Lord, and thou shalt walk in them; for I will give thee strength to fulfil them.

4 These commands are profitable to those who shall repent of the sins which they have formerly committed; if for the time to come they shall not continue in them.

5 Whosoever therefore ye be that repent, cast away from you the naughtiness of the present world; and put on all virtue, and righteousness, and so shall ye be able to keep these commands; and not sin from henceforth any more.

6 For if ye shall keep yourselves from sin for the time to come, ye shall cut off a great deal of your former sins. Walk in my commands, and ye shall live unto God: These things have I spoken unto you.

7 And when he, had said this, he added; let us go into the field, and I will show thee shepherds of sheep. I replied, sir, let us go.

8 And we came into a certain field, and there he showed me a young shepherd, finely arrayed, with his garments of a purple colour. And he fed large flocks; and his sheep were full of pleasure, and in much delight and cheerfulness; and they skipping, ran here and there.

9 And the shepherd took very great satisfaction in his flock; and the countenance of that shepherd was cheerful, running up and down among his flock.

10 Then the angel said unto me, Seest then this shepherd? I answered, sir, I see him. He said unto me, this is the messenger of delight and pleasure. He therefore corrupts the minds of the servants of God, and turns them from the truth, delighting them with many pleasures, and they perish.

ΔΙΔΑΧΗ ΤΩΝ ΔΩΔΕΚΑ ΑΠΟΣΤΟΛΩΝ

11 For they forget the commands of the living God, and live in luxury and in vain pleasures, and are corrupted by the evil angel, some of them even unto death; and others to a falling away.

12 I replied; I understand not what you mean, by saying unto death, and to a falling away. Hear, says he; all those sheep which thou sawest exceeding joyful, are such as have for ever departed from God, and given selves up to the lusts of this present time.

13 To these therefore there is no return, by repentance, unto life; because, to their other sins they have added this, that they have blasphemed the name of the lord: These kind of men are ordained unto death.

14 But those sheep which thou sawest not leaping, but feeding in one place; are such as have indeed given themselves up to pleasure and delights; but have not spoken anything wickedly against the Lord.

15 These therefore are only fallen off from the truth, and so have yet hope laid up for them in repentance. For such a falling off hath some hope still left of a renewal; but they that are dead, are utterly gone for ever.

16 Again we went a little farther forward, and he showed me a great shepherd, who had as it were a rustic figure; clad with a white goat's skin, having his bag upon his shoulder, and in his hand a stick full of knots, and very hard, and a whip in his other hand; and his countenance was stern and sour, enough to affright a man; such was his look.

17 He took from that young shepherd such sheep as lived in pleasures, but did not skip up and down; and drove them into a certain steep craggy place fall of thorns and briars, insomuch that they could not get themselves free from them:

18 But being entangled in them, fed upon thorns and briars, and were grievously tormented with his whipping. For he still drove them on, and afforded them not any place, or time, to stand still.

19 When therefore I saw them so cruelly whipped and afflicted, I was grieved for them; because they were greatly tormented, nor had they any rest afforded them.

20 And I said unto the shepherd that was with me: Sir, who is this cruel and implacable shepherd, who is moved with no compassion towards these sheep? He answered, This shepherd is indeed one of the holy angels, but is appointed for the punishment of sinners

21 To him therefore are delivered those who have erred from God, and served the lusts and pleasures of this world. For this cause he pun-

ishes them every one according to their deserts, with cruel and various kinds of pains.

22 Sir, said I, I would know what kind of pains they are which every one undergoes? Hearken, said he; The several pains and torments are those which men every day undergo in their present lives. For some suffer losses; others poverty; others divers sicknesses. Some are unsettled; others suffer injuries from those that are unworthy; others fall under many other trials and inconveniences.

23 For many with an unsettled design at many things, and it profiteth them not; and they say that they have not success in their undertakings.

24 They do not call to their mind what they have done amiss, and they complain of the Lord. When therefore they shall have undergone all kind of vexation and inconvenience; then they are delivered over to me for good instruction, and are confirmed in the Faith of the Lord, and serve the Lord all the rest of their days with a pure mind.

25 And when they begin to repent of their sins, then they call to mind their works which they have done amiss, and give honour to God, saying, that he is a just Judge, and they have deservedly suffered all things according to their deeds.

26 Then for what remains of their lives, they serve God with a pure mind; and have success in all their undertakings, and receive from the Lord whatever they desire.

27 And then they give thanks unto the Lord that they were delivered unto me; nor do they suffer any more cruelty.

28 I said unto him; Sir, I entreat you still to show me now one thing. What, said he, dost thou ask? I said unto him; Are they who depart from the fear of God, tormented for the same time that they enjoyed their false delight and pleasures? He answered me; they are tormented for the same time.

29 And I said unto him; They are then tormented but little; whereas they who enjoy their pleasures so as to forget God, ought to endure seven times as much punishment.

30 He answered me; Thou art foolish, neither understandest thou the efficacy of this punishment. I said unto him; Sir, if I understood it, I would not desire you to tell me.

31 Hearken, said he, and learn what the force of both is, both of the pleasure and of the punishment. An hour of pleasure is terminated within its own space: but one hour of punishment has the efficacy of thirty days. Whosoever therefore enjoys his false pleasure for one day, and is one day, tormented; that one day of punishment is equivalent to a whole year's space.

ΔΙΔΑΧΗ ΤΩΝ ΔΩΔΕΚΑ ΑΠΟΣΤΟΛΩΝ

32 Thus look how many days any one pursues his pleasures, so many years is he punished for it. You see therefore how that the time of worldly enjoyments is but short; but that of pain and torments, a great deal more.

33 I replied; Sir, forasmuch as I do not understand at all these times of pleasure and pain; I entreat you that you would explain yourself more clearly concerning them. He answered me, saying; Thy foolishness still sticks unto thee.

34. Shouldst thou not rather purify thy mind, and serve God? Take heed, lest when thy time is fulfilled, thou be found still unwise. Hear then, as thou desirest, that thou mayest the more easily understand.

35 He that gives himself up one day to his pleasures and delights, and does whatsoever his soul desires, is full of great folly, nor understands what he does, but the day following forgets what he did the day before.

36 For delight and worldly pleasure are not kept in memory, by reason of the folly that is rooted in them. But when pain and torment befall a man a day, he is in effect troubled the whole year after; because his punishment continues firm in his memory.

37 Wherefore he remembers it with sorrow the whole year; and then calls to mind his vain pleasure and delight, and perceives that for the sake of that he was punished.

38 Whosoever therefore have delivered themselves over to such pleasures, are thus punished; because that when they had life, they rendered themselves liable to death.

39 I said unto him; Sir, what pleasures are hurtful? He answered; That is pleasure to every man which he doth willingly.

40 For the angry man, gratifying his passion, perceives pleasure in it; and so the adulterer, and drunkard; the slanderer and liar; the covetous man and the defrauder; and whosoever commits anything like unto these, he followeth his evil disposition, because he receives a satisfaction in the doing of it.

41 All these pleasures and delights are hurtful to the servants of God. For these therefore they are tormented and suffer punishment.

42 There are also pleasures that bring salvation unto men. For many, when they do what is good, find pleasure in it, and are attracted by the delights of it.

43 Now this pleasure is profitable to the servants of God, and brings life to such men; but those hurtful pleasures, which were before mentioned, bring torments and punishment.

44 And whosoever shall continue in them, and shall not repent of what they have done, shall bring death upon themselves.

SIMILITUDE VII.

That they who repent, must bring forth, fruits worthy of repent once.

AFTER a few days I saw the same person that before talked with me, in the same field, in which I had seen those shepherds, And he said unto me; What seekest thou? Sir, said I, I came to entreat you that You would command the shepherd, who is the minister of punishment, to depart out of my house, because he greatly afflicts me.

3 And he answered, It is necessary for thee to endure inconveniencies and vexations; for so that good angel hath commanded concerning thee, because he would try thee.

4 Sir, said I; What so great offence have I committed, that I should be delivered to this messenger? Hearken, said he: Thou art indeed guilty of many sins, yet not so many that thou shouldest be delivered to this messenger.

5 But thy house hath committed many sins and offences, and therefore that good messenger being grieved at their doings commanded that for some time thou shouldst suffer affliction; that they may both repent of what they have done, and may wash themselves from all the lusts of this present world.

6 When therefore they shall have repented, and be purified, then that messenger which is appointed over thy punishment, shall depart from thee.

7 I said unto him; Sir, if they have behaved themselves so as to anger that good angel, yet what have I done? He answered: They cannot otherwise be afflicted, unless thou, who art the head of the family, suffer.

8 For whatsoever thou shalt suffer, they must needs feel it but as long as thou shalt stand well established, they cannot experience any vexation.

9 I replied; But, sir, behold they also now repent with all their hearts. I know, says he, that they repent with all their hearts; but dost thou therefore think that their offences who repent, are immediately blotted out.

10 No, they are not presently; but he that repents must afflict his soul and show himself humble in all his affairs, and undergo many and divers vexations.

ΔΙΔΑΧΗ ΤΩΝ ΔΩΔΕΚΑ ΑΠΟΣΤΟΛΩΝ

11 And when he shall have suffered all things that were appointed for him; then perhaps HE that made him, and formed all things besides, will be moved with compassion towards him, and afford him some remedy; and especially if HE shall perceive his heart who repents, to be free from every evil work.

12 But at present it is expedient for thee, and for thy house, to be grieved; and it is needful that thou shouldst endure much vexation, as the angel of the Lord who committed thee unto me, has commanded.

13 Rather give thanks unto the Lord, that knowing what was to come he thought thee worthy, to whom he should foretell that trouble was coming upon thee, who art able to bear it.

14 I said unto him; Sir, but be thou also with me, and I shall easily undergo any trouble. I will, said he, be with thee; and I will entreat the messenger who is set over thy punishment, that he would moderate his afflictions towards thee.

15 And moreover thou shalt suffer adversity but for a little time; and then thou shalt again be restored to thy former state; only continue on in the humility of thy mind.

16 Obey the Lord with a pure heart; thou, and thy house, and thy children; and walk in the commands which I have delivered unto thee; and then thy repentance may be firm and pure.

17 And if thou shalt keep these things with thy house, thy inconveniencies shall depart from thee.

18 And all vexation shall in like manner depart from those, whosoever shall walk according to these commands.

SIMILITUDE VIII.

That there are many kinds of elect, and of repenting sinners: and how all of these shall receive a reward proportionable to the measure of their repentance and good works.

AGAIN he shewed me a willow which covered the fields and the mountains, under whose shadow came all such as were called by the name of the Lord.

2 And by that willow stood an angel of the Lord very excellent and lofty, and did cut down bows from the willow with a great hook; and reached out to the people that were under the shadow of the willow, little rods, as it were about a foot long.

3 And when all of them had taken them, he laid aside his hook, and the tree continued entire, as I had before seen it; at which I wondered, and mused within myself.

4 Then that shepherd said unto me; Forbear to wonder that the tree continues whole, not-with-standing so many boughs have been cut off from it: but stay a little, for now it shall be shown thee, what that angel means, who gave those rods to the people.

5 So he again demanded the rods of them; and in the same order that every one had received them, was he called to him, and restored his rod; which when he had received, he examined them.

6 From some he received them dry and rotten, and as it were touched with the moth; those he commanded to be separated from the rest, and placed by themselves. Others gave in their rods dry indeed, but not touched with the moth: these also he ordered to be set by themselves.

7 Others gave in their rods half dry; these also were set apart, Others gave in their rods half dry and cleft; these too were set by themselves. Others brought in their rods half dry and half green, and these were in like manner placed by themselves.

8 Others delivered up their rods two parts green, and the third dry; and they too were set apart. Others brought their rods two parts dry, and the third green; and were also placed by themselves.

9 Others delivered up their rods less dry (for there was but a very little, to wit, their tops dry), but they had clefts, and these were set in like manner by themselves. In the rods of others there was but a little green, and the rest dry; and these were set aside by themselves.

10 Others came, and brought their rods green as they had received them, and the greatest part of the people brought their rods thus; and the messenger greatly rejoiced at these, and they also were put apart by themselves.

11 Others brought in their rods not only green, but full of branches; and these were set aside, being also received by the angel with great joy. Others brought their rods green with branches, and those also some fruit upon them.

12 They who had such rods, were very cheerful; and the angel himself took great joy at them; nor was the shepherd that stood with me, less pleased with them.

13 Then the angel of the Lord commanded crowns to be brought, and the crowns were brought made of palms; and the angel crowned those men in whose rods he found the young branches with fruit, and commanded them to go into the tower.

ΔΙΔΑΧΗ ΤΩΝ ΔΩΔΕΚΑ ΑΠΟΣΤΟΛΩΝ

14 He also sent those into the tower, in whose hands he found branches without fruit, giving a seal unto them. For they had the same garment, that is, one white as snow; with which he bade them go into the tower And so he did to those who returned their rods green as they had received them; giving them a white garment, and so sent them away to go into the tower.

15 Having done this, he said to the shepherd that was with me, I go my way; but do thou send these within the walls, every one into the place in which he has deserved to dwell; examining first their rods, but examine them diligently that no one deceive thee; and if any one shall escape thee, I will try them upon the altar. Having said this to the shepherd, he departed.

16 After he was gone, the shepherd said unto me; Let us take the rods from them, and plant them; if perchance they may grow green again. I said unto him; Sir, how can those dry rods ever grow green again?

17 He answered me; That tree. is a willow, and always loves to live. If therefore these rods shall be planted, and receive a little moisture, many of them will recover themselves.

18 Wherefore I will try, and will pour water upon them, and if any of them can live, I will rejoice with them; but if not, at least by this means I shall be found not to have neglected my part.

19 Then he commanded me to call them; and they all came unto him, every one in the rank in which he stood, and gave him their rods; which having received he planted every one of them in their several orders.

20 And after he had planted them all, he poured much water upon them, insomuch that they were covered with water, and did not appear above it. Then when he had watered them. he said unto me; Let us depart, and after a little time we will return and visit them.

21 For he who created this tree, would have all those live that received rods from it. And I hope now that these rods are thus watered, many of them receiving in the moisture, will recover.

22 I said unto him, Sir, tell me what this tree denotes? For I am greatly astonished, that after so many branches have been cut off, it seems still to be whole: nor does there any thing the less of it appear to remain, which greatly amazes me.

23 He answered, Hearken. This great tree which covers the plains and the mountains, and all the earth, is the law of God, published throughout the whole world.

24 Now this law is the Son of God, who is preached to all the ends of the earth. The people that stand under its shadow, are those which have heard his preaching, and believed.

25 The great and venerable angel which you saw, was Michael who had the power over his people, and governs them. For he has planted the law in the hearts of those who have believed: and therefore he visits them to whom lie has given the law, to see if they have kept it.

26 And he examines every one's rod; and of those, many that are weakened: for those rods are the law of the Lord. Then he discerns all those who have not kept the law, knowing the place of every one of them.

27 I said unto him, Sir, why did he send away some to the tower, and left others here to you? He replied, those who have transgressed the law, which they received from him, are left in my power, that they may repent of their sins: but they who fulfilled this law and kept it, are under his power.

28 But who then, said I, are those, who went into the tower crowned? He replied, all such as having striven with the devil, have overcome him, are crowned: and they are those, who have suffered hard things, that they might keep the law.

29 But they who gave up their rods green, and with young branches, but without fruit, have indeed endured trouble for the same law, but have not suffered death; neither have they denied their holy law.

30 They who delivered up their rods green as they received them, are those who were modest and just, and have lived with a very pure mind, and kept the commandments of God.

31 The rest thou shalt know, when I shall have considered those rods which I have planted and watered.

32 After a few days we returned, and in the same place stood that glorious angel, and I stood by him. Then he said unto me; Gird thyself with a towel, and serve me.

33 And I girded myself with a clean towel, which was made of coarse cloth. And when he saw me girded, and ready to minister unto him, he said, Call those men whose rods have been planted, every one in his order as he gave them.

34 And he brought me into the field, and I called them all, and they all stood ready in their several ranks. Then he said unto them; let every one pluck up his rod, and bring it unto me. And first they delivered theirs, whose rods had been dry and rotten.

35 And those whose rods still continued so, he commanded to stand apart. Then they came whose rods had been dry but not rotten. Some

ΔΙΔΑΧΗ ΤΩΝ ΔΩΔΕΚΑ ΑΠΟΣΤΟΛΩΝ

of these delivered. in their rods green; others dry and rotten, as if they had been touched by the moth.

36 Those who gave them up green, he commanded to stand apart: but those whose rods were dry and rotten, he caused to stand with the first sort. Then came they whose rods had been half dry, and cleft: many of these gave up their rods green, and uncleft.

37 Others delivered them up green with branches, like unto theirs who went crowned into the tower. Others delivered them up dry, but not rotten; and some gave them up as they were before, all dry, and cleft.

38 Every one of these he ordered to stand apart; some by themselves, others in their respective ranks.

32 Then came they whose rods had been green, but cleft. These delivered their rods altogether green, and stood in their own order. And the shepherd rejoiced at these, because they were all changed, and free from their clefts.

40 Then they gave in their rods, who had them half green and half dry. Of these some were found wholly green, others half dry: others green, with young shoots. And all these were sent away, every one to his proper rank.

41 Then they gave up their rods, who had them before two parts green, and the third dry. Many of those gave in their rods green; many half dry; the rest dry but not rotten. So these were sent away, each to his proper place.

42 Then came they who before had their rods two parts dry and the third green; many of these delivered up their rods half dry, others dry and rotten; others half dry and cleft: but few green. And all these were set every one in his own rank.

43 Then they reached in their rods, in which there was before but a little green, and the rest dry. Their rods were for the most part found green, having little boughs, with fruit upon them; and the rest altogether green.

44 And the shepherd upon sight of these rejoiced exceedingly, because he had found them thus; and they also went to their proper orders.

45 Now after he had examined all their rods, he said unto me, I told thee that this tree loved life thou seest how many have repented, and attained unto salvation. Sir, said I, I see it.

46 That thou mightest know saith he, that the goodness and mercy of the Lord is great, and to be had in honour; who gave his spirit to them that were found worthy of repentance.

THE THIRD PART OF THE BOOK OF HERMAS

47 I answered, Sir, why then did not all of them repent? He replied, Those whose minds the Lords foresaw would be pure, and that they would serve him with all their hearts, to them he gave repentance.

48 But for those whose deceit and wickedness he beheld, and perceived that they would not truly return unto him; to them he denied any return unto repentance, lest they should again blaspheme his law with wicked words.

49 I said unto him; Now, Sir, make known unto me, what is the place of every one of those, who have given up their rods, and what their portion; that when they may have not kept their seal entire, but have wasted the seal which they received, shall hear and believe these thins, and may acknowledge their evil deeds and repent;

50 And receiving again their seal from you, may give glory to God, that he was moved with compassion towards them, and sent you to renew their spirits.

51 Hearken, said he; they whose rods have been found and rotten, and as it were touched with the moth; are the deserters and the betrayers of the church;

52 Who with the rest of their crimes, have also blasphemed the Lord, and denied his name when he had called upon them. Therefore all these are dead unto God and thou seest that none of them have repented, although they have heard my commands which thou hast delivered unto them. From these men therefore life is far distant.

53 They also who have delivered up their rods dry, but not rotten, have not been far from them. For they have been counterfeits, and brought in evil doctrines, and have perverted the servants of God, especially those who had sinned; not suffering them to return unto repentance, but keeping them back by their false doctrines.

54 These therefore have hope; and thou seest that many of them have repented, since the time that thou hast laid my commands before them; and many more will yet repent. But they, that shall not repent; shall lose both repentance and life.

55 But they that have repented, their place is begun to be within the first walls, and some of them are even gone into the tower. Thou seest therefore, said he, that in the repentance of sinners there is life; but for those who repent not, death is prepared.

56 Hear now concerning those who gave in their rods half dry and full of clefts. Those whose rods were only half dry, are the doubtful; for they are neither living nor dead.

57 But they who delivered in their rods, not only half dry but also full of clefts, are both doubtful and evil speakers; who detract from

ΔΙΔΑΧΗ ΤΩΝ ΔΩΔΕΚΑ ΑΠΟΣΤΟΛΩΝ

those that are absent, and have never peace among themselves, and who envy one another.

58 Howbeit, to those also repentance is offered; for thou seest that some of these have repented.

59 Now all those of this kind who have quickly repented, shall have a place in the tower; and they who have been more slow in their repentance, shall dwell within the walls: but they that shall not repent, and shall continue on in their wicked doings, shall die the death.

60 As for those who had their rods green, but yet cleft; they are such as were always faithful and good, but they had some envy and strife among themselves concerning dignity and pre-eminence.

61 Now all such as are vain, and without understanding, contend with one another about these things.

62 Nevertheless, seeing they are otherwise good, if when they shall hear these commands they shall amend themselves, and shall at my persuasion suddenly repent; they shall at last dwell in the tower, like those who have truly and worthily repented.

63 But if any one shall again return to his dissension; he shall be shut out from the tower, and shall lose his life. For the life of those who keep the commandments of the Lord, consists in doing what they are commanded; not in principality, or in any other dignity.

64 For by forbearance and humility of mind, men shall attain unto life; but by seditions and contempt of the law, they shall purchase death unto themselves.

65 They who in their rods had half dry and half green, are those who are engaged in many affairs of the world, and are not joined to the saints. For which cause half of them liveth, and half is dead.

66 Wherefore many of these since the time that they have heard my commands, have repented, and begun to dwell in the tower. But some of them have wholly fallen away; to these there is no more place for repentance.

67 For by reason of their present interests, they have blasphemed and denied God: and for this wickedness they have lost life. And of these many are still in doubt, yet these may return; and if they shall quickly repent, they shall have a place in the tower; but if they shall be more slow, they shall dwell within the walls; but if they shall not repent, they shall die.

68 As for those who had two parts of their rods green, and the third dry; they have by manifold ways denied the Lord. Of these many have repented, and found a place in the tower: and many have altogether departed from God. These have utterly lost life.

THE THIRD PART OF THE BOOK OF HERMAS

69 And some being in a doubtful state, have raise up dissensions: these may yet return, if they shall suddenly repent and not continue in their lusts; but if they shall continue in their evil-doing they shall die.

70 They who gave in their rods two parts dry, and the other been, are those who have indeed been faithful, but withal rich and full of good things; and thereupon upon have desired to be famous among the heathen which are without, and have thereby fallen into great pride, and begun to aim at high matters, and to forsake the truth.

71 Nor were they joined to the saints, but lived with the heathen; and this life seemed the more pleasant to them. Howbeit they have not departed from God, but continued in the faith; only they have not wrought the works of faith.

72 Many therefore of these have repented; and begun to dwell in the tower. Yet others still living among the heathen people, and being lifted up with their vanities, have utterly fallen away from God, and followed the works and wickedness of the heathen. These kind of men therefore are reckoned among strangers to the Gospel.

73 Others of these began to be doubtful in their minds; despairing by reason of their wicked doings ever to attain unto salvation Others being thus made doubtful, did moreover stir up dissensions.

74 To these therefore, and to those who by reason of their doings are become doubtful, there is still hope of return; but they must repent quickly, that their place may be in the tower. But they that repent not, and continue still in their pleasures, are nigh unto death.

75 As for those who gave in their rods green, excepting their tops, which only were dry, and had clefts; these were always good, and faithful, and upright before God: nevertheless they sinned a little, by reason of their empty pleasures and trifling thoughts which they had within themselves.

76 Wherefore many of them when they heard my words, repented forthwith, and began to dwell in the tower. Nevertheless some grew doubtful, and others to their doubtful minds added dissensions. To these therefore there is still hope of return, because they were always good; but they shall not hardly be moved.

77 As for those, lastly, who gave in their rods dry, their tops only excepted, which alone were green; they are such as have believed indeed in God, but have lived in wickedness; yet without departing from God: having always willingly borne the name of the Lord, and readily received into their houses the servants of God.

78 Wherefore hearing these things they returned, and without delay repented, and lived in all righteousness. And some of them suffered

ΔΙΔΑΧΗ ΤΩΝ ΔΩΔΕΚΑ ΑΠΟΣΤΟΛΩΝ

death: others readily underwent many trials, being mindful of their evil doings.

79 If And when he had ended his explications of all the rods, he said unto me, Go, and say unto all men that they repent, and they shall live unto God; because the Lord being moved with great clemency hath sent me to preach repentance unto all:

80 Even unto those who by reason of their evil doings, deserve not to attain unto salvation. But the Lord will by patient, and keep the invitation that was made by his Son.

81 I said unto him, sir, I hope that all when they shall hear these things, will repent. For I trust that everyone acknowledging his crimes, and taking up the fear of the Lord, will return unto repentance.

82 He said unto me, Whosoever shall repent with all their hearts, and cleanse themselves from all the evils that I have before mentioned, and not add anything more to their sins, shall receive from the Lord cure of their former iniquities, if they do not make any doubt of these commands, and shall live unto God.

83 But they that shall continue to add to their transgressions, and still converse with the lusts of the present world, shall condemn themselves unto death. But do thou walk in these commands, and whosoever shall Walk in these, and exercise them rightly, shall live unto God.

84 And having showed me all these things, he said; I will show thee the rest in a few days.

SIMILITUDE IX.

The greatest mysteries of the militant and triumphant Church which is to be built.

AFTER I had Written the Commands and similitudes of the Shepherd, the Angel of Repentance came unto me, and said to me, I will show thee all those things which the Spirit spake with thee under the figure of the church. For that Spirit is the Son of God.

2 And because thou wert weak in body, it was not declared unto thee by the angel, until thou wert strengthened by the Spirit, and increased in force, that thou mightest also see the angel:

3 For then indeed the building of the tower was very well and gloriously shown unto thee by the church; nevertheless thou sawest all things shown unto thee as it were by a virgin.

THE THIRD PART OF THE BOOK OF HERMAS

4 But now thou art enlightened by the angel, and yet by the same Spirit. But thou must consider all things diligently; for therefore am I sent into thy house by that venerable messenger, that when thou shalt have seen all things powerfully, thou mayest not be afraid as before.

5 And he led me to the height of a mountain in Arcadia, and we sat upon its top. And he showed me a great plain, and about it twelve mountains in different figures.

6 The first was black as soot. The second was smooth, without herbs. The third was full of thorns and thistles. The fourth had herbs half dried; of which the upper part was green, but that next the root was dry; and some of the herbs, when the sun grew hot, were dry.

7 The fifth mountain was very rugged; but yet had green herbs. The sixth mountain was full of clefts, some lesser, and some greater; and in these clefts grew grass, not flourishing, but which seemed to be withering.

8 The seventh mountain had delightful pasture, and was wholly fruitful; and all kinds of cattle, and of the birds of heaven; fed upon it; and the more they fed on it, the more and better did the grass grow.

9 The eighth mountain was full of fountains, and from those fountains were watered all kinds of the creatures of Cod. The ninth mountain had no water at all, but was wholly destitute of it; and nourished deadly serpents, very destructive to men.

10 The tenth mountain was full of tall trees, and altogether shady; and under the shade of them lay cattle resting and chewing the cud.

11 The eleventh mountain was full of the thickest trees, and those trees seemed to be loaded with several sorts of fruits; that whosoever saw them could not choose but desire to eat of their fruit.

12 The twelfth mountain was altogether white, and of a most pleasant aspect, and itself gave a most excellent beauty to itself.

13 In the middle of the plain he showed me a huge white rock, which rose out of the plain, and the rock was higher than those mountains, and was square; so that it seemed capable of supporting the whole world.

14 It looked to me to be old, yet it had in it a new gate, which seemed to have been newly hewn out of it. Now that gate was bright beyond the sun itself; insomuch, that I greatly wondered at its light.

15 About the gate stood twelve virgins; of which four that stood at the corners of the gate, seemed to me to be the chiefest, although the rest were also of worth: and they stood in the four parts of the gate.

16 It added also to the grace of those virgins, that they stood in pairs, clothed with linen garments, and decently girded, their right

ΔΙΔΑΧΗ ΤΩΝ ΔΩΔΕΚΑ ΑΠΟΣΤΟΛΩΝ

arms being at liberty, as if they were about to lift up some burthen; for so they were adorned, and were exceeding cheerful and ready.

17 When I saw this, I wondered with myself to see such great and noble things. And again I admired upon the account of those virgins, that they were so handsome and delicate; and stood with such firmness and constancy, as if they would carry the whole heaven.

18 And as I was thinking thus within myself, the shepherd said unto me; What thinkest thou within thyself? Why art thou disquieted, and fillest thyself with care?

19 Do not seem to consider, as if thou wert wise, what thou doest not understand, but pray unto the Lord, that thou mayest have ability to understand it. What is to come thou canst not understand, but thou seest that which is before thee.

20 Be not therefore disquieted at those things which thou canst not see; but get the understanding of those which thou seest.

21 Forbear to be curious; and I will show thee all things that I ought to declare unto thee: but first consider what yet remains.

22 And when he had said this unto me I looked up, and behold I saw six tall and venerable men coming; their countenances were all alike, and they called a certain multitude of men; and they who came at their call were also tall and stout.

23 And those six commanded them to build a certain tower over that gate. And immediately there began to be a great noise of those men running here and there about the gate, who were come together to build the tower.

24 But those virgins which stood about the gate perceived that the building of the tower was to be hastened by them. And they stretched out their hands, as if they were to receive somewhat from them to do.

25 Then those six men commanded, that they should lift up stones out of a certain deep place, and prepare them for the building of the tower. And there were lifted up ten white stones, square, and not cut round.

26 Then those six men called the ten virgins to them, and commanded them to carry all the stones that were to be put into the building, and having carried them through the gate to deliver them to those that were about to build the tower.

27 Immediately the virgins began all of them together to lift up those stones, that were before taken out of the deep.

28 And they who also stood about the gate did carry stones in such a manner, that those stones which seemed to be the strongest were laid at the corners, and the rest were put into the sides;

29 And thus they carried all the stones, and bringing them through the gate delivered them to the builders, as they had been commanded: who receiving them at their hands, built with them.

30 But this building was made upon that great rock, and over the gate; and by these the whole tower was supported. But the building of the ten stones filled the whole gate, which began to be made for the foundation of that tower.

31 After those ten stones did five and twenty others rise up out of the deep; and these were placed in the building of the same tower; being lifted up by those virgins, as the others had been before.

32 After these did fire and thirty others rise up; and these were also in like manner fitted into the same work. Then forty other stones were brought up, and all these were added unto the building of that tower.

33 So there began to be four ranks in the foundation of that tower; and the stones ceased to rise out of the deep; and they also which built rested a little.

34 Again, those six men commanded the multitude, that they should bring stones out of those twelve mountains to the building of the same tower.

35 So they cut out of all the mountains stones of divers colours, and brought them and gave them to the virgins; which when they had received they carried them, and delivered them into the building of the tower.

36 In which when they were built they became white, and different from what they were before; for they were all alike, and did change their former colours. And some were reached up by the men themselves, which when they came into the building, continued such is they were put in.

37 These neither became white, nor different from what they were before; because they were not carried by the virgins through the gate. Wherefore these stones were disagreeable in the building; which, when these six men perceived they commanded them to be removed, and put again in the place from which they were brought.

38 And they said to those who brought these stones; Do not ye reach up to us any stones for this building, but lay them down by the tower, that these virgins may carry them and reach them to us.

39 For unless they shall be carried by these virgins through this gate, they cannot change their colours: therefore do not labour in vain.

40 So the building that day was done; howbeit the tower was not finished, for it was afterwards to be built; therefore now also there was some delay made of it.

ΔΙΔΑΧΗ ΤΩΝ ΔΩΔΕΚΑ ΑΠΟΣΤΟΛΩΝ

41 And these six men commanded those that built to depart, and as it were to rest for some time; but they ordered those virgins that they should not depart from the tower; so now they seemed to me to be left for the guarding of it.

42 When all were departed, I said unto the shepherd; Sir, why is not the building of the tower finished? Because it cannot, said he, be finished until its Lord comes, and approves of the building; that if he shall find any stones in it that are not good they may be changed; for this tower is built according to his will.

43 Sir, said I, I would know what the building of this tower signifies; as also I would be informed concerning this rock, and this gate;

44 And concerning the mountains, and the virgins, and the stones that did rise out of the deep, and were not cut, but put into the building just as they came forth; and why the ten stones were first laid in the foundation; then the twenty-five, then thirty- five; then forty?

45 Also concerning those stones that were put into the building, and again taken out, and carried back into their places? Fulfil, I pray, the desire of my soul as to all these things, and manifest all unto me.

46 And he said unto me; If thou shalt not be dull, thou shall know all, and shall see all the other things that are about to happen in this, tower: and shall understand diligently all these similitudes.

47 And after a few days we came into the same place where we had sat before; and he said unto me, Let us go unto the tower; for the Lord of it will come and examine it.

48 So we came thither, and found none but those virgins there. And he asked them whether the Lord of that tower was come thither? And they replied, that he would be there presently to examine the building.

49 After a very little while I saw a great multitude of men coming, and in the middle of them a man so tall, that he surpassed the tower in height.

50 About him were those six, who before commanded in the building, and all the rest of those who had built that tower, and many others of great dignity: and the virgins that kept the tower ran to meet him, and kissed him, and began to walk near unto him.

51 But he examined the building with so much care, that he handled every stone; and struck every one with a rod which he held in his hand:

52 Of which some being so struck turned black as soot; others were rough; some looked as if they had cracks in them; others seemed maimed; some neither black nor white; some looked sharp, and agreed not with the other stones, and others were full of spots.

THE THIRD PART OF THE BOOK OF HERMAS

53 These were the several kinds of those stones which were not found proper in the building; all which the Lord commanded to be taken out of the tower, and laid near it, and other stones to be brought and put in their places.

54 And they that built, asked him from which of the mountains he would have stones brought to put in the place of those that were laid aside. But he forbad them to bring any from the mountains, and commanded that they should take them out of a certain field that was near.

55 So they digged in the field, and found many bright square stones, and some also that were round. Howbeit, all that were found in that field were taken away, and carried through the gate by those virgins; and those of them that were square were fitted and put into the places of those that were pulled out.

56 But the round ones were not put into the building, because they were hard, and it would have required too much time to cut them but they were placed about the tower, as if they should hereafter be cut square, and put into the building; for they were very white.

57 When he who was chief in dignity, and lord of the whole tower saw this, he called to him the shepherd that was with me, and gave him the stones that were rejected and laid about the tower, and said unto him; cleanse these stones with all care, and fit them into the building of the tower, that they may agree with the rest; but those that will not suit with the rest, cast away afar off from the tower.

58 When he had thus commanded him, he departed, with all those that came with him to the tower but those virgins still stood about the tower to keep it.

59 And I said unto that shepherd; How can these stones, seeing they have been rejected, return into the building of this tower? He replied; I will cut off the greatest part from these stones, and will add them to the building, and they will agree with the rest.

60 And I said, Sir, how will they be able to fill the same place, when they shall be so much cut away? He answered; They that shall be found too little shall be put into the middle of the building, and the greater shall be placed without, and keep them in.

61 When he had said thus unto me, he added; Let us go, and after three days we will return, and I will put these stones, being cleansed, into the tower.

62 For all these that are about the tower must be cleansed, lest the master of the house chance to come upon the sudden, and find those which are about the tower unclean; and be so exasperated that these stones should never be put into the building of this tower, and I shall be looked upon to have been unmindful of my master's commands.

ΔΙΔΑΧΗ ΤΩΝ ΔΩΔΕΚΑ ΑΠΟΣΤΟΛΩΝ

63 When therefore we came after three days to the tower, he said unto me, Let us examine all these stones, and let us see which of them may go into the building. I answered, Sir, let us see.

64 And first of all we began to consider those which had been black; for they were found just such as they were when they were pulled out of the tower: wherefore he commanded them to be removed from the tower and put by themselves.

65 Then he examined those which had been rough; and commanded many of those to be cut round, and to be fitted by the virgins into the building of the tower; so they took them, and fitted them into the middle of the building and he commanded the rest to be laid by with the black ones, for they also were become black.

66 Next he considered those which were full of cracks, and many of those also he ordered to be pared away, and so to be added to the rest of the building, by the came virgins.

67 These were placed without because they were found entire; but the residue through the multitude of their cracks could not be reformed, and therefore were cast away from the building of the tower.

68 Then he considered those that had been maimed; many of these had cracks, and were become black; others had large clefts; these he commanded to be placed with those that were rejected;

69 But the rest being cleansed and reformed, he commanded to be put into the building. These therefore those virgins took up, and fitted into the middle of the building, because they were but weak.

70 After these he examined those which were found half white and half black, and many of those which were now black; these also he ordered to be laid among those that were cast away.

71 The rest were found altogether white; those were taken up by the virgins, and fitted into the same tower: and they were put in the outside, because they were found entire; that so they might keep in those that were placed in the middle, for nothing was cut off from them.

72 Next he looked upon those which had been hard and sharp; but few of these were made use of, because they could not be cut, for they were found very hard: but the rest were formed, and fitted by the virgins into the middle of the building, because they were more weak.

73 Then he considered those which had spots; of these a few were found black, and they were carried to their fellows. The rest were white and entire; and they were fitted by the virgins into the building, and placed in the outside, by reason of their strength.

THE THIRD PART OF THE BOOK OF HERMAS

74 After this he came to consider those stones which were white and round: and he said unto me, What shall we do with these stones? I answered, Sir, I cannot tell.

75 He replied, Canst thou think of nothing then for these? I answered, Sir, I understand not this art; neither am I a stone-cutter, nor can I tell anything.

76 And he said, seest thou not that they are very round? Now to make them square, I must cut off a great deal from them; howbeit, it is necessary that some of these should go into the building of the tower.

77 I answered; If it be necessary, why do you perplex yourself, and not rather choose, if you have any choice among them, and fit them into the building.

78 Upon this he chose out the largest and brightest, and squared them; which, when he had done the virgins took them up, and fitted them into the building.

79 And the rest that remained were carried back into the same field from which they were taken; howbeit, they were not cast away; because, said he, there is yet a little wanting to this tower, which is to be built; and perhaps the Lord will have these stones fitted into this building, because they are exceeding white.

80 Then there were called twelve very stately women, clothed with a black garment, girded, and their shoulders free, and their hair loose. These seemed to me to be country women.

81 And the shepherd commanded them to take up those stones which were cast out of the building, and carry them back to the mountains out of which they were taken.

82 And they took them all up joyfully, and carried them back to their places from whence they had been taken.

83 When not one stone remained about the tower, he said unto me, Let us go about this tower, and see whether anything be wanting to it.

84 We began therefore to go round about it; and when he saw that it was handsomely built, he began to be very glad; for it was so beautifully framed, that any one that had seen it must have been in love with the building.

85 For it seemed to be all but one stone, nor did a joint any where appear; but it looked as if it had all been cut out of one rock.

86 And when I diligently considered what a tower it was, I was extremely pleased: and he said unto me, Bring hither some lime and little shells, that I may fill up the spaces of those stones that were taken out of the building, and put in again; for all things about the tower must be made even.

ΔΙΔΑΧΗ ΤΩΝ ΔΩΔΕΚΑ ΑΠΟΣΤΟΛΩΝ

87 And I did as he commanded me, and brought them unto him and he said unto me, Be ready to help me, and this work will quickly be finished.

88 He therefore filled up the spaces of those stones, and commanded the place about the tower to be cleansed.

89 Then those virgins took besoms, and cleansed all the place around, and took away all the rubbish, and threw water on; which being done, the palace became delightful, and the tower beauteous.

90 Then he said unto me, All is now clean if the Lord should come to finish the tower, he will find nothing whereby to complain of us.

91 When he had said this he would have departed. But I laid hold on his bag, and began to entreat him for the Lord's sake, that he would explain to me all things that he had shown me.

92 He said unto me, I have at present a little business; but I will suddenly explain all things unto thee. Tarry here for me till I come.

93 I said unto him, Sir, what shall I do here alone? He answered, Thou art not alone, seeing all these virgins are with thee.

94 I said, Sir, deliver me then unto them. Then he called them and said unto them, I commend this man unto you until I shall come;

95 So I remained with those virgins: now they were cheerful and courteous unto me; especially the four, which seemed to be the chiefest among them.

96 Then those virgins said unto me, that shepherd will not return hither to-day. I said unto them, What then shall I do? They answered, Tarry for him till the evening, if perhaps he may come and speak with thee; but if not, yet thou shalt continue with us till he does come.

97 I said unto them, I will tarry for him till evening; but if he comes not by that time, I will go home, and return hither again the next morning.

98 They answered me, As thou art delivered unto us, thou mayest not depart from us. I said, Where shall I tarry?

99 They replied, Thou shalt sleep with us as a brother, not as a husband; for thou art our brother, and we are ready from henceforth to dwell with thee; for thou art very dear to us.

100 Howbeit I was ashamed to continue with them. But she that seemed to be the chiefest amongst them, embraced me, and began to kiss me. And the rest when they saw that I was kissed by her, began also to kiss me as a brother; and led me about the tower, and played with me.

THE THIRD PART OF THE BOOK OF HERMAS

101 Some of them also sung psalms, others made up the chorus with them. But I walked about the tower with them, rejoicing silently, and seeming to myself to be grown young again.

102 When the evening came on, I would forthwith have gone home, but they withheld me, and suffered me not to depart. Wherefore I continued with them that night near the same tower.

103 So they spread their linen garments upon the ground; and placed me in the middle, nor did they anything else, only they prayed.

104 I also prayed with them without ceasing, nor less than they. Who, when they saw me pray in that manner, rejoiced greatly: and I continued there with their till the next day.

105 And when we had worshipped God, then the shepherd came and said unto them: You have done no injury to this man? They answered, Ask him. I said unto him, Sir, I have received a great deal of satisfaction in that I have remained with them.

106 And he said unto me, How didst thou sup? I answered, Sir, I feasted the whole night upon the words of the Lord. They received thee well then, said he? I said, Sir, very well.

107 He answered, Wilt thou now learn what thou didst desire? I replied, Sir, I will: and first I pray thee that thou shouldest show me all things in the order that I asked them.

108 He answered, I will do all as thou wouldst have me, nor will I hide any thing from thee.

109 First of all, Sir, said I, tell me, what this rock and this gate denote? Hearken, said he; this rock, and this gate, are the Son of God. I replied, Sir, how can that be; seeing the rock is old, but the gate new?

110 Hear, said he, O foolish man! and understand. The Son of God is indeed more ancient than any creature; insomuch that he was in council with his Father at the creation of all things.

111 But the gate is therefore new, because he appeared in the last days in the fullness of time; that they who shall attain unto salvation, may by it enter into the kingdom of God.

112 You have seen, said he, those stones which were carried through the gate, how they were placed in the building of the tower; but that those which were not carried through the gate, were sent away into their own places? 113 I answered, sir, I saw it. Thus, said he, no man shall enter into the kingdom of God, but he who shall take upon him the name of the Son of God.

114 For if you would enter into any city, and that city should he encompassed with a wall, and had only one gate, could you enter into that city except by that gate?

ΔΙΔΑΧΗ ΤΩΝ ΔΩΔΕΚΑ ΑΠΟΣΤΟΛΩΝ

115 I answered, Sir, how could I do otherwise? As therefore, said he, there would be no other way of entering into that city but by its gate, so neither can any one enter into the kingdom of God, but only by the name of his Son, who is most dear unto him.

116 And he said unto me, Didst thou see the multitude of those that built that tower? Sir, said I, I saw it. He answered, All those are the angels, venerable in their dignity,

117 With these is the Lord encompassed as with a wall: but the gate is the Son of God, who is the only way of coming unto God. For no man shall go to God, but by his Son.

118 Thou sawest also, said he, the six men, and in the middle of them that venerable great man, who walked about the tower, and rejected the stones out of the tower?

119 Sir, said I, I saw them. He answered, that tall man was the Son of God; and those six were his angels of most eminent dignity, which stand about him on the right hand and on the left.

120 Of these excellent angels none comes in unto God without him. He added, Whosoever there, fore shall not take upon him his name, he shall nor enter into the kingdom of God.

121 Then I said, What is this tower? This, said he, is the church. And what, Sir, are these virgins? He said unto me, These are the holy spirits, for no man can enter into the kingdom of God, except these clothe him with their garment,

122 For it will avail thee nothing to take up the name of the Son of God, unless thou shalt also receive their garment from them. For these virgins are the powers of the Son of God. So shall a man in vain bear his name, unless he shall be also endued with his powers.

123 And he said unto me, sawest thou those stones that were cast away? They bore indeed the name, but put not on their garment. I said, Sir, what is their garment? Their very names, said he, are their garment.

124 Therefore whosoever beareth the name of the Son of God, ought to bear their names also; for the Son of God also himself beareth their names.

125 As for those stones, continued he, which being delivered by their hands, thou sawest remain in the building, they were clothed with their power; for which cause thou seest the whole tower of the same colour with the rock, and made as it were of one stone.

126 So also those who have believed in God by his Son, have put on his spirit. Behold there shall be one spirit, and one body, and one

THE THIRD PART OF THE BOOK OF HERMAS

colour of their garments; and all they shall attain this, who shall bear the names of these virgins.

127 And I said, Sir, why then were those stones cast away which were rejected, seeing they also were carried through the gate, and delivered by the hands of these virgins into the building of this tower?

128 Seeing, said he thou takest care to inquire diligently into all things, hear also concerning those stones which were rejected. All these received the name of the Son of God, and with that the power of these virgins.

129 Having therefore received these spirits, they were perfected, and brought into the number of the servants of God; and they began to be one body, and to have one garment, for they were endued with the same righteousness, which they alike exercised.

130 But after that they beheld those women which thou sawest clothed with a black garment, with their shoulders at liberty and their hair loose; they fixed their desires upon them, being tempted with their beauty; and were clothed with their power, and cast off the clothing of the virgins:

131 Therefore were they cast off from the house of God, and delivered to those women. But they that were not corrupted with their beauty, remained in the house of God. This, said he, is the signification of those stones which were rejected.

132 And I said, sir, what if any of these men shall repent, and cast away their desire of those women, and be converted, and return to these virgins, and put on again their virtue; shall they not enter into the house of God?

133 They shall enter, said he, if they shall lay aside all the works of those women, and shall resume the power of these virgins, and shall walk in their works.

134 And for this cause there is a stop in the building, that if they shall repent, they may be added to the building of this tower; but if they shall not repent, that others may be built in their places, and so they may be utterly cast away.

135 For all these things I gave thanks unto the Lord, that being moved with mercy towards all those upon whom his name is carried, he sent to us the angel of repentance to preside over us who have sinned against him; and that he has refreshed our spirits which were almost gone, and who had no hope of salvation, but are now refreshed to the renewal of life.

136 Then I said, Show me now sir, why this tower is not built upon the ground, but upon a rock, and upon the gate? He replied, Thou art foolish, and without understanding, therefore thou asketh this.

ΔΙΔΑΧΗ ΤΩΝ ΔΩΔΕΚΑ ΑΠΟΣΤΟΛΩΝ

137 And I said, sir, I must needs ask all things of you because I understand nothing at all. For all your answers are great and excellent; and which a man can hardly understand.

138 Hear, said he: The name of the Son of God is great and without bounds, and the whole world is supported by it. If therefore, said I, every creature of God be sustained by his Son, why should he not support those also who have been invited by him, and who carry his name, and walk in his commandments?

139 Seest thou not, said he, that he doth support them, who with all their heart, bear his name? He therefore is their foundation, and gladly supports those who do not deny his name, but willingly bear it.

140 And I said: Sir, tell me the names of these virgins; and of those women that were clothed with the black garment.

141 Hear, said he, the names of those virgins which are the more powerful, and stand at the corners of the gate. These are their names:

142 The first is called Faith; the second Continence; the third Power; the fourth Patience; the rest which stand beneath these are, Simplicity, Innocence, Chastity, Cheerfulness, Truth, Understanding, Concord, Charity.

143 Whosoever therefore bear these names, and the name of the Son of God, shall enter into the kingdom of God.

144 Hear now, said he, the names of those women, which were clothed with the black garment. Of these, four are the principal: the first is Perfidiousness; the second, Incontinence; the third, Infidelity; the fourth, Pleasure.

145 And the rest which follow are called thus, Sadness, Malice, Lust, Anger, Lying, Foolishness, Pride, and Hatred. The servant of God, which carries these spirits, shall see indeed the kingdom of God, but he shall not enter into it.

146 But, sir, what are those stones which were taken out of the deep and fitted into the building? The ten, said he, which were placed at the foundation, are the first age; the following five-and- twenty, are the second, of righteous men.

147 The next thirty-five, are the prophets and ministers of the Lord. And the forty, are the Apostles and doctors of the preaching of the Son of God.

148 And I said, sir, why did the virgins put even those stones into the building after they were carried through the gate? And he said, Because these first carried those spirits, and they departed not one from the other, neither the men from the spirits, nor the spirits from the men:

THE THIRD PART OF THE BOOK OF HERMAS

149 But the spirits were joined to those men even to the day of their death; who if they had not had these spirits with them, they could not have been useful to the building of this tower.

150 And I said, sir, show me this farther. He answered, What dost then ask? Why did these stones come out of the deep, and were placed into the building of this tower, seeing that they long ago carried those holy spirits?

151 It was necessary, said he, for them to ascend by water, that they might be at rest. For they could not otherwise enter into the kingdom of God, but by laying aside the mortality of their former life.

152 They therefore being dead, were nevertheless sealed with the seal of the Son of God, and so entered into the kingdom of God.

153 For before a man receives the name of the Son of God, he is ordained unto death; but when he receives that seal, he is freed from death, and assigned unto life.

154 Now that seal is the water of baptism, into which men go down under the obligation unto death, but come up appointed unto life.

155 Wherefore to those also was this seal preached, and they made use of it, that they might enter into the kingdom of God.

156 And I said, Why then, sir, did these forty stones also ascend with them out of the deep, having already received that seal?

157 He answered, Because these Apostles and teachers, who preached the name of the Son of God, dying after they had received his faith and power, preached to them who were dead before: and they gave this seal to them.

158 They went down therefore into the water with them, and again came up. But these went down whilst they were alive, and came up again alive: whereas those who were before dead, went down dead, but came up alive;

159 Through these therefore they received life, and knew the Son of God: for which cause they came up with them, and were fit to come into the building of the tower; and were not cut, but put in entire; because they died in righteousness, and in great purity; only this seal was wanting to them.

160 Thus you have the explication of these things.

161 I answered: Sir, tell me now what concerns those mountains; why are they so different, some of one form, and some of another?

162 Hear, said he; These twelve mountains which thou seest, are twelve nations, which make up the whole world. Wherefore the Son of God is preached to them, by those whom he sent unto them.

ΔΙΔΑΧΗ ΤΩΝ ΔΩΔΕΚΑ ΑΠΟΣΤΟΛΩΝ

163 But why, said I, are they different, and every one of a figure? He replied, Hearken. Those twelve nations which possess the whole world, are twelve people.

164 And as thou hast beheld these mountains different, so are they. I will therefore open to thee the meaning and actions of every mountain.

165 But first, sir, said I, show me this; Seeing these mountains are so different, how have they agreed in the building of this tower; and been brought to one colour; and are no less bright than those that came out of the deep?

166 Because, replied he, all the nations which are under heaven, have heard and believed in the same one name of the Son of God by whom they are called.

167 Wherefore having received his seal, they have all been made partakers of the same understanding and knowledge; and their faith and charity have been the same; and they have carried the spirits of these virgins together with his name.

168 And therefore the building of this tower appeared to be of the same colour, and did shine like the brightness of the sun.

169 But after that they had thus agreed in one mind, there began to be one body of them all; howbeit some of them polluted themselves, and were cast off from those of the righteous, and again returned to their former state, and became even worse than they were before.

170 How, air, said I, were they worse who knew the Lord? He answered: If he who knows not the Lord liveth wickedly, the punishment of his wickedness attends him;

171 But he who has known the Lord, ought to abstain altogether from all wickedness, and more and more to be the servant of righteousness.

172 And does not he then seem to thee to sin more who ought to follow goodness, if he shall prefer the part of sin; than he who offends without knowing the power of God?

173 Wherefore these are indeed ordained unto death; but they who have known the Lord, and have seen his wonderful works, if they shall live wickedly, they shall be doubly punished, and shall die for ever.

174 As therefore thou hast seen that after the stones were cast out of the tower, which had been rejected, they were delivered to wicked and cruel spirits; and thou beheldest the tower so cleansed, as if it had all been made of one stone:

175 So the church of God, when it shall be purified: (the wicked and counterfeits, the mischievous and doubtful, and all that have be-

THE THIRD PART OF THE BOOK OF HERMAS

haved themselves wickedly in it, and committed divers kinds of sin, being cast out) shall become one body, and there shall be one understanding, one opinion, one faith, and the same charity.

176 And then shall the Son of God rejoice among them, and shall receive his people with a pure will.

177 And I said; Sir, all these things are great and honourable; but now show unto me the effect and force of every mountain: that every soul which trusteth in the Lord, when it shall hear these things may honour his great, and wonderful, and holy name.

178 Hear, said he, the variety of these mountains, that is, of the twelve nations.

179 They who have believed of the first mountain, which is black, are those who have revolted from the faith, and spoken wicked things against the Lord; and betrayed the servants of God.

180 These are condemned to death; there is no repentance for them: and therefore they are black, because their kind is wicked.

181 Of the second mountain which was smooth, are the hypocrites, who have believed, and the teachers of naughtiness: and these are next to the foregoing, which have not in them the fruit of righteousness.

182 For as their mountain is barren and without fruit so also such kind of men have indeed the name of Christians, but are empty of faith; nor is there any fruit of the truth in them.

183 Nevertheless there is room left to them of repentance, if they shall speedily pursue it; but if they shall delay, they also shall be partakers of death with the foregoing kind.

184 I said, air, why is there room left to those for repentance, and not to the foregoing kind, seeing their sins are well nigh the same?

185 There is therefore, said he, to these a return unto life by repentance, because they have not blasphemed against their Lord, nor betrayed the servants of God: but by their desire of gain have deceived men, leading them according to the lusts of sinners; wherefore they shall suffer for this thing.

186 Howbeit there is still left them room for repentance, because they have not spoken any thing wickedly against the Lord.

187 They who are of the third mountain which had thorns and brambles, are those who believed, but were some of them rich; others taken up with many affairs: the brambles are their riches; the thorns, those affairs in which they were engaged.

188 Now they who are entangled in much business, and in diversity of affairs, join not themselves to the servants of God, but wander, being called away by those affairs with which they are choked.

ΔΙΔΑΧΗ ΤΩΝ ΔΩΔΕΚΑ ΑΠΟΣΤΟΛΩΝ

189 And so they which are rich, with difficulty yield themselves to the conversation of the servants of God; fearing lest any thing should be asked of them. These therefore shall hardly enter the kingdom of God.

190 For as men walk with difficulty bare-foot over thorns, even so these kind of men shall scarcely enter into the kingdom of God.

191 Nevertheless there is afforded to all these a return unto repentance, if they shall quickly return to it; because in their former days they having neglected to work, in the time that is to come they may do some good.

192 If therefore having repented they shall do the works of righteousness, they shall live; but if they shall continue in their evil courses, they shall be delivered to those women who will take away their lives.

193 As for the fourth mountain, which had many herbs, the upper part of which is green, but the roots dry, and some of which being touched with the heat of the sun, are withered;

194 It denotes the doubtful, who have believed, and some others who carry the Lord on their tongues, but have him not in their hearts: therefore their grass is dry, and without root; because they live only in words, but their works are dead.

195 These therefore are neither dead nor living, and withal are doubtful. For the doubtful are neither green nor dry; that is neither dead nor alive.

196 For as the herbs dry away at the sight of the sun, so the doubtful, as soon as they hear of persecution, and fear inconveniencies, return to their idols, and again serve them, and are ashamed to bear the name of their Lord.

197 This kind of men then is neither dead nor alive; nevertheless these also may live, if they shall presently repent; but if not, they shall be delivered to those women, who shall take away their lives.

198 As concerning the fifth mountain that is craggy, and yet has green grass; they are of this kind who have believed, and are faithful indeed, but believe with difficulty, and are bold and self-conceited; and would be thought to know all things, but really know nothing.

199 Wherefore, by reason of this confidence, knowledge is departed from them; and a rash presumption is entered into them.

200 But they carry themselves high, and as prudent men; and though they are fools, yet would seem to be teachers.

THE THIRD PART OF THE BOOK OF HERMAS

201 Now by reason of this folly many of them whilst they magnify themselves, are become vain and empty. For boldness and vain confidence is a very evil spirit.

202 Wherefore many of these are cast away; but others acknowledging their error, have repented, and submitted themselves to those who are knowing.

203 And to all the rest of this kind, there is repentance allowed; forasmuch as they were not so much wicked as foolish, and void of understanding.

204 If these therefore shall repent, they shall live unto God; but if not, they shall dwell with those women, who shall exercise their wickedness upon them.

205 For what concerns the sixth mountain having greater and lesser clefts, they are such as have believed; but those in which were lesser clefts are they who have had controversies among themselves; and by reason of their quarrels languish in the faith:

206 Nevertheless many of these have repented, and so will the rest when they shall hear my commands; for their controversies are but small, and they will easily return unto repentance.

207 But those who have the greater clefts, will be as stiff stones, mindful of grudges and offences, and full of anger among themselves. These therefore are cast from the tower, and refused to be put into its building; for this kind of men shall hardly live.

208 Our God and Lord, who ruleth over all things, and has power over all his creatures, will not remember our offences, but is easily appeased by those who confess their sins: but man being languid, mortal, infirm, and full of sins, perseveres in his anger against man; as if it were in his power to save or destroy him.

209 But I, as the angel who am set over your repentance, admonish you, that whosoever among you has any such purpose he should lay it aside, and return unto repentance; and the Lord will heal your former sins, if you shall purge yourself from this evil spirit; but if you shall not do it, ye shall be delivered to him unto death.

210 As for the seventh mountain in which the grass was green and flourishing, and the whole mountain faithful; and all kind of cattle fed upon the grass of it, and the more the grass was eaten, so much the more it flourished;

211 They are such as believed, and were always good and upright; and without any differences among themselves, but still rejoiced in the servants of God, having put on the spirit of these virgins; and been always forward to show mercy to all men, readily giving to all men of their labours without upbraiding, and without deliberation.

ΔΙΔΑΧΗ ΤΩΝ ΔΩΔΕΚΑ ΑΠΟΣΤΟΛΩΝ

212 Wherefore the Lord seeing their simplicity and innocence, has increased them in the works of their hands, and given them grace in all their works.

213 But I, who am the angel appointed over your repentance, exhort you, that as many as are of this kind would continue in the same purpose, that your seed may not be rooted out for ever.

214 For the Lord hath tried you, and written you into our number; and all your seed shall dwell with the Son of God; for ye are all of his spirit.

215 As concerning the eighth mountain in which were a great many springs, by which every kind of all the creatures of God was watered: they are such as have believed the Apostles which the Lord sent into all the world to preach;

216 And some of them being teachers have preached and taught purely and sincerely, and have not in the least yielded to any evil, desires, but have constantly walked in righteousness and truth.

217 These therefore have their conversations among the angels.

218 Again; as for what concerns the ninth mountain which is a desert, and full of serpents; they are such as have believed, but had many stains:

219 These are such ministers as discharge their ministry amiss; ravishing away the goods of the widows and fatherless; and serve themselves, not others, out of those things which they have received.

220 These, if they continue in this covetousness, have delivered themselves unto death, nor shall there be any hope of life for them. But if they shall be converted, and shall discharge their ministry sincerely, they may live.

221 As for those which were found rough, they are such as have denied the name of the Lord, and not returned again to the Lord, but have become savage and wild; not applying themselves to the servants of God; but being separated from them, have for a little carelessness lost their lives.

222 For as a vine that is forsaken in a hedge, and never dressed, perishes and is choked by the weeds, and in time becomes wild, and ceases to be useful to its lord; so this kind of men despairing of themselves, and being soured, have begun to be unprofitable to their Lord.

223 Howbeit, to these there is, after all, repentance allowed, if they shall not be found from their hearts to have denied Christ; but if any of these shall be found to have denied him from his heart, I cannot tell whether such a one can attain unto life.

THE THIRD PART OF THE BOOK OF HERMAS

224 I say therefore that if any one hath denied, he should in these days return unto repentance; for it cannot be that anyone who now denies the Lord, can afterwards attain unto salvation nevertheless repentance is promised unto them who have formerly denied.

225 But he who will repent must hasten on his repentance, before the building of this tower is finished; otherwise, he shall be delivered by those women unto death.

226 But they that are maimed, are the deceitful; and those who mix with one another, are the serpents that you saw mingled in that mountain.

227 For as the poison of serpents is deadly unto men, so the words of such persons infect and destroy men. They are therefore maimed in their faith, by reason of that kind of life which they lead.

228 Howbeit some of them, having repented, have been saved; and so shall others of the same kind be also saved, if they shall repent; but if not, they shall die by those women who power and force posses,

229 For what concerns the tenth mountain, in which were the trees covering the cattle, they are such as have believed; and some of them have been bishops, that is, governors of the churches.

230 Others, are such stones as have not feignedly, but with a cheerful mind entertained the servants of God.

231 Then, such as have been set over inferior ministries, and have protected the poor and the widows; and have always kept a chaste conversation: therefore they also are protected by the Lord.

232 Whosoever shall do on this wise, are honoured with the Lord; and their place is among the angels, if they shall continue to obey the Lord even unto the end.

233 As to the eleventh mountain in which were trees loaded with several sorts of fruit; they are such as have believed, and suffered death, for the name of the Lord; and have endured with a heavy mind, and have given up their lives with all their hearts.

234 And I said, Why then, sir, have all these fruit indeed, but yet some fairer than others?

235 Hearken, said he: Whosoever have suffered for the name of the Lord are esteemed honourable by the Lord; and all their offences are blotted out, because they have suffered death for the name of the Son of God.

236 Hear now, why their fruits are different, and some of them excel others. They who were brought before magistrates, and being asked, denied not the Lord, but suffered with a ready mind; these are more honourable with the Lord. The fruits therefore that are the most fair are these.

ΔΙΔΑΧΗ ΤΩΝ ΔΩΔΕΚΑ ΑΠΟΣΤΟΛΩΝ

237 But they who were fearful and doubtful, and have deliberated with themselves whether they should confess or deny Christ, and yet have suffered; their fruits are smaller, because that this thought came into their hearts.

238 For it is a wicked and evil thought for a servant to deliberate whether he should deny his master: Take heed therefore ye who have such thoughts, that this mind Pontinrie not in you, and ye die unto God.

239 But ye who suffer death for his name sake, ought to honour the Lord, that he has esteemed you worthy to bear his name; and that you should be delivered from all your sins.

240 And why therefore do you not rather esteem yourselves happy? Ye think verily that if any one among you suffer, he performs a great work! Yet the Lord giveth you life, and ye understand it not. For your offences did oppress you; and if you had not suffered for his name sake, ye would now be dead unto the Lord.

241 Wherefore I speak this unto you who deliberate whether ye should confess or deny him. Confess that ye have the Lord for your God, lest at any time denying him, ye be delivered up into bonds.

242 For if all nations punish their servants which deny their masters; what think you that the Lord will do unto you, who has the power of all things?

243 Remove therefore out of your hearts these doubts, that ye may live for ever unto God.

244 As for the twelfth mountain, which was white, they are such as have believed like sincere children, into whose thoughts there never came any malice, nor have they ever known what sin was, but have always continued in their integrity.

245 Wherefore this kind of men shall without all doubt inherit the kingdom of God; because they have never in any thing defiled the commandments of God, but have continued with sincerity in the same condition all the days of their lives.

246 Whosoever therefore, said he, shall continue as children without malice; shall be more honourable than all those of whom I have yet spoken: for all such children are honoured by the Lord, and esteemed the first of all.

247 Happy therefore are ye who shall remove all malice from you, and put on innocence; be. cause ye shall first see the Lord. 248 And after he had thus ended his explication of all the mountains, I said unto him, Sir, show me now also what concerns the stones that were

THE THIRD PART OF THE BOOK OF HERMAS

brought out of the plain, and put into the tower in the room of those that were rejected.

249 As also concerning those round stones which were added into the building of the tower; and also of those who still continued round.

250 Hear now, says he, concerning those stones which were brought out of the plain into the building of the tower, and placed in the room of those that were rejected: they are the roots of that white mountain.

251 Wherefore because those who have believed of that mountain, were very innocent; the lord of this tower commanded that they which were of the roots of this mountain should be placed into the building.

252 For he knew that if they were put into, this building they would continue bright; nor would any of them any more be made black.

253 But if he had added after this manner, from the rest of the mountains, he would almost have needed again to visit the tower, and to cleanse it.

254 Now all these white stones are the young men who have believed, or shall believe; for they are all of the same kind. Happy is this kind, because it is innocent.

255 Hear now also concerning those round and bright stones; all these are of this white mountain. But they are therefore found round, because their riches have a little darkened them from the truth, and dazzled their eyes.

256 Howbeit they have never departed from the Lord, nor has any wicked word proceeded out of their mouths; but all righteousness, and virtue, and truth.

257 When therefore the Lord saw their minds, and that they might adorn the truth; he commanded that they should continue good, and that their riches should be pared away:

258 For he would not have them taken wholly away, to the end they might do some good with that which was left, and live unto God; because they also are of a good kind.

259 Therefore was there little cut off from them, and so they were put into the building of this tower.

260 As for the rest which continued still round, and were not found fit for the building of this tower, because they have not yet received the seal; they were carried back to their place, be. cause they were found very round.

261 But this present world must be cut away from them, and the vanities of their riches; and then they will be fit for the kingdom of God. For they must enter into the kingdom of God, because God has blessed this innocent kind.

ΔΙΔΑΧΗ ΤΩΝ ΔΩΔΕΚΑ ΑΠΟΣΤΟΛΩΝ

262 Of this kind therefore none shall fall away: for though any of them being tempted by the devil should offend, he shall soon return to his Lord God.

263 I the angel of repentance esteem you happy, whosoever are innocent as little children, because your portion is good and honourable with the Lord.

264 And I say unto all you who have received this seal; keep simplicity, and remember not the offences which are committed against you, nor continue in malice, or in bitterness, through the memory of offences.

265 But become one spirit, and provide remedies for these evil rents, and remove them from you; that the lord of the sheep may rejoice at it; for he will rejoice, if he shall find all whole.

266 But if any of these sheep shall be found scattered away, Woe shall be to the shepherds; and if the shepherds themselves shall be scattered; what will they answer to the Lord of the sheep-fold? Will they say that they were troubled by the sheep? But they shall not be believed.

267 For it is an incredible thing that the shepherd should suffer by his flock; and he shall be the more punished for his life.

268 Now I am the shepherd; and especially must give an account of you.

269 Wherefore take care of yourselves whilst the tower is, yet building. The Lord dwells in those that love peace, for peace is beloved; but he is far off from the contentious, and those who are full of malice.

270 Wherefore restore unto him the Spirit entire, as ye received it. For if thou shalt give unto a fuller a garment new and whole, thou wilt expect to receive it whole again; if therefore the fuller shall restore it unto thee torn, wouldst thou receive it?

271 Wouldst thou not presently be angry, and reproach him, saying: I gave my garment to thee whole, why halt thou rent it, and made it useless to me? Now it is of no use to me, by reason of the rent which thou hast made in it. Wouldst thou not say all this to a fuller, for the rent which he made in thy garment?

272 If therefore thou wouldst be concerned for thy garment, and complain that thou hadst not received it whole; what thinkest thou that the Lord will do, who gave his Spirit to thee entire, and thou hast rendered him altogether unprofitable, so that he can be of no use unto his Lord? For being corrupted by thee, he is no longer profitable to him.

273 Will not therefore the Lord do the same concerning his Spirit, by reason of thy deed? Undoubtedly, said I, he will do the same to all those whom he shall find to continue in the remembrance of injuries.

274 Tread not then under foot he said, his mercy; but rather honour him, because he is so patient with respect to your offences, and not like one of you; but repent, for it will be profitable for you.

275 All these things which are above written, I the shepherd and angel of repentance, have shown and spoken to the servants of God.

276 If therefore ye shall believe and hearken to these words, and shall walk in them and correct your ways, ye shall live. But if ye shall, continue in malice, and in the remembrance of injuries, no such sinners shall live unto God.

277 All these things which were to be spoken by me, I have thus delivered unto you. Then the shepherd said unto me, Hast thou asked all things of me? I answered, sir, I have.

278 Why then, said he, hast thou not asked concerning the spaces of these stones that were put in the building, that I may explain that also unto thee? I answered, sir, I forgot it. Hear, then, said he, concerning these also.

279 They are those who have now heard these commands, and have repented with all their hearts;

280 And when the Lord saw that their repentance was good and pure, and that they could continue in it, he commanded their former sins to be blotted out. For these spaces were their sins, and they are therefore made even that they might not appear.

SIMILITUDE X.

Of Repentance and alms-deeds.

AFTER I had written this book, the angel which had delivered me to that shepherd, came into the house where I was and sat upon the bed, and that shepherd stood at his right hand.

2 Then he called me and said unto me; I delivered thee and thy house to this shepherd, that thou mightest be protected by him. I said, Yes, Lord.

3 If therefore, said he, thou wilt be protected from all vexations and from all cruelty, and have success in every good word and work, and have all virtue and righteousness; walk in those commands which he has given thee, and thou shalt have dominion over all sin.

ΔΙΔΑΧΗ ΤΩΝ ΔΩΔΕΚΑ ΑΠΟΣΤΟΛΩΝ

4 For if thou keepest those commands, all the lust and pleasure of this present world shall be subject to thee; and success shall follow thee in every good undertaking.

5 Take therefore his gravity and modesty towards thee, and say unto all, that he is in great honour and renown with God, and is a prince of great authority, and powerful in his office.

6 To him only is the power of repentance committed throughout the whole world. Does he not seem to thee to be of great authority?

7 But ye despise his goodness, and the modesty which he shows towards you.

8 I said unto him; Sir, ask him since the time that he came into my house whether I have done any thing disorderly, or have offended him in any thing?

9 I know, said he, that thou hast done nothing disorderly, neither wilt thou hereafter do any such thing, and therefore I speak these things with thee that then mayest persevere; for he has given me a good account concerning thee.

10 But thou shalt speak these things to others, that they who either have repented, or shall repent, may be like-minded with thee, and he may give me as good an account of them also; and that I may do the same unto the Lord.

11 I answered; Sir, I declare to all men the wonderful works of God; and I hope that all who love them, and have before sinned, when they shall hear these things, will repent, and recover life.

12 Continue therefore, said he, in this ministry, and fulfil it. And whosoever shall do according to the commands of this shepherd, he shall live; and shall have great honour both here and with the Lord.

13 But they that shall not keep his commands, flee from their life, and are adversaries to it. And they that follow not his commands, shall deliver themselves unto death; and shall be every one guilty of his own blood.

14 But I say unto thee, keep these commandments, and thou shalt find a cure for all thy sins.

15 Moreover, I have sent these virgins to dwell with thee; for I have seen that they are very kind to thee. Thou shalt therefore have them for thy helpers, that thou mayest the better keep the commands which he hath given thee; for these commands cannot be kept without these virgins.

16 And as I see how they are willing to be with thee, I will also command them that they shall not all depart from thy house.

THE THIRD PART OF THE BOOK OF HERMAS

17 Only do thou purify thy house; for they will readily dwell in a clean house. For they are clean and chaste, and industrious; and all of them have grace with the Lord.

18 If therefore thou shalt have thy house pure, they will abide with thee. But, if it shall be never so little polluted, they will immediately depart from thy house; for these virgins cannot endure any manner of pollution.

19 I said unto him; Sir, I hope that I shall so please them, that they shall always delight to dwell in my house. And as he to whom you have committed me, makes no complaint of me; so neither shall they complain.

20 Then he said to that shepherd: I see that the servant of God will live and keep these commandments, and place these virgins in a pure habitation.

21 When he had said this, he delivered me again to that shepherd, and called the virgins, and said unto them; Forasmuch as I see that ye will readily dwell in this man's house, I commend him and his family to you, that ye may not at all depart from his house. And they willingly heard these words.

22 Then he said unto me, Go on manfully in thy ministry; declare to all men the great things of God, and thou shalt find grace in this ministry.

23 And whosoever shall walk in these commands, shall live, and be happy in his life. But he that shall neglect them, shall not live, and shall be unhappy in his life.

24 Say unto all that whosoever can do well, cease not to exercise themselves in good works, for it is profitable unto them. For I would that all men should be delivered from the inconveniences they lie under.

25 For he that wants, and suffers inconveniences in his daily life, is in great torment and necessity. Whosoever therefore delivers such a soul from necessity, gets great joy unto himself.

26 For he that is grieved with such inconveniencies is equally tormented, as if he were in chains. And many upon the account of such calamities, being not able to bear them, have chosen even to destroy themselves.

27 He therefore that knows the calamity of such a man, and does not free him from it, commits a great sin, and is guilty of his blood.

28 Wherefore exercise yourselves in good works, as many as have received ability from the Lord; lest whilst ye delay to do them, the building of the tower be finished; because for your sakes the building is stopped.

ΔΙΔΑΧΗ ΤΩΝ ΔΩΔΕΚΑ ΑΠΟΣΤΟΛΩΝ

29 Except therefore ye shall make haste to do well, the tower shall be finished, and ye shall be shut out of it.

30 And after he had thus spoken with me, he rose up from the bed and departed, taking the shepherd and virgins with him.

31 Howbeit he said unto me, that he would send back the shepherd and virgins unto my house. Amen.

REFERENCES TO THE BOOK OF HERMAS, THE SHEPHERD.

[This book, divided into three parts, called his VISIONS, COMMANDS, and SIMILITUDES, is thus entitled, because it was composed by Hermas, brother to Pius, bishop of Rome; and because the Angel, who bears the principal part in it, is represented in the form and habit of a shepherd. Ireneus quotes it under the very name of Scripture. Origen thought it a most useful writing, and that it was divinely inspired; Eusebius says that, though it was not esteemed canonical, it was read publicly in the churches, which is corroborated by Jerome; and Athanasius cites it, calls it a most useful work, and observes, that though it was not strictly canonical, the Fathers appointed it to be read for direction and confirmation in faith and piety. Jerome, notwithstanding this, and that he applauded it in his catalogue of writers, in his comments upon it afterwards, terms it apocryphal and foolish. Tertullian praised it when a Catholic, and abused it when a Montanist. Although Gelasius ranks it among the apocryphal books, it is found attached to some of the most ancient MSS. of the New Testament; and Archbishop Wake, believing it the genuine work of an apostolical Father, preserves it to the English reader by the foregoing translation, in which he has rendered the three parts of it not only more exact, but in greater purity than they had before appeared. The archbishop procured Dr. Grabe to entirely collate the old Latin version with an ancient MS. in the Lambeth library; and the learned prelate himself still further improved the whole from a multitude of fragments of the original Greek never before used for that purpose.]

THE DIDACHE OR TEACHING OF THE APOSTLES

Translated by

J B Lightfoot

1

1:1 There are two ways, one of life and one of death, and there is a great difference between the two ways.

1:2 {The way of life} is this.

1:3 First of all, {thou shalt love the God} that made thee;

1:4 secondly, {thy neighbour as thyself.}

1:5 {And all things whatsoever thou wouldest not have befal thyself neither do thou unto another.}

1:6 Now of these words the doctrine is this.

1:7 {Bless them that curse you, and pray for} your enemies and fast for {them that persecute you;

1:8 for what thank is it, if ye love them that love you? Do not even the Gentiles the same? But do ye love them that hate you,} and ye shall not have an enemy.

1:9 Abstain thou from fleshly and bodily lusts.

1:10 {If any man give thee a blow on thy right cheek, turn to him the other also,} and thou shalt be perfect;

1:11 {if a man impress thee to go with him, one mile, go with him twain;

1:12 if a man take away thy cloak, give him thy coat also;

1:13 if a man take away from thee that which is thine own, ask it not back,} for neither art thou able.

1:14 {To every man that asketh of thee give, and ask not back;}

1:15 for the Father desireth that gifts be given to all from His own bounties.

1:16 Blessed is he that giveth according to the commandment;

1:17 for he is guiltless.

1:18 Woe to him that receiveth;

1:19 for, if a man receiveth having need, he is guiltless;

1:20 but he that hath no need shall give satisfaction why and wherefore he received;

THE DIDACHE OR TEACHING OF THE APOSTLES

1:21 and being put in confinement he shall be examined concerning the deeds that he hath done, and {he shall not come out thence until he hath given back the last farthing.}

1:22 Yea, as touching this also it is said;

1:23 {Let thine alms sweat into thine hands, until thou shalt have learnt to whom to give.}

2

2:1 And this is the second commandment of the teaching.

2:2 {Thou shalt do no murder, thou shalt not commit adultery,} thou shalt not corrupt boys, thou shalt not commit fornication, {thou shalt not steal,} thou shalt not deal in magic, thou shalt do no sorcery, thou shalt not murder a child by abortion nor kill them when born, {thou shalt not covet thy neighbour's goods, thou shalt not perjure thyself, thou shalt not bear false witness,} thou shalt not speak evil, thou shalt not cherish a grudge, thou shalt not be double-minded nor double-tongued;

2:3 for the double tongue is a snare of death.

2:4 Thy word shall not be false or empty, but fulfilled by action.

2:5 Thou shalt not be avaricious nor a plunderer nor a hypocrite nor ill-tempered nor proud.

2:6 Thou shalt not entertain an evil design against thy neighbour.

2:7 {Thou shalt not hate} any man, {but some thou shalt reprove,} and for others thou shalt pray, {and others thou shalt love} more than thy life.

3

3:1 My child, flee from every evil and everything that resembleth it.

3:2 Be not angry, for anger leadeth to murder, nor jealous nor contentious nor wrathful;

3:3 for of all these things murders are engendered.

3:4 My child, be not lustful, for lust leadeth to fornication, neither foul-speaking neither with uplifted eyes;

3:5 for of all these things adulteries are engendered.

3:6 My child, {be no dealer in omens,} since it leads to idolatry, nor an enchanter nor an astrologer nor a magician, neither be willing to look at them;

3:7 for from all these things idolatry is engendered.

ΔΙΔΑΧΗ ΤΩΝ ΔΩΔΕΚΑ ΑΠΟΣΤΟΛΩΝ

3:8 My child, be not a liar, since lying leads to theft, neither avaricious neither vainglorious;

3:9 for from all these things thefts are engendered.

3:10 My child, be not a murmurer, since it leadeth to blasphemy, neither self-willed neither a thinker of evil thoughts;

3:11 for from all these things blasphemies are engendered.

3:12 But be meek, since {the meek shall inherit the earth.}

3:13 Be long-suffering and pitiful and guileless and {quiet} and kindly {and} always {fearing the words} which thou hast heard.

3:14 Thou shalt not exalt thyself, neither shalt thou admit boldness into thy soul.

3:15 Thy soul shall not cleave together with the lofty, but with the righteous and humble shalt thou walk.

3:16 The accidents that befal thee thou shalt receive as good, knowing that nothing is done without God.

4

4:1 My child, {thou shalt remember him that speaketh unto thee the word of God} night and day, and shalt honour him as the Lord;

4:2 for whencesoever the Lordship speaketh, there is the Lord.

4:3 Moreover thou shalt seek out day by day the persons of the saints, that thou mayest find rest in their words.

4:4 Thou shalt not make a schism, but thou shalt pacify them that contend;

4:5 thou shalt judge righteously, thou shalt not make a difference in a person to reprove him for transgressions.

4:6 Thou shalt not doubt whether a thing shall be or not be.

4:7 {Be not thou found holding out thy hands to receive, but drawing them in as to giving.}

4:8 If thou hast ought passing through thy hands, thou shalt give a ransom for thy sins.

4:9 Thou shalt not hesitate to give, neither shalt thou murmur when giving;

4:10 for thou shalt know who is the good paymaster of thy reward.

4:11 Thou shalt not turn away from him that is in want, but shalt make thy brother partaker in all things, and shalt not say {that anything is thine own.}

4:12 For if ye are fellow-partakers in that which is imperishable, how much rather in the things which are perishable? Thou shalt not withhold thy hand from thy son or from thy daughter, but from their youth thou shalt teach them the fear of God.

4:13 Thou shalt not command thy bondservant or thine handmaid in thy bitterness, who trust in the same God as thyself, lest haply they should cease to fear the God who is over both of you;

4:14 for He cometh, not to call men with respect of persons, but He cometh to those whom the Spirit hath prepared.

4:15 But ye, servants, shall be subject unto your masters, as to a type of God, in shame and fear.

®LA1⁻4:16 Thou shalt hate all hypocrisy, and everything that is not pleasing to the Lord.

4:17 Thou shalt never forsake the commandments of the Lord;

4:18 but shalt keep those things which thou hast received, neither adding to them nor taking away from them.

4:19 In church thou shalt confess thy transgressions, and shalt not betake thyself to prayer with an evil conscience.

4:20 This is the way of life.

5

5:1 But the way of death is this.

5:2 First of all, it is evil and full of a curse murders, adulteries, lusts, fornications, thefts, idolatries, magical arts, witchcrafts, plunderings, false witnessings, hypocrisies, doubleness of heart, treachery, pride, malice, stubbornness, covetousness, foul-speaking, jealousy, boldness, exaltation, boastfulness;

5:3 persecutors of good men, hating truth, loving a lie, not perceiving the reward of righteousness, not {cleaving to the good} nor to righteous judgment, wakeful not for that which is good but for that which is evil;

5:4 from whom gentleness and forbearance stand aloof;

5:5 loving vain things, pursuing a recompense, not pitying the poor man, not toiling for him that is oppressed with toil, not recognizing Him that made them, murderers of children, corrupters of the creatures of God, turning away from him that is in want, oppressing him that is afflicted, advocates of the wealthy, unjust judges of the poor, altogether sinful.

5:6 May ye be delivered, my children, from all these things.

ΔΙΔΑΧΗ ΤΩΝ ΔΩΔΕΚΑ ΑΠΟΣΤΟΛΩΝ

6

6:1 See lest any man lead you astray from this way of righteousness, for he teacheth thee apart from God.

6:2 For if thou art able to bear the whole yoke of the Lord, thou shalt be perfect;

6:3 but if thou art not able, do that which thou art able.

6:4 But concerning eating, bear that which thou art able;

6:5 yet abstain by all means from meat sacrificed to idols;

6:6 for it is the worship of dead gods.

7

7:1 But concerning baptism, thus shall ye baptize

7:2 Having first recited all these things, baptize {in the name of the Father and of the Son and of the Holy Spirit} in living (running) water.

7:3 But if thou hast not living water, then baptize in other water;

7:4 and if thou art not able in cold, then in warm.

7:5 But if thou hast neither, then pour water on the head thrice in the name of the Father and of the Son and of the Holy Spirit.

7:6 But before the baptism let him that baptizeth and him that is baptized fast, and any others also who are able;

7:7 and thou shalt order him that is baptized to fast a day or two before.

8

8:1 And let not your fastings be with the hypocrites, for they fast on the second and the fifth day of the week;

8:2 but do ye keep your fast on the fourth and on the preparation (the sixth) day.

8:3 Neither pray ye {as the hypocrites,} but as the Lord commanded in His Gospel, {thus pray ye.

8:4 Our Father, which art in heaven, hallowed be Thy name;

8:5 Thy kingdom come;

8:6 Thy will be done, as in heaven, so also on earth;

8:7 give us this day our daily bread;

8:8 and forgive us our debt, as we also forgive our debtors;

8:9 and lead us not into temptation, but deliver us from the evil one;}

THE DIDACHE OR TEACHING OF THE APOSTLES

8:10 for Thine is the power and the glory for ever and ever.
8:11 Three times in the day pray ye so.

9

9:1 But as touching the eucharistic thanksgiving give ye thanks thus.
9:2 First, as regards the cup:
9:3 We give Thee thanks, O our Father, for the holy vine of Thy son David, which Thou madest known unto us through Thy Son Jesus;
9:4 Thine is the glory for ever and ever.
9:5 Then as regards the broken bread:
9:6 We give Thee thanks, O our Father, for the life and knowledge which Thou didst make known unto us through Thy Son Jesus;
9:7 Thine is the glory for ever and ever.
9:8 As this broken bread was scattered upon the mountains and being gathered together became one, so may Thy Church be gathered together from the ends of the earth into Thy kingdom;
9:9 for Thine is the glory and the power through Jesus Christ for ever and ever.
9:10 But let no one eat or drink of this eucharistic thanksgiving, but they that have been baptized into the name of the Lord;
9:11 for concerning this also the Lord hath said:
9:12 {Give not that which is holy to the dogs.}

10

10:1 And after ye are satisfied thus give ye thanks:
10:2 We give Thee thanks, Holy Father, for Thy holy name, which Thou hast made to tabernacle in our hearts, and for the knowledge and faith and immortality, which Thou hast made known unto us through Thy Son Jesus;
10:3 Thine is the glory for ever and ever.
10:4 Thou, Almighty Master, didst create all things for Thy name's sake, and didst give food and drink unto men for enjoyment, that they might render thanks to Thee;
10:5 but didst bestow upon us spiritual food and drink and eternal life through Thy Son.
10:6 Before all things we give Thee thanks that Thou art powerful;
10:7 Thine is the glory for ever and ever.

ΔΙΔΑΧΗ ΤΩΝ ΔΩΔΕΚΑ ΑΠΟΣΤΟΛΩΝ

10:8 Remember, Lord, Thy Church to deliver it from all evil and to perfect it in Thy love;

10:9 and {gather it together from the four winds}--even the Church which has been sanctified--into Thy kingdom which Thou hast prepared for it;

10:10 for Thine is the power and the glory for ever and ever.

10:11 May grace come and may this world pass away.

10:12 Hosanna to the God of David.

10:13 If any man is holy, let him come;

10:14 if any man is not, let him repent. Maran Atha. Amen.

10:15 But permit the prophets to offer thanksgiving as much as they desire.

11

11:1 Whosoever therefore shall come and teach you all these things that have been said before, receive him;

11:2 but if the teacher himself be perverted and teach a different doctrine to the destruction thereof, hear him not;

11:3 but if to the increase of righteousness and the knowledge of the Lord, receive him as the Lord.

11:4 But concerning the apostles and prophets, so do ye according to the ordinance of the Gospel.

11:5 Let every apostle, when he cometh to you, be received as the Lord;

11:6 but he shall not abide more than a single day, or if there be need, a 11:7 but if he abide three days, he is a false prophet.

11:8 And when he departeth let the apostle receive nothing save bread, until he findeth shelter;

11:9 but if he ask money, he is a false prophet.

11:10 And any prophet speaking in the Spirit ye shall not try neither discern;

11:11 for every sin shall be forgiven, but this sin shall not be forgiven.

11:12 Yet not every one that speaketh in the Spirit is a prophet, but only if he have the ways of the Lord.

11:13 From his ways therefore the false prophet and the prophet shall be recognized.

11:14 And no prophet when he ordereth a table in the Spirit shall eat of it;

11:15 otherwise he is a false prophet.

THE DIDACHE OR TEACHING OF THE APOSTLES

11:16 And every prophet teaching the truth, if he doeth not what he teacheth, is a false prophet.

11:17 And every prophet approved and found true, if he doeth ought as an outward mystery typical of the Church, and yet teacheth you not to do all that he himself doeth, shall not be judged before you;

11:18 he hath his judgment in the presence of God;

11:19 for in like manner also did the prophets of old time.

11:20 And whosoever shall say in the Spirit, Give me silver or anything else, ye shall not listen to him;

11:21 but if he tell you to give on behalf of others that are in want, let no man judge him.

12

12:1 But let every one {that cometh in the name of the Lord} be received;

12:2 and then when ye have tested him ye shall know him, for ye shall have understanding on the right hand and on the left.

12:3 If the comer is a traveller, assist him, so far as ye are able;

12:4 but he shall not stay with you more than two or three days, if it be necessary.

12:5 But if he wishes to settle with you, being a craftsman, let him work for and eat his bread.

12:6 But if he has no craft, according to your wisdom provide how he shall live as a Christian among you, but not in idleness.

12:7 If he will not do this, he is trafficking upon Christ.

12:8 Beware of such men.

13

13:1 But every true prophet desiring to settle among you {is worthy of his food.}

13:2 In like manner a true teacher {is} also {worthy,} like {the workman, of his food.}

13:3 Every firstfruit then of the produce of the wine-vat and of the threshing-floor, of thy oxen and of thy sheep, thou shalt take and give as the firstfruit to the prophets;

13:4 for they are your chief-priests.

13:5 But if ye have not a prophet, give them to the poor.

13:6 If thou makest bread, take the firstfruit and give according to the commandment.

ΔΙΔΑΧΗ ΤΩΝ ΔΩΔΕΚΑ ΑΠΟΣΤΟΛΩΝ

13:7 In like manner, when thou openest a jar of wine or of oil, take the firstfruit and give to the prophets;

13:8 yea and of money and raiment and every possession take the firstfruit, as shall seem good to thee, and give according to the commandment.

14

14:1 And on the Lord's own day gather yourselves together and break bread and give thanks, first confessing your transgressions, that your sacrifice may be pure.

14:2 And let no man, having his dispute with his fellow, join your assembly until they have been reconciled, that your sacrifice may not be defiled;

14:3 for this sacrifice it is that was spoken of by the Lord;

14:4 {In every place and at every time offer Me a pure sacrifice;

14:5 for I am a great king, saith the Lord and My name is wonderful among the nations.}

15

15:1 Appoint for yourselves therefore bishops and deacons worthy of the Lord, men who are meek and not lovers of money, and true and approved;

15:2 for unto you they also perform the service of the prophets and teachers.

15:3 Therefore despise them not;

15:4 for they are your honourable men along with the prophets and teachers.

15:5 And reprove one another, not in anger but in peace, as ye find in the Gospel;

15:6 and let no one speak to any that has gone wrong towards his neighbour, neither let him hear a word from you, until he repent.

15:7 But your prayers and your almsgivings and all your deeds so do ye as ye find it in the Gospel of our Lord.

16

16:1 {Be watchful} for your life;

16:2 {let your lamps not be quenched and your loins not ungirded, but be ye ready;

THE DIDACHE OR TEACHING OF THE APOSTLES

16:3 for ye know not the hour in which our Lord cometh.}

16:4 And ye shall gather yourselves together frequently, seeking what is fitting for your souls;

16:5 for the whole time of your faith shall not profit you, if ye be not perfected at the last season.

16:6 For in the last days {the false prophets} and corrupters shall be multiplied, and the sheep shall be turned into wolves, and love shall be turned into hate.

16:7 For as lawlessness increaseth, {they shall hate one another and shall persecute and betray.

16:8 And then} the world-deceiver {shall appear} as a son of God;

16:9 {and shall work signs and wonders,} and the earth shall be delivered into his hands;

16:10 and he shall do unholy things, which have never been since the world began.

16:11 Then all created mankind shall come to the fire of testing, and many shall be offended and perish;

16:12 {but they that endure} in their faith {shall be saved} by the Curse Himself.

16:13 {And then shall the signs} of the truth {appear;}

16:14 first a sign of a rift in the heaven, then a sign of a voice of a trumpet, and thirdly a resurrection of the dead;

16:15 yet not of all, but as it was said:

16:16 {The Lord shall come and all His saints with Him.

16:17 Then shall} the world {see the Lord coming upon the clouds of heaven.}

THE DIDACHE – IN GREEK

ΔΙΔΑΧΗ ΤΩΝ ΔΩΔΕΚΑ ΑΠΟΣΤΟΛΩΝ

Διδαχὴ κυρίου διὰ τῶν δώδεκα ἀποστόλων τοῖς ἔθνεσιν.

I

1. Ὁδοὶ δύο εἰσί, μία τῆς ζωῆς καὶ μία τοῦ θανάτου, διαφορὰ δὲ πολλὴ μεταξὺ τῶν δύο ὁδῶν.
2. Ἡ μὲν οὖν τῆς ζωῆς ἐστιν αὕτη· πρῶτον ἀγαπήσεις τὸν θεὸν τὸν ποιήσαντά σε, δεύτερον τὸν πλησίον σου ὡς σεαυτόν· πάντα δὲ ὅσα ἐὰν θελήσῃς μὴ γίνεσθαί σοι, καὶ σὺ ἄλλῳ μὴ ποίει.
3. Τούτων δὲ τῶν λόγων ἡ διδαχή ἐστιν αὕτη· εὐλογεῖτε τοὺς καταρωμένους ὑμῖν καὶ προσεύχεσθε ὑπὲρ τῶν ἐχθρῶν ὑμῶν, νηστεύετε δὲ ὑπὲρ τῶν διωκότων ὑμᾶς· ποία γὰρ χάρις, ἐὰν ἀγαπᾶτε τοὺς ἀγαπῶντας ὑμᾶς; οὐχὶ καὶ τὰ ἔθνη τὸ αὐτὸ ποιοῦσιν; ὑμεῖς δὲ ἀγαπᾶτε τοὺς μισοῦντας ὑμᾶς, καὶ οὐχ ἕξετε ἐχτρόν. 4. ἀπέχου τῶν σαρκικῶν καὶ σωματικῶν ἐπιθυμιῶν· ἐὰν τίς σοι δῷ ῥάπισμα εἰς τὴν δεξιὰν σιαγόνα, στρέψον αὐτῷ καὶ τὴν ἄλλην, καὶ ἔσῃ τέλειος· ἐὰν ἀγγαρεύσῃ σέ τις μίλιον ἕν, ὕπαγε μετ' αὐτοῦ δύο· ἐὰν ἄρῃ τις τὸ ἱμάτιόν σου, δὸς αὐτῷ καὶ τὸν χιτῶνα· ἐὰν λάβῃ τις ἀπὸ σοῦ τὸ σόν, μὴ ἀπαίτει· οὐδὲ γὰρ δύνασαι. 5. παντὶ τῷ αἰτοῦντί σε δίδου καὶ μὴ ἀπαίτει· πᾶσι γὰρ θέλει δίδοσθαι ὁ πατὴρ ἐκ τῶν ἰδίων χαρισμάτων. μακάριος ὁ διδοὺς κατὰ τὴν ἐντολήν· ἀθῷος γάρ ἐστιν. οὐαὶ τῷ λαμβάνοντι· εἰ μὲν γὰρ χρείαν ἔχων λαμβάνει τις, ἀθῷος ἔσται· ὁ δὲ μὴ χρείαν ἔχων δώσει δίκην, ἱνατί ἔλαβε καὶ εἰς τί· ἐν συνοχῇ δὲ γενόμενος ἐξετασθήσεται περὶ ὧν ἔπραξε, καὶ οὐκ ἐξελεύσεται ἐκεῖθεν, μέχρις οὗ ἀποδῷ τὸν ἔσχατον κοδράντην. 6. ἀλλὰ καὶ περὶ τούτου δὲ εἴρηται· Ἱδρωσάτω ἡ ἐλεημοσύνη σου εἰς τὰς χεῖράς σου, μέχρις ἂν γνῷς τίνι δῷς.

THE DIDACHE – IN GREEK

II

1. Δευτέρα δὲ ἐντολὴ τῆς διδαχῆς· 2. οὐ φονεύσεις, οὐ μοιχεύσεις, οὐ παιδοφθορήσεις, οὐ πορνεύσεις, οὐ κλέψεις, οὐ μαγεύσεις, οὐ φαρμακεύσεις, οὐ φονεύσεις τ'κνον ἐν φθορᾷ, οὐδὲ γεννηθὲν ἀποκτενεῖς, οὐκ ἐπιθυμήσεις τὰ τοῦ πλησίον. 3. οὐκ ἐπιορκήσεις, οὐ ψευδομαρτυρήσεις, οὐ κακολογήσεις, οὐ μνησικακήσεις. 4. οὐκ ἔσῃ διγνώμων οὐδὲ δίγλωσσος· παγὶς γὰρ θανάτου ἡ διγλωσσία. 5. οὐκ ἔσται ὁ λόγος σου ψευδής, οὐ κενός, ἀλλὰ μεμεστωμένος πράξει. 6. οὐκ ἔσῃ πλεονέκτης οὐδὲ ἅρπαξ οὐδὲ ὑποκριτὴς οὐδὲ κακοήθης οὐδὲ ὑπερήφανος. οὐ λήψῃ βουλὴν πονηρὰν κατὰ τοῦ πλησίον σου. 7. οὐ μισήσεις πάντα ἄνθρώπον, ἀλλὰ οὓς μὲν ἐλέγξεις, περὶ δὲ ὧν προσεύξῃ, οὓς δὲ ἀγαπήσεις ὑπὲρ τὴν ψυχήν σου.

III

1. Τέκνον μου, φεῦγε ἀπὸ παντὸς πονηροῦ καὶ ἀπὸ παντὸς ὁμοίου αὐτου. 2. μὴ γίνου ὀργίλος, ὁδηγεῖ γὰρ ἡ ὀργὴ πρὸς τὸν φόνον, μηδὲ ζηλωτὴς μηδὲ ἐπιστικὸς μηδὲ θυμικός· ἐκ γὰρ τούτων ἁπάντων φόνοι γεννῶνται. 3. τέκνον μου, μὴ γίνου ἐπιθυμητής, ὁδηγεῖ γὰρ ἡ ἐπιθυμία πρὸς τὴν πορνείαν, μηδὲ αἰσχχρολόγος μηδὲ ὑψηλόφθαλμος· ἐκ γὰρ τούτων ἁπαντων μοιχεῖαι γεννῶνται. 4. τέκνον μου, μὴ γίνου οἰωνοσκόπος, ἐπειδὴ ὁδηγεῖ εἰς τὴν εἰδωλοατρίαν, μηδὲ ἐπαοιδὸς μηδὲ μαθηματικὸς μηδὲ περικαθαθαίρων, μηδὲ θέλε αὐτὰ βλέπειν· ἐκ γὰρ τούτων ἁπάντων εἰδωλολατρία γεννᾶται. 5. τέκνον μου, μὴ γίνου ψεύστης, ἐπειδὴ ὁδηγεῖ τὸ ψεῦσμα εἰς τὴν κλοπήν, μηδὲ φιλάργυρος μηδὲ κενόδοξος· ἐκ γὰρ τούτων ἁπάντων κλοπαὶ γεννῶνται. 6. τέκνον μου, μὴ γίνου γόγγυσος, ἐπειδὴ ὁδηγεῖ εἰς τὴν βλασφημίαν, μηδὲ αὐθάδης μηδὲ πονηρόφρων· ἐκ γὰρ τούτων ἁπάντων βλασφημίαι γεννῶνται. 7. ἴσθι δὲ πραΰς, ἐπεὶ οἱ πραεῖς κληρονομήσουσι τὴν γῆν. 8. γίνου μακρόθυμος καὶ ἐλεήμων καὶ ἄκακος καὶ ἡσύχιος καὶ ἀγαθὸς καὶ τρέμων τοὺς λόγους διὰ παντός, οὓς ἤκουσας. 9. οὐχ ὑψώσεις σεαυτὸν οὐδὲ δώσεις τῇ ψυχῇ σου θράσος. οὐ κολληθήσεται ἡ ψυχή σου μετὰ ὑψηλῶν, ἀλλὰ μετὰ δικαίων καὶ ταπεινῶν ἀναστραφήσῃ. 10. τὰ συμβαίνοντά σοι ἐνεργήματα ὡς ἀγαθὰ προσδέξῃ, εἰδὼς ὅτι ἄτερ θεοῦ οὐδὲν γίνεται.

ΔΙΔΑΧΗ ΤΩΝ ΔΩΔΕΚΑ ΑΠΟΣΤΟΛΩΝ

IV

1. Τέκνον μου, τοῦ λαλοῦντός σοι τὸν λόγον τοῦ θεοῦ μνησθήσῃ νυκτὸς καὶ ἡμέρας, τιμήσεις δὲ αὐτὸν ὡς κύριον· ὅθεν γὰρ ἡ κυριότης λαλεῖται, ἐκεῖ κύριός ἐστιν. 2. ἐκζητήσεις δὲ καθ' ἡμέραν τὰ πρόσωπα τῶν ἁγίων, ἵνα ἐπαναπαῇς τοῖς λόγοις αὐτῶν. 3. οὐ ποθήσεις σχίσμα, εἰρηνεύσεις δὲ μαχομένους· κρινεῖς δικαίως, οὐ λήψῃ πρόσωπον ἐλέγξαι ἐπὶ παραπτώμασιν. 4. οὐ διψυχήσεις, πότερον ἔσται ἢ οὔ. 5. Μὴ γίνου πρὸς μὲν τὸ λαβεῖν ἐκτείνων τὰς χεῖρας, πρὸς δὲ τὸ δοῦναι συσπῶν. 6. ἐὰν ἔχῃς διὰ τῶν χειρῶν σου, δώσεις λύτρωσιν ἁμαρτιῶν σου. 7. οὐ διστάσεις δοῦναι οὐδὲ διδοὺς γογγύσεις· γνώσῃ γάρ, τίς ἐστιν ὁ τοῦ μισθοῦ καλὸς ἀνταποδότης. 8. οὐκ ἀποστραφήσῃ τὸν ἐνδεόμενον, συγκοινωνήσεις δὲ πάντα τῷ ἀδελφῷ σοῦ καὶ οὐκ ἐρεῖς ἴδια εἶναι· εἰ γὰρ ἐν τῷ ἀθανάτῳ κοινωνοί ἐστε, πόσῳ μᾶλλον ἐν τοῖς θνητοῖς;
9. Οὐκ ἀρεῖς τὴν χεῖρα σου ἀπὸ τοῦ υἱοῦ σου ἢ ἀπὸ τῆς θυγατρός σου, ἀλλὰ ἀπὸ νεότητος διδάξεις τὸν φόβον τοῦ θεοῦ. 10. οὐκ ἐπιτάξεις δούλῳ σου ἢ παιδίσκῃ, τοῖς ἐπὶ τὸν αὐτὸν θεὸν ἐλπίζουσιν, ἐν πικρίᾳ σου, μήποτε οὐ μὴ φοβηθήσονται τὸν ἐπ' ἀμφοτέροις θεόν· οὐ γὰρ ἔρχεται κατὰ πρόσωπον καλέσαι, ἀλλ' ἐφ' οὓς τὸ πνεῦμα ἡτοίμασεν. 11. ὑμεῖς δὲ οἱ δοῦλοι ὑποταγήσεσθε τοῖς κυρίοις ὑμῶν ὡς τύπῳ θεοῦ ἐν αἰσχύνῃ καὶ φόβῳ.
12. Μισήσεις πᾶσαν ὑπόκρισιν καὶ πᾶν ὃ μὴ ἀρεστὸν τῷ κυρίῳ. 13. οὐ μὴ ἐγκαταλίπῃς ἐντολὰς κυρίου, φυλάξεις δὲ ἃ παρέλαβες, μήτε προστιθεὶς μήτε ἀφαιρῶν. 14. ἐν ἐκκλησίᾳ ἐξομολογήσῃ τὰ παραπτώματά σου, καὶ οὐ προσελεύσῃ ἐπὶ προσευχήν σου ἐν συνειδήσει πονηρᾷ· αὕτη ἐστὶν ἡ ὁδὸς τῆς ζωῆς.

V

1. Ἡ δὲ τοῦ θανάτου ὁδός ἐστιν αὕτη· πρῶτον πάντων πονηρά ἐστι καὶ κατάρας μεστή· φόνοι, μοιχεῖαι, ἐπιθυμίαι, πορνεῖαι, κλοπαί, εἰδωλολατρίαι, μαγεῖαι, φαρμακίαι, ἁρπαγαί, ψευδομαρτυρίαι, ὑποκρίσεις, διπλοκαρδία, δόλος, ὑπερηφανία, κακία, αὐθάδεια, πλεονεξία, αἰσχρολογία, ζηλοτυπία, θρασύτης, ὕψος, ἀλαζονεία. 2. διῶκται ἀγαθῶν, μισοῦντες ἀλήθειαν, ἀγαπῶντες ψεῦδος, οὐ γινώσκοντες μισθὸν δικαιοσύνης, οὐ κολλώμενοι ἀγαθῷ οὐδὲ κρίσει δικαίᾳ ἀγρυπνοῦντες οὐκ εἰς τὸ ἀγαθόν, ἀλλ' εἰς τὸ πονηρόν· ὧν μακρὰν πραΰτης καὶ ὑπομονή, μάταια ἀγαπῶντες, διώκοντες ἀνταπόδομα, οὐκ ἐλεοῦντες πτωχόν, οὐ πονοῦντες ἐπὶ καταπονουμένῳ, οὐ γινώσκοντες τὸν ποιήσαντα αὐτούς, φονεῖς

τέκνων, φθορεῖς πλάσματος θεοῦ, ἀποστρεφόμενοι τὸν ἐνδεόμενον, καταπονοῦντες τὸν θλιβόμενον, πλουσίων παράκλητοι, πενήτων ἄνομοι κριταί, πανθαμάρτητοι· ῥυσθείητε, τέκνα, ἀπὸ τούτων ἁπάντων.

VI

1. Ὅρα, μή τίς σε πλανήσῃ ἀπὸ ταύτης τῆς ὁδοῦ τῆς διδαχῆς, ἐπεὶ παρεκτὸς θεοῦ σε διδάσκει. 2. εἰ μὲν γὰρ δύνασαι βαστάσαι ὅλον τὸν ζυγὸν τοῦ κυρίου, τέλειος ἔσῃ· εἰ δ' οὐ δύνασαι, ὃ δύνῃ, τοῦτο ποίει. 3. περὶ δὲ τῆς βρώσεως, ὃ δύνασαι βάστασον· ἀπὸ δὲ τοῦ εἰδωλοθύτου λίαν πρόσεχε· λατρεία γάρ ἐστι θεῶν νεκρῶν.

VII

1. Περὶ δὲ τοῦ βαπτίσματος, οὕτω βαπτίσατε· ταῦτα πάντα προειπόντες, βαπτίσατε εἰς τὸ ὄνομα τοῦ πατρὸς καὶ τοῦ υἱοῦ καὶ τοῦ ἁγίου πνεύματος ἐν ὕδατι ζῶντι. 2. ἐὰν δὲ μὴ ἔχῃς ὕδωρ ζῶν, εἰς ἄλλο ὕδωρ βάπτισον· εἰ δ' οὐ δύνασαι ἐν ψυχρῷ, ἐν θερμῷ. 3. ἐὰν δὲ ἀμφότερα μὴ ἔχῃς, ἔκχεον εἰς τὴν κεφαλὴν τρὶς ὕδωρ εἰς ὄνομα πατρὸς καὶ υἱοῦ καὶ ἁγίου πνεύματος. 4. πρὸ δὲ τοῦ βαπτίσματος προνηστευσάτω ὁ βαπτίζων καὶ ὁ βαπτιζόμενος καὶ εἴ τινες ἄλλοι δύνανται· κελεύεις δὲ νηστεῦσαι τὸν βαπτιζόμενον πρὸ μιᾶς ἢ δύο.

VIII

1. Αἱ δὲ νηστεῖαι ὑμῶν μὴ ἔστωσαν μετὰ τῶν ὑποκριτῶν. νηστεύουσι γὰρ δευτέρᾳ σαββάτων καὶ πέμπτῃ· ὑμεῖς δὲ νηστεύσατε τετράδα καὶ παρασκευήν. 2. μηδὲ προσεύχεσθε ὡς οἱ ὑποκριταί, ἀλλ' ὡς ἐκέλευσεν ὁ κύριος ἐν τῷ εὐαγγελίῳ αὐτοῦ, οὕτω προσεύχεσθε· Πάτερ ἡμῶν ὁ ἐν τῷ οὐρανῷ, ἁγιασθήτω τὸ ὄνομά σου, ἐλθέτω ἡ βασιλεία σου, γενηθήτω τὸ θέλημά σου ὡς ἐν οὐρανῷ καὶ ἐπὶ γῆς· τὸν ἄρτον ἡμῶν τὸν ἐπιούσιον δὸς ἡμῖν σήμερον, καὶ ἄφες ἡμῖν τὴν ὀφειλὴν ὡς καὶ ἡμεῖς ἀφίεμεν τοῖς ὀφειλέταις ἡμῶν, καὶ μὴ εἰσενέγκῃς ἡμᾶς εἰς πειρασμόν, ἀλλὰ ῥῦσαι ἡμᾶς ἀπὸ τοῦ πονηροῦ· ὅτι σοῦ ἐστιν ἡ δύναμις καὶ ἡ δόξα εἰς τοὺς αἰῶνας. 3. τρὶς τῆς ἡμέρας οὕτω προσεύχεσθε.

ΔΙΔΑΧΗ ΤΩΝ ΔΩΔΕΚΑ ΑΠΟΣΤΟΛΩΝ

IX

1. Περὶ δὲ τῆς εὐχαριστίας, οὕτως εὐχαριστήσατε· 2. πρῶτον περὶ τοῦ ποτηρίονυ Εὐχαριστοῦμεν σοι, πάτερ ἡμῶν, ὑπὲρ τῆς ἁγίας ἀμπέλου Δαυεὶδ τοῦ παιδός σου· σοὶ ἡ δόξα εἰς τοὺς αἰῶνας. 3. περὶ δὲ τοῦ κλάσματος· Εὐχαριστοῦμέν σοι, πάτερ ἡμῶν, ὑπὲρ τῆς ζωῆς καὶ γνώσεως, ἧς ἐγνώρισας ἡμῖν διὰ Ἰησοῦ τοῦ παιδός σου. σοὶ ἡ δόξα εἰς τοὺς αἰῶνας. 4. ὥσπερ ἦν τοῦτο τὸ κλάσμα διεσκορπισμένον ἐπάνω τῶν ὀρέων καὶ συναχθὲν ἐγένετο ἕν, οὕτω συναχθήτω σου ἡ ἐκκλησία ἀπὸ τῶν περάτων τῆς γῆς εἰς τὴν σὴν βασιλείαν. ὅτι σοῦ ἐστιν ἡ δόξα καὶ ἡ δύναμις διὰ Ἰησοῦ Χριστοῦ εἰς τοὺς αἰῶνας. 5. μηδεὶς δὲ φαγέτω μηδὲ πιέτω ἀπὸ τῆς εὐχαριστίας ὑμῶν, ἀλλ᾽ οἱ βαπτισθέντες εἰς ὄνομα κυρίου· καὶ γὰρ περὶ τούτου εἴρηκεν ὁ κύριος· Μὴ δῶτε τὸ ἅγιον τοῖς κυσί.

X

1. Μετὰ δὲ τὸ ἐμπλησθῆναι οὕτως εὐχαριστήσατε· 2. Εὐχαριστοῦμέν σοι, πάτερ ἅγιε, ὑπὲρ τοῦ ἁγίου ὀνόματός σου, οὗ κατεσκήνωσας ἐν ταῖς καρδίαις ἡμῶν, καὶ ὑπὲρ τῆς γνώσεως καὶ πίστεως καὶ ἀθανασίας, ἧς ἐγνώρισας ἡμῖν διὰ Ἰησοῦ τοῦ παιδός σου· σοὶ ἡ δόξα εἰς τοὺς αἰῶνας. 3. σύ, δέσποτα παντοκράτορ, ἔκτισας τὰ πάντα ἕνεκεν τοῦ ὀνόματός σου, τροφήν τε καὶ ποτὸν ἔδωκας τοῖς ἀνθρώποις εἰς ἀπόλαυσιν, ἵνα σοι εὐχαριστήσωσιν, ἡμῖν δὲ ἐχαρίσω πνευματικὴν τροφὴν καὶ ποτὸν καὶ ζωὴν αἰώνιον διὰ τοῦ παιδός σου. 4. πρὸ πάντων εὐχαριστοῦμέν σοι, ὅτι δυνατὸς εἶ· σοὶ ἡ δόξα εἰς τοὺς αἰῶνας. 5. μνήσθητι, κύριε, τῆς ἐκκλησίας σου, τοῦ ῥύσασθαι αὐτὴν ἐν τῇ ἀγάπῃ σου, καὶ σύναξον αὐτὴν ἀπὸ τῶν τεσσάρων ἀνέμων, τὴν ἁγιασθεῖσαν, εἰς τὴν σὴν βασιλείαν, ἣν ἡτοίμασας αὐτῇ· ὅτι σοῦ ἐστιν ἡ δύναμις καὶ ἡ δόξα εἰς τοὺς αἰῶνας. 6. ἐλθέτω χάρις καὶ παρελθέτω ὁ κόσμος οὗτος. Ὡσαννὰ τῷ θεῷ Δαυείδ. εἴ τις ἅγιός ἐστιν, ἐρχέσθω· εἴ τις οὐκ ἔστι, μετανοείτω· μαρὰν ἀθά· ἀμήν. 7. τοῖς δὲ προφήταις ἐπιτρέπετε εὐχαριστεῖν ὅσα θέλουσιν.

XI

1. Ὅς ἂν οὖν ἐλθὼν διδάξῃ ὑμᾶς ταῦτα πάντα τὰ προειρημένα, δέξασθε αὐτόν· 2. ἐὰν δὲ αὐτὸς ὁ διδάσκων στραφεὶς διδάσκῃ ἄλλην διδαχὴν εἰς τὸ καταλῦσαι, μὴ αὐτοῦ ἀκούσητε· εἰς δὲ τὸ προσθεῖναι δικαοσύνην καὶ γνῶσιν κυρίου, δέξασθε αὐτὸν ὡς κύριον.

3. Περὶ δὲ τῶν ἀποστόλων καὶ προφητῶν, κατὰ τὰ δόγμα τοῦ εὐαγγελίου οὕτω ποιήσατε. 4. πᾶς δὲ ἀπόστολος ἐρχόμενος πρὸς ὑμᾶς δεχθήτω ὡς κύριος· 5. οὐ μενεῖ δὲ εἰ μὴ ἡμέραν μίαν· ἐὰν δὲ ᾖ χρεία, καὶ τὴν ἄλλην· τρεῖς δὲ ἐὰν μείνῃ, ψευδοπροφήτης ἐστίν. 6. ἐξερχόμενος δὲ ὁ ἀπόστολος μηδὲν λαμβανέτω εἰ μὴ ἄρτον, ἕως οὗ αὐλισθῇ· ἐὰν δὲ ἀργυριον αἰτῇ, ψευδοπροφήτης ἐστί. 7. Καὶ πάντα προφήτην λαλοῦντα ἐν πνεύματι οὐ πειράσετε οὐδὲ διακρινεῖτε· πᾶσα γὰρ ἁμαρτία ἀφεθήσεται, αὕτη δὲ ἡ ἁμαρτία οὐκ ἀφεθήσεται. 8. οὐ πᾶς δὲ ὁ λαλῶν ἐν πνεύματι προφήτης ἐστίν, ἀλλ' ἐὰν ἔχῃ τοὺς τρόπους κυρίου. ἀπὸ οὖν τῶν τρόπων γνωσθήσεται ὁ ψευδοπροφήτης καὶ ὁ προφήτης. 9. καὶ πᾶς προφήτης ὁρίζων τράπεζαν ἐν πνεύματι οὐ φάγεται ἀπ' αὐτῆς, εἰ δὲ μήγε ψευδοπροφήτης ἐστί. 10. πᾶς δὲ προφήτης διδάσκων τὴν ἀλήθειαν, εἰ ἃ διδάσκει οὐ ποιεῖ, ψευδοπρφήτης ἐστί. 11. πᾶς δὲ προφήτης δεδοκιμασμένος, ἀληθινός, ποιῶν εἰς μυστήριον κοσμικὸν ἐκκλησίας, μὴ διδάσκων δὲ ποιεῖν, ὅσα αὐτὸς ποιεῖ, οὐ κριθήσεται ἐφ' ὑμῶν· μετὰ θεοῦ γὰρ ἔχει τὴν κρίσιν· ὡσαύτως γὰρ ἐποίησαν καὶ οἱ ἀρχαῖοι προφῆται. 12. ὃς δ' ἂν εἴπῃ ἐν πνεύματι· δός μοι ἀργύρια ἢ ἕτερά τινα, οὐκ ἀκούσεσθε αὐτοῦ· ἐὰν δὲ περὶ ἄλλων ὑστερούντων εἴπῃ δοῦναι, μηδεὶς αὐτὸν κρινέτω.

XII

1. Πᾶς δὲ ὁ ἐρχόμενος ἐν ὀνόματι κυρίου δεχθήτω· ἔπειτα δὲ δοκιμάσαντες αὐτὸν γνώσεσθε, σύνεσιν γὰρ ἕξετε δεξιὰν καὶ ἀριστεράν. 2. εἰ μὲν παρόδιός ἐστιν ὁ ἐρχόμενος, βοηθεῖτε αὐτῷ, ὅσον δύνασθε· οὐ μενεῖ δὲ πρὸς ὑμᾶς εἰ μὴ δύο ἢ τρεῖς ἡμέρας, ἐὰν ᾖ ἀνάγκη. 3. εἰ δὲ θέλει πρὸς ὑμᾶς καθῆσθαι, τεχνίτης ὤν, ἐργαζέσθω καὶ φαγέτω. 4. εἰ δὲ οὐκ ἔχει τέχνην, κατὰ τὴν σύνεσιν ὑμῶν προνοήσατε, πῶς μὴ ἀργὸς μεθ' ὑμῶν ζήσεται Χριστιανός. 5. εἰ δ' οὐ θέλει οὕτω ποιεῖν, χριστέμπορός ἐστι· προσέχετε ἀπὸ τῶν τοιούτων.

XIII

1. Πᾶς δὲ προφήτης ἀληθινὸς θέλων καθῆσθαι πρὸς ὑμᾶς ἄξιός ἐστι τῆς τροφῆς αὐτοῦ. 2. ὡσαύτως διδάσκαλος ἀληθινός ἐστιν ἄξιος καὶ αὐτὸς ὥσπερ ὁ ἐργάτης τῆς τροφῆς αὐτοῦ. 3. πᾶσαν οὖν ἀπαρχὴν γεννημάτων ληνοῦ καὶ ἅλωνος, βοῶν τε καὶ προβάτων λαβὼν δώσεις τὴν ἀπαρχὴν τοῖς προφήταις· αὐτοὶ γάρ εἰσιν οἱ ἀρχιερεῖς ὑμῶν. 4. ἐὰν δὲ μὴ ἔχητε προφήτην, δότε τοῖς πτωχοῖς. 5. ἐὰν σιτίαν ποιῇς, τὴν ἀπαρχὴν λαβὼν δὸς κατὰ τὴν ἐντολήν. 6. ὡσαύτως κεράμιον οἴνου ἢ

ΔΙΔΑΧΗ ΤΩΝ ΔΩΔΕΚΑ ΑΠΟΣΤΟΛΩΝ

ἐλαίου ἀνοίξας, τὴν ἀπαρχὴν λαβὼν δὸς τοῖς προφήταις· 7. ἀργυρίου δὲ καὶ ἱματισμοῦ καὶ παντὸς κτήματος λαβὼν τὴν ἀπαρχήν, ὡς ἄν σοι δόξῃ, δὸς κατὰ τὴν ἐντολήν.

XIV

1. Κατὰ κυριακὴν δὲ κυρίου συναχθέντες κλάσατε ἄρτον καὶ εὐχαριστήσατε, προεξομολογησάμενοι τὰ παραπτώματα ὑμῶν, ὅπως καθαρὰ ἡ θυσία ὑμῶν ᾖ. 2. πᾶς δὲ ἔχων τὴν ἀμφιβολίαν μετὰ τοῦ ἑταίρου αὐτοῦ μὴ συνελθέτω ὑμῖν, ἕως οὗ διαλλαγῶσιν, ἵνα μὴ κοινωθῇ ἡ θυσία ὑμῶν. 3. αὕτη γάρ ἐστιν ἡ ῥηθεῖσα ὑπὸ κυρίου· Ἐν παντὶ τόπῳ καὶ χρόνῳ προσφέρειν μοι θυσίαν καθαράν. ὅτι βασιλεὺς μέγας εἰμί, λέγει κύριος, καὶ τὸ ὄνομά μου θαυμαστὸν ἐν τοῖς ἔθνεσι.

XV

1. Χειροτονήσατε οὖν ἑαυτοῖς ἐπισκόπους καὶ διακόνους ἀξίους τοῦ κυρίου, ἄνδρας πραεῖς καὶ ἀφιλαργύρους καὶ ἀληθεῖς καὶ δεδοκιμασμένους· ὑμῖν γὰρ λειτουργοῦσι καὶ αὐτοὶ τὴν λειτουργίαν τῶν προφητῶν καὶ διδασκάλων. 2. μὴ οὖν ὑπερίδητε αὐτούς· αὐτοὶ γάρ εἰσιν οἱ τετιμημένοι ὑμῶν μετὰ τῶν προφητῶν καὶ διδασκάλων.
3. Ἐλέγχετε δὲ ἀλλήλους μὴ ἐν ὀργῇ, ἀλλ' ἐν εἰρήνῃ ὡς ἔχετε ἐν τῷ εὐαγγελίῳ· καὶ παντὶ ἀστοχοῦντι κατὰ τοῦ ἑτέρου μηδεὶς λαλείτω μηδὲ παρ' ὑμῶν ἀκουέτω, ἕως οὗ μετανοήσῃ. 4. τὰς δὲ εὐχὰς ὑμῶν καὶ τὰς ἐλεημοσύνας καὶ πάσας τὰς πράξεις οὕτω ποιήσατε, ὡς ἔχετε ἐν τῷ εὐαγγελίῳ τοῦ κυρίου ἡμῶν.

XVI

1. Γρηγορεῖτε ὑπὲρ τῆς ζωῆς ὑμῶν· οἱ λύχνοι ὑμῶν μὴ σβεσθήτωσαν, καὶ αἱ ὀσφύες ὑμῶν μὴ ἐκλυέσθωσαν, ἀλλὰ γίνεσθε ἕτοιμοι· οὐ γὰρ οἴδατε τὴν ὥραν, ἐν ᾗ ὁ κύριος ἡμῶν ἔρχεται. 2. πυκνῶς δὲ συναχθήσεσθε ζητοῦντες τὰ ἀνήκοντα ταῖς ψυχαῖς ὑμῶν· οὐ γὰρ ὠφελήσει ὑμᾶς ὁ πᾶς χρόνος τῆς πίστεως ὑμῶν, ἐὰν μὴ ἐν τῷ ἐσχάτῳ καιρῷ τελειωθῆτε. 3. ἐν γὰρ ταῖς ἐσχάταις ἡμέραις πληθυνθήσονται οἱ ψευδοπροφῆται καὶ οἱ φθορεῖς, καὶ στραφήσονται τὰ πρόβατα εἰς λύκους, καὶ ἡ ἀγάπη στραφήσεται εἰς μῖσος. 4. αὐξανούσης γὰρ τῆς ἀνομίας μισήσουσιν ἀλλήλους καὶ διώξουσι καὶ παραδώσουσι, καὶ τότε φανήσεται ὁ κοσμοπλανὴς ὡς υἱὸς θεοῦ, καὶ ποιήσει σημεῖα καὶ τέρατα, καὶ ἡ γῆ παραδοθήσεται εἰς χεῖρας αὐτοῦ, καὶ ποιήσει ἀθέμιτα, ἃ οὐδέποτε γέγονεν ἐξ αἰῶνος. 5. τότε ἥξει ἡ

κτίσις τῶν ἀνθρώπων εἰς τὴν πύρωσιν τῆς δοκιμασίας, καὶ σκανδαλισθήσονται πολλοὶ καὶ ἀπολοῦνται, οἱ δὲ ὑπομείναντες ἐν τῇ πίστει αὐτῶν σωθήσονται ὑπ' αὐτου τοῦ καταθέματος. 6. καὶ τότε φανήσεται τὰ σημεῖα τῆς ἀληθείας· πρῶτον σημεῖον ἐκπετάσεως ἐν οὐρανῷ, εἶτα σημεῖον φωνῆς σάπιγγος, καὶ τὸ τρίτον ἀνάστασις νεκρῶν. 7. οὐ πάντων δέ, ἀλλ' ὡς ἐρρέθη· Ἥξει ὁ κύριος καὶ πάντες οἱ ἅγιοι μετ' αὐτοῦ. 8. τότε ὄψεται ὁ κόσμος τὸν κύριον ἐρχόμενον ἐπάνω τῶν νεφελῶν τοῦ οὐρανοῦ.

On the Christian Life
John Calvin
Benediction Classics, 2011
58 pages
ISBN: 978-1-84902-426-6

Available from www.amazon.com,
www.amazon.co.uk

John Calvin (1509 - 1564) was an influential French theologian and pastor during the Protestant Reformation. This book is an abridged version of Calvin's "Institutes". The language has been translated into crisper English, making it very readable. Calvin's positive theological statements and arguments are included, while the bitter polemics that Calvin often used have been removed. Hence, it is possible to see the flow of Calvin's arguments without being distracted by the denunciations of those who disagreed with him. The abridgement has been skilfully executed, enabling the reader to see the coherent argument at the centre of Calvin's theology. This edition comes complete with the original title page, outline of the book, an index of scriptures and an index of French words and phrases.

The Imitation Of Christ - with indexes of Biblical References, People Names and Subject Matter
Thomas à Kempis
Benediction Classics, 2011
190 pages
ISBN: 978-1-78139-038-2

Available from www.amazon.com,
www.amazon.co.uk

The Imitation of Christ by Thomas à Kempis is the most widely read Christian devotional book next to the Bible. It was written in Latin five hundred years ago and now brings comfort to millions of readers in over fifty languages. The Imitation is based on meditations on the life and teachings of Jesus, and emphasises the interior life and the centrality of the Eucharist rather than an active imitation of Christ. This version has an index of Biblical references, an index of names and an index of subjects.

The Pilgrim's Progress From This World to That Which is to Come;Delivered under the Similitude of a Dream
John Bunyan
Benediction Classics, 2012
316 pages
ISBN: 978-1-78139-097-9

Available from www.amazon.com, www.amazon.co.uk

John Bunyan's 'The Pilgrim's Progress from This World to That Which Is to Come" is one of the most famous books written in the English Language. It is a Christian allegory written and was published in February, 1678. It is without doubt one of the most significant works of religious English literature, translated into over 200 languages, it has never been out of print. It traces the spiritual journey of Christian as he learns lessons that help him to grow in Christian maturity. It is thought that Bunyan wrote it during his imprisonment from 1660-1672 in the Bedfordshire county gaol for violations of the Conventicle Act, which prohibited the holding of religious services that were not under the auspices of the Church of England. This version has a beautiful cover from the early 1900s and contains over 80 back and white illustrations engraved by the Dalziel Brothers.and created by, among others, Frederick Barnard, J.D. Linton, W. Small.

Also from Benediction Books …
Wandering Between Two Worlds: Essays on Faith and Art
Anita Mathias
Benediction Books, 2007
152 pages
ISBN: 0955373700

Available from www.amazon.com, www.amazon.co.uk

In these wide-ranging lyrical essays, Anita Mathias writes, in lush, lovely prose, of her naughty Catholic childhood in Jamshedpur, India; her large, eccentric family in Mangalore, a sea-coast town converted by the Portuguese in the sixteenth century; her rebellion and atheism as a teenager in her Himalayan boarding school, run by German missionary nuns, St. Mary's Convent, Nainital; and her abrupt religious conversion after which she entered Mother Teresa's convent in Calcutta as a novice. Later rich, elegant essays explore the dualities of her life as a writer, mother, and Christian in the United States-- Domesticity and Art, Writing and Prayer, and the experience of being "an alien and stranger" as an immigrant in America, sensing the need for roots.

About the Author

Anita Mathias is the author of *Wandering Between Two Worlds: Essays on Faith and Art*. She has a B.A. and M.A. in English from Somerville College, Oxford University, and an M.A. in Creative Writing from the Ohio State University, USA. Anita won a National Endowment of the Arts fellowship in Creative Nonfiction in 1997. She lives in Oxford, England with her husband, Roy, and her daughters, Zoe and Irene.

Anita's website:
   http://www.anitamathias.com, and
Anita's blog Dreaming Beneath the Spires:
   http://dreamingbeneaththespires.blogspot.com

The Church That Had Too Much
Anita Mathias
Benediction Books, 2010
52 pages
ISBN: 9781849026567

Available from www.amazon.com, www.amazon.co.uk

The Church That Had Too Much was very well-intentioned. She wanted to love God, she wanted to love people, but she was both hampered by her muchness and the abundance of her possessions, and beset by ambition, power struggles and snobbery. Read about the surprising way The Church That Had Too Much began to resolve her problems in this deceptively simple and enchanting fable.

About the Author

Anita Mathias is the author of *Wandering Between Two Worlds: Essays on Faith and Art*. She has a B.A. and M.A. in English from Somerville College, Oxford University, and an M.A. in Creative Writing from the Ohio State University, USA. Anita won a National Endowment of the Arts fellowship in Creative Nonfiction in 1997. She lives in Oxford, England with her husband, Roy, and her daughters, Zoe and Irene.

Anita's website:
    http://www.anitamathias.com, and
Anita's blog Dreaming Beneath the Spires:
    http://dreamingbeneaththespires.blogspot.com

www.ingramcontent.com/pod-product-compliance
Lightning Source LLC
Chambersburg PA
CBHW020631230426
43665CB00008B/126